Microeconomic Theory

Microeconomic Theory
Basic Principles and Extensions

Walter Nicholson
Amherst College

The Dryden Press Inc.
Hinsdale, Illinois

Preface

This book is intended for use by undergraduates who have some command of basic economic concepts and by graduate students who want a systematic review. It should also provide an introduction to several important topics in modern economic theory which are not covered in traditional microeconomics courses.

The formal requirements for using the book are modest. No previous training in microeconomic theory has been assumed by the author, although some acquaintance with simple supply-demand analysis would be desirable. The student should have taken a one-semester course in elementary calculus, or should at least understand what a derivative is.

More important than formal prerequisites, however, is the student's ability to follow somewhat abstract arguments. Because this ability is difficult to quantify with a detailed list of courses, it is perhaps best to let each instructor use his own judgment in this matter when selecting his students.

The book covers most of the material usually presented in microeconomics courses, but it contains two important additions: its use of mathematics and the breadth of subjects covered. While the level of mathematical presentation is not particularly advanced, nevertheless calculus methods are used throughout the text. My own experience is that the use of calculus increases rather than inhibits a student's understanding of the marginalist principles which form the basis of most microeconomic theory. The book's use of mathematics is not excessively formal, and most arguments are presented initially in an intuitive and graphic manner. It is hoped that such a dual approach will succeed both in getting students to think intuitively about the subject and to appreciate the precise shorthand which mathematical analysis provides.

The technique of partial differentiation is developed in detail in Chapter 2; this technique is used throughout the remainder of the book. Also in Chapter 2 the Lagrangian Multiplier method of maximization is discussed on an elementary level. This method is used to develop alternative proofs of the principle theoretical results in the text. Some emphasis is given to the interpretation of Lagrangian Multipliers as dual variables. A few other mathematical topics (such as the mathematics of compound interest) are introduced as they are needed. Problems are presented at the end of each major section in the text; these (some of which are fairly difficult) require the use of calculus for solution.

There are two reasons why it was thought desirable to treat a larger number of topics than is usual in a price theory text. First, the additional topics covered represent those areas in which most current economic research is being undertaken. To investigate only "core" topics would be to limit unnecessarily the student's understanding of the questions which modern microeconomics addresses. Second, and a related reason for this expansion in topics, is a reaction to students' demands for greater "relevance" in price theory courses. By showing the applicability of economic logic to a wide variety of subjects the book hopes to force students to think beyond traditional graphic analyses of price determination and to see the generality of microeconomic methodology. Some attempt is also made to point out the major unsolved questions in economics.

Specifically, the book presents a far more detailed treatment of consumer theory than usual (the economic theories of labor force participation, consumption allocation over time, and behavior under uncertainty are discussed in detail in separate chapters), a careful examination of pricing in factor markets (a chapter is devoted to capital theory and its relationship to the theory of the firm), a detailed presentation of some of the principle results of general equilibrium theory and welfare economics (including an appendix which examines some recent mathematical techniques), and four chapters devoted to the role of government (including discussions of public goods, cost-benefit analysis, externalities and property rights, and the distribution of income).

It is hoped that these special sections will introduce students to topics in price theory which are intrinsically interesting but which are usually only available in a much more difficult form. By examining these extensions, students should be in a better position to understand both the analytical richness of microeconomic methods and the limitations of these methods.

I have used various drafts of this book both at Amherst College and the University of Massachusetts. It is possible, I know, to cover the entire book in a one-semester course while maintaining a high retention rate on the part of students. Yet complete coverage in one semester may seem too rushed. In this case only the "core" topics and a selected few of the special sections might be used; these basic chapters (excluding appendices) might be included: Chapters 1–6, 10–17, 20, and 22. They could be supplemented with additional material from the text on the theory of consumer demand, the theory of factor pricing, welfare economics, or the role of government. Such sections are relatively distinct from one another and may therefore be covered selectively.

Acknowledgments

No book is the product of a single individual and this is especially true of the present one. Certainly my most important intellectual debt is to the members of the economics department at M.I.T. where I learned most of what I know about economic theory. The intellectual stamp of that department is visible throughout the book. The department is not responsible for what I did not learn; I take full responsibility for all errors, both those of commission and of omission.

The students who have used the various versions of this book have been most helpful. They have forced me to make things clear and, occasionally, to get my analysis right. A roomful of puzzled faces is a most effective demand for clarification. I am grateful to those who kept after me to demand an improved presentation.

Donald A. Nichols of the University of Wisconsin read the entire manuscript and made numerous suggestions which have been incorporated into the text. His insistence on intuitive explanations led to substantial improvements in the readability of the book. Charles E. Metcalf (University of Wisconsin), G. Hartley Mellish (University of South Florida), Edward J. Ray (Ohio State University), Joseph Stiglitz (Yale University), and Jack E. Triplett (Washington University) also read the manuscript and made numerous contributions both in the theoretical presentation and in matters of pedagogy. Their influences can be seen in many places. My colleagues at Amherst College were most helpful and encouraging, and particular thanks are extended to Heinz Kohler and Hugh Aitken for their suggestions.

Seibert Adams of The Dryden Press is in many ways responsible for the existence of this book. I appreciate his support, his interest, and his highly productive prodding. Louise Waller edited the manuscript. Although she may never wish to see another subscript, her work is excellent and her stylistic improvements most welcome.

Dorothy Ives typed the entire manuscript (more than once). Her ability to bring order out of chaos is exceptional. As is the case for most of the books written in the economics department at Amherst College, she should probably be listed here as a co-author.

My wife, Susan, helped in many ways in the creation of this book. As she well knows, this help is most appreciated. Although my daughter Katherine arrived after the book was completed, she too would want to be mentioned.

—W.N.

Princeton, New Jersey
April 1972

Contents

PART I
Introduction

Outline of the Book: Some Recurrent Themes

The primary purpose of this book is to examine the way in which individual tastes and productive technology interact to determine how resources are allocated in a society. Some attention is also given to defining what an "optimal" or "ideal" allocation of resources might be. The book is not exclusively concerned with the American economy, or with any other particular organization of society, although many of the problems which are examined were suggested by recent experience in the United States. Rather, the central concern here is with the basic economic problems which face all societies, and particularly with those that arise in an economy in which most goods are traded among individuals in organized markets.

Three basic themes are developed throughout the book which are relevant to a broad range of social questions. These are:

1. *The beneficial nature of free exchange.* If Smith has something Jones wants and Jones has something Smith wants, then they both can be made better off by exchanging these goods. Many of the results in this book are specific applications of this common-sense idea.

2. *The limitations of exchange.* There are many situations, however, in which individuals left on their own to exchange goods freely will not produce socially desirable results. Some measure of coercion must be imposed on the members of society if such desirable results are to be achieved. For example, it is doubtful that individuals left on their own would provide a desirable level of public-health facilities. Each person, acting in his own self-interest, would adopt the principle of "let the other guy do it," hoping to benefit from his neighbors' expenditures. Since everyone (or almost everyone) would adopt this position, adequate facilities would never be built. Free exchange is not sufficient to guarantee that all desirable exchanges will be accomplished, and there is room for governmental coercion.

3. *The value of the "maximization hypothesis" in explaining behavior.* In order to understand why economic agents (firms, individuals, labor unions, and others) act as they do, it is frequently useful to assume that these agents are rationally pursuing some goal. Among a number of actions open to him the agent will choose that one which best achieves (that is, maximizes) his goal. Perhaps the most familiar example of this hypothesis is the assumption that firms act so as to maximize profits. From this one basic behavioral assumption a number of interesting implications about a firm's behavior can be derived, and these implications can then be contrasted to phenomena observed in the real world. In this book similar assumptions will be made about most economic agents, and it will be shown that these assumptions can give considerable insights into the ways in which choices are made.

Part I of this book develops some important groundwork for a further consideration of the themes mentioned above. First, a brief historical overview of the development of microeconomics is presented so that the reader may place the "modern" analysis which follows into a broader context. Chapter 2 outlines the methodological approach and the mathematical tools which will be used throughout the body of the text. In many respects Part I provides an introduction to the book.

In Parts II and III the actions of two important types of participants in the economic process are examined. Part II develops in detail the economic theory of individual behavior. Simply put, the purpose of this part is to explain how economists treat individuals' tastes, and how they assume that these tastes affect decisions. A similar development is presented in Part III for the decisions which firms make. This part represents an attempt to quantify the important aspects of productive technology. Even if a society were organized without entities called *firms* many of the tools which are developed here would be equally relevant to those production activities which are undertaken in this society.

In Parts IV and V it is shown how individual tastes and productive technologies interact to create markets. The allocation of goods and resources takes place in such markets. Part IV specifically discusses the market for goods and investigates the various ways in which these markets are organized. A similar analysis is presented in Part V for the market for productive resources. Both of these parts build directly on the analysis of individuals' and firms' decisions which was presented in Parts II and III.

Parts VI and VII raise more general questions about the desirability of certain ways of integrating tastes and technology. General concepts of social welfare are developed in Part VI, and a theoretically optimal exchange situation is described. Possible departures from this "ideal" are discussed in Part VII, and the role of government as an agent for dealing with these departures is investigated in some detail.

CHAPTER 1
An Historical Overview

Economics can be defined as the study of the allocation of scarce resources among competing ends. This definition stresses two important aspects of the study of economics: First, resources are "scarce" in that they are not available in sufficient quantities to satisfy all human wants; second, because resources are scarce, we must be judicious in allocating them among alternative ("competing") end uses. The definition is therefore broad enough to include not only narrow questions about possible optimum methods for making steel or bread but more generally to include questions about the "good life" and the welfare of man. In this sense economics is a branch of more general philosophic investigations into how society operates and how society *should* operate. Economists, in attempting to answer these questions, have centered their attention on the activities of men as consumers, producers, suppliers of resources, and — to a more limited extent — as voters. The interactions of men in these various roles is the subject matter of economics.

Many of these interactions take place through markets. The allocation of goods and of factors of production among competing ends takes place in and is determined by the operation of markets. Similarly, voting can be regarded as participating in a political "market" in order to affect government allocational policies. Economists have therefore spent a great deal of their energy in an attempt to understand how markets operate and how this operation might be improved. To do this it has been necessary to construct relatively simple models which attempt to explain the very complex real world. These theoretical models are the subject matter of this book.

Two important general questions might be raised about this abstract theoretical approach to explaining the real world: First, what is a theory and what does it mean to "prove" a theory? Second, how does the current state of economic theory fit into the historical development of the subject. An extended treatment of the first of these questions will be presented in Chapter 2; Chapter 1 places the theory which is developed in the remainder of the book into historical perspective.

To give a brief discussion of the development of economic thinking seems desirable for several reasons. Of primary importance is the aid to understanding current theory which is provided by an examination of its historical predecessors. Only by understanding some of the difficulties previous authors have had can one comprehend the current methods and appreciate the advances that have been made in the analysis of economic phenomena. Similarly, it should be recognized that any theory is historically relative. Economic theory is constantly evolving and coming to grips with more difficult issues. To omit a study of historical thinking on economic issues would be, in a sense, to accept current theory as "proven" for all time. On the other hand, if the current state of economic thinking is seen in historical perspective, the possibilities for future expansion may be more fully appreciated.

This book is about economic theory as it stands today, not about the history of economic thought. Therefore, the discussion of the evolution of this theory must be brief and so only one area of economic study will be examined in its historical setting. This subject is called the *theory of value* and has been of interest to economists — or to their philosopher predecessors — from the earliest times to the present day.

The theory of value, not surprisingly, concerns the determinants of the "value" of a commodity. The study of this subject is at the center of modern microeconomic theory and is closely intertwined with the subject of the allocation of scarce resources for alternative ends. One major purpose of this book is to develop this interconnection. Only recently have the theoretical interrelationships between the determinants of value and the optimal allocation of resources been made clear. Earlier economists were concerned primarily with explaining the determinants of "value," and it is these efforts which are outlined in this chapter.

The logical place to start is with a definition of the word *value*. Unfortunately, the meaning of this term has not been consistent throughout the development of the subject. Today we regard value as being synonymous with the price of a commodity.[1] Modern value theory is price theory. Earlier philosopher-economists, however, made a distinction between the market price of a commodity and its value. The term value was then thought of as being in some sense synonymous with importance, essentiality, or (at times) godliness. Since price and value were separate concepts they could differ, and most early economic discussions centered on these divergences.

St. Thomas Aquinas believed value to be divinely determined. Since prices were set by men it was possible for the price of a commodity to differ from this value. A man accused of charging a price in excess of a good's value was guilty of charging an "unjust" price. For example, St. Thomas believed the "just" rate of interest to be 0. Any lender who demanded a payment for the use of money was charging an unjust price and could be—and often was—prosecuted by church officials.

Controversies over the *just price* for a commodity dominated the economic discussions of the Middle Ages. Such discussions were fruitful in that they served to lay some analytical foundations for the economic advances of the eighteenth and nineteenth centuries. However, the idea of a just price gradually came to have less importance in economic discussions as the general methods of analysis moved away from the concept of natural law toward the scientific method. Rather than attempting to ascertain a divine pattern in economic affairs, emphasis shifted toward an effort to understand economic phenomena in their own right. The scientific method of proposing and testing hypotheses became the predominant means of investigation in the Age of Reason.

The early scientific economists, such as Adam Smith (1723–1790) and David Ricardo (1772–1823), continued to make a distinction between value and price. To Smith, for example, the value of a commodity meant its "value in use," whereas the price represented its "value in exchange." The distinction between these two concepts was illustrated

[1] This, in a sense, is not completely true (*see* Part VII of this text, especially Chapter 25).

by the famous water-diamond paradox. Water, which obviously has great value in use, has little value in exchange; diamonds are of little practical usefulness but have a great value in exchange. This paradox was never specifically resolved by either Smith or Ricardo. Rather, the concept of value in use was left for philosophers to argue over while the economists turned their attention to explaining the determinants of value in exchange. An obvious possible explanation is that exchange values of goods are determined by what it costs to produce them. Costs of production are primarily influenced by labor costs—at least in the times of Smith or Ricardo—and therefore it was a short step to embrace a labor theory of value. For example, to paraphrase an example from Smith, if it takes twice the number of man hours to kill a deer as to kill a beaver, then 1 deer should exchange for 2 beaver.

A difficulty with this explanation of exchange value is how to deal with other productive resources: How does payment for rent and for capital equipment enter into the determination of price? Ricardo answered this problem with an ingenious analysis. The cost of using capital could also be regarded as labor costs, with the labor being invested some years ago. In this way any capital cost can ultimately be traced back to some primary labor input. Ricardo disposed of rent by theorizing that rent is not a determinant of price (*see* Ricardo's analysis of rent in Chapter 17). Therefore, one is left with a pure labor theory of value: The relative price of two commodities is determined by the direct and indirect labor input used in each good.

To anyone with even a passing knowledge of what we now call the law of supply and demand, Ricardo's explanation must seem strange. Didn't he recognize the effects of demand on price? The answer to this question is both "yes" and "no." He did observe both periods of rapidly rising and rapidly falling prices and attributed such changes to demand shifts. However, he classed such changes as being abnormalities which produced only a temporary divergence of market price from labor value. Because he had not really solved the paradox of value in use, he was unwilling, or unable, to assign demand any more than a transient role in determining exchange value.

Karl Marx (1818–1883) used Ricardo's analysis of the determinants of value as a cornerstone for his theory of political economy. Since labor is the source of all value, Marx reasoned, labor deserves to receive the total proceeds of the productive process. Capitalists and landowners syphon off value that only labor can create, which makes Capitalists and landowners exploiters. This notion of exploitation is most notable for the central role it plays in Marxian political theories. However, by placing a theory of value at the heart of his system Marx was also laying down a challenge to future economists to prepare some alternative explanation of exchange value which would serve as a cornerstone for a different theory of the allocation of economic goods.

In the period 1850–1880 it became clear to many scholars that in order to construct an adequate alternative to Ricardo's theory of value one had to come to grips with the paradox of value in use. In an almost simultaneous revelation numerous economists discovered that it is not the total usefulness of a commodity that gives it exchange value but rather the usefulness of the last unit consumed. In the aggregate, water is certainly very useful to an individual, but, since water is relatively plentiful, *one more* gallon has very little use. By redefining the concept of value in use from an idea of aggregate usefulness to one of *marginal* usefulness – the usefulness of an additional unit of a commodity – the paradox of value had been solved.

This "marginalist revolution" in the later part of the nineteenth century produced an important synthesis of the concepts of demand and supply which, although it has been greatly elaborated upon, remains the cornerstone of modern economic analysis. The clearest statement of these principles was presented by the English economist Alfred Marshall (1842–1924) in his *Principles of Economics* published in 1890. Marshall showed that demand and supply simultaneously operate to determine price – the effects cannot be separated, just as one cannot ask which blade of a scissors actually does the cutting. This analysis is illustrated by the famous Marshallian cross shown in Figure 1.1. In this diagram the quantity of a good purchased per period is shown on the horizontal axis and its price appears on the vertical axis. The curve *DD* represents

Figure 1.1　The Marshallian Supply-Demand Cross

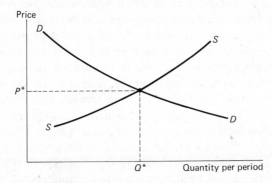

Marshall theorized that demand and supply interact to determine the equilibrium price (P^*) and quantity (Q^*) which will be traded in the market. Just as one cannot say which blade of a scissors does the cutting, it is not possible to say that either demand or supply alone determines price or, therefore, that costs of usefulness alone determines exchange value.

the quantity of the good demanded per period at each possible price. The curve is negatively sloped to reflect the marginalist principle that as quantity increases people are willing to pay less and less for the last unit purchased. It is the value of this last unit which sets the price for all units purchased. The curve SS shows how production costs rise as more output is produced. This, as we will show later on, reflects the increasing scarcity of those resources which are used relatively intensively in the particular industry. The two curves intersect at P^*, Q^*. This is an equilibrium point where both buyers and sellers are content with the quantity which is being traded and the price at which it is traded. If one of the curves should shift this equilibrium point would shift; price and quantity are simultaneously determined by the joint operation of supply and demand.

To a major extent this book is simply an explanation and elaboration of the Marshallian cross analysis. It will be seen that more recent work has led both to a greater understanding of the factors underlying the rather casually drawn supply and demand curves and to the application of supply-demand analysis in a much wider range of circumstances than are at first glance obvious from the simple diagram. For example, with only slight modifications the Marshallian model can handle not only the market for ordinary goods but also the market for resources, the market for goods delivered in the future, and the market for goods involving uncertainty (lottery tickets, common stocks, and so on). These applications will be discussed later in the text.

While the Marshallian model is an extremely useful and versatile tool, it is a *partial equilibrium model;* it looks at only one market at a time. For some questions this narrowing of perspective gives valuable insights and analytical simplicity. For other, broader questions about the efficiency and welfare implications of economic activities, such a narrow viewpoint may prevent the discovery of important interrelations. To answer more general questions one must have a model of the whole economy which suitably mirrors the interrelationships between various markets and various economic agents. The French economist Leon Walras (1834–1910), building on a long Continental tradition in such analysis, created the basis for modern investigations into these broad questions. His method of representing the economy by a large number of simultaneous equations forms the basis for an understanding of the interrelationships implicit in *general equilibrium* analysis. It is obvious from using such a representation that one cannot legitimately talk about raising the demand for one commodity in isolation. Rather, it is necessary to take account of the secondary and tertiary effects of such a change. In mathematical terms the equations must be solved simultaneously.

Most recent theoretical developments in economics have been in the field of general equilibrium analysis.[2] Questions about the efficiency of economic systems, the role of government, and the distribution of income have come to the forefront. The analytical viewpoint of economists has been extended from questions of how the system works to the related though broader question of why it doesn't work better. Microeconomic techniques have proved to be extremely valuable in giving insights into such questions and two parts of this book, VI and VII, will discuss these techniques in some detail.

Over the past two hundred years great advances have been made in scientific economics. By using the framework of Marshall and Walras we now understand, in a general way, how value in exchange is determined. This is not to imply, however, that economics is a closed subject. Three vast areas of interest are just beginning to be explored by economists.

First, many of the elementary supply-and-demand models which have been developed must be made more realistic in order to take account of important real-world departures from simple theoretical models. In this regard also it has become increasingly important to know the precise form of the supply-and-demand relationships in certain markets. The increasing use of statistical methods in economics will undoubtedly add to our knowledge of these relationships.

A second important area of recent investigations is the consideration of nonmarket interactions. Many of the effects of one economic agent on another are not completely represented by market prices, and these situations raise important questions about the allocation of resources. For example, the production and use of automobiles may involve such nonmarket "externalities" since the market price of a car does not adequately reflect the pollution and physical destruction it causes. Hence, although we may understand the determinants of the value in exchange of an automobile (this itself is a thorny issue), we might still wish to distinguish this concept from an automobile's value in use. In this sense economics has returned to re-examine the fundamental dichotomy proposed by Adam Smith.

Finally, a third important area of investigation in modern economics (which in actuality includes those previously mentioned as subcases) is the study of those factors which influence general social welfare. This subject is the central concern of all social scientists, and in this sense economics represents just a minor branch of a vast area of inquiry. The tools of economics, however, can illuminate many aspects of such investigations, and future developments in economic understanding will undoubtedly prove to be even more productive in this regard.

---

[2] In a sense modern macroeconomics is simply an example of applied general equilibrium analysis.

CHAPTER 2
Methodology and Mathematics

Modern microeconomics seeks to understand the behavior of various economic agents (individuals, firms, governments) and to analyze the interactions of these agents. When one looks at the world one is struck by the vast complexity of economic motivations and interactions. It would be impossible to develop a theory which could portray all the specific details of economic behavior. For this reason economists have chosen to abstract from many real-world complexities and to concentrate on "essentials."[1] Economists build rather simplified models (usually

---

[1] Investigators may differ on what the "essentials" really are. This, in a sense, is why different social science disciplines have been developed.

mathematical) which are intended, more or less, to represent reality. All scientific theorizing involves the creation of models (the idea of a "perfect" gas or vacuum in chemistry, the notion of an atom in nuclear physics or, indeed, the concept of a "culture" in anthropology), for without some abstraction, all investigation is merely descriptive. Among the social sciences economics has probably gone the farthest in the construction of precisely defined and empirically testable models. Many of these have certain conceptual and technical similarities. The purpose of this chapter is to discuss these similarities and to develop some tools which will be used throughout the rest of the book.

The Maximization Hypothesis

An hypothesis central to many economic models is that an agent is seeking to maximize something. Firms may operate so as to achieve the highest level of profits possible. Or, alternatively, firms may forsake maximum profits in pursuit of some maximum level of sales. Individuals might be assumed to maximize their consumption, or, more generally, to maximize their happiness (utility). Governments, if they are beneficial, may try to maximize the social welfare of the citizens they represent.

All such hypotheses of maximization are obviously abstracting from reality. They take no account of such "irrational" behavior as some firms' observed tendencies to build overly lush office buildings, nor of an individual's "impulse" buying of an overpriced car, nor of the government's being riddled with graft and corruption. However, one should not be too hasty in condemning a theory simply because it "ignores the real world." The ultimate test of a theory is how well it explains a variety of real-world phenomena. An a priori condemnation of a theory as being "unrealistic" would seem to be unwarranted, since all theories, by their nature, are "unrealistic." One must see how useful a theory is before offering such a judgment.

The maximization hypothesis has proved to be very useful indeed. Two factors account for its application to a wide variety of economic problems. First, the concept of maximization is precise. One may argue about what in fact is maximized (this is the case in the theory of the firm for example, as will be discussed in Chapter 10), but the alternative behavioral assumptions to maximization have proved to be imprecise and unquantifiable. For example, if consumers, or firms, are assumed to strive toward "satisfactory" performance in certain endeavors one is forced to specify exactly what "satisfactory" means, and the theory may lose much of its simplicity.[2]

A second factor accounting for the widespread application of the maximization hypothesis is the extent to which mathematical techniques have been developed to investigate maximum problems. Since maximization (and minimization) problems occur quite often in the natural sciences, mathematicians have long been interested in general solutions to these problems. Fortunately, economists have been able to make use of those mathematical developments and have found that such analyses give many insights into economic behavior.

Before beginning a detailed investigation of the mathematics of maximization, however, it is important to make one further methodological distinction. The study of economics has two rather different aspects. The first of these is sometimes called the *positive*, or *scientific*, mode of analysis. In this type of analysis economic phenomena are taken as given, and some attempt is made to understand the causes of those phenomena. Emphasis is placed on the predictive value of the hypotheses which are formulated. In a sense this method of analysis is "value free": No implication of "good" or "bad" is carried by the analysis. For example, the assumption might be made that firms act so as to maximize profits. No implication is to be drawn from this assumption that such behavior is to be considered desirable. Rather, the assumption is made for its predictive usefulness.

A second set of questions which economists investigate might be called *normative*. These investigations take a definite moral stance on what "should be." In such studies there are explicit attempts at proposing value judgments. Under a normative framework it would therefore be proper to argue that firms *should* maximize their "social responsibility," even though this assumption would be of little usefulness from a predictive point of view.

The maximization hypothesis is useful for both the normative and positive modes of economic analysis. If one is interested in positive questions the maximization assumption has proven quite valuable for predicting behavior. For normative questions the maximization hypothesis may provide clearcut guidelines for what actions should be taken to achieve desired results. In the remainder of this chapter we will discuss maxi-

---

[2] The distinction between maximization and "satisfaction" is not so clear as is here implied. In many respects satisfaction can be regarded as merely an example of maximization subject to constraints. For example, a firm which seems to achieve only satisfactory profits might be assumed to be maximizing something else (perhaps the prestige of its manager) subject to the constraint of earning a certain level of profits.

mization as a purely mathematical problem. The reader should keep in mind the two rather different ways in which the tools developed will be utilized in the remainder of the book.

Maximization as a Mathematical Problem: The One Variable Case

Suppose a firm manager desires to maximize the profits he receives from selling a particular good. Suppose also that the profits (π) which he receives depend only on the quantity (Q) of the good sold. Mathematically:

$$\pi = f(Q). \tag{2.1}$$

Figure 2.1 shows a possible relationship between π and Q. Clearly, to achieve maximum profits, the manager should produce output Q^* for which he receives profits π^*. If he were to produce more or less than this amount he would not be maximizing profits. How will the manager find this point of maximum profits? If he has a graph such as that of Figure 2.1 this would seem to be a simple matter.

Figure 2.1 Hypothetical Relationship between Quantity Produced and Profits

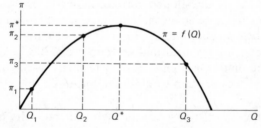

If a manager wishes to produce that level of output which maximizes his profits he should produce Q^*. Notice that at Q^*, $d\pi/dQ = 0$.

Suppose, as is more likely, he doesn't have such an accurate picture of his market. He may then try varying Q to see where he gets maximum profit. For example, he may start selling Q_1 and observe his profits from sales, π_1. Next he may try output Q_2 and observe that profits have increased to π_2. The common-sense idea that profits have increased in response to an increase in Q can be stated formally as:

$$\frac{\pi_2 - \pi_1}{Q_2 - Q_1} > 0 \quad \text{or} \quad \frac{\Delta\pi}{\Delta Q} > 0 \tag{2.2}$$

where the Δ notation is used to mean "the change in" π or Q. So long as $\Delta\pi/\Delta Q$ is positive, profits are increasing and the manager will continue to increase output. For increases in output to the right of Q^*, however, $\Delta\pi/\Delta Q$ will be < 0 and the manager will realize he made a mistake by increasing his output; he should return to the previous output level.

In calculus, mathematicians study the limit of ratios such as $\Delta\pi/\Delta Q$ for very small changes in Q. This limit is called the *derivative* of the profit function, $\pi = f(Q)$, and is denoted by $d\pi/dQ$ or df/dQ or $f'(Q)$. More formally, the derivative of a function $\pi = f(Q)$ at the point Q_1 is defined as:

$$\frac{d\pi}{dQ} = \frac{df}{dQ} = \lim_{h \to 0} \frac{f(Q_1 + h) - f(Q_1)}{h} \qquad [2.3]$$

where the symbol $\lim\limits_{h \to 0}$ means that we are interested in the ratio

$$\frac{f(Q_1 + h) - f(Q_1)}{h}$$

as h becomes small. Notice that the value of this ratio obviously depends on the point Q_1 which is chosen. Also notice the close similarity between this definition and the Δ notation developed earlier.

A notational convention should be mentioned: Sometimes one wishes to note explicitly the point at which the derivative is to be evaluated. For example, if one wishes to evaluate the derivative at the point $Q = Q_1$, it could be denoted by:

$$\left.\frac{d\pi}{dQ}\right|_{Q = Q_1}. \qquad [2.4]$$

At other times one is interested in the value of $d\pi/dQ$ for all possible values of Q and no explicit mention of a particular point of evaluation is made.

In the example of Figure 1.1 $\left.\dfrac{d\pi}{dQ}\right|_{Q = Q_1}$ is > 0, whereas $\left.\dfrac{d\pi}{dQ}\right|_{Q = Q_3}$

is < 0. What is the value of $d\pi/dQ$ at Q^*? It would seem to be 0, since the value is positive for values of Q less than Q^* and negative for values greater than Q^*. The derivative is then simply the slope of the curve in question; to the left of Q^* this slope is positive, to the right of Q^* it is negative. At the point Q^* the slope of $f(Q)$ is 0.

This result is quite general. For a function to attain its maximum value at a point, the derivative evaluated at that point must be 0. Hence, even if the manager didn't have a graph such as Figure 2.1 at his disposal, he might know the function $f(Q)$ and (using the techniques discussed below) be able to find the point where $df/dQ = 0$. For example, he could graph all the values of df/dQ for alternative values of Q as shown in Figure 2.2. Then all he has to do is to choose the point Q^* where:

$$\frac{df}{dQ}\bigg|_{Q = Q^*} = 0. \qquad\qquad [2.5]$$

The manager would choose the point at which the slope of his profit function is equal to 0.

Figure 2.2   Graph of df/dQ from Figure 2.1.

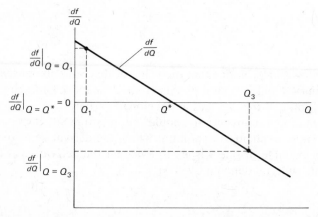

The value of df/dQ depends on the value of Q. For values of Q to the left of Q^*, df/dQ is positive: An increase in output would cause profits to increase. For Q to the right of Q^*, df/dQ is negative: Increases in Q would decrease profits (a decrease in Q would, on the other hand, increase profits). At Q^*, df/dQ is equal to 0 and profits are at a maximum.

The unsuspecting manager could, however, be tricked by a naïve application of this rule alone. For example, suppose the profit function looks like that shown in either Figure 2.3a or 2.3b. If the profit function is that shown in Figure 2.3a, the manager will, by producing where $d\pi/dQ = 0$, choose point Q_a^*. This point in fact yields minimum, not maximum, profits for the manager. Similarly, if the profit function is that shown in Figure 2.3b, the manager will choose point Q_b^* which, while it yields a profit greater than that for any output lower than Q_b^*, is certainly inferior to any output greater than Q_b^*. These situations point up the mathematical fact that $d\pi/dQ = 0$ is a *necessary* condition for a maximum, but not a *sufficient* condition. To insure that the chosen point is indeed a maximum point an additional condition must be imposed.

Figure 2.3 Two Profit Functions which Give Misleading Results if the First Derivative Rule Is Applied Uncritically

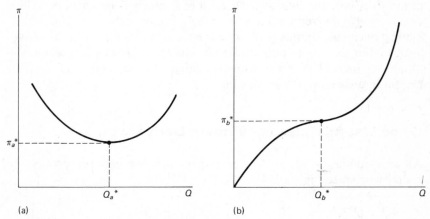

(a) (b)

In (a) the application of the first derivative rule would result in point $Q_a{}^*$ being chosen. This point is in fact a point of minimum profits. Similarly, in (b) output level $Q_b{}^*$ would be recommended by the first derivative rule, but this point is inferior to all outputs greater than $Q_b{}^*$. This graphically demonstrates that finding a point at which the derivative is equal to 0 is a necessary but not a sufficient condition for a function to attain its maximum value.

Intuitively this additional condition is clear: The profit available by producing either a bit more or a bit less than Q^* must be smaller than that available from Q^*. If this is not true the manager can do better than Q^*. Mathematically this means $d\pi/dQ$ must be greater than 0 for $Q < Q^*$ and must be less than 0 for $Q > Q^*$. Therefore, at Q^*, $d\pi/dQ$ must be decreasing. Another way of saying this is that the derivative of $d\pi/dQ$ must be negative at Q^*.

The derivative of what is already a derivative is called a *second derivative* and is denoted by:

$$\frac{d^2\pi}{dQ^2} \quad \text{or} \quad \frac{d^2f}{dQ^2} \quad \text{or} \quad f''(Q).$$

The additional condition for Q^* to represent a true maximum is therefore:

$$\left.\frac{d^2\pi}{dQ^2}\right|_{Q=Q^*} = \left.f''(Q)\right|_{Q=Q^*} < 0 \qquad [2.6]$$

where the notation is again a reminder that this second derivative is to be evaluated at Q^*. The reader should check the slopes of the curves in Figure 2.3 to see that the "second order" condition of Equation 2.6[3] does not hold at those points where $d\pi/dQ = 0$.

Equations 2.5 and 2.6 therefore represent the necessary and sufficient conditions for a function of one variable to achieve a maximum at Q^*. It is possible that by a series of trials the manager may be able to decide on Q^* by relying on market information rather than on mathematical reasoning. In this book we will be less interested in how he arrives at this point than in its properties and how the point changes when conditions change. The present mathematical development will be very helpful in answering these questions.

Some Useful Rules for Finding Derivatives

As an example, suppose the specific relationship between profits and quantity produced is given by:

$$\pi = 4Q - Q^2. \tag{2.7}$$

One could try to graph this (it would look much like Figure 2.1) or try several guesses in order to find that Q which gives maximum profits. However, the most straightforward method is to apply Equations 2.5 and 2.6 to calculate the derivatives of this profit function.

By the definition of a derivative, Equation 2.3:

$$\frac{d\pi}{dQ} = \lim_{h\to 0} \frac{4(Q + h) - (Q + h)^2 - 4Q + Q^2}{h}$$

$$= \lim_{h\to 0} \frac{4Q + 4h - Q^2 - 2Qh - h^2 - 4Q + Q^2}{h} \tag{2.8}$$

$$= \lim_{h\to 0} \frac{4h - 2Qh - h^2}{h} = \lim_{h\to 0} 4 - 2Q - h$$

$$= 4 - 2Q$$

and therefore $d\pi/dQ = 0$ when $Q = 2$.

---

[3] It might also be instructive to draw graphs of $d\pi/dQ$ for the functions in Figure 2.3. Notice that at Q^* the slope of $\left.\dfrac{d\pi}{dQ}\right|_{Q = Q^*}$ is positive for 2.3a and is 0 for 2.3b.

To check whether this is a true maximum we must compute $d^2\pi/dQ^2$. Applying the definition of a derivative to $d\pi/dQ$ (which was shown to be $4 - 2Q$) gives:

$$\frac{d^2\pi}{dQ^2} = \lim_{h \to 0} \frac{4 - 2(Q + h) - 4 + 2Q}{h}$$

[2.9]

$$= \lim_{h \to 0} \frac{-2h}{h} = -2 < 0.$$

Therefore Equation 2.6 is satisfied and $Q = 2$ is a true maximum (notice that $d^2\pi/dQ^2$ is negative at every point, not just at $Q = 2$).

The repeated application of the definition of a derivative can be tedious. For this reason several elementary derivatives are presented below. The proof of these results is left to the reader, or can be found in any book on elementary calculus.

1. If b is a constant, then $\dfrac{db}{dx} = 0$.

2. If a and b are constants and $b \neq 0$ then $\dfrac{dax^b}{dx} = bax^{b-1}$.

3. $\dfrac{d \log_e x}{dx} = \dfrac{1}{x}$,

   where $\log_e$ signifies the logarithm to the base e $(= 2.71828)$.

Such logarithms are generally used in calculus because of property 3. These are called *natural* logarithms.

4. $\dfrac{da^x}{dx} = a^x \log_e a$ for any constant a.

A particular case of this rule is $de^x/dx = e^x$.

Now suppose $f(x)$ and $g(x)$ are two functions of x and that $f'(x)$ and $g'(x)$ exist. Then:

5. $\dfrac{d[f(x) + g(x)]}{dx} = f'(x) + g'(x)$.

6. $d[f(x) \cdot g(x)] = f(x)g'(x) + f'(x)g(x)$.

7. $d\left(\dfrac{f(x)}{g(x)}\right) = \dfrac{f'(x)g(x) - f(x)g'(x)}{[g(x)]^2}$

   provided $g(x) \neq 0$.

Finally, if $y = f(x)$ and $x = g(z)$ and if both $f'(x)$ and $g'(z)$ exist, then:

8. $\dfrac{dy}{dz} = \dfrac{dy}{dx} \cdot \dfrac{dx}{dz} = \dfrac{df}{dx} \cdot \dfrac{dg}{dz}$.

This result is sometimes called the *chain rule*.

Functions of Several Variables

Economic problems seldom involve functions of only a single variable. Most goals of interest to economic agents depend on several variables which are more or less controlled by the agent. For example, the *utility* an individual receives from his activities as a consumer depends on the amount of each good he consumes. For a firm's *production function* the amount produced depends on the quantity of labor, capital, and land devoted to the production process. In these circumstances this dependence of one variable (y) on a series of other variables $(x_1, x_2,..., x_n)$ is denoted by:

$$y = f(x_1, x_2,..., x_n). \qquad\qquad [2.10]$$

We are interested in the point at which y reaches a maximum and how an economic agent might find that point. It is again convenient to picture this agent as changing the variables at his disposal (the x's) in order to locate a maximum. Again, there is interest in how y changes as one or several of the x's are changed. Unfortunately, for a function of several variables, the idea of *the* derivative is not well defined. Just as in climbing a mountain the steepness of ascent depends on which direction you go, so does the slope (or derivative) of the function depend on the direction in which it is taken. Usually the only directional slopes of interest are those which are obtained by increasing one of the x's while holding all the other variables constant (the analogy of mountain climbing might be to measure slopes only in a north-south, or east-west direction). These directional slopes are called *partial derivatives*. The partial derivative of y with respect to (that is, in the direction of) x_1 is denoted by:

$$\frac{\partial y}{\partial x_1} \quad \text{or} \quad \frac{\partial f}{\partial x_1} \quad \text{or} \quad f_{x_1} \quad \text{or} \quad f_1.$$

It is understood that in calculating this derivative all of the other x's are held constant. Again it should be emphasized that the numerical value of this slope depends on the value of x_1 and on the (preassigned) values of $x_2,\ldots, x_n$.

A somewhat more formal definition of the partial derivative is:

$$\left.\frac{\partial f}{\partial x_1}\right|_{\bar{x}_2,\ldots,\bar{x}_n} = \lim_{h\to 0} \frac{f(x_1 + h, \bar{x}_2,\ldots, \bar{x}_n) - f(x_1, \bar{x}_2,\ldots, \bar{x}_n)}{h} \qquad [2.11]$$

where the notation is intended to indicate that $x_2,\ldots, x_n$ are all held constant at the preassigned values $\bar{x}_2,\ldots, \bar{x}_n$.

Using the rules developed for finding derivatives in the previous section, it is easy to calculate some simple partial derivatives. The calculation proceeds as for the usual derivative by *treating the $x_2,\ldots, x_n$ as constants* (which indeed they are by the definition of a partial derivative). Consider the following examples:

1. If $y = f(x_1, x_2) = ax_1{}^2 + bx_1x_2 + cx_2{}^2$

then $\dfrac{\partial f}{\partial x_1} = f_1 = 2ax_1 + bx_2$

and $\dfrac{\partial f}{\partial x_2} = f_2 = bx_1 + 2cx_2.$

Notice that $\partial f/\partial x_i$ is in general a function of both x_1 and x_2 and will therefore depend on the particular values assigned to these variables.

2. If $y = f(x_1, x_2) = e^{ax_1+bx_2}$

then $\dfrac{\partial f}{\partial x_1} = f_1 = ae^{ax_1+bx_2}$

and $\dfrac{\partial f}{\partial x_2} = f_2 = be^{ax_1+bx_2}.$

3. If $y = f(x_1, x_2) = a \log x_1 + b \log x_2$

then $\dfrac{\partial f}{\partial x_1} = f_1 = \dfrac{a}{x_1}$

and $\dfrac{\partial f}{\partial x_2} = f_2 = \dfrac{b}{x_2}.$

Notice that the treatment of x_2 as a constant in the derivation of $\partial f/\partial x_1$ causes the term $b \log x_2$ to disappear upon differentiation since it is a constant.

Partial derivatives generally obey the same rules as do the more familiar total derivatives. For example, the chain rule holds; that is:

$$\frac{\partial f}{\partial x_1} = \frac{\partial f}{\partial z} \cdot \frac{\partial z}{\partial x_1}.$$

The partial derivative of a partial derivative is directly analogous to the second derivative of a function of one variable and is called a *second order partial derivative*. This may be written as:

$$\frac{\partial(\partial f/\partial x_i)}{\partial x_j} \qquad\qquad [2.12]$$

or more simply as:

$$\frac{\partial^2 f}{\partial x_i \partial x_j} \quad \text{ or } f_{ij}.$$

For the examples above:

1. $\dfrac{\partial^2 f}{\partial x_1 \partial x_1} = f_{11} = 2a$

$$f_{12} = b$$
$$f_{21} = b$$
$$f_{22} = 2c.$$

This example points out the rather general result that under "normal" conditions: $f_{ij} = f_{ji}$.

2. $f_{11} = a^2 e^{ax_1 + bx_2}$
$f_{12} = abe^{ax_1 + bx_2}$
$f_{21} = abe^{ax_1 + bx_2}$
$f_{22} = b^2 e^{ax_1 + bx_2}$

3. $f_{11} = \dfrac{-a}{x_1{}^2}$
$f_{12} = 0$
$f_{21} = 0$
$f_{22} = \dfrac{-b}{x_2{}^2}$

Using these concepts it is possible to discuss the agents' search for a maximum rigorously. To understand the mathematics used in solving this problem an analogy to the one variable case is helpful. In this one variable case we can picture an agent varying x by a small amount dx and observing the change in y (call this dy). This change is given by:

$$dy = f'(x) \; dx. \qquad [2.13]$$

The identity of Equation 2.13 then records the fact that the change in y is equal to the change in x times the slope of the function. This formula is equivalent to the *point-slope* formula used for linear equations in high-school algebra. The necessary condition for a maximum can be regarded as being given by $dy = 0$ for small changes in x. But since dx does not necessarily equal 0 this must (by Equation 2.13) imply that at the desired point $f'(x) = 0$. This is another way of getting the result already derived in the section for finding derivatives.

Using this analogy, it is possible to envision the decisions made by an economic agent with more than one variable at his command. Suppose this agent wishes to find a set of x's which will maximize the value of $y = f(x_1, x_2, ..., x_n)$. The agent might consider changing only one of the x's, say x_1, while holding all the others constant. The change in $y(dy)$ which would result from this change in x_1 is given by:

$$dy = \frac{\partial f}{\partial x_1} \; dx_1 = f_1 \; dx_1. \qquad [2.14]$$

This says that the change in y is equal to the change in x_1 times the slope measured in the x_1 direction. Using the mountain analogy again, this would say that the gain in altitude a climber heading north would achieve is given by the distance northward he travels times the slope of the mountain measured in a northward direction.

If all the x's are varied by a small amount the total effect on y will be the sum of effects such as that shown above. Therefore the total change in y is defined to be:

$$dy = \frac{\partial f}{\partial x_1} \; dx_1 + \frac{\partial f}{\partial x_2} \; dx_2 + ,..., + \frac{\partial f}{\partial x_n} \; dx_n$$
$$= f_1 dx_1 + f_2 dx_2 + ,..., + f_n dx_n. \qquad [2.15]$$

This expression is called the *total differential* of y (or of f) and is directly analogous to the expression for the single variable case given in Equation 2.13. The equation is intuitively sensible: The total change in y is the sum of changes brought about by varying each of the x's.

By an argument similar to that given in the section for finding derivatives, a necessary condition for a maximum is that $dy = 0$ for any combination of small changes in the x's. The only way this can happen is if, at the point being considered:

$$f_1 = f_2 = ,..., = f_n = 0. \tag{2.16}$$

A point where Equation 2.16 holds is called a *critical point*. Equation 2.16 is the necessary condition for a maximum. To see this intuitively note that if one of the partials (say f_i) were greater (or less) than 0 then y could be increased by increasing (or decreasing) x_i. An economic agent then could find this maximal point by finding the spot where y does not respond to very small movements in any of the x's. This is an extremely important result for economic analysis. It says that any activity (that is, the x's) should be pushed to the point where its "marginal" contribution to the objective (that is, y) is 0. The mathematical derivation of this condition permits a clear understanding of what this marginal principle means: The additional contribution of a particular x_i to the objective must be 0 when all other x's are held constant. If this is not true, the chosen point is not a maximum.

Again, however, the conditions of Equation 2.16 are not sufficient to insure a maximum. This can be illustrated by returning to an already overworked analogy: All hilltops are (more or less) flat, but not every flat place is a hilltop. A second-order condition similar to Equation 2.6 is needed to insure that the point found by applying Equation 2.16 is a true maximum. Intuitively, for a true maximum y should be decreasing for any small changes in the x's away from the critical point. This then necessarily involves looking at the second-order partial derivatives of the function f. These second-order partials must obey certain restrictions (analogous to the restriction which was derived in the single variable case) if the critical point found by applying Equation 2.16 is to be a true maximum.[4]

Since only functions of certain shapes satisfy these restrictions everywhere, it is only in these circumstances that the necessary conditions of Equation 2.16 are also automatically sufficient. Conveniently (or perhaps by design) most functions we will encounter in this book do obey these restrictions, and we will only be interested in applying the

---

[4] Technically, it is required that, at the critical point:

$$\sum_{i=1}^{n} \sum_{j=1}^{n} f_{ij} \, dx_i \, dx_j < 0$$

for all possible combinations of small changes in x_i and x_j. This means that y should be decreasing for any movement away from the critical point.

first-order conditions. This should not, however, be taken to imply that second-order conditions are somehow unimportant. As will be seen in several portions of the book, second-order conditions have a great deal of economic significance. Such examples will, however, be discussed in exposition rather than in a formal, mathematical way.

Constrained Maximization

Previously, attention has been centered on finding the maximum value of the function f without restricting the choices of the x's available. We have been investigating the properties of a "global" maximum for the function. In most economic problems not all values for the x's are permissible. In many problems it is required, for example, that all the x's be positive. This would be true for the problem faced by the manager in the section on finding derivatives; a negative output would have no meaning. In other instances the x's may be constrained by other economic considerations. For example, in choosing the items he will consume, an individual is not able to choose any quantities he desires. Rather, his choices must be constrained by the amount of purchasing power he has, that is, by his budget constraint. Such constraints necessarily lower the maximum value for the function we are seeking to maximize. Because we are not able to choose freely among all the x's, y will not be as large as it can be. If this were not true the constraints would be said to be "ineffective," since we could obtain the same level of y with or without imposing the constraint.

One method for solving constrained maximization problems is the *Lagrangian Multiplier method*. This method involves a clever mathematical trick which also turns out to have a useful economic interpretation. The rationale of this method is quite simple, although no rigorous presentation will be attempted here. In the previous section the necessary conditions for a maximum were discussed. It was shown that at the optimal point all the partial derivatives of f must be 0. There are therefore n equations ($f_i = 0$ for $i = 1,\ldots, n$) in n unknowns (the x's). Generally these equations can be solved for the optimal x's. When the x's are constrained, however, there is at least one additional equation (the constraint) without there being any additional variables. The set of equations is therefore overdetermined. The Lagrangian technique introduces an additional variable (the Langrangian Multiplier) which not only helps to solve the problem at hand (since there are now $n + 1$ equations in $n + 1$ unknowns) but also has an interesting interpretation.

More specifically, suppose we wish to find the values of $x_1, x_2,\ldots, x_n$ which maximize:

$$f(x_1, x_2,..., x_n)$$

subject to the constraint:[5]

$$g(x_1, x_2,..., x_n) = 0.$$

The Lagrangian technique sets up the expression:

$$L = f(x_1, x_2,..., x_n) - \lambda g(x_1, x_2,..., x_n)$$ [2.17]

where λ is an additional variable called the *Lagrangian Multiplier*. Notice that when the constraint is satisfied (that is, when $g[x_1, x_2,..., x_n] = 0$), L and f have the same value.

Among those x's which satisfy the constraint we wish to choose that set which makes f as large as possible. But this set of x's will also make the function L in Equation 2.17 as large as possible from among the values of the x's satisfying the constraint. This, then, suggests that we should look at the critical points of the function L. We should choose $x_1, x_2,..., x_n$ *and* λ so that the partial derivatives of L are equal to 0. From Equation 2.17:

$$\frac{\partial L}{\partial x_1} = f_1 - \lambda g_1 = 0$$

$$\frac{\partial L}{\partial x_2} = f_2 - \lambda g_2 = 0$$

$$\vdots$$ [2.18]

$$\frac{\partial L}{\partial x_n} = f_n - \lambda g_n = 0$$

$$\frac{\partial L}{\partial \lambda} = g(x_1,..., x_n) = 0$$

are the $n + 1$ necessary conditions for a maximum.[6] Notice that the final equation is simply the constraint. Any set of $x_1, x_2,..., x_n$, λ which obeys Equation 2.18 will therefore not only be a candidate for a maximum point

---

[5] This equation is written in "implicit" form for convenience. Any equation relating $x_1, x_2,..., x_n$ can be written in this form.

[6] Strictly speaking these are the necessary conditions for an interior maximum. In some economic problems it is necessary to amend these conditions (in fairly obvious ways) to take account of the possibility that some of the x's may be on the boundary of the region of permissible x's. For example, if all the x's are required to be non-negative, it may be that the conditions of Equation 2.18 will not hold exactly, since these may require negative x's. We will not detail the ways in which these conditions must be modified to take account of such problems, although some of these modifications will be hinted at throughout the book.

of the function f but will also obey the constraint. The Lagrangian technique is therefore seen to be a rather simple (albeit useful) trick.

Equation 2.18 is again only necessary for a maximum. There are sufficient conditions which are broadly similar to those discussed in the unconstrained case.[7] These conditions will not be examined here, although some simple examples of cases where the necessary conditions are not sufficient will be shown in later chapters.

It is interesting to rewrite Equation 2.18 as:

$$\frac{f_1}{g_1} = \frac{f_2}{g_2} = ,..., = \frac{f_n}{g_n .} = \lambda. \qquad [2.19]$$

Equation 2.19 says that, for the function to be a maximum, the ratio of f_i to g_i should be the same for all x_i. To interpret this condition it is necessary to repeat what f_i and g_i represent. The additional amount of y which would be yielded by increasing x_i slightly is f_i. This partial derivative represents the "marginal benefit" of slightly more x_i. On the other hand, g_i represents how additional x_i will affect the constraint. In this sense g_i can be regarded as the "marginal cost" of additional x_i. What Equation 2.19 says is that the *ratio of the marginal benefit to the marginal cost should be the same for all of the* x's.

To see that this is an obvious condition for a maximum, suppose it were not true: Suppose that the "benefit-cost ratio" were higher for x_1 than for x_2. In this case slightly more x_1 should be used in order to achieve a maximum. This can be shown by considering employing additional x_1 but giving up enough x_2 to keep g (the constraint) constant. Hence, the marginal cost of the additional x_1 used would equal the cost released by using less x_2. But, since the benefit-cost ratio (the amount of benefit per unit of cost) is greater for x_1 than for x_2, the additional benefits from using more x_1 would exceed the loss in benefits from using less x_2. The use of more x_1 and appropriately less x_2 will then increase y since x_1 provides more "bang for your buck." Only if the marginal benefit-marginal cost ratios are equal for all the x's will this choice of x's be a true maximum. Concrete applications of this basic principle are developed in many places in this book. The result is a fundamental one for the microeconomic theory of maximizing behavior.

The Lagrangian Multiplier (λ) may also be given an interesting interpretation in the light of this discussion. λ is the common benefit-cost ratio for all the x's. Loosely speaking, then, λ represents how much additional

---

[7] For a rigorous treatment of the sufficient conditions for a maximum for both the constrained and the unconstrained cases *see* Paul A. Samuelson, *Foundations of Economic Analysis* (Cambridge, Mass.: Harvard University Press, 1947), Mathematical Appendix A.

benefit (how much additional y) would accrue if the constraint were relaxed slightly. Since $\lambda = (\partial f/\partial x_i)/(\partial g/\partial x_i)$ for every x_i it is in some sense true that $\lambda = \Delta f/\Delta g$. Broadly speaking, the Lagrangian Multiplier tells one "how important" the constraint is. In particular, if the constraint is not effective, then λ will equal 0. No additional f will accrue from relaxing the constraint slightly since the constraint is not lowering the maximum value of f anyway: When λ equals 0 it is clear that maximizing Equation 2.17 is identical to maximizing an unconstrainted f.

Economists have studied this relationship between the "primary" problem of maximization and the "dual" problem of assigning values to constraints closely. It is often of interest to know how important a constraint is. A by-product of the Lagrangian technique is that such values are calculated. Most constrained maximization problems, whether solvable by calculus or by other methods, turn out to have this interesting "duality" property. In solving a problem in constrained maximization one automatically solves the problem of how to value the constraints.[8] This purely mathematical feature of maximization problems turns out to have a vast number of important economic applications as we shall see in the remainder of the book.

An Example of a Constrained Maximization Problem

Although the concepts outlined in the previous section will probably only become familiar as they are used in later chapters, it is instructive to present a noneconomic example which points out the techniques' major features. Consider the following geometric problem:

> Prove that a rectangle with a fixed perimeter encloses the maximum possible area when it is a square.

To demonstrate that this is a simple constrained maximization problem, let X be the length of one side of the rectangle and Y be the length of the other side. The problem then is to choose X and Y so as to maximize the area of the rectangle (given by $A = X \cdot Y$) subject to the constraint that the perimeter is fixed at $P = 2X + 2Y$.

We can solve this problem in two ways. The first method involves

---

[8] The discussion in the text concerns problems involving a single constraint. In general, one can handle m constraints ($m < n$) by simply introducing m new variables (Lagrangian Multipliers) and proceeding in an analogous way to that discussed above.

substitution. Use the perimeter constraint to solve for X:

$$P = 2X + 2Y$$

or

$$2X = P - 2Y \qquad\qquad [2.20]$$

or

$$X = \frac{P}{2} - Y.$$

Now substitute this value for X into the formula for the area of the rectangle:

$$A = X \cdot Y$$

$$A = \left(\frac{P}{2} - Y\right)Y = \frac{PY}{2} - Y^2. \qquad\qquad [2.21]$$

Since A is now simply a function of one variable (Y) and the fixed parameter (P), it is possible to apply the rule for finding the maximum of a function. This involves computing dA/dY and setting this equal to 0:

$$\frac{dA}{dY} = \frac{P}{2} - 2Y = 0$$

or

$$Y = \frac{P}{4}.$$

Substituting this result back into Equation 2.20 gives:

$$X = \frac{P}{2} - Y = \frac{P}{2} - \frac{P}{4} = \frac{P}{4}. \qquad\qquad [2.22]$$

Hence,

$$X = Y = \frac{P}{4}$$

and we have shown that the maximum area occurs when the rectangle is in fact a square.

A second way of proving this theorem involves using the Lagrangian Multiplier technique. We wish to choose X and Y so as to maximize:

$$A = X \cdot Y$$

subject to the constraint:

$$P = 2X + 2Y.$$

Setting up the Lagrangian expression as in Equation 2.17 gives:

$$L = X \cdot Y - \lambda(2X + 2Y - P) \tag{2.23}$$

where λ is an unknown Lagrangian Multiplier. The first-order conditions for a maximum are:

$$\frac{\partial L}{\partial X} = Y - 2\lambda = 0$$

$$\frac{\partial L}{\partial Y} = X - 2\lambda = 0 \tag{2.24}$$

$$\frac{\partial L}{\partial \lambda} = 2X + 2Y - P = 0.$$

The three equations in 2.24 must now by solved simultaneously for X, Y, and λ. Such a solution will obey the constraint and find a way for choosing X and Y so that area is a maximum. The first two equations say that $Y/2 = X/2 = \lambda$. This shows that X must be equal to Y. It also shows that X and Y should be chosen so that the ratio of marginal benefits to marginal cost is the same for both variables. The benefit (in terms of area) of 1 more unit of X is given by Y (area is increased by $1 \cdot Y$) and the marginal cost (in terms of perimeter) is 2 (the available perimeter is reduced by 2 for each unit that the length of side X is increased). The maximum conditions then state that this ratio should be equal for each of the variables.

Since we have shown $X = Y$ we can use the constraint to prove that:

$$X = Y = \frac{P}{4},$$

and because $Y = 2\lambda$ it must be the case that:

$$\lambda = \frac{P}{8}.$$ [2.25]

It is possible to use this solution for λ to show how much more area would be obtained if the perimeter of the rectangle were increased by one unit. For example, suppose a farmer were interested in knowing how much more field he could fence by adding an extra yard of fence. He could solve this problem by simply calculating the present perimeter and dividing by 8. Some specific numbers might make this clear. Suppose the field currently has a perimeter of 32 yards. If the farmer has planned "optimally" the field will be a square with 8 yards ($= P/4$) on a side. The enclosed area will be 64 square yards. Suppose now that the perimeter were enlarged by 1 yard. Equation 2.25 would then "predict" that the total area would be increased by approximately 4 ($= P/8$) square yards.[9] That this is indeed the case can be shown as follows: Since the perimeter is now 33 yards, each side of the square will be 33/4 yards. The total area of the square is then 1089/16 [$= (33/4)^2$]. But this fraction is approximately 68.1. The enclosed area has therefore increased by 4.1 square yards ($= 68.1 - 64$), which is what was initially predicted by Equation 2.25.

While this examples does not embody any great economic truths it does provide a useful illustration of the maximization procedure. It also shows the interesting interpretation which can be assigned to the Lagrangian Multipliers that are calculated along with solving the constrained-maximum problem. Most of the problems examined in this book will have features similar to those demonstrated in this problem.

Maximization Without Calculus

Not all economic maximization problems can be solved using the calculus methods outlined above.[10] For example, the manager of a firm may not know his profit function exactly but only be able to approximate parts of it by straight lines. This situation is illustrated in Figure 2.4a. Here Q^* is clearly the quantity which produces maximum profits, but this point cannot be found by calculus methods since $dQ/d\pi$ does not

---

[9] The word "approximately" is used here because the result, as is true for all calculus type of analysis, holds only for "small" changes. An addition of 1 yard to a 32-yard perimeter (a 3 percent increase) is not really a small change.

[10] It should be clear that although all the discussion has concerned problems of maximization directly analogous results hold for minimization. One way to see this is to note that to minimize a function $f(x_1 \ldots x_n)$ one need only maximize $-f(x_1 \ldots x_n)$.

exist[11] at Q^*. Some other method must be found in order to locate a point such as Q^* systematically.

Figure 2.4 Possible Profit Functions for which the Calculus Maximization Techniques Would Be Inappropriate

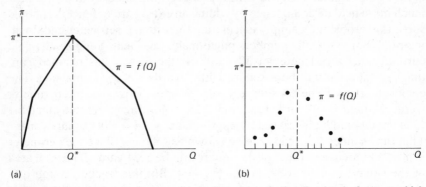

(a)   (b)

In Figure 2.4a calculus methods would not succeed in finding that level of output which yields maximum profits (Q^*) since the derivative is not defined at such a point. Similarly, in Figure 2.4b the manager may only choose integral values for Q. In this case the small changes required to apply calculus reasoning cannot be made. In order to find either of these maximum points various kinds of "programming" techniques must be utilized.

A second example of the failure of traditional calculus methods is illustrated in Figure 2.4b. Here the manager can only produce integral units of Q — it makes no sense to produce 4 1/3 cars. In this case again $d\pi/dQ$ is not defined at Q^* — calculus will not provide a systematic method for finding Q^*.

Specific mathematical "programming" techniques have been developed for dealing with problems such as those illustrated in Figure 2.4. The example illustrated in 2.4a is an extremely simple case of a problem which can be solved by "linear programming" methods; that illustrated in 2.4b can be solved by "integer programming" methods.[12] These techniques provide powerful tools for solving constrained maximization problems, and have proved extremely useful in analyzing difficult real-world situations. In this book, however, we will be concerned primarily with calculus methods of solving constrained-maximization problems. This choice is made both for simplicity and because calculus methods and programming techniques have numerous similarities. Most eco-

[11] To see this, note that the slope of $f(Q)$ changes very abruptly at Q^*.

[12] For a simple discussion of these methods *see* R. Dorfman, P. A. Samuelson, and R. M. Solow, *Linear Programming and Economic Analysis* (New York: McGraw-Hill, Inc., 1958).

nomically interesting aspects of programming techniques are illustrated by the calculus methods.[13]

One similarity between most maximization procedures should be mentioned – the concept of duality. The vast majority of constrained maximization problems yield, as a concomitant of their solution, dual variables which assign values to the constraints. These are directly analogous to the Lagrangian Multipliers discussed above. They indicate how much is added to the objective by relaxing a constraint slightly. If the constraint is ineffective the value of its corresponding dual variable is 0. Otherwise, the dual variable can give an indication of how "binding" the constraint is. Using these methods for assigning values to constraints provides a variety of important economic insights, as will be seen throughout the text.

A Concluding Note

Despite the formidable appearance of Chapter 2, this is not a mathematics book. The mathematical tools developed here will yield a great many insights into the analysis of certain economic problems, but purely formal analysis is not an end in itself. Rather, the study of economic phenomena must also rely on empirical observations, educated guesses, and perhaps a large degree of introspection. Using mathematics provides a convenient mental shorthand which permits us to concentrate on the essential aspects of a problem. In this way it is possible to describe many seemingly dissimilar problems in an identical format. We can therefore solve many different problems at one time. Mathematics can add logic and precision to economic investigations; it cannot suggest the relevant questions to be investigated. For this reason the mathematics developed in this chapter should be regarded as nothing more than a useful tool which may, in some cases, be appropriately applied.

---

[13] A brief discussion of the technique of linear programming is presented in the Appendix to Chapter 12.

DISCUSSION QUESTIONS AND PROBLEMS
FOR PART I

Discussion Questions

1. The application of mathematical models and the tools of maximization to economic analysis is in many ways a methodology borrowed from the physical sciences. Some social scientists object to this "pseudoscientific" approach to social phenomena and claim it obscures rather than enlightens. Does the use of these scientific tools inhibit one's ability to understand what is really going on in the world?

2. As was mentioned in Chapter 2 some economists draw a distinction between *positive* and *normative* economic analysis. Positive analysis seeks to explain "what is" (that is, how the economic system works), whereas normative analysis asks "what should be." Is this distinction a valid one or might we, by answering how the system works, also answer how it should work (or at least better understand how it should work)?

3. Can you think of an alternative, quantifiable way to define value other than market price? Even if you cannot, do you object to making these two concepts synonymous?

Problems

1. Suppose $f(X, Y) = XY$. Find the maximum value for f if X and Y are constrained to sum to 1. Solve this problem in two ways: by substitution, and by using the Langrangian Multiplier method.

2. Show that a solid rectangular block with a given volume has minimum surface area when it is a cube.

3. Suppose $f(X, Y) = -X^2 + 2X - 2XY + 2Y - 2Y^2$. Find the point where f has a maximum value. Prove that the second-order conditions for a maximum are also satisfied at this point; do this by showing that the equation in Footnote 4 of the text implies that f_{XX} must be < 0 and that $(f_{XX} f_{YY} - f^2_{XY})$ must be > 0 for a true maximum. This equation obeys these conditions everywhere.

4. Solve the following constrained-maximization problem using the Lagrangian technique:

    Choose x_1, x_2, and x_3 to maximize:

$$M = 5 \log x_1 + 3 \log x_2 + 2 \log x_3$$

subject to the constraint:

$$10 \, x_1 + 2 \, x_2 + 4 \, x_3 = 100.$$

Solve for the value of the Lagrangian Multiplier and give an interpretation of this solution.

5.   Choose X and T to maximize:

$$M = X^{1/3} \, Y^{2/3}$$

subject to the constraint:

$$3/4 \, X + 12/27 \, Y = 18.$$

(*Hint:* The math here may get burdensome. Just show that $X = 8$, $Y = 27$ are the optimal values.)

PART II
Individual
Behavior

Introduction

In Part II we will investigate the economic theory of individual behavior. The concept of utility is introduced in Chapter 3 and the remainder of this part deals with applications of the hypothesis that individuals make choices so as to maximize the utility of those choices. In a wide variety of situations this hypothesis can yield insights into the behavior of individuals.

Chapters 4, 5, and 6 develop the theory of consumer demand. One final product of these three chapters is the Marshallian market demand curve which was first depicted in Figure 1.1. Although it is possible to start a discussion of microeconomic theory by simply postulating the existence of such a (negatively sloped) market demand curve, the philosophy here is that the theoretical foundations of demand theory provide valuable insights into both individual and market behavior. The demand curve is therefore built up from more basic concepts. It is hoped that by this process the reader will gain a strong understanding of some fundamental aspects of the problem of choice.

The role of individuals as providers of productive resources is examined in Chapters 7 and 8. The individual's decision to offer labor services is examined in Chapter 7. Work and leisure are competing demands for the individual's time. The utility-maximizing hypothesis provides a useful model of how the choice between these two activities will be made. Chapter 8 investigates the individuals' saving decision. By abstaining from current consumption the individual encourages capital formulation; hence this chapter can be regarded as an investigation of individuals' decisions to supply capital. The role of interest rates in this decision is examined in some detail. These two chapters show that the utility-maximization hypothesis is useful not only for gaining an understanding of the behavior of individuals as demanders of goods but also for an understanding of their role as suppliers of the basic productive resources of any economy.

In Chapter 9 it is recognized that uncertainty and lack of information are pervasive economic problems. The chapter serves as a brief description of some of the analytical techniques which have been proposed for dealing with the problem of individual choice in uncertain situations. Again the hypothesis of utility maximization proves to be productive in this analysis.

Part II presents a broad-ranging, though elementary, survey of the way economists treat the individual's problem of choice. Since any society is no more than a collection of individuals, this seems the obvious place to start an investigation of economic behavior. It is hoped that the broad coverage presented here will serve the purpose of introducing economic methodology, and will also demonstrate many of the conceptual clarifications which this methodology permits.

CHAPTER 3
Individuals and Utility

Introduction

The individual is at the center of the economic system. Desires of individuals determine what goods will be demanded; what level of productive services will be supplied; and, through voting, what governmental objectives will be pursued. Thus, each individual operates in the role of at least three economic agents.

1. *The individual is a consumer.* Individuals demand a variety of consumption goods and services. Presumably they derive some welfare

from those items which they demand. There may be a "higher order" of demands for the necessities of life than for the luxuries, but this dividing line is a difficult one to draw in practice. A major assumption of economic theory is that individual tastes are taken as given, and attempts are made to analyze choices which are made based on these tastes.

2. *The individual provides productive services.* The most obvious resource provided by the individual is labor. He must decide how much labor he will trade in the market in exchange for goods or services. Individuals by their saving (that is, abstaining from current consumption) also provide capital as a productive resource to the economic system. Savings may be invested by the individual directly in tangible capital, or they may be used to buy financial assets which in turn permit the borrower of these funds to invest in tangible capital goods. An individual may also decide to invest in his own education. In this respect he invests in "human" capital. Recognizing that this decision to invest in human capital may change the quality of labor service offered by the individual creates a certain fuzziness in the distinction between labor and capital.

3. *The individual participates in the political process.* By his voting and other political activities the individual expresses his preferences regarding the government's provision of goods and services (national defense, police, trash collection, for example). He also expresses his willingness to pay for these services by paying taxes. Individuals express their tastes in regard to other major political issues, and the social consensus which emerges sets the framework in which the economic system operates.

It is important to recognize that these roles cannot be separated from one another. Any decision an individual makes as a consumer, say to buy a new car, will undoubtedly have an effect on his decisions as a provider of resources (he may save less or work harder) and on his decisions as a voter (he may favor spending for new highways on which to drive his new car). Economic texts used to refer to "economic man" *(homo economicus)* and center attention on the individual's role as a consumer only. Most authors recognized other roles, but those were never explicitly discussed. Modern microeconomics explicitly recognizes this mixture of roles and has developed tools to aid in understanding these interrelationships. The analysis of the individual in these various roles is the subject matter of Part II[1] of this book. Before beginning this analy-

---

[1] The discussion of the individual as a participant in the political process is reserved until Part VII.

sis, however, we must talk about individual tastes and the concept of utility. That is the principle purpose of this chapter, which concludes with a very brief discussion of some broader issues regarding individual choice.

The Concept of Utility

Economists assume that individuals act in their various roles so as to maximize their own satisfaction or *utility*. In some sense the utility which is perceived by an individual is determined by his attitudes about all the stimuli which act on him over his lifetime. This definition is obviously too general to be of much analytical usefulness. Therefore, economists have chosen to center their attention on quantifiable economic magnitudes and to investigate how individuals choose among them. It is not that economists assign no role to nonquantifiable magnitudes (tastes, love, character, and so on). Rather, these aspects of human behavior are assumed to be held constant throughout the analysis. This is one example of the principle of *ceteris paribus* (other things being equal) in economics. In order to make the analysis manageable it is necessary to hold certain aspects of individual behavior constant, leaving them outside the analysis. The choice of what to hold constant will depend on the particular area of investigation and on the length of time being examined.

As an important example of the *ceteris paribus* assumption, consider the individual's problem of choosing, at a single point in time, among n consumption goods $x_1, x_2, \ldots, x_n$. We will assume that he seeks to maximize a utility "function" of the form:

$$\text{Utility} = U(x_1, x_2, \ldots, x_n; c, t) \qquad [3.1]$$

where the "; c, t" notation is to remind the reader that many aspects of individual welfare are being held constant in the analysis. Not only must we hold "tastes" constant but we must hold constant such quantifiable items as the individual's consumption in some future time periods, the number of hours he will work (this amounts to holding his income constant), and the amount of his income he is saving. All these quantifiable aspects of individual behavior can be (and will be) investigated in their own right. But in the most common utility-maximization problem they are held constant.

Quite often it is easier to write Equation 3.1 as:

$$\text{Utility} = U(x_1, x_2, \ldots, x_n) \qquad [3.2]$$

where it is clear that everything is being held constant (that is, outside the frame of analysis) except the goods currently consumed, $x_1, x_2, \ldots, x_n$. It would be tedious to remind the reader at each step what is being held constant in the analysis, but it should be remembered that there will always be some form of the *ceteris paribus* assumption in operation.

The utility function notation will therefore be used to indicate how an individual ranks (that is, how he feels about) the particular arguments of the function being considered. In the most usual case the utility function Equation 3.2 will be used to represent how an individual ranks certain bundles of goods which are available at one point of time. On occasion it will be useful to use other arguments in the utility function, and it is best to clear up certain conventions at the outset. For example, it may be useful to talk about the utility an individual receives from his real income (Y). Therefore we will use the notation:

$$\text{Utility} = U(Y). \tag{3.3}$$

Unless the individual is a rather peculiar Scrooge type of person, income in its own right gives no direct utility. Rather, it is only when this income is spent on consumption goods that any utility results. For this reason Equation 3.3 will be taken to mean that the utility from income is in fact derived by spending that income in a way so as to yield as much utility as possible. Equation 3.3 is therefore an "indirect" utility function, because those things which really provide utility (the consumption items which real income buys) are obscured from view.

Two other utility functions of this aggregated type will be used in later chapters. In Chapter 7 we will be concerned with the individual's labor-leisure choice and will therefore have to consider the presence of leisure in the utility function. A function of the form:

$$\text{Utility} = U(Y, H) \tag{3.4}$$

will be used. Here Y represents income and H represents leisure. This function is also an indirect representation of utility because income provides no direct utility. Indeed, "leisure" is an equally indirect concept because it is the uses to which leisure time is put which directly provide utility.

In Chapter 8 we will be interested in the individual's consumption decisions in different time periods. In that chapter we will use a utility function of the form:

$$\text{Utility} = U(c_1, c_2) \tag{3.5}$$

where c_1 is consumption in this period and c_2 is consumption in the next period. This extremely simple case will prove to be useful in analyzing important aspects of an individual's behavior over time. It should be recognized that the use of an aggregate such as "consumption next period" is based on the assumption that such a magnitude is allocated optimally (so as to maximize utility) over a collection of specific individual goods.

A final note of warning should be offered in regard to the *ceteris paribus* assumption. Often we will want to analyze the response of an individual to changing prices. In order to make this analysis correct we must assume that prices do not enter into the utility function. An individual gains utility from consuming a good, but not from knowing how much it costs.[2] By making this assumption individuals are assumed to be rational buyers, not "conspicuous consumers." It is assumed that people buy Cadillacs because they provide superior transportation and other services, not because they are expensive. Goods are regarded as purely physical commodities distinct from the prices attached to these items. There are situations in which prices do affect an individual's perception of the desirability of a good (consider a novice choosing from among a bewildering assortment of cameras and being forced, to some extent, to "judge quality by price"). It is possible to develop theories which take such behavior into account. Because the explicit treatment of this problem involves considerable analytical complications without adding appreciably to an understanding of the theory of choice, the problem will not be pursued here. This omission can be rationalized by observing that prices do not affect the utility obtained from "most" consumption items; and in those cases which are exceptions, the traditional analysis is only slightly changed.

The Measurability of Utility

The first economists to deal with the concept of utility thought that it might be measurable. Indeed, some early psychological experiments on individuals' responses to various stimuli gave some premature hopes that all individual reactions were not only quantifiable but also of the same general type.[3] If utility were measurable, many economic questions could be easily answered. Not only could we understand and predict individual

[2] This rules out a phenomenon reportedly observed in a 5¢ and 10¢ store where a 50¢ lipstick failed to sell until its price was raised to the "luxury" level of $1.00.

[3] In particular it was thought that people responded in proportion to the logarithm of the stimulus (*see* Chapter 9 for a more extended discussion of the logarithmic utility function).

consumer behavior, for example, but we could also make judgments between people in order to produce a "fair" distribution of goods among people.

Unfortunately, the obstacles to measuring utility have proved to be insurmountable. The major problems seem to be of two general types. The first of these is what to use for a unit of measurement. We have no very good psychological idea of what a *util* might be. Similarly there is no way to determining how one man's utils compare to another's. A second class of problems in measuring utility is in the attempts to impose the *ceteris paribus* assumption. Whereas in simple psychological experiments it may, to a first order of approximation, be possible to hold everything except the stimulus under question constant (that is, to provide an adequate "control"), in economics this has proven to be unfeasible. The myriad of factors affecting an individual are impossible to list and quantify. To attempt to hold some of them constant while trying to measure an economically relevant concept of utility is out of the question.

Consequently, we must expect much less than measurability from a utility theory. All that can be assumed is that individuals rank bundles of commodities in some consistent way. To say that the utility of a bundle of goods $A[U(A)]$ is greater than that of another bundle $B[U(B)]$ only means that A is preferred to B. We cannot answer the question by "how much" A is preferred to B, since a hard-and-fast measure of utility is beyond our grasp.[4] Fortunately, this does not prove to be too great a problem in economic analysis. Most observable economic behavior can be explained without the necessity of having measurable utility functions. As a substitute for measurability we can inquire into the general shape of the utility function by examining how individuals feel about various bundles of goods. This is the purpose of the next section.

The Shape of the Utility Function: Some Assumptions

The first obvious assumption one might make about individual preferences is that more of a good is preferred to less. In Figure 3.1 all points in the shaded area are preferred to the amounts X^* of good X and Y^* of good Y. This assumes that individuals are not satiated (at least not in all goods). Movement from point X^*, Y^* to any point in the shaded area is an unambiguous improvement, since the individual (at least) obtains more of one good without being forced to accept less of any other. This idea of preferences is implicit in the definition of "goods" as items which

---

[4] Mathematically we can assume that utility is unique only up to a monotonic (order preserving) transformation. Most utility functions used in later chapters are assumed to be unique only up to such a transformation.

yield positive utility. A more important aspect of individual taste which must be conceptualized is how individuals feel about getting more of some good when they must give up an amount of some other good. This would involve an ambiguous increase in utility. It is necessary to develop some additional terminology if one is to investigate such situations. We will proceed to do just that in some detail since ambiguous changes of this kind are very common in economics. Giving up units of one commodity to get back some other commodity is what trade and markets are all about.

Figure 3.1   More of a Good Is Preferred to Less

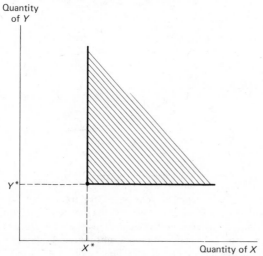

The shaded area represents those combinations of X and Y which are unambiguously preferred to the combination X^*, Y^*. In a sense this is why goods are called "goods"; because, *ceteris paribus*, individuals prefer more of any good rather than less.

An intuitive assumption which could be made involves the trades an individual might be willing to make from his current situation. Suppose we asked an individual how many hamburgers he would give up to get an additional soft drink. The answer to this question might be very different depending on whether he had just finished drinking a soft drink or eating a hamburger. We might assume he gets tired of eating hamburgers, and that he might, say, give up two hamburgers for a soft drink if he had just finished a hamburger, whereas he would only give up one hamburger for an additional soft drink if he had just finished the drink. This is an example (admittedly gastronomically inane) of an assumption economists make about the shape of the utility function called the assumption of *a diminishing marginal rate of substitution*. The assumption will be made far more precisely below by using a mathematical derivation. This technique will permit a formal statement of the simple notion that individuals prefer some variety in their fare of goods; some balance in consumption is desirable.

Figure 3.2 A Single Indifference Curve

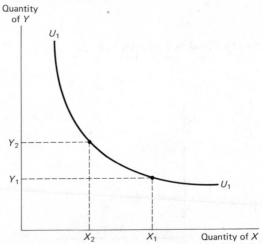

The curve U_1 represents those combinations of X and Y from which the individual derives the same utility. The slope of this curve represents the rate at which the individual is willing to trade X for Y while remaining equally well off. This slope (or, more properly, the negative of the slope) is termed the marginal rate of substitution. In the figure the indifference curve is drawn on the assumption of a diminishing marginal rate of substitution.

To discuss rigorously the principle of a diminishing marginal rate of substitution it is easiest first to develop the idea of an *indifference curve*. In Figure 3.2 the curve U_1 represents all the alternative combinations of X and Y for which an individual is equally well off (remember again that all other arguments of the utility function are being held constant). The individual is equally happy consuming, for example, either the combination of goods X_1, Y_1 or the combination X_2, Y_2. This curve representing the trade-off between good X and good Y is called an indifference curve (because, by definition, the individual is indifferent about where he is on this curve). The slope of the curve is negative, showing that if the individual is forced to give up some Y he must be compensated by an additional amount of X to keep him indifferent between the two bundles of goods. The curve is also drawn so that the slope increases as X increases (that is, the slope starts at negative infinity and increases toward 0). This is a graphical representation of the assumption of a diminishing marginal rate of substitution. Let the slope of curve U_1 be denoted by:

$$\frac{dY}{dX}\bigg|_{U\,=\,constant} \qquad\qquad [3.6]$$

where the notation is to indicate that utility is being held constant along the curve. We define the *marginal rate of substitution* (of X for Y) *MRS* to be the negative of this slope:

$$MRS = -\frac{dY}{dX}\bigg|_{U\,=\,constant.} \qquad\qquad [3.7]$$

As has been remarked before, the value of the *MRS* diminishes as X increases. For very low X an individual is willing to give up a large amount of Y to get one more unit of X — the *MRS* is a large positive number. For a high level of X the *MRS* is small — the individual is willing to give up only a small amount of Y for an additional unit of X.

The hamburger-soft drink example with which we started this discussion can be seen as a special case of this general principle. If we let X represent soft drinks and Y represent hamburgers it is easy to see that an individual at a point such as X_1, Y_1 (with relatively few hamburgers) will be unwilling to give up many hamburgers to get an additional soft drink. The *MRS* (of soft drinks for hamburgers) is low. At X_2, Y_2, on the other hand, the individual has relatively many hamburgers and is more willing to trade these for soft drinks while staying on the same indifference curve.

The assumption of a diminishing marginal rate of substitution is both analytically important and accords well with an intuitive notion that people are progressively less willing to consume more of a commodity as they acquire more of it. An individual's psychic rate of trade-off between commodities depends on how much of those commodities he is currently consuming. We will see in Chapters 4 and 5 how the assumption of a diminishing marginal rate of substitution permits many intuitively plausible results concerning individual behavior to be derived. In later chapters we will examine other psychic trade-offs for the individual. In these situations the two-commodity analogy will prove to be quite useful.

In Figure 3.2 only one indifference curve was drawn. The X, Y quadrant, however, is full of such curves, each corresponding to a different level of utility. Since every bundle of goods yields some level of utility, each point in Figure 3.2 must have an indifference curve passing through it. Indifference curves are similar to contour lines on a map in that they represent lines of equal "altitude" of utility. In Figure 3.3 several indifference curves are shown, to indicate that there are infinitely many in the plane. The level of utility represented by these curves increases as we move in a northeast direction—the utility of curve U_1 is less than that of U_2, which is less than that of U_3. This is because of the assumption made in Figure 3.1: that more goods are preferred to less. As was discussed earlier, we have no way to measure the utility of these curves precisely except to note that the combinations of goods on U_3 are preferred to those on U_2, which are preferred to those on U_1.

Figure 3.3   There Are Many Indifference Curves in the X-Y Plane

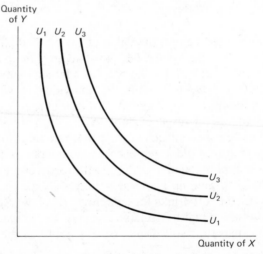

There is an indifference curve passing through each point in the X-Y plane. Each of these curves records combinations of X and Y from which the individual receives a certain level of satisfaction. Movements in a northeast direction represent movements to higher levels of satisfaction.

As an exercise in examining the notion of consistency in tastes, consider the following question: Can an individual's indifference curves intersect? Two intersecting indifference curves are shown in Figure 3.4. We wish to know if this is possible if the individual is to exhibit consistent tastes. Examine the three bundles of goods A, B, and C. Since combination C falls on the indifference curve U_1, it must be the case that C is indifferent to A. Similar reasoning also leads to the result that C is indifferent to B. If the individual is to be consistent, therefore, A and B should be regarded by the individual as yielding equal amounts of utility, since they are both indifferent to combination C. But this is plainly a contradiction of our initial assumption (pictured in Figure 3.1), since point B includes more of both goods than does point A and therefore must be preferred to A. Hence we can conclude that indifference curves cannot intersect if we assume rational and consistent tastes.

Figure 3.4 Intersecting Indifference Curves Imply Inconsistent Tastes

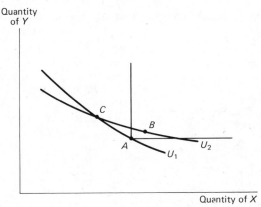

By the definition of indifference curves the individual should regard A, B, and C as all equally desirable. However, point B is plainly preferred to point A by the assumption of nonsatiation (*see* Figure 3.1). Therefore this situation cannot occur if we assume individuals exhibit consistent tastes.

It is possible to develop these notions of individual preferences in many ways. For example, an interesting alternative way of stating the principle of a diminishing marginal rate of substitution uses the mathematical notion of a convex set. A set of points is said to be *convex* if any two points within the set can be joined by a straight line which is contained completely within the set. The assumption of a diminishing MRS is equivalent to the assumption that all combinations of X and Y, which are preferred to or indifferent to a particular combination X^*, Y^*, form a convex set.[5] This is illustrated in Figure 3.5, where all combinations

---

[5] This definition is equivalent to the assumption that the utility function is assumed to be "quasiconcave." What the assumption does *not* say is that the increment to utility gets less and less as we increase X and Y together. Utility functions which possess that property are called "concave" and are a subclass (that is, a special case of) quasiconcave functions. This distinction is important for some economic problems, although these problems will not be encountered in this book. For a more complete discussion *see* Alain C. Enthoven, "Appendix: The Simple Mathematics of Maximization" in Charles J. Hitch and Roland N. McKean, *The Economics of Defense in the Nuclear Age* (Cambridge, Mass.: Harvard University Press, 1960).

preferred to or indifferent to X^*, Y^* are in the shaded area. Any two of these combinations — say X_1, Y_1 and X_2, Y_2 — can be joined by a straight line also contained in the shaded area. In Figure 3.5b this is not true. A line joining X_1, Y_1 and X_2, Y_2 passes outside the shaded area. Therefore the indifference curve through X^*, Y^* in 3.5b does not obey the assumption of a diminishing MRS, since the set of points preferred or indifferent to X^*, Y^* is not convex.

Figure 3.5   The Notion of Convexity as an Alternative Definition of a Diminishing MRS

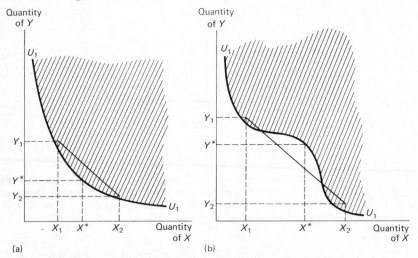

In 3.5a the indifference curve is *convex* (any line joining two points above U_1 is also above U_1). In 3.5b this is not the case, and the curve shown here does not everywhere have a diminishing MRS.

By using the notion of convexity we can show an interesting implication of the assumption that the MRS diminishes as the ratio of X to Y increases. Suppose an individual is indifferent between the combination X_1, Y_1 and X_2, Y_2. What the assumption of a diminishing MRS means then is that the combination $(X_1 + X_2)/2$, $(Y_1 + Y_2)/2$ will be preferred[6] to either of the initial combinations. Intuitively, "well-balanced" bundles of commodities are preferred to bundles which are heavily weighted toward one commodity. This fact is illustrated in Figure 3.6. Since the indifference curve is assumed to be convex, all points on the straight line joining (X_1, Y_1) and (X_2, Y_2) are preferred to or indifferent to these

[6] The combination will be preferred unless the indifference curve is a straight line (a degenerate case of the diminishing MRS assumption), in which case the individual is indifferent between all three combinations.

initial points. This will therefore be true of the point $(X_1 + X_2)/2$, $(Y_1 + Y_2)/2$ which lies at the midpoint of such a line. Indeed, if the indifference curve is strictly convex (not a straight line), any proportional combination of the two indifferent bundles of goods will be preferred to the initial bundles, since it will represent a more balanced combination. Thus strict convexity is equivalent to the assumption of a diminishing *MRS*, and either assumption rules out the possibility of an indifference curve being straight over any portion of its length.

Figure 3.6   Balanced Bundles of Goods Are Preferred to Extreme Bundles

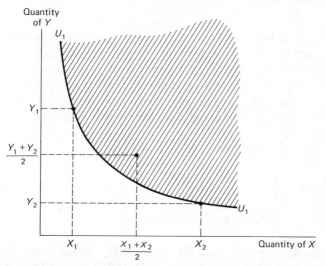

If indifference curves are convex (if they obey the assumption of a diminishing *MRS*), then the line joining any two points which are indifferent will contain points preferred to either of the initial combinations. Intuitively, balanced bundles are preferred to unbalanced ones.

An Alternative Derivation of the *MRS* Using the Concept of Marginal Utility

The development of the *MRS* given here is the preferred one in modern economic discussions because the concepts involved are, at least in principle, observable. It is possible to conceive of asking an individual about his psychic rate of trade-off over various combinations of commodities. The assumption of a diminishing *MRS* can be discussed without the necessity of ever referring to *the* utility function.[7] Originally, however, the concept of the *MRS* was developed using the ideas of utility and

---

[7] *See* the Appendix to Chapter 5 for an elaboration of this point.

marginal utility. Since this derivation provides both insights and some practice in mathematical manipulation, it is presented here.

Suppose an individual ranks goods by a utility function of the form:

Utility $= U(x_1, x_2,..., x_n)$ [3.8]

where $x_1, x_2,..., x_n$ are the amounts of each of n goods he consumes. By the marginal utility of good x_1 we mean the function:

Marginal utility of $x_1 = MU_{x_1} = \dfrac{\partial U}{\partial x_1}$. [3.9]

The marginal utility of x_1 is the extra utility obtained from slightly more x_1 while holding the amount of all other commodities constant. Obviously the value of the marginal utility depends on the point at which the partial derivative is to be evaluated — it depends on how much $x_1, x_2,..., x_n$ the individual is currently consuming. The idea of marginal utility has no very good practical usefulness because of the measurement problems discussed earlier.

We can write the total differential of U as:

$$dU = \frac{\partial U}{\partial x_1} dx_1 + \frac{\partial U}{\partial x_2} dx_2 + \cdots + \frac{\partial U}{\partial x_n} dx_n$$ [3.10]

$$= MU_{x_1} dx_1 + MU_{x_2} dx_2 + \cdots + MU_{x_n} dx_n.$$

Equation 3.10 says that the extra utility obtainable from slightly more $x_1, x_2,..., x_n$ is simply the sum of the additional utility provided by each of these increments.

To develop the concept of MRS consider changing only the level of two goods, X and Y, so as to keep the individual indifferent (that is, $dU = 0$). By Equation 3.10 therefore:

$$dU = 0 = \frac{\partial U}{\partial X} dX + \frac{\partial U}{\partial Y} dY = MU_X dX + MU_Y dY.$$ [3.11]

Notice that all other goods are held constant, hence dU is only affected by changing the quantities of the two goods in question. This is the same assumption which was used in the development of indifference curves in the previous section.

Rearranging terms a bit gives:

$$-\frac{dY}{dX}\bigg|_{U = \text{constant}} = \frac{MU_X}{MU_Y} = \frac{\partial U/\partial X}{\partial U/\partial Y}$$ [3.12]

where the notation is a reminder that Y and X are constrained to change so as to hold the level of utility constant.[8] But Equation 3.12 is simply the definition of the MRS given in Equation 3.7. Hence the result of this section is that the marginal rate of substitution (of X for Y) is equal to the ratio of the marginal utility of X to the marginal utility of Y.[9]

In Chapter 1 it was shown how the assumption of diminishing marginal utility was used by Marshall to solve the paradox of value. Marshall theorized that it is the marginal valuation that an individual places on a good which determines its value: It is the amount that an individual is willing to pay for one more pint of water which determines the price of water. Since it might be thought that this marginal value declines as the quantity of water which is consumed increases, Marshall had shown why water has a low exchange value. Intuitively, it seems clear that the assumption of the decreasing marginal utility of a good is related to the assumption of a decreasing MRS; both concepts refer to the same common-sense idea of an individual tiring of some good as he consumes more of it. Unfortunately, exhibiting the interrelationship between the two concepts involves some degree of mathematical complication and this will not be pursued here.[10] In modern usage the concept of a decreasing rate of trade-off has replaced Marshall's idea, since a discussion of the MRS does not require utility measurement.

Marshall's conception of a diminishing marginal utility plays little

---

[8] Equation 3.12 defines, for a constant level of utility, a relationship between X and Y. This equation is sometimes called the *implicit function theorem* because of this implied relationship.

[9] Using Equation 3.12, it is possible to see why the concept of an MRS is independent of how utility is measured. Suppose an individual's utility function is given by U. Consider any monotonic transformation of U. Call this transformation $F(U)$. Under this new utility function the marginal utility of a particular good, say X, has been changed to:

$$MU'_X = \frac{\partial F}{\partial X} = \frac{dF}{dU} \cdot \frac{\partial U}{\partial X} = F' \cdot MU_X$$

where MU_X is the marginal utility of X according to the original utility function.

However, the MRS (a measure of the individuals' psychic rate of trade-off) has not been changed by this transformation since:

$$MRS \ (X \text{ for } Y) = \frac{MU'_X}{MU'_Y} = \frac{\partial F/\partial X}{\partial F/\partial Y} = \frac{F'\partial U/\partial X}{F'\partial U/\partial Y} = \frac{MU_X}{MU_Y}.$$

[10] The reason for these complications is that the marginal utility of a good, say X, depends not only on the quantity of X consumed but also depends on the quantities of all other goods. Since, in moving along an indifference curve, the quantities of both X and Y, say, are changing, exactly what is happening to the marginal utility of good X alone is unclear. These matters are discussed in detail in J. R. Hicks, *Value and Capital* (Oxford: The Clarendon Press, 1962), Chapters II and III and the Mathematical Appendix. A similar question is discussed in Chapter 11, where the relationship between diminishing marginal "usefulness" and the rate of trade-off is examined mathematically.

more than a tangential role in the development of the theory of individual behavior in this book. Most of the results exhibited by Marshall can be demonstrated without resort to measurability.

Conclusion: Some Broader Issues

In the mass of detail in this chapter one should not lose track of its essential focus on individual tastes. The analysis has attempted to make precise the idea of a psychic trade-off between alternative goods. It is a simple matter to extend this idea to talk about the trade-off between various other individual goals. There are presumably a large number of such trade-off relationships embodied in the broadly defined utility functions discussed earlier in the section on "The Concept of Utility." Economists have chosen to center their attention on those trade-offs which are, at least in principle, quantifiable. Other aspects of individual behavior could conceivably be handled in the same manner if they could be quantified.

A question which has not been specifically posed is: "How are tastes formulated?" Economists assume individuals know their own minds and act in accordance with such preferences. It should be recognized that these tastes are formed by a vast variety of social and biological stimuli. To recognize that tastes are affected by advertising, governmental persuasion, or family relationships is not to negate the theory we have developed. It is hard to imagine what "pure" or "unaffected" tastes might be. It would be interesting to study how tastes are formulated, but this subject has traditionally been outside the purview of economics. Even if it were well known how tastes are formulated and if some of these tastes could be changed, we would still need an analysis of the type developed here to investigate how a person acts given his new set of tastes.

Economists sometimes use the term *consumer sovereignty* to indicate that individuals act in accordance with their own tastes. The use of this term should not, however, be taken to imply that individuals are somehow blessed with an ideal free will. Rather, economists have traditionally elected to examine how choices are made within a given set of tastes. Tastes are assumed to change so slowly and so unpredictably that holding them constant does not great affect the validity of the analysis. Besides, we have found no generally accepted way to analyze how tastes are formed. The development of models of taste formation which shed some light on men's behavior is an important area for future research in both psychology and economics.

CHAPTER 4
Individual Utility Maximization

Introduction

In this chapter we will investigate some of the conclusions which are implied by the assumption that an individual makes choices so as to maximize his utility. This assumption (the first example of the maximization hypothesis to be encountered) is central to most of the theory of the individual that has been developed by economists. To explain consumer behavior it is necessary to assume some measure of rationality in the choices which individuals make. The utility-maximization assumption is both sufficiently flexible to accommodate a wide variety of taste patterns and sufficiently precise to permit interesting results to be derived. It is therefore an important aspect of the theory of choice.

The particular problem studied in this chapter will be how an individual allocates a fixed amount of money in purchasing n goods so as to maximize his utility from these goods. We will first investigate this problem in a graph using two goods, and then will treat the general n good case. The results in both instances will be identical and can be explained at the outset.

In order to maximize his utility, given a fixed amount of money to spend, an individual will buy those quantities of goods for which the psychic rate of trade-off between any two goods (the MRS) is equal to the rate at which the goods can be traded one for the other in the market place.

Since the rate at which one good can be traded for another in the market is given by the ratio of their prices, this result can be restated to say that the individual will equate his MRS (of X for Y) to the ratio of the price of X to the price of Y (P_X/P_Y). This equating of a *psychic trade-off rate* to a *market trade-off rate* is a result common to all individual utility-maximization problems (and to many other types of maximization problems). It will occur again and again throughout this text.

To see the intuitive reasoning behind this result, assume that it were not true that the individual had equated his MRS to the ratio of the prices of goods. Specifically assume that the individual's MRS is equal to 1, that he is willing to trade 1 unit of X for 1 unit of Y and remain equally well off. Assume also that the price of X is $2 per unit and of Y $1 per unit. It is easy to show in this case that the individual can be made better off. Let him give up 1 unit of X and trade it in the market for 2 units of Y. But he only needed 1 extra unit of Y to keep him as happy as before the trade—the second unit of Y is a net addition to his welfare. Therefore, he could not have been allocating his money rationally in the first place. A similar method of reasoning can be used whenever the MRS and the price ratio P_X/P_Y differ. The condition for maximum utility must be the equality of these two magnitudes.

This discussion seems eminently reasonable, but it can hardly be called a proof. Rather, we must now show the result in a rigorous manner, and at the same time illustrate several other important attributes of the maximization process.

The Two-good Case: A Graphic Analysis

Assume[1] the individual has I dollars to allocate between good X and good

[1] The symbol I is used with the obvious implication that it is to represent income. However, I represents only funds which are to be consumed currently. This is to differentiate it from the symbol Y we will use in later chapters for income which can be consumed or saved.

Y. If P_X is the price of good X and P_Y is the price of good Y, then the individual is constrained by:

$$P_X X + P_Y Y \leq I. \qquad\qquad [4.1]$$

He can spend no more than I on the two goods in question. This budget constraint is shown graphically in Figure 4.1. The individual is able to choose only combinations of X and Y in the shaded triangle of the figure.

Figure 4.1   The Individual's Budget Constraint for Two Goods

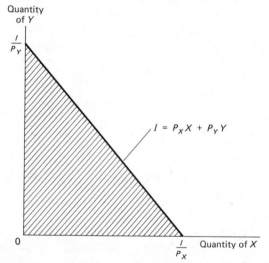

Those combinations of X and Y which the individual can afford are shown in the shaded triangle. If, as we usually assume, the individual prefers more rather than less of every good, the outer boundary of this triangle is the relevant constraint where all of the available funds are spent either on X or on Y. The slope of this straight line boundary is given by $-P_X/P_Y$.

If he spends all of I on good X he can buy I/P_X units of X. Similarly, if he spends all of I on Y he can buy I/P_Y units of Y. The slope of the constraint is easily seen to be $-P_X/P_Y$. For example, suppose hamburgers (Y) cost 20¢, soft drinks (X) cost 10¢, and that the individual has \$1.00 (I) which he must spend on these two goods. In this situation he can buy five hamburgers (I/P_Y), or ten soft drinks (I/P_X), or a variety of combinations of the goods (such as three hamburgers and four soft drinks). The rate at which he can trade soft drinks for hamburgers is two for one, since this is the ratio of the prices of the goods. Economists would say that the *opportunity cost* of one hamburger is two soft drinks.

This budget constraint can be imposed on the individual's indifference curve map to show the utility maximization process. Figure 4.2 illustrates this procedure. The individual would be irrational to choose a point such as A — he can get to a higher utility level just by spending some of the unspent portion of I. Similarly, by reallocating his expenditures he can do better than point B. Point D is out of the question because I is not large enough to permit him to purchase D. It is clear that the position of maximum utility will be at point C where the combination X^*, Y^* is chosen. This is the only point on indifference curve U_2 which can be bought with I dollars; no higher utility level can be bought. C is a point of tangency between the budget constraint and the indifference curve. Therefore:

$$\text{Slope of budget constraint} = \frac{P_X}{P_Y} = \text{slope of indifference curve}$$

$$= \frac{dY}{dX}\bigg|_{U\,=\,\text{Constant}}$$

or

$$\frac{P_X}{P_Y} = -\frac{dY}{dX}\bigg|_{U\,=\,\text{Constant}} = MRS \text{ (of } X \text{ for } Y). \qquad [4.2]$$

Therefore the result is proved — for a utility maximum the MRS should equal the ratio of the prices of the goods. It is obvious from the diagram that if this condition is not fulfilled, the individual could be made better off by reallocating his expenditures.

Figure 4.2 can be given a concrete interpretation by returning to the hamburger-soft drink example. Point A might represent a choice of two hamburgers and three soft drinks. This choice would be plainly inefficient since some part of the individual's dollar will not be spent. With the 30¢ (= $1.00 − 2 × 20¢ − 3 × 10¢) which is left over it would be possible for the individual to buy more of either good and thereby increase his utility. Point B (four hamburgers, two soft drinks) is also inefficient, even though the entire dollar is spent. At this point relatively too much of the dollar has been allocated to hamburger purchases. The individual could enjoy a higher level of utility by trading hamburgers for soft drinks in the market. He would do so until he reaches a point such as C (three hamburgers, four soft drinks) at which the entire dollar is spent *and* his psychic rate of trade-off between soft drinks and hamburgers is exactly equal to that rate which is provided in the market (two for one). Notice that combinations such as D (four hamburgers, five soft drinks), although

Figure 4.2   A Graphic Demonstration of Utility Maximization

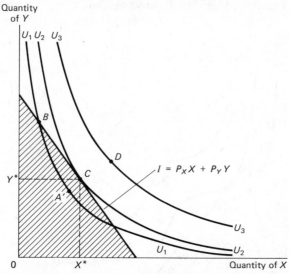

Point C represents the highest utility level which can be reached by the individual, given his budget constraint. The combination X^*, Y^* is therefore the rational way for the individual to allocate his purchasing power. Only for this combination of goods will two conditions hold: All available funds will be spent; and the individuals' psychic rate of trade-off (MRS) will be equal to the rate at which the goods can be traded in the market (P_X/P_Y).

preferred to point C, are unattainable because their total costs exceed $1.00.

The tangency rule is only a necessary condition for a maximum. To see that it is not a sufficient condition consider the indifference curve map shown in Figure 4.3. Here a point of tangency (C) is inferior to a point of nontangency (B). The true maximum is indeed at another point of tangency (A). The failure of the tangency condition to produce an unambiguous maximum can be attributed to the peculiar shape of the indifference curves in Figure 4.3. If the indifference curves are shaped as are those in Figure 4.2, no such problem can arise. But in Chapter 3 it was shown that "normally" shaped indifference curves are a result of the assumption of a diminishing MRS. Therefore, if the MRS is assumed to be diminishing, the condition of tangency (Equation 4.2) is both a necessary and sufficient condition for a maximum. Without this assumption one would have to be very careful in applying the tangency rule.

The n Good Case

The results derived in the case of two goods carry over directly for the case of n goods. Again it can be shown that the MRS between any two

Figure 4.3 Example of an Indifference Curve Map for Which the Tangency
Condition Does Not Insure a Maximum

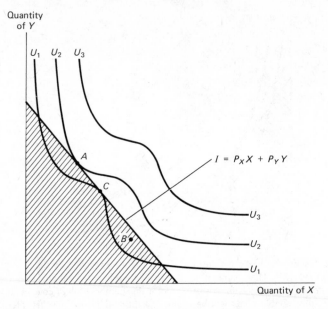

If indifference curves do not obey the assumption of a diminishing MRS, not all points of
tangency (points for which $MRS = P_X/P_Y$) may truly be points of maximum utility. In this
example tangency point C is inferior to many other points, which can also be purchased
with the available funds. In order that the necessary conditions for a maximum (that is, the
tangency conditions) also be efficient, one must assume that the MRS is diminishing.

goods must equal the ratio of the prices of these goods for a utility maximum. However, because the case of n goods cannot be presented graphically, we will adopt a mathematical proof, which provides additional
insights into the maximization assumption.

When there are n goods to choose from the individual's objective is
to maximize his utility from these n goods:

$$\text{Utility} = U(X_1, X_2,..., X_n) \qquad\qquad [4.3]$$

subject to the budget constraint:[2]

[2] The budget constraint has been written as an equality here because, given the assumption of nonsatiation, it is clear that the individual will spend all his income. Remember, the
alternative to spending one's income is not to save it (since this would involve using it in
some future time period which is not explicitly considered) but rather to throw it away.

$$I = P_1X_1 + P_2X_2 + \cdots + P_nX_n. \qquad [4.4]$$

Following the techniques developed in Chapter 2 for maximizing a function subject to a constraint, we set up the Lagrangian expression:

$$L = U(X_1, X_2, \ldots, X_n) - \lambda(P_1X_1 + P_2X_2 + \cdots + P_nX_n - I) \qquad [4.5]$$

Setting the partial derivatives of L (with respect to $X_1, X_2, \ldots, X_n$ and λ) equal to 0 yields $n + 1$ equations representing the necessary conditions for a maximum:

(1.) $\qquad \dfrac{\partial L}{\partial X_1} = \dfrac{\partial U}{\partial X_1} - \lambda P_1 = 0$

(2.) $\qquad \dfrac{\partial L}{\partial X_2} = \dfrac{\partial U}{\partial X_2} - \lambda P_2 = 0$

$$\vdots \qquad\qquad [4.6]$$

(n.) $\qquad \dfrac{\partial L}{\partial X_n} = \dfrac{\partial U}{\partial X_n} - \lambda P_n = 0$

($n + 1$.) $\qquad \dfrac{\partial L}{\partial \lambda} = P_1X_1 + P_2X_2 + \cdots + P_nX_n - I = 0.$

These $n + 1$ equations can now be solved for the optimal $X_1, X_2, \ldots, X_n$ and for λ (*see* the example in the next section to be convinced that such a solution is possible).

Equation 4.6 is necessary only for a maximum. The second-order conditions which insure a maximum are relatively complex. However, the assumption of a diminishing *MRS* (as in the two-good case) is sufficient to insure that any point obeying Equation 4.6 is in fact a true maximum. Hereafter, therefore, only necessary conditions will usually be discussed, with the implication that the assumption of a diminishing *MRS* assures that these conditions are also sufficient.

Equation 4.6 can be rewritten in a variety of interesting ways. For example, for any two goods X_i and X_j we have by Equation 4.6:

$$\frac{\dfrac{\partial U}{\partial X_i}}{\dfrac{\partial U}{\partial X_j}} = \frac{P_i}{P_j}. \qquad [4.7]$$

But in Chapter 3 it was shown that the ratio of the marginal utilities of two goods is in fact identical to the marginal rate of substitution between the two goods. Therefore, the conditions for an optimal allocation of income become:

$$MRS \ (X_i \text{ for } X_j) = \frac{P_i}{P_j}. \tag{4.8}$$

This is exactly the result derived earlier in this chapter; in order to maximize utility the individual should equate his psychic rate of trade-off to the market trade-off rate.

Another result can be derived by solving Equation 4.6 for λ:

$$\lambda = \frac{\dfrac{\partial U}{\partial X_1}}{P_1} = \frac{\dfrac{\partial U}{\partial X_2}}{P_2} = \cdots = \frac{\dfrac{\partial U}{\partial X_n}}{P_n}$$

or $\hspace{6cm}$ [4.9]

$$\lambda = \frac{MU_{X_1}}{P_1} = \frac{MU_{X_2}}{P_2} = \cdots = \frac{MU_{X_n}}{P_n}.$$

This equation says that at the utility-maximizing point each good should yield the same marginal utility per dollar spent on that good. Each good should therefore have an identical (marginal) benefit to (marginal) cost ratio. If this were not true one good would promise more "marginal enjoyment per dollar" than some other good, and funds would not be optimally allocated.

Although the reader is again warned against talking very confidently about marginal utility, what Equation 4.9 says is that an extra dollar should yield the same "additional utility" no matter which good it is spent on. The common value for this extra utility is given by the Lagrangian Multiplier of I (that is, by λ). Therefore, λ can be regarded as the marginal utility of an extra dollar of consumption expenditure (the marginal utility of "income").

One final way to rewrite the necessary conditions for a maximum is:

$$P_i = \frac{MU_i}{\lambda} \tag{4.10}$$

for every good i.[3] This equation says that for every good which an indi-

---

[3] It should be pointed out that this equation (and the others which have been derived from the necessary conditions) holds only if the good in question is actually consumed. (*See* Problem 4 at the end of Part II for an illustration of why certain goods may not be consumed at all and how the necessary conditions must be modified to take account of this possibility.)

vidual buys, the price of that good represents his evaluation of the utility of the last unit consumed. The price (obviously) represents how much he is willing to pay for that last unit.

An Example of Constrained Utility Maximization

This analysis of utility maximization can be illustrated with a specific numerical example. Suppose that an individual receives utility from the amount of food, clothing, and shelter he consumes. Let:

X_1 = the amount of food consumed
X_2 = the amount of clothing consumed
X_3 = the amount of shelter consumed

and suppose

$$\text{Utility} = U(X_1, X_2, X_3) = 5 \log X_1 + 3 \log X_2 + 2 \log X_3. \qquad [4.11]$$

Assume the individual has \$100 to spend on these items and that the price of each item is:

P_1 = Price of food = \$10
P_2 = Price of clothing = \$2
P_3 = Price of shelter = \$4.

The individual's "budget constraint" is given by:

$$\begin{aligned} 100 &= P_1 X_1 + P_2 X_2 + P_3 X_3 \\ &= 10 X_1 + 2 X_2 + 4 X_3. \end{aligned} \qquad [4.12]$$

He could calculate all possible combinations of X_1, X_2, and X_3 which obey the budget constraint, and then choose the one which gives U its highest value. It is much easier, however, to use the Lagrangian Multiplier method. In this problem the Lagrangian expression is given by:

$$L = 5 \log X_1 + 3 \log X_2 + 2 \log X_3 - \lambda(10X_1 + 2X_2 + 4X_3 - 100). \quad [4.13]$$

The necessary conditions for a maximum are (using the rules for partial differentiation introduced earlier):

$$\frac{\partial L}{\partial X_1} = \frac{5}{X_1} - 10\lambda = 0$$

$$\frac{\partial L}{\partial X_2} = \frac{3}{X_2} - 2\lambda = 0$$

$$\frac{\partial L}{\partial X_3} = \frac{2}{X_3} - 4\lambda = 0$$ [4.14]

$$\frac{\partial L}{\partial \lambda} = - (10X_1 + 2X_2 + 4X_3 - 100) = 0.$$

There are four equations in four unknowns, X_1, X_2, X_3, and λ. These are easily worked by solving for X_1, X_2, and X_3 in terms of λ:

$$X_1 = \frac{1}{2\lambda}$$

$$X_2 = \frac{3}{2\lambda}$$ [4.15]

$$X_3 = \frac{1}{2\lambda}$$

for $\lambda \neq 0$

and plugging these into the budget constraint:

$$10\left(\frac{1}{2\lambda}\right) + 2\left(\frac{3}{2\lambda}\right) + 4\left(\frac{1}{2\lambda}\right) = 100$$

or

$$\frac{5}{\lambda} + \frac{3}{\lambda} + \frac{2}{\lambda} = 100$$

or

$$100\lambda = 10$$

or

$$\lambda = \frac{1}{10}.$$

Hence,

$$X_1 = \frac{1}{2\left(\frac{1}{10}\right)} = 5$$

$$X_2 = \frac{3}{2\left(\frac{1}{10}\right)} = 15 \qquad\qquad [4.16]$$

$$X_3 = \frac{1}{2\left(\frac{1}{10}\right)} = 5.$$

The individual will maximize his utility, given his \$100 budget, by buying 5 units of food, 15 units of clothing, and 5 units of shelter. Here $\lambda = 1/10$ — an extra dollar of income would yield approximately $1/10$ "units" of additional utility. If the extra dollar were spent on, say, clothing, this would buy $1/2$ unit of clothing. Since $\partial U/\partial X_2 = 3/X_2 = 3/15 = 1/5$, this $1/2$ additional unit of clothing could be translated into $1/10$ ($= 1/2 \times 1/5$) unit of additional utility.

This example is not realistic for a variety of reasons. The most important of these is that the utility function chosen assumes that the goods are "independent" in the sense that the marginal utility of any one good does not depend on the quantities of the other goods consumed. Intuitively this assumption appears unreasonable. Surely the extra utility which an individual obtains, say, from one more piece of clothing will depend on how much shelter he currently has. Since the assumption of independence rules out such important interrelationships among goods, the assumption may be of questionable usefulness in real-world investigations.[4]

A second (and related) unrealistic feature of the utility function is that the optimal solution requires a fixed proportion of income always to be spent on food, clothing, and shelter. These proportions are $1/2$, $3/10$, and $2/10$ respectively, and will not change if either income or the goods prices change. This assumption seems unreasonable from an empirical point of view (surely a rich man spends less than half of his income on food) and again indicates the artificial nature of the example.

The problem is useful, however, in that it demonstrates in a convincing fashion that the Lagrangian method can indeed be used to solve for the optimal consumption quantities. While more "realistic" examples can also be solved, they would be considerably less tractable.

[4] Several interesting theoretical curiosities result from the assumption of independence, however (*see* Problem 5 of Part II).

Demand Functions

In principle it will always be possible to solve the necessary conditions of a utility maximum (*see* Equation 4.6) for the optimal levels of X_1, $X_2,..., X_n$ (and λ) as functions of all the prices and income. As was clear from the graph analysis of the two-good case, the optimal quantities chosen will depend only on the position of the budget constraint and on the shape of the individual's indifference curves. This geometrical result can be generalized for the case of n goods to conclude that the quantities of $X_1, X_2,..., X_n$ "demanded" by the individual will depend on the shape of his utility function and on $P_1, P_2,..., P_n$ and I. Written mathematically this can be expressed as n "demand functions" of the form:

$$X_1 = D_1(P_1, P_2,..., P_n, I)$$
$$X_2 = D_2(P_1, P_2,..., P_n, I)$$

[4.17]

$$X_n = D_n(P_1, P_2,..., P_n, I).$$

Once we know the functions $D_1, D_2,..., D_n$ and the values of P_1, $P_2,..., P_n$ and I we can "predict" how much of each good the individual will buy. In the next chapter we will be interested in what happens to the optimal amount of, say, X_1 when P_1 changes. We will also investigate what happens to X_1 when the price of another good changes or when I changes. Such questions involve the study of "comparative statics" — we are interested in comparing the optimal allocation of I under alternative circumstances. Such questions are of obvious interest in analyzing individual economic behavior.

One comparative statics "theorem" can easily be demonstrated here. If we were to double all prices and I (indeed if we were to multiply them all by any positive constant) the optimal quantities demanded would remain unchanged. Doubling all prices and I only changes the units we count in, not the "real" quantity of goods demanded.[5] This result can be seen in a number of ways, although perhaps the easiest is through a graphic approach. Referring to Figures 4.1 and 4.2, it is clear that if we double P_X and P_Y and I we will not affect the graph of the budget constraint. Hence X^*, Y^* will still be the combination which is chosen. $P_X X + P_Y Y = I$ is the same constraint as $2P_X X + 2P_Y Y = 2I$. Somewhat more technically we can write this result as saying that for any good X_i:

$$X_i = D_i(P_1, P_2,..., P_n, I) = D_i(tP_1, tP_2,..., tP_n, tI)$$

[4.18]

[5] Note that the assumption that prices do not enter into the utility function plays a role here.

for any $t > 0$. Functions which obey the property illustrated in Equation 4.18 are said to be homogeneous of degree 0.[6] Hence we have shown that individual *demand functions are homogeneous of degree 0 in all prices and income*. Changing all prices and income in the same proportions will not affect the physical quantities of goods demanded.

Conclusion and Summary

This chapter presents the primary result that can be derived from the assumption of individual utility maximization: An individual will equate his MRS for any two goods to the price ratio of these goods. This tangency condition, when combined with the assumption of a diminishing MRS, assures a true maximum. In the following chapters we will use this result of the maximization principle in a number of ways to illustrate individual behavior. The reader should keep in mind several general assumptions which underlie this principle:

1. The individual can rationally order his preferences and attempts to maximize his own welfare.

2. The individual is assumed to have a diminishing MRS between any two goods. If this were not true our tangency solutions might not be true maximum points.

3. The scope of the *ceteris paribus* assumption holds constant all factors affecting individual welfare except those specifically being analyzed.

4. The individual is assumed to be a *price taker* in that he accepts market prices as given and adjusts his behavior to these prices.

5. The individual has full information about those options open to him. If he had only partial information we would have to inquire how much he would be willing to pay to obtain further information. This problem will be explicitly considered in Chapter 9.

---

[6] More generally, a function $f(X_1, X_2,..., X_n)$ is said to be homogeneous of degree k if $f(tX_1, tX_2,..., tX_n) = t^k f(X_1, X_2,..., X_n)$ for any $t > 0$. The most common cases of homogeneous functions are $k = 0$ and $k = 1$. If f is homogeneous of degree 0, doubling all of its arguments leaves f unchanged in value. If f is homogeneous of degree 1 doubling all its arguments will double the value of f.

CHAPTER 5

Comparative Statics Analyses of Utility Maximization

Introduction

In this chapter we will study the change in the quantity demanded of a particular good as a result of changed "conditions." In particular, the effect of changes in income, the effect of changes in the price of the good, and the effect of changes in the price of some other good will be investigated. We will be interested in comparing the new utility-maximizing choices which are made with those which prevailed before conditions changed. Because we are only interested in comparing these two optimal positions, not in studying the "dynamics" of movement from one position to the next, this type of investigation is called *comparative statics* analysis.

Two warnings about comparative statics analysis should be offered at the outset. First, the importance of the *ceteris paribus* assumption must be clearly recognized. We are only changing one variable at a time; everything else is being held constant. Not only are all other variables in the demand function being held constant but the tastes of the individual are also held constant. In graphic terms, we will be keeping the individual's *indifference curves fixed* and studying the effects of *shifting the budget constraint* to alternative positions.

Second, the reader is warned about the general notion of changing "conditions." Ideally, we would like to explain why conditions have changed. Instead of hypothesizing that, say, the price of potatoes has risen, we would be more interested in asking *why* the price of potatoes has risen. This chapter is only a first step in answering this larger question, which cannot be discussed in detail until Part IV.

Changes in Income

As total expenditures rise, it is natural to expect that the quantity of each good purchased will also increase. This situation is illustrated in Figure 5.1. As expenditures increase from I_1 to I_2 to I_3, the quantity of X demanded increases from X_1 to X_2 to X_3. Also the quantity of Y increases from Y_1 to Y_2 to Y_3. Notice that the budget lines I_1, I_2, and I_3 are all parallel reflecting the fact that we are only changing income not the relative prices of X and Y. Since the ratio P_X/P_Y stays constant, the utility-maximizing conditions also require that the MRS stay constant as the individual moves to higher levels of satisfaction. The MRS is therefore the same at point X_3, Y_3 as it is at X_1, Y_1.

The information from Figure 5.1 can be used to construct *Engel Curves*. These curves record the relationship between the quantity of X purchased and total expenditures.[1] In Figure 5.2 these Engel Curves are drawn. Notice that these curves are not necessarily straight lines. The demand for some "luxury" goods may increase proportionately more rapidly than income, whereas the demand for "necessities" may grow proportionately less rapidly than income.

In Figures 5.1 and 5.2 both X and Y increase as income increases — $\partial X/\partial I$ and $\partial Y/\partial I$ are both positive. This might be considered the usual situation, and goods which exhibit this property are called *normal goods*.

[1] The curves are named for the Prussian economist Ernst Engel (1821–1896) who was one of the first persons to study systematically the relation between the quantity of a good demanded and income. His finding that the percent of income spent on food declines as incomes rises is called "Engel's Law."

Figure 5.1 Effect of Increasing Income on Quantities of X and Y Chosen

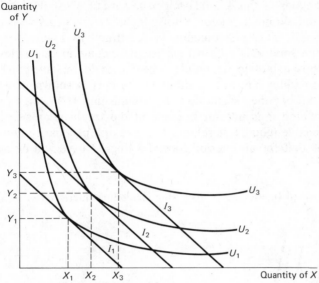

As income increases from I_1 to I_2 to I_3 the optimal (utility-maximizing) choices of X and Y are shown by the successively higher points of tangency. Notice that the budget constraint shifts in a parallel way because its slope (given by P_X/P_Y) does not change.

Figure 5.2 Engel Curves Derived from the Individual's Indifference Curves

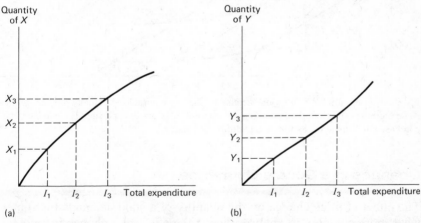

(a)

(b)

Engel Curves depict the relationship between total expenditures and the quantity of a particular good purchased. In the two panels of this figure both goods are normal because the quantity purchased increases as income increases. The good pictured in 5.2a is, however, a "necessity" in the sense that the *fraction* of expenditures devoted to X declines as income increases. On the other hand, good Y (5.2b) is a "luxury."

There are goods, however, where quantity decreases as income increases. Some examples of these goods might be rot-gut whiskey, potatoes, and second-hand clothing. A good Z for which $\partial Z/\partial I$ is negative is called an *inferior good*. This phenomenon is illustrated in Figure 5.3. In this diagram the good Z is inferior because as income increases less of it is actually chosen. Notice that indifference curves do not have to be "oddly" shaped to exhibit inferiority; although the curves shown in Figure 5.3 continue to obey the assumption of a diminishing MRS, they exhibit inferiority. Good Z is inferior because of the way it relates to the other goods available (good Y here), not because of a peculiarity unique to it.[2] It is clear that for an inferior good the Engel Curve will be negatively sloped.

Figure 5.3   An Indifference Curve Map Exhibiting Inferiority

Quantity of Y

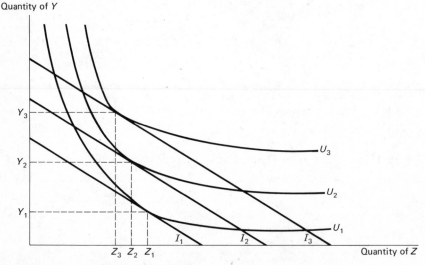

In this diagram good Z is inferior because the quantity purchased actually declines as income increases. Y is a normal good (as it must be if there are only two goods available), and purchases of Y increase as total expenditures increase.

Changes in a Good's Own Price

The effect of price change on the quantity of a good demanded is somewhat more complex to analyze than is the effect of a change in income.

[2] If there are only two goods to choose from, however, both of them cannot be inferior. A rise in income must, by our assumption of nonsatiation, be spent on something. In Figure 5.3 purchases of Y will increase markedly when income increases.

Geometrically this is because changing a price involves not only changing the level of the budget constraint but also changing its slope. Consequently, moving to the new utility-maximizing choice will involve not only moving to another indifference curve but will also necessitate changing the *MRS*. When a price changes, therefore, two analytically different effects come into play. One of these is a *substitution effect*—even if the individual were to stay on the *same* indifference curve he would reallocate his consumption pattern in order to equate his *MRS* to the new price ratio. A second effect, the *income effect,* arises because a price change necessarily changes an individual's "real" income—he, in fact, will not stay on the same indifference curve on which he started.

Figure 5.4   A Demonstration of the Income and Substitution Effects of a Fall in the Price of X

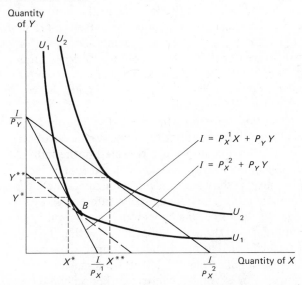

When the price of X falls from P_X^1 to P_X^2, the utility-maximizing choice shifts from X^*, Y^* to X^{**}, Y^{**}. This movement can be broken down into two analytically different effects; first, a movement along the initial indifference curve to point B where the *MRS* is equal to the new price ratio (the substitution effect); second (the income effect), involves a movement to a higher level of utility since real income has increased. In the diagram both the substitution and income effects cause more X to be bought when its price declines. Notice that the point I/P_Y is the same as before. This is because P_Y has not changed, and so the point I/P_Y appears on both the old and new budget constraints.

These two effects are illustrated in Figure 5.4. The individual is initially maximizing his utility (subject to his total expenditures, I) by consuming the combination X^*, Y^*. The initial budget constraint is

$I = P_X^1 X + P_Y Y$. Now suppose that the price of X falls to P_X^2. The new budget constraint is given by the equation $I = P_X^2 X + P_Y Y$ in Figure 5.4. It is clear that the new position of maximum utility is at X^{**}, Y^{**} where the new budget line is tangent to the indifference curve U_2. The movement to this new point can be viewed as being composed of two effects. First, the change in the slope of the budget constraint would have motivated the individual to move to point B even if he had to stay on his original indifference curve U_1. The dashed line in Figure 5.4 has the same slope as the new budget constraint $(I = P_X^2 X + P_Y Y)$, but is drawn to be tangent to U_1 because we are conceptually holding his "real" income (that is, utility) constant. A relatively lower price for X causes the individual to move from X^*, Y^* to B if we do not allow him to be made better off as a result of the lower price. This movement is a graphic demonstration of the *substitution effect*. The further move from B to the optimal point X^{**}, Y^{**} is analytically identical to the kind of change exhibited in Figure 5.1. for changes in income. Because the price of X has fallen, the individual has a greater "real" income and can afford a utility level (U_2) which is greater than that he could previously attain. If X is a normal good the individual will demand more of it in response to this increase in purchasing power. This observation explains the origin of the term *income effect* for the movement.

It is important to realize that the individual does not actually move from X^*, Y^* to B and then to X^{**}, Y^{**}. We never observe the point B; only the two optimal positions are reflected in the individual's behavior. However, the notion of income and substitution effects is analytically valuable because it shows that a price change affects the quantity of X which is demanded in two conceptually different ways.

In order to reinforce this conceptual distinction it is useful to return to the hamburger-soft drink example. Suppose that the price of soft drinks fell to 5¢ (remember that previously soft drinks were assumed to sell for 10¢). This price change has the effect of increasing the individual's purchasing power. For example, whereas earlier he could buy ten soft drinks with his dollar he can now buy twenty. He will probably not choose such an unbalanced consumption bundle, but he could, and therefore the price decline represents an increase in his welfare. The individual will, however, choose some different combination of hamburgers and soft drinks than he did before—if only because his previous selection (three hamburgers, four soft drinks) now leaves him with 20¢ extra in purchasing power. In moving to this new preferred consumption choice two different effects come into play. First, even if we conceptually hold constant the individual's "real income" (that is if we *compensate* for the positive effect that the price change has on purchasing power), he will still adjust his expenditures so that his MRS is brought into line with the new price ratio (now four to one). This compensated response we call the *substitution effect*. Even at a constant real income there is an incentive to substitute soft drinks for hamburgers. In actuality, real income has also increased, and in order to assess the total effect of the price change on the demand for soft drinks we must also investigate the income effect.

Figure 5.5   A Demonstration of the Income and Substitution Effects of an Increase in the Price of Good X

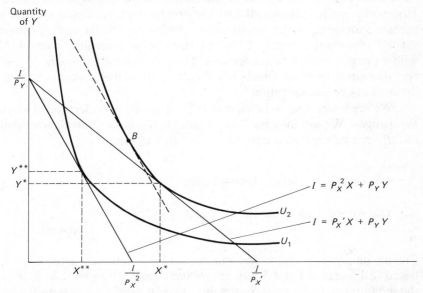

When the price of X increases, the budget constraint shifts inward. The movement from the initial utility maximizing point (X^*, Y^*) to the new point (X^{**}, Y^{**}) can be analyzed as two separate effects. The substitution effect would be depicted as a movement to point B on the initial indifference curve (U_2). The price increase would, however, also create a loss of purchasing power and a consequent movement to a lower indifference curve. This is the income effect. In the diagram both the income and substitution effects cause the quantity of X to fall as a result of the increase in its price. Again, the point I/P_Y is not affected by the change in the price of X.

If the price of good X were to increase, a similar analysis would be used. In Figure 5.5 the budget line has been shifted inward because of an increase in the price of X from P_X^1 to P_X^2. The movement from the initial point of utility maximization (X^*, Y^*) to the new point (X^{**}, Y^{**}) can be decomposed into two effects. First, even if the individual could stay on his initial indifference curve (U_2) he would substitute Y for X and move along U_2 to point B. However, because he has less purchasing power after the price of X rises, the individual must move to a lower level of utility. This movement is again called the income effect. Notice in Figure 5.5 that both the income and substitution effects work in the same direction and cause the quantity of X demanded to be reduced in response to an increase in its price.

Substitution and income effects can be derived mathematically. The mathematics utilized in this derivation is rather difficult because it involves taking the derivative of the first-order conditions for a maximum. A complete mathematical proof will not, therefore, be attempted here. However a written, quasimathematical proof will be presented because a precise statement of the income and substitution effects can illuminate several important aspects of the reactions of an individual confronted with a price change. The reader should bear in mind that the strictly correct derivation of these effects is a direct result of the assumption of individual utility maximization.

We are interested in the change in the quantity of X demanded when P_X changes: We are interested in $\partial X/\partial P_X$. It has been shown above that $\partial X/\partial P_X$ can be separated into the sum of two effects:

$$\frac{\partial X}{\partial P_X} = \text{Substitution effect} + \text{Income effect.} \qquad [5.1]$$

The substitution effect can be denoted by $\left.\dfrac{\partial X}{\partial P_X}\right|_{U\,=\,\text{Constant.}}$

This is simply a mathematical statement of the definition already illustrated in Figures 5.4 and 5.5. It is relatively easy to see that, so long as the indifference curves are "normally" shaped (again the assumption of a diminishing MRS), this effect is *always negative*. If P_X falls then P_X/P_Y decreases and, for a utility maximum, the MRS (of X for Y) must also decrease. The only way for this to happen, when utility is held constant, is for X to rise (and Y to fall). Similarly, if P_X rises, P_X/P_Y increases and the conditions for a maximum require that the MRS (of X for Y) must also increase. Again, since utility is held constant, the only way for this to happen is for X to fall. The assumption of a diminishing MRS therefore implies that the substitution effect is negative. The reader should check this result graphically for himself.

A mathematical statement of the income effect is somewhat more difficult to derive. What we are interested in is the movement from point B in Figures 5.4 and 5.5 to the optimal combination X^{**}, Y^{**}. For small changes this is equal to $\partial X/\partial I$ times the change in real income that results from a change in P_X. But the change in real income resulting from a change in P_X is proportional to how important X is in the individual's total expenditure. If expenditure on X is large then the effect of a price change on the individual's real income will be large. If X is a relatively unimportant good then the effect on the individual's real income of a price change will be correspondingly small. Therefore the income effect of a price change is approximately equal to $-X\, \partial X/\partial I$ where the minus sign indicates that P_X and real income move in opposite directions. The sign of the income effect is not determinate. By referring back to the section on "Changes in Income" it can be seen that if good X is a normal good $\partial X/\partial I$ is positive. Hence the total income effect is negative[3] (since $-X$ times a positive number is negative). This says a rise in the price of X will reduce real income which will lead the individual to reduce his purchases of X (since it is a normal good). On the other hand, if X is an inferior good ($\partial X/\partial I < 0$) then the income effect will be positive. A price increase, by lowering real income, induces the individual to buy *more* of the inferior good.

Using the results of the two previous paragraphs, it is possible to rewrite Equation 5.1 as:[4]

$$\frac{\partial X}{\partial P_X} = \frac{\partial X}{\partial P_X}\bigg|_{U\,=\,\text{Constant}} - X\frac{\partial X}{\partial I} \qquad [5.2]$$

where the first term is the substitution effect and the second term is the income effect.

Equation 5.2 can be used to investigate the likely sign of $\partial X/\partial P_X$. So long as X is a normal good, both the income and substitution effects are negative, hence $\partial X/\partial P_X$ is negative. The *ceteris paribus* result of an increase in the price of X is to decrease the quantity of X demanded. This result must be considered the usual case. It forms the basis for the belief that most demand curves are negatively sloped—that price and quantity move in opposite directions.

If X is an inferior good, the sign of $\partial X/\partial P_X$ is indeterminate. The substitution effect is negative whereas the income effect is positive. It is possible that this positive income effect is large enough to produce the "perverse" result that $\partial X/\partial P_X$ becomes positive—that is, that the demand

[3] Some authors refer to "the income effect" as being defined as $X\, \partial X/\partial I$ (without the minus sign). In this case "positive" and "negative" income effects will be defined in a reversed way from those developed here. The definition in the text is adopted so that there is no ambiguity in statements such as "the income and substitution effects work in the same direction."

[4] Equation 5.2 is sometimes referred to as the "Slutsky Equation" after the Russian statistician Eugen Slutsky who first discovered it. For a detailed derivation of this equation *see* Paul A. Samuelson, *Foundations of Economic Analysis* (Cambridge, Mass.: Harvard University Press, 1947), Chapter 5.

curve is positively sloped. While such a result is rare, it is not impossible. For example, the English economist Robert Giffen is said to have observed that in nineteenth-century Ireland, when the price of potatoes rose, people consumed *more* of them.[5] This peculiar result can be explained by referring to Equation 5.2. Potatoes were not only inferior goods but made up a large portion of the Irish people's expenditures.

Figure 5.6   Giffen's Paradox

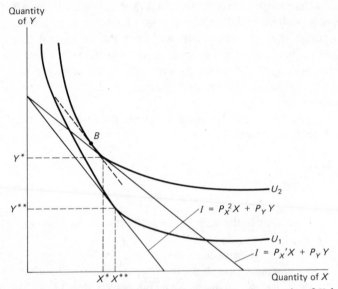

The total effect of an increase in the price of X is to *increase* the quantity of X demanded. This happens because the negative substitution effect (the movement from X^*, Y^* to point B) is outweighed by a strong positive income effect resulting from the inferiority of good X (compare Figure 5.3). Not every inferior good need exhibit Giffen's Paradox.

A rise in the price of potatoes therefore reduced real income substantially. Because of this, the Irish were forced to cut back on "luxury" food consumption and, in fact, buy more potatoes. The possibility of $\partial X/\partial P_X$ being positive has come to be known as Giffen's Paradox. The Paradox is illustrated graphically in Figure 5.6. In response to a rise in the price of good X actually more of it is demanded. Even though the substitution effect is (as always) negative, the "perverse" income effect is sufficiently strong

[5] Whether Giffen's Paradox was actually observed is subject to considerable debate. There is some evidence that the story is completely apocryphal. In any case, as George Stigler points out in *The Theory of Price*, third edition (New York: Macmillan and Company, pp. 24 and 62–63) it *could* have happened. The Paradox does provide a useful example in understanding income and substitution effects, and perhaps the myth should be maintained for its pedagogic value.

to make the total effect of the price change positive. Real income *falls* and, since X is an inferior good, the demand for X *increases*. The occurrence of this Paradox in the real world is extremely rare — not only must the good under consideration be inferior but the positive income effect must be large enough to outweigh the negative substitution effect. Such strong income effects will not occur unless the good in question occupies a major position in the individual's expenditures (as was the case for potatoes in Ireland) or the good is "extremely" inferior. As a general rule, then, we can regard $\partial X/\partial P_X$ as being negative without much chance of being contradicted by experience.[6]

Changes in the Price of Another Good

It is obvious from Figure 5.4 that a change in the price of X also affects the quantity of Y demanded. An expression directly analogous to Equation 5.2 can be derived for the change in Y when P_X changes:

$$\frac{\partial Y}{\partial P_X} = \left.\frac{\partial Y}{\partial P_X}\right|_{U = \text{Constant}} - X\frac{\partial Y}{\partial I}. \qquad [5.3]$$

The first term is the substitution effect; the second term is the income effect. The income effect here is slightly different from that in Equation 5.2; it represents $\partial Y/\partial I$ times the change in income as a result of changing P_X. Again the sign of $\partial Y/\partial P_X$ is indeterminate. In the two-good case the substitution effect *must* be positive, as can be seen in Figure 5.4. When utility is held constant an increase in the price of X will tend to cause purchases of Y to increase. This is again a result of the assumption of a diminishing MRS. If Y is a normal good the income effect is negative. Therefore $\partial Y/\partial P_X$ may be either positive or negative depending on the relative strength of these two effects. In Figure 5.4 $\partial Y/\partial P_X$ happens to be negative (the quantity of Y chosen increases from Y^* to Y^{**} in response to a decrease in the price of X, since the income effect of this change outweighs the substitution effect), but it would be an easy matter to draw a situation where the reverse was the case.

The importance of Equation 5.3 is to show clearly the implications of utility maximization. Whenever a price changes this will affect all goods demanded, not only the good whose price has changed. These changes can always be broken down into substitution and income components, and one must analyze the strength and sign of these two components to determine the total change in the quantity demanded.

---

[6] Remember that such cases as the cheap lipstick example have been ruled out as being "irrational."

For example, consider once again the changing quantities chosen of hamburgers and soft drinks as the price of a soft drink falls from 10¢ to 5¢. We have already discussed the substitution and income effects that such a change will have on the number of soft drinks bought. Similar effects come into play when examining the change in the number of hamburgers chosen. The substitution effect predicts that fewer hamburgers will be purchased. Since hamburgers are now relatively more expensive (that is, soft drinks are now relatively cheaper) the initial level of utility can be achieved at minimal cost by substituting soft drinks for hamburgers. However, to calculate the total effect on hamburger purchases the income effect of the price change must also be taken into account. As a result of the fall in the price of soft drinks the individual now has a higher real income and may use some of this increased purchasing power to buy more hamburgers. The total effect of the price change on hamburger purchases is therefore ambiguous. The substitution effect works to decrease hamburger purchases, whereas the income effect works to increase such purchases.

Substitutes and Complements

For the case of n goods, equations identical to 5.2 and 5.3 apply to each good. Specifically, it can be shown that:

$$\frac{\partial x_i}{\partial p_j} = \frac{\partial x_i}{\partial p_j}\bigg|_{U = \text{Constant}} - x_j \frac{\partial x_i}{\partial I} \qquad [5.4]$$

for any i and j (including $i = j$). This simply says that the change in the price of any good (here good j) induces income and substitution effects which may change the quantity of every good which is demanded. Equation 5.4 can be used to discuss the idea of substitutes and complements. Intuitively these ideas are rather simple. Two goods are *substitutes* if one good may, as a result of changed conditions, replace the other in use. Some examples are: tea and coffee, hamburgers and hot dogs, or, alcohol and drugs. *Complements,* on the other hand, are goods which "go together" such as: coffee and cream, fish and chips, or brandy and cigars. In some sense "substitutes" substitute for one another in the utility function, whereas "complements" complement each other.

There are two different ways of making these intuitive ideas precise. The most direct definition would seem to be to define x_i to be a substitute for x_j if:

$$\frac{\partial x_i}{\partial p_j} > 0 \qquad [5.5]$$

and a complement if:

$$\frac{\partial x_i}{\partial p_j} < 0.$$

Two goods are substitutes (complements) if a rise in the price of one causes the demand for the other to increase (decrease). For example, if the price of coffee rises, the demand for tea might be expected to increase (they are substitutes), whereas the demand for cream might decrease (coffee and cream are complements). Equation 5.4 makes it clear that this definition is a "gross" definition in that it includes both income and substitution effects. Since these effects are in fact combined in any real-world observation we can make, it might be reasonable always to speak only of "gross" substitutes and "gross" complements.

There are, however, several things which are undesirable about the definitions in Equation 5.5. Most important of these failures is that the definitions are not symmetric. It is possible by the definitions for X to be a substitute for Y and at the same time for Y to be a complement of X. The presence of income effects can produce paradoxical results. For example, consider two consumption items: food (X) and yo-yos (Y). If the price of food (P_X) rises, it may be that $\partial Y / \partial P_X < 0$. Because food is an important item in consumption, a rise in its price will substantially reduce real income and may reduce the demand for Y even though there may be a substitution effect favoring an increase in yo-yo consumption as a replacement for food. On the other hand, if the price of yo-yos (P_Y) changes, it is quite likely that $\partial X / \partial P_Y$ will be positive. A change in the price of yo-yos will not induce important income effects and the principal effect may be a substitution of food for yo-yos. Consequently, Y would be termed a "complement" for X, whereas X would be classed as a "substitute" for Y. Clearly this assymetry can lead to possible confusion. For this reason an alternative definition of substitutes and complements is sometimes used: x_i and x_j are said to be substitutes in the "Hicksian" sense[7] if:

$$\left.\frac{\partial x_i}{\partial p_j}\right|_{U = \text{Constant}} > 0 \qquad\qquad [5.6a]$$

and complements in the Hicksian sense if:

$$\left.\frac{\partial x_i}{\partial p_j}\right|_{U = \text{Constant}} < 0. \qquad\qquad [5.6b]$$

---

[7] Named for John R. Hicks, who developed these ideas in his *Value and Capital, op. cit.*

The definitions of Equation 5.6 look only at the substitution terms to determine whether two goods are substitutes or complements. This definition is both intuitively appealing (because it looks only at the shape of an indifference curve) and theoretically desirable (because it is a symmetric definition). Once x_i and x_j have been discovered to be substitutes they stay substitutes, no matter in which direction the definition is applied. As a matter of fact, it can be shown that the definitions are identical in that:

$$\frac{\partial x_i}{\partial p_j}\bigg|_{U \,=\, \text{Constant}} = \frac{\partial x_j}{\partial p_i}\bigg|_{U \,=\, \text{Constant}} \qquad [5.7]$$

Cross-substitution effects are completely symmetric—the substitution effect of a change in p_i on good x_j is identical to the substitution effect of a change in p_j on the quantity of x_i chosen. This symmetry is important in both theoretical and empirical work. Unfortunately, the symmetry arises out of the sufficient conditions for a utility maximum, and it is difficult to present an intuitive explanation of why this should be so. For a mathematical derivation of the symmetry condition, the reader should consult the works by Samuelson and Hicks cited previously.

Referring back to Figure 5.4 the differences between the two definitions of substitutes and complements are easily demonstrated. In this figure X and Y are gross complements, but they are substitutes by the Hicksian definition. $\partial Y/\partial P_X$ turns out to be negative (X and Y are gross complements) because the (positive) substitution effect is outweighed by the (negative) income effect (a fall in the price of X causes real income to increase greatly and consequently actual purchases of Y increase). As the figure makes clear, if there are only two goods from which to choose, they must be Hicksian substitutes. This fact is obvious when a simple geometric argument is used identical to that used to prove the own-price substitution effect is negative. Because we have assumed a diminishing MRS, the own-price substitution effect must be negative, and consequently the cross-price substitution effect must be positive when only two goods are considered. By Equation 5.6a the two goods would then be classified as Hicksian substitutes. Indeed, it can be shown that there can only be a "few" complementary relationships in the Hicksian sense.[8] Hicksian substitution is the prevalent relationship among goods.

Although it would be necessary to use three goods (and a three-dimensional graph) to exhibit Hicksian complementarity between goods, the simple indifference curves shown in Figure 5.7 may give some intuitive feeling for the difference between substitutes and complements.

[8] *See* Hicks, *op. cit.*, p. 312.

The relatively flat indifference curves shown in Figure 5.7a imply that X and Y are nearly perfect substitutes. One of these goods may be traded for the other without significantly affecting the MRS between them. It is geometrically clear that small price changes will induce large movements along these indifference curves, and that substitution effects will therefore be quite large. Since X and Y are close substitutes the individual will be willing to utilize one of the goods for the other in response to changing conditions.

Figure 5.7   Differing Sizes of Substitution Effects

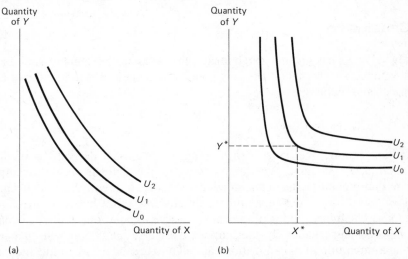

(a)   (b)

For the indifference curves shown in Figure 5.7a substitution effects will be large, and we might call X and Y "substitutes." In this case small price changes will cause relatively large reallocations in expenditures. For the curves shown in 5.7b, however, substitution effects will be small. The proportions in which X and Y are chosen will stay relatively fixed even if the ratio of their prices changes greatly.

In Figure 5.7b, on the other hand, sharply curved (L-shaped) indifference curves are shown. In this case the individual desires to use X and Y in relatively fixed proportions, and will not change these proportions very much in response to changing prices. It is intuitively clear that no matter what the slope of the budget constraint the utility maximizing point will occur in the vicinity of X^*, Y^* if we keep the individual on indifference curve U_1. In some sense X and Y go together, and the individual is unwilling to replace one with the other. Although the goods pictured in Figure 5.7b cannot properly be called "complements" (complementary goods in Hicks' sense can only arise when three or more goods are considered), these goods are certainly less viable substitutes for one another than are the goods pictured in 5.7a.

In many respects these distinctions between substitutes and complements are purely formal; they don't adequately describe real-world relationships such as those between coffee and cream or coffee and tea. A truly adequate definition would stress the attributes of coffee and cream which "fit well together." It would also point out why, in many respects, tea and coffee fulfill similar human needs and hence may substitute for one another. One weakness of traditional utility theory is its inability to capture such relationships in any simple way.[9]

Conclusion

This chapter has given a rough idea of the shape of the demand functions developed in Chapter 4. For any good, x_i, we know x_i is a function of all prices and income;

$$x_i = D_i(p_1, p_2, \ldots, p_n, I). \qquad [5.8]$$

In this chapter we have been looking at the partial derivatives of the function D_i. We have repeatedly conducted the analysis on the assumption that the individual is maximizing his utility. Many of the conclusions have been based on an assumed diminishing MRS between any two goods. The many details of the chapter serve to point out that when conditions change, generally the individual's entire allocation will change. The assumption of maximization can tell us a great deal about the qualitative and quantitative nature of these allocational changes. In particular, we have shown that for any good X, $\partial X/\partial I$ will be positive unless X is an inferior good. We have also shown that a change in any price induces both income and substitution effects which will affect the quantity of X demanded in analytically different ways. It is likely that $\partial X/\partial P_X$ will be negative since, for a normal good, both income and substitution effects work in the same direction. However, the sign of $\partial X/\partial P_Y$ (for some other good Y) is ambiguous, and we must conduct a closer analysis of the signs and relative magnitudes of the income and substitution effects.

---

[9] For an interesting alternative approach to utility theory which mitigates this problem *see* K. J. Lancaster, "A New Approach to Consumer Theory," *Journal of Political Economy*, vol. 74 (April 1966), pp. 132–157.

APPENDIX TO CHAPTER 5
Foundations of Utility Analysis

The analysis in Chapters 3, 4, and 5 has made liberal use of the twin concepts of utility functions and indifference curves. It seems somewhat strange that so much analysis should be based on a concept so intangible and unproven as the utility function. Economists have recognized the weak theoretical foundations of utility analysis and have made a variety of attempts to secure these foundations. The earliest attempts to confirm the utility approach to individual choice dealt mainly with attempts to measure utility. As has already been mentioned, these attempts met with failure. More recently, two different approaches have been developed which go a long way toward improving our understanding of the utility assumption. Both of these approaches were first discussed rigorously in Samuelson[1] and the interested reader is directed to this source for a more complete exposition than can be presented here.

The first proposed method for deriving information about utility functions from more basic (and perhaps observable) information relates to the marginal rate of substitution. Conceptually we can offer an individual a variety of price ratios and income levels and observe the quantities of X and Y purchased. We know he will equate the price ratio to his MRS; therefore each choice he makes tells us a bit about the shape of his indifference curve map. The situation is illustrated in Figure 5A.1.

Figure 5A.1   Map of MRS Segments

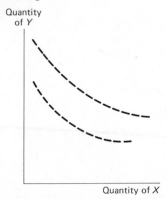

By presenting individuals with different price-income combinations it might be experimentally possible to observe a series of MRS segments. Whether these can be pieced together to form a meaningful utility function is a difficult mathematical question.

If the observed trade-off rates change "smoothly" as X increases, it might be possible to "piece them together" to get a whole set of indifference curves. Since it seems reasonable to assume an individual's MRS does change rather smoothly, it was initially thought that this sort of piecing together of indifference curves was a highly believable "proof" of the fact that individuals act as if they are maximizing a utility function.

Samuelson showed that this piecing together of small MRS segments to form indifference curves of a utility function was not so simple as a diagram such as Figure 5A.1 seems to imply. In more than two dimensions, the observed MRS's have to obey certain other conditions before they can be pieced together into an indifference curve. These conditions are somewhat mathematical and have no recognized economic content. There seems to be no particular reason why an individual should obey these conditions as a consequence of his "rational" behavior. Samuelson

[1] Samuelson, *Foundations of Economic Analysis, op. cit.*

called this difficulty the "integrability" problem because of the nature of the purely mathematical strictures placed on the MRS segments. Since no economic rationale has yet been found to justify the assumptions needed to construct indifference curves in more than two dimensions, the search for a firm foundation to utility analysis went in other directions.

The other direction, also proposed by Samuelson, has proved to be both intuitively attractive and very powerful in its ability to get results. This development is called the *theory of revealed preference*. The basic idea of the theory is very simple. We first define a "principle of rationality" and then show how this principle of rationality allows us to approximate any indifference curve as closely as we like. In this sense a person who obeys the principle of rationality is operating as if he had consulted a utility function.

The principle of rationality in the theory of revealed preference is as follows: Consider two bundles of goods, A and B. If at some prices and income level the individual can afford both A and B, but chooses A, we say A has been "revealed preferred" to B. The principle of rationality states that under any different price-income arrangement, B can never be revealed preferred to A. If B is in fact chosen at some price-income configuration, it must be because the individual cannot afford A. The principle is illustrated in Figure 5A.2. Suppose that when the budget constraint is given by I_1, point A is chosen even though B could have also been purchased. A has then been revealed preferred to B. If for some other budget constraint B is in fact chosen, it must be a case such as that represented by I_2 — where A could not have been bought. If B were chosen when the budget constraint is I_3, this would be a violation of the principle of rationality, since with I_3 both A and B can be bought. With budget constraint I_3 it is likely that some point other than either A or B, say, C will be bought.

Mathematically,[2] let $P_X{}^A$, $P_Y{}^A$ be the prices which prevail when A is revealed preferred to B. This means that:

$$P_X{}^A X_A + P_Y{}^A Y_A \geq P_X{}^A X_B + P_Y{}^A Y_B \qquad [5A.1]$$

that is, the purchaser can afford either A or B. The principle of rationality states that it must be the case that if $P_X{}^B$, $P_Y{}^B$ are the prices which prevail when B is chosen, then:

$$P_X{}^B X_B + P_Y{}^B Y_B < P_X{}^B X_A + P_Y{}^B Y_A \qquad [5A.2]$$

that is, he cannot now afford A.

[2] The definitions of revealed preference are discussed here for only two goods. The generalization to n goods is trivial.

Figure 5A.2   Demonstration of the Revealed Preference Axiom of Rationality

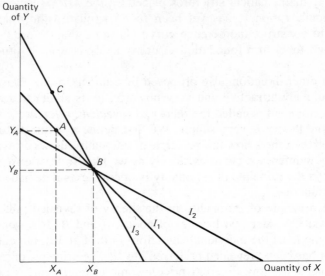

If the individual has income I_1 he can afford both points A and B. If he then chooses A, A is revealed preferred to B. It would be irrational for B to be revealed preferred to A in some other price-income configuration.

This principle of rationality can be used to show a variety of results about individual behavior. Perhaps the most instructive example would be to use the principle of revealed preference to show that the pure substitution effect must be negative. Suppose an individual is *indifferent* between two bundles, C (composed of X_C and Y_C) and D (composed of X_D and Y_D). Let P_X^C, P_Y^C be the prices at which bundle C is chosen and P_X^D, P_Y^D be the prices at which bundle D is chosen.

Since the individual is indifferent between C and D it must be the case that when he chose C, he could not afford D. Hence:

$$P_X^C X_C + P_Y^C Y_C < P_X^C X_D + P_Y^C Y_D. \qquad [5A.3]$$

A similar statement holds for the case when D is chosen:

$$P_X^D X_D + P_Y^D Y_D < P_X^D X_C + P_Y^D Y_C. \qquad [5A.4]$$

Rewriting Equations 5A.3 and 5A.4 gives:

$$P_X^C (X_C - X_D) + P_Y^C (Y_C - Y_D) < 0 \qquad [5A.3']$$

$$P_X^D (X_D - X_C) + P_Y^D (Y_D - Y_C) < 0. \qquad [5A.4']$$

Adding these together we get:

$(P_X^C - P_X^D)(X_C - X_D) + (P_Y^C - P_Y^D)(Y_C - Y_D) < 0.$

Now suppose only the price of X changes; assume $P_Y^C = P_Y^D$. Then:[3]

$(P_X^C - P_X^D)(X_C - X_D) < 0.$ $\hspace{3cm}$ [5A.5]

But Equation 5A.5 simply says that price and quantity move in the opposite direction when utility is held constant. This is precisely a statement of the negative substitution effect given in Chapter 5:

$$\left.\frac{\partial X}{\partial P_X}\right|_{U\ =\ \text{Constant}} < 0. \hspace{3cm} [5A.6]$$

We have arrived at the result by an approach which requires neither the existence of a utility function nor the assumption of a diminishing MRS.

Several other properties which have already been developed using the concept of utility can be proved using the revealed preference axiom instead. For example, it is an easy matter to show that demand functions are homogeneous of degree 0 in all prices and income,[4] and to show that the Hicksian cross-substitution terms are identical (Equation 5.7). It therefore is apparent that the revealed preference axiom and the existence of "well-behaved" utility functions are somehow equivalent conditions. That this is in fact the case was first shown by H. Houthakker in 1950. Houthakker showed that a set of indifference curves can always be derived from the revealed preference axiom.[5] Hence the revealed preference axiom provides a somewhat more tangible base for utility theory.

The theory of revealed preference has also proved to be quite useful in its own right. In practical applications it has proved invaluable as a tool in understanding the construction and evaluation of certain index

---

[3] This proof follows that developed by Samuelson (*op. cit.*, p. 109). It should be pointed out that the proof is not strictly correct and is presented for pedagogic purposes only. The principal problem in the development of a complete proof is that the concept of "indifference" is not defined in revealed preference theory.

[4] Homogeneity of degree 0 is a direct result of the principle of rationality. If a particular bundle, say, C is chosen when P_X, P_Y, and I prevail, it must also be chosen when the price-income set becomes $2P_X$, $2P_Y$, $2I$. At this new set, C can be afforded and any other bundle is either too expensive (as it was in the initial price-income configuration) or was already revealed to be inferior to C. Consequently, C must be chosen in this new situation and "demand functions" remain unchanged.

[5] H. Houthakker, "Revealed Preference and the Utility Function," *Economica*, vol. 17 (May 1950), pp. 159–174. Actually the version of the revealed preference axiom stated here is the "weak" version. In order to prove Houthakker's result one must assume a "strong" version of the axiom.

numbers (such as the Consumer Price Index or GNP measured in constant prices).

As a simple example of these applications consider the problem of deciding whether or not an individual is better off in 1970 than he was in 1960. For simplicity, suppose there are only two consumption goods[6] (X and Y) and let P_X^{70}, P_Y^{70} and P_X^{60}, P_Y^{60} be the prices of these two goods which prevailed in 1970 and 1960 respectively. We wish to have some way to compare the quantities purchased in 1970 (X^{70}, Y^{70}) with those purchased in 1960 (X^{60}, Y^{60}). Ideally we would compare the utility level obtainable from the goods consumed in 1970 with that from the 1960 goods. Unfortunately we do not have such information on individual tastes, so we must develop some approximation.

One common procedure is to use a *fixed-price index* to compare the two bundles of goods. For example, we could use 1960 prices and compute a *Laspeyres* (base year) measure of output change. The computation of this index proceeds as follows. First, compute 1960's GNP in 1960 prices:

$$G^{60} = P_X^{60} X^{60} + P_Y^{60} Y^{60} \qquad\qquad [5A.7a]$$

also compute 1970's GNP *in 1960 prices:*

$$G^{70} = P_X^{60} X^{70} + P_Y^{60} Y^{70}. \qquad\qquad [5A.7b]$$

The usual comparison then is to compute:

$$L = \frac{G^{70}}{G^{60}} \qquad\qquad [5A.8]$$

and if this figure is greater than 1 conclude that welfare has improved. That this is an overly optimistic statement is demonstrated in Figure 5A.3 in which the 1960 combination of goods is shown as point E and the indifference curve through E is labeled U_1. The 1960 "budget constraint" is labeled G^{60} in the diagram. If in 1970 we are at some point below G^{60}, the index L would say things have gotten worse, and indeed they have. Point E has been revealed preferred to all points below G^{60}. However, a value of L greater than 1 is not necessarily an improvement. Some points to the right of G^{60} (such as point M) are in fact inferior to point E even though the Laspeyres index would say welfare has improved. L is therefore an overly optimistic measure of true welfare improvement.

---

[6] For index number "problems" to arise there must be at least two goods. The essence of such problems is that relative prices change over time and we have no common measuring rod for adding up quantities of different goods. If there were only one good this problem would not arise because (at least in principle) we could compare physical quantities.

Figure 5A.3 Problems in Judging Welfare Improvement

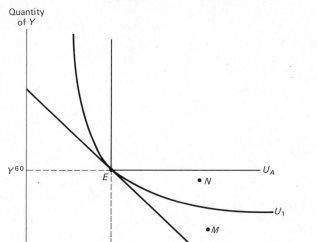

Neither the right-angle curve U_A nor the fixed price index curve G^{60} provide an unambiguous approximation to the true indifference curve U_1.

A slightly different approach may make this argument more transparent. We want an approximation to the indifference curve U_1 so as to be able to make welfare judgments. One possible approximation would be the combination of unambiguous improvements from point E. Any point above the right-angle curve U_A is definitely superior to E. But using U_A as an approximation to U_1 is overly pessimistic: There exist points (such as N) which are better than E but which would be disqualified by the U_A criterion. On the other hand, the use of G^{60} as an approximation to U_1 is overly optimistic as has been shown. This problem is intrinsic to the nature of comparing different quantities of goods when prices change. Without knowledge of the true indifference curve all approximations will be ambiguous.[7]

---

[7] The reader may wish to show that using current year prices when constructing an index raises similar problems of ambiguity. In this case use of the index will lead to unduly pessimistic statements about the improvement in welfare. Such an index is called a Paasche quantity index.

CHAPTER 6
Market Demand

Introduction: The Individual's Demand Curve

In Chapter 4 it was shown that an individual's demand for a good (say x_1) depends on the shape of his utility function (his tastes) and on all prices and his income:

$$x_1 = D_1(p_1, p_2,..., p_n, I). \qquad [6.1]$$

Frequently it is convenient to graph x_1 as simply a function of its own price (p_1), with the understanding that all other prices and income are being held constant. Such a graph is called a demand curve and is illustrated in Figure 6.1. This curve can be derived from the individual's indifference curve map by noting how the quantity of x_1 changes as its price changes. The reader may wish to attempt this construction for himself. It would proceed in the same way as the graphic discussion of income and substitution effects in Chapter 5. Indeed the notion that income and substitution effects are both operative as an individual moves along his demand curve is central to the economic theory of individual behavior.

Figure 6.1 Individual's Demand Curve for x_1

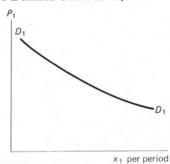

The curve D_1 records how much of good x_1 the individual will demand at each price. It is drawn with a negative slope because of the discussion about the likely sign of $\partial x_1/\partial p_1$ in Chapter 5. In drawing this curve it is assumed that all other prices and income remain constant. If one of these variables were to change, the curve would shift.

Curve D_1 in Figure 6.1 is drawn downward sloping because of the discussion in Chapter 5, which points out that it is very likely that $\partial x_1/\partial p_1$ will be less than 0. *Ceteris paribus,* as p_1 increases, less x_1 will be demanded. Remember, this curve is drawn on the assumption that $p_2,\ldots, p_n$ and I are held constant. If one of these variables were to change, the curve in Figure 6.1 would shift. For example, if I were to increase the curve would shift upward (provided $\partial x_1/\partial I > 0$—that is, that the good is a "normal" good). More x_1 would be demanded at *each* price. If another price, say p_2, were to increase then the curve shown in Figure 6.1 would shift upward if x_2 and x_1 were gross substitutes (an increase in the price of coffee shifts the demand curve for tea upward). On the other hand, if x_2 and x_1 were gross complements, then an increase in p_2 would shift the demand curve downward (an increase in the price of coffee shifts the demand curve for cream downward). As this discussion makes clear, one must remember that the demand curve drawn in Figure 6.1 is only a simplification of the true demand function (Equation 6.1) and that it is only stable if other things in fact stay constant. It is important to keep clearly in mind the difference between a movement along a given demand curve caused by a change in p_1 and a shift in the entire curve caused by a change in income or in one of the other prices. Traditionally, the term "an increase in demand" is reserved for an outward shift in the demand curve, while the term "an increase in the quantity demanded" refers to a movement along a given curve.

In this chapter we will be interested in summing up all individuals' demands for a single good. It should be evident that the total demand for a good, because it is the sum of each individual's demand, will depend on all prices and on the income *each person* has. We will discuss market demand functions and their associated market demand curves. Some ways of measuring the responsiveness of market demand to changing conditions will also be developed.

Market Demand Functions

Suppose there are only two individuals in society. Let the first individual's demand function for good x_1 be given by:

$$x_1^1 = D_1^1(p_1,..., p_n, I_1) \tag{6.2}$$

and the second individual's demand for x_1 be:

$$x_1^2 = D_1^2(p_1,..., p_n, I_2) \tag{6.3}$$

where I_1 and I_2 are the incomes of individuals 1 and 2. Notice that D_1^1 and D_1^2 may very well be different functions and that each individual's demand depends on all prices and on his own income.

If we let Q_1 equal the total market demand for x_1, then:

$$Q_1 = x_1^1 + x_1^2 = D_1^T(p_1,..., p_n, I_1, I_2) \tag{6.4}$$

where D_1^T means the total demand for x_1. It is important to notice that Q_1 depends on both I_1 and I_2. It is not true in general that Q_1 depends on the sum $I_1 + I_2$. For example, if individual 1 loves pizza and individual 2 is revolted by it, then we would expect to have a very different total demand for pizza if we gave all available income to individual 1 than if we gave it to individual 2. Clearly the demand for pizza depends on how total income is distributed.

Equation 6.4 is easily generalized to m individuals:

$$Q_1 = x_1^1 + x_1^2 + \cdots + x_1^m = D_1^T(p_1, p_2,..., p_n, I_1, I_2,..., I_m) \tag{6.4'}$$

Thus total demand depends on all prices and on the distribution of income among individuals. It is important to recognize that the total demand for any commodity does depend on the distribution of income. As we will see in later chapters, these total demand functions to a large extent determine what and how much will be produced. Those individuals with larger incomes (more "dollar votes") will have a larger say in this interaction because of their greater influence on total demand.

Market Demand Curves

It is possible to graph a demand curve from Equation 6.4′ by holding all variables other than p_1 constant. This curve is shown in Figure 6.2, and is drawn downward sloping because of the likelihood that most individuals will, *ceteris paribus,* increase their demand for x_1 when its price falls. This, then, is the theoretical foundation of the Marshallian idea of a negatively sloped market demand curve.

Figure 6.2   Market Demand Curve for x_1

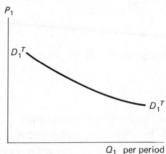

The market demand curve is drawn on the assumption that all other prices and all incomes of individuals are held constant. This curve has a negative slope because of the fact that most individual demand curves will be downward sloping. Consequently, the lower the price of good 1, the more total quantity will be demanded.

The market demand curve can also be graphically constructed by horizontally summing each individual's demand curve. This is exhibited in Figure 6.3. In this figure $Q_1{}^* = x_1{}^{1*} + x_1{}^{2*}$ and $Q_1{}^{**} = x_1{}^{1**} + x_1{}^{2**}$. The curve $D_1{}^T$ is therefore a horizontal sum. This market demand curve is identical in meaning to that in Figure 6.2. Again the *ceteris paribus* nature of the curve should be pointed out. If total income is reallocated toward x_1 lovers, the curve will shift upward. The curve will shift downward if income is allocated to x_1 haters. If p_2 increases and x_2 is for "most people" a gross substitute for x_1, then the curve will shift upward. If x_2 is a gross complement for most people then the curve will shift downward.

Figure 6.3 Construction of Market Demand Curve from Individual Demand
Curves

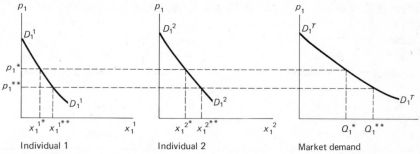

Individual 1   Individual 2   Market demand

The market demand curve can be seen to be a horizontal sum of each individual's demand
curve. At any price the curve is constructed by summing the quantity each individual demands. For example, at p_i^*; $x_1^{1*} + x_1^{2*} = Q_1^*$.

This overly tedious rendition of the results has been presented because: they are often neglected; and they are important in empirical investigations. Most data which are available only pertain to an entire
market. If we wish to draw inferences about how the market demand
curve has shifted over time, it is important to recognize the various factors which may cause it to shift. In the analysis which follows we will
be interested in the market demand curve for a particular good and will
denote its quantity by Q and price by P. The previous discussion about
the *ceteris paribus* nature of any market demand curve should be kept in
mind during this analysis.

The Concept of Elasticity

Often economists are interested in how quantity demanded responds to
changes in a good's price. A common way of summarizing this response
is by using the concept of elasticity. The *price elasticity of demand* for
a good is defined to be the percentage change in the quantity of a good
purchased divided by the concomitant percentage change in the good's
price. Mathematically:

Elasticity of Q with respect to $P = E_{Q,P} = \dfrac{\text{percent change in } Q}{\text{percent change in } P}$

$$= \frac{\dfrac{\Delta Q}{Q}}{\dfrac{\Delta P}{P}} = \frac{\Delta Q}{\Delta P} \cdot \frac{P}{Q} = \frac{\partial Q}{\partial P} \cdot \frac{P}{Q}. \qquad [6.5]$$

Since in the usual case $\partial Q/\partial P < 0$, elasticity will usually be negative. A distinction is often made between whether $E_{Q,P}$ is less than, equal to, or greater than minus 1. Specifically the terminology used is:[1]

Table 6.1

Value of $E_{Q,P}$ at a point:	Curve at this point is said to be:
$E_{Q,P} < -1$	Elastic
$E_{Q,P} = -1$	Unit elastic
$E_{Q,P} > -1$	Inelastic

For an elastic curve, a price increase is met by a more than proportionate quantity decrease. For a unit elastic curve the price increase and the quantity decrease are of identical proportional magnitudes. For an inelastic curve price increases proportionally more than quantity decreases. If a curve is elastic, price therefore affects quantity "a lot"; if a curve is inelastic, price does not have as much of an effect on quantity demanded. One might classify goods by their elasticities of demand. For example, the quantity of medical services demanded is undoubtedly very inelastic. The market demand curve may be almost vertical in this case, indicating that the quantity demanded is not responsive to price. On the other hand, it is likely that price changes will have a great effect on the quantity of candy bought (the demand is elastic). Here the market demand curve would be nearly horizontal. If market price were to change even slightly the quantity demanded would change significantly.

There is, therefore, the presumption that goods for which substitutes are plentiful have an elastic demand ($E_{Q,P} < -1$) whereas for goods where there are no good substitutes demand is inelastic ($E_{Q,P} > -1$).

The concept of elasticity is easy to generalize. If X and Y are any two variables such that Y depends on X, then the elasticity of Y with respect to X is calculated as:

$$E_{Y,X} = \frac{\text{percent change in } Y}{\text{percent change in } X} = \frac{\frac{\Delta Y}{Y}}{\frac{\Delta X}{X}} = \frac{\Delta Y}{\Delta X} \cdot \frac{X}{Y} = \frac{\partial Y}{\partial X} \cdot \frac{X}{Y}. \qquad [6.6]$$

[1] Sometimes the elasticity of demand is defined as the absolute value of the definition in Equation 6.5. Consequently, under this alternative definition, elasticity is never negative and curves are classified as elastic, unit elastic, or inelastic depending on whether $|E_{Q,P}|$ is greater than, equal to, or less than 1. The reader should recognize this distinction in examining empirical work, since there is no consistent usage in economic literature.

Two particular applications of this definition are the income elasticity of demand $(E_{Q,I})$ and an "other" price elasticity of demand $(E_{Q,P'})$ where P' is the price of some other good. By definition (Equation 6.6) these concepts are given by:

$$E_{Q,I} = \frac{\partial Q}{\partial I} \cdot \frac{I}{Q}$$

$$E_{Q,P'} = \frac{\partial Q}{\partial P'} \cdot \frac{P'}{Q}.$$

[6.7]

When Q is a normal good $E_{Q,I}$ will be positive. For "luxuries" $E_{Q,I} > 1$, whereas for "necessities" it is likely that $E_{Q,I} < 1$. The income elasticity of demand therefore provides some information about the shape of the Engel Curve for the good in question. The sign of $E_{Q,P'}$ is indeterminate: It depends on whether Q and the other good in question are gross substitutes or gross complements.[2]

Forms of Demand Curves

A straight line demand curve is certainly the easiest to draw and the type which appears most frequently in textbook graphs. In a sense this is unfortunate because the behavior implied by a straight line demand curve seems unrealistic. Along a straight line $\partial Q/\partial P$ is constant. This means that a price change from, say, 25¢ to 50¢ (a doubling of price) will have the same effect on Q as a change from \$5.00 to \$5.25 (an increase of 5 percent). Behavior of this type would seem unreasonable on the basis of the information we have about market reactions.

This problem with straight line demand curves can be rephrased to state that elasticity is not constant along a straight line demand curve. At low price levels demand is inelastic; at high price levels it is elastic.

---

[2] The notion presented here of elasticity is a market concept. In this sense, strictly speaking, $E_{Q,I}$ has no meaning unless some condition is imposed on how the distribution of income changes as I changes. This distinction is usually not mentioned in practice. The concepts of elasticity also apply to the individual's demand function. Since most measurement of elasticity is in a market context and since the terms presented can easily be applied to individual behavior, this development is not presented here. It should be pointed out, however, that there are numerous mathematical relationships between the various elasticities. For example, by using the fact that demand functions are homogeneous of degree 0 in all prices and income, it can be shown that the *sum of all* elasticities for a particular good (those with respect to its own price, all other prices, and income) is equal to 0. This is a direct result of Euler's Theorem (*see* Chapter 17 for a discussion of this theorem).

This result can be shown mathematically as follows:

If $Q = a + bP \qquad b < 0$

then [6.8]

$$E_{Q,P} = \frac{\partial Q}{\partial P} \cdot \frac{P}{Q} = b \cdot \frac{P}{Q}.$$

As P/Q increases, the demand curve becomes more elastic. Figure 6.4 illustrates this fact. The reader should show for himself that $E_{Q,P} = -1$ at a price exactly halfway between 0 and where the demand curve hits the P axis $(-a/b)$.

Figure 6.4 The Elasticity of Demand Varies Along a Straight Line Demand Curve

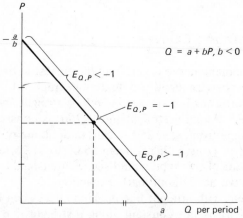

A straight line demand curve may be inappropriate for empirical work because it implies individual behavior in reaction to price changes which is difficult to believe.

Assuming a straight line demand curve can lead to difficulties, especially if prices and quantities are varying by significant amounts over time. Economists generally feel that it is more reasonable to deal with demand curves which have constant elasticity. This assumes that individuals respond to proportionate rather than absolute changes in prices. A curve which does have the same elasticity at every point is:

$Q = aP^b \qquad b < 0, P \neq 0$ [6.9]

or, equivalently:

$$\log Q = \log a + b \log P. \qquad\qquad [6.10]$$

For this curve:

$$E_{Q,P} = \frac{\partial Q}{\partial P} \cdot \frac{P}{Q} = \frac{baP^{b-1} \cdot P}{aP^b} = b. \qquad\qquad [6.10']$$

Therefore the elasticity of this curve is constant (and $= b$) along its entire length. For example, if $E_{Q,P} = -1.5$, then a 1 percent increase in price is always met by a 1.5 percent fall in quantity. This kind of behavior seems more reasonable than that implied by a straight line curve. A constant elasticity curve is pictured in Figure 6.5. Notice that the curve is not defined for $P = 0$.

Figure 6.5 A Constant Elasticity Demand Curve

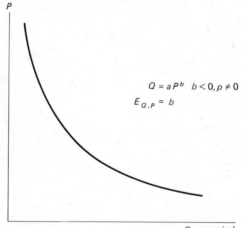

$$Q = aP^b \quad b < 0, p \neq 0$$
$$E_{Q,P} = b$$

Q per period

A curve of this mathematical form (or, equivalently, one which is linear in the logarithms of P and Q) exhibits a constant elasticity of demand along its entire length. This feature may make such curves more suitable for empirical work since demand functions of this form seem to fit historical data rather well.

Ultimately, the choice among alternative functional forms for demand curves cannot be made on pure theoretical grounds. Some forms seem to fit certain data rather well, whereas alternative shapes seem appropriate for different sets of data. Most recent empirical investigations into consumer demand have tended to use the log-linear formulation[3] (Equation 6.10). In theoretical work, the problem of choosing among functional forms is most often resolved by choosing the form with which it is easiest to work.

Conclusion

In a sense this chapter forms a link between Part II and later parts of the book. The derivation of a downward sloping market demand curve is a first step in the development of the Marshallian model of supply and demand. Although it is not directly relevant to the next three chapters on individual behavior, the material has been presented here because it draws directly on the model of utility maximization developed in Chapters 3–5. This use of the fundamentals of the theory of individual choice permits a clearer understanding of exactly where a market demand curve comes from, and illustrates some of the technical difficulties of using aggregate tools which may obscure basic microeconomic relationships.

[3] One reason for this choice is that certain theoretical restrictions on individual demand functions can most easily be imposed if a log-linear function is used. For example, *see* Henri Theil, *Economics and Information Theory* (Skokie, Ill.: Rand McNally & Company, 1967) Chapters 6 and 7.

CHAPTER 7

The Labor-Leisure Choice and Income Taxation

Introduction: Time in Economic Theory

The previous discussion of utility maximization has not mentioned time. It was assumed that the allocation process took place during one "period," and we asked questions about what would happen in the "next period" if conditions changed. This concept of a period is unfortunately vague. We might take the typical period to be one year, one hour, or any other convenient length of time. More scientifically, perhaps, we might choose one period to be that length of time over which a market equilibrium can be established. However a suitable period is chosen, the utility an individual receives from consuming a certain quantity of a good will depend on the length of the time period we are using. The utility obtained from consuming forty hamburgers is rather different if these are to be consumed over a period of one year than if they are to be consumed over a period of one hour. We should therefore be careful to keep a consistent idea throughout our investigations of exactly what the period of analysis is.

Once a suitable period is chosen (say one year is chosen as a useful length), we can regard an individual as living through a succession of periods. In the next chapter we will discuss the individual's problem of allocating goods among these periods. This problem is the most important way in which time enters into economic analysis. A second and often neglected way in which time enters into such analysis occurs within a single period. The amount of time an individual has within one period is absolutely fixed. He must somehow decide how to allocate this fixed amount of time to many alternative uses. He must decide how many hours to work, how many hours to sleep, how many hours to spend in consumption and cultural activities, and how many hours to remain "idle." The utility analysis developed in earlier chapters can aid in understanding the factors which go into determining this allocation of time. This study is a primary purpose of Chapter 7.

Suppose an individual can allocate his fixed amount of time between only two uses—work and nonwork ("leisure"). It is undoubtedly the case that leisure enters into his utility function. This is true not because idleness is necessarily cherished in its own right but because "leisure time" is needed in order to consume.[1] Consumption takes time: Television sets and bowling balls are worthless without the time devoted to using them. Time is probably complementary to most consumption goods—the greater free time one has, the more utility one can derive from using these goods. With the rising level of consumption goods time has become an increasingly scarce commodity. Time cannot be stored up; we must use it as it "passes by." The division of one's time between work and leisure (or among other goals) has therefore become an important allocational

---

[1] This section draws on the fascinating analysis presented by S. B. Linder in *The Harried Leisure Class* (New York: Columbia University Press, 1970). The author investigates various demands on leisure time and the increasing scarcity of time in developed nations. His discussions of cooking, religion, and sexual practices are particularly recommended.

A more theoretical treatment of the allocation of time is given by G. S. Becker in "A Theory of the Allocation of Time," *The Economic Journal*, vol. LXXV (September 1965), pp. 493–517. The author treats the household as both a provider of labor services and a producer of utility, which is made by combining time with goods. The household is then seen to be bound by a time constraint and must allocate available time between a number of activities. The implications drawn by Becker are far-reaching and affect most of the traditional theory of individual behavior.

question. The widespread use of datebooks and appointment calendars attests to this fact.

Although an individual is relatively free to decide how he will allocate his leisure time, it is not so clear that he is perfectly free in allocating his time between work and nonwork. Hours of work are usually fixed by the employer and the individual has no real choice in this matter. Over the past fifty years the work week has been shortened considerably and this undoubtedly represents a substitution of leisure for potential income. But in the short run it is likely that an individual will be somewhat constrained by institutional considerations in his choice of hours of work. In this chapter, however, we will avoid such complications and assume that an individual is perfectly free to choose his number of hours of work so as to maximize his utility. This treatment may perhaps be justified by noting that individuals are free to choose many other conditions associated with their jobs in addition to the number of hours worked. By choosing among the amenities associated with particular jobs, the individual may be thought of as making a marginal choice even though the hours of "work" are institutionally fixed. For example, a person who accepts a low-paying job as a surfing instructor can be viewed as accepting a leisure component in his occupation and thereby adjusting his hours of "actual work." In addition, opportunities for parttime work, seasonal work, home repairs, searching for bargains, and learning how to make money permit almost anyone to spend as much time working as he wants.

The Labor-Leisure Choice: Simple Utility Maximization

Assume an individual has a utility function of the form:

$$\text{Utility} = U(Y, H) \qquad [7.1]$$

where Y represents real income over the period and H represents hours of leisure over the period. He desires to maximize Equation 7.1 subject to the constraint that he only earns income for those hours he works. If D is the total number of hours available in the period and the prevailing real wage rate is w, then this constraint is given by:

$$Y = w(D - H) = wL \qquad [7.2]$$

where $L = $ hours worked.

Anyone who has studied the analysis of Chapter 4 should recognize the conditions which must prevail if Equation 7.1 is to be maximized subject to Equation 7.2. The individual should choose H so that the psychic trade-off rate between leisure and income[2] (the *MRS* of leisure for income) is equal to the rate at which he can trade one for the other in the market place (the wage rate). This result can be shown either mathematically or graphically. The mathematical proof is presented here. A graphic description of other aspects of the problem is presented below.

Set up the Lagrangian expression for the maximization of Equation 7.1 subject to Equation 7.2:

$$L = U(Y, H) - \lambda[Y - w(D - H)].$$ [7.3]

The first-order conditions for a maximum are:

$$\frac{\partial L}{\partial Y} = \frac{\partial U}{\partial Y} - \lambda = 0$$

[7.4]

$$\frac{\partial L}{\partial H} = \frac{\partial U}{\partial H} - w\lambda = 0.$$

Dividing the two equations in 7.4 we get:

$$\frac{\dfrac{\partial U}{\partial H}}{\dfrac{\partial U}{\partial Y}} = w = MRS \ (H \text{ for } Y).$$ [7.4']

Thus the first-order conditions for a maximum are those discussed in the preceding paragraph: The utility maximizing individual should equate his psychic rate of trade-off between leisure and income to the rate at which he can exchange these in the market. This point will be a true maximum providing the individual exhibits a diminishing marginal rate of substitution of leisure for income. Two interesting aspects of these first-order conditions should be pointed out. First, Equation 7.3 shows, as would be expected, that λ can be interpreted as the marginal utility of income. The equations also show that $w\lambda$ is equal to the marginal utility of leisure. Therefore, in a sense w represents the value that an individual puts on his "free time" at the margin. We will discuss this observation somewhat more fully in Chapter 24 when we discuss the problem of assigning an economic value to time.

A second observation is that w must be regarded as a "real" wage rate. The individual is not interested in the dollar magnitude of his income but rather in how income translates into consumption goods. Hence Y and w are both to be thought of as being expressed in real terms. If the

---

[2] Remember the convention adopted in Chapter 3. Income has no utility in itself. Rather, utility comes once the income is optimally spent on consumption goods.

prices of all goods were to double, the individual's real wage rate would be halved and we would expect him to reallocate his time in view of these changed circumstances.[3]

The Income and Substitution Effects of a Change in w

A change in the real wage rate (w) can be analyzed in a manner identical to that used in Chapter 5. When w rises, the "price" of leisure becomes higher—the individual must give up more in lost wages for each hour of leisure he consumes. The substitution effect of an increase in w on the hours of leisure will therefore be negative. As leisure becomes more expensive there is reason to consume less of it. However, the income effect will be positive—since leisure is a normal good, the higher income resulting from a higher w will increase the demand for leisure. Hence the income and substitution effects work in the opposite direction. It is impossible to predict on a priori grounds whether an increase in w will increase or decrease the demand for leisure time. Since leisure and work are mutually exclusive ways to spend one's time, it is also true that it is impossible to predict what will happen to the number of hours worked. The substitution effect tends to increase hours worked when w increases; whereas the income effect, because it increases the demand for leisure time, tends to decrease the number of hours worked. Which of these two effects is the stronger is an important empirical question.[4]

The two possible reactions to a change in w are illustrated in Figure 7.1. In both graphs the initial wage is w_0 and the initial optimal choices of Y and H are given by the point Y_0, H_0. When the wage rate increases to w_1 the optimal combination moves to point Y_1, H_1. This movement can be considered as the result of two effects. The substitution effect can be represented by the movement of the optimal point form Y_0, H_0 to S and the income effect by the movement from S to Y_1, H_1. In Figures 7.1a and 7.1b these two effects combine to produce different results. In 7.1a the substitution effect of a change in w outweighs the income effect, and the individual demands less leisure ($H_1 < H_0$). Another way of saying this is that the individual will work longer hours when w rises.

---

[3] Although in theory a person's labor-leisure choice depends on the real wage, it may be the case that, empirically, individuals pay more attention to money wages without recognizing concomitant price changes. Although such "money illusion" may be an important short-run phenomenon, it is likely that individuals will react only to real wages over longer time periods.

[4] If the family is taken to be the relevant decision unit even more interesting questions arise about the income and substitution effects that changes in the wages of one family member, say the husband, will have on the labor force behavior of other family members, for example, the wife.

Figure 7.1 Income and Substitution Effects of a Change in the Wage Rate

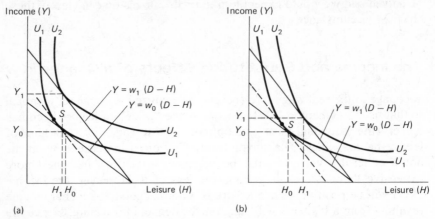

(a)   (b)

Since the individual is a supplier of labor the substitution and income effects of a changing wage rate work in opposite directions in their effect on hours of leisure (or hours worked). In 7.1a the substitution effect (that is, movement to point S) is stronger and a higher wage decreases the number of hours of leisure (and increases the number of hours worked). In 7.1b the income effect is stronger and hours of leisure actually increase in response to an increase in w.

In 7.1b the situation is reversed. The income effect of a change in w more than offsets the substitution effect and the demand for leisure increases $(H_1 > H_0)$. The individual works shorter hours when w rises. In the cases examined in Chapter 5 this would have been considered an unusual result—when the "price" of leisure rises the individual demands more of it. For the case of normal consumption goods the income and substitution effects work in the same direction. Only for "inferior" goods do they differ in sign. In the case of leisure and income, however, the income and substitution effects always work in opposite directions. An increase in w makes an individual better off because he is a *supplier* of labor. In the case of a consumption good an individual is made worse off when a price rises because he is a *consumer* of that good.

In light of this discussion either $\partial H/\partial w > 0$ or $\partial H/\partial w < 0$ must be considered plausible. A reasonable hypothesis might be that for low wage rates $\partial H/\partial w < 0$, but for higher wage rates $\partial H/\partial w > 0$. At low wage levels an increase in w causes an individual to work more hours, whereas for "affluent" wage levels an increase in w causes an individual to demand more leisure time in which to enjoy his yachts and ski cabins. This possibility is illustrated by the labor supply curve shown in Figure 7.2. Hours of work $(D - H)$ are graphed against the real wage rate w. The supply curve is "backward bending" under the assumption that $\partial H/\partial w$ becomes positive at a high wage rate.

Figure 7.2   Individual Labor Supply Curve

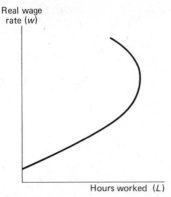

The individual's supply of labor curve may be "backward bending" if, at low levels of w, the substitution effect outweighs the income effect, whereas at higher wage rates the income effect is stronger.

Whether the actual labor supply curve for an individual is backward bending has been the basis for many empirical investigations. The most important piece of evidence is the substantial decline in the work week during the twentieth century in the face of rapidly increasing real wages. Another bit of supporting evidence is that lower-paid workers (often paid by the hour) are generally offered increased wages for overtime work and seem willing (even eager) to accept the loss of leisure time. On the other hand, higher-paid workers are usually salaried and offered no specific monetary inducements for overtime work. This may be because such inducements would be ineffective in prompting the individual to give up his leisure time. Hence, a backward-bending supply curve for labor services provided seems to accord well with much of the available evidence.[5]

Taxes and Subsidies: The "Lump-Sum" Principle

Income from labor services is taxed in many countries. In the United States income taxation is the largest source of governmental revenue. There are three reasons which account for the popularity of such taxes: they are relatively easy to collect; they are broad-based and can be used to make living conditions more "equitable"; they are an economically "efficient" way of gathering revenue. The second of these reasons will

---

[5] The shape of the total supply of labor curve for all individuals is more difficult to predict because of the tendency for people who were not formerly in the labor force (women and children) to enter the labor force as w rises.

be discussed at length in the section on " 'Fair' Income Taxation" which follows. Here we will examine the assumed "efficiency" of income taxation. It is important to be precise in this examination because the correct result is frequently misstated.

Figure 7.3   An Illustration of the Efficiency of Income Taxation

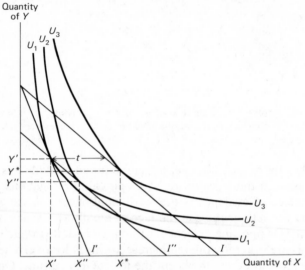

An excise tax on good X shifts the budget constraint to I'. A "lump sum" income tax which takes in the same revenue could be represented by the budget constaint I''. But with I'' a higher level of utility can be reached than with I', and hence the income tax is more efficient from the individual's point of view.

A theoretically correct statement is that taxes which produce general changes in purchasing power are superior to those which raise an equal amount of money by taxing one particular good (or a group of goods). This result is illustrated in Figure 7.3. Suppose the purchase of good X is taxed. This will raise its price to a buyer, and will shift his budget constraint to I'. With this new constraint the individual will consume the combination X', Y' and will pay as a tax the distance between lines I and I' (the tax is therefore measured in units of good X). Now an income tax which raises the same amount of money can be represented by a budget line (I'') parallel to the initial line but passing through point X', Y'. In both cases the tax collected is given by the length $t-t$ units of X are lost under both taxes. However, the income constraint I'' permits an individual to reach a higher indifference curve than does I'; and point X'', Y'' will be chosen because it is preferred to X', Y'. Hence it has been shown that an income tax permits the individual to reach a higher level of utility than does an excise (that is, sales) tax which produces equal revenue.

The intuitive explanation for this result is that an excise tax causes a loss in utility not only from a loss in general purchasing power but also because the individual has been forced to reallocate his income in a certain way by the distorted prices resulting from the tax. An "income" tax, on the other hand, takes away the same amount of purchasing power, but does not distort the individual's consumption choices.[6] "Lump-sum," nondistorting taxes are therefore, on efficiency grounds, to be preferred to distorting excise taxes. An identical argument can be made for subsidies (that is, negative taxes). It is more efficient to provide individuals with general purchasing power and let them make their own decisions than to distort their decisions by providing them with certain goods at below market prices.[7] Again the "lump-sum" approach is to be favored on efficiency grounds.

This analysis is correct as it is stated. However, care should be exercised in applying these concepts to the real world. Income taxes, for example, by changing the relevant "take-home" wage rate will (by the analysis of the section, "The Income and Substitution Effects of a Change in w") certainly affect the individual's labor-leisure choice. Whereas such taxes may be "nondistorting" in regard to choices among consumption goods,[8] they are at best an approximation to an ideal "lump-sum" tax because of this other distorting effect. A similar argument holds for subsidies: "Negative income tax" type of subsidies might be preferred over subsidized prices on specific goods because the income grant does not affect the choice between commodities. However, it must be recognized that all the negative income tax schemes which have been proposed do in fact change the relevant wage rate and thus distort the labor-leisure

---

[6] This result can be also demonstrated using the revealed preference theory developed in the Appendix to Chapter 5. Under an excise tax the individual chooses the bundle X', Y'. With an income tax he can also afford X', Y', but will likely choose some other point (here X'', Y''). Hence X'', Y'' is revealed preferred to X', Y'. This shows that an income tax is more efficient.

[7] This argument assumes individuals are better than taxing bodies at deciding what's good for them. Frequently the taxation of cigarettes or liquor, and the provision of free school lunches and subsidized housing, are supported on the presumption that in fact individuals don't know what is good for them. These matters are discussed briefly in Chapter 26.

[8] Changes in tax rates may indeed distort consumption decisions when the necessary time component of consuming is recognized. For example, consider a tax increase: This lowers the take-home wage rate and makes leisure less expensive. In turn this may promote a substitution effect toward goods which take relatively more time to consume. There will also be a negative income effect tending to reduce all consumption, but this analysis would tentatively suggest that time-saving type of consumption (convenience foods, electrical appliances) would be cut back to the greatest extent.

choice. In spite of these observations it might be reasonable to accept income taxes and subsidies as adequate approximations to the ideal lump-sum principle, although there is no unambiguous evidence on this point.

"Fair" Income Taxation

Two principles of equity ostensibly underlie the present income tax system in the United States:

1. People with equal income should pay the same taxes.
2. Taxation should be based on an "equal sacrifice" principle when deciding on the tax rates to be assessed against individuals with different incomes.

The first of these will not be discussed here. The interested reader is urged to consult the numerous exposés and serious analytical works which detail the failure of this principle in practice.[9] The concept of fairness in income taxation, however, can be readily discussed using the tools developed so far.

For simplicity, assume an individual derives utility only from after-tax income (Y).[10] The utility function for the ith individual is then given by:

Utility of individual $i = U_i(Y_i)$. [7.5]

Also assume that the utility functions for all individuals are the same. In the absence of any detailed knowledge about individual's utility functions this is a reasonable first approximation, although more detailed work would probably find that this was not true.[11] Hence it is assumed that:

Utility of individual $i = U(Y_i)$ [7.6]

---

[9] Three obvious situations where people with equal incomes may pay different taxes are: when part of income is in the form of "capital gains"; when the individuals have different numbers of children; or where some portion of income is tax free (for example, interest on municipal bonds or the imputed income one receives by living in his own home).

[10] This assumption is obviously only an approximation. In particular, we cannot really expect the individual's quantity of leisure to stay constant as we talk about changing income tax rates.

[11] If all utility of income functions are the same, this would imply that individuals behave the same particularly in regard to risk (*see* Chapter 9). This does not in fact seem to be true.

where the function U is the same for all individuals. Now let B_i represent the individual's before-tax income and let his income tax be given by T_i. Then:

$$Y_i = B_i - T_i \qquad\qquad [7.7]$$

and

$$U(Y_i) = U(B_i - T_i) \qquad\qquad [7.7']$$

for all individuals.

We are interested in arriving at some sort of "fair" relationship between B_i and T_i. More specifically we might question whether income taxes should be *proportional* (T_i/B_i the same for all levels of income), *progressive* (T_i/B_i increases as income increases), or *regressive* (T_i/B_i decreases as income increases). To answer this question it is necessary to define what we mean by "fair." One definition might be that everyone pays the same dollar amount in taxes. This would be a very regressive tax and contrary to some people's basic sense of equity. Surely, they would argue, $1000 in taxes hurts a poor man more than it hurts a rich man. What we may mean by "equal sacrifice" is not equal dollar sacrifice but rather equal loss of utility. One possible presumption (subject to empirical verification) might be that the marginal utility of income decreases as income increases. The principle of equal sacrifice of utility would then imply that a rich man should pay more in taxes than a poor man.

This observation does not, however, give us any guide to whether taxes should be proportional, regressive, or progressive. If the marginal utility of income decreases very rapidly, progressive taxation is called for; if the marginal utility of income declines rather slowly, regressive taxation is required (although the rich still pay more dollars in taxes than the poor do). Which taxing system we use depends on the specific shape of the utility of income function. It is rather easy to show that the dividing line between progressive and regressive taxation under the equal sacrifice of utility criterion occurs when:

$$\text{Utility} = U(Y_i) = a \log Y_i \qquad\qquad [7.8]$$

where a is some constant. For a utility function of this type proportional taxation is required. This can be shown as follows.

The equal utility sacrifice criterion states that:

$$\text{Loss of utility} = U(B_i) - U(Y_i) = U(B_i) - U(B_i - T_i) \qquad\qquad [7.9]$$

should be the same for all individuals. But if the utility function is given by Equation 7.8 this says:

$$a \log (B_i) - a \log (B_i - T_i) = a \log \frac{B_i}{B_i - T_i} \qquad [7.10]$$

should be the same for all individuals.

This means that $B_i/B_i - T_i$ is a constant for all i, or that T_i/B_i is constant for all i. Hence we have shown that proportional taxation is implied (by the equal sacrifice principle) for utility functions of the form shown by Equation 7.8. Under this principle, utility functions which rise more rapidly than Equation 7.8 imply regressive taxation, whereas functions which rise less rapidly imply progressive taxation. This is illustrated in Figure 7.4.

Figure 7.4   The Shape of the Utility of Income Function and Its Relationship to Fair Taxation under the Equal Utility Loss Criterion

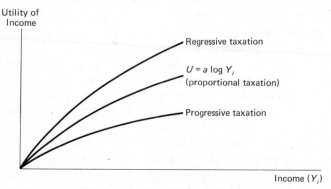

The tax schedule required by the principle of fair taxation depends on what we mean by "fair," and what the utility of income function looks like. If an equal loss of utility criterion is adopted, then progressive taxation will be fair only if the marginal utility of income declines rather rapidly.

The fact that so many governments of the world favor progressive taxation must mean either that they believe utility rises less rapidly than $a \log Y_i$, or that they are operating under some more egalitarian principle than the equal utility sacrifice principle.[12] In any case, this discussion illustrates the desirability of stating explicitly the principles of fairness underlying a tax system. Only by doing so can a consistent tax rate schedule be developed.

---

[12] *See* Problem 7 at the end of this part.

Conclusion

This chapter has discussed two closely related issues: the individual's labor-leisure choice and income taxation. Since individuals respond to after-tax wage rates, it is clear that these two subjects are integrally connected and that only the barest outlines of these interconnections have been sketched. One interesting aspect of the chapter has been an avoidance of assigning any "disutility" to work. The reason people choose not to work is not that they hate work; rather, that there are competing demands for the use of their limited time. It was seen that the marginal value people put on leisure is given by the (after-tax) wage rate, and that changes in this rate produce income and substitution effects which are similar to those which operate when the price of a consumption good changes.

CHAPTER 8

Time and the
Savings Decision

Introduction

Because an individual lives through several periods he has the opportunity to reallocate goods between these periods. He may transfer some
current purchasing power into the future by saving, or he may transfer
some future purchasing power to the present by borrowing, with the intention of paying off the loan in the future. This sort of reallocation is a
prevalent phenomenon. Figure 8.1 shows hypothetical consumption and
income streams for a typical individual (or family "unit"). In early adult
years consumption exceeds income $(C > Y)$. The individual borrows so

that he may purchase the "necessities" of family life. He is in effect transferring purchasing power from his middle years, where it is needed less, to his early years, when the establishment of a family necessitates large expenditures. In middle years income exceeds consumption $(Y > C)$. With this excess of purchasing power the individual can either pay off past loans or save for future needs. In later years earnings fall off and consumption again exceeds income as the individual uses past savings to consume during retirement.

Figure 8.1   Hypothetical Consumption and Income Stream for an Individual

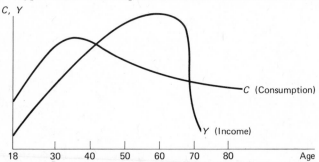

Because an individual's desired consumption pattern may not agree with the pattern of his income there is an opportunity for a reallocation of expenditures over time. In this diagram a "typical" pattern of reallocation is shown. The individual uses the income in his peak earning years to finance his consumption on either side of those years.

Figure 8.1 is not intended either as an exact representation of the way in which all individuals plan their lives nor as a prescription for how one should allocate his consumption expenditures. Rather it is merely intended to illustrate the general manner in which individuals do in fact reallocate their purchasing power over time, and that they do so in what seems to be a reasonable way. They utilize possibilities for borrowing and lending (that is, saving) to turn a rather arbitrary stream of income[1] into an "optimal" pattern of consumption (and presumably of utility). In this chapter we will analyze several principles of this reallocation in some detail.

We will assume that the individual is attempting to maximize a utility function of the general form:

$$\text{Utility} = U(C_0, C_1, C_2, ..., C_n) \tag{8.1}$$

---

[1] The individual is free also to determine his income stream in the way discussed in Chapter 7. However, the stream of possible earnings available to an individual will quite likely fail to match his desired consumption stream exactly, and reallocation by borrowing or saving will prove to be useful.

where C_0 is consumption in this period, C_1 is consumption in the next period, and C_n is consumption in the final period.[2,3] As a simple example we will study allocational problems in the case of a two-period utility function:

$$\text{Utility} = U(C_0, C_1) \qquad [8.2]$$

where it will be assumed that all other periods' consumption levels are held constant. The natural result for an individual who maximizes Equation 8.1 subject to a budget constraint (the form of which will be discussed later) is that he will equate his psychic rate of trade-off of C_0 for C_1 to the ratio of the "prices" at which they can be traded in the market. It will be shown that interest rates play the role of prices in such allocational problems over time. Therefore, the decision regarding consumption now versus consumption in the next period is importantly influenced by the interest rate prevailing between now and the next period. In the section on "Two-period Analysis" below several examples of this allocation are analyzed.

By referring to his own tastes and market interest rates the individual arrives at an optimal (utility-maximizing) plan of consumption. If his optimal consumption in year 0, say C_0^*, falls short of his income, he will borrow. On the other hand, if $C_0^* < Y_0$, he will have excess funds which may be saved for use in some future period.

The decision to borrow or to save raises the issue of exactly how to borrow, and how to invest one's savings. Some very simple aspects of this problem are discussed below. It will be shown that various monetary assets perform the task of reallocating consumption in different ways. The problem of "durable goods" (goods which last more than one period) is also discussed in relation to the more general issue of savings. Because many real-world goods (automobiles, washing machines, and so on) are not consumed during only one period, this section is important to any understanding of actual savings decisions.

Finally, the section on "Education and Human Capital" will examine a rather special investment an individual can make—in himself. To invest in one's own education may lead to a higher stream of future earnings and is therefore a very important aspect of the individual's allocational decision. Some simple economic principles can aid in an understanding of this decision to purchase *human capital*. Again, interest rates are shown to be important prices which enter into this allocational decision.

---

[2] The reader is reminded of the problems involved in using such aggregates. These are not discussed explicitly here.

[3] C_n might also include bequests (that is, gifts to future generations).

Interest Rates as Prices

Interest rates play a role in the maximizing of Equations 8.1 or 8.2 which is similar to that played by prices in the single-period model used in earlier chapters. Interest rates can be regarded as the "prices" which relate purchases between various time periods. Suppose the interest rate between period 0 and period 1 is given by $r_{0,1}$. Then, if I invest $1 this period, I will receive $1 \times (1 + r_{0,1})$ next period. Another way of saying this is that the *present value* of $1 of consumption goods next period is $1/1 + r_{0,1}$. If I invest $1/1 + r_{0,1}$ this period, I will be returned $1 in the next period. This is the simplest of the price relationships which connect expenditures this period with expenditures next period.[4]

As an illustration, consider the case where an individual has a fixed amount this period (W) to spend on either C_0 or C_1; the budget constraint would be:

$$C_1 = (W - C_0)(1 + r_{0,1})$$

or   [8.3]

$$C_0 + \frac{C_1}{1 + r_{0,1}} = W.$$

Equation 8.3 says that the rate at which the individual can trade C_0 for C_1 in the market is given by $1 + r_{0,1}$; for each unit of C_0 he gives up he can obtain $1 + r_{0,1}$ units of C_1. Hence $1 + r_{0,1}$ plays the same role here as relative prices did earlier. $1/1 + r_{0,1}$ is in fact the price of C_1 in terms of C_0. It will be shown below that an individual who is seeking to maximize Equation 8.2 subject to Equation 8.3 will in fact equate his *MRS* of C_0 for C_1 to the ratio of their "prices" (that is, to $1 + r_{0,1}$); the analogy between the two constrained-maximization problems is exact.

A similar analysis holds between any two periods. If $r_{0,k}$ is the interest rate which prevails between this period and period k, then the present value of $1 of consumption in period k is $1/1 + r_{0,k}$ and the relative price of consumption in the two periods is given by $1 + r_{0,k}$. By using the market for savings, he can exchange one unit of C_0 for $1 + r_{0,k}$ units of C_k. By similar reasoning it can be shown that for any two periods,

---

[4] The appendix to this chapter discusses several mathematical results about interest rates. These may be helpful in gaining a deeper understanding of some of the issues discussed here.

i and j, that $1 + r_{i,j}$ represents the rate at which C_i can be traded for C_j in the market.[5]

This discussion has implicitly assumed that prices for consumption goods remain constant between the two periods under investigation. This assumption permitted us to talk interchangeably about either exchanging C_0 for C_1 or exchanging \$1 in period 0 for \$1 in period 1. For the allocational problem we are interested in, clearly the former notion is the important one. Individuals are interested in the "real" rate of interest — in how they can exchange C_0 for C_1. Most interest rates which are in common usage (for example, the rate on savings accounts or on home mortgages), however, are "monetary" rates. They only record how \$1 in this period can be exchanged for \$1 in some future period. In periods of general inflation of prices this rate may not be very indicative of the real possibilities for trading consumption goods between the periods. More specifically if $R_{0,k}$ is the monetary rate of interest, and $P_{0,k}$ is the *percentage change* in prices between period 0 and period k, then the real rate of interest $(r_{0,k})$ is given by:[6]

$$r_{0,k} = R_{0,k} - P_{0,k}. \qquad [8.4]$$

In the next section of this chapter only real interest rates[7] will be used as these are the important magnitudes in allocational decisions. It is a simple matter to translate the analysis which is presented from real interest rate terms into monetary rate terms.

Two-period Analysis

Most of the important aspects of individual allocation over time can be illustrated using only two-period analysis. We will be interested in maxi-

[5] A k period savings decision can be looked at as a sequence of one-period decisions. If I wish to save now (period 0) for consumption in period k, this is equivalent to saving now for period 1, then reinvesting my accumulated savings in period 1 until period 2, and so forth. There is a necessary relationship between the "long-period rate" $r_{0,k}$ and the various short-term rates:
$1 + r_{0,k} = (1 + r_{0,1}) \times (1 + r_{1,2}) \times \cdots \times (1 + r_{k-1,k})$.

[6] A numerical example may help. If the one-period savings account rate is 5 percent, but prices are rising at 3 percent, then the real interest rate is only 2 percent. \$1 invested today yields \$1.05 in the next period, but the 3 percent inflation means that this sum will only buy what \$1.02 would buy today. One unit of C_0 trades for \$1.02 units of C_1. Notice that by Equation 8.4 it is at least possible for the real interest rate to be negative if the rate of inflation exceeds the monetary interest rate. It is also possible for prices to be falling $(P_{0,k} < 0)$, and in this case the real rate will exceed the monetary rate.

[7] Interest rates should also be defined as net of taxes, since it is the real, after-tax interest rate which truly represents the possibilities for reallocation over time.

mizing $U(C_0, C_1)$ in two separate situations: where the individual has a fixed amount of money today to allocate between C_0 and C_1, and where the individual has income in each period and must decide whether to borrow or save in the first period. Both of these cases will yield the same qualitative result: A utility-maximizing individual will equate his MRS (of C_0 for C_1) to $1 + r_{0,1}$. However, the budget constraints and the comparative statics results will differ in the two situations.

Consider first an individual who has a certain amount of money (W) to allocate between two periods. His budget constraint is given by Equation 8.3. If we let $r = r_{0,1}$ for simplification, then this constraint can be written as:

$$C_0 + \frac{C_1}{1 + r} = W \qquad [8.5]$$

or

$$C_1 = S(1 + r) \qquad [8.5']$$

where $S = (W - C_0)$ and is meant to represent current period savings. The individual can spend all of W on C_0 (implying $C_1 = 0$), or can spend $W(1 + r)$ on C_1 and nothing on C_0. More likely, however, if we assume there is a diminishing MRS of C_0 for C_1, he will spend some of W on C_0 and save some of it for use next period. This situation is illustrated in Figure 8.2. The budget constraint has slope $- (1 + r)$; this is the rate at which C_0 can be traded for C_1 in the market. The utility-maximizing point is $C_0{}^*$, $C_1{}^*$ where the budget constraint is tangent to the highest indifference curve. Here $S^* = W - C_0{}^*$ is the optimal amount saved.

From Figure 8.2 the result that the MRS (of C_0 for C_1) should equal $1 + r$ for a utility maximum is obvious. The result is exactly the same as that of Figure 4.2. A mathematical derivation would be an equally trivial application of the analysis previously presented.

The comparative statics analysis of a change in W is simple. Presumably both C_0 and C_1 will increase when W increases. It would be hard to conceive of either C_0 or C_1 being inferior goods.

The reaction to a change in r is more interesting. If r increases, then the substitution effect moves the optimal point in a northwest direction along U_2. In effect, the relative price of C_1 has declined and there is an incentive to increase C_1 and to decrease C_0. The income effect is positive for both periods' consumption since neither is inferior; a rise in r means the individual could (if he chose to) consume more in both periods. Therefore, for C_1 both income and substitution effects work in the same direction and $\partial C_1/\partial r$ must be positive. As before, a decline in the price of a

Figure 8.2   Optimal Allocation of a Fixed Sum of Money between Two Periods

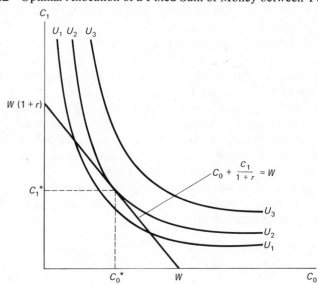

The budget constraint in this diagram represents the individual's possibilities for trading consumption this period (C_0) for consumption next period (C_1). The condition of utility maximization then is that the MRS (of C_0 for C_1) should equal the rate at which these can be traded in the market $(1 + r)$.

commodity (C_1) means that more of it will be consumed. The sign of $\partial C_0/\partial r$ is, however, ambiguous. The income and substitution effects work in opposite directions in this case, and the outcome depends on the relative strength of the two. In this simple situation, then, the effect of a change in r on savings $(W - C_0)$ is indeterminate.[8]

In a real-world savings situation the analysis is slightly different from that already outlined. Rather than having a fixed sum to allocate over present and future periods, the individual expects to earn some income in each period and must decide whether to borrow or save in the current period. If Y_0 is the individual's income in the current period and Y_1 is the income he will receive next period then his budget constraint is:

---

[8] Consider a numerical example: Suppose $W = \$100$ and that when $r = .05$, $C_0 = \$50$. Therefore $S = \$50$ and $C_1 = \$50 \times (1.05) = \$52.50$. Now if r rises to .10 the individual can keep C_1 at $\$52.50$ by reducing S to $\$47.73$ ($\$47.73 \times (1.10) = \$52.50$); alternatively he may keep $S = \$50$ (hence $C_1 = \$50 \times (1.10) = \$55.00$); or he may increase S and decrease C_0 in which case C_1 would exceed $\$55.00$. Either of these seems plausible, although the latter two are probably more likely (*see* Problem 8).

$$(Y_0 - C_0)(1 + r) = S(1 + r) = C_1 - Y_1 \tag{8.6}$$

or

$$C_1 = Y_1 + Y_0(1 + r) - C_0(1 + r). \tag{8.6'}$$

If $C_0 = 0$, then $C_1 = Y_1 + Y_0(1 + r)$; the individual can consume in the next period all of Y_1 and Y_0 plus the interest earned on Y_0. On the other hand, if $C_1 = 0$, then $C_0 = Y_0 + Y_1/1 + r$; in the current period he can consume all of Y_0 and can borrow $Y_1/1 + r$ with the intention of repaying the loan with his income in the next period. Since we assume there is a diminishing MRS between C_0 and C_1, the actual solution decided upon will be somewhere between these two extremes.

It is instructive to write out the first-order conditions for the maximization of $U(C_0, C_1)$ subject to the constraint Equation 8.6. The relevant Lagrangian expression is:

$$L = U(C_0, C_1) - \lambda[(Y_0 - C_0)(1 + r) - C_1 + Y_1]. \tag{8.7}$$

Differentiating with respect to C_0, C_1, and λ gives:

$$\frac{\partial L}{\partial C_0} = \frac{\partial U}{\partial C_0} + (1 + r)\lambda = 0$$

$$\frac{\partial L}{\partial C_1} = \frac{\partial U}{\partial C_1} + \lambda = 0 \tag{8.7'}$$

$$\frac{\partial L}{\partial \lambda} = (Y_0 - C_0)(1 + r) - C_1 + Y_1 = 0.$$

The first-order conditions state that:

$$MRS \ (C_0 \text{ for } C_1) = \frac{\frac{\partial U}{\partial C_0}}{\frac{\partial U}{\partial C_1}} = 1 + r \tag{8.8}$$

which is exactly the condition derived earlier. From Equation 8.7 it can be seen that λ has the interpretation of the marginal utility of C_1 whereas, at the maximum point, the marginal utility of C_0 is greater than this [that is, $(1 + r)\lambda$]. Somewhat loosely speaking, a utility-maximizing individual will consume "relatively less" now than in the future. Future goods are cheaper than are present goods due to the effect of interest payments.[9]

---

[9] This statement suggests that individuals prefer present to future consumption and must be paid some reward to postpone consumption into the future. This possibility is an important aspect of the study of the determination of the rate of interest which is taken up in Chapter 19.

A similar statement applies to income received in the two periods: An extra dollar of income this period adds more to utility than would an extra dollar of income next period. Present dollars are more desirable than future dollars because one has the opportunity to earn interest on present dollars.

A comparative statics analysis of the present case can only be briefly mentioned. In Figure 8.3 the initial budget constraint is shown as a solid line AA'. The initial equilibrium (which is not drawn) will be a tangency similar to that drawn in Figure 8.2. If this optimal point is a point such as 1, the individual will choose to be a saver $(Y_0 - C_0 > 0)$. On the other hand, if a point such as 2 is chosen, the individual borrows $C_0 - Y_0$ this period and pays it back next period. Whether point 1 or 2 will be selected obviously will depend on the individual's preferences between C_0 and C_1.

Figure 8.3 Possible Reactions to a Change in r when the Individual Has Income in Both Periods

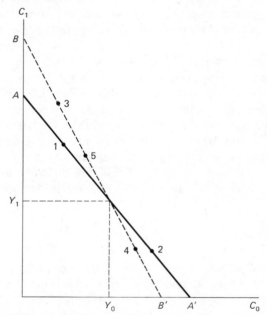

This diagram shows schematically how a person with income in both periods may react to an increase in r. The initial budget constraint is given by the solid line, whereas the new constraint is shown as a dashed line. If point 1 were initially chosen, it would be irrational to choose a point such as 4 when the interest rate rises.

Now suppose the interest rate rises. This can be illustrated by rotating the budget line about the point (Y_0, Y_1). The new budget constraint is given by the dashed line BB'. With a higher r the individual can, if he allocates all his current income to future purchases, increase the total amount he can buy in period 1 $(B > A)$. If all consumption is to be done in this period, total possible C_0 must fall because of the higher interest charges the individual must repay next period $(B' < A')$.

By using some geometrical and economic intuition it is possible to derive some comparative statics results from Figure 8.3. For example, if the individual is initially a saver, say at point 1, then saving can either increase (point 3) or decrease (point 5) in response to an increase in r. The income and substitution effects (as before) work in opposite directions in their effect on saving, and the ultimate result depends on the strength of these two effects. One thing is clear, however: The individual cannot, if he is acting rationally, respond to an increase in r by going from a net saver position (point 1) to a net borrower position (point 4, for example). Points such as 4 have already been revealed inferior to point 1 because they lie below the initial budget constraint AA'. Consequently we would not expect to observe savers become borrowers in response to a rise in r, nor would we expect borrowers to become savers when r falls.

This extended analysis is really nothing more than an elaboration of the two-good analysis presented in Chapters 3–5.[10] It has been developed in some detail here both for its value in illustrating certain aspects of individual allocation over time and because it provides some added facility with the utility-maximization hypothesis. We will also see (in the Appendix to Chapter 9) that this two-period analysis can be given another useful interpretation in the study of individual behavior under uncertainty. In the concluding sections of this chapter some applications of this analysis to real-world savings decisions will be developed.

Monetary Assets

Most of the reallocation of income that individuals engage in is through the use of monetary assets and liabilities. This is so because it is a great convenience to lend and borrow readily accepted units, such as dollars, which can then be traded for consumption goods. It is conceivable that one could lend or borrow actual consumption goods (indeed people do), but it is much simpler to deal with a common monetary unit and this is the most widespread practice.

Major monetary assets include money (demand deposits and cur-

[10] Diagrams such as those illustrated in Figures 8.2 and 8.3 are directly applicable to the two-good case when individuals start out with initial supplies of the goods and trade these in the market to bring about preferred results.

rency), savings accounts, life insurance, corporate stock, and bonds. All of these represent uses to which current savings can be put, so that purchasing power can be transferred into the future. In choosing among these assets the individual will both pay attention to the yield they promise[11] and to the special features of the asset. These special features differentiate one asset from another and make the real-world study of individual saving both complicated and interesting. A brief outline of these features is presented below. It is hoped that the reader will try to fit each of these into the general allocation problems discussed earlier in this chapter.

1. *Money* includes demand deposits (checking accounts) and currency. By law, neither of these yields a monetary return. Money is, however, extremely useful in conducting transactions (the alternative, trade by barter, would be extremely time-consuming), and it must be assumed that money yields a psychic return to its holder. Some people regard holding money (perhaps in a mattress) as the only "safe" form of savings. This is due to its *liquidity* — the ability to transform it rapidly into any other asset. As was pointed out in the section "Interest Rates as Prices," however, it is the real yield on any asset which determines its usefulness in reallocating consumption. In inflationary periods the real monetary yield on money will be negative and therefore its "safety" is not obvious.

2. *Savings accounts* come in a variety of forms ranging from small savings and loan accounts to large denomination (over $100,000) negotiable certificates of deposit. All of these yield a monetary return but are somewhat less liquid than money (that is, they cannot be so easily transferred into other assets as money can). Because the definition of "money" is not clearcut, some authors classify savings accounts as money also. However one chooses to define money, it is probably the case that cash and savings accounts are close substitutes. Because savings accounts yield a monetary return they are superior to cash for pure savings motives.

3. *Life insurance* is really two products in one: a savings asset and insurance against a particular risk. In some cases the individual can choose a policy which mixes these two elements to suit his own tastes. The yield on life insurance is therefore difficult to measure because some valuation must be assigned to the utility an individual receives from protection. The actual monetary yield earned on any

---

[11] The question of choosing among assets with different yields is of necessity a problem involving uncertainty. In a certain situation the choice would be a simple one — choose that asset with the highest yield (where "yield" is taken to include psychic returns in addition to monetary yield).

policy depends on an uncertain event (that is, the time of death), and therefore must be handled as a part of the theory of individual behavior under uncertainty.

4. *Corporate stock* is a claim on a portion of the earnings of some firm. These earnings are either paid out to the stock owner in the form of dividends or reinvested in the company. The yield on a stock is made up of two components; dividends and increases in the price of a share (capital gains). Since the individual is interested in after-tax yields, the latter of these is the preferred way to receive returns on stock because capital gains are taxed at a lower rate than are dividends. Since the earnings of a corporation are uncertain, the yield on a stock is also uncertain. Many of the studies of individual behavior under uncertainty which have been undertaken look at the market for stocks in drawing their conclusions.

5. A *bond* is a promise to pay certain fixed sums at various dates in the future. Bonds are issued in maturities ranging from three months through thirty years. For some savers short maturities are desired because of the greater liquidity provided, whereas other savers may prefer the assured interest payments provided by very long-term maturities. A saver may choose to match the bond's characteristics to his desired consumption stream. The mathematics used in the computation of bond yields is developed in the appendix to this chapter.

Just as the individual can use monetary assets to reallocate present income to future consumption, he can also borrow (contract for "negative assets" or liabilities) in order to transfer future income to the present for consumption purposes. The loan can then be repaid out of future income with the repayment being made either in several installments or in one sum. The two most common liabilities of individuals are mortgages and consumer credit. Mortgages are long-term loans (perhaps twenty years) which are repaid in regular installments. Often the obtaining of a mortgage is associated with the purchase of a house (*see* the next section below), but this should not obscure the basic fact that the primary function of a mortgage is to reallocate income over time. Consumer credit comes in a variety of forms, but is basically a short-term loan (less than two years) usually associated with the purchase of a major consumption item (an automobile is the most common case). The loan is either repaid monthly or in a single payment. Again the primary function of this liability in reallocating income should be stressed; the fact that it is generally closely tied to the purchase of a specific good is primarily an institutional peculiarity. The yield on a liability is negative (it is a cost) and is calculated in a manner similar to that used for the case of an asset. A rational individual will make decisions based on this yield,[12] although the actual computation of the yield may be made difficult because of the unusual terminology in which some liability contracts are phrased.

Durable Goods

In the theory of individual behavior developed so far it has been assumed that all goods which are purchased during a particular period are totally consumed in that period. In the real world some consumption goods are only consumed over a considerable length of time (houses are probably the most long-lived example), and the theory must be modified to take this into account. Theoretically, we are interested in the amount an individual consumes in each period. This consumption may be derived either from using up the good completely (for example, by eating a steak), or it may represent the consumption of the services provided by a "durable" good which will still physically exist in the next period. Some obvious examples of these durable goods are houses, automobiles, furniture, household appliances, and sports equipment.[13] Each of these has the property that its services are consumed over several periods.

The distinction between durable and nondurable goods is a difficult one to make in practice. First, the distinction depends on the length of the period being used and on the rate at which the good depreciates. Most clothing would be considered "durable" if a time period of one month were being used, while it would clearly be "nondurable" if a period of ten years were used. Durability (or lack of it) may also depend on the degree to which a good is used. A car which is only driven occasionally will obviously be more "durable" than one which is continuously driven at high speeds. Finally, a good may be treated as durable by some people and as nondurable by others. Consider a prize fish which has just been caught. This can be either eaten immediately (and hence be nondurable), or it may be preserved and hung in the living room, thus providing consumption (in the form of pride and admiring glances from guests) for many periods into the future. For these reasons any definition of durable goods will be to some extent arbitrary. The principle, however, is clear: Durable goods, once purchased, provide a stream of services over several future

---

[12] Again it is real, after-tax yields which are relevant in this case, since the ultimate aim is the reallocation of consumption.

[13] An intriguing analysis can be conducted by considering children to be durable goods subject to the same decision processes as are more conventional goods. It might be interesting for the reader to try to place fertility and family planning decisions into the general framework of individual utility maximization. For example, is it reasonable to say that the "demand" for children depends on all prices and income? How will changing prices and income affect this demand?

periods. For this reason the purchase of a durable good represents current savings to some extent. A durable good is a means of transferring current purchasing power into future consumption.

An important question is how to measure the consumption services yielded by a given durable good during a particular period. Conceptually, an answer to this question might be given by asking how much it would cost to rent the good for this period. For example, the value of consumption services yielded by a car during one year might be approximated by what it would cost to rent an identical car for that year. The value of the consumption services provided by any durable good could be estimated in a similar way.[14] Unfortunately the rental market for most durable goods is either underdeveloped (as in the case of major household appliances) or totally nonexistent (as in the case of "durable" clothing). Estimation of an accurate value to be assigned to the consumption services of a particular durable good is therefore very difficult.[15] Such services clearly do exist, and represent a major source of an individual's reallocation of consumption over time. In Chapter 19 a possible way of estimating an appropriate value for the services of a durable asset during a particular period is mentioned in connection with a more general discussion of capital theory.

Education and Human Capital

Education serves two distinct purposes for an individual. First, it presumably makes an individual a "better" person, in that his intellectual senses are sharpened; he is made more culturally aware; and he becomes more socially "acceptable." In this sense education is much like a durable good for it yields a stream of consumption services over an individual's lifetime. Second, education raises an individual's productivity, and therefore may raise his future income. In this sense investing in one's own education is similar to investing in a monetary asset: A monetary return is yielded in future periods. This second aspect of education has been intensively studied under the general heading of investment in "human capital." Looking at education in this way gives insights both into indi-

---

[14] The only important attempt which is currently made at estimating the consumption services yielded by durable goods is the estimate made in the National Income and Products Accounts of the value of services which accrue to the owners of homes. This estimation is made somewhat easier by the existence of a fairly well-developed rental market in housing.

[15] Because the "yield" on a durable good is much more difficult to estimate than is the yield on a monetary asset, frequently the latter is included in income to be taxed, whereas the former is not. This may create a bias toward the purchase of durable goods at the expense of monetary assets.

vidual decisions regarding the purchase of education and into questions about the optimal educational level for the population as a whole.

Conceptually, it is an easy matter to compute the yield on investment in human capital. If E_0 is the current cost of education and $I_1, I_2, ..., I_n$ are the *increments* to income attributable to this education in n future periods, then the present discounted value[16] of the benefits to educational expenditure is:

$$\frac{I_1}{(1 + i)} + \frac{I_2}{(1 + i)^2} + \cdots + \frac{I_n}{(1 + i)^n}.$$ [8.9]

Equating this to E_0 and solving for i, one can estimate the yield on these present educational expenditures. In this sense investment in human capital is formally identical to buying a bond. A current sum is invested and a stream of "pay-offs" is received in future periods. A yield on this investment would be calculated in exactly the same way that bond yields can be calculated. Unfortunately, in the real world two very difficult problems interfere with this calculation. One must differentiate between that portion of E_0 which goes toward pure consumption and that part which represents investment in human capital. Presumably it is only the latter which is relevant in computing the monetary yield on education. Even more important, however, is the difficulty in estimating the income increments (the I's). These are not only uncertain but also must represent only that portion of income directly attributable to the educational expenditure. To separate this factor from the other factors which enter into determining an individual's income might prove to be extremely difficult.

The analogy between human capital and monetary assets should not, however, be stretched too far. Human capital has a number of very special properties which make it unique among the assets an individual can purchase. First, contrary to other assets human capital (in the absence of slavery) cannot be sold. Human capital and its "owner" are necessarily tied together and cannot be separated. Therefore this is the most illiquid of assets. Second, human capital depreciates in a rather unusual way. Forgetfulness may produce some depreciation, but the death of an individual causes his accumulated human capital immediately to disappear. Sudden losses of substantial capital investments are possible. Finally, the acquisition of human capital takes considerably more time than does the acquisition of other assets. During this time substantial earnings may be foregone. These foregone earnings should be considered a cost of acquisition.

These observations point out both the difficulties in adequately

---

[16] See the appendix to this chapter for a definition of this term.

studying human capital and the insights which simple economic analysis can give. Education is an extremely important subject in current policy discussions, and viewing it as part of a general allocational problem over time aids greatly in clarifying many conceptual problems.

Conclusion

This chapter has expanded greatly on the simple model of utility maximization. By focusing attention on consumption in future periods various real-world aspects of individual behavior can be made more easily understood. The utility-maximization hypothesis remains central to the analysis and forms a convenient starting point for more detailed investigations. Specifically, we have shown that interest rates play the role of prices in individual decisions. This is true because interest rates indicate the terms at which the market allows consumption items in different periods to be exchanged. Any multiperiod decision an individual makes must take these prices into account.

The Mathematics of Compound Interest

Introduction

The purpose of this appendix is to gather together some simple results concerning the mathematics of compound interest. These results will not only be useful in several later sections of this book but also have applications in a wide variety of economic problems ranging from macroeconomic policy to the optimal way to raise Christmas trees (*see* Problem 5 of Part V).

We assume that there is a current prevailing market interest rate of i per period, say one year. This interest rate is assumed to be both certain and constant[1] over all future periods. If $1 is invested at this rate i, and the interest is compounded (that is, future interest is paid on past interest earned), then:

at the end of 1 period $1 will be ... $1 \times (1 + i)$

at the end of 2 periods $1 will be ... $1 \times (1 + i) \times (1 + i) = $1 \times (1 + i)^2$

$$\vdots$$

and

at the end of n periods $1 will be ... $1 \times (1 + i)^n$.

Similarly, N grows like:

$N \times (1 + i),$
$N \times (1 + i)^2$

$$\vdots$$

$N \times (1 + i)^n$.

Present Discounted Value

The *present value* of $1 payable one period from now is:

$$\frac{$1}{(1 + i)}.$$

This is simply the amount that an individual would be willing to pay now for the promise of $1 at the end of one period. Similarly, the present value of $1 payable n periods from now is:

$$\frac{$1}{(1 + i)^n}$$

and the present value of N payable n periods from now is:

$$\frac{$N}{(1 + i)^n}.$$

[1] The assumption of a constant i is obviously unrealistic. Since the problems introduced by considering an interest rate which varies from period to period greatly complicate the notation without adding a commensurate degree of conceptual knowledge, such an analysis is not undertaken here. In many cases the generalization to a varying interest rate is merely a trivial application of the equation given in Footnote 5 of Chapter 8.

The *present discounted value* of a stream of payments $N_0, N_1, N_2,...,$ N_n (where the subscripts indicate the period in which the payment is to to be made) is:

$$PDV = N_0 + \frac{N_1}{(1+i)} + \frac{N_2}{(1+i)^2} + \cdots + \frac{N_n}{(1+i)^n}. \qquad [8A.1]$$

PDV is the amount that an individual would be willing to pay in return for a promise to receive the stream $N_0, N_1,..., N_n$. It represents the amount that would have to be invested now if one wished to duplicate the payment stream.

Annuities and Perpetuities

An *annuity* is a promise to pay N dollars in each period for n periods, starting next period. The *PDV* of such a contract is:

$$PDV = \frac{N}{(1+i)} + \frac{N}{(1+i)^2} + \cdots + \frac{N}{(1+i)^n}. \qquad [8A.2]$$

Let $D = 1/(1+i)$, then:

$$
\begin{aligned}
PDV &= N(D + D^2 + \cdots + D^n) \\
&= ND(1 + D + D^2 + \cdots + D^{n-1}) \qquad [8A.3] \\
&= ND\left(\frac{1-D^n}{1-D}\right).
\end{aligned}
$$

Notice that $\lim_{n\to\infty} D^n = 0$.

Therefore, for an annuity of infinite duration:

$$PDV \text{ of infinite annuity} = \lim_{n\to\infty} PDV = ND\left(\frac{1}{1-D}\right), \qquad [8A.4]$$

which, by the definition of D:

$$
\begin{aligned}
&= N\left(\frac{1}{1+i}\right)\left(\frac{1}{1-\frac{1}{1+i}}\right) \\
&= N\left(\frac{1}{1+i}\right)\left(\frac{1+i}{i}\right) = \frac{N}{i}.
\end{aligned}
\qquad [8A.5]
$$

This case of an infinite period annuity is sometimes called a *perpetuity* or a *consol*. Such annuities are rare (indeed technically illegal) in the United States, but are common in Canada and the United Kingdom. The formula simply says that the amount that must be invested if one is to obtain $N per period forever is simply N/i, since this amount of money would earn $N in interest each period ($i \cdot \$N/i = \$N$).

The Special Case of a Bond

An n period *bond* is a promise to pay N dollars each period (starting next period) for n periods. It also promises to return the principal (face) value of the bond at the end of n periods. If the principal value of the bond is P dollars (usually $1000 in the United States bond market) then the present discounted value of such a promise is:

$$PDV = \frac{N}{(1+i)} + \frac{N}{(1+i)^2} + \cdots + \frac{N}{(1+i)^n} + \frac{P}{(1+i)^n}. \qquad [8A.6]$$

Again let $D = 1/(1+i)$, then:

$$PDV = ND + ND^2 + \cdots + (N+P)D^n. \qquad [8A.7]$$

Equation 8A.7 can be looked at in another way. Suppose we knew the price at which the bond is currently trading, say B. Then we could ask what value of i gives the bond a *PDV* equal to B. To find this i we set:

$$B = PDV = ND + ND^2 + \cdots + (N+P)D^n. \qquad [8A.8]$$

Since B, N, and P are known, we can solve this equation for D and hence for i.[2] The i which solves the equation is called the *yield* on the bond, and is the best measure of the return actually available from the bond. The yield of a bond represents the return available both from direct interest payments and from any price differential between the initial price (B) and the maturity price (P).

Notice that as i increases, *PDV* decreases. This is a precise way of formulating the well-known concept that bond prices (*PDV*'s) and interest rates (yields) are inversely correlated.

---

[2] Since this equation is really an nth degree polynomial, there are in reality n solutions (roots). Only one of these solutions is the relevant one reported in bond tables. The other solutions are either imaginary or are unreasonable. In the present example there is only one real solution.

Continuous Time

So far this appendix has dealt with discrete time — the analysis has been divided into periods. Often it is more convenient to deal with continuous time. In such a case the interest on an investment is compounded "instantaneously" and growth over time is "smooth." This facilitates the analysis of maximization problems because certain functions are more easily differentiated.

Suppose that i is given as the (nominal) interest rate per year, but that half this nominal rate is compounded every six months. Then, at the end of one year, the investment of $1 would have grown to:

$$\$1 \times \left(1 + \frac{i}{2}\right)^2. \tag{8A.9}$$

Notice that this is superior to investing for one year at the simple rate, i, because interest has been paid on interest; that is:

$$\left(1 + \frac{i}{2}\right)^2 > (1 + i). \tag{8A.10}$$

Consider the limit of this process — for the nominal rate of i per period consider the amount that would be realized if i were in fact "compounded n times during the period"; let $n \to \infty$:

$$\lim_{n \to \infty} \left(1 + \frac{i}{n}\right)^n. \tag{8A.11}$$

This limit exists and is simply e^i, where e is the base of natural logarithms (the value of e is approximately 2.72). It is important to note that $e^i > (1 + i)$ — it is much better to have continuous compounding over the period than to have simple interest.

We can ask what continuous rate, r, yields the same amount at the end of one period as the simple rate i. We are looking for the value of r which solves the equation:

$$e^r = (1 + i). \tag{8A.12}$$

Hence:

$$r = \log_e(1 + i). \tag{8A.12'}$$

Using this formula, it is a simple matter to translate from discrete interest rates into continuous ones. If i is measured in percent per year, then r is a yearly continuous rate.

One dollar invested at r will become:

$$V = \$1 \cdot e^{rT} \tag{8A.13}$$

after T years. This growth formula is a very convenient one to work with. For example, it is easy to show that the instantaneous relative rate of change in V is, as would be expected, simply given by r:

$$\text{Rate of change} = \frac{\dfrac{dV}{dt}}{V} = \frac{re^{rt}}{e^{rt}} = r. \tag{8A.14}$$

Continuous interest rates are also convenient for calculating present discounted values. Suppose we wished to calculate the *PDV* of \$1 to be paid T years from now. This would be given by:[3]

$$\frac{\$1}{e^{rT}} = \$1 \cdot e^{-rT}. \tag{8A.15}$$

The logic of this calculation is exactly the same as that used in the discrete time analysis of the section, "Interest Rates as Prices"; future dollars are worth less than present ones.

One interesting application of continuous discounting occurs in calculating the *PDV* of \$1 paid *each instant* from today (time 0) until period T. Since there would be an infinite number of payments, the mathematical tool of integration must be used to compute this result.

$$PDV = \int_0^T e^{-rt}\, dt. \tag{8A.16}$$

All this statement says is that we are adding all the discounted dollars over the time period 0 to T.

The value of this definite integral is given by:

$$PDV = \left. \frac{-e^{-rt}}{r} \right|_0^T \tag{8A.17}$$

$$= \frac{-e^{-rT}}{r} + \frac{1}{r}.$$

---

[3] In physics this formula occurs as an example of "radioactive decay." If one unit of a substance decays continuously at the rate δ then, after T periods, $e^{-\delta T}$ will remain. This amount never exactly reaches 0 no matter how large T is.

If we let T go to infinity this value becomes:

$$PDV = \frac{1}{r} \qquad \text{[8A.18]}$$

as was the case for the infinitely long annuity considered above.

Continuous discounting is particularly convenient for calculating the PDV of an arbitrary stream of payments over time. Suppose $f(t)$ records the number of dollars to be paid at time t. Then the PDV of the payment at time T is:

$$e^{-rT} f(T) \qquad \text{[8A.19]}$$

and the PDV of the entire stream from the present time (year 0) until year T is given by:

$$\int_0^T f(t)\, e^{-rt}\, dt. \qquad \text{[8A.20]}$$

CHAPTER 9
Individual Behavior under Uncertainty

Introduction

In previous chapters it has been implicitly assumed that the individual makes his decisions in an environment characterized by certainty. When an individual purchases a good he knows exactly what he is getting and how much utility this will yield. Once the allocation of his budget is determined, there is no uncertainty associated with the utility he will derive.

In a variety of real-world situations this assumption cannot be considered tenable. First, some goods which individuals purchase are in the nature of games or lotteries in which the outcome is uncertain. Racetrack

143

bets, craps, insurance purchases, and stock market transactions all fit into this general category: The purchase of the good does not guarantee any particular outcome. A second way in which uncertainty affects individual behavior is in dealings with others. Many encounters between individuals are in the form of adversary proceedings in which the reward that anyone receives will depend on what the others do. This type of uncertainty is manifest in numerous situations ranging from poker games to the conduct of diplomacy.

A final way in which the individual is confronted by uncertainty is because of a lack of understanding or of information concerning the problem he is trying to solve. An individual is not able to predict the weather with any degree of certainty, nor is he able to decide specifically which refrigerator offers the best quality for his money. In such situations he is faced by a lack of knowledge and might be willing to pay something for additional information.

Of these three types of uncertainty the first is the most easily investigated and will occupy the major portion of this chapter. The analysis used to study this first type of uncertainty also is extremely useful in analyzing the other two types, and some of these interactions will be mentioned. In an appendix to this chapter an alternative and all-encompassing approach to the problem of uncertainty which has only recently been developed will be discussed briefly.

The study of individual behavior under uncertainty and the mathematical study of probability and statistics has a common historical origin in attempts to understand (and presumably to win) games of chance. The study of simple coin-flipping games, for example, has been unusually productive in the mathematics which has been developed from these games and in illuminating certain characteristics of human behavior which they exhibit. Two statistical concepts which originated in such games, and will be quite useful in the remainder of this chapter, are *probability* and *expected value*. These are discussed below.

The *probability* of an event happening is, roughly speaking, the relative frequency with which it will occur. For example, to say that the probability of a head on the flip of a fair coin is 1/2 means that one would expect that, if a fair coin were flipped a large number of times, a head would appear in approximately 1/2 of the trials. Similarly, the probability of rolling a two on a single die is 1/6. In approximately one out of every six rolls a two will come up.

Suppose a lottery offers n prizes (some of which may be 0) $X_1, X_2, \ldots, X_n$ and that the probabilities of winning these prizes are $\pi_1, \pi_2, \ldots, \pi_n$. If we assume one and only one prize will be awarded to a player it must be the case that:

$$\sum_{i=1}^{n} \pi_i = 1. \tag{9.1}$$

Equation 9.1 simply says that some outcome has to occur. The *expected value* (or *mean value*) of this lottery is defined as:[1]

$$\text{Expected value} = \pi_1 X_1 + \pi_2 X_2 + \cdots + \pi_n X_n = \sum_{i=1}^{n} \pi_i X_i. \tag{9.2}$$

The expected value of the lottery is a weighted sum of the prizes where the weights are the respective probabilities. It is simply the size of the prize that the player will win, on average. As an example, suppose Jones and Smith agree to flip a coin once. If the coin comes up heads, Jones pays Smith \$1; if the coin comes up tails, Smith pays Jones \$1. From Smith's point of view there are two prizes in this game: If the coin is heads $X_1 = +\$1$; if it comes up tails $X_2 = -\$1$, where the minus sign indicates that Smith must pay. From Jones' point of view the game is exactly the same except that the signs of the outcomes are reversed. The expected value of the game is then:

$$\frac{1}{2} X_1 + \frac{1}{2} X_2 = \frac{1}{2} (\$1) + \frac{1}{2} (-\$1) = 0. \tag{9.3}$$

The game has expected value 0. If the game were to be played a large number of times, it is not likely that either player would come out very far ahead.

Now suppose the prizes of the game were changed slightly so that (again from Smith's point of view) $X_1 = \$10$, $X_2 = -\$1$. Smith will win \$10 if a head comes up, but will lose only \$1 if it is a tail. The expected value of this game is:

$$\frac{1}{2} X_1 + \frac{1}{2} X_2 = \frac{1}{2} (\$10) + \frac{1}{2} (-\$1) = \$5 - \$.50 = \$4.50. \tag{9.4}$$

If this game is played many times Smith will certainly end up the big winner. In fact, Smith might be willing to pay Jones something for the privilege of playing the game. He might even be willing to pay as much as \$4.50 for a chance to play. Games such as that in Equation 9.3 which have expected value 0, or games such as Equation 9.4 which do cost their expected values (here \$4.50) for the right to play are called (actuarially)

---

[1] It is an easy matter to define the expected value of a game with continuous outcomes by generalizing Equation 9.2 to an integral.

fair games. A common observation is that, in many situations, people will refuse to play actuarially fair games. This point is central to an understanding of developments in the theory of uncertainty and is taken up in the next section.

Fair Games and the Expected Utility Hypothesis

People are generally unwilling to play fair games.[2] I may at times agree to flip a coin for small amounts of money, but if I were offered the chance to wager $1000 on one coin flip I would undoubtedly refuse. Similarly, I would probably not be willing to pay $4.50 for the right to participate in the game of Equation 9.4 even though this price is actuarially fair. An even more convincing example is the "St. Petersburg Paradox," which was first rigorously investigated by the mathematician Daniel Bernoulli in the eighteenth century.[3] In the St. Petersburg Paradox the following game is proposed: A coin is flipped until a head appears. If a head first appears on the nth flip, the player is paid $\$2^n$. This game has an infinite number of outcomes (a coin might be flipped from now 'til doomsday and never come up heads although the likelihood of this is small), but the first few can easily be written down. If X_i represents the prize awarded when the first head appears on the ith trial, then:

$$X_1 = \$2$$
$$X_2 = \$4$$
$$X_3 = \$8$$
$$\vdots$$

$$X_n = \$2^n \qquad\qquad\qquad\qquad [9.5]$$
$$\vdots$$

The probability of getting a head for the first time on the ith trial is $1/2^i$; it is the probability of getting $(i-1)$ tails and then a head. Hence the probabilities of the prizes given in Equation 9.5 are:

[2] The games discussed here are assumed to yield no utility in their play other than the prizes. Hence, the observation that many individuals gamble at "unfair" odds (for instance, in the game of roulette where there are 38 possible outcomes but the house only pays 36 to 1 for a winning number) is not necessarily a refutation of this statement. Rather, such individuals can reasonably be assumed to be deriving some utility from the circumstances associated with the play of the game. It is conceptually possible therefore to differentiate the consumption aspect of gambling from the pure risk aspect.

[3] The original Bernoulli article is well worth reading. It has been reprinted as D. Bernoulli, "Exposition of a New Theory on the Measurement of Risk," *Econometrica*, vol. 22 (January 1954), pp. 23–36.

$$\pi_1 = \frac{1}{2}$$

$$\pi_2 = \frac{1}{4}$$

$$\pi_3 = \frac{1}{8}$$

$$\vdots$$

$$\pi_n = \frac{1}{2^n}$$

$$\vdots$$

[9.6]

Notice that the sum of the probabilities is equal to 1 since some outcome must occur:

$$\sum_{i=1}^{\infty} \pi_i = \sum_{i=1}^{\infty} \frac{1}{2^i} = \frac{1}{2}\left(1 + \frac{1}{2} + \frac{1}{4} \cdots\right)$$

$$= \frac{1}{2} \cdot \left(\frac{1}{1 - \frac{1}{2}}\right) = \frac{1}{2} \cdot 2 = 1.$$

[9.7]

The expected value of the St. Petersburg Paradox game is infinite:

$$\text{Expected value} = \sum_{i=1}^{\infty} \pi_i X_i = \sum_{i=1}^{\infty} 2^i \frac{1}{2^i}$$

$$= 1 + 1 + 1 + \cdots + 1 \cdots = \infty.$$

[9.8]

Some introspection, however, should convince anyone that no player would pay very much (much less than infinity) to play this game. If I charged $1 billion to play the game, I would surely have no takers despite the fact that $1 billion is still considerably less than the expected value of the game. This, then, is the paradox — Bernoulli's game is in some sense not worth its (infinite) expected dollar value.

Bernoulli's solution to this paradox was to argue that individuals do not really care about the dollar prizes of a game; rather they respond to the utility which these dollars provide. If it is assumed that the marginal utility of income declines as income increases, the St. Petersburg game may converge to a finite *expected utility* value which players would be willing to pay for the right to play. Bernoulli termed this expected utility value the "moral value" of the game, since it represents how much the game is worth to the individual. Because utility may rise less rapidly than income it is possible that a game's moral value will fall short of its monetary expected value.

More specifically, Bernoulli proposed a particular utility function:

$$U(Y) = a \log Y \qquad [9.9]$$

where a is some positive constant. The prizes of the game must then be expressed in terms of this utility measure. If the utility prizes of the game are denoted by X_i^*, then:

$$X_i^* = a \log X_i \qquad [9.10]$$

or

$$
\begin{aligned}
X_1^* &= a \log 2 \\
X_2^* &= a \log 2^2 = 2 \, a \log 2 \\
&\vdots \\
X_n^* &= a \log 2^n = n \, a \log 2 \\
&\vdots
\end{aligned}
\qquad [9.10']
$$

and the expected utility (or moral value) of the game is:

$$
\begin{aligned}
\text{Expected utility} &= \sum_{i=1}^{\infty} \pi_i X_i^* = \sum_{i=1}^{\infty} \frac{i}{2^i} \cdot i \, a \log 2 \\
&= a \log 2 \sum_{i=1}^{\infty} \frac{i}{2^i} = 2 \, a \log 2 \\
&= 1.39 \, a.
\end{aligned}
\qquad [9.11]
$$

Therefore the expected utility of the game is finite and may (for small values of a) be a very "reasonable" number. Since this theoretical solution agrees with intuitive ideas about what people might be willing to pay for the right to participate in the St. Petersburg game, it can be claimed that Bernoulli solved the paradox. In studying individual's choices among uncertain ventures emphasis must be placed on the utility of outcomes rather than on dollar values.

While Bernoulli's basic observation is extremely important to any discussion of individual behavior under uncertainty, he did not really solve the St. Petersburg Paradox. So long as there is no upper bound on utility function,[4] the prizes in the game can be suitably redefined so as to regenerate the paradox. (In the problems to Part II the reader is asked to speculate on other, perhaps "noneconomic," explanations for the paradox.) However, Bernoulli clearly had an important observation about individual behavior, and the hypothesis that individuals look at expected utility rather than at expected dollar values has a great intuitive appeal.

The principal problem with the Bernoulli expected utility hypothesis is that it assumes measurable utility. As was pointed out in Chapter 3 theoretical advances since Bernoulli's time cast great doubt on the validity of this assumption. For this reason, until rather recently the expected utility hypothesis was only an interesting theoretical curiosity. In 1944, however, J. von Neumann and O. Morgenstern laid the foundations for a new way of looking at individual behavior in uncertain situations which returned the expected utility hypothesis (somewhat revised) to the center of attention. The next section will briefly discuss Von Neumann's and Morgenstern's results.

The Von Neumann-Morgenstern Theorem

In their book, *The Theory of Games and Economic Behavior*,[5] Von Neumann and Morgenstern developed mathematical models for examining relationships among individuals under conditions of uncertainty. To examine these interactions it was necessary first to investigate the motives of the participants in such "games." Since the hypothesis that individuals make choices in uncertain situations based on expected utility seemed intuitively reasonable, the authors set out to show that this hypothesis could be derived from more basic axioms of "rational" behavior. We will not investigate these axioms in any detail. The axioms represent an attempt by the authors to generalize some of the foundations of the theory of individual choice to cover uncertain situations. While most of these axioms seem eminently reasonable at first glance, many

---

[4] This problem and several others have prompted many investigators to adopt the assumption of a bounded utility function. It is assumed that there is some income level above which utility no longer increases with further increases in income.

For example, suppose that the level of bliss is taken to be 2^{42} (which is about the total value of all physical assets in the United States). Then prizes greater than this are worth no more than 2^{42}. Under this assumption the *expected value* of the St. Petersburg game is a "reasonable" $43. This level of "bliss" is so far above any observable level of income as to be irrelevant to real-world problems. In this case the assumption of boundedness is merely a convenient assumption without any stringent empirical content.

[5] J. von Neumann and O. Morgenstern, *The Theory of Games and Economic Behavior* (Princeton, N.J.: Princeton University Press, 1944). The axioms of rationality in uncertain situations are discussed in the appendix.

important questions about their tenability have been raised.[6] Generally it seems to be quite difficult to develop a universally agreed upon set of principles of rational behavior under conditions of uncertainty.

Even without discussing the axioms in detail, it is possible to show how Von Neumann and Morgenstern were able to avoid the problem of utility measurement. Suppose there are n possible prizes which an individual might win by participating in a game. Let these prizes be denoted by $X_1, X_2,..., X_n$ and assume (without loss of generality) that these have been arranged in order of ascending desirability. X_1 is therefore the least preferred prize for the individual, and X_n is his most preferred prize. Now assign arbitrary utility numbers to these two extreme prizes. For example, it might be convenient to assume:

$$U(X_1) = 0$$
$$U(X_n) = 1$$

[9.12]

but any other pair of numbers would do equally well.[7] Using these two values of utility, the point of the Von Neumann-Morgenstern Theorem is to show that a reasonable way exists to assign specific utility numbers to the other prizes available. Suppose we choose any other prize, say X_i. Consider the following experiment. Ask the individual at what probability, say π_i, he would be indifferent between X_i with *certainty* and a *gamble* offering prizes of X_n with probability π_i and X_1 with probability $(1 - \pi_i)$. It seems reasonable (although again this is a questionable axiom) that such a probability will exist: The individual will always be indifferent between a gamble and a sure thing providing that a high enough probability of winning the best prize is offered. It also seems likely that π_i will be higher the more desirable X_i is; the better X_i is, the better a chance of winning X_n must be offered to get the individual to gamble. In some sense the probability π_i represents how desirable the prize X_i is. In fact, the Von Neumann-Morgenstern technique is to define the utility of X_i to be the expected utility of the gamble which the individual considers to be equally desirable to X_i:

---

[6] An excellent summary of these axioms, together with an elementary (but insightful) discussion of the debate over the axioms, is presented in R. D. Luce and H. Raiffa, *Games and Decisions* (New York: J. Wiley & Sons, Inc., 1957), Chap. 2.

[7] Technically, a Von Neumann-Morgenstern utility index is unique only up to a choice of scale and origin—only up to a "linear transformation." This is also true, for example, of temperature scales (Centigrade, Fahrenheit, Kelvin).

Notice that the requirement that these utility numbers be unique up to a linear transformation is more stringent than the requirement, discussed in Chapter 3, that a utility function be unique up to a monotonic transformation.

$$U(X_i) = \pi_i \cdot U(X_n) + (1 - \pi_i) \cdot U(X_1)$$
$$= \pi_i \cdot 1 + (1 - \pi_i) \cdot 0 \qquad [9.13]$$
$$= \pi_i.$$

By judiciously choosing the utility numbers to be assigned to the best and worst prizes, we have been able to show that the utility number attached to any other prize is simply the probability which was defined above. This choice of utility numbers is totally arbitrary. Any other two numbers could have been used in Equation 9.12 and hence $U(X_i)$ would have to be redefined using Equation 9.13.

By means of these methods we can assign utility numbers to every prize. In line with the choice of scale and origin represented by Equation 9.13 suppose that some probability π_i has been asigned to represent the utility of every prize X_i. Notice in particular that $\pi_1 = 0$ and $\pi_n = 1$ and that the other utility values range between these extremes. Using these utility numbers it is possible to show that a "rational" individual will choose among gambles based on their expected "utilities" (that is, based on the expected value of these Von Neumann-Morgenstern numbers).

As an example, consider two gambles. One gamble offers X_2 with probability q and X_3 with probability $(1 - q)$. The other offers X_5 with probability t and X_6 with probability $(1 - t)$. We want to show that the individual will choose gamble 1 if and only if the expected utility of gamble 1 exceeds that of gamble 2. Now for the gambles:

$$\text{Expected utility (1)} = q \cdot U(X_2) + (1 - q) \cdot U(X_3)$$
$$\text{Expected utility (2)} = t \cdot U(X_5) + (1 - t) \cdot U(X_6). \qquad [9.14]$$

Substituting the utility index numbers (that is, π_2 is the "utility" of X_2, and so forth) gives:

$$\text{Expected utility (1)} = q \cdot \pi_2 + (1 - q) \cdot \pi_3$$
$$\text{Expected utility (2)} = t \cdot \pi_5 + (1 - t) \cdot \pi_6. \qquad [9.15]$$

We wish to show that the individual will prefer gamble 1 to gamble 2 if and only if:

$$q \cdot \pi_2 + (1 - q) \cdot \pi_3 > t \cdot \pi_5 + (1 - t) \cdot \pi_6. \qquad [9.16]$$

To show this, recall the definitions of the utility index. The individual is indifferent between X_2, say, and a gamble promising X_1 with probability

$(1 - \pi_2)$, and X_n with probability π_2. Now use this fact to substitute gambles involving X_1 and X_n for the utilities in Equation 9.15 (even though the individual is indifferent between these, the assumption that this substitution can be made is another of the important Von Neumann-Morgenstern axioms).

$$
\begin{aligned}
\text{Expected utility (1)} &= q[\pi_2 \cdot U(X_n) + (1 - \pi_2) \cdot U(X_1)] + (1 - q)[\pi_3 \cdot \\
&\quad U(X_n) + (1 - \pi_3) \cdot U(X_1)] \\
&= [q\pi_2 + (1 - q)\pi_3] \cdot U(X_n) + [q(1 - \pi_2) + (1 - q) \\
&\quad (1 - \pi_3)] \cdot U(X_1). \\
\text{Expected utility (2)} &= t[\pi_5 \cdot U(X_n) + (1 - \pi_5) \cdot U(X_1)] + (1 - t)[\pi_6 \cdot \\
&\quad U(X_n) + (1 - \pi_6) \cdot U(X_1)] \\
&= [t\pi_5 + (1 - t)\pi_6] \cdot U(X_n) + [t(1 - \pi_5) + (1 - t) \\
&\quad (1 - \pi_6)] \cdot U(X_1).
\end{aligned}
$$

$$[9.17]$$

Consequently, gamble 1 is equivalent to a gamble promising X_n with probability $q\pi_2 + (1 - q)\pi_3$, and gamble 2 is equivalent to a gamble promising X_n with probability $t\pi_5 + (1 - t)\pi_6$. The individual will presumably prefer that gamble with the highest probability of winning the best prize. Consequently, he will choose gamble 1 if and only if:

$$q\pi_2 + (1 - q)\pi_3 > t\pi_5 + (1 - t)\pi_6. \qquad [9.18]$$

But this was what was asked to be shown in Equation 9.16. Consequently, we have proved that an individual will choose from among gambles that one which provides the highest level of expected (Von Neumann-Morgenstern) utility.

In a sense then the Von Neumann-Morgenstern ordering plays the role of a utility function and individuals can be shown to maximize expected "utility." Since much debate and confusion has centered on the exact relationship, if any, between Von Neumann-Morgenstern "utility" and the more traditional concept it is best to keep the two ideas distinct. In the remainder of this chapter the "utility" functions which are used will in fact represent Von Neumann-Morgenstern orderings. It will be assumed that the basic Von Neumann-Morgenstern axioms hold, and therefore that it is possible to talk about individuals maximizing *expected utility*. While this is the most productive way to investigate individual decisions under uncertainty, it is not the only way, as is pointed out in the sections "Other Types of Uncertainty" and "Games against Nature."

Risk Aversion

Two lotteries may have the same expected monetary value, but may differ in their riskiness. For example, flipping a coin for $1 and flipping a coin for $1000 are both fair games and both have the same expected value (0). However, the latter is in some sense more "risky" than the former, and fewer people would participate in the game for which the prize was winning or losing $1000. The purpose of this section is to discuss the meaning of the term "risky" and to explain the widespread aversion to risk.

The term *risk* refers to the variability of the outcomes of some uncertain activity.[8] If variability is high the outcome of the activity must be considered risky; if variability is low the activity may be approximately a sure thing. With no more precise notion of variability than this, it is possible to show why individuals, when faced with a choice between two gambles with the same expected value, will usually choose the one with a smaller variability of return. Intuitively, the reason behind this is that we usually assume that the marginal utility from extra dollars of prize money (that is, income) declines as the prizes get larger. A flip of a coin for $1000 promises a relatively small gain of utility if you win, but a large loss of utility if you lose. A bet of only $1 is "inconsequential" and the gain in utility from a win approximately counterbalances the decline in utility from a loss.

This argument is illustrated in Figure 9.1. Here Y^* represents the individual's current income and $U(Y)$ is a Von Neumann-Morgenstern utility function which reflects how the individual feels about various levels of income. $U(Y)$ is drawn as a concave function of Y to reflect the assumption of a diminishing marginal utility of income. It is assumed that obtaining an extra dollar adds less to enjoyment as total income increases. Now suppose the individual is offered two fair gambles: a fifty-fifty chance of winning or losing h or a fifty-fifty chance of winning or

---

[8] Often risk or variability is used synonymously with the statistical concept of "variance." If the outcomes of a lottery are $X_1, X_2,..., X_n$ with probabilities $\pi_1, \pi_2,..., \pi_n$ and the expected value of the game is denoted by μ_X (that is, $\mu_X = \sum_{i=1}^{n} \pi_i X_i$), then the variance of the game is defined as:

$$\text{Variance} = \sum_{i=1}^{n} (X_i - \mu_X)^2 \pi_i.$$

If many of the X_i are far from μ_X the outcome of the lottery will be highly variable and the variance will be high. If most of the X's are close to μ_X the mean prize (μ_X) will be nearly assured and the variance will consequently be small. Sometimes the square root of the variance, the "standard deviation," is used as a measure of riskiness.

losing $2h$. The utility of his present income is $U(Y^*)$. His expected utility if he participates in gamble 1 is given by $U^h(Y^*)$:

$$U^h(Y^*) = \frac{1}{2} U(Y^* + h) + \frac{1}{2} U(Y^* - h) \qquad\qquad [9.19]$$

and the expected utility of gamble 2 is given by $U^{2h}(Y^*)$:

$$U^{2h}(Y^*) = \frac{1}{2} U(Y^* + 2h) + \frac{1}{2} U(Y^* - 2h). \qquad\qquad [9.20]$$

It is geometrically clear from the figure that:

$$U(Y^*) > U^h(Y^*) > U^{2h}(Y^*). \qquad\qquad [9.21]$$

Figure 9.1   Utility of Income from Two Fair Bets of Differing Variability

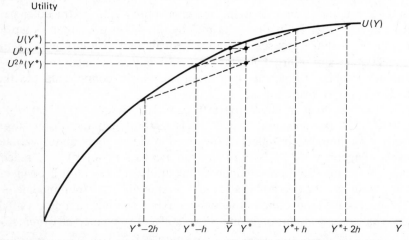

If the individual's utility of income function is concave (that is, exhibits a diminishing marginal utility of income) he will refuse fair bets. A fifty-fifty bet of winning or losing h dollars, for example, yields less utility $[U^h(Y^*)]$ than does refusing the bet. The reason for this is that winning h dollars means less to such an individual than does losing h dollars.

The individual will therefore prefer his current income to his current income combined with a fair gamble, and will prefer a small gamble to a large one. The reason for this is that winning a fair bet adds to the individual's enjoyment less than losing hurts him. Although the prizes are equal in dollar terms, in utility terms the loss is more serious. As a matter of fact the individual might be willing to pay some amount of his current income to avoid participating in a gamble. Notice that a certain income of $\bar{Y}$ provides the same utility as does participating in gamble 1. The individual will be willing to pay anything up to $Y^* - \bar{Y}$ to avoid participating in the gamble. This undoubtedly explains why people buy insurance; they are giving up a small amount of certain income (the premium) to avoid the risky outcome which is insured against. It also may explain why individuals place person-to-person phone calls. They are paying a higher cost to avoid the gamble inherent in calling station-to-station, even though they may believe there is a 95 percent chance that the person called will be there anyway.

An individual who is characterized by a diminishing marginal utility of income is therefore a *risk averter*.[9] He will pay some amount of money to avoid gambles; or, phrased another way, he will only take a chance of winning or losing $h if the odds are slanted in his favor. Even if it is accepted that risk-aversion is the prevalent attitude toward risk, there are many pieces of evidence which suggest that it is not an absolute rule. Many instances which purport to show that individuals are risk-takers (casino gambling, racetrack betting, buying penny stocks) have substantial consumption (as opposed to pure risk) aspects associated with them and thus are not a clearcut contradiction to risk aversion. However, individuals do participate in unfair games (for example, state lotteries

---

[9] Sometimes it is desirable to have a measure of exactly how averse to risk an individual is. It might be desirable to look at the second derivative $[U''(Y)]$ of the utility function for this information, but this is not a scale-free measure; the value taken by $U''(Y)$ depends on which particular Von Neumann-Morgenstern ranking we use. Since no ranking has any particular claim on being the "correct" one (any linear transformation satisfies the axioms of rationality) this is a clearly undesirable state of affairs. For this reason a measure of (absolute) risk aversion $[r(Y)]$ has been defined as:

$$r(Y) = \frac{-U''(Y)}{U'(Y)}.$$

It is easy to show that this measure is independent of the particular ordering used. If $U^* = a + bU$, then for this transformed utility function:

$$r(Y) = \frac{-U^{*\prime\prime}(Y)}{U^{*\prime}(Y)} = \frac{-bU''(Y)}{bU'(Y)} = \frac{-U''(Y)}{U'(Y)}.$$

It can be demonstrated that $r(Y)$ has a number of intuitively pleasing properties. In particular $r(Y)$ is approximately proportional to the amount an individual will pay to avoid a small fair bet. If the individual becomes more risk averse $[r(Y)$ rises] this amount of money will also increase.

An important theoretical question is what happens to $r(Y)$ as income increases. There is some presumption that $r'(Y) < 0$. This says that the amount one is willing to pay for insurance against a particular risk declines as income increases.

such as that which exists in New Hampshire) where the consumption aspects of participation must be regarded as minimal. To explain such behavior two assumptions are possible: People act irrationally (that is, not in their own best interest) in some risky situations; or there are segments of individuals' utility of income function which are not concave, and in these convex sections individuals will be risk-takers. The latter assumption seems more amenable to investigation and has been extensively examined by Friedman and Savage[10] and by others.

The Mean-Variability Approach to Investment Decisions

Investments generally offer uncertain returns which individuals project to have a mean (that is, expected value) and variability. Some "safe" investments, say savings accounts, offer a low mean return combined with a low variability of this return; whereas other "speculative" investments may offer a high expected value of return, but this return may be quite variable. In making investment decisions the individual must weigh these two aspects and decide on a proper allocation of his assets among those available. Since an individual generally prefers higher mean returns, but dislikes variability of returns, it might be possible to draw a set of indifference curves[11] for alternative combinations of mean and variability of the return on his portfolio. This possibility is illustrated in Figure 9.2. The indifference curves have a positive slope to indicate that an individual will accept a greater variability of return only if he is compensated by a higher mean return. In fact, it should be clear that if individuals are risk averse (and therefore demand a higher rate of return on a very risky investment than on a less risky one), then risky investments will have to yield a high rate of return if they are to be sold. Since risky investments do indeed yield higher rates of return than nonrisky ones do, we can be quite certain that investors are, on the average, averse to risk.

---

[10] M. Friedman and L. J. Savage, "The Utility Analysis of Choices Involving Risk," *Journal of Political Economy*, vol. 56 (August 1948), pp. 279–304.

[11] There is much theoretical controversy over the mean-variability approach (where variability is now taken in a technical sense to mean variance). The assumption that utility depends only on the mean return and the variance of return can be justified by assuming that the returns from investments are Normally distributed, or that individuals have utility functions which are quadratic in income. The first of these assumptions does not seem to be empirically true, whereas the latter leads to many theoretically undesirable properties. In spite of these theoretical shortcomings the mean-variability approach is widely used in practice.

Figure 9.2   Indifference Curves for the Mean and Variability or Returns from
Investments

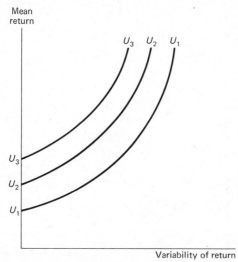

These curves show alternative combinations of mean return and variability of return about
which the individual is indifferent. Movement in a northwest direction leads to a higher level
of utility because such investments promise a higher mean return with lower risk. Whether
these indifference curves can be justified on theoretical grounds is dubious, but they are
important for applied work.

An indifference curve diagram such as that in Figure 9.2 can be used
to illustrate the maxim "don't put all your eggs in one basket" as it applies
to investment decisions. Suppose there are only two assets, A and B.
The mean return of these assets can be designated by M_A and M_B respectively, and their variability by V_A and V_B. The possible combinations of
mean return and variability of return by holding either A or B alone are
illustrated by the two points in Figure 9.3. If an individual is forced to
choose an undiversified portfolio consisting of only A or only B, he will
choose that point which lies on his highest indifference curve. Notice
that an asset such as C is clearly inferior to A because it offers a lower
mean return at greater risk.

If the individual is allowed to hold a mixture of A and B, however,
he can obtain a mean return somewhere between M_A and M_B. The exact
value of the mean return on the portfolio will depend on the proportions
in which the two assets are held. The variability of return on this mixture
will depend not only on the proportions in which the assets are held but
also on how the returns are related. For example, if the returns on the
two assets are independent, the possible combinations of mean and variability available from a mixed portfolio are given by the solid line AB.

Figure 9.3   Alternative Combinations of Mean and Variability Obtainable from a Mixed Portfolio of Two Assets

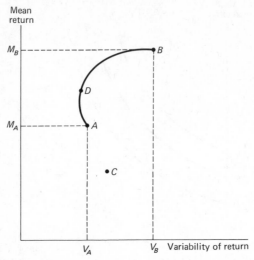

The curve AB represents those combinations of mean and variability of return which are attainable by mixing the pure assets A and B. Because of the shape of individuals' tastes (*see* Figure 9.2) it is likely that a point such as D will be preferred to either of the pure assets. Mixed portfolios will be preferred.

Notice that there are points on this line which are clearly superior to asset A because they offer both a higher mean return and a lower variability.[12] Therefore the individual in maximizing his utility, using the assets available, will choose some point such as D which represents a diversified portfolio.[13] Diversification is an important manifestation of

[12] A numerical example may help. Suppose $M_A = 5$ (that is, 5 percent), $V_A = 1$, $M_B = 7$, and $V_B = 2$. Then a portfolio which has 1/2 invested in A and 1/2 in B will have:

$$M_{1/2A + 1/2B} = \frac{1}{2}(5) + \frac{1}{2}(7) = 6$$

$$V_{1/2A + 1/2B} = \frac{1}{4}(1) + \frac{1}{4}(2) = \frac{3}{4}$$

where the final line is a result of the definition of variance given in footnote 8. Clearly this mixed investment is preferable to a portfolio consisting of A alone, since it has a higher mean return and a lower variability of return.

[13] If the assets have returns which are negatively correlated (in periods when one return is high the other is low and vice-versa), the line of possible combinations of mean and variability would be even more bowed than line AB. Hence diversification is even more likely to occur. If the assets have returns which are positively correlated, the curve will be less bowed and diversification is not so likely.

of the four outcomes might occur, rationality on the part of both players will lead each of them to play tails. These strategies are *equilibrium strategies* in that if either player is told with certainty that his opponent will play tails, he will also play tails. Nothing is gained by departing from the equilibrium strategy when the opponent's move becomes known.

The coin-matching game is a simple example of a class of two-person, noncoöperative games called *zero-sum games*. The term "zero-sum" is used to indicate that the game is constructed so that whatever player 2 loses, player 1 wins and vice-versa. The net sum of the prizes is 0. While much interesting work has been done in the theory of zero-sum games, even more relevant economic examples arise in the case of non-zero-sum games. A simple but analytically rich example of a non-zero-sum is provided by the *Prisoner's Dilemma*.[17] This section concludes with a discussion of this very important game.

In the Prisoner's Dilemma two men, say Smith and Jones again, are arrested for a crime and interrogated separately. Since the district attorney has little substantive evidence, he is anxious for both prisoners to confess to the crime. In isolation from his companion each suspect is told: If you confess and your companion doesn't, I can promise you a short (six-month) sentence, whereas your companion will get ten years. If you both confess then your sentences will be three years." At the same time both suspects realize that if they both don't confess the lack of substantive evidence will mean that they will be tried for a lesser crime, and will each receive only a two-year sentence. The question then is: What is the likely outcome of this situation, and will this outcome be a desirable one from among those which are open to the suspects.

In order to clarify this game it is helpful to write out its payoff matrix. Each player has only two strategies open to him: "confess" or "not confess," so the possible outcomes are:[18]

Table 9.2   Outcomes of the Prisoner's Dilemma

| | | Smith's strategies | |
		Confess	Not confess
Jones' strategies	Confess	Smith — 3 years Jones — 3 years	Smith — 10 years Jones — 6 months
	Not confess	Smith — 6 months Jones — 10 years	Smith — 2 years Jones — 2 years

[17] The Prisoner's Dilemma was first rigorously discussed by A. W. Tucker in the late 1940's.

[18] Again it is assumed that the length of sentences is an adequate measure of the disutility of the respective strategy decisions. In particular, any disutility from being branded a stoolpigeon is not taken into account.

Both suspects can avoid any possibility of getting a ten-year sentence by confessing and, if each has little faith in his companion, this is the outcome which will result. If Smith knows that Jones will confess under pressure, he has no choice other than to confess also. In a sense, then, this outcome is an equilibrium. But notice that this outcome is not the best which is available to the suspects. If they could enter into an iron-clad agreement not to confess their sentences would be cut from three years to two. The problem with this twin "not confess" strategy is that it is not stable. Even if Smith knows that Jones will not confess, he can improve his position by confessing and reduce his sentence from two years to six months. This "not confess" point is not a stable equilibrium in that there is always an incentive to cheat on one's companion.

For these reasons both suspects will probably confess and the district attorney's ploy will have been successful. Each suspect, by following his own self-interest has decided on a course of action which is in a larger sense irrational. Conspiring before the play of the game could have made both men better off. The Prisoner's Dilemma is the prototype for many economic problems in which individual rationality in an uncertain situation can lead to an outcome which is collectively irrational. It will be seen in later chapters that this type of problem arises in such diverse situations as the U.S. farm problem, the behavior of oligopolistic industries, and in the problem of financing governmental services on a voluntary payment basis.

Games against Nature

In games against nature it is assumed that in the future the world will be in exactly one "state." There may be either a large or small number of states of the world, but the states should be distinct and the list should include all possible situations which can arise. As a simple example of this idea consider the question of whether or not to go on a picnic tomorrow. Suppose it is decided that the only factor which affects the desirability of this planned picnic is the weather tomorrow. It might be possible to consider only two states-of-the-world: "It is raining tomorrow"; or "It is not raining tomorrow." These two states are mutually exclusive (assuming it has been agreed how the term "it is raining" is to be defined), and together they include all possible outcomes. This is a very gross definition of the possible future states-of-the-world and in any complex problem one would want to have a much finer gradation.[19] However, for the purposes of this section, this simple two-state description will suffice.

[19] For example, one could define states-of-the-world by the percent of sunshine or by the inches of rain.

Faced with these two possible states of the world the individual must choose either the strategy go on the picnic or stay home. It will be assumed that once he has decided to go on the picnic there is no possibility for changing his plans in response to more recent information about the weather. Suppose that the utilities he receives from a picnic in the various states-of-the-world are those given in Table 9.3.[20]

Table 9.3   Utilities from a Picnic

| | States of the world | |
	Rain	No rain
Picnic	0	20
No picnic	5	10

In choosing a strategy the individual can no longer be guided by the assumption that his "opponent" will maximize his own welfare. Nature must be regarded as neutral in this problem, and there is no a priori information on the "strategy" nature will choose.

A variety of decision rules have been proposed for dealing with games against nature, but no one of these has proved to be desirable in all instances. Only the two most common rules will be discussed. It will be shown that the two rules can lead to the selection of different strategies.

A first decision rule is called the *maximin* (or sometimes *minimax*) rule. This rule states that the individual should choose that strategy for which the minimum possible return is the greatest. This rule is basically a pessimistic rule which implicitly assumes that the worst will happen no matter which strategy is chosen. Hence the strategy with the "least bad" possible outcome should be chosen. In the picnic example this rule would choose the "no picnic" strategy because the lowest possible utility from this strategy (5) exceeds the lowest possible utility from the "picnic" strategy (0).

This decision rule can be criticized both because it disregards the other entries in the table and because it gives no room for the individual's subjective views as to how likely it is to rain. For example, if the individual receives a great level of utility from a rain-free picnic and he believes there is practically no possibility of rain (say he lives in the Sahara Desert) then it seems unnecessarily pessimistic to choose the "no picnic" strategy. There may be situations where the maximin rule is a reasonable choice. For example, if one is competing against a particularly malevo-

---

[20] Again, "utility" is not really an observable quantity and the numbers in the table are intended for illustrative purposes only.

lent opponent (or if I consider myself to be the unluckiest person alive) the maximin rule can lead to a prudent choice of strategies.

A second decision rule which is in common use is the *Bayesian Decision Rule*. This rule assumes that an individual has "subjective" views of the probabilities that certain states-of-the-world will occur and that he uses these probabilities to calculate the expected utility from pursuing each of the available strategies. The individual then chooses that strategy which provides him with the greatest (subjective)[21] expected utility. As an illustration of this decision rule, suppose the individual believes there is a fifty-fifty chance of rain tomorrow: The state-of-the-world "rain tomorrow" has subjective probability 1/2 and the state-of-the-world "no rain tomorrow" has subjective probability 1/2. The expected utility from the strategy choice "picnic" is:

$$\frac{1}{2}(0) + \frac{1}{2}(20) = 0 + 10 = 10$$

and the expected utility from the strategy choice "no picnic" is:

$$\frac{1}{2}(5) + \frac{1}{2}(10) = 2\frac{1}{2} + 5 = 7\frac{1}{2}.$$

Therefore, by the Bayesian Decision Rule, the individual will choose to go on the picnic.

The Bayesian approach has the desirable property that it uses all the information in the payoff table to reach a decision. Our friend in the Sahara Desert would undoubtedly choose to go on a picnic if he employed this decision rule. An even more desirable property of this rule, from a theoretical point of view, is that it is the only rule which agrees in spirit with the Von Neumann-Morgenstern axioms of rational choice. If an individual is to be an expected utility maximizer, it can be shown (by adding a few extremely reasonable axioms to those proposed by Von Neumann and Morgenstern) that he must also operate in a Bayesian manner when objective probabilities are unknown.[22] Thus there are strong reasons for favoring this decision rule.

The Bayesian approach is not a totally satisfactory solution to the problem of choice in games against nature. The rule necessitates the introduction of the notion of subjective probabilities. This introduction

---

[21] The term "subjective" is emphasized here to differentiate this situation from the "objective" probabilities discussed in the coin-flipping examples earlier in the chapter. It should be pointed out that some authors deny the validity of this distinction and regard all probabilities as being subjective.

[22] For a more complete discussion of this point *see* Luce and Raiffa, *op. cit.*, Chap. 13.

raises the whole question of how an individual formulates his views of subjective probabilities. We may, as was the case with utility theory, adopt the assumption that an individual acts *as if* he based his decisions on subjective probabilities and calculated expected utilities. This approach is still considerably less concise than the theory of behavior when "objective" probabilities which are known to everyone exist.

Conclusion: The Individual's Search for Information

This chapter has surveyed a number of approaches to the problem of individual decision making under uncertainty. Two aspects of such behavior have been repeatedly emphasized. First, the individual is concerned with the utilities from uncertain events. The dollar magnitudes of events are important only in that they reflect utilities. Second, individuals in general dislike uncertainty and may be willing to pay some amount to avoid being subjected to uncertainty. Individuals, for example, buy automobile insurance to avoid the small probability of a very large claim against them.

In a sense all individual behavior in uncertain situations can be regarded as a lack of information. If the individual knew that a coin were going to come up heads, or knew that it was not going to rain tomorrow, he would be better off. He may, in fact, be willing to pay for additional information, and will do so as long as the expected gains from this information exceed its cost. For example, the individual trying to decide whether or not to go on a picnic may invest in the price of a phone call to the weather bureau to help him in deciding on a strategy.

More important illustrations of the willingness of persons to pay for additional information when faced with uncertainty are easy to find. For example, better weather forecasting undoubtedly has reduced the uncertainty associated with crop cultivation and mitigated the dangers of living on the Gulf Coast. A similar service is provided by Consumer's Union in that it supplies additional information on consumer goods; and this information presumably permits more rational purchase decisions. The study of the interplay between the theory of individual decision making under uncertainty and information theory is an interesting and fertile new field in economics.

The State-Preference
Approach to Uncertainty

While the analysis of Chapter 9 gives many insights into individual behavior in uncertain situations, the treatment seems in some ways to be unsatisfactory. A principal reason for this is that the techniques used differ so greatly from the rather elegant and consistent utility theory developed in previous chapters. In the vast detail of expected returns, variability, and strategy choices the essential point of choosing a collection of goods so as to maximize utility seems to have been lost. In this appendix an alternative approach to uncertainty (the "state-preference" theory) will be examined which, in a very clever way, permits the standard utility methods to be applied to uncertain situations. Unfortunately, this new approach is not a panacea, for it raises many extremely difficult (perhaps intractible) issues which must be solved before it can have the usefulness of the tools developed in Chapter 9. As a conceptual aid to understanding uncertainty, and as a theoretical problem-solving tool, however, this approach has proved to be an exciting discovery.

States-of-the-world and Contingent Commodities

The state-preference theory starts with the notion of *states-of-the-world,* which has been previously mentioned in Chapter 9. We cannot tell what will happen in a future period, say tomorrow, but we may be willing to accept the idea that the world will be in some definable "state." For example, we might make the very crude approximation of saying that the world will be in only one of two possible states tomorrow: It will be either "good times" or "bad times." One could make a much finer gradation of states-of-the-world (involving even millions of possible states), but most of the essentials of the theory can be developed using only two states; therefore, no more complex definition will be used here.

A conceptual idea which can be developed concurrently with the notion of states-of-the-world is that of *contingent commodities,* which are goods delivered only if a particular state-of-the-world occurs. "$1 in good times" is an example of a contingent commodity which promises the individual $1 in good times but nothing should tomorrow turn out to be bad times. It is even possible, by stretching one's intuitive ability somewhat, to conceive of being able to purchase this commodity — I might be able to buy from someone the promise of $1 if tomorrow turns out to be good times. If someone were also willing to sell me the contingent commodity "$1 in bad times" then I could assure myself of having $1 tomorrow by buying the two contingent commodities "$1 in good times" and "$1 in bad times." Notice that even though I buy both of these commodities today, only one will "pay off" tomorrow, since tomorrow will be either good times or bad times but not both. Similarly, it is possible to guarantee a winner in a horse race by betting on all the horses. Some horse has to come in ahead and therefore some winnings are generated.

This concept of a contingent commodity can be extended to include claims on any good in the future. One can envision a hamburger to be delivered tomorrow with certainty as in reality the combination of two contingent claims: "A hamburger if tomorrow is good times" plus "a hamburger if tomorrow is bad times." There may be markets for these two distinct contingent goods, and conceivably an individual could buy one without buying the other. If an individual did buy a contingent claim on "one hamburger in good times," then, if tomorrow turned out to be bad times he would receive nothing.

Utility Analysis and Risk Aversion

A utility analysis involving the choice of contingent commodities proceeds formally in much the same way as did the analysis of individual choices over time in Chapter 8. The principal difference is that in choosing goods over time the individual actually consumes both goods, whereas in choosing contingent commodities he will only ultimately consume one of the goods. This distinction makes possible a simple assumption which might be made about the form of the utility function for contingent commodities. This assumption is illuminating in what it shows about individual behavior in uncertain situations. Specifically, denote consumption in good times by C_g and in bad times by C_b. The individual will choose among these contingent commodities in a way so as to maximize an expected utility function of the form $U(C_g, C_b)$. The assumption to be made about this function is that the utility an individual receives from consumption is *independent of the state-of-the-world*. Formally this assumes that:

Utility in state $g = V(C_g)$

and   [9A.1]

Utility in state $b = V(C_b)$

where the function V is the same in both states of the world. If π_g is the probability of good times and π_b is the probability of bad times, then the expected utility of any bundle of contingent consumption choices is given by:

$$U(C_g, C_b) = \pi_g \cdot V(C_g) + \pi_b \cdot V(C_b).$$ [9A.2]

Given assumption 9A.1, it is an easy matter to show that if the market for contingent commodities is "fair" the individual will be a "risk averter." To make this clear some definitions are necessary. By a "fair market" for contingent commodities we simply mean that the prices of the contingent commodities (call them P_g and P_b) are proportional to the probabilities (π_g and π_b) of the two states-of-the-world:

$$\frac{P_g}{P_b} = \frac{\pi_g}{\pi_b}.$$ [9A.3]

Equation 9A.3 is simply the assumption that buying contingent commodities is a fair game. This may be true if there are a large number of buyers and sellers in the market, and if the probabilities are known to all. In the racetrack example Equation 9A.3 is satisfied when the odds on each horse reflect the true probability of its winning the race.

A possible definition of "risk averter" in this model (one we will cast some doubt on below) is that the individual prefers to insure himself of the same level of consumption in all states-of-the-world: that he will choose $C_g = C_b$ so that it doesn't matter what state actually occurs. Using assumptions 9A.1 and 9A.3, it can be shown that the individual is a risk averter in this sense. To maximize Equation 9A.2 subject to the budget constraint $I = P_g C_g + P_b C_b$ (where I is the amount the individual has decided to devote to the purchase of contingent commodities), the first-order conditions for a maximum require that the individual equate his MRS (of C_g for C_b) to the ratio of the prices P_g/P_b:

$$\frac{P_g}{P_b} = \frac{\partial U/\partial C_g}{\partial U/\partial C_b} = \frac{\pi_g V'(C_g)}{\pi_b V'(C_b)} \qquad\qquad [9A.4]$$

but by Equation 9A.3 this means that:

$$\frac{V'(C_g)}{V'(C_b)} = 1 \quad \text{or} \quad V'(C_g) = V'(C_b) \qquad\qquad [9A.5]$$

and by assumption 9A.1 this implies that:

$$C_g = C_b. \qquad\qquad [9A.6]$$

This result can also be presented graphically. In Figure 9A.1 the individual's indifference map for C_g and C_b is drawn. In this figure the 45° line is labeled the "certainty line" since this is the locus of points for which $C_g = C_b$. Now assumption 9A.1 means that along the certainty line the MRS is simply $-\pi_g/\pi_b$. But if the market is fair (that is, if Equation 9A.3 holds) this will also be the slope of the individual's budget constraint, and hence maximization of expected utility will involve moving to the certainty line. The individual will act in this case so as to insure himself of the same consumption level in all eventualities.

Risk Preference and Movement Away from the Certainty Line

There are many situations where individuals are observed to choose points off the certainty line. For example, very few individuals buy flight insurance. Those who don't are choosing to buy high consumption for themselves and their families in good times (no crash), but very low consumption in bad times (a crash). Should this be considered an example of risk preference? There are two reasons for rejecting such a conclusion. First, the market for flight insurance may not be actuarially fair. There is some evidence that flight insurance is in fact far more costly than is actuarially justified. In such a case the slope of the individual's budget constraint will be flatter than it "should be" (the price of C_b is higher than is necessitated by the probabilities), and the individual's maximizing position will be to the right of the certainty line.

Figure 9A.1　Utility Maximization for Contingent Commodities

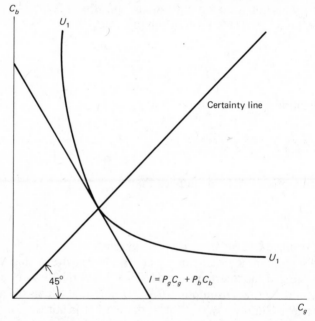

The indifference curve U_1 represents alternative combinations of "consumption in good times (C_g)" and "consumption in bad times (C_b)" about which the individual is indifferent. The 45° line is a certainty line, since along it $C_g = C_b$; along this line the individual gets the same quantity whichever state-of-the-world comes about. If the market for contingent commodities is fair, and if the utility an individual gets from consumption is independent of the state-of-the-world, then the utility maximizing point will be on the certainty line and the individual will be a "risk averter."

Even if the market for flight insurance were fair, there might be reasons to expect a point off the certainty line to be chosen. This would be the case if assumption 9A.1 did not hold. In particular, suppose the individual valued consumption in good times far more highly than in bad times. Utility might not be independent of the state-of-the-world, because in bad times the individual won't be around to enjoy his consumption. Movement away from the certainty line should not, in this case, be considered risk preference but merely a rational example of utility maximization. The individual could be the most cautious man alive and still choose a point off the certainty line. In a realistic situation then, risk aversion actually has little to do with choosing points on the certainty line. It is quite likely that the utility of a contingent commodity will depend on the state-of-the-world which actually comes about.

To take a trivial example, the utility from an umbrella will depend on whether the state "rain" or "no rain" is realized, and even in a fair market for "contingent umbrellas" I would not choose to buy one for clear days.

Conclusion

It might be argued that this analysis is both trivial and unnecessary. Certainly the reasons for not purchasing flight insurance could be adequately discussed without the cumbersome tools which have been developed. Perhaps so, but the analysis which has been presented adds greatly to our conceptual understanding of the nature of decisions made in uncertain situations. Much of the fuzziness which is usually associated with the analysis of these decisions has been eliminated. The traditional model of utility maximization has proved to be quite useful in a situation for which it was not originally intended, and most of the well-known results for the certain case could be carried over to this analysis.[1] All of the problems of economic behavior under uncertainty can be rephrased in the language of the choice of contingent commodities. This must be regarded as a major theoretical advance.

As was stated at the outset, the contingent commodity, state-preference approach is not a panacea. There really do not exist adequate markets in contingent commodities and there is no general agreement on how to break down the future into distinct states-of-the-world. If I walked into a drive-in and asked to buy a "hamburger in good times," I would surely be regarded as an eccentric.

Although work is progressing on clarifying some of the basic concepts of the state-preference theory, it has only just begun, and any significant empirical application is in the distant future.

[1] For a summary of some of the analytical simplifications made possible by the state-preference theory *see* J. Hirshleifer, "The Investment Decision under Uncertainty: Choice Theoretic Approaches," *Quarterly Journal of Economics,* vol. 79 (November 1965) pp. 509–536; and "The Investment Decision under Uncertainty: Applications of the State-Preference Approach," *Quarterly Journal of Economics,* vol. 80 (May 1966), pp. 252–277. Several of the examples given in the text draw on Hirshleifer's analysis.

DISCUSSION QUESTIONS AND PROBLEMS FOR PART II

Discussion Questions

1. Most people believe that advertising affects tastes (if it doesn't, why do companies have such large advertising budgets?). How does this observation affect the theory developed in this part of the book?

2. Some recent work has questioned the notion that utility depends on the quantity of "goods" consumed. Rather, it is claimed, utility depends on the quantities of certain "attributes" which are consumed. For example, a blanket is not viewed as a provider of utility in itself; it is the quantities of various attributes (warmth, beauty, feel, and so on) which provide utility. How might utility theory be modified to take account of this different way of looking at individual rankings of consumption goods, and what special complications might arise?

3. Thorstein Veblen invented the term "conspicuous consumption" to describe the "invidious" comparisons people make between their own consumption and that of others. There are two theoretical ways to incorporate this idea into utility analysis. The first is to assume prices enter the utility function: The utility one gets from a Rolls Royce in part depends on its automotive superiority and in part on its "conspicuous" price. Another possible way to incorporate Veblen's ideas would be to assume that utility depends on relative rather than on absolute consumption levels. How might one develop utility theory using either of these two approaches?

4. The theory developed in Part II has centered on the individual as the relevant decision unit. Perhaps a more realistic approach is to regard the family (or extended family) as the relevant decision unit. Would a theory of family decision making be different from the individual decision theory developed in this part? In particular, how might the tastes of individual family members be taken into account? (This question raises a number of issues which are also relevant to governmental decision making, since government is simply a very extended family. Such issues are discussed in much greater detail in Part VII.)

5. Following the ideas of Question 4, one important type of reallocation of consumption within families is intergenerational bequests. Presumably the utility of the family head depends not only on his own consumption but also on the utility experienced by other family members in the future. For this reason he will have some incentive (depending on relative "prices") to shift some consumption from his own use toward other family members. Can you make up a simple

model of this bequest motive? What variables play the role of prices in this allocational decision? How might inheritance taxes affect the allocation?

6. Should the "imputed income" from durable goods be taxed? What problems do you see in such taxation?

7. Is Bernoulli's "solution" to the St. Petersburg Paradox really a solution? Show that by suitably redefining the prizes of the game the paradox can be made to reappear if the Bernoulli utility function is used. Are there factors other than Bernoulli's observation of the necessity for using utility in game calculations which can explain the paradox?

8. How does advertising fit into the discussion of the individual's problem of information gathering? It has been estimated that the average American is subject to about 10,000 commercial messages per year. What can you make of this statistic? Is this seeming bombardment of one's senses a good or a bad thing?

Problems

1. An indifference map is "vertically parallel" if the marginal rate of substitution is constant for a fixed level of X_1. Graphically this says that a vertical line cuts all indifference curves at points of equal slope (*see* Figure II.1a).

Figure II.1   Indifference Maps for Problems 1 and 2.

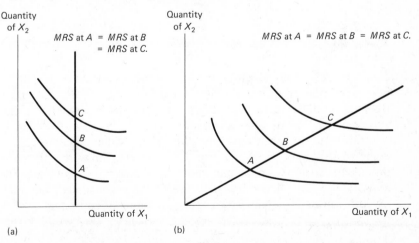

(a)   (b)

(a)   What implications does this assumption have for individuals' behavior? Show that $\partial X_1 / \partial P_1$ must be negative.

(b) Show that an indifference map is both "vertically parallel" and "horizontally parallel" (analogously defined) if and only if X_1 and X_2 are perfect substitutes (that is, the MRS is constant for all X_1 and X_2).

2. An indifference map is *homothetic* if any straight line through the origin cuts all indifference curves at points of equal slope: The MRS depends on the ratio X_2/X_1 (*see* Figure II.1b).

(a) Prove that the Engel Curves for a homothetic indifference map are straight lines.

(b) Prove that if an individual's tastes can be represented by a homothetic indifference map $\partial X_1/\partial P_1$ must be negative.

3. Show that if an individual is forced to spend a fixed amount of his income on a particular good his utility level will be lower than if he could freely allocate his income.

4. Suppose an individual consumes three goods—food, clothing, and automobiles. Denote the quantities of these goods consumed by X_1, X_2, and X_3. Suppose the individual's utility function is given by:

$$U = 5 \log X_1 + 4 \log X_2 + \log (1 + X_3),$$

that the prices of the goods are given by:

$$P_1 = 1$$
$$P_2 = 2$$
$$P_3 = 2000,$$

and that the individual's total income is $9000. Automobiles, however, have the property that they must be bought in discrete units (that is, X_3 must equal 0, 1, 2, and so on). It is impossible, in this simple model, to buy one-half of a car.

Given these constraints, how will an individual allocate his income so as to maximize his utility. This problem shows that the conditions for a utility maximum must be reinterpreted to read that $MU_i/P_i = \lambda$ for all goods which are actually consumed, but that MU_i/P_i can be less than λ for a good not actually consumed.

5. A utility function $U(X_1, X_2,..., X_n)$ is said to be independent in its arguments if:

$$U(X_1, X_2,..., X_n) = U_1(X_1) + U_2(X_2) + \cdots + U_n(X_n).$$

It is also reasonable to assume:

$$U_i'(X_i) > 0 \quad \text{and} \quad U_i''(X_i) < 0.$$

Suppose the individual's budget constraint is given by:

$$I = P_1 X_1 + P_2 X_2 + \cdots + P_n X_n.$$

   (a)   What are the first-order conditions for a maximization of this utility function subject to the budget constraint?
   (b)   Show that $\partial X_i / \partial P_i < 0$ for all goods.
   (c)   Can any good in this set be an inferior good?
   (d)   Suppose that the demand for X_1 is elastic, that the quantity purchased of X_1 responds more proportionally to any change in P_1. Show that all other goods are gross substitutes for X_1.

   This problem illustrates how important the general functional notation $U(X_1, X_2,..., X_n)$ is. It is only because goods interact with one another in individuals' preferences that many results can occur. If independence is assumed, demand theory becomes both easier and less realistic.

6. Generalize the revealed preference axiom of rationality to three goods (or to n goods if you prefer).
   Now consider the three-good case. Suppose $X_1 = 4$, $X_2 = 6$, and that $X_3 = 9$ is the chosen bundle of commodities when $P_1 = 1$, $P_2 = 2$, and $P_3 = 3$. Assume that these prices change to $P_1 = 2$, $P_2 = 3$, $P_3 = 1$. Would it be a violation of the axiom of reationality for the individual to choose $X_1 = 10$, $X_2 = 6$, and $X_3 = 5$? Can you explain why this would turn out to be irrational?

7. As an alternative to the "equal absolute sacrifice" criterion of income tax fairness, consider the following criterion: Taxes should be levied so that for any given amount of dollars that must be raised in taxes aggregate loss of utility should be minimized. The aggregate loss of utility is taken here to be the sum of the utilities lost by each individual. If it is assumed that every individual has the same utility function for (after-tax) income, what would such a principle dictate for a tax rate structure?

8. Using a simple two-period model, show that the statement that $\partial S / \partial r$ (where S denotes saving) is less than 0 is equivalent to observing that consumption in the next period is price inelastic (where the "price" of consumption next period is taken to mean $1/1 + r$).

9. The Prisoner's Dilemma discussed in Chapter 9 suggests that pre-

game discussions will always aid both players. This may not really be the case when the possibility of threats is examined. Consider the following game between Smith and Jones: Each has two strategies to choose from. The pay-offs of the game are shown in Table II.1 (a minus sign indicates a loss).

Table II.1

		Smith's strategies	
		1	2
Jones' strategies	1	Jones 4 Smith 1	Jones 3 Smith 2
	2	Jones 2 Smith −50	Jones 1 Smith −25

Show first that strategy 2 is a dominant one for Smith, whereas 1 is dominant for Jones. Consequently, Jones should end up with a pay-off of 3 and Smith with a pay-off of 2.

Suppose, however, you were in Jones' position and could "consult" with Smith before the game. What would you do?

If, on the other hand, you were Smith, what would you do to counteract Jones' ploys?

PART III
Production and the Firm

Introduction

In Part II the demand side of the market for goods was developed. There was also some emphasis on the role of individuals as suppliers of productive resources. As a first step toward an analysis of the way in which productive resources are bought from some individuals and turned into goods for other individuals, Part III centers on the middleman, the firm. Firms, quite simply phrased, turn inputs into outputs. In this process numerous decisions have to be made, and we will analyze some of these decisions.

A first step in treating the firm as a decision-making unit is to discuss the goals it can be assumed to pursue. Do firms strive toward maximization of profits? Or perhaps they seek to maximize revenues. Or does it make any sense to speak of a single goal? These issues are discussed in Chapter 10; it is concluded that profit maximization can serve as a reasonable first approximation to the goal of the firm. It is recognized that alternative assumptions may be very useful in particular applications.

Chapter 10 does not discuss either the firm's goals over several time periods or in uncertain situations. The analysis of these questions would be basically similar to that presented in Chapters 8 and 9 (perhaps firms maximize the present discounted value of future profits, or the expected value of uncertain profits). In order to avoid unnecessary repetition, the reader will be left on his own to fill in these details. One aspect of the firm's decision making over time, the investment decision, will be covered in some detail in Chapter 19.

After having decided on a satisfactory conceptual way of treating the firm and its goals, it is necessary to specify the technical relationships between inputs and outputs. This general question has two aspects which are examined in Chapters 11 and 12. In Chapter 11 the problem of specifying the purely physical relationship between inputs and outputs is investigated. It is shown that the economists' concept of a production function provides a useful abstraction of real-world production processes. This discussion of the physical aspects of production is followed in Chapter 12 by using the production function concept to discuss cost minimization. Some conceptual problems in the definition of costs are also examined.

Part III serves the purpose of introducing the concept of a firm and of analyzing some of the firm's technical problems. Although the discussion does not analyze the specific question of the quantity of output which a firm will supply, it does provide the necessary prerequisites to investigating this question. The tools of this part will be used heavily in Part IV to analyze pricing (the interaction of supply and demand) in the market for goods and in Part V to analyze pricing in markets for the factors of production.

CHAPTER 10

The Firm:
Definitions and Goals

Basic Concepts

A *firm* is here defined to be any entity which produces economic goods. This definition is sufficiently broad to include a wide variety of organizations ranging from single craftsmen and local cottage industries through the giant collections of men and machinery which characterize modern industrial society. A reasonable way to approach the theory of the firm might be as a special case of individual behavior. If this approach were followed, interest would center on the general sort of utility analysis which has been presented earlier in this book and on the theory of individuals' interactions in groups. Some economists have adopted this *behavioral* approach to studying firms' operations and have achieved great insights into intrafirm decision making. However, most economists have regarded the behavioral theory as being too complex for any general approach to the theory of production. They have therefore been led to adopt a *holistic* theory of the firm in which firms are treated as single decision-making units. A firm is viewed as being run by an entrepreneur who has total dictatorial powers over its operation. Such a view is an obvious oversimplification of decision processes in real-world firms. However, since any theory necessarily involves some abstraction, the relevant question is whether the benefits of this holistic approach in terms of greater analytic simplicity exceed its costs. In a wide variety of situations, this has clearly been the case.

The firm or its entrepreneur owner (we shall use the terms somewhat interchangeably) must then decide on which goods to produce and on how much of each good to produce.[1] It must also decide on the technical questions of how best to combine various inputs (labor, machine hours, raw materials) into the production of its outputs. In making such decisions the firm is constrained by the existing productive technology. This technology can be represented by a *production function* of the form:

$$Q = f(L, K, M,...) \tag{10.1}$$

where Q represents the output of a particular good during some period, L represents the input of labor during the period, K represents the machine usage during the period, and M is the amount of raw materials used in the productive process. The ellipsis in Equation 10.1 indicates that many other factors (such as the weather or entrepreneurial effort) enter into the production relationship which f is intended to symbolize. It is important to emphasize that the production function is a purely technical relationship which represents the current best state-of-the-art method of combining inputs to produce outputs. It is a constraint on how the entrepreneur can trade some goods or services with "nature" to produce other goods. Many technical details of the production function are discussed in Chapter 11.

Given this simplified view of a firm and its productive relationships, we must now ask what goal it wishes to pursue. A reasonable first approximation might be to assume that the entrepreneur operates the firm in a way so as to maximize his own utility. If this assumption is accepted, then the whole body of analysis presented in Chapters 3 through 9 be-

---

[1] A firm could be directed in these matters by some overall planning board. The analysis in either situation would essentially be the same.

comes relevant and we must ask questions about the entrepreneur's utility of income, his labor-leisure preferences, his time preferences, and his attitudes toward risk. Although such an examination is possible,[2] we will further simplify the goals of the entrepreneur here and assume that he desires to operate the firm so as to maximize his own income or, what amounts to the same thing, to maximize the profits of the firm.

The assumption that firms operate in a manner so as to maximize profits has a long history in economic literature. The assumption has much to recommend it: It seems intuitively reasonable; it is simple; it has been analytically productive; and, perhaps most important, it has never been unambiguously disproved. Nonetheless, the assumption has been attacked on a number of fronts. Some of these attacks will be discussed below. First it is useful to point out some of the implications of the profit-maximization assumption for the behavior of a firm.

Profit Maximization and Marginalism

If firms are strict profit maximizers they will make decisions in a "marginal" way. The entrepreneur will perform the conceptual experiment of adjusting those variables under his control until it is impossible to increase profits further. This involves, say, looking at the incremental (or "marginal") profit obtainable from producing one more unit of output, or the additional profit available from hiring one more laborer. So long as this incremental profit is positive he will produce the extra output or hire the extra laborer. When the incremental profit of an activity becomes 0, the entrepreneur has pushed that activity far enough and it would not be profitable to go farther.

The twin concepts of profit maximization and marginal decision making are straightforward applications of the mathematical problem of maximization discussed in Chapter 2. For example, consider the entrepreneur's decision of how much to produce. Since profits are defined to be revenues minus costs of production,[3] and since both revenues and costs can be taken to be dependent on the quantity produced, one can write:

$$\pi(Q) = R(Q) - C(Q). \tag{10.2}$$

[2] For example, in studies of the banking industry it is sometimes assumed that these firms seek to maximize some utility function of profits and liquidity.

[3] The term "costs" has a somewhat different meaning in economic usage than in everyday language. This distinction will be discussed at length in Chapter 12.

Here profits (π) depend on the quantity produced (Q) and are in turn simply defined as the difference between revenues (R) and costs (C). The necessary condition for choosing that value of Q which maximizes profits is found by setting the derivative of Equation 10.2 with respect to Q equal to 0:

$$\frac{d\pi}{dQ} = \pi'(Q) = \frac{dR}{dQ} - \frac{dC}{dQ} = 0 \tag{10.3}$$

or the first-order condition for a maximum is that:

$$\frac{dR}{dQ} = \frac{dC}{dQ}. \tag{10.4}$$

Equation 10.4 says that at the maximum point the extra (marginal) revenue obtained from selling slightly more Q should exactly equal the extra (marginal) cost of producing that extra output. More simply, Equation 10.4 is a mathematical representation of the well-known maxim that if a firm is to maximize profits, it should produce that quantity for which *marginal revenue equals marginal cost.*

We will discuss these important concepts in considerable detail later. The following section of this chapter will focus on the idea of marginal revenue, whereas a treatment of marginal cost will be postponed until Chapter 12. It is important to recognize at the outset that the marginal revenue equals marginal cost rule is a direct result of the profit-maximization assumption. If a firm decided to produce an output level for which marginal revenue exceeded marginal cost, it could not be maximizing profits, since the production of one more unit of output would yield more in additional revenue than it would cost to produce. Similarly, if marginal revenue were less than marginal costs, reducing output by one unit would lower costs by a greater amount than it would lower revenue, and this action would increase profits. Assuming it is in fact possible for the firm to make "small" adjustments, marginalism and profit maximization are synonymous.

Equations 10.3 or 10.4 are only the necessary conditions for a maximum. For sufficiency, it is required that:

$$\left.\frac{d^2\pi}{dQ^2}\right|_{Q=Q^*} = \left.\frac{d\pi'(Q)}{dQ}\right|_{Q=Q^*} < 0 \tag{10.5}$$

or that "marginal" profit must be decreasing at the optimal level of Q. For Q less than Q^* (the optimal level of output) profit must be increasing

$[\pi'(Q) > 0]$ and for Q greater than Q^* profit must be decreasing $[\pi'(Q) < 0]$. Only if this condition holds is it the case that a true maximum of profits has been achieved.

Figure 10.1   Marginal Revenue Must Equal Marginal Cost for Profit Maximization

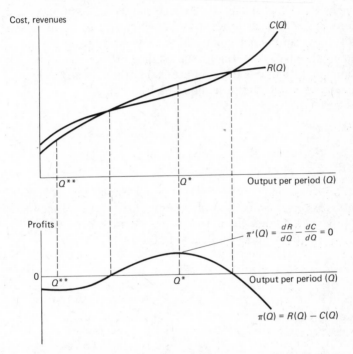

Since profits are defined to be revenues (R) minus costs (C), it is clear that profits reach a maximum when the slope of the revenue function (marginal revenue) is equal to the slope of the cost function (marginal cost). This equality is only a necessary condition for a maximum, as may be seen by comparing points Q^* (a true *maximum*) and Q^{**} (a true *minimum*).

These relationships are illustrated in Figure 10.1. In this figure the top panel depicts typical cost and revenue functions. For low levels of output costs exceed revenue and therefore profits are negative. In the middle ranges of output revenues exceed costs; this means that profits are positive. Finally, at high levels of output costs rise sharply and again exceed revenues. This relationship between the revenue and cost curves is shown in the bottom panel of Figure 10.1, where it can be seen that profits reach a maximum at Q^*. At this level of output it is also true that the slope of the revenue curve (marginal revenue) is equal to the slope of the cost curve (marginal cost). It is clear from the figure that the sufficient conditions for a maximum are also satisfied at this point, since profits are increasing to the left of Q^* and decreasing to the right of Q^*. Output level Q^* is therefore a true profit maximum. This is not true for output level Q^{**}. Even though marginal revenue is equal to marginal cost at this output, profits are in fact a minimum at that point.

An analysis similar to that for choosing an optimal output is also possible for the problem of choosing inputs so as to maximize profits. Intuitively, additional productive inputs should be hired so long as the goods these additional inputs produce yield more in revenue than the inputs themselves cost. Inputs should then be hired up to the point where marginal contributions to profit are 0. This result can be derived mathematically by combining Equations 10.1 and 10.2:

$$\pi(Q) = \pi[f(L, K, M,...)] = R(Q) - C(Q)$$
$$= R[f(L, K, M,...)] - C[f(L, K, M,...,)]. \qquad [10.6]$$

This rather complex expression merely states the obvious fact that profits, revenues, and costs all depend on the level of inputs used. The first-order conditions for a maximum are found by setting the partial derivatives of Equation 10.6 equal to 0:

$$\frac{\partial \pi}{\partial L} = \frac{\partial R}{\partial L} - \frac{\partial C}{\partial L} = 0$$

$$\frac{\partial \pi}{\partial K} = \frac{\partial R}{\partial K} - \frac{\partial C}{\partial K} = 0 \qquad [10.7]$$

$$\frac{\partial \pi}{\partial M} = \frac{\partial R}{\partial M} - \frac{\partial C}{\partial M} = 0$$
$$\vdots$$

or

$$\frac{\partial R}{\partial L} = \frac{\partial C}{\partial L}$$

$$\frac{\partial R}{\partial K} = \frac{\partial C}{\partial K} \qquad [10.8]$$

$$\frac{\partial R}{\partial M} = \frac{\partial C}{\partial M}$$
$$\vdots$$

Equation 10.8 says that the use of each input in the productive process should be expanded to the point where the extra cost of one more unit of that input is exactly balanced by the revenue it produces.[4] In Chapters 17 and 18 the conditions of Equation 10.8 will be explained more fully, and will be examined for a variety of different market organizations. The essential point to be made here is that the adoption of marginal principles in the employment of inputs is also a necessary corollary of the assumption of profit maximization.

Marginal Revenue

It is the revenue obtained from selling one more unit of output which is relevant to the profit-maximizing firm. If the firm can sell all it wishes without having any effect on market price, the market price will indeed be the extra revenue obtained from selling one more unit. Phrased in another way, if a firm's output decisions will not affect market price, marginal revenue is equal to price.

A firm may not always be able to sell all it wants at the prevailing market price, however. If it faces a downward sloping demand curve, more output can be sold only by reducing market price. In this case the revenue obtained from selling one more unit will be less than the price of that unit because, in order to get consumers to take the extra unit, the price of all other units must be lowered. This result can be easily demonstrated. Total revenue (R) is simply the product of the quantity sold (Q) times the price at which it is sold (P):

$$\text{Total revenue} = R(Q) = P \cdot Q. \hspace{2cm} [10.9]$$

Marginal revenue (MR) is then defined to be the change in R resulting from a change in Q:

$$\text{Marginal revenue} = MR(Q) = \frac{dR}{dQ} = \frac{d(P \cdot Q)}{dQ} = P + Q \cdot \frac{dP}{dQ}. \hspace{0.5cm} [10.10]$$

Notice that the marginal revenue is a function of output. In general, MR will be different for different levels of Q. From Equation 10.10 it is

[4] The reader is reminded, perhaps to the point of tedium, that Equations 10.7 or 10.8 are only necessary conditions. Appropriate second-order conditions are required to insure the existence of a true maximum. It should also be emphasized that all the equations in 10.8 must be solved simultaneously for the optimal levels of L, K, M, and so forth. The conditions must all hold—a haphazard solution of only one or two of the equations will not insure a profit maximum.

easy to see that if price does not change as quantity increases ($dP/dQ = 0$) then marginal revenue will be equal to price. On the other hand, if price falls as quantity increases ($dP/dQ < 0$), marginal revenue will be less than price. A profit-maximizing entrepreneur must know how increases in output will affect the price he receives before he can make an optimal output decision. If increases in Q cause market price to fall, he must take this into account.

The concept of marginal revenue can be related to the concept of demand elasticity which was developed in Chapter 6. Remember that the elasticity of demand ($E_{Q,P}$) was defined as the percentage change in quantity which results from a 1 percent change in price:

$$E_{Q,P} = \frac{dQ/Q}{dP/P} = \frac{dQ}{dP} \cdot \frac{P}{Q}. \qquad [10.11]$$

This definition can be combined with Equation 10.10 to give:

$$MR = P + Q\frac{dP}{dQ} = P\left(1 + \frac{Q}{P} \cdot \frac{\partial P}{\partial Q}\right) = P\left(1 + \frac{1}{E_{Q,P}}\right). \qquad [10.12]$$

If the demand curve is negatively sloped, $E_{Q,P} < 0$ and marginal revenue will be less than price, as we have already shown. If demand is elastic ($E_{Q,P} < -1$) marginal revenue will be positive. If demand is elastic the sale of one more unit will not affect price "very much" and hence more revenue will be yielded by the sale. In fact, if demand is infinitely elastic ($E_{Q,P} = -\infty$) marginal revenue will equal price. However, if demand is inelastic ($E_{Q,P} > -1$) marginal revenue will be negative. Increases in Q will cause "large" declines in market price and these declines will actually cause total revenue to decrease.[5]

The relationship between marginal revenue and elasticity is summarized by Table 10.1:

Table 10.1

$E_{Q,P} < -1$	$MR > 0$	
$E_{Q,P} = -1$	$MR = 0$	[10.13]
$E_{Q,P} > -1$	$MR < 0$	

[5] In this light it might be pointed out that so long as marginal costs are positive a profit-maximizing firm will not produce at a point on the demand curve for which demand is inelastic. In such a case marginal revenue (negative) could not be equated to marginal cost (positive).

These relationships can be pictured graphically by using a linear demand curve such as the one first developed in Chapter 6 (*see* Figure 6.4). Suppose the demand curve is given by:

$$Q = a + bP \qquad b < 0$$

or   [10.14]

$$P = \frac{1}{b} Q - \frac{a}{b}.$$

Since $R = P \cdot Q$, we have:

$$R = \frac{1}{b} Q^2 - \frac{a}{b} Q$$

and, by the definition of marginal revenue:

$$MR = \frac{dR}{dQ} = \frac{2}{b} Q - \frac{a}{b}. \qquad\qquad [10.15]$$

Figure 10.2   Marginal Revenue Curve Associated with a Linear Demand Curve

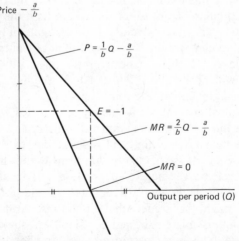

If a demand curve is negatively sloped, the marginal revenue curve will fall below the demand ("average revenue") curve. The linear case shown exhibits the relationship between marginal revenue and the elasticity of demand. Notice in particular that when $E_{Q,P} = -1$, $MR = 0$. Since a percentage increase in quantity is met by an identical percentage drop in price, total revenue stays constant for such an elasticity of demand.

The demand curve, Equation 10.12, and this marginal revenue curve are graphed in Figure 10.2. Notice that the marginal revenue curve lies below the demand curve (since the demand curve has a negative slope) and that, when $E_{Q,P} = -1$, MR is equal to 0.

A similar construction could be made for any demand curve. So long as additional output can be sold only by decreasing market price, the marginal revenue curve will lie below the demand curve. Profit-maximizing firms will recognize this fact and will base output decisions on information about marginal revenue.

The Controversy over the Profit-maximization Hypothesis

The so-called "marginalist controversy," although usually dormant in the economics profession, occasionally has a revival which spurs a wide variety of theoretical and empirical research.[6] Over the years a vast amount of evidence has been marshaled against the profit-maximization hypothesis, but, primarily because no suitable alternative has been found, the hypothesis has withstood these assaults. The attacks on the marginalist approach can be classed into three general types: that the profit-maximization approach is too simple; that there exist alternative, equally simple hypotheses which can better explain reality; and that real-world firms don't have suitable information to be able to maximize profits, nor would they particularly want to maximize profits if they had such information. Because it has been decided to investigate only simple hypotheses of firm behavior here, the first point will not be pursued. Some other simple hypotheses which have been proposed as substitutes for profit maximization will be mentioned in the next section. This section will summarize the arguments of the third type.

Certainly most economists would agree that real-world firms do not have adequate information to maximize profits in any exact sense. For most firms the demand and marginal revenue curves they face are only vaguely understood. It is also likely that firms do not have adequate information on their cost structure so as to be able to make delicate and precise marginal calculations. In defense of the profit-maximization hypothesis, it might be argued that only those firms which are able reasonably to approximate marginal decisions will survive in a competitive atmosphere. This *survivorship principle* implies that any firms we

[6] Perhaps the most interesting of these debates over the goals of the firm was conducted by Richard A. Lester and Fritz Machlup in the *American Economic Review* during the years 1946 and 1947.

observe are likely to be profit maximizers (simply because they are still in business) even though their technical knowledge of revenue and cost factors may be minimal.

The empirical evidence on whether firms maximize profits is unclear. Firms in answering questionnaires seldom rank profits as their major goal. Similarly they often deny making marginal decisions.[7] On the other hand, economists have found the profit-maximization hypothesis to be extremely accurate in predicting certain aspects of firms' behavior. For example, many firms seem eager to enter into the most profitable industries, and some of the larger, stagnant firms seek to diversify to increase profitability. Attempts to reconcile these two seemingly contradictory findings about profit maximization have centered on the methodological question of the role of assumptions in economic theory. Friedman[8] argues that one cannot judge the assumption of profit maximization either by a priori logic or by asking firms what they do. Rather the ultimate test is the predictive ability of the hypothesis. Friedman uses the analogy of the expert pool player who has no knowledge of the rules of physics which determine the movements of the balls on the table. This ignorance on the part of the player, however, does not prevent an observer from accurately predicting the player's behavior by applying physical principles. Just as Molière's Monsieur Jourdain spoke prose all his life without knowing it, firms may in fact maximize profits despite their protests that they have no such intentions. In a sense the argument again rests on the survivorship principle: Firms are led by the rigors of the market toward profit maximization.

The alternative to Friedman's positivist position is to argue that much more can be learned about a firm's motives by studying the behavior of its managers. Profit maximization is claimed to be too simple an hypothesis to be useful in understanding the complex workings of a modern corporation. A resolution of these conflicting methodological views may never be achieved. Clearly, both views have elements of truth and each can be valuable for certain applications. The position taken here will be that the profit-maximization hypothesis is the single most acceptable starting point for a theory of firm behavior. It will also be shown in later chapters that firms which operate in a profit-maximizing way (or firms which are forced to do so by the state) may perform the task of production in an efficient manner. Hence, for a theoretical overview of microeconomic behavior profit maximization seems a reasonable and useful assumption to make.

[7] Recent advances in managerial education and sophistication have, however, brought "incremental" thinking into the foreground in some decisions.

[8] See Milton Friedman, "The Methodology of Positive Economics" in *Essays in Positive Economics* (Chicago, Illinois: The University of Chicago Press, 1953).

Simple Alternatives to Profit Maximization

Although no simple alternative to the profit-maximization hypothesis has won widespread acceptance, several have been proposed and a brief discussion of a few of these will suggest the general flavor of the debate. A first, rather obvious, generalization of the marginalist approach is to assume firms act so as to maximize "long-run" profits. Under this hypothesis the observation, say, that firms build luxury office buildings is not taken as evidence which disproves the profit-maximization hypothesis. Rather, the cultivation of a suitable image is viewed as integral to a strategy of maximizing long-run profits. Similarly, charitable contributions by firms certaintly do not increase short-run profits, but, in a more general sense, they may maximize long-run profits by building up a favorable public climate. The objection to the long-run maximization hypothesis is that it is too general; it is not able to be refuted by any evidence. Any conceivable behavior might be consistent with very long-run maximization goals. If the firm goes out of business because it cannot afford to pay to have its luxury windows washed, this could be claimed not to refute the hypothesis since, after all, no one can accurately predict the future.

A second variation on the profit-maximization hypothesis is the assumption that firms seek to maximize profits subject to constraints. These constraints keep firms from operating in a strictly marginalist way since any constraint, if it is effective, will lower the maximum profit achievable. For example, it has been proposed that firms may maximize profits subject to the constraint of maintaining their share of the market.[9] They may therefore, in the interest of maintaining market share, continue to produce unprofitable items, or may introduce new lines which are not immediately profitable. Other constraints which have been suggested are: maximization of profits subject to a liquidity constraint (this applies mainly to banks); maximization of profits subject to the desire of the entrepreneur to maintain control of his company (high profits may attract some greedy, unwanted merger partner); or profit maximization subject to the desire to keep the firm a "nice place to work." Each of these assumptions undoubtedly has explanatory ability in some situations. To the extent these constraints are effective, the firm may not satisfy the marginal conditions of Equations 10.4 or 10.8.

A third alternative hypothesis has been proposed by William J. Baumol.[10] In his consulting work Baumol noticed that most managerial

[9] It has also been suggested that maintaining market share is a reasonable long-run profit-maximizing strategy in an uncertain market environment.

[10] A clear statement of this hypothesis is in Chapter 6 of William J. Baumol, *Business Behavior, Value and Growth,* rev. ed. (New York: Harcourt, Brace & World, Inc., 1967).

Figure 10.3 A Comparison of Profit Maximization and Revenue Maximization

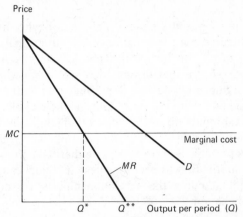

For simplicity it has been assumed that each unit of output can always be produced at a cost of MC. A profit-maximizing firm will therefore produce output level Q^* for which $MR = MC$. If the firm were devoted to the goal of revenue maximization, however, it would proceed to output level Q^{**}, since at this level of output *marginal* revenue is 0.

incentives are tied to increasing sales rather than profits. For example, higher salaries are paid to the managers of the largest corporations (ones with a high volume of sales) than to managers of the most profitable ones. Other pieces of evidence (for example, that bank credit is more easily available to large firms) also suggested to Baumol that sales volume might be the relevant goal. A strictly revenue-maximizing firm would produce that quantity of output for which marginal revenue equals 0 (the quantity Q^{**} in Figure 10.3).[11] Output will be expanded so long as any additional revenue is obtainable. Baumol suggests that a firm may not go this far in pursuing sales volume, but may in fact be bound by a profit constraint imposed by the firm's owners. Hence Baumol's firm would probably produce some quantity between that which a profit maximizer would (Q^*) and that which a revenue maximizer would (Q^{**}). The Baumol hypothesis has inspired much empirical research. A difficult question in such investigations has been how to specify exactly what the relevant profit constraint is for a firm. Even accepting the rather questionable assumptions which have been made on this point, the constrained-revenue-maximization hypothesis has not proved an unambiguously better predictor of firm behavior than has the profit-maximization hypothesis. Nonetheless, it is probably the most interesting simple alternative which has been proposed.

[11] In the figure it has been assumed for simplicity that marginal costs are constant at level MC.

Summary and Conclusion

This chapter has proposed a general definition of the firm and has presented a brief summary of the debate over the firm's goals. Emphasis has centered on the profit-maximization hypothesis as a useful simplification of reality. It was shown that firms which seek to maximize profits will operate in a marginal way: They will produce that output for which marginal revenue equals marginal cost; and, in their choice of inputs, will employ additional inputs up to the point at which the additional revenue from hiring one more unit of input is exactly balanced by its additional cost. While it is possible that firms may neither have the necessary information nor the motivation to perform these marginal calculations, it was shown that understanding these relationships is a useful first step in analyzing firm behavior.

CHAPTER 11

The Physical Aspects
of Production

The Concept of a Production Function

Firms are in business for the purpose of turning inputs into outputs. In many respects this process presents an engineering problem of determining the technically best way of producing particular goods. Because economists are interested in the choices a firm makes regarding input and output, but are not particularly interested in specific techniques of production, they have chosen to abstract from the engineering problems of production. The economist's production function (first discussed in Chapter 10) provides such an abstraction by centering attention on the relationship between inputs and outputs. The reader is reminded that the production function has the form:

$$Q = f(K, L, M,...) \tag{11.1}$$

where Q represents the output of a particular good during a period,[1] K represents the machine (that is, capital) usage during the period, L represents hours of labor input,[2] M represents raw materials used, and the notation indicates the possibility of other variables affecting the production process.[3] The function 11.1 is assumed to provide, for any conceivable set of inputs, the engineer's solution to the problem of how best to combine these inputs to get output. In this sense the economist's production function already represents an optimization process. The important question from an economic point of view is how the levels of Q, K, L, and M are chosen by the firm. This question is taken up in detail in the next several chapters.

This chapter will not touch on these questions of optimal choice. Rather the intention is to describe a few concepts which have been developed for the purpose of understanding the relationship between inputs and outputs. The chapter centers on purely physical relationships in contrast to later chapters, which will concentrate on costs and profit maximization. Production functions represent constraints on the activities of producers which are imposed by the existing technology. Our purpose is to examine the way in which these constraints can be formalized.

Variations in One Input

In this section we will study the change in output which is brought about by a change in one of the productive inputs. For the purposes of this examination (and indeed for most of the purposes of this book) it will be more convenient to write Equation 11.1 as:

---

[1] The terms "output of a particular good" are here used to indicate that we are only considering productive processes which produce identical goods. For example, "cheap" shoes and "good" shoes are two different goods, and presumably have different production functions. We shall see in later chapters that it may be difficult in some productive processes to specify exactly what output is (for example, consider the problem of defining the output of a hospital).

[2] Capital and labor inputs are assumed to be homogeneous. This is a great simplification since there are in reality numerous kinds of labor and many types of machines. The recognition that these inputs are in fact inhomogeneous raises many technical problems in the theory of aggregation which cannot be elaborated here. For a brief discussion of some of the issues involved in the aggregation of capital *see* the appendix to Chapter 19.

[3] In a purely formal way technical progress can be accommodated within the formulation of Equation 11.1 by assuming that variable "time" enters into the production function (*see* the appendix to this chapter for an elaboration of this point).

$$Q = f(K, L) \qquad\qquad [11.2]$$

with the understanding that all inputs other than K and L are being held constant during the analysis.[4] Most of the analysis to be presented will hold true for any two inputs which might be investigated.

The *marginal physical productivity* of an input is defined to be the additional output which can be obtained by the employment of one additional unit of that input. Mathematically:

$$\text{Marginal product of capital} = MP_K = \frac{\partial Q}{\partial K} = f_K \qquad\qquad [11.3]$$

and

$$\text{Marginal product of labor} \quad = MP_L = \frac{\partial Q}{\partial L} = f_L. \qquad\qquad [11.3']$$

As a physical example of these definitions consider the case of a farmer hiring one more man to harvest his crop but holding all other inputs constant. The extra output which this man produces is his marginal physical productivity. The marginal physical productivity of this labor input is measured in physical quantities (such as bushels of wheat, crates of oranges, or heads of lettuce). This magnitude would be expected to depend on the quantity of other factors employed. An extra worker might be very productive if he had a great amount of capital to work with, whereas a poorly equipped worker would have a low marginal productivity.

It might also be expected that the marginal physical productivity of an input depends on how much of that input is used. Labor, for example, cannot be added indefinitely to a given field (while keeping the amount of equipment, fertilizer, and so forth fixed) without eventually exhibiting some deterioration in its productivity. This possibility is illustrated in Figures 11.1a and 11.1b. The relationship between the quantity of a particular input (labor) and total output is recorded in Figure 11.1a as TP_L. For small amounts of L, output increases rapidly as additional L is added. However, because *other inputs are held constant,* eventually the ability of additional labor to generate additional output begins to deteriorate. Finally, at L^* output reaches its maximum level. Any additional labor added beyond this point actually decreases output.

[4] Often in empirical investigations the form of Equation 11.2 is used, and output is defined to be the "value added" by the particular firm being investigated. In this way inputs such as natural resources are assumed to be transformed into output, and the application of capital and labor to these resources produces added value. Similarly each stage of the productive process adds value to those intermediate inputs it uses.

Figure 11.1 (a) Total Product of Labor Curve; (b) Average and Marginal Product Curves for Labor

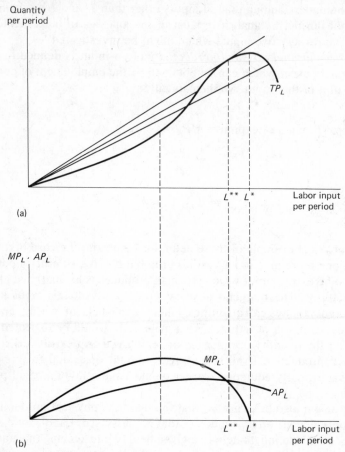

These curves show how the average and marginal product of labor curves can be derived from the total product curve. The curve TP_L in 11.1a represents the relationship between labor input and output, on the assumption that all other inputs are held constant. The slope of this curve is the marginal product of labor (MP_L), and the slope of a chord joining the origin to a point on the TP_L curve gives the average product of labor (AP_L). The relationship between the AP_L and MP_L curves is geometrically obvious from the figures.

From this total labor productivity curve both average and marginal productivity curves can be constructed. The marginal physical product of labor is simply the slope of the curve TP_L. This should be clear from definition 11.3. In Figure 11.1b the marginal product curve (MP_L) is drawn. Notice that MP_L reaches a maximum at that level of L for which TP_L has a point of inflexion, and that MP_L is equal to 0 at the point L^* for which TP_L reaches a maximum. Beyond L^* further additions of labor input actually reduce output. The point L^* is sometimes called the *intensive margin* of production. Production will not take place beyond L^* since using more labor (which is presumably costly) will result in less output for the firm.

In common usage the term "labor productivity" usually means *average productivity*. When it is said that a certain industry has experienced productivity increases, this is taken to mean that output per unit of labor input has increased. Although this concept of average productivity is not nearly so important in theoretical economic discussions as is marginal productivity, it is a simple matter to derive average productivity relationships from the total product curve. This is also done in Figure 11.1. We define the average product of labor (AP_L) to be:

$$AP_L = \frac{\text{Output}}{\text{Labor input}} = \frac{Q}{L}.$$ [11.4]

Geometrically the value of AP_L for any quantity of labor input is the slope of the chord drawn from the origin in Figure 11.1a to the relevant point on the TP_L curve. By recognizing this relationship it is easy to see that AP_L reaches a maximum where AP_L equals MP_L (at the point L^{**}). At this point the chord is exactly tangent to the TP_L curve. Consequently, by the definition of tangency, the AP_L (the slope of this chord) is equal to MP_L (the slope of the total product curve).[5] It is also geometrically obvious that for $L < L^{**}$, MP_L exceeds AP_L and for $L > L^{**}$, AP_L exceeds MP_L. So long as $MP_L > AP_L$, the average product of labor is rising. The output of the marginal laborer exceeds the average product which previously prevailed, so the average must be increased by the addition of this extra worker. A similar argument would show that when $MP_L < AP_L$,

---

[5] Mathematically we wish to find that L for which $AP_L(= Q/L)$ is a maximum. Differentiating AP_L with respect to L gives:

$$\frac{L \cdot \frac{\partial Q}{\partial L} - Q}{L^2} = \frac{L \cdot MP_L - Q}{L^2} = 0$$

as the condition for a maximum. But this says:

$$L \cdot MP_L - Q = 0$$

or

$$MP_L = \frac{Q}{L} = AP_L$$

at the maximum point.

the average product must be falling. The point L^{**} is sometimes called the *extensive margin* of production since labor added beyond this point will cause *average* productivity to fall.

Many price theory textbooks build a substantial amount of analysis around the average, marginal, and total productivity curves exhibited in Figure 11.1.[6] Although it was thought important to discuss these curves for historical interest, no more complete analysis will be presented here. There are two reasons for giving these venerable curves such brief attention. First, the curves are drawn on the assumption that all other inputs are held constant and this must be recognized as a very limiting assumption. In any empirical observation we are likely to make, all inputs will be changing. Since changing the quantity of some other input, say K, will change both the location and shape of the curves in Figure 11.1, we will not observe one single set of these curves. Discussing specifically how the curves shift when K changes can be a tedious and unnecessary exercise.

Second, we in fact know very little about their actual shape. While the shapes of the curves drawn in Figure 11.1 seem reasonable, any additional analysis should not be based simply on hunches about these shapes.

For these related reasons the strategy adopted in this chapter for studying the technology of production will be to investigate the form of the production function as a whole rather than to look only at some particular set of average and marginal product curves. In any case, once the production function is known exactly the curves in Figure 11.1 can be easily derived by using their mathematical definitions.

Isoquant Maps and the Rate of Technical Substitution

One way to picture a production function in two dimensions is by using its *isoquant map*. We will again use a production function of the form $Q = f(K, L)$ with the understanding that "capital" and "labor" are simply convenient examples of any two inputs which might happen to be of interest. An isoquant (from *iso* meaning equal) records those combinations of K and L which are able to produce a given level of output. For example, all those combinations of K and L which fall on the curve labeled "$Q = 10$" in Figure 11.2 are capable of producing ten units of output per period. This isoquant then records the fact that there are many alternative ways of producing ten units of output. One way might be

---

[6] For example, such analysis might be used to show that production must take place between the extensive and intensive margins; the quantity of labor chosen must be between L^{**} and L^*. We have already seen why a level of labor input greater than L^* will never be chosen. We will not show why the quantity of labor chosen must exceed L^{**}, but the reader may wish to do so after completing Chapter 17.

represented by point A: We would use L_A and K_A to produce ten units of output. Alternatively, we might prefer to use relatively less capital and more labor and would therefore choose a point such as B.

Figure 11.2   An Isoquant Map

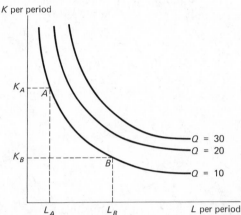

Isoquants record the alternative combinations of inputs which can be used to produce a given level of output. The slope of these curves shows the rate at which L can be substituted for K while keeping output constant. The negative of this slope is called the (marginal) rate of technical substitution (RTS). In the figure the RTS is positive, and it is diminishing for increasing inputs of labor.

There are many isoquants in the K-L plane. Each isoquant represents a different level of output. Isoquants record successively higher levels of output as we move out in a northeasterly direction. Presumably using more of each of the inputs will permit output to increase. Several other isoquants (for $Q = 20$ and $Q = 30$) are shown in Figure 11.2. These record those combinations of inputs which can produce the required output. The reader will probably notice the similarity between an isoquant map and the individual's indifference curve map discussed in Part II. These are indeed similar ideas, since both represent "contour" maps of the particular function of interest. For isoquants, however, the labeling of the curves is measurable (an output of ten units has a quantifiable meaning), and we will therefore be somewhat more interested in studying the shape of these curves than we were in examining the exact shape of indifference curves.

The slope of an isoquant shows how one input can be traded for another while holding output constant. Examining the slope will give us some information about the technical possibility for substituting labor for capital. Because of this, the slope of an isoquant (or, more properly, its negative) is called the *marginal rate of technical substitution* (RTS) of labor for capital. Mathematically, we define:

$$RTS \ (L \ \text{for} \ K) = \frac{-dK}{dL}\bigg|_{Q \ = \ \text{Constant}} \qquad\qquad [11.5]$$

where the notation is intended as a reminder that output is to be held constant as L is substituted for K. The particular value of this trade-off rate will depend not only on the level of output but also on the quantities of capital and labor being used. Its value depends on the point on the isoquant map at which the slope is to be measured.

In order to examine the shape of production function isoquants it is useful to prove the following result: The RTS (of L for K) is equal to the ratio of the marginal product of labor (MP_L) to the marginal product of capital (MP_K). The proof of this assertion proceeds by setting up the total differential of the product function:

$$dQ = \frac{\partial f}{\partial L} \cdot dL + \frac{\partial f}{\partial K} \cdot dK = MP_L \cdot dL + MP_K \cdot dK. \qquad\qquad [11.6]$$

Along an isoquant $dQ = 0$ (output is constant) so:

$$MP_L \cdot dL = -MP_K \cdot dK. \qquad\qquad [11.7]$$

This says that along an isoquant the gain in output from increasing L slightly is exactly balanced by the loss in output from suitably decreasing K. Rearranging terms a bit gives:

$$\frac{-dK}{dL}\bigg|_{Q \ = \ \text{Constant}} = RTS \ (L \ \text{for} \ K) = \frac{MP_L}{MP_K} \qquad\qquad [11.8]$$

as was to be shown.

We can use the result of Equation 11.8 to see that those isoquants which we observe must be negatively sloped. Since both MP_L and MP_K will be positive (no firm would choose to produce where a marginal productivity is negative), the RTS will also be positive. Because the negative of the RTS is the slope of an isoquant the slopes of these isoquants which are observed must be negative.[7] An increase in L must be met by a decrease in K if output is to be held constant. If both L and K had to be increased to keep output constant, one of these inputs would of necessity have a negative marginal productivity.

---

[7] It is possible for an isoquant to have a positive slope: It is easy to dream up functions which do. The importance of this discussion is to indicate that such positively sloped portions will not be observed.

The isoquants in Figure 11.2 are not only drawn with a negative slope (as they should be) but they are also drawn as convex curves. Along any one of the curves the *RTS is diminishing*. For high ratios of K to L the RTS is a large positive number indicating that a great deal of capital can be given up if one more unit of labor becomes available. On the other hand, when a lot of labor is already being used, the RTS is low, signifying that only a small amount of capital can be traded for an additional unit of labor if output is to be held constant. This shape seems intuitively reasonable: The more labor (relative to capital) that is used, the less able labor is to substitute for capital. In some sense labor becomes less potent as a substitute as more of it is used. Since this idea seems reasonable, it would be nice if it could be derived as a fundamental rule built on some more basic foundation. For example, using Equation 11.8, it might be thought that the convex shape of the isoquants could be derived as a corollary to the assumption that the marginal productivity of an input is likely to be decreasing for increases in that input. Unfortunately, no such general rule can be derived.[8] Nonetheless, the assumption of a diminish-

---

[8] To see why no general conclusion can be drawn, assume $Q = f(K, L)$ and that f_K and f_L are positive (that is, the marginal productivities are positive). Assume also that $f_{KK} < 0$ and $f_{LL} < 0$ (that the marginal productivities are decreasing). In order to show that isoquants are convex, we would like to show $d(RTS)/dL < 0$. Since, by Equation 11.6, $RTS = f_L/f_K$ we have:

$$\frac{dRTS}{dL} = \frac{d(f_L/f_K)}{dL}.$$

Because f_L and f_K are functions of both K and L we must take the total derivative of this expression:

$$\frac{dRTS}{dL} = \frac{\left[f_K \left(f_{LL} + f_{LK} \cdot \frac{dK}{dL} \right) - f_L \left(f_{KL} + f_{KK} \cdot \frac{dK}{dL} \right) \right]}{(f_K)^2}.$$

Using the fact that $dK/dL = -f_L/f_K$ along an isoquant, and the fact that $f_{KL} = f_{LK}$ we have:

$$\frac{dRTS}{dL} = \frac{(f_K^2 f_{LL} - 2f_K f_L f_{KL} + f_L^2 f_{KK})}{(f_K)^3}.$$

Since we have assumed $f_K > 0$, the denominator of this function is positive. Hence the whole fraction will be negative providing the numerator is. Because f_{LL} and f_{KK} are both assumed negative, the numerator will definitely be negative if f_{KL} is positive. If we can assume this, we have shown that $dRTS/dL < 0$ (that the isoquants are convex).

Although it will frequently be the case that f_{KL} is positive (that an increase in L will increase MP_K), this will not necessarily always be so, and consequently we cannot prove the existence of a diminishing RTS unambiguously. However, for "most" production functions, and for all constant returns to scale production functions (*see* below), f_{KL} will be positive, and therefore the assumption of diminishing marginal productivities will insure a diminishing RTS.

ing RTS seems a reasonable one, and we will adopt this assumption for later applications.

Classifying Production Functions: Returns to Scale

Because production functions represent tangible productive processes, more attention has been paid to the particular form of these functions than has been given to characterizing the shape of an ethereal utility function. Knowledge of the shape and properties of a firm's production function is important for a variety of policy reasons,[9] and in the remainder of this chapter a brief taxonomy of some functional types will be presented.

The first important question which might be asked about production functions is how does output respond to increases in all inputs together. For example, suppose all inputs were doubled, then would output double or would the relationship not be quite so simple? This is a question of the *returns to scale* exhibited by the production function that has been of interest to economists ever since Adam Smith intensively studied the production of pins. Smith identified two forces which came into operation when the conceptual experiment of doubling all inputs was performed. First, a doubling of scale permits a greater division of labor, and hence there is some presumption that efficiency might increase—production might more than double. Second, doubling of the inputs also entails some loss in efficiency, because managerial overseeing may become more difficult. Which of these two tendencies will have a greater effect is an important empirical question.

Presenting a technical definition of these concepts is misleadingly simple. If the production function is given by $Q = f(K, L)$, then we say that this function exhibits *constant returns to scale* if:

$$f(mK, mL) = mf(K, L) = mQ \text{ for } m > 0. \tag{11.9}$$

This definition says that if we multiply all the inputs by some constant m, we multiply output by that constant also.[10]

Similarly, a production function is said to exhibit *decreasing returns to scale* if output is increased proportionally less than are inputs:

[9] Of the two characteristics of the production function examined here, the question of returns to scale is an important one for governmental regulation of industry, and the elasticity of substitution sheds light on the question of how income will be distributed between capital and labor. We will examine these policy issues in later chapters.

[10] Mathematically such functions are said to be "homogeneous of degree one" or, sometimes, "linear homogeneous" (*see* Footnote 6 of Chapter 4 for a rigorous definition of these terms).

$$f(mK, mL) < m f(K, L) = mQ \qquad\qquad [11.10]$$

and to exhibit *increasing returns to scale* if output increases more than proportionally:

$$f(mK, mL) > m f(K, L) = mQ. \qquad\qquad [11.11]$$

These definitions are clearcut, and it should be possible to determine which type of production function one has.

The simplicity of these definitions may be somewhat misleading, however, when it is recognized that inputs other than K and L enter into the production function. What is to be done with these inputs when K and L are doubled? Does it make sense to talk of doubling "all" inputs, or must some necessarily be regarded as fixed? For example, suppose climatic conditions are an important argument in a production function. What sense could be made out of the stipulation that we "double the weather"? Alternatively, if we hold the weather "constant," we have violated the rigorous definition of returns to scale which requires that all inputs increase proportionately. The reader may wish to suggest several other inputs which cannot in actuality be increased proportionally. Such "problem" inputs are both difficult to deal with conceptually and extremely important in empirical investigations. However, because the methods used will depend on the particular productive process under investigation, the subject will not be pursued here. In later chapters (notably Chapter 15) we will see how a slightly different notion of returns to scale is sometimes used in dealing with policy questions. In the remainder of this chapter we will get around this problem of fixed inputs by assuming K and L are the *only* inputs in the production function.

Constant returns to scale production functions occupy an important place in economic theory. This is not only because such functions occupy a mathematical middle ground between increasing and decreasing returns but also because there are economic reasons for expecting an industry's production function to exhibit constant returns. If all production in the industry is carried on in plants of an "efficient" size, then doubling all inputs could most reasonably be accomplished by doubling the number of these plants. But this would presumably double output since there are now exactly twice as many plants. Hence the *industry* would have a constant returns to scale production function. So long as doubling of inputs is brought about by doubling the number of optimally sized plants, this will be the case.

Constant returns to scale production functions also have the interesting theoretical property that the RTS between two factors, say K and L, depends only on the *ratio of K to L*, but not on the scale of production.[11] This can be shown with a simple argument. Suppose that we have a constant returns to scale production function such that when $K = 10$ and $L = 10$, $Q = 20$. Suppose also that at this point the *RTS* of L for K is equal to 2. Therefore 8 units of K and 11 units of L will also yield $Q = 20$. Now consider doubling all inputs. What we want to show is that the *RTS* at the new input configuration ($K = 20$, $L = 20$) is also equal to 2. We know, because of the assumption of constant returns to scale, that the input combination ($K = 20$, $L = 20$) will produce 40 units of output, but so will the input combination ($K = 16$, $L = 22$). Therefore the *RTS* at ($K = 20$, $L = 20$) is given by $-(-4)/2 = 2$. That was the result to be shown: The *RTS* does not depend on the scale of production, only on the ratio of K to L.

Figure 11.3   Isoquant Map for a Constant Returns to Scale Production Function

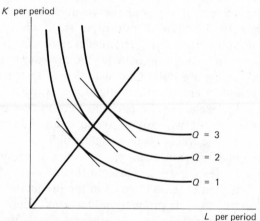

K per period

$Q = 3$

$Q = 2$

$Q = 1$

L per period

For a constant returns to scale production function the *RTS* depends only on the ratio of K to L, but not on the scale of production. Consequently, each isoquant will simply be a radial blowup of the unit isoquant. Along any ray through the origin (a ray of constant K/L) the *RTS* will be the same on all isoquants.

Geometrically, all the isoquants of a constant returns to scale production function are "radial blowups" of the unit isoquant. Along any ray through the origin (a line along which K/L is constant), the slope of

---

[11] A technical proof of this assertion rests on the mathematical theorem that if $f(K, L)$ is homogeneous of degree 1, then the partial derivatives of f are homogeneous of degree 0. If we double both K and L, the marginal productivities of f stay constant and therefore depend only on the ratio K/L. Hence by Equation 11.8 the *RTS* also depends only on K/L.

the isoquants is the same. This is illustrated in Figure 11.3, which also shows that the isoquants are equally spaced as output expands, thus exhibiting the constant proportional relationship between increases in all inputs and increases in output. If the production function exhibited increasing returns, the isoquants would get closer together as the quantity of inputs expanded, since proportional increases in quantity require less than proportional increases in inputs. On the other hand, the isoquants of a decreasing returns to scale production function would move further apart, since proportional increases in quantity require more than proportional increases in inputs. It is conceivable for a production function to exhibit all three of these effects in different output ranges. Such a possibility is illustrated in Figure 11.4.

Figure 11.4   A Production Function with Increasing, Decreasing, and Constant
Returns to Scale

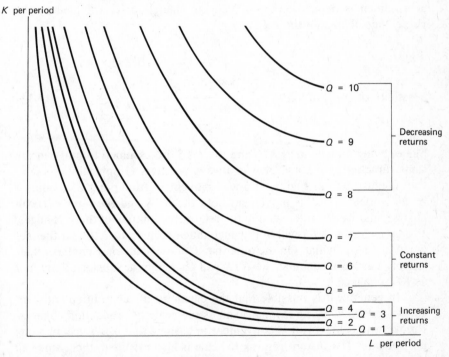

The returns to scale of a production function dictate how the isoquants will be spaced. When returns to scale are increasing, isoquants are getting closer together. When returns to scale are decreasing, the isoquants get further apart, since proportional increases in inputs yield less than proportional increase in output. A production function may exhibit both types of returns to scale, as the isoquant map shows.

Classifying Production Functions: The Elasticity of Substitution

Another important characteristic of the production function is how "easy" it is to substitute capital for labor. This is essentially a question of the shape of a single isoquant rather than a question about the whole isoquant map. Along one isoquant it has been assumed that the rate of technical substitution will decrease as the capital-labor ratio decreases (that is, as K/L decreases), and we wish to define some parameter which measures this degree of responsiveness. If the RTS does not change at all for changes in K/L we might say that substitution is easy (we will see in Chapter 12 exactly why the term "easy" is used). Whereas if the RTS changes rapidly for small changes in K/L we would say substitution is difficult. A scale-free measure of this responsiveness is provided by the *elasticity of substitution*. Technically, the elasticity of substitution along an isoquant is defined as the percentage change in K/L divided by the percentage change in the RTS:

$$\text{Elasticity of substitution} = \sigma = \frac{\text{percent } \Delta \frac{K}{L}}{\text{percent } \Delta RTS} = \frac{\dfrac{d(K/L)}{\dfrac{K}{L}}}{\dfrac{d(RTS)}{RTS}} \qquad [11.12]$$

Since, along an isoquant, K/L and the RTS are assumed to move in the same direction, the value of σ is always positive. Graphically this concept is illustrated in Figure 11.5 as a movement from point A to point B on an isoquant. In this movement both the RTS and the ratio K/L will change, and we are interested in the relative magnitude of these changes. If σ is high, the RTS will not change much relative to K/L and the isoquant is relatively flat. On the other hand, a low value of σ implies rather sharply curved isoquants: the RTS will change by a substantial amount as K/L changes.[12]

In general, it is possible that the elasticity of substitution will vary as one moves along an isoquant and as the scale of production changes. Frequently, however, it is convenient to assume that σ is constant along an isoquant. If constant returns to scale is also assumed, then, since all the isoquants are merely radial blowups of each other, σ will be the same

---

[12] Mathematically it can be shown that σ is inversely related to the "curvature" of the isoquant. Sharply curved isoquants have low values for σ. For a derivation of this fact and some other interesting properties of the elasticity of substitution *see* R. G. D. Allen, *Mathematical Analysis for Economists* (New York: St. Martin's Press, 1938), pp. 340–343.

Figure 11.5 Graphic Derivation of the Elasticity of Substitution

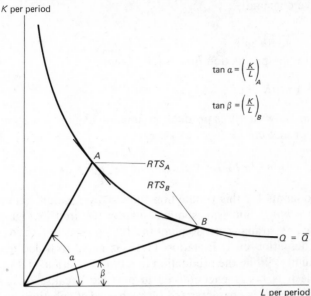

$$\tan \alpha = \left(\frac{K}{L}\right)_A$$

$$\tan \beta = \left(\frac{K}{L}\right)_B$$

In moving from point A on the $Q = \bar{Q}$ isoquant to point B both the capital labor ratio (K/L) and the RTS will change. The elasticity of substitution (σ) is defined to be the ratio of these proportional changes. It is a measure of how curved the isoquant is.

along all isoquants. Most investigations of real-world production functions have centered on this *constant returns to scale, constant elasticity of substitution* type. Some of the most important of these are discussed in detail in the next section.[13]

Some Common Constant Returns to Scale Production Functions

In this section four constant returns to scale production functions will be discussed. Each of these is characterized by a different elasticity of

---

[13] Allen (*ibid.*, p. 343) shows that for the constant returns to scale case σ can be defined in terms of the production function as:

$$\sigma = \frac{\dfrac{\partial Q}{\partial L} \cdot \dfrac{\partial Q}{\partial K}}{Q \cdot \dfrac{\partial^2 Q}{\partial L \partial K}}.$$

substitution. The choices for σ will be: $\sigma = \infty$, $\sigma = 0$, $\sigma = 1$, and σ equals any positive constant:

Case 1: $\sigma = \infty$.

Suppose the production function is given by:

$$Q = f(K, L) = aK + bL.$$ [11.13]

It is easy to show that this production function exhibits constant returns to scale: For any $m > 0$:

$$f(mK, mL) = amK + bmL = m(aK + bL) = mf(K, L).$$ [11.14]

All isoquants for this production function are parallel straight lines with slope $-b/a$.[14] Such an isoquant map is pictured in Figure 11.6a. Since along any straight-line isoquant the RTS is constant, the denominator in the definition of σ, Equation 11.12, is equal to 0 and hence σ is equal to infinity. While the production function, Equation 11.13, is a useful example it is rarely encountered in practice because there are few production processes characterized by such ease of substitution. Indeed, in this case capital and labor can be thought of as perfect substitutes for each other. Using the analysis of Chapter 12, the reader is asked to show that an industry characterized by such a production function would use *only* capital or *only* labor (*see* Problem 4 of Part III). It is hard to envision such a production process: Every machine needs someone to press its buttons, and every laborer requires some capital equipment however modest.

Case 2: $\sigma = 0$.

The production function characterized by $\sigma = 0$ is the important case of a *fixed-proportions production function*. Capital and labor must always be used in a fixed ratio. The isoquants for this production function are "L"-shaped and are pictured in Figure 11.6b. A firm characterized by this production function will always operate along the ray where the ratio K/L is fixed at b/a. To operate at some point other than at the vertex of the isoquants would be inefficient, since the same output could be produced with less inputs by moving along the isoquant toward the vertex. Because K/L is a constant it is easy to see from the definition of the elasticity of substitution that σ must equal 0.

---

[14] The production function, Equation 11.13, provides a simple case in which to show that the slope of an isoquant (that is, the negative of the RTS) is equal to $-MP_L/MP_K$ since in this case $MP_L = \partial Q/\partial L = b$ and $MP_K = \partial Q/\partial K = a$.

Figure 11.6   Isoquant Maps for Production Functions with Various Values
for σ

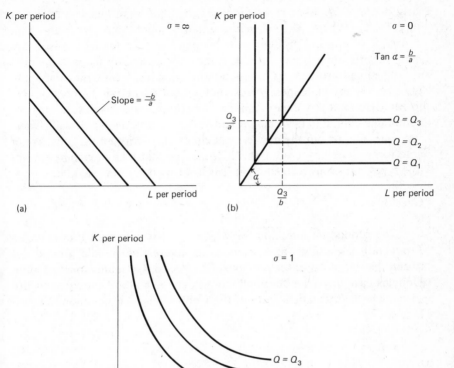

(a)

(b)

(c)

Three possible values for the elasticity of substitution are illustrated in these figures. In
11.6a capital and labor are perfect substitutes. In this case the RTS will not change as the
capital-labor ratio changes. In 11.6b, the fixed proportions case, no substitution is possible.
The capital-labor ratio is fixed at b/a. A case of limited substitutability is illustrated in 11.6c.

The mathematical form of the fixed proportions production function
is given by:

$$Q = \min(aK, \ bL) \hspace{4cm} [11.15]$$
$$a, \ b > 0$$

where the operator "min" means that Q is given by the smaller of the
two values in parentheses. For example, suppose $aK < bL$, then $Q = aK$
and we would say that capital is the binding constraint in this production

process. The employment of more labor would not raise Q, and hence the marginal product of labor is 0; labor is superfluous in this case. Similarly if $aK > bL$ labor is the binding constraint on output and capital is superfluous. When $aK = bL$ neither input is superfluous. When this happens $K/L = b/a$ and production takes place at a vertex on the isoquant map. If both inputs are costly this is the only reasonable place to operate.

The fixed-proportions production function has a wide range of applications.[15] Many machines, for example, require a certain number of men to run them, but any excess labor is superfluous. For example, consider combining capital (a lawn mower) and labor to mow a lawn. It will always take one man to run the mower, and either input without the other is not able to produce any output at all. It may be that many machines are of this type—requiring a fixed complement of workers per machine.[16]

Case 3: $\sigma = 1$.

The production function for which $\sigma = 1$ is called a *Cobb-Douglas Production Function*[17] and provides an interesting middle ground between the two polar cases previously discussed. Isoquants for the Cobb-Douglas case have the "normal" convex shape and are shown in Figure 11.6c. The mathematical form of the Cobb-Douglas production function is given by:

$$Q = f(K, L) = AK^aL^b \qquad [11.16]$$

where A, a, and b are all positive constants.

For $a + b = 1$ the Cobb-Douglas function exhibits constant returns to scale:

$$f(mK, mL) = A(mK)^a(mL)^b = Am^{a+b}K^aL^b$$
$$= mAK^aL^b = mf(K, L). \qquad [11.17]$$

---

[15] The fixed-proportions production function exhibits constant returns to scale since:
$$f(mK, mL) = \min(amK, bmL) = m \cdot \min(aK, bL)$$
$$= mf(K, L) \quad \text{for any } m > 0.$$

[16] The lawn mower example points up another possibility, however. Presumably there is some leeway in choosing what size of lawn mower to buy. Hence, prior to the actual purchase, the capital-labor ratio in lawn-mowing can be considered variable: Any device, from a pair of clippers to a gang mower, might be chosen. Once the mower is purchased, however, the capital-labor ratio becomes fixed.

Several authors have adopted this general "putty-clay" view of productive processes. In the planning stage there may be substantial possibilities for substituting capital for labor. Once investment decisions have been made (the "putty" has hardened into "clay"), the machines have to be used with a specified amount of labor.

[17] Named after C. W. Cobb and P. H. Douglas [*see* P. H. Douglas, *The Theory of Wages* (New York: The Macmillan Company, 1934), pp. 132–135].

If $a + b > 1$ then this function exhibits increasing returns to scale; similarly, if $a + b < 1$ it shows decreasing returns.

A direct proof that when $a + b = 1$, the elasticity of substitution for the Cobb-Douglas production function equals 1 is rather formal and will be relegated to a footnote.[18] A more interesting, intuitive proof that $\sigma = 1$ for the Cobb-Douglas case will be presented in Chapter 17 when the distribution of income between factors is discussed. Notice that, as for all constant returns to scale production functions, the marginal productivities in the Cobb-Douglas case depend only on the *ratio* K/L:

since

$$Q = AK^aL^{1-a}$$

$$MP_L = \frac{\partial Q}{\partial L} = (1 - a)AK^aL^{-a} = (1 - a)A\left(\frac{K}{L}\right)^a \qquad [11.18]$$

and

$$MP_K = \frac{\partial Q}{\partial K} = aAK^{a-1}L^{1-a} = aA\left(\frac{K}{L}\right)^{a-1}.$$

As with all the production functions discussed in this section notice also that the marginal productivities for both K and L are nonnegative for all values of the ratio K/L.

The Cobb-Douglas function has proved to be quite useful in many applications since it is linear in logs:

$$\log Q = \log A + a \log K + b \log L. \qquad [11.19]$$

The constant a is then the elasticity of output with respect to capital input, and b is the elasticity of output with respect to labor input. Numerous studies have found that a is approximately $1/4$, and b is approximately $3/4$ for a variety of data. There is much controversy over the exact meaning to be attributed to such findings, and these values are mentioned only

---

[18] Using Allen's definition from Footnote 13 of this chapter, when $Q = AK^aL^{1-a}$:

$$\sigma = \frac{(1 - a)\frac{Q}{L} \cdot a\frac{Q}{K}}{\frac{Q^2(1 - a)(a)}{KL}} = 1.$$

so that the reader might have some indication of the orders of magnitude involved.

Case 4: σ = Some positive constant.

Although 0, 1, and ∞ are important constants there is little reason to believe that production processes would be characterized by any of these elasticities of substitution. Rather, it is desirable to have a general production function which permits σ to take on any positive value. Such a function is provided by the *constant elasticity of substitution* (*CES*) *production function* first developed by Arrow, Chenery, Minhas, and Solow.[19] The complex mathematical form of this production function is given by:

$$Q = \gamma[\delta\, K^{-\rho} + (1 - \delta)L^{-\rho}]^{-1/\rho}$$

where $\gamma > 0$,

$$0 \le \delta \le 1,$$ [11.20]

and $\rho \ge -1$.

These parameters have been given the following interpretation: γ is an efficiency parameter in that it merely shifts the whole production function; δ is a distribution parameter; and ρ is a substitution parameter because it can be shown that $\sigma = 1/1 + \rho$. The *CES* production function therefore includes $\sigma = 1$, $\sigma = 0$, and $\sigma = \infty$ as special cases. When $\rho = 0$, $\sigma = 1$;[20] when $\rho = \infty$, $\sigma = 0$; and when $\rho = -1$, $\sigma = \infty$. Proof of the third of these statements is trivial. The other two require a rather complicated limiting argument; the proof is therefore not presented here.

The isoquant map of the general *CES* production function is much like that of the Cobb-Douglas. It is easy to show that the *CES* function exhibits constant returns to scale:

---

[19] K. J. Arrow, H. B. Chenery, B. S. Minhas, and R. M. Solow, "Capital Labor Substitution and Economic Efficiency," *The Review of Economics and Statistics* (August 1961), pp. 225–250.

[20] In particular for $\rho = 0$, the *CES* production function approaches a Cobb-Douglas function of the form:

$$Q = \gamma K^{\delta}L^{1-\delta}.$$

As will be pointed out in Chapter 17, this explains the use of the term *distribution parameter* for the parameter δ.

$$f(mK, mL) = \gamma[\delta(mK)^{-\rho} + (1 - \delta)(mL)^{-\rho}]^{-1/\rho}$$

$$= \gamma[m^{-\rho}]^{-1/\rho} [\delta K^{-\rho} + (1 - \delta)L^{-\rho}]^{-1/\rho} \qquad [11.21]$$

$$= mf(K, L) \qquad \text{for any } m > 0.$$

The *CES* production function has proved to be extremely useful in empirical studies in which the investigator prefers to let the data determine σ rather than specifying σ to take some particular value a priori. The most generally encountered case has been found to be that characterized by a positive ρ. By the definition of ρ, this means that the value of σ lies somewhere between 0 and 1. This in turn implies that, while some substitution is possible, production is not as flexible as is suggested by the Cobb-Douglas function and not nearly so flexible as in the straight-line isoquant case.

Conclusion

This chapter has presented a brief summary of the way economists have chosen to investigate the purely technical aspects of production. The concept of a production function was introduced as a useful abstraction of the way in which inputs can be combined to produce outputs. Although engineers would undoubtedly cringe at this kind of abstraction, it serves the economist's purpose of isolating in some simple way the technology of production.

Several characteristics of production functions have been investigated. It was shown that it is commonly assumed that production functions are characterized by constant returns to scale and a constant elasticity of substitution. Two particularly important cases are $\sigma = 0$ (fixed proportions) and $\sigma = 1$ (Cobb-Douglas). These are widely used in empirical work.

This chapter is rather different from most others in this book in that it does not present any aspects of a theory of choice. Technology is given by "nature," and the firm must operate within the constraints set by the available productive processes. In the next few chapters we will see how the entrepreneur, when constrained by these technical relationships, will make input and output choices so as to maximize profits.

Technical Progress and the Production Function

What Is Technical Progress?

The study of technical progress starts with the observation that output per man hour (the average physical product of labor) has risen rapidly over the past two hundred years. Some portion of this rise can undoubtedly be attributed to an increasing amount of capital per worker, but some major portion must be ascribed to the development of better productive techniques. Today we can get more output from the same level of man hours and machine hours than was possible in the past. In formal terms, the production function has changed over time. In this brief appendix we will explore some of the issues which have been raised in an attempt to understand these phenomenal increases in productive technology. Unfortunately, because the study of technical progress is inextricably tied to empirical research, the treatment must be essentially of a taxonomic nature. It is hoped that the interested reader will investigate the wide variety of empirical evidence for himself.[1]

The first observation to be made about technical progress is that the rate of growth of output over time has exceeded the growth rate which can be attributed to the growth in conventionally defined inputs. Suppose we let:

$$Q = A(t) f(K, L) \tag{11A.1}$$

be the production function for some good (or perhaps for society's output as a whole). The term $A(t)$ in the function represents all the factors which go into determining Q besides K (machine hours) and L (man hours). Changes in A over time could represent technical progress. For this reason A is shown as a function of time.

Differentiating Equation 11A.1 with respect to time gives:

$$\frac{dQ}{dt} = \frac{dA}{dt} \cdot f(K, L) + A \cdot \frac{df(K, L)}{dt}$$

$$= \frac{dA}{dt} \cdot \frac{Q}{A} + \frac{Q}{f(K, L)} \left(\frac{\partial f}{\partial K} \cdot \frac{dK}{dt} + \frac{\partial f}{\partial L} \cdot \frac{dL}{dt} \right). \tag{11A.2}$$

Dividing by Q gives:

$$\frac{\frac{dQ}{dt}}{Q} = \frac{\frac{dA}{dt}}{A} + \frac{\frac{\partial f}{\partial K}}{f(K, L)} \cdot \frac{dK}{dt} + \frac{\frac{\partial f}{\partial L}}{f(K, L)} \cdot \frac{dL}{dt}$$

or $\tag{11A.2'}$

$$\frac{\frac{dQ}{dt}}{Q} = \frac{\frac{dA}{dt}}{A} + \frac{\partial f}{\partial K} \cdot \frac{K}{f(K, L)} \cdot \frac{\frac{dK}{dt}}{K} + \frac{\partial f}{\partial L} \cdot \frac{L}{f(K, L)} \cdot \frac{\frac{dL}{dt}}{L}.$$

---

[1] A useful starting point is two books by E. F. Denison, *The Sources of Economic Growth in the United States and the Alternatives before Us* (New York: Committee for Economic Development, 1962) and *Why Growth Rates Differ: Postwar Experience in Nine Western Countries* (Washington, D.C.: The Brookings Institution, 1967). For a detailed bibliography *see* M. I. Nadiri, "Some Approaches to the Theory and Measurement of Total Factor Productivity: A Survey," *Journal of Economic Literature,* vol. VII, no. 4 (December 1970), pp. 1137–1177.

Now, for any variable x, $(dx/dt)/x$ is simply the geometric rate of growth of x per unit of time. We will denote this by G_x. Hence Equation 11A.2 can be written:

$$G_Q = G_A + \frac{\partial f}{\partial K} \cdot \frac{K}{f(K, L)} \cdot G_K + \frac{\partial f}{\partial L} \cdot \frac{L}{f(K, L)} \cdot G_L$$

but

$$\frac{\partial f}{\partial K} \cdot \frac{K}{f(K, L)} = \frac{\partial Q}{\partial K} \cdot \frac{K}{Q} = \text{Elasticity of output with respect to capital input}$$
$$= E_{Q,K}$$

and

$$\frac{\partial f}{\partial L} \cdot \frac{L}{f(K, L)} = \frac{\partial Q}{\partial L} \cdot \frac{L}{Q} = \text{Elasticity of output with respect to labor input}$$
$$= E_{Q,L}.$$

Therefore Equation 11A.2 finally becomes:

$$G_Q = G_A + E_{Q,K} G_K + E_{Q,L} G_L. \tag{11A.3}$$

This says that the rate of growth in output can be broken down into the sum of two components: growth attributed to changes in inputs (K and L), and other growth (that is, changes in A). Given estimates[2] of $E_{Q,K}$, $E_{Q,L}$ and the three growth rates G_Q, G_K, G_L, it would be possible to compute G_A from Equation 11A.3. This would then give an estimate of that portion of growth to be attributed to factors other than the growth of quantities of inputs. Many researchers have found this "residual" to be substantial, accounting for perhaps 40 percent, or more, of the growth in output. Technical progress is therefore a real phenomenon which must be explained. Increases in output have been the result of the shifting of prevailing isoquant maps rather than simply moving out on a given isoquant map as K and L increase.

Classifying Technical Progress

The empirical question to answer then is in what precise way does the technical change factor $[A(t)]$ enter into the production function. Three possible ways that this might happen are:

[2] In Chapter 17 it will be shown that under certain assumptions these elasticities can be estimated as the share of capital income and the share of labor income in total output.

1. *Neutral technical progress*

$$Q = A(t) f(K, L). \qquad [11A.4]$$

Here technical progress affects all the factors of production equally.

2. *Capital augmenting technical progress*

$$Q = f[A(t)K, L]. \qquad [11A.5]$$

In this case technical progress affects only capital. Machine hours (K) become more productive over time.

3. *Labor augmenting technical progress*

$$Q = f[K, A(t)L]. \qquad [11A.6]$$

This is the case in which technical progress affects only the quality of man hours which enter into the production function. The productive power of labor is "augmented" over time.

Each of these three types of technical progress has the effect of shifting the production function. Over time, more output can be obtained from any given combination of inputs. In graphic terms the isoquant map shifts toward the origin as the productive technology improves. Equations 11A.4-11A.6 provide a way of classifying those shifts which do take place. It is quite likely that all three types of technical progress occur simultaneously. One important role of empirical investigations is to identify the relative importance of each of these types so that policy makers can appraise the possible effects of input changes on the increase in productivity.

The Embodiment Hypothesis and Endogenous Technical Progress

Although the classification of technical progress presented above is in general use, several authors have questioned its descriptive realism. The formulas picture technical progress as an all-enveloping blanket which spreads over all the units of the particular factor affected. For example, both old and new machine hours are assumed to be affected equally by capital augmenting technical progress. Similarly, neutral technical progress is pure manna in that it spreads over the entire productive process. This is surely unrealistic. Most technical progress comes about through the development of new productive technologies. The productivity of a windmill may improve slightly over time, but the major portion of progress takes place as better machines are introduced. In this alternative view technical progress is *embodied* in only the latest additions to the capital stock (the most recent investments); machines which were inherited from the past do not experience technical progress. At any point of time, then, the stock of productive capital is in reality a collection of machines of different "vintages," and each vintage embodies a different level of technical progress. Similarly "new" labor (laborers just entering the labor force) may have a different level of productivity than those already at work. Whether these technical differences stem from better education (new labor may be more productive than old) or from the fact that a worker's productivity increases while he is on a job ("learning by doing") is an interesting empirical question.

These descriptions of technical progress are certainly more realistic than those presented earlier. This increase in descriptive realism is not without cost, however. No longer is it possible to speak of homogeneous labor and homogeneous capital. There are now a large number of different types of labor and capital, and one must somehow add these up into meaningful totals. This aggregation presents numerous conceptual and empirical difficulties since we no longer can speak of "man hours" and "machine hours" as being homogeneous units of measurement.

The stylized production function approach to technical progress exhibits a second conceptual weakness. In this simple approach technical change is *exogenous:* It is outside the economic system. Progress proceeds smoothly over time without regard to the efforts of economic agents. The whole spirit of invention and innovation which permeates any study of the history of technology is missing. It is hard to see the hand of James Watt or Thomas A. Edison in the function $A(t)$. Recognizing this, some recent investigations have attempted to treat technical progress as being *endogenous* to the economic system. Technical advances depend on how much investment in new capital equipment is made, on how many resources are devoted to research and development, and on the emphasis given to the education of the labor force. It may even be possible to picture a "technical progress production function" which formalizes the relationship between inputs devoted to obtaining technical advances and the ultimate improvements in technology which emerge.

CHAPTER 12
The Theory of Costs

Introduction

Having developed some concepts which describe the technical aspects of production, it is now possible to discuss the firm's costs in a rigorous way. In this chapter two basic questions will be investigated: First, how should the firm choose its inputs so as to produce any given level of output as cheaply as possible; and, second, how will this process of cost minimization differ between the *short run* and the *long run*. In a sense these questions are still of a technical nature. There will be in this chapter no mention of demand: We are still skirting the crucial issue of how a firm chooses the level of output it will supply. A development of the theory of costs is, however, a necessary prerequisite to any understanding of the nature of the supply decision.

Before we can discuss the theory of costs some conceptual difficulties about the proper definition of "costs" must be cleared up. At least three different concepts of costs can be distinguished: opportunity cost, accounting cost, and "economic" cost. For economists the most important of these is *social* or *opportunity cost*. Because resources are limited, any decision in our economy to produce some good necessitates doing without some other good. When an automobile is produced, for example, an implicit decision has been made to do without the, say, fifteen bicycles which could have been produced using the labor, metal, chrome, and glass which went into the automobile. The opportunity cost of one automobile is then fifteen bicycles.[1] It is often inconvenient to express opportunity costs in terms of physical goods; we may sometimes choose monetary units instead. Indeed the price of a car may adequately reflect the goods which were given up by its being produced. If this were true we would say the opportunity cost of an automobile is $3000 worth of other goods. This may not always be the case, however. If, for example, the car were produced with resources which couldn't be usefully employed elsewhere, the opportunity cost of its production might have been close to zero.

The opportunity cost doctrine is extremely important in economic analysis. Many problems of social choice are made conceptually clearer by recognizing the alternatives inherent in the economic process. Because the concept, in its most general statement, is directly relevant to social decisions, a full discussion will be postponed until Part VII. In this chapter we will be primarily interested in the definition of costs which is relevant to the firm's decision-making process.

The two other concepts of cost are both directly related to the firm's theory of choice. These are the accountant's concept of cost and the economist's concept of the firm's costs. The accountant's view of cost stresses out-of-pocket expenses, historical costs, depreciation, and other bookkeeping entries. The economist's definition (which draws in obvious ways on the idea of opportunity cost) defines cost to be that payment necessary to keep a resource in its present employment. The best way to make the distinction between these two views is to consider how the costs of various resources (labor, capital, and entrepreneurial services) are defined under each system.

Economists and accountants both regard labor costs in much the same way. To the accountant, expenditures on labor are current expenses

---

[1] The notion of opportunity cost in a general sense pervades all applications of a theory of choice. For example, an individual by choosing to purchase a hamburger is at the same time foregoing, say, two soft drinks.

and hence are costs of production. For economists labor is an *explicit cost*. Labor services (man hours) are purchased at some wage rate (w) and it might be assumed that this is the amount which the labor services would earn in their next best alternative employment. Thus both definitions of costs look at wages although there is a slight distinction in that accountants tend to stress the total wage bill, whereas economists look at the cost of the marginal man hour.

In the case of capital services (machine hours), the two concepts of cost differ greatly. Accountants in calculating capital costs use the historical price of the particular machine under investigation and apply some more-or-less arbitrary depreciation rule to determine how much of that machine's original price to charge to current costs. Economists regard the historical price of a machine as a "sunk cost," which is basically irrelevant to the productive process. They, instead, regard the *implicit cost* of the machine to be what someone else would be willing to pay for its use. Thus the cost of one machine hour is the *rental rate* for that machine in the best alternative use. By continuing to use the machine itself, the firm is implicitly forgoing the rental rate someone else would be willing to pay for its use. This rental rate for one machine hour will be denoted by v.[2]

The concept of entrepreneurial income provides a final illustration of the divergencies which arise between economists and accountants on the definition of costs. Much of what accountants term "profits" would be called "entrepreneurial income" by economists. Profits are a payment to the owner of a firm, and that part of the payment which is necessary to keep the owner in the particular business, economists would argue, is a cost of that business. For an economist, *economic profits* would be defined as that amount of entrepreneurial income in excess of the earning capacity of the entrepreneur's abilities in some other employment. Indeed, if the owner of a firm earns only a nominal "profit" despite his great skills, an economist might conclude that the economic profits of the enterprise are negative.[3]

In this book, not surprisingly, we will use the economist's definition of cost. This is not meant to imply that the accountant's concepts are irrelevant to economic behavior, however. Indeed, bookkeeping methods are integrally important to any manager's decision-making process because they can greatly affect the rate of taxation to be applied against

[2] In most other texts the symbol r is chosen to represent the rental rate on capital. Since this variable is often confused with the related though distinct concept of the interest rate, an alternative symbol was chosen here. The exact relationship between v and the interest rate is examined in Chapter 19.

[3] An interesting application of these concepts occurs in the debate between economists and historians over whether slavery was "profitable" in the economy of the antebellum South.

profits. Accounting costs also have the desirable property of being readily available sources of data. Since the "economic profits" and "costs" of General Motors are never calculated (perhaps not even unambiguously defined), it is usually necessary to use some accounting concepts for empirical work. The economist's definitions do, however, have the desirable features of being broadly applicable to all firms[4] and of forming a conceptually consistent system. They are therefore best suited for a general theoretical analysis.

Two simplifications will initially be made in this chapter about the inputs a firm uses. First it will be assumed, as before, that there are only two variable inputs: homogeneous labor (L, measured in man hours) and homogeneous capital (K, measured in machine hours). Cases of more than two inputs can be handled in an analogous way to that used here — most of the proofs carry over directly.[5] The use of only two inputs is simply a graphic convenience.

A second simplification will be that the inputs to the firm are bought in perfectly competitive markets.[6] Firms can buy (or sell) all the labor or capital they want at the prevailing rental rates (w and v). In graphic terms the supply curve for these resources which faces the firm is horizontal at the prevailing factor prices. Both w and v are treated as "parameters" in the firm's decisions; there is nothing the firm can do to affect them. These conditions will be relaxed in later chapters (notably Chapter 18), but for the moment the perfectly competitive assumption is a convenient and useful one to make.

The Cost-minimizing Input Choice

Because of the assumptions made so far, the total costs for the firm are given by:

$$\text{Total costs} = TC = wL + vK. \tag{12.1}$$

The problem for the firm is to choose K and L so as to minimize Equation 12.1 for each level of output. Mathematically this is a constrained minimization problem, but before proceeding with a rigorous solution it might be useful to state the result to be derived with an intuitive argu-

---

[4] In fact, in recent years accountants have moved toward economists' definitions in their work. For example, the conceptual model of economic costs has been applied to several topics in depreciation accounting and to the calculation of the profits of life insurance companies.

[5] But see the Appendix to Chapter 19 for some dissenting views.

[6] A more complete description of the assumptions of a perfectly competitive market is given in Chapter 22.

ment. In order to minimize the cost of producing a given level of output a firm should choose that point on the isoquant for which the rate of technical substitution of L for K is equal to the ratio w/v: It should equate the rate at which K can be traded for L in the productive process to the rate at which they can be traded in the market place. Suppose this were not true. In particular, suppose the firm were producing output level Q_0 using $K = 10$, $L = 10$; and assume that the RTS were 2 at this point. Assume also that $w = \$1$, $v = \$1$, and hence that $w/v = 1$ (which is unequal to 2). At this input combination the cost of producing Q_0 is \$20. It is easy to show this is not the minimal input cost. Q_0 can also be produced using $K = 8$ and $L = 11$; we can give up two units of K and keep output constant at Q_0 by adding one unit of L. But at this input combination the cost of producing Q_0 is \$19 and hence the initial input combination was not optimal. A proof similar to this one can be demonstrated any time the RTS and the ratio of the factor costs differ.

Mathematically we seek to minimize Equation 12.1 given $Q = f(K, L) = Q_0$. Setting up the Lagrangian expression:

$$\mathscr{L} = wL + vK - \lambda[f(K, L) - Q_0],$$

the first-order conditions for a constrained minimum are:

$$\frac{\partial \mathscr{L}}{\partial L} = w - \lambda \frac{\partial f}{\partial L} = 0$$

$$\frac{\partial \mathscr{L}}{\partial K} = v - \lambda \frac{\partial f}{\partial K} = 0 \qquad\qquad [12.2]$$

$$\frac{\partial \mathscr{L}}{\partial \lambda} = f(K, L) - Q_0 = 0$$

or

$$\frac{w}{v} = \frac{\partial f/\partial L}{\partial f/\partial K} = RTS \ (L \text{ for } K). \qquad\qquad [12.3]$$

This says that the cost minimizing firm should equate the RTS for the two inputs to the ratio of their prices.[7] The result is shown graphically in Figure 12.1. Given the output isoquant Q_0 we wish to find the least costly point on the isoquant. From Equation 12.1 all lines of equal cost are

[7] Equation 12.3 also shows that $\dfrac{1}{\lambda} = \dfrac{\partial f/\partial L}{w} = \dfrac{\partial f/\partial K}{v}$. This means that the marginal productivity per dollar spent should be the same for all inputs used. In other words, the ratio of marginal benefit (that is, increased output) to marginal cost should be the same for all inputs.

parallel straight lines with slopes $-w/v$. Three lines of equal total cost are shown in Figure 12.1: $TC_1 < TC_2 < TC_3$. It is clear from the figure that the minimum total cost for producing Q_0 is given by TC_1 where the total cost curve is just tangent to the isoquant. The cost minimizing input combination is L^*, K^*. This point will be a true minimum if the isoquant is convex (if the RTS diminishes for increases in L/K).

Figure 12.1 Minimization of Costs Given $Q = Q_0$

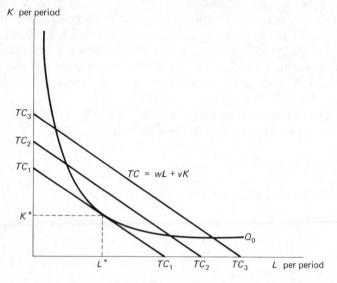

A firm is assumed to choose K and L to minimize total costs. The condition for this minimization is that the rate at which K and L can be technically traded (while keeping $Q = Q_0$) should be equal to the rate at which these inputs can be traded in the market. In other words, the RTS (of L for K) should be set equal to the price ratio w/v. This tangency is shown in the figure; costs are minimized at TC_1 by choosing inputs K^* and L^*.

Figure 12.1 exhibits the formal similarity between the firm's cost-minimization problem and the individual's utility-maximization problem. In both cases we took prices as fixed parameters and derived the tangency conditions. In Chapter 5 we then asked the comparative statics question of how the utility-maximizing choice of goods would change if a price were to change. The analysis of this change permitted the construction of the familiar downward sloping demand curve. An interesting question is whether an analogous development could be made here for the firm's demand for an input. Could we change some input price (change the slope of the TC curves) and then trace out the effects of this price change on the quantity of the factor demanded? The analogy to the individual's utility-maximization process can be misleading at this point. In order to analyze what happens to K^*, say, as v changes, we also have to know what happens to Q_0. The demand for K is a *derived demand* based on the demand for the firm's output. We cannot answer questions about K^* without looking at the interaction of supply and demand in the goods market. While the analogy to the theory of individual behavior is useful in pointing out basic similarities, it is not an exact analogy—the derivation of a firm's demand for an input is considerably more complex. An analysis of the firm's demand for inputs is presented in Part V of this book.

The Lagrangian Multiplier, λ, in Equation 12.2 can be given an interesting interpretation:

$$\lambda = \frac{w}{\partial f/\partial L} = \frac{v}{\partial f/\partial K} = \frac{\partial TC/\partial L}{\partial f/\partial L} = \frac{\partial TC/\partial K}{\partial f/\partial K} = \frac{dTC}{dQ} \qquad [12.4]$$

where the final equality can be derived from the implicit function theorem or, less rigorously, can be understood as a mathematical statement of the fact that the Lagrangian Multiplier represents the change in the objective function (here TC) brought about by a relaxation of the constraint (here $Q = Q_0$). λ can therefore be interpreted as the *marginal cost;* it is the extra cost of producing one more unit of output. We will wish to investigate this concept more completely below.

The Firm's Expansion Path

A firm can perform an analysis such as that presented above for each level of output: For each Q it finds that input choice which minimizes the cost of producing Q. If input costs (w and v) remain constant for all amounts the firm may demand, we can easily trace out this locus of cost-minimizing choices. This procedure is shown in Figure 12.2. The line OE records the cost-minimizing tangencies for successively higher levels of Q. For example, the minimum cost for producing output level Q_1 is given by TC_1 and inputs K_1 and L_1 are used. Other tangencies in the figure can be interpreted in a similar way. The locus of these tangencies is called the firm's *expansion path* because it records how input usage expands as output expands while holding the prices of the inputs constant.

As shown in Figure 12.2, the expansion path need not be a straight line. The use of some inputs may increase faster than others as output expands. Which inputs expand more rapidly will depend on the shape of the production isoquants. Since cost minimization requires that the RTS always be set equal to the ratio w/v, and since the w/v ratio is assumed to be constant, the shape of the expansion path will be determined by where a particular RTS occurs on successively higher isoquants.[8]

[8] Using this discussion it should be easy for the reader to show that the expansion path for a firm with a constant returns to scale production function is a straight line.

Figure 12.2   The Firm's Expansion Path

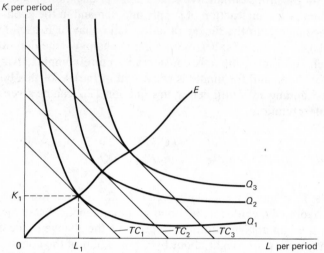

The firm's expansion path is the locus of cost-minimizing tangencies. On the assumption of fixed input prices the curve shows how input usage increases as output increases.

Figure 12.3   Factor Inferiority

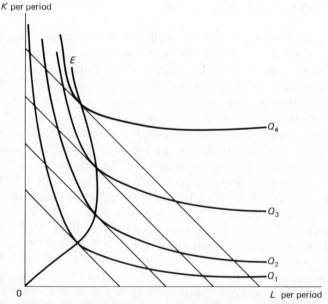

With this particular set of isoquants labor is an inferior input since less L is chosen as output expands beyond Q_2.

It would seem reasonable to assume that the expansion path will be positively sloped, that successively higher output levels will require more of both inputs. This need not be the case, however, as Figure 12.3 illustrates. Increases of output beyond Q_2 actually cause the quantity of labor used to decrease. In this range labor would be said to be an *inferior input*.[9] The occurrence of inferior inputs is then a theoretical possibility which may happen even when isoquants have their usual convex shape.

Much theoretical discussion has centered on the analysis of factor inferiority. Whether inferiority is likely to occur in real-world production functions is a difficult empirical question to answer. It seems unlikely that such comprehensive magnitudes as "capital" and "labor" could be inferior, but a finer classification of inputs may bring inferiority to light. For example, the employment of "unskilled labor" may decline as output increases. In this book we will not be particularly concerned with the analytical complications raised by this possibility.

The Short-run Total Cost Curve

It is traditional in the economic theory of the firm to differentiate between the *short run* and the *long run*. The distinction to be made concerns the length of time over which the firm has a chance to alter its decisions. If only a short period of time is allowed, it may be necessary for the firm to treat some inputs as fixed. It may be technically impossible to change such inputs in the short run. For example, if a period of only one month is to be examined, it may be necessary to treat the size of a firm's physical plant as absolutely fixed. Similarly, an entrepreneur may be committed to a particular business in the short run and it would be impossible (or extremely costly) for him to retire. Over a longer time period (the long run), however, we might not want to treat either of these inputs as fixed, since it is clear that a firm's plant can eventually be enlarged and an entrepreneur can indeed leave the industry. The distinction to be made is between a period over which some inputs are fixed and a longer period over which all inputs become variable.

To make this distinction clear we will add a third productive input to our production function. This input will be called *plant size* (S) for the sake of concreteness, but will in fact stand for all inputs which are fixed in the short run. The production function will now be written as:

$$Q = f(K, L, S) \qquad [12.5]$$

[9] Inferior inputs have many graphic similarities to inferior consumption goods, for example, compare Figures 5.3 and 12.3.

with the understanding that S is absolutely fixed in the short run. We will then seek to examine the differences in a firm's behavior depending on whether we are interested in short-run or long-run reactions.

In the short run plant size is fixed at some level, say S_1. The short-run production function for this firm is then given by:

$$Q = f(K, L, S_1).$$ [12.6]

Associated with plant size S_1 will be a certain level of *fixed costs*. These would include the costs of plant maintenance and depreciation and more generally would include all those costs which would be incurred even if output were 0. This level of fixed costs associated with plant size S_1 will be called F_1.

Equation 12.1 for total costs must now be amended to take fixed costs into account. *Short-run total costs* (*STC*) for plant size S_1 are therefore given by:

$$STC_1 = wL + vK + F_1.$$ [12.7]

Sometimes the expression $(wL + vK)$ is given the name *variable costs* to make it clear that these costs do change with changes in output. The firm could set $L = K = 0$ and incur 0 variable costs (and also produce no output). Fixed costs of F_1 would still be incurred, however. Using the notation SVC_1 for variable costs, Equation 12.7 can be rewritten as:

$$STC_1 = SVC_1 + F_1$$ [12.8]

where it is clear that SVC_1 (and hence STC_1) depends on the level of output, but that F_1 does not change as output changes in the short run. One result of Part IV will be to show that the level of fixed costs is almost irrelevant to profit-maximizing behavior. However, the notion of fixed costs is "excess baggage" which must be carried around a bit before this irrelevance can be shown.

The relationship between short-run variable costs and output can be derived from the firm's expansion path. Returning to Figure 12.2, suppose the isoquants in this diagram have been drawn on the assumption that plant size is fixed at S_1. What were labeled "total costs" in Figure 12.2 should therefore be interpreted as short-run variable costs. These are the costs of the variable factors used in production. Consequently, we would say that Q_1 can be produced at variable costs SVC_{11} ($= TC_1$ in Figure 12.2) where the first subscript refers to the fixed plant size (S_1) and the second subscript represents output level. Similarly SVC_{12} and SVC_{13} are the variable costs of producing outputs Q_2 and Q_3 with plant size S_1. We can now graph this relationship between output and (mini-mized) variable costs in Figure 12.4a. This graph is drawn on what seem to be "reasonable" assumptions about the way in which costs respond to output changes when some inputs are of necessity held fixed. It might be expected that variable costs would rise rather rapidly for low levels of output since plant size is underutilized. There would initially be "excess" capacity. In middle output ranges variable costs would not rise so rapidly with output increases since the firm would be operating in the output range for which the plant was built. Finally, for even higher levels of out-put it might be expected that total variable costs would again start to rise rapidly as the existing plant became overutilized. The production of out-puts greater than Q_3, say, would require crowding of capital and labor into the existing plant and these conditions might cause costs to rise sharply.

Figure 12.4 Hypothetical Short-run Variable and Total Cost Curves

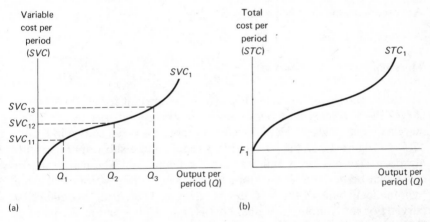

(a) (b)

These curves illustrate a possible relationship between various output levels and the total costs of producing these output levels. The variable costs of producing Q are recorded in Figure 12.4a. These can be derived directly from the firm's expansion path (Figure 12.2) and represent costs which vary systematically with output level. Figure 12.4a is drawn on the assumption that some inputs ("plant size") are held fixed in the short run at S_1. The costs associated with these fixed inputs are denoted by F_1 and these are added to variable costs in 12.4b to show short-run total costs (STC_1) associated with the plant size.

This scenario seems reasonable: The notion that some inputs are fixed in the short run would seem to imply that these inputs could in some sense be under- or overutilized. However, it must be stressed that the actual shape of the SVC_1 curve can only be determined by empirical in-vestigations of the firm's underlying production function. The shape shown in Figure 12.4 is commonly assumed, and we shall continue to use it here.

In Figure 12.4b the short-run total cost curve (STC_1) for plant size S_1 is drawn. This curve is derived by simply adding fixed costs (F_1) to each level of variable costs in 12.4a. The STC_1 curve therefore has exactly the same shape as the SVC_1 curve except that it is higher by the amount F_1.

Other Short-run Cost Curves

Although the short-run total cost curve summarizes all the relevant information about the firm's cost structure, it is frequently convenient to use a set of short-run curves which can be derived from this basic curve. These curves are defined as:

Average fixed cost $= SAFC = F/Q$

Average variable cost $= SAVC = SVC/Q$ [12.9]

Average total cost $= SATC = STC/Q$

Marginal cost $= SMC = \dfrac{dSTC}{dQ} = \dfrac{d(SVC + F)}{dQ} = \dfrac{dSVC}{dQ}$

where the final equality holds because F is constant for all Q. Of these curves the two most important ones are average total cost ($SATC$) and marginal cost (SMC). The derivation of these curves is shown in Figure 12.5. In Figure 12.5a the STC curve is redrawn (the subscript representing plant size has been omitted here for simplicity). The marginal cost curve can be derived as the slope of this STC curve.[10] Notice that the hypothetical shape of the STC curve yields a "U-shaped" marginal cost curve. For low outputs marginal cost is diminishing, but at the point of inflexion of the STC curve (Q^{**}), marginal cost reaches its minimum value and then rises as the STC curve becomes increasingly steep. The cost of producing one more unit is hypothesized to fall initially, but ultimately it will start to rise, since to increase output with a given plant size becomes more difficult.

The construction of the average total cost curve can be derived as the slope of the chord joining the origin with the relevant point on the STC curve. This curve (labeled $SATC$) is also U-shaped. Average costs diminish up to the point Q^*, and then increase for levels of output beyond

---

[10] The reader will recognize that this concept of marginal cost is precisely that which was discussed in Chapter 10. It is also the same concept as was derived in Equation 12.4 as the Lagrangian Multiplier in the derivation of the minimum-cost combination of inputs. In theoretical work it is frequently convenient to work with this mathematical interpretation of marginal cost.

Figure 12.5   Derivation of Short-run Cost Curves from the Short-run Total Cost Curve

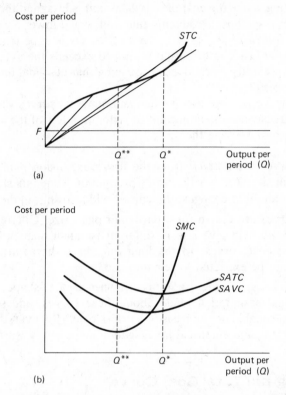

The STC curve from Figure 12.4 is used to construct a set of average and marginal curves. All these curves are constructed on the assumption that plant size is fixed, but the subscript has been omitted for notational simplicity. Marginal cost (MC) is defined as the slope of the STC curve: It represents the cost of producing one more unit of output. The average total cost curve (ATC) and the average variable cost curve (AVC) can also be constructed from the STC curve. Because of the hypothesized shape of the STC curve, all three of these derived curves will be U-shaped.

this point. The output Q^* is therefore that output for which unit (that is, average) costs are minimized for the particular plant size. The average variable cost curve is derived in a similar manner (the chords would start from the F intercept on the STC curve), and this curve (labeled $SAVC$) appears in Figure 12.3b. $SAVC$ always lies below $SATC$ (they differ by the average fixed cost), and $SAVC$ approaches $SATC$ as output increases (F/Q decreases as Q increases).

It is no accident that the SMC curve is drawn passing through the low points of the $SATC$ and $SAVC$ curves. The construction of these curves from the STC curve makes this obvious.[11] That this must logically be the case can be shown as follows. For $SMC < SATC$, the $SATC$ curve must be falling, since the cost of one more unit is less than the previously prevailing average cost. Producing that unit would lower $SATC$. On the other hand for $SMC > SATC$, the $SATC$ curve must be rising, because the cost of the last unit of output produced exceeds the average cost of those units previously produced. Producing that marginal unit of output would raise $SATC$.[12]

Because we will use the average and marginal curves shown in Figure 12.5 extensively it is important to reiterate a few of the assumptions which went into deriving them:

1. The curves are derived from the firm's expansion path. Since this path will shift if either the firm's production isoquants shift or if the price of an input changes, the curves will also shift in these cases.

2. The curves are drawn for a particular plant size. Different levels of fixed inputs will give rise to different isoquant maps and therefore different cost curves. In the long run, then, short-run cost curves would not be expected to remain fixed.

3. The curves in Figure 12.5b are drawn with a U-shape. This is the traditional assumption made about these curves, and such shapes seem reasonable on the basis of a priori logic. However, this need not be the case, and empirical investigation is certainly warranted.

The Long-run Total Cost Curve

In the long run the entrepreneur has the possibility of changing those inputs which were constant in the short run. In choosing to minimize the

---

[11] Mathematically we wish to find the Q for which $SATC$ is a minimum. The first-order condition for a minimum is:

$$\frac{dSATC}{dQ} = \frac{d\left(\frac{STC}{Q}\right)}{dQ} = \frac{Q \cdot \frac{dSTC}{dQ} - STC}{Q^2} = \frac{Q \cdot SMC - STC}{Q^2} = 0$$

or for the minimum point on $SATC$:

$$SMC = \frac{STC}{Q} = SATC.$$

The property of the $SAVC$ curve is proved in an analogous manner.

[12] An analogy which is perhaps closer to home may help. Suppose you have a certain quiz average. If you really blew the more recent (marginal) quiz (received a score lower than your previous average) then your average will fall. If you aced the quiz your average will rise.

cost of producing a given level of output he now can select the minimum cost plant size in addition to selecting the optimal input proportions. This added flexibility means that the long-run cost of producing any output level will be as low or lower than the cost of producing that level in the short run. In Figure 12.6 this possibility is illustrated. Consider the cost of producing output level Q_0. For plant size S_1 the Q_0 isoquant is shown in Figure 12.6, together with the cost-minimizing choice of inputs for

Figure 12.6   Effect of Changing Plant Size on an Isoquant Map

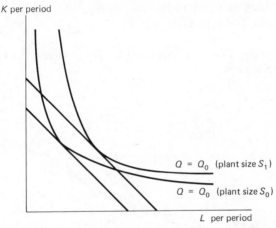

In moving from plant size S_1 to S_0 the isoquant map will shift. This will entail a new cost-minimizing choice of inputs and a different expansion path.

this plant size. In the long run plant size is variable and some other size of plant, say S_0, may be more suited to producing output Q_0. The firm could keep producing with plant size S_1, but by changing to S_0 it can produce Q_0 more cheaply (when both fixed and variable costs are included). The new Q_0 isoquant (for plant size S_0) is also shown in the diagram. Changing to the new plant size will mean the introduction of a new isoquant map and also a new expansion path.[13]

The relationship between long-run total costs and short-run total costs is shown in detail in Figure 12.7. Here several short-run total cost curves are shown; STC_1 represents the total cost curve associated with plant size S_1 and so forth. The *long-run total cost curve* is then constructed as the locus of lowest points from among those on the various

[13] The diagram has been drawn so that the variable costs of producing Q_0 with plant size S_0 are less than those for producing Q_0 with plant size S_1. Though this will quite likely be the case, it need not be so. It is only necessarily true that the *total* costs of producing Q_0 will be less when plant size S_0 is adopted.

short-run curves. For any given Q_0 the long-run total cost of producing Q_0 is the minimum total cost chosen from all those plant sizes which are available. This long-run total cost curve (technically called an *envelope curve*) is labeled *LTC* in Figure 12.7. For any level of Q the *LTC* curve is tangent to some short-run curve and the plant size represented by this short-run curve might be said to be the "correct" size for producing this level of output. For example, Q_1 should be produced with plant size S_1, Q_2 with plant size S_2, and Q_3 with plant size S_3. There are many relationships between short-run and long-run curves and these can all be derived by using this tangency relationship (*see* the next section and Problems 8 and 9 of Part III).

Figure 12.7   Using Short-run Total Cost Curves to Derive the Long-run Total Cost Curve

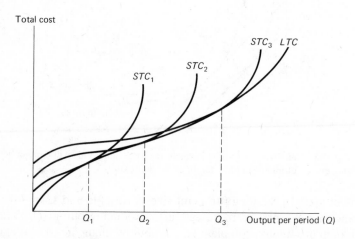

Various short-run total cost curves are shown for several plant sizes. The long-run total cost curve (*LTC*) is constructed as the locus of the lowest extremities of these short-run curves.

Again, the specific shape of the *LTC* curve is an interesting empirical question. A first observation one might make about its shape is that the curve passes through the origin. In the long run there are no fixed costs since plants can be scrapped and entrepreneurs may leave the business. It is likely that the curve will have a positive slope throughout; it always costs more to produce more output. Two possible shapes for the curve are shown in Figure 12.8. In 12.8a the curve is drawn to resemble a short-run curve. The assumption behind such a shape is that long-run costs of production may rise slowly at first, but eventually increasing costs may set in. A reason for this segment of increasing costs might be that even in the long run some inputs are fixed (for example, available land), and these will prove to be constraining on output if production is raised to a very high level.

Figure 12.8   Hypothetical Long-run Total Cost Curves

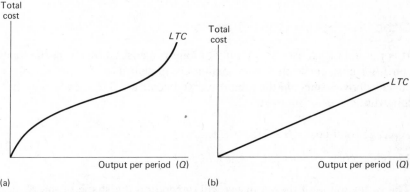

(a)   (b)

These figures represent two possible shapes for the firm's long-run total cost curve. In 12.8a the long-run curve resembles the shape which was assumed for the short-run total cost curve. One reason which might account for such a shape would be that even in the long run there are some fixed inputs. Figure 12.8b on the other hand exhibits the long-run total cost curve for a production function which exhibits constant returns to scale. Since a doubling of output is brought about by a doubling of all inputs to such a production function, costs are linearly related to output.

A second possibility might be that the long-run production function, Equation 12.5, exhibits constant returns to scale. In this case, doubling capital, labor, and plant size will exactly double output.[14] To see what this would imply about the long-run total cost curve, assume that plant size can be measured in some convenient units and that s is the cost per period of a "unit" of plant size. Suppose also that the firm can buy all the plant size it wants at this rate. Then long-run total costs would be:

$$LTC(Q) = vK + wL + sS. \qquad [12.10]$$

Now, in the long run Q can be doubled by doubling all these inputs. Hence:

$$LTC(2Q) = v2K + w2L + s2S$$
$$= 2LTC(Q). \qquad [12.11]$$

[14] It is important in this discussion to recognize that *all* outputs must be doubled. If it were not possible to do this we could not speak precisely of constant returns to scale. In this type of long-run analysis some authors may define capital to include both machines and plant and consequently deal with a production function of the form $f(K, L)$ which is assumed to be constant returns to scale. How one adds together plants and machines to obtain this aggregate capital is a difficult conceptual question.

Long-run total costs are therefore seen to be simply a linear function of quantity produced. A doubling of Q will, in the long run, simply double total costs. This long-run total cost curve for such a constant returns to scale production function is shown in Figure 12.8b.

Other Long-run Cost Curves

It is possible to construct a family of long-run cost curves from the long-run total cost curve in a way analogous to that used for the short-run curves above. Since, in the long run, fixed costs are 0, there are only two long-run curves of interest:

$$\text{Average total cost} = LATC = LTC/Q$$
$$\text{Marginal cost} \quad = LMC \quad = d\,LTC/dQ. \qquad [12.12]$$

The exact shape of these curves will depend on the shape of the related LTC curve. If the LTC curve has the shape shown in Figure 12.8a, the long-run average and marginal cost curves will have the familiar U-shape. Should the LTC curve be a straight line, as in Figure 12.8b, average cost and marginal cost would be equal and constant for all values of output: The $LATC$ and LMC curves would be the same horizontal straight line.

Long-run and short-run curves can be superimposed on one another to show the relationships between these sets of curves. The derivation of all of these relationships is rather tedious (see Problem 8 of Part III and Figure III.1), but the most important set of the curves is shown in Figure 12.9. In this figure the $LATC$ and LMC curves are drawn. These curves have been drawn with the conventional U-shape on the assumption that the firm has a long-run total cost curve such as that shown in Figure 12.8a. Long-run average costs initially fall as output increases and we might (somewhat imprecisely)[15] say that the firm initially exhibits increasing returns to scale. Let Q_k be that level of output for which $LATC$ is a minimum and let S_k be the plant size which is optimal for producing Q_k. Now superimpose the short-run cost curves ($SATC_k$, SMC_k) associated with plant size S_k onto the figure. Notice first that all four curves ($LATC$, LMC, $SATC_k$, SMC_k) intersect at the low point of the LTC curve. This is a result of the fact that the curves LTC and STC_k are tangent at output level Q_k.[16] The long-run curves in Figure 12.9 are flatter

---

[15] We use the terms "somewhat imprecisely" to indicate that our definition of increasing returns to scale cannot be strictly applied if the reason for the curve's shape is that one of the productive inputs is fixed even in the long run.

[16] $LMC = SMC$ because the total cost curves are tangent (their slopes are equal). $LATC = SATC$ since $LTC = STC$ at Q_k. The average curves are tangent because each takes on its minimum value at Q_k (hence they each have 0 slope). As before, the marginal curves pass through these low points on the average curves.

than are their short-run analogies. This is a graphic demonstration of the greater flexibility of the adjustment of costs in the long run. Capacity constraints are a primary cause of increasing unit costs in the short run, but these constraints are not operative in the long run. Costs will therefore tend to rise less slowly as output levels move away from the "optimal" (minimum $LATC$) point. In fact, some empirical evidence indicates that in many cases the $LATC$ curve (and hence the LMC curve) is nearly horizontal over a relatively broad range of output levels. In such cases firms may relatively easily adapt plant size to a variety of output levels. We might say that these firms exhibit constant returns to scale over a broad range of possible outputs.

Figure 12.9   Relationship between Long-run and Short-run Cost Curves at the Minimum Point of the $LATC$ Curve

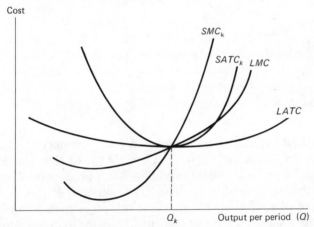

If Q_k is that output level for which the $LATC$ curve reaches a minimum this graph shows the relationship between the long-run cost curves and the short-run cost curves for a plant size appropriate for producing Q_k. All of these curves intersect at the low point of the $LATC$ curve. The long-run curves are flatter than their short-run counterparts.

Multiple Outputs and the Production Possibility Frontier

Firms may produce more than one output. An entrepreneur will therefore not only have to make choices about which inputs to use in the production process but will also have to decide how to allocate inputs to alternative output uses. In reality input and output choices are made simultaneously. The firm decides how much labor, capital, and other inputs to hire, and at the same time decides how much of each of its outputs to produce. We will find it convenient here, however, to regard these two decisions separately. In particular it will be assumed that the firm already has a certain quantity of inputs on hand and can allocate these to the production of several outputs. We want to examine the output choices open to firms.

Suppose the firm can produce two outputs (X and Y) and that the production of these involves only labor as an input.[17] Assume also that the total amount of labor available is given by L^* and that the two goods' production functions are given by:

$$X = f(L_X)$$
$$Y = g(L_Y) \qquad [12.13]$$

where L_X and L_Y are the amounts of labor devoted to the production of X and Y respectively. Since:

$$L_X + L_Y = L^* \qquad [12.14]$$

we may rewrite the production functions as:

$$X = f(L_X)$$
$$Y = g(L^* - L_X). \qquad [12.15]$$

Now if all available labor is devoted to the production of X it will be possible to obtain an output of $X^* = f(L^*)$. In this situation no Y would be produced since all labor is utilized in X production. Conversely, if all the labor were used to produce Y, an output of $Y^* = g(L^*)$ would be produced (but no X would be). These two production possibilities are indicated by the points $(X^*, 0)$ and $(0, Y^*)$ on the axes in Figure 12.10. By considering all possible allocations of L^* between X and Y production it is possible to trace out those combinations of X and Y which might be produced. These possibilities are shown by the curve X^*, Y^* in Figure 12.10. This curve is called the *production possibility frontier.*

The slope of the production possibility frontier shows how, by reallocating labor input, output of X may be traded for output of Y. The

---

[17] This discussion can readily be generalized to any number of variable inputs (*see* Chapter 20). However, the recognition that some inputs may be fixed in the short run raises difficulties in the allocation of the fixed costs of these inputs to particular outputs. Because variable costs are related to output levels, they may be properly allocated to the production of particular goods. Fixed costs occur regardless of the composition of the output mix and some more-or-less arbitrary rules must be developed if these costs are to be assigned to particular goods. We will not investigate these issues here.

Figure 12.10 The Production Possibility Frontier

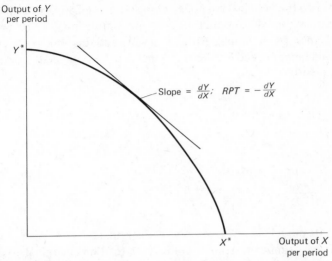

Output of Y
per period

Y^*

Slope $= \dfrac{dY}{dX}$; $RPT = -\dfrac{dY}{dX}$

X^*

Output of X
per period

This curve shows the alternative combinations of X and Y which can be produced with a fixed quantity of inputs. The slope of the curve represents the rate at which X output may be traded for Y output. This slope (or, more correctly, its negative) is called the marginal rate of product transformation (RPT).

negative of this slope is called the (marginal) *rate of product transformation* (RPT). Mathematically:

$$RPT = \frac{-dY}{dX} \qquad\qquad [12.16]$$

where it is understood that total labor input is being held constant as the mix of output is changed. In Figure 12.10 the production possibility frontier is drawn as a concave curve. Along this curve the RPT increases as the output mix includes more X and less Y. This shape seems intuitively reasonable. It assumes that for points near Y^* a small reduction in Y will cause a great increase in X output. This would be the case, for example, if labor exhibited a diminishing marginal productivity in the production of both X and Y; moving some labor out of Y production would only decrease Y output slightly whereas using this labor in X production would increase the output of this good significantly. Conversely, it would be true that when X/Y is high, relatively little additional X could be obtained even if the output of Y were contracted sharply. At such a point the RPT would be high. An increasing RPT then seems to be in accord with a general expectation that it is possible to push the production of one good "too far."

It is easy to show that the RPT is equal to the ratio of the marginal cost of X to the marginal cost of Y. Consider reallocating some labor from Y production into X production. The amount of labor given up by this cutback in Y production is $-(dL/dY) \cdot dY$, and this should exactly equal the added labor needed for the additional X to be produced: $(dL/dX) \cdot dX$. Consequently:

$$-\left(\frac{dL}{dY}\right) \cdot dY = \left(\frac{dL}{dX}\right) \cdot dX$$

or   [12.17]

$$\frac{-dY}{dX} = \frac{dL/dX}{dL/dY}.$$

But in this model, dL/dX is simply the marginal cost (in terms of labor) of X (MC_X); a similar statement holds for Y (call this marginal cost MC_Y). Hence we have shown that:[18]

$$RPT = \frac{-dY}{dX} = \frac{MC_X}{MC_Y}.$$ [12.18]

Intuitively this result should be obvious. The rate at which we can trade X for Y while holding costs (here labor input) constant is given by the ratio of the extra costs involved in making these output changes. If the cost of an extra unit of X were high relative to the cost of an extra unit of Y, Equation 12.18 would say we could trade "a lot" of Y for a small amount of X while still holding costs constant. This would suggest that Equation 12.18 holds not only for the simple case of a single input but also holds more generally for any number of inputs. This is indeed the case.

Part IV of this book will not be particularly concerned with analyzing multiproduct firms. Much of the material to be presented, however, can be generalized to cover such cases. We will, on several occasions, in later chapters wish to use the concept of the production possibility frontier; it will be useful to keep this concept (and the related one of the rate of production transformation) in mind. This production possibility frontier summarizes another notion of cost: The cost of additional X production can be measured by the concomitant reduction in Y production. The

[18] The fact that the RPT is increasing for increases in X can be seen from Equation 12.18. If both production functions exhibit a diminishing marginal product of labor, then, as labor is shifted from Y to X production, MC_X rises and MC_Y falls. Consequently, the RPT rises.

idea that different outputs can be traded one for the other in the productive process is an additional type of trade-off relationship we will want to examine in more detail.

Conclusion

One assumption underlies most of the analysis of this chapter: the assumption of cost minimization. Minimizing the cost of producing a given level of output is a necessary but not sufficient condition for profit maximization. To truly maximize profits the firm also has to choose the "right" level of output (that level for which marginal revenue equals marginal cost). This choice will be discussed in Part IV. The analysis of this part may also be relevant to firms which do not seek maximum profits. Even if a Q other than the profit-maximizing level is chosen, it still may make sense to choose inputs so as to minimize the cost of producing this level of output. The analytical tools of this chapter may therefore be useful in analyzing a variety of behavior of firms even if these firms are not strict profit maximizers.

Optimal Choice of Output, Linear Programming, and Duality

Introduction

The principal purpose of the appendix is to discuss a useful maximization technique: linear programming. In recent years this technique has come to be widely used in both theoretical and empirical problems. While the technique was initially regarded as an esoteric mathematical curiosity, today it is an integral element of the set of tools used by economists, business planners, and other researchers. A detailed treatment of linear programming is, however, beyond the scope of this book. We will be content to investigate only one problem, choosing the optimal (that is, profit maximizing) output combination for a multiproduct firm, which can be solved by linear programming methods. Most of the major features of linear programming can be illustrated in this application.

Before approaching the problem of optimal output choice in a linear programming context, however, it may be useful to develop the analysis in a more traditional way so that some analogies can be drawn. Suppose that a firm has a fixed level of inputs, and with these inputs produces various combinations of two outputs. We shall call these outputs cars (C) and trucks (T). Because inputs are in fixed quantities costs of production will be the same no matter what output combination of cars and trucks is chosen. The firm's goal is to maximize the revenues it receives from its activities. Since costs are fixed, this revenue maximization is necessarily equivalent to profit maximization.

Figure 12A.1   Choosing the Revenue-maximizing Point

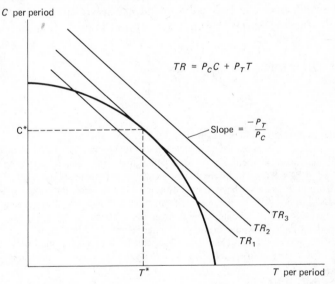

In choosing that combination of C and T to maximize revenues, the firm is constrained by its production possibility frontier. The highest line of equal revenue which just touches this frontier is the line TR_2. The point of tangency (T^*, C^*) is the optimal output choice for the firm. At this point RPT (trucks for cars) $= P_T/P_C$.

We will also assume here that the firm can sell all the cars and trucks it wants at the prevailing market prices, P_C and P_T. Consequently, total revenue is given by:

$$TR = P_C C + P_T T \qquad\qquad [12A.1]$$

and the firm will choose C and T to maximize this magnitude. In making this choice the firm is constrained to choose among only those combinations of cars and trucks it is technically able to produce. In other words it is constrained by its production possibility frontier.

The profit-maximization process is most easily demonstrated by a graphic analysis. In Figure 12A.1 the production possibility curve for cars and trucks is drawn. Again this curve is drawn with a concave shape to indicate the increasing relative marginal cost of trucks as truck production expands. Several parallel lines representing combinations of C and T which yield equal revenue are also drawn in the figure. These lines have a slope given by $-P_T/P_C$. This is the rate at which cars may be traded for trucks in the market while keeping revenues constant. It is clear from the drawing that the highest revenues (and, by our assumptions, profits) are obtained at the output combination T^*, C^*. At this point the rate at which cars can technically be traded for trucks (the RPT) is equal to the rate at which they can be traded in the market (P_T/P_C). Stated mathematically, the necessary condition for a profit maximum is that:[1]

$$RPT \text{ (cars for trucks)} = \frac{-dC}{dT} = \frac{P_T}{P_C}. \qquad [12A.2]$$

[1] This result can be demonstrated in two other interesting ways:

First, since a profit-maximizing firm will choose that output for which marginal revenue is equal to marginal cost, the firm will produce that combination of cars and trucks for which $P_C = MC_C$ and $P_T = MC_T$. The prices P_C and P_T are equal to the marginal revenue from selling one more unit, since we have assumed the firm has no effect on price. Consequently, $P_T/P_C = MC_T/MC_C = RPT$ by the results of Chapter 12. Notice that although total costs are fixed, marginal costs still have importance for the firm's decisions.

Second, let the production possibility frontier be written in implicit functional notation as $f(C, T) = 0$. Then the problem becomes a constrained-maximization problem: Maximize $P_C C + P_T T$ subject to $f(C, T) = 0$. Setting up the Lagrangian expression:

$$L = P_C C + P_T T - \lambda f(C, T)$$

gives

$$P_C - \lambda \frac{\partial f}{\partial C} = 0$$

$$P_T - \lambda \frac{\partial f}{\partial T} = 0$$

$$f(C, T) = 0$$

as the necessary conditions for a maximum. But these equations can be rewritten as:

$$\frac{P_T}{P_C} = \frac{\partial f/\partial T}{\partial f/\partial C} = \frac{-dC}{dT} = RPT.$$

It seems clear from the diagram that Equation 12A.2 will insure a true maximum, providing that the production possibility frontier is concave (as we have assumed it to be).

A Linear Programming Solution to the Problem

This problem in optimal output combinations can also be solved using linear programming techniques. In real-world applications, for example, we may not know the exact form of the production possibility frontier but may be able to approximate it with straight-line segments derived from engineering data. Linear programming methods then provide a systematic way of finding the optimal point on this approximate production possibility frontier.[2] In this appendix we will not be concerned with showing exactly how linear programming problems are solved (most larger problems are solved by computer routines) but rather with pointing out some of the qualitative properties which the optimal solutions will have.

The technique of linear programming is necessarily "linear" — it is a method for maximizing linear functions subject to linear constraints. For our cars and trucks example it is necessary to assume that the underlying production functions are of the fixed-proportion type. Specifically, suppose there are three productive inputs: man years (L), machine hours (K), and steel (S), and that the production functions are given by:

$$\text{Production of trucks} = T = \min\left|\frac{L_T}{1}, \frac{K_T}{3}, \frac{S_T}{5}\right|$$

$$\text{Production of cars} \quad = C = \min\left|\frac{L_C}{2}, \frac{K_C}{1}, \frac{S_C}{4}\right|$$

[12A.3]

where L_C, K_C, S_C are the inputs used in the production of cars, and L_T, K_T, S_T are the inputs used in the production of trucks. Equation 12A.3 records the fact that it takes one man year of labor, three machine hours, and five tons of steel to build a truck; and two man years, one machine hour, and four tons of steel to build a car.

Suppose now that the inputs which the firm has on hand are: 720 man years, 900 machine hours, and 1800 tons of steel. Then C and T must satisfy the following constraints:

$$1T + 2C \leq 720$$
$$3T + 1C \leq 900 \qquad\qquad [12A.4]$$
$$5T + 4C \leq 1800.$$

---

[2] It should be pointed out that linear approximations to what are truly nonlinear functions may give misleading or even wrong optimal solutions. This would be the case if the approximations were in some sense not very "close."

These constraints only record the fact that the firm cannot use more inputs in both production activities than it has on hand. Suppose further that $P_T = \$4000$ and $P_C = \$5000$. The problem for the firm is to maximize:

$$TR = 4000\,T + 5000\,C \qquad\qquad [12A.5]$$

subject to the constraints of Equation 12A.4.[3]

This problem is most easily solved by graphic techniques. In Figure 12A.2 the three input constraints are shown. The heavy line in the figure represents the production possibility frontier for this problem: It is the perimeter of the set of all combinations of C and T which satisfies *all three* input constraints. Notice that this frontier is made up of three linear segments. This is a reflection of the inflexible fixed proportions production functions assumed here, as opposed to the smooth substitution of factors assumed previously.

Figure 12A.2 Construction of the Production Possibility Frontier for the Linear Programming Problem

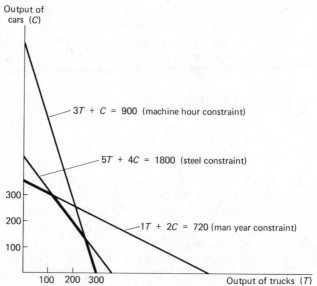

The heavy line in this diagram is the production possibility frontier for cars and trucks implied by the input constraints. It is the perimeter of the set of output combinations which satisfies all the constraints.

The production possibility frontier can be used to find the point of maximum revenues. In Figure 12A.3 this point can be seen to be the

[3] Notice that the costs of inputs are not mentioned here. For the initial discussion of this problem we assume the firm has some inputs on hand and seeks to obtain maximum revenues from these inputs. We will have far more to say about input prices later on.

Figure 12A.3   Maximization of Revenue in the Linear Program

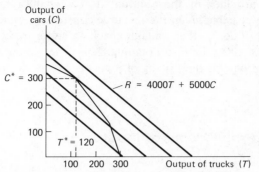

By superimposing several lines of equal revenue on the production possibility frontier the point of maximum revenue can be found. This point occurs where the man year and steel constraints intersect.

combination C^*, T^*, where the man year constraint and the steel constraint intersect.[4] Solving the two constraints for C^* and T^* gives:

$$1T + 2C = 720$$
$$5T + 4C = 1800$$

or   [12A.6]

$$T = 720 - 2C.$$

Therefore, by substitution:

$$5(720) - 10C + 4C = 1800$$
$$- 6C = -1800$$

Hence

$$C = 300$$ [12A.7]

and

$$T = 120.$$

---

[4] This point in a sense satisfies the rule that the RPT should equal the ratio P_T/P_C. The RPT along the man year constraint is $-1/2$; along the steel constraint the RPT is $-5/4$. The vertex at C^*, T^* includes all slopes between $-1/2$ and $-5/4$. But the ratio $-P_T/P_C$ is given by $-4/5$, which lies between these two values. Hence C^*, T^* is the revenue-maximizing point. In linear programming problems the optimal solutions will always occur at corners such as the one illustrated.

This means that 120 trucks should be produced along with 300 cars. The revenue provided by these outputs is $1,980,000; this is the maximum revenue possible given the resource constraints. Notice that at this production level not all the available machine hours are being used: The machine hours constraint is not binding. This observation will have interesting implications for the pricing of inputs.

Duality and the Pricing of Inputs

In this linear programming problem nothing was said about the price of inputs. The firm had these inputs on hand and set about the task of maximizing revenues. A linear programming problem which is related to the *primal* problem above is the *dual* linear programming problem of finding input prices associated with the optimal choice of C and T. Formally, these dual input prices solve the following linear programming problem:
    Minimize:

$$M = 720\ P_L + 900\ P_K + 1800\ P_S \tag{12A.8}$$

subject to

$$\begin{aligned} P_L + 3\ P_K + 5\ P_S &\geq 4000 \\ 2\ P_L + P_K + 4\ P_S &\geq 5000 \end{aligned} \tag{12A.9}$$

where P_L, P_K and P_S are the (non-negative) per unit prices of labor, capital, and steel. This dual problem can be given an economic interpretation. We are asked to find prices for the inputs which minimize the total value of all inputs available, but which also have the property that the production of neither cars nor trucks earns a pure profit (this is stated by the inequalities of Equation 12A.9 of the dual). For example, the first inequality says that the costs of producing one truck (that is, the cost of one unit of labor, three machines, and five tons of steel) should not be less than the price of a truck. If constraints such as those of Equation 12A.9 were not imposed, the minimization problem of Equation 12A.8 could be trivially solved by setting $P_L = P_K = P_S = 0$.

Without going into formal detail it is clear that the dual problem is related in some way to the original problem. All the constants which appeared in the primal problem also appear in the dual, but in different places. In particular, notice that quantities which appeared in the original constraints now appear as parameters in the dual objective function (M)

and vice-versa. Also the constraints of the primal problem seem to have been "turned on their side" in the dual.

A graphic solution to the dual linear programming problem will not be presented here because it would require a three-dimensional graph. It must be taken on faith that the solution to the dual program turns out to be:

$$P_L = \$1500$$
$$P_K = \$0 \qquad\qquad\qquad\qquad\qquad\qquad [12A.10]$$
$$P_S = \$500.$$

There are several important features to be noted about this solution:

1. With these input prices Equation 12A.9 is exactly satisfied. Neither good is produced at a loss. Hence both goods can be produced.

2. The value of M with these input prices is \$1,980,000. It is no coincidence that this is identical to the maximum value for TR found in the primal problem. Such a relationship holds between the primal and the dual solutions of all linear programs. Here this equality resembles the income-output identity in the *National Income and Product Accounts*.

3. The input which was not a binding constraint in the primal problem (machine hours) is given a price of 0 in the dual problem. In a sense the dual input prices can be given a Lagrangian Multiplier interpretation – if the machine hour constraint were relaxed slightly, it would have no effect on TR. Hence P_K is assigned the value 0 in the dual. The other input constraints are both binding. The positive prices assigned to these inputs in the dual solution indicate how much an extra unit of the inputs would add to TR.

Some Further Observations on Duality

These linear programming problems clearly demonstrate the relationship between the optimal choice of outputs and the correct choice of input prices. If, instead of using the example of a firm's choices of output, we had developed the problem as one of society choosing what proportion of cars and trucks to produce, the analysis would have been the same, but a broader interpretation could have been applied. The optimal allocation of a fixed amount of inputs to the production of a variety of possible outputs has as its associated dual problem the optimal pricing of those inputs available. The solution of one problem is equivalent to the solving of the other.[5]

All constrained-maximization (and minimization) problems have duality properties. This is true not only of linear programming problems but is also true of the calculus-type of maximization processes used throughout this book. Occasionally the solutions to dual problems have price interpretations, although this is not always the case. It may also at times be mathematically more convenient to solve a dual problem than to attack the primal. Certain theoretical properties which are difficult to examine when attacked head-on become tractible by using the "backdoor" approach of the dual.

Two examples, previously discussed as "primal" maximization problems, have interesting and mathematically tractable dual problems. First, consider the problem of utility maximization subject to a total expenditures constraint. The dual to this familiar problem is to consider minimizing total expenditure, given that utility must be at least at some fixed level. The symmetry between these two problems is clear. Certain properties of individual demand theory can be more easily demonstrated using this dual approach.

Second, consider duality involving production functions. A production function in fact represents a maximization problem — we are asking to maximize output given the quantities of inputs to be used. In certain cases (for constant returns to scale production functions) the dual to this problem is to minimize the cost of producing, say, one unit of output. The two problems are formally identical.[6]

In this book, because there is a conscious effort to minimize the use of complex mathematics, we will not discuss duality in any detail. However, it will occasionally be instructive to examine the duals associated with certain constrained-maximization problems. The reader is urged to follow up these discussions with investigations of his own.

---

[5] Linear programming problems may not always have solutions. If a linear programming problem and its associated dual have "feasible" solutions (solutions which satisfy the constraints of the problems) then they each have optimal solutions which have the qualitative properties listed above. For an elegant and concise discussion of the relationship between primal and dual linear programming problems with applications to a variety of allocational problems *see* D. Gale, *The Theory of Linear Economic Models* (New York: McGraw-Hill Book Company, 1960).

[6] For an example of this approach *see* Paul A. Samuelson, "Parable and Realism in Capital Theory: The Surrogate Production Function," *Review of Economic Studies,* vol. XXIX, no. 3 (June 1962), pp. 193–206.

DISCUSSION QUESTIONS AND PROBLEMS FOR PART III

Discussion Questions

1. Can you think of any pieces of evidence which either tend to support or to refute the profit-maximization hypothesis? For example, what can you say about the following observations? Do they seem consistent with profit maximization?
   (a.) Firms make donations to charities, educational institutions, and foundations.
   (b.) Firms such as AT & T advertize when it is obvious that you'll use the telephone whether or not you see an ad.
   (c.) Some firms provide golf courses, resorts, and free coffee for their employees.
   (d.) Firms have sculptures and fountains outside of their offices, and antiques and art collections inside.
   (e.) Salesmen are usually promoted because they are successful sellers with no regard to the profitability of their sales.

2. Obviously profit maximization involves uncertainty. How might uncertainty affect the decisions a firm makes? What goals might be reasonable for a firm in uncertain situations? In particular, might sales maximization be a reasonable strategy in an uncertain world?

3. Identify the inputs and outputs of the following firms. Can you imagine what the production function of these firms would look like?
   (a.) an oil pipeline
   (b.) a college
   (c.) an airline
   (d.) a professional baseball team
   (e.) a supermarket
   (f.) a fire prevention unit
   (g.) a bookie
   (h.) an opera company.

4. Does the economist's distinction between "profits" and "entrepreneurial income" make any sense in a world where most corporations are owned by a widely dispersed group of stockholders?

5. Can you draw an analogy between the problem of calculating the rental rate on a machine owned by a firm and that of calculating the consumption services one receives from a durable good?

6. Does the marginal cost concept make any sense for a firm such as a ship builder which may produce only two or three ships per year?

Problems

1. Suppose Mr. Entrepreneur is the only decision maker in his firm. The profits of this firm depend solely on the amount of time Mr. Entrepreneur spends on the job:

$$\pi = f(H)$$

where H is the number of hours on the job. However, Mr. E. is a harsh boss and gets on everyone's nerves if he is around too long. Hence π reaches a maximum long before H reaches twenty-four hours per day.

Suppose also that Mr. E. has a utility function for profits and leisure $(L = 24 - H)$ of the form:

$$U = U(\pi, L).$$

(a.) In this situation will the number of hours of work corresponding to profit maximization be the same number that maximizes Mr. E's utility? What special condition must hold for this to be true? Is this condition "reasonable"?

(b.) In fact, profits (π) should, according to Marshall, be defined to exclude that portion of entrepreneurial income necessary to keep Mr. E. in the business. Hence economic profits $= \pi' = \pi - w$, where w is the amount of income necessary to keep Mr. E. in the business (that is, the wage to make him indifferent between working and staying home). Clearly w depends on H.

With this new definition of profits, will the profit-maximizing position agree with Mr. E's utility-maximizing position? Show that in order for this to be true Mr. E must have indifference curves like those in Problem 1 of Part II — there is no income effect in the demand for hours worked.*

2. Would a lump-sum profits tax affect the profit-maximizing quantity of output? How about a proportional tax on profits? How about a tax assessed on each unit of output?

3. Contrast the concepts of diminishing returns to scale and diminishing

---

* This problem is abstracted from T. Scitovsky, "A Note on Profit Maximization and Its Implications," *Review of Economic Studies,* vol. 11, no. 1 (1943), pp. 57–60.

constant returns to scale and diminishing returns to a factor? Can a production function exhibit diminishing returns to scale but not have diminishing returns to a factor?

4. Show that for a production function with $\sigma = \infty$, the cost-minimizing input ratio, if it is unique, will necessitate the use of only capital or only labor. Show also that for $\sigma = 0$ the cost-minimizing input ratio will be constant no matter what w/v is.

5. Is it possible that isoquants might have positive slopes? Can you interpret this occurrence? Show that positively sloped sections of isoquants will never be observed because they do not represent cost-minimizing positions.

6. Prove that for a *CES* production function:

$$Q/L = c(\partial Q/\partial L)^\sigma$$

where $c = (1 - \delta)^\sigma$.
Hence

$$\log \left(\frac{Q}{L}\right) = \log c + \sigma \log \left(\frac{\partial Q}{\partial L}\right).$$

The latter equality is useful in empirical work, since in some cases we may approximate $\partial Q/\partial L$ by the competitively determined wage rate.

7. The "expansion path" was defined to be the locus of least-cost input combinations for all possible output levels. Use an isoquant map to show that the expansion path for a constant returns to scale production function is a straight line so long as w and v are constant.

8. Show that for any output Q_j the *SATC* curve associated with plant size S_j (where S_j is the "optimal" size for producing Q_j) is tangent to the *LATC* curve at Q_j, and that $LMC = SMC_j$ at Q_j. If Q_k is the point where *LATC* reaches a minimum, show $SMC_j < SATC_j$ for $Q_j < Q_k$ and that $SMC_j > SATC_j$ for $Q_j > Q_k$ (*see* Figure III.1).

Figure III.1 Relation between Short-run and Long-run Cost Curves

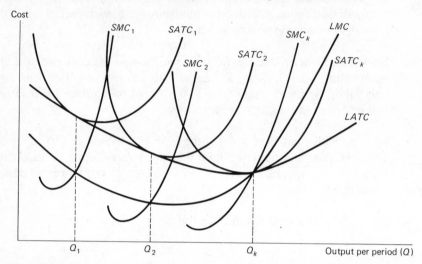

This graph is derived from the relationship between the firm's long- and short-run total cost curves. The graph is an extension of Figure 12.9 in that short-run average and marginal curves, in addition to those associated with plant size S_k, are shown. In Problem 8 of Part III the reader is asked to show that these curves are indeed related to each other in the way shown above.

9. In a famous article [J. Viner, "Cost Curves and Supply Curves," *Zeitschrift für Nationalökonomie,* vol. 3 (September 1931) pp. 23–46] Viner criticized his draftsman because he could not draw a family of *SATC* curves whose points of tangency with the *LATC* curve were also the minimum points on each *SATC* curve. The draftsman protested that such a drawing was impossible to construct. Who would you support in this debate?

PART IV
Pricing in the Goods Market

Introduction

In the previous chapters of this book we have developed some concepts which make precise various aspects of individual tastes and productive technology. Part IV presents an analysis of the ways in which tastes and technology interact to determine the prices of goods. The analysis is in many ways simply an elaboration of the Marshallian supply-demand cross mentioned in Chapter 1. These notions of supply and demand will be made more precise as various types of market organization are examined.

There are several assumptions which underlie the analysis of Part IV. First, we will only be looking at the market for 1 good. We are consciously ignoring the secondary effects which in fact spread through the economy whenever conditions in one market change. The analysis is therefore of a "partial equilibrium" nature; "general equilibrium" analysis will be studied in Part VI.

Second, we will assume that there are a large number of individuals demanding the good under examination. Although the actions of demanders as a group have a great deal to do with the market price of a good, it will be assumed here that no one individual is able to have any effect on price by his own actions. Each individual therefore takes the price of the good as given: There is nothing he can do about the price except to adjust his consumption patterns to it. This is the assumption we made throughout Part II, and therefore the analysis of individual and market demand carries over here.

While this assumption of individual "impotence" may be justified in a large and complex economy, an analogous assumption cannot be made about the supply side of the market. It is an obvious fact of economic life that there are many goods which are produced by only a few sellers. The behavior of General Motors, for example, certainly has an effect on the price of cars. A major purpose of Part IV is to investigate the differences in the behavior of markets characterized by "one," "few," or "many" sellers. It will be concluded that most real-world situations cannot be characterized as either having one or many sellers but that the case of few sellers is by far the most prevalent. Unfortunately, the case of a few sellers is difficult to analyze; we will often have to rely on the two other polar cases for insights.

It has been said that one can teach a parrot to be an economist by teaching him the words "supply" and "demand." There is a sense in which this is true. Starting the analysis of an economic problem by asking about the demand and supply characteristics of the market is an obvious and productive way to begin. The insights to be gained from even a cursory examination of supply and demand can be great. At the same time one should be aware of the limitations of simple supply-demand analysis and be aware of the extensions of this analysis which can be made. The purpose of this part and, indeed, of the remainder of this book is to demonstrate these limitations and extensions.

CHAPTER 13

Alternative Forms of Market Organization

Introduction: Homogeneous and Differentiated Products

In order to analyze pricing in the goods market it is first necessary to describe what is meant by the terms *good* and *market*. For example, how precisely is the notion of a good to be defined? Possible definitions extend from the very general ("consumption," "investment") to the uniquely specific ("1 pound of 10X confectioner's cane sugar delivered at 9:00 A.M. on January 21, 1971, in Amherst, Massachusetts"). Obviously neither of these extremes is a useful definition for the purpose of studying pricing. The first is too general a definition: Individuals' and firms' decisions on total consumption are in reality a multitude of decisions on more specifically defined goods. To use such an aggregate would be to obscure any understanding of market interactions. On the other hand, the very specific definition is useless because it represents a unique transaction which will never again take place. Clearly some middle ground must be chosen and the particular choice made will depend on the interests of the investigator.

We will define goods to be either "homogeneous" or "differentiated." All suppliers of a *homogeneous good* produce the identical good. Individuals are indifferent about which firm they will buy from. In this case (assuming perfect knowledge and costless mobility of goods), the market for this good must obey the *law of one price*. All trades of the good between seller and buyer must be conducted at the same price. If the price for a homogeneous good were to differ between firms, everyone would flock to the less expensive seller. Hence only a single price can prevail. Examples of strictly homogeneous goods are hard to find. Some tentative examples might be steel girders, concrete pipe, work clothes, gasoline, and club soda.[1]

For *differentiated products,* on the other hand, it does make a difference which firm one buys from. The goods produced are not identical (although the differences may be more apparent than real) and firms may strive to differentiate their products from those of their competitors. Most consumer goods fall in this category. This creates some problem in defining exactly what we mean by a good. For example, suppose we wished to study the demand for automobiles. Several questions then arise about the exact products we should include in the study. Should station wagons be included? How about jeeps? Or pickup trucks? Or taxis? And so on. Even in the category of what are usually considered automobiles, there is a huge variation of possible models. Should all these be considered the same basic good?

This line of questions could be extended indefinitely, but the point should now be clear. In order to get some theoretical grasp of the factors which influence pricing, we must of necessity make some simplification about what we mean by a good. It will be assumed that it is possible to delimit a well-defined good and its respective market. Homogeneous goods, because they can be most easily handled, will occupy the major portion of the analysis, but occasional mention will be made of the complications presented by differentiated products.

[1] Even for these goods firms make valiant efforts to differentiate their products by providing "service" or "brand identification."

Integrating Demand and Supply

A "market" is a hypothetical "place" where the producers of a good (suitably defined) get together with the demanders to haggle about price.[2] In order to analyze the behavior of the agents entering into these bargains it is necessary to look at matters through their eyes. For individuals this is easy. Individuals are so numerous that any one of them can have no effect on the outcome of the price-setting process. Each is a *price taker* being forced to accept the price which the market dictates. The actual quantities that any one individual (and that individuals as a group) will demand depends on this price.

The way a firm looks at the market is not so simple. If there are so many firms that any particular one of them feels that it must accept the price of its product as given by the market, then the firm believes it is faced by a horizontal demand curve. It can sell all it wants at the prevailing price because its actions, if taken alone, will have no effect on price. In this case the firm too is a *price taker*.

At the other extreme, if a firm is the only producer of some good it will face the entire market demand. Its actions will obviously affect price. If the market demand curve is downward sloping it will have to charge a lower price to get people to buy a high level of output than it would if it produced less.

Between these two possibilities is the case of a market with a "few" sellers. In this case it is difficult to say exactly what kind of a demand curve faces the firm. The firm's actions will have some effect on price so it is not a price taker. On the other hand, its competitors are also absorbing some of the total demand for the product, so the total market demand curve is not relevant either. The demand curve facing the firm is therefore uncertain. The firm must make decisions while being in some ignorance about what its competitors will do. Analyzing firm behavior in such situations raises challenging and interesting problems.

A Taxonomy of Market Types

As the above discussion makes clear, to study pricing in the market for a good we must first ask how the market is organized. The approach

---

[2] This is a simplification. In reality, most trading is through middlemen such as supermarkets, department stores, trading companies, or auto dealerships. The buyer of a good purchases the services of these middlemen together with purchasing the actual product. This distinction creates some difficulties in the analysis which will not be pursued here.

taken in explaining a firm's actions will depend on how many other firms there are in the market: It will depend on the type of *demand curve which faces the firm*. Markets are usually classified by whether there are many, few, or one producer. A cross-classification is also made as to whether the good under investigation is homogeneous or differentiated. There are therefore six possible market types (although we will see below that one of these is not relevant). The names which have been given to these types are recorded in Table 13.1 and are discussed below.

Table 13.1   Market Types

Number of firms \ Type of product	Homogeneous	Differentiated
Many	Perfect competition	Differentiated or monopolistic competition
Few	Pure oligopoly	Differentiated oligopoly
One	Monopoly	Not used

Perfect competition. A perfectly competitive market is characterized by a large number of firms each producing an identical product. None of these firms is large relative to the market as a whole. Hence each firm in a perfectly competitive industry operates as if it were faced by a horizontal (that is, infinitely elastic) demand curve. Its individual decision on output will not affect price. Entry into the industry by other firms is assumed to be costless. In the long run new firms will be able to enter the market in response to opportunities for profit. Perfect competition is the prototype for a major portion of economic analysis. Although it is difficult to identify a market which is perfectly competitive in a strict sense, the closest example is provided by the market for most agricultural crops.

Differentiated competition or monopolistic competition.[3] A market characterized by a large number of producers in which each producer supplies a good slightly different from his competitors' is termed monopolistic competition. Although each firm in such a market is small, relative to total demand, because it sells a slightly different product, its actions will affect the price which it receives. The firm is therefore faced by a negatively sloped demand curve. It must be careful in its decisions, however, because there are many close substitutes for its product which are offered by competitors. Again, entry into the market is assumed to be costless, and it is presumed that new firms will be brought into the market by the prospect of profits. An example of a monopolistically competitive market is provided by the construction industry. There are many relatively small firms in this industry and the product of each is slightly different from that of its competitors principally because of locational advantages. There are obvious limits on the ability of firms in this industry to take advantage of any beneficial location they might have.

Pure oligopoly. A market in which relatively few[4] firms produce a homogeneous product is termed a pure oligopoly. A firm in an oligopoly market can, because it produces a large share of the total output, have some effect on the price it will receive. However, to give a precise idea of the kind of demand curve one firm faces is difficult. This is so not only because there are close substitutes (indeed the identical product) being produced by others but also because the firm must explicitly take account of how its competitors will react to any decisions which it makes. This feature of the market makes decision making in oligopoly markets subject to great uncertainties. Most observed behavior can be rationalized as a reaction to these uncertainties. Consequently, the analysis of these markets has a certain lack of precision and an absence of definitive results. Nonetheless, since numerous markets (steel, aluminum, glass, chemicals to name a few) can be classified as pure oligopolies, such studies are extremely important to any understanding of the details of how the United States economic system works.

Differentiated oligopoly. Most ordinary consumer products (toothpaste, soft drinks, frozen food, automobiles — the list is endless) are produced in markets which can be described as differentiated oligopolies; there are a relatively few firms each producing a slightly different product.

[3] The term "monopolistic competition" was made widely known by E. Chamberlin in *The Theory of Monopolistic Competition* (Cambridge, Mass.: Harvard University Press, 1933).

[4] The meaning of "few" is necessarily ambiguous and will vary from case to case. Entry into the market by others can be either assumed to be impossible or to be relatively costly. If the latter assumption is made (as would usually be the case) then those firms already in the market will not only pay attention to the actions of their rivals but they may also adopt strategies which discourage potential entrants.

All of the comments made about pure oligopoly markets apply to this case. In this type of market firms have the additional strategy of product differentiation available. Whereas it may be hard to impart a special identity to brands of concrete pipe, this is not the case for deodorants or toothpastes. For these products much effort goes into developing "product identification" and "brand loyalty." Certainly some of these efforts can be regarded as socially wasteful. However, an out-of-hand condemnation is not possible because a wider variety of products is provided than might otherwise be the case. In evaluating the societal desirability of differentiated oligopoly one must be careful to estimate both the benefits and the costs of purposeful product differentiation.

Monopoly. A monopoly market is one in which there is only a single supplier. This single firm then faces the entire market demand. It has relative freedom in its pricing policies because there are no other firms to worry about. The monopoly is in a general competition for the consumer's dollar, but this does not lead to the great uncertainties which are present in oligopolies. Entry into a monopoly market is difficult, perhaps entailing high initial investment costs. Nonetheless, most monopolies are aware of the possibility of entry and may adopt strategies which make it more difficult. For example, companies which obtain monopoly power in a market by owning patents may not strive for huge profits for fear of attracting successful imitators.

The term "differentiated monopoly" is conceivable as a market type, but the meaning to be applied to this is unclear, since in a sense the firm would only be competing against itself. A monopoly may produce several versions of the same basic product, but these might be either regarded as attempts to enter separate markets or as a device to inhibit entry. In any case this market type is usually not investigated separately but is rather considered to be one aspect of the general theory of monopoly markets.

Conclusion

Contrary to the analytical spirit of this book, this chapter has been concerned primarily with classification. The argument might be made that this classification is peculiarly unproductive (say from a regulatory point of view) because every market imaginable can be regarded as a differential oligopoly. Every good is differentiated in some respects and every firm has only a few competitors producing relatively close substitutes. In this view the other entries of Table 13.1 are in reality empty boxes, so why learn about nonexistent market types?

The answer to this argument is essentially pragmatic. An adequate general theory of oligopoly behavior has not as yet been developed. The most useful approach has been a case-by-case analysis of real-world markets. In order to develop a generally applicable model we must either study the perfect competition or the monopoly cases. The theory of these market types is both well developed and analytically insightful. The questions raised in the study of these two "ideal" types provide a framework within which to analyze more "realistic" market structures. Since, presumably, most markets lie somewhere between the two polar cases of perfect competition and monopoly one can use aspects of both theories in studying these markets. For this reason Chapters 14 and 15 will investigate these two ideal types in detail. In Chapter 16 a brief analysis of markets with "few" producers will be presented. This chapter will draw on the tools developed in 14 and 15 and will hopefully form a bridge into the analysis of real-world market organization.

CHAPTER 14

Pricing in a Perfectly Competitive Market

Introduction

In this chapter the determination of price in perfectly competitive markets will be discussed in some detail. The theory developed is an elaboration of the familiar Marshallian supply-demand analysis and, conversely, the Marshallian analysis is strictly appropriate only in markets characterized by perfect competition. The perfectly competitive model is the basis of all microeconomic analysis. Many insights are provided by this model into the way in which equilibrium market prices are established; these insights transcend the narrow bounds of a strictly defined perfectly competitive market.

Before beginning the analysis it may be useful to repeat the assumptions of the perfectly competitive model. There are assumed to be a large number of firms each producing a product identical to that produced by its competitors. Each firm is "small" relative to the total market demand, in the sense that each firm acts as a price taker. Therefore, in its decisions, each firm believes it cannot affect the market price of its product. Over the long run the number of firms may change in response to differing profit opportunities. In the long run the number of firms in the industry is an additional variable which must be considered in the analysis of pricing. The only costs faced by new firms are the same costs of production already faced by existing firms: There are no special costs of entry. Finally, all goods are assumed to be completely mobile, and there are assumed to be no costs associated with making transactions. Given all these assumptions, we will be able to investigate the theory of price determination in some detail. In later chapters we may wish to relax many of the restrictive perfectly competitive assumptions.

Figure 14.1   Pricing in the Very Short Run

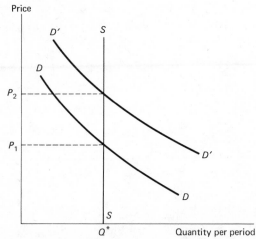

When quantity is absolutely fixed in the very short run price acts only as a device to ration demand. With quantity fixed at Q^*, price P_1 will prevail in the market place if D is the market demand curve. At this price individuals are willing to consume exactly that quantity available. If demand should shift upward to D' the equilibrium market price would rise to P_2.

In the analysis of pricing it is important to decide the length of time which is to be allowed for a *supply response* to changing demand conditions. The establishment of equilibrium prices will be different if we are talking about a very short period of time during which supply is absolutely fixed or if we are envisioning a very long-run process in which it is possible for entirely new firms to enter an industry. For this reason we will conduct analyses of pricing in the *very short run,* pricing in the *short run,* and pricing in the *long run.* While it is not possible to give these terms an exact chronological definition the essential aspect of these distinctions is the nature of the response by firms which is assumed to be possible.

In the very short run (or the *market period*) there is no supply response. The goods are already "in" the market place and must be sold for whatever the market will bear. In this situation price acts as a device to ration demand, but not as a signal for increasing production, since output is fixed. This situation is pictured in Figure 14.1. Market demand is represented by the curve D. Supply is fixed at Q^* and the price which clears the market is P_1. At P_1 individuals are willing to take all that is offered in the market. Sellers want to dispose of Q^* without regard to price (suppose the good in question is perishable and will be worthless if not sold in the very short run). Hence P_1, Q^* is an equilibrium price-quantity combination. If demand should shift to D', the equilibrium price would increase to P_2, but Q^* would stay fixed since no supply response is possible. The *supply curve* in this situation then is a vertical straight line at output Q^*.

The analysis of the very short run is not particularly useful for most markets. While such a theory may adequately represent some situations in which goods are perishable[1] or in which goods must be sold on a given day for other reasons (as in an auction), the far more usual case involves some degree of supply response to changing demand. The remainder of this chapter will investigate these more flexible situations.

Competitive Pricing in the Short Run

In Chapter 10 we saw that a profit-maximizing firm will produce that quantity for which marginal revenue is equal to marginal cost. For a firm in a perfectly competitive market marginal revenue is simply the prevailing market price. The firm can sell one extra unit at this price and, since the firm is a small part of the market, the selling of one more unit will have no effect on price.[2] Profit maximization for a firm in perfect competition

---

[1] For example, the very short run model may represent the pricing mechanism at work when fishing boats return to port to sell their catch.

[2] Remember that total revenue (TR) is equal to $P \cdot Q$. Marginal revenue (MR) was defined as $\partial TR / \partial Q$. Hence, as was shown in Chapter 10:

$$MR = \frac{\partial TR}{\partial Q} = \frac{\partial P \cdot Q}{\partial Q} = P + Q \cdot \frac{\partial P}{\partial Q}$$

but for a perfectly competitive firm, $\partial P / \partial Q = 0$: The firm's output has no effect on market price. Therefore, $MR = P$.

then dictates that it should produce that quantity for which *marginal cost equals price*. In the short run it is the short-run marginal cost curve which is relevant to this decision.

The individual firm's short-run decision is shown in Figure 14.2. The market price is given by P^*. The demand curve facing the firm is therefore a horizontal line through P^*. This line is labeled $P = MR$ to remind the reader that an extra unit can be sold by the perfect competitor without affecting market price. Output level q^* provides maximum profits, since at q^* price is equal to marginal cost. The profits earned by the firm in the short run can be read off Figure 14.2 as the area P^*EAC. This is simply the amount by which price exceeds average cost (EA) times the total quantity produced (q^*). Notationally, if q represents the individual firm's output, we have:

$$\pi = TR - TC$$

or

$$\pi = q \cdot \left(\frac{TR}{q} - \frac{TC}{q} \right)$$

$$= q \cdot (P - AC).$$

[14.1]

Figure 14.2   Short-run Equilibrium for a Perfectly Competitive Firm

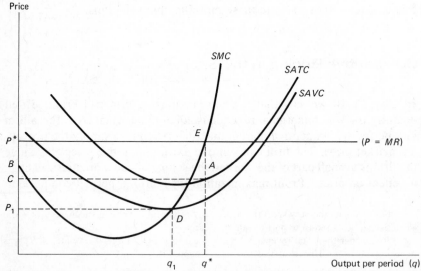

In the short run the firm will produce that quantity for which price is equal to short-run marginal cost. The short-run marginal cost curve is therefore the firm's supply curve. Should price fall below P_1, however, the firm will choose to produce nothing, since at such prices it is not even covering its variable costs.

In the figure it can be seen that profits are a true maximum. For $q < q^*$ profits would be less than those at q^* since the revenue lost would exceed the reduction in costs. Similarly, increasing q beyond q^* would cost more than the additional revenues which would be brought in. In other words, the necessary conditions for a profit maximum (price equals marginal cost) are also sufficient because the marginal cost curve cuts the marginal revenue curve from below.

The short-run marginal cost curve is therefore the *short-run supply curve* for a perfectly competitive firm. The curve shows how much the firm will produce for every possible market price. One exception must be made to this statement, however. Should market price fall below P_1, the profit-maximizing decision would be to produce nothing. Prices less than P_1 do not cover variable costs: There is a loss on each unit produced in addition to the loss of all fixed costs. By shutting down production the firm still must pay fixed costs, but avoids the loss incurred on the units produced. Since, in the short run the firm cannot leave the industry and avoid all costs, its best decision is to produce no output. On the other hand, a price only slightly above P_1 will cause production to take place. Even though profits may be negative (which they will be if price falls short of average total costs), so long as variable costs are covered, the profit-maximizing decision is to continue production. Fixed costs must be paid in any case, and any price which covers variable costs will provide revenue as an offset to these fixed costs. The conclusion of these observations then is that the firm's short-run supply curve is its marginal cost curve above the point of minimum average variable cost (point D in Figure 14.2). At price P_1 the firm is indifferent between producing output q_1 or producing no output.

Given information on each firm's short-run supply curve, it would seem possible to sum these curves horizontally to obtain a short-run *market supply curve*. This would be directly analogous to the technique used to construct the market demand curve in Chapter 6. Such a market supply curve would then show how much all firms, in the short run, are willing to supply at each market price. Because each firm is operating on a positively sloped segment of its marginal cost curve, it is reasonable to assume that the short-run market supply curve also has a positive slope.[3]

---

[3] The calculation of the total market supply curve may not be such a simple matter. Whereas each firm considers the costs of its inputs to be given, this may not be true at all levels of output for the industry as a whole. If increasing industry output causes the price of inputs to be bid up for all firms, the relevant cost curves for the firms will shift upward. Such "interaction effects" may cause the market supply curve to be more steeply sloped than simply the sum of each firm's supply curve. As an example of this sort of interaction consider what would happen if the jewelry industry tried to increase the output of precision-cut diamonds significantly in the short run. Surely the wages of diamond cutters would be bid up sharply (there is no excess of diamond cutters merely waiting to be put to work) and this would shift up the cost curves for each firm in the industry. Whereas each firm may have been a "small" demander of a specialized input (here diamond cutters), this is not the case for the industry as a whole.

Figure 14.3 The Interactions of Many Individuals and Firms Determine Market Price in the Short Run

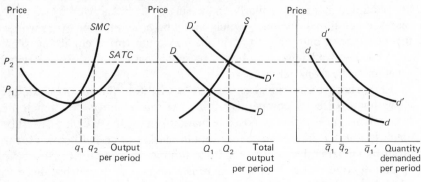

(a) A typical firm   (b) The market   (c) A typical individual

Market demand curves and market supply curves are each the horizontal sum of numerous components. These market curves are shown in (b). Once price is determined in the market each firm and each individual treats this price as a fixed parameter in its decisions. Although individual firms and persons are impotent in determining price, their interaction as a whole is the sole determinant of price. This is illustrated by a shift in an individual's demand curve to d'. This will not affect market price if only one individual reacts in this way. However, if everyone exhibits an increased demand, market demand will shift to D' and, in the short run, price will rise to P_2.

It is the interaction of this supply curve with the demand curve which determines market price in the short run.

Short-run market equilibrium is pictured schematically in the three panels of Figure 14.3, where 14.3a shows the situation for a "typical" firm, 14.3b depicts the interaction of supply and demand in the whole market, and 14.3c represents the demand curve for a typical individual. Price is determined in the market shown in 14.3b. With a demand curve represented by D and a market supply curve by S, the price-quantity combination P_1, Q_1 is an equilibrium. At this combination, suppliers and demanders are satisfied. The typical firm will respond to the market price P_1 by producing output q_1. Similarly, the typical individual (whose demand curve is labeled d) will respond to this market price by purchasing $\bar{q}_1$. The total amount purchased by individuals will be exactly equal to the quantities offered by firms.

Figure 14.3 clearly shows that although individuals and firms acting alone must accept market price as given, the simultaneous decisions of large numbers of buyers and sellers in fact determine this price. As an example, suppose one individual's demand curve shifted to d'. Because each individual is a small part of the market this shift will not affect the total market demand curve D. Therefore, market price remains at P_1.

The individual whose demand has shifted will purchase more at P_1 (say $\bar{q}_1'$) than he did previously.[4]

A different analysis would be appropriate if the individual's increased desire for the product were shared by a large segment of the public. In this case many individuals' demand curves would shift to d'. This action would cause the market demand to shift to D' and a new price-quantity equilibrium would be established at P_2, Q_2. At this new, higher price the typical firm would produce more (q_2), and this output would yield (at least in the short run) a higher profit.

Special Features of Perfectly Competitive Pricing in the Long Run

In the long run the firm will base its decisions on its long-run marginal cost curve. In response to a given market price the firm may now choose its optimal plant size, in addition to choosing its profit-maximizing level of output. Both of these decisions are accounted for by using the long-run marginal cost curve. However, one further complication must be taken into account when analyzing the reactions of an industry in the long run: the possibility of the entry of new firms. If profits[5] are positive in the long run, new firms, because entry is free, will be lured into the industry. This will cause the short-run market supply curve to shift to the right (at any price now more firms are producing), and the market price will fall. This process will continue until it is impossible for a new firm entering the industry to make a profit. If the assumption is made that the cost curves for all firms in the industry are identical,[6] this means that in equilibrium no firm in the industry will be making long-run economic profits. A similar argument can be made for the case in which price is so low that it yields a long-run loss. In this case firms will leave the industry, causing the

---

[4] It might properly be asked where the extra quantity $\bar{q}_1' - \bar{q}_1$ comes from since nothing has happened to cause firms to change their output decisions. If, prior to the increase in demand, supply and demand were in balance, now there will be a shortage. The answer to this question lies in the extremely small magnitude $\bar{q}_1' - \bar{q}_1$ represents when compared to the market as a whole. It is not literally true that nothing changes when one individual's demand curve shifts, but for all practical purposes this will be the case. The effect of one individual on market price is inconsequential. For a convincing example, see Problem 2 of Part IV.

[5] We are using the economists' definition of profit as the return in excess of that which is necessary to keep the entrepreneur (and his capital investment) in the business. Hence when we talk about "zero" profits we mean zero economic profits. The firms' cost curves are defined to include a normal payment for entrepreneurial services.

[6] The interesting case of firms with differing cost structures will be discussed in Chapter 17.

market supply curve to shift to the left, and this will cause price to rise. Therefore, in the long run no firm will operate at a loss either. The long-run equilibrium position for a perfectly competitive industry made up of identical firms is a situation in which every firm earns exactly zero in economic profits. In graphic terms this means that the long-run equilibrium price will settle at the level of *minimum long-run average cost,* for only at this point do the two equilibrium conditions $P = LMC$ *(profit maximization)* and $P = LATC$ *(zero profit)* hold.

As an example which may make this short-run, long-run distinction clear, consider the market for wheat. Suppose that the market demand for wheat increases as a result of a change in individuals' tastes. In the short run the effect of this increase in demand will be to increase the market price of wheat. As a result of this increase in price farmers' profits will also increase. Each farmer may respond to this increased profitability by increasing his output (he may, for example, work harder and thereby provide more labor input) but, in the short run, he is limited as to the types of adjustment he can make. When the view shifts to the long run several additional possibilities for adjustment must be considered. First, individual farmers can decide to increase the land which they have under cultivation. They may also buy additional farm equipment. In other words, those farmers already in the industry can adjust the size of their "plant." The possibility of profits may also lure other farmers into the wheat-growing business. The entry of these new "firms" will have a depressing effect on price, and entry will continue until the possibility for profit disappears. The industry will be in long-term equilibrium only when it has fully adjusted to the initial increase in demand.

In Figure 14.4 this long-run equilibrium for an industry is demonstrated. The initial market demand curve is given by curve D. At P_1 there is no incentive to enter or leave the industry, and at this price the typical firm will produce output level q_1 and earn exactly 0 in economic profits on these sales. The market price-quantity combination (P_1, Q_1) is a long-run equilibrium in that it will tend to persist until either tastes or technologies change.

Suppose now that tastes do change. Specifically assume that the market demand curve shifts upward to D'. If SS is the relevant short-run supply curve for the industry, then in the short run price will rise to P_2. The typical firm will, in the short run, choose to produce q_2, and will earn profits on this level of output. In the long run these profits will attract new firms into the market. The ultimate equilibrium which is established depends on how the cost structure of the industry is affected by the entry of these new firms. One possibility is the *constant cost industry* case in which the entry of the new firms will have no effect on cost structure. In this situation new firms will continue to enter the market until price is

Figure 14.4 Long-run Equilibrium for a Perfectly Competitive Industry: Constant Cost Case

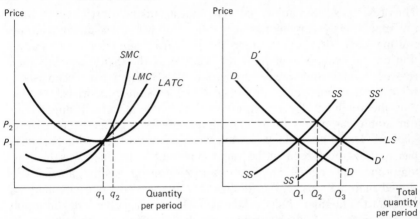

(a) A typical firm　　　　　　　　(b) Total market

An increase in demand from D to D' will cause price to rise from P_1 to P_2 in the short run. This higher price will create profits in the industry and new firms will be drawn into the market. If it is assumed that the entry of these new firms has no effect on the cost curves of the firms in the industry, new firms will continue to enter until price is pushed back down to P_1. At this price economic profits are 0. The long-run supply curve (LS) will therefore be a horizontal line at P_1. Along LS output is increased by increasing the number of firms each producing q_1.

forced down to the level at which there are again no pure economic profits. The entry of new firms will therefore shift the short-run supply curve to SS' where the equilibrium price (P_1) is reestablished. At this new long-run equilibrium the price quantity combination P_1, Q_3 will prevail in the market. The typical firm will again produce at output level q_1, although now there will be more firms than there were in the initial situation.

We have shown that the *long-run supply curve* for a constant cost industry will be a horizontal straight line at price P_1. This curve is labeled LS in Figure 14.4b. No matter what happens to demand, the twin equilibrium conditions of 0 long-run profits (since free entry is assumed) and profit maximization[7] will insure that no price other than P_1 can prevail in the long run. If the constant-cost assumption is abandoned, the long-run supply curve need not be horizontal. This possibility is examined in the next section.

―――――――――

[7] These equilibrium conditions also point out what seems to be, somewhat imprecisely, an "efficient" aspect of the long-run equilibrium in perfectly competitive markets: The good under investigation will be produced at minimum average cost.

The Shape of the Long-run Supply Curve

The previous section points out that, contrary to the short-run case, long-run supply analysis really has very little to do with the shape of the long-run marginal cost curve. Rather, the zero profit condition centers attention on the low point of the $LATC$ curve as the factor which is most relevant to long-run price determination. This distinction has been used to solve a major point of controversy among economic theorists.[8] To simplify the argument, the contention was made that negatively sloped long-run supply curves are a theoretical impossibility in perfectly competitive markets. Using an analogy to what we have called "short-run analysis," past authors theorized that the long-run marginal cost curve was the firm's long-run supply curve. The first observation made was that a negatively sloped marginal cost curve implies that average cost exceeds marginal cost (for the familiar U-shaped curves). Hence a negatively sloped supply (or marginal cost) curve would mean that the firms in the industry, by equating price to marginal cost, would be losing money. In the long run firms would leave the industry because of this lack of profitability. Therefore, a negatively sloped long-run supply curve, the argument concluded, is incompatible with perfect competition: Eventually only one firm (or a few firms) would remain.

The long-run, short-run analysis helps to point out the fallacy in this argument. In the long run the shape of the perfectly competitive industry's supply curve is not determined by the individual firms' marginal cost curves. In fact, there are conditions under which a negatively sloped long-run supply curve may occur even though each firm has a positively sloped marginal cost curve. Consider the example diagrammed in Figure 14.5. The initial long-run equilibrium is at P_1, Q_1. Suppose now demand shifts to D'. In the short run output will increase to Q_2 and price will increase to P_2. Each typical firm will also increase its output and will show short-run profitability. New firms will enter the industry. Instead of the entry of these new firms being made at constant cost, however, suppose their entry lowers the cost structure of every firm in the industry. This may occur because the new firms create the possibility for better training of labor, or because they lead to the development of better transportation

---

[8] This famous debate over "empty economic boxes" is still fascinating and enjoyable reading (*see* the articles by Clapham, Pigou, and D. H. Robertson which originally appeared in *The Economic Journal* between 1922 and 1924 and are reprinted in G. J. Stigler and K. E. Boulding, eds., *Readings in Price Theory* (Homewood, Ill.: Richard D. Irwin, Inc., 1952).

and communications networks.[9] Whatever the source of these cost reductions their result can be easily demonstrated in Figure 14.5. The new cost curves for the typical firm are labeled $LATC'$, LMC' and SMC'. These curves are below those which prevailed previously, thus showing the extent of the cost reductions. With this new set of cost curves it is clear that the long-run equilibrium – where the zero profit condition holds – will be at price P_3. The long-run supply curve is the locus of similar equilibrium points for a variety of different demand shifts. This locus (labeled LS in the figure) will be downward sloping, representing the cost reductions which stem from the entry of new firms. An industry characterized by this pattern of supply response is said to be a *decreasing cost industry*.

Figure 14.5   A Negatively Sloped Long-run Supply Curve for a Decreasing Cost Industry

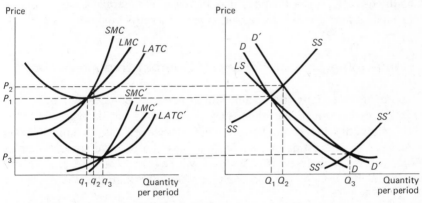

(a) A typical firm

(b) The market

An increase in demand to D' causes new firms to enter the industry. If the entry of these new firms causes the industry's cost structure to shift downward, the long-run equilibrium price will shift downward to P_3. The curve LS traces out the resultant set of equilibria for various demand shifts. Thus LS can turn out to be a negatively sloped long-run supply curve if costs do in fact shift downward.

Although a decreasing cost industry is a logical possibility, this should not be regarded as a common situation. Conditions favorable to cost-reducing externalities are probably quite rare, especially in well-developed economies. On the other hand, *increasing cost industries* may be frequently encountered. If the entry of new firms engendered by an

[9] Cost reductions of this nature are called *external economies* because the benefits not only accrue to the new firms entering the industry but also to those already in it. These external economies form a theoretical basis for the "infant industry" defense of the use of protective tariffs and quotas. If an industry can be protected in the short run from cheaper foreign competition, the argument runs, then in the long run external economies in the development of the industry will eventually permit domestic producers to compete at the lower foreign price.

increase in demand causes the cost structure of the industry to shift upward this result will occur. For example, new firms may bid up the prices of relatively scarce inputs or they may impose other costs, such as pollution, on previously existing firms. Since these situations are probably fairly common, long-run supply curves may often be positively sloped. The reader should use a construction similar to that in Figure 14.5 to demonstrate this increasing cost phenomenon for himself.

The conclusion is that the long-run industry supply curve may have a positive slope, a negative slope, or (in the constant cost case) it may be horizontal. The precise shape of the curve will depend on the way in which the entry of new firms affects the low point of the *LATC* curve of the firms in the industry.[10] In short-run analysis it is increasing marginal costs which give the short-run supply curve its positive slope. In perfectly competitive long-run analysis it is increases in average costs as output expands which gives the long-run supply curve its positive slope.

Some Examples of Perfectly Competitive Analysis

The analysis of long-run equilibrium in perfectly competitive markets is very precise. Given the underlying assumptions of this type of market structure, the tools which have been developed permit almost exact answers to interesting economic questions. To provide some examples of this type of analysis two questions will be investigated here: the effect of a specific tax on long-run competitive equilibrium; and the effects on

---

[10] Perhaps it is worth emphasizing the difference between the concepts of increasing, decreasing, and constant cost industries and the concepts of increasing, decreasing, or constant returns to scale.

Usually the notion of returns to scale refers to the productive technology of a single firm. Hence we may say that a firm exhibits increasing, decreasing, or constant returns to scale over various ranges of output. Alternatively, the concepts of increasing, decreasing, or constant costs refer to an industry and how the costs of firms in an industry are affected by the entry and exit of other firms. In perfectly competitive industries it is this latter concept which is relevant to discussions of the shape of the long-run supply curve. The two concepts are not the same. For example, an industry may exhibit increasing costs and increasing returns to scale at the same time. This can happen if production economies are offset by higher factor prices when industry output expands.

Occasionally these terminological conventions are violated in economic discussions. For example, some firms are said to exhibit "decreasing costs" in the long run. This means that the long-run average cost curve is negatively sloped over some range and might result from what would more properly be called increasing returns to scale. An even more important example is provided by discussions of industry (or even economy-wide) "production functions." Such production functions are frequently assumed to exhibit "constant returns to scale." What this may mean is that the industries are constant cost, and that (by the analysis of this chapter) a doubling of industry output is brought about by a doubling of optimally sized firms.

a perfectly competitive market of the development of new, lower-cost production techniques. Both of these cases will be analyzed using the assumptions of a constant cost industry. The reader is asked to work out for himself the analysis in the increasing or decreasing cost cases.

The Effect of a Specific Tax

A *specific tax* is a tax of a fixed amount per unit of output on a firm's production. It is a cost per unit of output which is (in appearance) paid by the firm to the government. If a per unit specific tax of t dollars is levied, the total costs of a firm are therefore increased by tq. The average and marginal cost curves of the firm are similarly shifted upward by t. There is, however, another way of analyzing a specific tax which will be more convenient here. The demand curve relevant to an industry's behavior is in fact an "after-tax" demand curve. A specific tax merely shifts the demand curve which is relevant to the firms in the industry downward by the amount t. Any quantity which is produced will sell at some market price P, but the after-tax amount received by firms in the industry will be $P - t$. The after-tax demand curve is labeled D' in Figure 14.6. This is the demand curve on which industry output decisions will be based, although the market price of any output produced will still be determined by the original market demand curve D.

Figure 14.6   Effect of the Imposition of a Specific Tax on a Perfectly Competitive, Constant Cost Industry

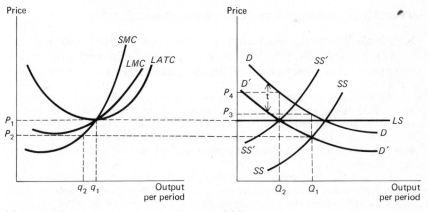

(a) A typical firm   (b) The market

A specific commodity tax of amount t lowers the after-tax demand curve to D'. With this "new" demand curve Q_2 will be produced in the short run at an after-tax price of P_2. The market price will be P_3. In the long run firms will leave the industry and the after-tax price will return to P_1. The entire amount of the tax is shifted onto consumers in the form of a higher market price (P_4).

The initial equilibrium in the market is given by the intersection of the long-run supply curve (LS) and the market demand curve. At this initial point market price is P_1, the quantity exchanged in the market is Q_1, and the typical firm will produce output level q_1. With the imposition of the tax, the after-tax demand curve becomes D'. In the short run industry output will be determined by the intersection of the curve D' with the industry short-run supply curve SS. This intersection occurs at output level Q_2 and price P_2. The after-tax price received by the firm is now P_2, and the typical firm will (assuming P_2 exceeds average variable cost) produce output level q_2. In the market, total output Q_2 will sell for P_3. Notice that $P_3 - P_2 = t$. In the short run, then, the tax is borne partially by the consumers of the good (market price has risen from P_1 to P_3) and partially by the firms in the industry who are operating at a short-term loss.

In the long run firms will not continue to operate at a loss. Some firms will leave the industry bemoaning the role of an oppressive government in bringing about their demise. The industry short-run supply curve will therefore shift leftward as fewer firms remain in the market. A new long-run equilibrium will be established at Q_3 where the after-tax price received by the firm enables it to earn exactly 0 in economic profits. Those firms left in the industry will return to producing output level q_1. The price paid by individuals in the market will now be P_4. In the long run the entire amount of the tax has been shifted into increased prices. Even though the firm ostensibly "pays" the tax, in fact the burden is borne by individuals.[11]

The Introduction of Low-cost Equipment

Suppose a new productive technique is developed which is characterized by a lower $LATC$ than that currently prevailing. In the very long run it is clear that this new technique will displace the previous one and the lower

[11] It should be emphasized that this result depends crucially on the assumptions of perfect competition and free entry and exit. If either or both of these do not hold, the result must be modified. Similarly, the prediction that price will rise by exactly the amount of the tax depends on the assumption of constant costs. If the industry is characterized by increasing costs, price will ultimately rise by less than t, and will rise by more than t in the decreasing cost case. Why?

This analysis is perhaps the simplest example of tax incidence theory. It clearly shows that in order to determine who ultimately pays a tax, it is necessary to investigate market responses. It is incorrect to argue that the agent who writes his check to the government actually bears the burden of the tax. Two other interesting possibilities of tax shifting occur in the cases of the corporate income tax and in employers' contributions for social security. Even though firms "pay" both taxes it has been argued that the true burden of the profits tax is shifted to consumers in the form of higher prices, and that the burden of the social security tax is shifted onto workers in the form of lower wages. Each of these assertions deserves extensive empirical investigation.

Figure 14.7 The Introduction of Low-cost Techniques into a Perfectly Competitive Industry

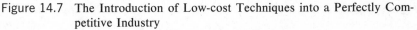
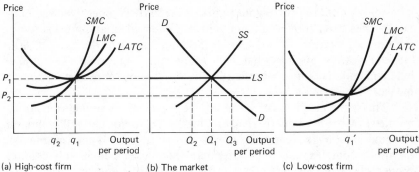

(a) High-cost firm   (b) The market   (c) Low-cost firm

With the entry of new low-cost firms market price will be forced down to P_2. At this price Q_3 is demanded in the market. Since the high-cost firms are stuck in the industry, they will continue to produce; their total output will be Q_2. The remaining output $(Q_3 - Q_2)$ will be supplied by the low-cost firms. In the very long run all firms will adopt the low-cost technique.

$LATC$ minimum will set the long-run price. However, in the short run this may not be the case. The older, high cost firms are "stuck" in the industry. There is nothing they can do with their now-outmoded techniques, except to continue producing. This situation is pictured in Figure 14.7. In 14.7a the older, higher cost firms' cost curves are drawn; 14.7c shows the cost curves for the low-cost firms. Suppose that the initial market equilibrium is given by the price-quantity combination P_1, Q_1. Assume that the low-cost firms can enter the industry freely and in a much shorter time interval than those already in can get out. Low-cost firms will be lured in so long as they envision a long-run profit—so long as price exceeds P_2. Entry will therefore continue until price falls to P_2. If P_2 exceeds the average variable cost for the high-cost firms they will continue to produce as indicated by their short-run supply curve SS. At P_2 they are, in the short run, willing to supply Q_2 (the typical firm produces q_2). But at P_2 total demand calls for Q_3, and therefore the amount $Q_3 - Q_2$ will be supplied by the new low-cost firms. The low-cost firms cannot produce more than this. If they did, price would fall below P_2 and they would suffer a loss. In the very long run the high-cost firms will be forced to adapt to the new technology.[12] In the short run, however, their production serves the useful function of providing output during this transitional phase.

[12] The reader may wish to apply this analysis to his own decision to purchase a new car (or any durable good) when an older, higher cost one is already owned. If the car owner is not tempted by Detroit's advertising prowess, the new car will not be bought until the average total cost of its operation is less than the average variable cost of the old junker.

Conclusion

The analysis of long-run equilibrium in a perfectly competitive, free-entry market has been shown to be definitive. Given adequate information on the cost structures of firms and on the interactions of the costs of firms we can always predict what will happen in equilibrium. The pricing mechanism is well understood, and only relatively "minor" questions of measurement remain.

This conclusion must, however, be regarded as premature, to say the least. Most markets (perhaps all markets) are not perfectly competitive and most have some costs of entry. Any real-world analysis must be far more complex and imprecise than that developed in this chapter. Nonetheless, the insights about entry, output decisions, and pricing provided by the chapter have a great value in understanding operations in less-perfect markets.

Short-run Supply-Demand Dynamics

Introduction

Chapter 14 presented numerous examples of what we have called "comparative statics analysis." The conditions of supply-demand equilibrium for a particular situation were demonstrated and then we asked what new equilibrium would emerge as a result of changed conditions. There was always the implicit assumption that price and quantity would move promptly to their new short-run equilibrium[1] levels whenever a move-

---

[1] This appendix discusses only the establishment of short-run equilibrium prices. Since the functioning of markets in the long run is a succession of short-run equilibria, the analysis to be presented is also relevant to that case.

ment from one equilibrium to another was necessary. While this assumption may be suitable in an elementary analysis a more detailed investigation raises several difficult issues. For example, how is it that suppliers and demanders are able to settle on a new equilibrium price? The only information available to them must come from the market, and no trading is permitted except at equilibrium prices. It would seem that some crucial element of the adjustment process has been left out of the analysis. Unless an omniscient figure is overseeing the operation of markets, it is hard to envision exactly how a new equilibrium is established. It is the purpose of this appendix to discuss briefly the ways in which economists have attempted to formalize those economic adjustment processes which are necessary to any complete supply-demand model.

Adjustment Processes: Basic Concepts

The problem to be investigated can be stated most precisely in a mathematical way. Consider a demand function in which quantity depends on price, $D(P)$, and a (short-run) supply function in which quantity also depends on price, $S(P)$. An equilibrium price, P^*, has the property that:

$$D(P^*) = S(P^*)$$

or   [14A.1]

$$D(P^*) - S(P^*) = 0.$$

Suppose now that the price initially starts at P_0 (perhaps this was an equilibrium before conditions changed, but that is not a necessary condition of the problem). Are there economic forces which cause the market price to move from P_0 to P^*? Related to this basic question are several others such as: How long will it take for price to get to P^*? Will prices "midway" between P_0 and P^* be observed in the market? What meaning are we to assign to any nonequilibrium prices which do occur? Only the initial question will be answered in any detail; the others will be discussed in a cursory manner at the end of the appendix.

To explain the movement of price to its equilibrium level economists have relied on the fictitious notion of an *impartial auctioneer*. The auctioneer is charged with calling out prices and recording the actions of buyers and sellers. Only when the auctioneer calls a price for which the quantity demanded is identical to that which is supplied will he permit trading to take place.[2] Presumably the auctioneer will use information about the market supply and demand curves to guide his pricing decisions, but precise rules for this operation are seldom spelled out.

The abstract idea of an auctioneer seems too far removed from reality to be an acceptable representation of the way in which prices are actually set. There have been numerous attempts, therefore, to give this fictional concept a behavioral interpretation. One such interpretation is the idea of *recontracting*. Buyers and sellers are assumed to enter into provisional contracts before the exchange of goods actually takes place. Each of these provisional contracts is voided if it is discovered that at the agreed upon price the market is not in equilibrium. Only when market clearing prices for all markets are discovered will exchange take place. Recontracting is then a form of haggling over price.

A second suggestion, which is similar to recontracting, was proposed by Walras.[3] In this scheme equilibrium prices are a goal toward which the market gropes. Changes in price are motivated by information from the market about the degree of *excess demand* at any particular price. Mathematically, the Walrasian adjustment mechanism specifies that the change in price over time is given by:

$$\frac{dP}{dt} = k[D(P) - S(P)] = k[ED(P)] \qquad k > 0 \qquad\qquad [14A.2]$$

where $ED(P)$ is used to represent excess demand at price P. Equation 14A.2 says that price will increase if there is positive excess demand, and decrease if excess demand is negative. Such a mechanism is called a *tâtonnement* (literally "groping") *process*. This mechanism is pictured graphically in Figure 14A.1. For any price above the equilibrium price (P^*) the *tâtonnement* process operates to lower price. Similarly, for prices less than P^* the process raises price. In 14A.1 the equilibrium price P^* is *stable;* there are forces which move P toward P^*. That this may not be the case is illustrated in 14A.1b. In this case the *tâtonnement* rule causes price to move away from its equilibrium level. It is easy to

---

[2] Real-world analogies to this notion are rare. One interesting Middle Eastern custom has an auctioneer sit between buyer and seller holding the hand of each. The auctioneer then calls off prices and the buyer and seller indicate their willingness to trade at these prices by pressing the hand of the auctioneer. When the auctioneer calls a price to which both parties agree, he announces that the trade has been completed.

[3] L. Walras, *Elements of Pure Economics*, translated by W. Jaffee (Homewood, Ill.: Richard D. Irwin, Inc., 1954). *See* the Appendix to Chapter 22 for a more complete discussion of Walras' ideas in a general equilibrium setting.

see that if the supply curve has a positive slope the equilibrium price P^* is stable.[4]

Figure 14A.1   Two Possible Supply-Demand Configurations and Their Walrasian Stability

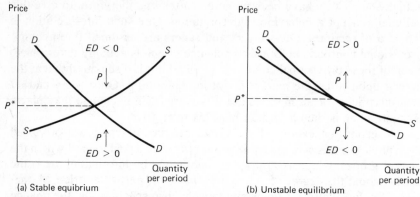

(a) Stable equibrium

(b) Unstable equilibrium

The Walrasian definition of stability specifies that prices will adjust in response to excess demand. If at some price quantity demanded exceeds quantity supplied, price is assumed to rise. Conversely, if quantity demanded is less than that supplied, price falls. In 14A.1a these rules insure that the equilibrium price P^* will be stable. Starting anywhere, there are forces moving price toward P^*. This is not true for the demand-supply configuration shown in 14A.1b. There the Walrasian mechanism will cause price to move away from P^*.

Another way to see the Walrasian result is to examine the excess demand function, $ED(P)$. Three possible shapes for the excess demand

---

[4] Actually if the supply curve were more negatively sloped than the demand curve the equilibrium would also be stable in the Walrasian sense. Another definition of stability, proposed by Marshall, would have quantity rather than price adjust in response to excess demand. We define an equilibrium quantity to be some quantity, Q^* such that the price demanders are willing to pay for Q^* $[= D^{-1}(Q^*)$ where the symbol D^{-1} indicates we are regarding P as a function of $Q]$ equal to what suppliers wish to receive $[= S^{-1}(Q^*)]$. The Marshallian adjustment mechanism is then given by:

$$\frac{dQ}{dt} = m[D^{-1}(Q) - S^{-1}(Q)] \qquad m > 0.$$

If, at some quantity, "demand price" exceeds "supply price," Q will rise. Similarly, if demand price falls short of supply price, quantity will fall. By this definition the situation pictured in Figure 14A.1a is stable (as it is by the Walrasian definition); but the situation of 14A.1b is stable also in contradiction to the Walrasian analysis. In the case of negatively sloped supply curves, Walrasian and Marshallian analyses differ on their assessments of stability. However, since the likelihood of either negatively sloped short-run supply curves or positively sloped demand curves is small, the situation pictured in 14A.1a must be considered to be the most usual one.

function are shown in Figure 14A.2. For each of these shapes equilibrium prices exist at those points where excess demand equals 0. In 14A.2a the equilibrium price P_1 is a stable equilibrium in the Walrasian sense. If price initially starts above P_1, the Walrasian process will tend to move it downward toward P_1. Similarly if the initial price is less than P_1, it will be adjusted upward.[5] The excess demand function in 14A.2b is unstable. The Walrasian process will tend to move price in the wrong direction. In 14A.2c there are multiple equilibria: P_1, P_2, and P_3 all cause excess demand to be 0. However, only P_1 and P_3 are stable in the Walrasian sense. There are no forces moving price toward P_2 (although if price started exactly at P_2 it would stay at this equilibrium position).

Figure 14A.2   Using Excess Demand Curves to Show Walrasian Stability

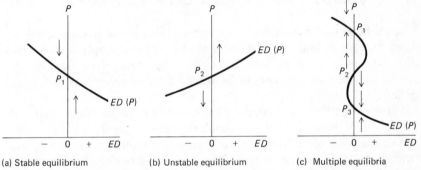

(a) Stable equilibrium   (b) Unstable equilibrium   (c) Multiple equilibria

Using the excess demand function $[ED(P) = D(P) - S(P)]$ we can investigate the stability of various equilibrium prices. These equilibrium prices occur whenever $ED(P) = 0$. However, only if the slope of the excess demand curve is negative $[ED'(P) < 0]$ at the equilibrium point will the Walrasian adjustment mechanism insure stability. Notice, for example, in 14A.2c that stable and unstable equilibria alternate.

The Walrasian idea is then a relatively precise way of classifying stability in a single market.[6] By looking at the supply and demand curves (or, equivalently, by looking at the excess demand curve) we will be able to tell whether the adjustment process specified by Walras will insure that prices move toward their equilibrium levels. The difficult conceptual problem with this process is in understanding physically how it is assumed to work. It does seem reasonable to assume that sellers will re-

---

[5] It is worth noting that a curve such as that shown in 14A.1a will occur whenever the supply curve has a positive slope (assuming the demand curve is always negatively sloped), or when the supply curve is more negatively sloped than the demand curve.

[6] The *tâtonnement* device can also be applied to multimarket adjustments. Although the basic ideas behind this application are virtually identical to those developed here, the mathematics used in multimarket stability analysis is beyond the scope of this book.

spond to positive excess demand by raising price and will try to stimulate demand by lowering price when *ED* is negative. But exactly how firms perceive the level of excess demand if trading is only permitted at equilibrium is not clear. On the other hand, if equilibrium prices are to be understood only as a goal toward which price moves, (with nonequilibrium prices occurring along the way), then a theory of nonequilibrium pricing is needed. Such a theory is not provided by this model. The Walrasian mechanism, therefore, is far from a totally satisfactory answer to conceptualizing the adjustment process. In the next section we will investigate one simple model which permits an explanation of how nonequilibrium prices might arise.

Other Approaches to Equilibrium Adjustment

One problem which interferes with the specification of a realistic adjustment process is that the traditional model pictures supply and demand decisions as being made simultaneously. There are two equations (the supply and demand curves) to be solved for two unknowns (price and quantity).

Imagining how this solution is discovered presents conceptual difficulties.[7] If it were possible to assume that the supply decision preceded the demand decision, this problem would be simplified. For example, if firms based their current output decisions on the market price occurring in the previous period, then output in the current period could be regarded as fixed; there will be no current period supply response. The analysis of pricing in the "very short-run" would then be the relevant model to study. The mechanisms for pricing in such situations are relatively well understood (auctions[8] are the primary example): Here price acts only as a rationing device for demand; it has no influence on production in the current period. In the next period the market price established in this period will be the one relevant to output decisions and there is thus some (lagged) response of output to price changes.

These ideas can be shown most clearly by a simple *cobweb model* of price determination. Suppose firms' supply decisions in period t depend only on the market price which prevailed in period $t - 1$:

Supply in period $t = Q_t^S = a + bP_{t-1}$. [14A.3]

---

[7] This simultaneity also presents numerous statistical difficulties in any attempt to estimate demand curves. For a discussion of this "identification problem" *see* Discussion Question 4 of Part IV.

[8] For an interesting survey of a variety of auction techniques and the institutional peculiarities of these systems *see* R. Cassady, Jr., *Auctions and Auctioneering* (Berkeley, Calif.: University of California Press, 1967).

The total quantity supplied is then sold in the market for whatever it will bring. Market demand depends on current price:

Demand in period $t = Q_t^D = c - dP_t$ [14A.4]

and equilibrium in the market at time t necessitates that:

$$Q_t^S = Q_t^D.$$ [14A.5]

This view of the market assumes the following sequence of events: Firms decide on Q_t^S by referring to P_{t-1}; demanders (perhaps by auction) bid for Q_t^S and in so doing establish P_t. Firms' output decisions in period $t + 1$ are then based on P_t. An equilibrium price in this system is one which will be repeated each period: $P^* = P_t = P_{t-1}$. This equilibrium price can be found by setting $Q_t^S = Q_t^D$:

$$a + bP_{t-1} = c - dP_t$$ [14A.6]

or, at an equilibrium price, P^*:

$$a + bP^* = c - dP^*$$

and

$$P^* = \frac{c - a}{b + d}.$$ [14A.6']

Also, any price, P_t, can be "predicted" from the market clearing Equation 14A.6 by:

$$P_t = \frac{-b}{d} P_{t-1} + \frac{c - a}{d}.$$ [14A.7]

Hence, for any arbitrary initial price P_0:

$$P_1 = \frac{-b}{d} P_0 + \frac{c - a}{d},$$

$$P_2 = \frac{-b}{d} P_1 + \frac{c - a}{d}$$ [14A.8]

$$= \left(\frac{-b}{d}\right)^2 P_0 + \frac{c - a}{d} \left[1 + \left(\frac{-b}{d}\right)\right]$$

and by repeated substitution:

$$P_t = \left(\frac{-b}{d}\right)^t P_0 + \frac{c - a}{d} \left[1 + \frac{-b}{d} + \left(\frac{-b}{d}\right)^2 + \cdots + \left(\frac{-b}{d}\right)^{t-1}\right]$$ [14A.8']

Therefore:[9]

$$P_t = \left(\frac{-b}{d}\right)^t P_0 + \frac{c-a}{d}\left[\frac{d}{b+d}\left(1 - \left(\frac{-b}{d}\right)^t\right)\right]$$

$$= \left[P_0 - \frac{c-a}{b+d}\right]\left(\frac{-b}{d}\right)^t + \frac{c-a}{b+d}.$$

[14A.9]

Finally, then, by substitution from Equation 14A.6':

$$P_t = [P_0 - P^*]\left(\frac{-b}{d}\right)^t + P^*.$$

[14A.10]

Equation 14A.10 says that market price will oscillate around P^* (since the factor $(-b/d)^t$ is alternatively positive and negative). P_t will approach P^* provided that $(-b/d)^t$ goes to 0 for large values of t. This will be the case if $b/d < 1$ or, equivalently, if $b < d$. On the other hand, if $b > d$, the price oscillations will become wider over time.[10] These two possibilities are illustrated in the "cobweb" supply-demand graphs in Figure 14A.3. In 14A.3a the demand curve is flat relative to the supply curve $(b < d)$.[11] By Equation 14A.10 this means that any price (say P_0) will ultimately converge to P^*. The sequence of events depicted in this diagram would be: P_0 dictates the amount supplied in period 1 (Q_1); this determines period 1's price (P_1) by reference to the demand curve. P_1 then is used in firms' decisions to set Q_2, and the process is repeated. From the diagram it is clear that the market price will work its way toward P^*. In 14A.3b, however, this does not happen. Here the oscillations of price are explosive, since $d > b$. The reason for this is that demand is relatively inelastic. Hence prices change rather greatly in response to quantity changes. But these price changes interact with a fairly elastic supply curve to produce

[9] This line is a result of the mathematical formula:

$$\frac{1}{1-X} = 1 + X + X^2 + \cdots + X^n + \cdots$$

Let $X = -b/d$. Therefore, $1/1 - X = d/b + d$.

[10] These conditions are much more strict than those discussed previously. They require that the slopes of the supply and demand curves have a precise relationship to one another. Since prices seldom exhibit explosive oscillations, yet there is no obvious reason why the slopes should bear such a relationship to each other, the feature points out the oversimplified nature of this cobweb model.

[11] The reader should be warned that the demand and supply curves are expressed here with the dependent variable on the horizontal axis rather than in the "usual" way of having the dependent variable on the vertical axis. Consequently, somewhat more care must be employed in thinking about what the words "flat" and "steep" imply.

even greater quantity changes, and the whole process quickly becomes explosive.[12]

This model, although it is an obvious oversimplification of reality, may approximate the way in which markets make adjustments to equilibrium. It would take a peculiar lack of sophistication on the part of buyers and sellers to accept such a regularly oscillating price for long, and some kinds of expectational adjustments are bound to be made. The model does, however, introduce the idea of "feedback" in a precise way and, by adopting a time sequence to the supply-demand process, it eliminates the simultaneity problem.

Figure 14A.3   Cobweb Model of Price Determination

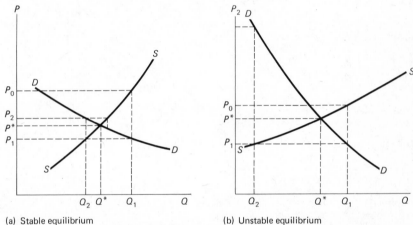

(a) Stable equilibrium   (b) Unstable equilibrium

In the cobweb model of lagged response to price by firms a theory of nonequilibrium pricing can be established. Whether these prices will approach an equilibrium level will depend on the relative slopes of the demand and supply curves. In the configuration shown in 14A.3a convergence will take place, whereas in 14A.3b it will not. A third possibility (not shown) would be for the supply and demand curves to have slopes so that the price perpetually oscillates at about P^*.

[12] A third possibility would be that $b = d$. In this case $-b/d = -1$ and (by Equation 11A.10) market price would oscillate perpetually at about P^*.

CHAPTER 15

Pricing in Monopoly Markets

Introduction

The market for a particular good is described as a monopoly if there is only one producer of the good.[1] This single firm faces the entire market demand curve. Using its knowledge of this demand curve, the monopoly makes a decision on how much to produce. Unlike the perfectly com-

---

[1] It should be recognized at the outset that no monopoly is totally without competition. The good in question will always have some substitutes available, if only because it is in competition for the consumer's dollar.

petitive firm's output decision (which has no effect on market price), the monopoly's output decision will, in fact, determine the good's price. In this sense monopoly markets are the opposite polar case from markets characterized by perfect competition. Some authors treat monopolies as having the power to set price and, in a sense, monopolies do have this power. Technically, a monopoly can choose that point on the market demand curve at which it prefers to operate: It may choose either market price or quantity (but not both). In this chapter it will be convenient to assume monopolies choose that quantity of output which maximizes profits. It would be a simple matter to rephrase the discussion in terms of price setting, although the wording of some results would be more complex.

Causes of Monopoly

The reason monopolies exist is that other firms find it unprofitable or impossible to enter the market. *Barriers to entry* are therefore the source of all monopoly power: If other firms could enter the market, there would, by definition, no longer be a monopoly. There are two general types of barriers to entry: technical barriers and legal barriers. A primary technical barrier is that the production of the good in question may exhibit decreasing marginal (and average) cost over a wide range of output levels. The technology of production is such that relatively large-scale firms are efficient. In this situation one firm may find it profitable to drive others out of the industry by price-cutting. Similarly, once a monopoly has been established, entry will be difficult because any new firm must produce at relatively low levels of output and therefore at relatively high costs. It is important to stress that the range of declining costs need only be "large" relative to the market in question. Declining costs on some absolute scale are not necessary. For example, the manufacture of concrete does not exhibit declining marginal costs over a broad range of output when compared to the total United States market. However, in any particular small town declining marginal costs may permit a monopoly to be established. The high costs of transportation in this industry tend to isolate one market from another.

A further technical basis of monopoly is special knowledge of a low-cost productive technique. The problem for the monopoly fearing entry is to keep this technique uniquely to itself. When matters of technology are involved this may be extremely difficult, unless the technology can be protected by a patent (*see* below). Ownership of unique resources (mineral deposits, land locations) or the possession of unique managerial talents may also be a lasting basis for maintaining a monopoly.[2]

Many pure monopolies are created as a matter of law rather than as a matter of economic conditions. One important example of a government-granted monopoly position is in the legal protection of a productive technique by a patent. Situations of this sort are numerous; Xerox machines and Polaroid cameras are the most notable examples. Because the basic technology for these products was uniquely assigned to one firm, a monopoly position was established. The defense made of the patent system is that is allows productive innovations to be more profitable and therefore acts as a spur to invention. This argument can be expressed in more precise terms by using the concept of *social benefit*. It is argued that the social benefits from an innovation exceed the benefits which would normally accrue to the innovator. Hence the workings of the price system will underallocate resources to research and development. By granting monopoly rights for a period of years (usually seventeen), private and social benefits can be brought into closer agreement and a greater amount of resources will be devoted to innovation.

A second example of a legally created monopoly is in the awarding of an exclusive franchise to serve a market. These franchises are awarded in cases of public utility (gas and electric) service, communications services, the post office, some airline routes, some television and radio station markets, and a variety of other situations. The argument usually put forward in favor of creating these franchised monopolies is that having only one firm in the industry is somehow "more desirable" than permitting open competition. In that this rationale has an economic basis the one usually proposed is that the industry in question is a *natural monopoly:* marginal cost is diminishing over a broad range of output levels and minimum average cost can be achieved only by organizing the industry as a monopoly. The argument in the early part of this section may convince the reader that a monopoly might emerge in such a market even without the legislative sanction of a franchise. The public utility and communications industries can be considered representative of these natural monopolies. It would seem to be extremely undesirable to have two overlapping telephone or electricity distribution systems. Other cases of gov-

---

[2] High costs of entry into a market are sometimes mentioned as a basis for monopoly. Whereas there are undoubtedly cases in which this is correct, it is important to be careful in distinguishing these cases. In a world of certainty and perfect capital markets a firm would enter a market so long as the present discounted value of future profits exceeded the fixed costs of entry. In the real world uncertainty (particularly about the behavior of the firm already in the industry) and imperfect capital markets undoubtedly make high entry costs a real barrier.

ernment franchises (certain airline routes, the post office) do not appear to be clearcut natural monopolies and it is more difficult to specify the rationale for franchising in these instances. Whatever the rationale of the government franchise, it serves the function of eliminating the possibility of entry into the market in question. Frequently the pricing policy of the franchised monopoly is regulated by the government[3] to make up for this lack of actual or potential competition.

Profit Maximization in Monopoly Markets

In order to maximize profits a monopoly will choose to produce that output level for which marginal revenue is equal to marginal cost. Since the monopoly, in contrast to a perfectly competitive firm, faces a negatively sloped market demand curve, marginal revenue will be less than price in this situation. To sell an additional unit the monopoly must lower its price on all units to be sold, if it is to generate the extra demand necessary to absorb this marginal unit. The profit-maximizing output level for a firm is then the level Q^* in Figure 15.1.[4] At this level marginal revenue is equal to marginal costs and profits are maximized. The price which will clear the market in this situation is given by P^*. The price-quantity combination observed in the market is therefore P^*, Q^*.[5]

Profits earned by the monopolist can be read directly from Figure 15.1. These are shown by the rectangle P^*CAE and again represent the profit per unit (price minus average cost) times the number of units sold. These profits will be positive if market price exceeds average total cost. Since no entry is possible into a monopoly market, these monopoly profits can exist even in the long run. For this reason some authors refer to those profits which a monopoly earns in the long run as *monopoly rents*. These profits can be regarded as a return to that factor which forms the basis of the monopoly (a patent, a favorable location, a dynamic entrepreneur), hence another possible owner might be willing to pay that amount in rent for the right to the monopoly. Profits can therefore be treated as an im-

---

[3] *See* Chapter 23 for a brief discussion of this function of government.

[4] In Figure 15.1, and in the other diagrammatic analyses of this chapter, no distinction is made between the behavior of a monopoly in the short run and in the long run. The analysis is the same in both cases, except that different sets of cost curves would be used depending on the possibilities for adjustment which are assumed to be feasible for the firm. Notice though that in the long run a monopoly will not in general choose that plant size for which long run average cost is a minimum. The only situation in which this would occur would be if MR and LMC happened to intersect at the low point of the $LATC$ curve. These observations are further discussed in the section "What's Wrong with Monopoly?" below.

[5] This combination will be on an elastic section of the demand curve so long as $MC > 0$. This will be true because $MC > 0$ implies that for a profit maximum $MR > 0$. Hence $E_{Q,P} < -1$, since we have shown that $MR = P(1 + 1/E_{Q,P})$.

plicit rental cost. In this sense one could argue that there is never such a thing as "pure profits." This distinction is purely an exercise in semantics and the analysis would be unchanged if we treated the entrepreneur as seeking to maximize the quasi-rents of his monopoly position.

In the theory of perfectly competitive markets presented earlier it was possible to speak of an industry supply curve. This curve was constructed by allowing the market demand curve to shift and observing the supply curve which was traced out by the series of equilibrium points.

Figure 15.1 Profit Maximization and Price Determination in a Monopoly Market

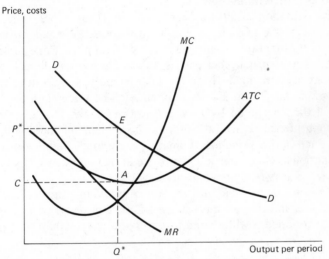

A profit-maximizing monopolist produces that quantity for which marginal revenue is equal to marginal cost. In the diagram this quantity is given by Q^* which will yield a price of P^* in the market. Monopoly profits can be read as the rectangle P^*CAE.

For monopoly markets this type of construction is not possible. With a fixed market demand curve the supply "curve" for a monopoly will be only one point, namely that quantity for which $MR = MC$. If the demand curve should shift, the marginal revenue curve would also shift, and a new profit-maximizing output would be chosen. However, to connect the resulting series of equilibrium points on the market demand curves would have little meaning. This locus might have a very strange shape, depending on how the market demand curve's elasticity (and hence its associated MR curve) changes as the curve is shifted.[6] In this sense the monopoly firm has no well-defined supply curve.

[6] *See* Problem 5 of Part IV for some exercise in analyzing these shifts.

Market Separation and Price Discrimination

It may sometimes be the case that a firm will have a monopoly position in two different markets for the same good. If these markets are effectively separated so that buyers cannot shift from one market to the other there may be the possibility for the monopolist to increase his profits further by practicing *price discrimination*. The profit-maximizing decision would be to produce that quantity in each market for which marginal revenue equals marginal cost.[7] This may lead to different prices for the same good in the two markets, and, if the markets are effectively separated, these price differentials can persist.

This situation is shown graphically in Figure 15.2. The figure is drawn so that the market demand (and marginal revenue) curves in the two separated markets share the same vertical axis. For simplicity it is also assumed that marginal cost is a constant over all levels of output. The profit-maximizing decision for the monopoly is to produce Q_1^* in the first market and Q_2^* in the second market. The prices in these two markets will then be given by P_1 and P_2, respectively. It is clear from the figure that the market with the more inelastic demand curve will have the higher price in this price-discriminating example.[8] The price-discriminating monopolist will charge a higher price in that market in which quantity purchased is less responsive to price changes.

There are many examples in the real world of a firm selling an identical product in different markets at different prices. For example, bulk chemical producers will charge less to large buyers than to small ones;

---

[7] A mathematical proof of this assertion can be shown as follows. Let Q_1 be the quantity sold in one market and Q_2 the quantity sold in the other. Then $\pi(Q_1, Q_2) = R_1(Q_1) + R_2(Q_2) - C(Q_1 + Q_2)$ where R_1 and R_2 are the revenues obtained from selling Q_1 and Q_2 in their respective markets.

The first-order conditions for a maximum are:

$$\frac{\partial \pi}{\partial Q_1} = \frac{\partial R_1}{\partial Q_1} - \frac{\partial C}{\partial Q_1} = 0$$

$$\frac{\partial \pi}{\partial Q_2} = \frac{\partial R_2}{\partial Q_2} - \frac{\partial C}{\partial Q_2} = 0.$$

But, since the cost of producing output in the two markets is the same, $\partial C/\partial Q_1 = \partial C/\partial Q_2 = MC$. Therefore, for a profit maximum the firm should choose Q_1 and Q_2 so that $MR_1 = MR_2 = MC$.

[8] *Proof:* Since $MR = P(1 + 1/E)$, $MR_1 = MR_2$ implies $P_1(1 + 1/E_1) = P_2(1 + 1/E_2)$. If $E_1 > E_2$ (if the demand in market 1 is less elastic), then P_1 must exceed P_2 for this equality to hold.

Figure 15.2   Separated Markets Raise the Possibility of Price Discrimination

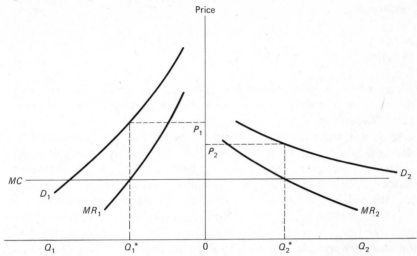

Quantity in Market 1   Quantity in Market 2

If two markets are separate a monopolist can maximize profits by selling his product at different prices in the two markets. This would entail choosing that output for which $MC = MR$ in each of the markets. The diagram shows that the market which has a less elastic demand curve will be charged the higher price by the price discriminator.

electric utilities usually charge lower rates to industrial and commercial users than to consumers; and supermarkets may charge higher prices to central city purchasers than to suburban buyers. Each of these situations presents the firm with the possibility of separating markets to maximize profits. Similarly, the results which emerge might have been predicted by the simple price discrimination model: Large chemical buyers presumably have a more elastic demand because they can more easily take their business elsewhere, or even go into the production business themselves; industrial and commercial users of electricity have a more elastic demand because they use electricity on a scale where it might be profitable for them to generate their own; and central city residents are generally less mobile than their suburban counterparts and may therefore have a less elastic demand for the services of a particular supermarket. Nonetheless, these situations are not exactly analogous to the textbook price-discriminating model. The markets are not pure monopolies as we have defined them, and entry is possible in a number of ways. Marginal costs may differ between the two markets and these cost differentials could lead to differing prices, even if the markets were perfectly competitive. To draw any definitive conclusions about price discrimination from such simple a priori arguments can therefore be unwarranted. A careful investigation of demand and cost data is required before making such an assessment.

What's Wrong with Monopoly?

Firms which occupy a monopoly position in a market are frequently damned for a variety of reasons. It has been argued that monopolies earn "excess" profits; give poor, unresponsive service; "exploit" their employees; stifle technical progress; and distort the allocation of resources. While each of these complaints undoubtedly has some analytic truth to it, only two of the claims will be discussed here: the profitability of monopoly and the effect of monopoly on resource allocation. Some of the other claims will be investigated in other sections of this book.

Since perfectly competitive firms earn no pure profits in the long run, it is true that a firm in a monopoly market can earn higher profits than if the market were competitive. This does not imply, however, that monopolies necessarily earn huge profits. Two equally "strong" monopolies may differ greatly in their profitability.

To see this it is necessary to define what is meant by a strong monopoly. One definition, proposed by Lerner,[9] defines the *degree of monopoly* to be:

$$D = \frac{\text{Price} - \text{Marginal cost}}{\text{Price}} \qquad [15.1]$$

The distinguishing characteristic of monopoly is a divergence between price and marginal cost, and Lerner's definition measures this divergence. Notice that for a perfectly competitive firm $D = 0$.

For two firms with similar degrees of monopoly power (as measured by Lerner's criterion), the degree of profitability may differ greatly. The level of profits will depend on the relative positions of the average cost curve and the demand curve, but not necessarily on the degree of monopoly. Figure 15.3 exhibits the cost and demand possibilities for two firms

---

[9] A. P. Lerner, "The Concept of Monopoly and the Measurement of Monopoly Power," *Review of Economic Studies*, vol. 1 (June 1934), pp. 157–175. For a profit-maximizing monopoly $MR = MC$, and therefore Lerner's definition becomes:

$$D = \frac{P - MR}{P} = -\frac{1}{E_{Q,P}}.$$

The closer $E_{Q,P}$ is to -1, the closer D will be to 1, which is its maximum value (in view of Footnote 5 of this chapter).

with essentially the same degree of monopoly power. In this diagram the monopoly in 15.3a earns a high level of profits, whereas the one illustrated in 15.3b actually earns 0 in profits. The primary objection to monopoly profits, then, is not based on the inevitability of huge profits but rather rests on an objection to the *distributional effects of monopoly profits.* If these profits go to relatively wealthy owners at the expense of less well-to-do consumers there may be valid objections to monopoly profits no matter what their size. This may not necessarily be the case. For example, consider the decision of Navajo blanket makers to form a monopoly in the sale of their products to tourists. This is clearly a situation in which monopoly profits would make the income distribution more equal.

Figure 15.3   Monopoly Profits Depend on the Relationship between the Demand and Average Cost Curves

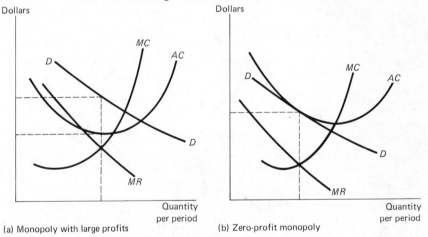

(a) Monopoly with large profits   (b) Zero-profit monopoly

Both of the monopolies in this figure are equally "strong," if by this we mean they produce similar divergences between market price and marginal cost. However, because of the location of the demand and average cost curves, it turns out that the monopoly in 15.3a earns huge profits, whereas that in 15.3b earns no profits. Consequently, the size of profits is not a measure of the strength of a monopoly.

A second objection to monopoly markets is that the existence of these markets distorts the allocation of resources. Monopolies intentionally restrict their level of output in order to maximize profits. The discrepancy between price and marginal cost reflects the fact that at the monopoly's preferred output level consumers are willing to pay more for one more unit of output than it would cost to produce that output. From a social point of view, therefore, output is too low. This observation is illustrated in Figure 15.4 by comparing the output which will be produced in a market characterized by perfect competition with that which will be produced in the same market when there is only one firm in it. In the figure it is assumed that both the monopoly and the perfectly competitive firms would produce under conditions of constant marginal costs. In this situation a perfectly competitive industry would choose output level Q^* where price is equal to marginal cost. A monopoly would choose output level Q^{**} for which marginal revenue is equal to marginal cost. The restriction in output $(Q^* - Q^{**})$ is then some measure of the allocational harm done by monopoly.[10]

Figure 15.4 Differential Effects of Perfect Competition and Monopoly in a Market

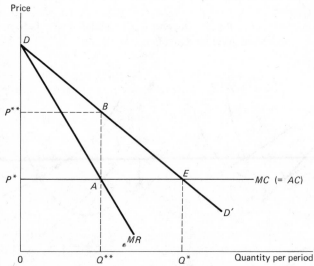

A perfectly competitive industry would produce output level Q^* for which price equals marginal cost. A monopoly, by recognizing the downward slope of the demand curve, would produce Q^{**} where marginal revenue equals marginal cost. This output reduction is a measure of the allocational "evil" of monopolies. In some cases it may be possible to place a value on this loss in output.

Under rather restrictive assumptions it is possible to evaluate the loss suffered by consumers as a result of the output restriction by a monopoly. Such a measure relies on the concept of *consumer's surplus.* Simply put, the surplus received by consumers from the purchase of some quantity of a good is the difference between the value of the utility they

---

[10] *See* Chapter 22 for a more precise discussion of the allocational distortions from monopolized markets.

receive from that quantity of the good and the actual cost of that quantity. One possible measure of the value of the total utility from the purchase of, say, Q^* of a good is the area under the demand curve from $Q = 0$ to $Q = Q^*$. If a firm were a *perfect price discriminator* and could dole out one unit at a time to consumers for the highest price they were willing to pay for that unit its revenues would equal this area under the demand curve. The perfect price discriminator could force consumers to pay the total value they place on a particular good. Because perfect price discrimination is not usually possible, goods are sold at one price. Those who value these goods more highly than the prevailing market price receive a "bonus" because price is determined by the marginal buyer.[11,12]

Figure 15.4 can be used to demonstrate these ideas. When the market is perfectly competitive the price-quantity combination P^*, Q^* prevails. An approximation to the value of the total utility from this quantity is given by the area DOQ^*E. But the individual pays P^*OQ^*E for these goods, and therefore consumer's surplus for this equilibrium position is given by the triangle DP^*E. If the market has only one monopoly producer the value of the total utility from consuming Q^{**} is given by $DOQ^{**}B$. For this consumers pay $P^{**}OQ^{**}B$ and obtain consumer's surplus of $DP^{**}B$. Consumer's surplus has therefore been reduced by $P^{**}P^*EB$ as a result of the introduction of a monopoly. Not all of this is a net loss, however. The area $P^{**}P^*AB$ represents the profits of the monopoly: It is a measure of the redistribution from consumer's surplus

---

[11] A semimathematical treatment may illuminate these ideas. For an individual to be maximizing his utility he will equate marginal utility to $P \cdot \lambda$ where λ is the marginal utility of income. Now assume that all individuals have the same utility function and that λ is constant for all individuals and for all levels of P. Then the total utility from purchasing Q^* is

$$\int_0^{Q^*} MU(Q)\,dQ = \int_0^{Q^*} \lambda \cdot P(Q)\,dQ = \lambda \cdot (\text{Area under demand curve from 0 to } Q^*),$$ since λ is

constant. Because λ is the marginal utility of income, $1/\lambda$ is a measure of the value of utility. Hence (Total utility)$/\lambda$ = Value of utility from the good = Area under the demand curve.

For a more rigorous discussion of the concept of consumer's surplus see J. R. Hicks, "A Rehabilitation of Consumer's Surplus," *Review of Economic Studies,* vol. 8 (February 1941), pp. 108–116.

[12] Using the notion of consumer's surplus it has sometimes been claimed that perfect price discrimination may be desirable. By being a perfect discriminator a firm is able to expropriate all (or almost all) the "value" of his product. If perfect price discrimination were possible, therefore, the good might be provided even though cost considerations could prevent its being provided if the firm had to obey a one-price pricing policy. For example, it might be argued that the ability of small-town doctors to practice price discrimination among their patients is beneficial because otherwise there would be no medical service at all.

The notion of consumer's surplus provides some quantification of what earlier economists may have had in mind by "value in use." Because of the rigid assumptions necessary to justify the measure presented here, however, this observation should not be pressed too far.

to monopoly profits. To make a judgment on the desirability of this transfer it is necessary to investigate the particular nature of the redistributional effect. There is no ambiguity about the loss of consumer's surplus represented by the triangle BAE. This is a *dead weight loss* occasioned by the monopolization of the market. If the market were organized as a competitive one instead, individuals would be better off by this amount.[13]

This allocational argument relies on the theoretically suspect notion of consumer's surplus. A more definitive analysis of the welfare loss from monopoly is not possible. However, the output reduction brought about by monopolization is probably the best single reason for condemning such markets. Not only does this reduction lead to a situation in which individuals are willing to pay more for an extra unit of the good than it would cost to produce but it also leads to the likelihood that the good will not be produced at minimum average total cost. There is no economic force (as there is in perfectly competitive markets) driving a monopoly toward the low point on its average cost curve. Thus, there is the possibility that monopolies will be unnecessarily high cost producers.

Conclusion: A Broader View of Monopoly

To conclude that monopolies are an unambiguous evil would be to place too much credence on the simple, static analyses of this chapter. In order to evaluate any market arrangement properly one must compare the evolution of several alternatives over time. Although a monopoly market may be in a static sense inefficient, over time it may be that monopolies are a dynamic element of the economy. For example, monopolies may use their profits to engage in research and development. A desire to stay one step ahead of potential entrants may also promote innovation and cost-saving advances. Schumpeter[14] proposed the argument that the monopolization of a market provides a degree of stability. Given such stability, firms are better able to plan future growth and are in a better position to take a long-term view of the need for research, which is more profitable for a monopoly because such a firm is in a better position to capture all the profits generated by its discoveries.

These observations on the possible beneficial aspects of monopoly

[13] Notice that in moving from Q^{**} to Q^* more resources must be brought into this industry. This will mean that output elsewhere must be reduced. It is possible that the total value of this lost output can be represented by area $AQ^{**}Q^*E$ if these shifted inputs are drawn away "at the margin" from other perfectly competitive industries. But this area also represents additional utility value to consumers from the good being investigated. Hence the loss from transferring resources is totally compensated for and the net gain is in fact BAE.

[14] J. A. Schumpeter, *Capitalism, Socialism and Democracy*, 3rd ed. (New York: Harper & Row, 1950). *See* especially Chapter 8 on monopolistic practices.

raise important empirical issues which cannot be answered confidently by a priori assertions. In the next chapter several other interesting questions about industrial organization in the real world will be mentioned. Although such difficult empirical issues can only be discussed in a most cursory manner, the tools developed here will form a framework within which to conduct the analysis.

CHAPTER 16

Topics in the Theory of Industrial Organization

Introduction

Having developed the theoretical polar cases of perfect competition and monopoly, there are two possible approaches to discussing intermediate types. One method would be to present and criticize several of the oligopoly models which have been developed. This traditional approach would center attention on duopoly (two-firm) markets and on markets characterized by monopolistic competition. While some of the Problems for Part IV ask the reader to develop such analyses, standard oligopoly models will not be analyzed in any detail in this text. Rather, a second, more descriptive method will be used to investigate those real-world situations which fall between the extremes of monopoly and perfect competition.

The vocabulary and mode of analysis to be used is that which has been developed in the field of economics called the *theory of industrial organization*. In recent years this field has expanded rapidly and this chapter can only hint at the sophisticated and thought-provoking questions which have been asked. The purpose of these investigations, in a broad sense, has been to evaluate the performance of certain industries. The standards by which these industries are to be judged vary from study to study, but they generally fall into two categories: *static efficiency* and *dynamic efficiency*. By static efficiency is usually meant how closely the industry in question approximates the perfectly competitive model. Questions which are raised include: How close is price to marginal cost? Are prices flexible in response to changing demand conditions? Is entry relatively costless (are there long-run forces which assure that the low point on the average cost curve will be approached)? Finally, the general issue of private versus social costs in production and whether markets are providing a socially desirable allocation of resources is of concern. These investigations use the competitive model as a standard against which to measure actual performance. An industry which approximates the perfectly competitive ideal is sometimes described as *workable competition*.

The concept of dynamic efficiency has no such clearly defined standards. Rather, this category represents a catch-all for many difficult real-world problems of evaluation. A brief taste of this sort of analysis was presented in the previous chapter when Schumpeter's views of the innovative potential of monopoly were discussed. It is not clear whether perfect competition or monopoly (or some combination of the two) is more amenable to technical innovation, and empirical research must be used to investigate this issue. Similar problems occur when attempting to evaluate the desirability of product differentiation (Can there be too many kinds of toothpaste?) or of advertising (Is it persuasive or informative?). One must of necessity step beyond the perfectly competitive model (and perhaps beyond the traditional bounds of economics) to answer such questions. Another departure from the competitive model's stress on allocative efficiency is the study of what Leibenstein[1] has termed *X-efficiency*. Leibenstein uses this term to refer to the ability of firms' managements to lessen costs within the confines of existing technology. Examples of this would include entrepreneurial organizational ability, increases in worker motivation, and other sources of productivity

---

[1] H. Leibenstein, "Allocative Efficiency v. X-Efficiency," *American Economic Review*, vol. 56 (June 1966), pp. 392–415.

increase which are not easily handled by the usual methods of concentrating on the productivity of specific factors.

The development of the theory of industrial organization to be presented in this chapter will be essentially a priori and taxonomic: There is no attempt here at an empirical discussion. Instead, the purpose is to indicate how economists have modified many of the tools which have been developed earlier in this text to investigate difficult real-world issues.

Concentration in Markets

A first question one might pose about industrial structure is which markets[2] are generally characterized by a small number of firms and which by a large number. One concept which is commonly used for measuring this is the *concentration ratio*. Concentration ratios measure the percent of the output in a particular market that is produced by the four largest firms.[3] For example, such markets as flat glass, breakfast cereals, primary aluminum, and cigarettes have very high concentration ratios. The top four firms in these industries account for more than 80 percent of the total domestic output. On the other hand, markets such as men's suits, dresses, ready-mixed concrete, household furniture, and soft drinks are relatively unconcentrated, having concentration ratios of 15 percent or less.[4]

It is important to point out that one should be very careful in interpreting these concentration ratios. For example, imports are not considered in the published figures. The possibility of imports may have significant effects on particular markets (for example, consider the cases of automobiles and primary steel production, both "highly concentrated"

[2] Economists have been most interested in concentration within one market. This is the relevant consideration for questions about pricing strategy and related allocational matters. Sociologists and political scientists, on the other hand, have had considerable interest in the question of the general concentration of manufacturing industry. For example, much analysis has been devoted to examining what has been happening to the percent of manufacturing assets controlled by the top two hundred corporations. While there is no general agreement on the direction of the trend in the level of overall concentration, nor in the meaning to be attached to any trend which is finally determined, the discussion has engendered much debate. For an interesting analysis of this debate and some discussion of the concept of market concentration *see* S. Rose, "Bigness Is a Numbers Game," *Fortune*, vol. LXXX, no. 6 (November 1969), pp. 112–115ff.

[3] The definition is rather arbitrary. It is possible to use value added or to use total assets as a measure of size rather than sales. Similarly there is nothing particularly significant about the number four, although this one has been traditionally used in government studies.

[4] These data come from the United States Census Bureau, *Concentration Ratios in Manufacturing Industry, 1958,* prepared for the Subcommittee on Antitrust and Monopoly of the Committee on the Judiciary (Washington, D.C.: U.S. Government Printing Office, 1963).

industries) and the published concentration ratios may overestimate the strength of firms in the market. Low concentration ratios need not imply lack of market power. The case of ready-mixed concrete has already been mentioned as an example of an industry which appears to be unconcentrated on a national sacle; but, in fact, many firms in this industry occupy strong local monopolies. Similarly the toilet preparations market appears to be relatively unconcentrated (a ratio of 38 percent was reported in 1963). Yet some segments of this market (toothpaste and deodorants, for example) are far more highly concentrated. Additional problems in interpretation are raised by firms which sell in more than one product market and by licensing arrangements (as in the soft-drink market) which are not represented in the available data. Consequently, published figures on concentration must be regarded as indicative rather than as a definitive scheme for locating markets on the continuum between perfect competition and monopoly.

In view of the unsatisfactory nature of the available data on market concentration it is not surprising that there have been few specific findings about the behavior of firms in concentrated markets. For example, while there is some agreement that firms in highly concentrated markets are more profitable than firms in unconcentrated ones, there is wide disagreement as to the extent of these differences.[5] There are many markets which appear to be concentrated in which profitability is below average. Another question which has not been answered satisfactorily is whether concentrated industries produce goods (or services) of a quality which is inferior to that produced in unconcentrated markets. Again, there is evidence on both sides. Many questions about pricing and price flexibility in concentrated markets are similarly unsettled. These will be discussed later in this chapter.

The question can properly be raised: "If concentration is so hard to define, and if those ratios which can be calculated are able to tell us very little about behavior, then why bother about the concept in the first place?" There are two possible answers to this assertion — one pragmatic, the other theoretical. On pragmatic grounds the data currently available on concentration ratios, although far from perfect, are all that we have on industrial structure. It is necessary to use those data which are available until something better comes along.

From a theoretical point of view concentration ratios may in fact indicate the types of interactions among firms which prevail in a market. In highly concentrated industries actions by one firm cannot be taken

---

[5] *See* G. Stigler, *Capital and Rates of Return in Manufacturing Industry* (Princeton, N.J.: Princeton University Press, 1963).

without regard to possible reactions by rivals. On the other hand, firms in less concentrated markets may regard possible reactions of other firms as being of secondary importance and may omit the consideration of these reactions in their decisions. Hence concentration ratios may be quite useful in indicating the proper method of analysis to be used in the study of any particular market. For example, an analysis of an automobile company's decisions to produce a small car might be very different from an analysis of a dress company's decision to produce a new line of low-cost dresses. In the former case we might want to consider feedback effects: The decision to produce a small car will undoubtedly cause the producer's rivals to adopt some competitive strategy (they, too, might enter the small-car field) which would affect the demand curve facing the firm. For the dress firm these feedback effects may be small. Because there are many small firms in the industry, there will not be a general reaction to the decisions of a single firm.[6]

[6] We can make this distinction in a mathematical way. Suppose there are two auto firms and n dress firms. Assume also that we can write the profits of one auto firm (π_A) as a function of its own output (q_1) and that of its rival as (q_2). Hence:

Profits $= \pi_A(q_1, q_2)$.

In deciding how much to produce, the firm will look at $d\pi_A/dq_1$. But in order to evaluate this derivative it must also consider feedback effects. Therefore:

$$\frac{d\pi_A}{dq_1} = \frac{\partial \pi_A}{\partial q_1} + \frac{\partial \pi_A}{\partial q_2} \cdot \frac{dq_2}{dq_1}$$

where $dq_2/dq_1 \neq 0$ because of other firms' reactions. Consequently, it would be incorrect to look only at $\partial \pi_A/\partial q_1$.

For the dress firm we may assume that the profits of the firm π_D depend on its own output (q_1) and on the outputs of the other $n - 1$ firms ($q_2,..., q_n$). Therefore:

Profits $= \pi_D(q_1, q_2,..., q_n)$.

Taking the derivative with respect to q_1 gives:

$$\frac{d\pi_D}{dq_1} = \frac{\partial \pi_D}{\partial q_1} + \frac{\partial \pi_D}{\partial q_2} \cdot \frac{dq_2}{dq_1} + ..., + \frac{\partial \pi_D}{\partial q_n} \cdot \frac{dq_n}{dq_1},$$

but if we assume there are no feedback effects (that $dq_i/dq_1 = 0$ for $i = 2,..., n$) then:

$$\frac{d\pi_A}{dq_1} = \frac{\partial \pi_A}{\partial q_1}$$

and the dress firm need only take its own actions into account.

For a numerical example of these types of feedback effects *see* Problem 8 of Part IV.

Other Choice Variables:
Product Differentiation and Advertising

Even if it is agreed that the sole goal of the firm is profit maximization, in imperfectly competitive markets there often are decision variables in addition to quantity which must be taken into consideration. Not only will the quantity produced determine profits for the firm but profits will also depend on how successful the firm is in differentiating its product from that of its competitors and on the extent to which advertising can affect the demand curve faced by the firm. Profit maximization is therefore a problem in maximizing a function of several variables. For example, suppose that both costs and revenues depend on output (q), the extent of product differentiation (d), and on advertising expenditures (A). Then profits will also depend on these three magnitudes:

$$\pi(q, d, A) = \text{Revenues} - \text{Costs}$$

$$= R(q, d, A) - C(q, d, A).$$

The first-order conditions for a maximum are:

$$\frac{\partial \pi}{\partial q} = \frac{\partial R}{\partial q} - \frac{\partial C}{\partial q} = 0$$

$$\frac{\partial \pi}{\partial d} = \frac{\partial E}{\partial d} - \frac{\partial C}{\partial d} = 0 \qquad [16.1]$$

$$\frac{\partial \pi}{\partial A} = \frac{\partial R}{\partial A} - \frac{\partial C}{\partial A} = 0.$$

This result, as would be expected, states that any activity (quantity, product differentiation, or advertising) should be expanded to the point where the marginal revenue from the activity is equal to the marginal cost of the activity. Because both product differentiation and advertising are carried on in most markets it would seem to be the case that each of these activities provides some positive increment to profits.[7]

As a more specific example of the sort of calculation a profit-maxi-

[7] In some cases advertising (and indeed product differentiation) may be, in reality, defensive strategies. One firm advertises only because others do. Not to advertise would be to lose out to competitors. Although it may be irrational for the industry as a whole to advertise (an effective ban on advertising might increase total profits), it is rational for each firm, acting individually, to advertise. This is one example in the theory of industrial organization for which the Prisoner's Dilemma (first discussed in Chapter 9) has some relevance. Further examples are mentioned in the section "More General Treatments of Strategy" below.

mizing firm might carry on, consider a monopoly for which quantity demanded depends on the market price (P) and level of advertising $(A$, measured in dollars):

$$Q = f(P, A). \qquad [16.2]$$

Then total revenues are given by:

$$P \cdot Q = P \cdot f(P, A). \qquad [16.3]$$

Suppose costs are given by:

$$\text{Costs} = C(Q) + A = C[f(P, A)] + A. \qquad [16.4]$$

Profits are therefore a function of market price and advertising expenditures:

$$\text{Profits} = \pi(P, A) = P \cdot f(P, A) - C[f(P, A)] - A. \qquad [16.5]$$

The firm will choose P and A to maximize profits (notice it is more convenient here to treat this monopoly as a price setter). The conditions for a maximum are:

$$\frac{\partial \pi}{\partial P} = P \frac{\partial Q}{\partial P} + Q - \frac{\partial C}{\partial Q} \cdot \frac{\partial Q}{\partial P} = 0$$

$$\frac{\partial \pi}{\partial A} = P \frac{\partial Q}{\partial A} - \frac{\partial C}{\partial Q} \cdot \frac{\partial Q}{\partial A} - 1 = 0. \qquad [16.6]$$

The first equation in 16.6 is simply the marginal revenue equals marginal cost rule stated with respect to price rather than quantity. By rewriting the second condition in Equation 16.6 as:

$$\left[P - \frac{\partial C}{\partial Q}\right] \frac{\partial Q}{\partial A} = (P - MC)\frac{\partial Q}{\partial A} = 1 \qquad [16.6']$$

it can be seen that profit maximization requires that an additional dollar be spent on advertising so long as the profits on the additional quantity prompted by this advertising exceed one dollar.

In a formal sense a similar analysis could be carried out for any other decision variable under the firm's control. Such analyses can only be considered to be of limited conceptual value, however. In concentrated markets the demand curve facing a firm is not so well known as these examples imply. Rather, interactions among firms create a vagueness on the part of any one firm in discovering the demand curve it faces. In addition, the recognition of advertising and product differentiation as widely used strategies creates an ambiguity about the definitions of a "market" and of "market demand." Some of the problems associated with this ambiguity were already discussed in Chapter 13.

Entry Conditions

One of the desirable features of the perfectly competitive model is that the assumption of costless entry assures that firms will produce at the low points of their long-run average cost curves. This observation is not merely an interesting theoretical result but considerations of ease of entry have become a fundamental aspect of antitrust law.[8] Courts often ask how a proposed merger will affect entry conditions in a market. If entry will remain relatively easy following the merger then the merger may be permitted with the supposition that potential entrants will keep the merged companies from exercising undesirable power. For this reason much research has centered on the identification and quantification of barriers to entry.

The barriers to entry which were mentioned in regard to monopoly in Chapter 15 apply with equal force here and will not be repeated. Additional entry barriers which might be discussed include those stemming from product differentiation, economies of scale, and pricing policies. The first of these is undoubtedly the most important.[9] Consumers faced with uncertainty rely heavily on brand identification to judge quality. It may be difficult for new firms to break through this attachment. The possibility of product differentiation is not always unfavorable to entry, however, and some firms have been very successful in gaining entry to a market by satisfying a demand not currently being met by those firms already in the market. Volkswagens and the variety of small electronic calculators currently available are prominent examples.

Economies of scale may be a significant barrier to entry. This is undoubtedly a factor limiting entry in such cases as the automobile and primary aluminum markets. In these industries the total market size permits only a few optimally sized plants. It is important, however, to be careful in assigning great importance to this barrier to entry. Often bar-

---

[8] The classic treatment of the entry issue is presented by J. S. Bain in *Barriers to New Competition* (Cambridge, Mass.: Harvard University Press, 1956).

[9] *See* Bain, *op. cit.,* p. 127. Bain estimates that a new product in a differentiated market may have to sell for 10–25 percent less than one already established in the market in order to win customer acceptance.

riers which appear to be related to economies of scale are in fact caused by an inability to differentiate one's product successfully from that of an existing firm, or by a high cost of capital to potential entrants. Recent diversification by "conglomerate" firms may indicate the failure of economies of scale to be an effective barrier to entry in many markets where this was previously thought to be the case.

A final possible barrier to entry which is frequently mentioned is that the firms already in a particular market may settle for less than maximum profits in order to discourage potential entrants. For example, firms may pursue maximum sales rather than profits in the short run in order to maintain control over a share of the market. In a similar vein firms may adopt a strategy of *limit pricing*: charging a price below that which would result in profit maximization in order to discourage entrants. Certainly limit pricing would seem to be a more successful method for discouraging entry than would be, say, engaging in wasteful business practices to keep profits low. The latter strategy would only encourage the entry of more efficient firms, whereas limit pricing combined with efficient operations may be a true barrier to entry.[10] Empirical research on limit pricing has served to clarify many issues in the theory of entry by new firms, but there is no hard evidence of the widespread use of this technique.

Pricing in Oligopoly Markets

Neither the Marshallian supply-demand analysis nor the simple monopoly model are strictly appropriate for analyzing pricing in markets characterized by a few firms. While these models may yield some insights (certainly demand and cost conditions have some relevance to pricing in any market), the absence of any notion of interaction among firms severely limits these models' predictive ability in the real world. Unfortunately, there are no generally applicable models of oligopoly pricing. Rather, several models have been proposed as explanations of certain aspects of observed oligopoly behavior, but none of these has won widespread acceptance. In this section only one such model will be investigated: the *kinked demand curve* model. Because this model has features common to many oligopoly pricing models it can be considered to be generally representative.

The kinked demand curve model was first developed by Sweezy[11] in 1939 to explain the fact that prices in oligopoly markets tended to be

---

[10] These comments point out that some strategies open to firms to prevent entry are not necessarily "bad."

[11] P. M. Sweezy, "Demand under Conditions of Oligopoly," *Journal of Political Economy*, vol. 47 (August 1939), pp. 568–573.

inflexible. It was asserted that changes in costs were only rarely met by changes in market prices and that, when changes in market price did occur in oligopoly markets, these changes tended to be of rather large magnitudes. Sweezy explained these observations by asking about the demand curve which is faced by a firm in an oligopoly market. He hypothesized that firms make their decisions in a cautious and pessimistic way. When contemplating lowering its price a firm believes all its rivals will follow. Hence demand is relatively inelastic for price decreases. If a firm were to try to raise its price in isolation Sweezy assumes that others would not follow. For price increases, therefore, the firm will find demand very elastic, since its customers will switch to competitors' products whose prices have not been raised. This kinked demand curve possibility is labeled D in Figure 16.1. The prevailing market price is P^* and the firm sells quantity q^*. Quantity sold would not be increased greatly by lowering price (since rivals are assumed to follow) but would be decreased markedly by attempting to raise price.

Figure 16.1   The Kinked Demand Curve

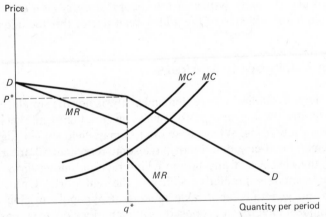

A firm in an oligopoly industry may believe it is faced by a demand curve (D) with a kink at the prevailing price (P^*). If the firm considers raising its price others would not follow and demand would appear to be very elastic since customers would shift to its competitors. Conversely, the firm may believe that if it lowered price all its competitors would do the same. Demand would be relatively inelastic below P^*. The kink at P^* means that the MR curve will be discontinuous at this point. Therefore firms may not respond to shifts in their marginal cost curves.

If the firm believes it is faced by a kinked demand curve it may not react to small changes in costs. This can be seen by examining the marginal revenue curve associated with the kinked demand curve. The MR curve is drawn in Figure 16.1. Notice that it is discontinuous at q^*, reflecting the kinked nature of the assumed demand curve. Suppose marginal cost were initially MC and that cost increases have shifted this curve to MC'. With this new marginal cost curve there will be no incentive to change either price or quantity because marginal revenue is still "equal to" marginal costs and profits are being maximized. Hence prices will tend to remain fixed until some unifying event can get all firms to raise prices in concert.

This view of oligopoly pricing tends to accord with many real-world observations. For example, in some markets *price leadership* is a prevalent phenomenon. In such markets one firm or group of firms is looked upon as the leader in pricing and all firms will adjust prices when the leader does. These general price changes are relatively infrequent, but are generally of substantial magnitude. The price leadership technique can then be seen as a way of creating market discipline and as a way of providing a signal to firms (which believe they are faced by a kinked demand curve) when the "right" time to raise prices has arrived. Two examples of price leadership are the steel industry (where United States Steel or Bethlehem play the role of a leader) and the commercial banking industry (where the prime rate tends to be determined by the major New York City banks). In both of these industries cost changes are not manifested by price changes until the leaders decide to move.

There is one major theoretical weakness of the kinked demand curve model: The model gives no real guidance about where prices will settle if they are disturbed from the "kink." Similarly, if price changes are assumed to be initiated by a leader, it is not clear how a leader is chosen nor why other firms may not initiate price increases if the leader has been successful in the past. The theory must at least be made more complete if it is to represent a general theory of oligopoly pricing.

Empirically, a closer examination of oligopoly pricing behavior reveals a surprising lack of rigidity. For example, while the banking "prime rate" may change only occasionally, other conditions associated with borrowing (the riskiness of those loans granted, the balance a borrower must hold with the bank, and so on) tend to be far more flexible in responding to changing cost conditions. In manufacturing industries rigidity of list prices is by no means indicative of actual market prices. There is considerable evidence[12] that various forms of discounts from list prices vary greatly in response to supply and demand conditions in the market.

From this discussion it should be clear that any theory which attempts to explain pricing in oligopoly markets must be a hybrid of simpler economic theories. As always, a reasonable place to start is with a careful analysis of market demand and cost conditions. The specific content of any theory will then be determined by the particular institutional setting under investigation.

[12] *See* G. J. Stigler and J. K. Kindahl, *The Behavior of Industrial Prices* (New York: National Bureau of Economic Research, distributed by Columbia University Press, 1970).

More General Treatments of Strategy

Currently existing theories of oligopoly behavior must be regarded as unsatisfactory. Some economists[13] believe that this area will be a most fertile one for new and interesting investigations. Simple price theory models may be overshadowed in these investigations by the use of the tools of game theory. In many ways oligopoly behavior provided the impetus for the development of game theory, and it is possible that the next few years will see this theory providing rich analytic insights.

N-person game theory is particularly suited to the study of oligopoly. Generally there are N players (firms) in the game and each has a number of strategies available. The game is played by each person choosing a strategy; the outcome (profits) received by each player will depend on the set of strategies chosen. The most interesting possibility in the play of N-person games is that *coalitions* may develop among the players. The players in a particular coalition may synchronize their strategies so as to yield a more favorable outcome than if they approached the game individually. For example, the largest coalition possible in an oligopoly market would be for all the firms to synchronize their policies to act as a multiplant monopoly (*see* Problem 7 of Part IV). This would assure the firms as a group of the maximum profits possible for a given market demand. One problem which arises is how to split up the profits which accrue to a coalition. Clearly some firms will have to be bribed to restrict output in the interest of overall profit maximization. In the language of game theory *side payments* must be made to assure the success of a coalition.

The formation of coalitions in the real world faces two obstacles. First, some coalitions are not legal (are outlawed by the "rules of the game"). The Sherman Anti-trust Act at least makes the formation of coalitions more difficult. Even in the absence of legal restrictions, however, the establishment and maintenance of an effective coalition can be very difficult. There will often be a temptation for a member of a coalition to "cheat" on his partners and this may cause coalitions to break down. In the case of oligopoly theory this is especially true because it is very difficult to impose sanctions on a firm which violates the strategy decided upon by the coalition.

One particularly interesting aspect of oligopoly behavior which is illustrated by the game theory approach is that oligopoly "games" are generally *not zero-sum*. The total level of profits which an industry can receive is not fixed but will depend on the particular strategies chosen and the particular coalitions which are established. A perfectly coordinated strategy can achieve that level of profits which a monopoly could earn,

---

[13] *See* M. Shubik, "A Curmudgeon's Guide to Microeconomics," *Journal of Economic Literature,* vol. VIII (June 1970), pp. 405–434.

whereas, if each firm is on its own as in the perfectly competitive model, long-run industry profits may be 0. Because coalitions are difficult to enforce industry profits may turn out to be considerably lower than they would be with perfect coordination. For example, consider the United States agricultural industry. A monopoly (or an all-inclusive coalition) in this industry could undoubtedly earn large profits, but most attempts at enforcing discipline in this industry have resulted in failure. It is just too attractive for the individual farmer to plant more acreage or sell more milk. What is individually rational to the farmer proves to be irrational from the point of view of the profits of the industry as a whole.

This case is one example of the paradox of the Prisoner's Dilemma (*see* Chapter 9) which occurs in the theory of oligopoly. Each firm's profits depend on the actions of its competitors, but no firm can be certain what its competitors will do. Firms may, therefore, adopt strategies which do not maximize industry profits.

Other instances of this type of problem are not hard to find. For example, consider the major automobile companies' decisions to produce a small car. This may result in lower profits for the industry as a whole even though, given that its rivals are also building a small car, any one of the auto companies has no other choice.[14] Similar examples are provided by the supermarket industry's move toward "discount pricing," the growing popularity of "free" checking accounts, and the showing of motion pictures and serving of "gourmet" meals on airline flights. As these examples show, while difficulty in enforcing discipline may be detrimental to the total profits of the industry in question, it may, in a broader sense, represent desirable forces of competition.

Conclusion

In contrast to the concise analysis of other chapters in this book, the present one must seem depressingly vague. The real world of industrial structure does not conform to any textbook example. If the reader carries away from this chapter the message that there are no easy answers to hard policy problems then the chapter will have served its purpose.

This conclusion does not imply that simple models have no usefulness, however. Without such models all analysis would be merely descriptive. By using economic models it is possible to isolate the important issues to be investigated. Such a simple idea as the Marshallian supply-demand cross provides a logical starting place for the analysis of far more complex questions. Only by understanding both the strengths and the limitations of basic economic models can one hope to comprehend these more realistic cases.

[14] The presence of the import market for small cars complicates this analysis to some extent.

DISCUSSION QUESTIONS AND PROBLEMS FOR PART IV

Discussion Questions

1. It might be argued that the only useful chapter in this part is Chapter 16 and that it is only valuable when it departs from the perfect competition-monopoly dichotomy. The study of markets as classified by number of firms is not only overly simplistic but can be analytically misleading. Discuss the benefits and costs of studying such polar cases.

2. In the market period price acts as a device to ration a fixed supply. One method of arriving at this equilibrium price is by means of an auction, in fact, there are many different auction systems in use. The three most important of these are the English (ascending bid) system, the Dutch (descending price) system, and the Japanese (simultaneous bid) system. What are the relative merits of each of these systems and which one most closely approximates the theoretical concepts of supply-demand analysis?

3. Demand curves and supply curves are never absolutely fixed for a period of time. Rather, they are constantly shifting in response to changing tastes and technologies. Use this observation to discuss the notion of a "teacher shortage" which was widely publicized in the early 1960's (although more recently "teacher glut" might be a better term) and to analyze the United States housing "shortage." How would you interpret the concept of shortage in the usual static framework?

4. A common empirical problem is to estimate the demand curve for a good from data on its price and quantity. Since price and quantity are in fact jointly determined by the interaction of supply and demand; obtaining an unambiguous estimation of a demand curve from such data is very difficult. In order to be certain that the price-quantity combinations which were observed do represent a demand curve one must assume either that the demand curve is fixed and has no random component; or, since the first condition is quite unlikely, that the supply curve, during the period of observation, shifted around "a lot" relative to the demand curve. Use a simple supply-and-demand diagram to discuss these aspects of the "identification problem."

5. Can you evaluate the desirability of government-created monopolies? Do the benefits which are claimed to result from these protected positions outweigh the costs of the static inefficiency of monopoly?

6. What problems are there in proposing a definition of the "concentra-

tion" of an industry? Even if an unambiguous definition could be formulated, of what use would it be?

7. Use the analysis developed in this part to explain the following pricing behavior:

    (a)   Doctors charge poor patients less for identical services than they charge rich patients.

    (b)   Banks announce a widely publicized "prime rate" and change it only occasionally.

    (c)   Blacks pay more than whites for identical houses.

    (d)   Insurance companies continue to solicit automobile insurance business in spite of their plea that "we lose money on every policy we write."

    (e)   Seats on the New York Stock Exchange are very expensive. They also fluctuate greatly in price.

    (f)   A certain brand of beer used to be sold in cans and returnable bottles (with a deposit required). It was less expensive to buy beer in bottles and throw them away than to buy the beer in cans.

Problems

1. Suppose there are one hundred identical firms in a perfectly competitive industry. Each firm has a short-run total cost curve of the form:

$$C = 0.0033Q^3 + 0.2Q^2 + 4Q + 10.$$

    (a)   Calculate the firm's short-run supply curve with Q as a function of market price (P).

    (b)   On the assumption that there are no interaction effects between costs of the firms in the industry calculate the industry supply curve.

    (c)   Suppose market demand is given by $Q = -200P + 8000$. What will be the short-run equilibrium price-quantity combination?

2. A perfectly competitive market has one thousand firms. In the very short run each of the firms has a fixed supply of one hundred units. The market demand is given by:

$$Q = 160,000 - 10,000P.$$

    (a)   Calculate the equilibrium price in the very short run.

(b) Calculate the demand schedule facing any one firm in this industry.

(c) Calculate what the equilibrium price would be if one of the sellers decided to sell nothing or if one seller decided to sell two hundred units.

(d) At the original equilibrium point calculate the elasticity of the industry demand curve and the elasticity of the demand curve facing any one seller.

Suppose now that in the short run each firm has a supply curve which shows the quantity the firm will supply (q_i) as a function of market price. The specific form of this supply curve is given by:

$$q_i = -200 + 50P.$$

Using this short-run supply response answer questions (a)-(d) above.

3. A perfectly competitive industry has a large number of potential entrants. Each firm has an identical cost structure such that long-run average cost is minimized at an output of twenty units $(q_i = 20)$. The minimum average cost is $10 per unit. Total market demand is given by:

$$Q = 1500 - 50P.$$

(a) What is the industry's long-run supply schedule?

(b) What is the long-run equilibrium price (P^*), the total industry output (Q^*), the output of each firm (q_i^*), the number of firms, and the profits of each firm?

(c) The short-run total cost curve associated with each firm's long-run equilibrium output is given by:

$$C = .5q^2 - 10q + 200.$$

Calculate the short-run average and marginal cost curves. At what output level does short-run average cost reach a minimum?

(d) Calculate the short-run supply curve for each firm and the industry short-run supply curve.

(e) Suppose now that the market demand function shifts upward to $Q = 2,000 - 50P$. Using this new demand curve, answer Question (b) for the very short run when firms cannot change their outputs.

(f) In the short run use the industry short-run supply curve to recalculate the answers to (b).

(g) What is the new long-run equilibrium for the industry?

4. Suppose the market demand for a particular product is given by:

$$Q_D = -2P + 13$$

and the industry supply curve by:

$$Q_S = 2P^2 - 12P + 21.$$

What are the equilibrium prices for this market? Which of these prices is stable by the Walrasian criterion?

5. Consider a monopoly market in which the market demand curve has shifted outward. Would you expect both quantity and price to increase in this situation (as would be the case in the "normal" supply-demand analysis) or is the final result indeterminate?

   Use similar reasoning to discuss the effect of a specifix tax on the firm in a monopoly market.

6. Suppose a monopoly market has a demand function in which quantity demanded depends not only on market price (P) but also on the amount of advertising the firm does (A, measured in dollars). The specific form of this function is:

$$Q = (20 - P)(1 + .1A - .01A^2).$$

The monopoly firm's cost function is given by:

$$C = 10Q + 15 + A.$$

   (a) Suppose there is no advertising ($A = 0$), what output will the profit-maximizing firm choose? What market price will this yield? What will be the monopoly's profits?
   (b) Now let the firm also choose its optimal level of advertising expenditure. In this situation what output level will be chosen? What price will this yield? What will the level of advertising be? What are the firm's profits in this case?

   (*Hint:* Question (b) can be worked out most easily by assuming the monopoly chooses the profit-maximizing price rather than quantity.)

7. Suppose a monopoly produced its output in several different plants and that these plants have differing cost structures. How should the firm decide how much total output to produce? How should it distribute this output among its plants in order to maximize profits?

8. A monopolist can produce at constant average (and marginal) costs of $AC = MC = 5$. The firm faces a market demand curve given by: $Q = 53 - P$.

    (a) Calculate the profit-maximizing price-quantity combination for this monopolist. Also calculate the monopolist's profits.

    (b) Suppose a second firm enters the market. Let q_1 be the output of the first firm and q_2 the output of the second. Market demand is now given by:

$$q_1 + q_2 = 53 - P.$$

On the assumption that this second firm has the same costs as the first, calculate the profits of firms 1 and 2 as functions of q_1 and q_2.

    (c) Suppose (after Cournot) that each of these two firms chooses its level of output so as to maximize profits on the assumption that the other's output is fixed. Calculate each firm's "reaction function" which expresses desired output of one firm as a function of the other's output.

    (d) On the assumption in Question (c) what is the only level for q_1 and q_2 with which both firms will be satisfied (what q_1, q_2 combination satisfies both reaction curves)?

    (e) With q_1 and q_2 at the equilibrium level specified in Question (d) what will be the market price, the profits for each firm, and the total profits earned?

    (f) Suppose now that there are n firms in the industry. If each firm adopts the Cournot strategy toward all its rivals, what will be the profit-maximizing output level for each firm? What will the market price be? What will the total profits earned in the industry be? (All these will depend on n.)

    (g) Show that when n approaches infinity, the output levels, market price, and profits approach those which would "prevail" in perfect competition.

9. Consider an industry in which a large number of firms produce a slightly differentiated product. Each firm has the same total cost schedule of the form:

$$c_i = 9 + 4q_i.$$

Each firm also faces a demand curve for its product of the form:

$$q_i = -.01(n - 1)p_i + .01 \sum_{j \neq i} p_j + \frac{303}{n}$$

where the p_j are the prices charged by other firms and n is the number of firms in the industry. In equilibrium for this industry all prices must be equal ($p_i = p_j$ for all i and j).

(a) What is the equilibrium output for each firm and the total output? (Your answer will depend on n.)

(b) What are the profits of the ith firm as a function of p_i, p_j, and n?

(c) If the firm maximizes its profits on the assumption that p_j and n are constant, how will the optimal p_i depend on p_j and n?

(d) Since, in equilibrium, $p_i = p_j$ for all j, show how these equilibrium values depend on n.

(e) In the long run (assume long-run and short-run costs are the same) the number of firms will adjust so that every firm will earn 0 economic profits. What is this equilibrium number of firms?

(f) With this long-run equilibrium number of firms what will p_i and q_i be?

(g) At the long-run equilibrium, graph:

(i)   The demand curve facing a firm
(ii) The associated marginal revenue curve
(iii) The average cost curve for this firm
(iv) The marginal cost curve for this firm.

[*Note:* This problem is an example of the analysis presented by E. Chamberlin in *The Theory of Monopolistic Competition (op. cit.).*]

PART V
Pricing in the Factor Market

Introduction

Factors of production also have prices. Labor services are purchased for a wage rate per man hour, machines have rental rates, and one must pay something for the use of land. In this part we will investigate how these prices are determined. As a starting point it might be assumed that these prices (as is the case for the prices of goods) are established by the forces of supply and demand. Individuals supply labor services and these services are demanded by firms. Owners of capital and land are similarly willing to rent these resources to a firm for a price. In some way, then, prices are determined by the operation of the market.

The supply-demand analysis of factor pricing in perfectly competitive markets is examined in some detail in Chapter 17. There are several aspects of this analysis which differ from the supply-demand analysis used for the goods market, and these differences are stressed. Particularly important in this regard are the observations that: factor demands are *derived demands* (the demand depends indirectly on the demand for the good which the factor produces); and that the concept of *economic rent* plays an important role in the theoretical development. In Chapter 17 the *marginal productivity theory* of factor pricing is discussed, and several applications of this theory are developed.

The two major factors of production, labor and capital, are treated in Chapters 18 and 19 respectively. Chapter 18 examines the labor market and centers attention on the possibility of imperfect competition in this market. Although it is conceivable for any factor market to be imperfectly competitive, some of the most important cases occur in the labor market. For example, unions may make the labor market depart from the assumptions of perfect competition on the supply side. On the other hand, "one-company towns" and other situations where there are only a few demanders of labor may make the market noncompetitive on the demand side. This latter possibility raises the issue of labor "exploitation," and this term is discussed systematically in Chapter 18. Finally, a particularly interesting aspect of labor markets is that they may be imperfectly competitive on both sides. Negotiations between large companies and large unions have become common-place, and the strict perfectly competitive model is inappropriate for studying such confrontations. Chapter 18 therefore concludes with a brief examination of bargaining.

One of the most important and most difficult areas of economic analysis is capital theory. Chapter 19 isolates some of the strands of modern capital theory for a brief investigation. An attempt is made to answer two very basic questions: What is capital? How is its price determined? The chapter answers these questions by stressing the close interconnection between "time" and "capital."

The theory presented in the three chapters of this part is not as widely accepted by economists as are the theories of pricing in the goods market which were examined in Part IV. Although the analyses appear in many ways to be formally identical, far more objections have been raised about the application of supply-demand analysis to factor markets. Since this has been particularly true of the capital market the appendix to Chapter 19 investigates these objections. Many of the observations of this appendix are equally valid for the labor market.

In *The Principles of Political Economy and Taxation* David Ricardo wrote:

> The produce of the earth ... is divided among three classes of the community, namely, the proprietor of the land, the owner of the stock of capital necessary for its cultivation, and the laborers by whose industry it is cultivated. To determine the laws which regulate this distribution is the principal problem in Political Economy.[1]

The study of this pricing of factors and of the associated distribution of income between factors of production is the purpose of Part V. Hopefully, the analysis to be presented will raise many issues in a form which permits the reader to carry forward a discussion of this question on his own.

---

[1] David Ricardo, *The Principles of Political Economy and Taxation* (London: J. M. Dent and Son, 1817, last reprinted 1965), p. 1.

CHAPTER 17

Pricing in Perfectly Competitive Factor Markets

Introduction: Supply and Demand in Factor Markets

A reasonable place to start a discussion of pricing in factor markets is to assume that prices are established by the interaction of supply and demand. Figure 17.1 depicts this Marshallian concept. The factor supply curve (labeled S) is drawn positively sloped on the assumption that higher factor rewards (v) will induce suppliers to offer more factor services (F) in the market place. Similarly the demand curve for the factor is drawn with a negative slope on the assumption that demanders (principally firms) will hire a smaller quantity of the factor at higher levels of v.

The price v^* is therefore an equilibrium price at which the total quantity of factor services supplied is exactly equal to that quantity which is demanded. At a price above v^* supply would exceed demand and there would be "unemployment"; for a price below v^* there would be excess demand for the factor.

Figure 17.1   Supply and Demand in the Factor Market

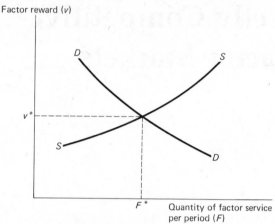

By analogy to the theory of pricing in the goods market the supply and demand curves for a productive factor (F) have been drawn. It has been assumed that the quantity of the factor service supplied is an increasing function of the factor payment (v) and that the quantity demanded is a decreasing function of v. The factor reward v^* is an equilibrium price, since at this price the quantity supplied is equal to the quantity demanded.

The curves in Figure 17.1 are rather casually drawn. As was the case in the examination of pricing in the goods market the most interesting aspects of the analysis arise when we inquire into the more basic determinants of the shape of these curves. In this chapter we will be primarily interested in the demand side of the market, therefore initially it might be useful to discuss the supply assumptions which will be made here. Basically it will be assumed that there are a large number of suppliers of the resource in question. Any single supplier cannot affect the price to be received and therefore he will treat factor price as a fixed parameter in his decisions. The market supply curve can assume a wide variety of possible shapes. For example, the supply curve for land might be assumed to be very inelastic, whereas the supply of certain other factors may be very elastic.[1] It is at least a theoretical possibility that the supply curve for a factor may be negatively sloped. This possibility was mentioned in

---

[1] Although this section is rather vague in defining exactly what a "factor of production" is, the analysis is intended to apply to major aggregates such as land, labor, and capital. It might be thought that a similar analysis could be used for more refined categories such as

Chapter 7, where it was shown that at high wage rates the income effect of still higher wage rates may outweigh the substitution effect and an individual may choose to work shorter hours. For the market as a whole, however, the likelihood of this happening can be considered remote. It is more likely that a higher v will induce an increase in the total quantity of F offered in the market. Whatever the shape of the market supply curve this curve will be assumed to be the horizontal sum of numerous individual curves, and the curve will be assumed to be fixed during the analysis of factor pricing which is presented in this chapter.

The demand for a factor of production is a *derived demand:* It is related to the demand for the product which the factor is used to produce. Firms do not demand labor, capital, or land simply to have these factors around. Rather, the factor rewards a firm is willing to pay are determined by how productive the factor is. If factor markets are reasonably competitive, firms will bid against each other for factors until that firm which can most productively use a particular factor eventually wins out. In order to investigate the shape of the market demand curve for a factor, therefore, it is first necessary to analyze the individual firm's decisions. Although we will examine this question in detail in the section "The Marginal Productivity Theory of Factor Demand" below, it is possible to indicate here briefly why a firm might demand more of F when its price falls. A fall in the price of F will cause the firm to substitute F for other inputs in the production of its original output level. At a constant output, therefore, there will be a *substitution effect* tending to increase the quantity of F hired. But this is not the end of the story. A lower price for F will also change the firm's cost curves and will consequently affect its output decisions. One plausible scenario would be that a fall in the cost of F would shift both the total and marginal cost curves downward. Possibly this decrease in marginal cost would cause the profit-maximizing level of output to increase from its original level. This would in turn create an *output effect* prompting the purchase of even more F with which to produce the additional output. Consequently, there is a second reason to expect that a single firm's demand for F would be negatively sloped.[2] A horizontal summation of these demand curves would yield a negatively

---

"unskilled labor," "risk capital," or "farm land." Indeed, we might be willing to disaggregate even further and talk about the supply and demand for plumbers or teachers. There would be nothing intrinsically wrong with this procedure; in fact such analyses are frequently undertaken. The concept of supply in these disaggregated studies is rather ambiguous, however. For example, while the analysis of Chapter 7 indicates how a model of individual labor supply might be developed, no such well-defined analysis for the labor supplied to particular occupations has as yet been developed. In developing such an analysis it would certainly be necessary to take account of an individual's education and training which may channel him into one [or a few] well-defined occupational category.

[2] It should be emphasized that this is only one possible story. A more complete analysis is presented below.

sloped market demand curve in much the same way that the individual demand curves for a good can be summed to generate a market demand curve. The shapes of the demand and supply curves in Figure 17.1 therefore seem reasonable on the basis of a priori arguments.

Economic Rent and Ricardian Rent

The *economic rent* earned by any factor is defined to be that portion of total payments to the factor which is in excess of what is needed to keep the factor in its current occupation. The *economic profit* of an entrepreneur (*see* Chapter 12) is one example of this concept. In Figure 17.2 the concept is illustrated as a general case. Since the supply curve records that amount of factor service which would be supplied at each price, the total dollar amount which is necessary to retain the level F^* in this occupation is given by the area SOF^*E. Total factor payments are given by the area v^*OF^*E. The economic rent of this factor is represented by the shaded area v^*SE. Because the equilibrium factor price is determined by the "marginal supplier," other suppliers, in the aggregate, receive a surplus benefit of this amount.[3] If a firm could act as a perfectly discriminating buyer it could avoid paying v^*SE by offering each individual supplier only what was necessary to lure him into the market.

It is easy to see that the more elastic the supply curve for a factor is, the smaller the area which represents economic rent is. If a supply curve were infinitely elastic (a horizontal line at the prevailing price) there would in fact be no economic rent. At the other extreme, all of the return to a factor which is in fixed supply is in the nature of an economic rent.[4] The factor payments in such a situation are determined solely by demand, and there is no notion of sacrifice on the part of the supplier of this fixed factor. It will always be supplied no matter what factor reward is offered. Any return which is received is a result of the "accident" of where the demand curve happens to be.

The most commonly encountered example of this analysis of economic rent is in the case of a fixed land supply. This situation is represented in Figure 17.3 by the vertical supply curve at the existing level of

---

[3] This analysis is very similar to that presented in Chapter 15 when the notion of consumer's surplus was discussed. Any such concepts are subject to numerous theoretical strictures and must be regarded as approximations of theoretically correct magnitudes at best.

[4] Some authors make a distinction between short-run and long-run rents. In the short run, when supply curves tend to be more inelastic, rent is referred to as "quasi-rent" to indicate that it may disappear when long-run supply response is permitted. The profits of perfectly competitive firms in the short run would be one example of quasi-rent.

Figure 17.2   Economic Rent

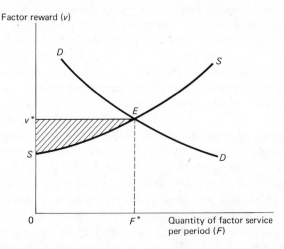

The shaded area represents total factor payments which exceed those necessary to keep F^* in its present employment. This quantity is the difference between total factor payments (v^*OF^*E) and those payments a perfectly discriminating hirer might pay (SOF^*E).

Figure 17.3   All the Returns to a Fixed Supply of Land Are Economic Rent

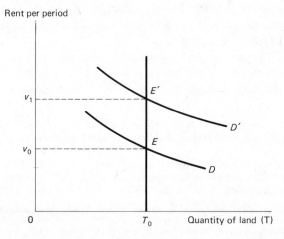

With land in absolutely fixed supply (at T_0) the rental rate will be determined solely by demand conditions. A lump-sum tax on land owners would not affect the quantity of land supplied.

land (T_0). No matter what the level of demand is, this supply will be fixed. If demand were given by curve D the rental rate on the land will be v_0 and the total return to the owner of the land will be v_0OT_0E. If, on the other hand, demand were given by the curve D', the equilibrium rental rate would be v_1 and total rentals would be v_1OT_0E'. It is clear that the increase in demand from D to D' has no effect other than to enrich the land owner. The nineteenth-century American economist Henry George[5] noted this fact and proposed that those rents accruing to such fortunate land owners be taxed at a very high level, since this taxation would have no effect on the quantity of land provided. While there are numerous complications in this proposal,[6] George's idea of a single tax on land still has many adherents, particularly in the British Labour Party.

A somewhat more comprehensive explanation of the determinants of land rent had been provided earlier by David Ricardo, who recognized that the rent on land was derived from the demand for the produce of the land and that rents on land varied according to the quality of the land. By recognizing that land was not a homogeneous factor Ricardo both added a degree of realism to the discussion of the determinants of rent and made the analysis more complex, since the simple supply and demand models of Figures 17.2 and 17.3 are no longer appropriate when the factor is not of uniform quality. Ricardo theorized that additional land (of inferior quality) would be cultivated up to the point at which the last acre planted earned exactly 0 in economic profits. The more productive parcels of land would earn high economic profits (or rent), and these profits could be considered a return for their superior fertility. Since price is determined by the costs of the marginal producer, and since at the margin rents are 0, Ricardo had demonstrated that rent was not a determinant of price but should more properly be considered as resulting from demand and fertility conditions.

Ricardo's argument can be most readily demonstrated using a graphic analysis. Assume there are many parcels of land suitable for growing wheat. These parcels range from very fertile (low costs of production)

---

[5] *See* Henry George, *Progress and Poverty: An Inquiry into the Cause of Industrial Depressions and of Increase of Want with Increase of Wealth* (New York: Henry George, 1881).

[6] For example, consider the problem of separating that portion of the income from a New York City office building which represents land rent (pure economic rent) from that portion which represents rent on the physical structure (in large part not pure economic rent). If the rent on land were heavily taxed, there would be an added incentive to own buildings and land together and to attempt to hide the true value of land rent.

It might also be questioned why land is singled out as a target for taxation of its economic rent. Surely the payments which Elizabeth Taylor receives for a movie or which Joe Frazier or Muhammad Ali received for their championship fight are also primarily economic rent.

to rather poor quality (high cost). The long-run supply curve for wheat can be constructed as follows: At low prices only the best land is cultivated; as price rises, production continues on the fertile land and additional crops are planted on land of poorer quality. At still higher prices it will be profitable to utilize lower quality land in production. The market equilibrium is pictured in the four panels of Figure 17.4. At the equilibrium price P^* owners of low-cost land parcels earn large economic profits (rent); those less favorably situated earn smaller rents; the marginal farm earns 0 in rents. If it were possible to earn any rents on additional pieces of land these would be brought into cultivation. Those acres which are left unplanted must be of lower quality than those of the marginal farm. Notice that the equilibrium described in Figure 17.4 is stable in the long run. It is impossible for new entrants to earn a profit even though those farms already in the market, by virtue of controlling the best land, are able to do so. This analysis shows how the demand for land is a demand derived from the product market; this notion permits the previous discussion of homogeneous land (Figure 17.3) to be generalized. It might be argued that the rents earned by low-cost farmers should be accounted as implicit costs since this is what someone else would pay for the right to farm the land. Hence all farms in reality have the same cost curves: Those of low-cost producers have a large element of implicit rental cost. This is a purely semantic distinction and would not change the analysis of the way in which superior fertility determines rent.

Figure 17.4 The Creation of Ricardian Rent on Land of Differing Fertility

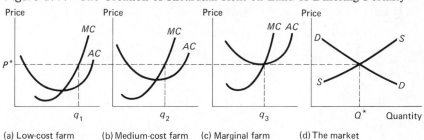

(a) Low-cost farm   (b) Medium-cost farm   (c) Marginal farm   (d) The market

Because land differs in quality, farms with the most fertile land will have lower costs. Since price will be determined by the costs of the marginal supplier low-cost firms will earn pure economic profits. These profits might be called rent and will persist even in the long run since fertile land is in fixed supply.

Ricardo's observation about rent not being a determinant of price is easily seen in Figure 17.4. It is the fact that land differs in quality and that land of high quality is in fixed supply which creates the conditions making rent possible. The location of the demand curve will determine exactly how much will be earned in total rents.[7] However, the shape of the supply curve is determined by the technical relationship between the farms' cost curves. Rent does not affect the location of the supply-demand intersection.

The Marginal Productivity Theory of Factor Demand

Ricardian rent theory was an important predecessor of the development of "marginalist" economics. Ricardo's hypothesis that price is determined by the costs of the marginal producer in many ways represents the seed from which modern price theory grew. One major generalization of this hypothesis took place in the development of the marginal productivity theory of factor demand. Since this is in many respects *the* theory of factor pricing the rest of this chapter will investigate it in detail.

The basic concept of the marginal productivity theory of factor demand has already been stated in Chapter 10 when profit maximization was discussed. There it was shown that a firm will hire any factor up to the point at which the extra revenue to be obtained from hiring one more unit of that factor is equal to the cost of hiring that unit. If we are willing to assume that perfect competition holds in all markets we can be somewhat more precise about what this statement means. In particular, assume a firm uses only labor (L) to produce some output $[Q = f(L)]$. Assume also that this output is sold in a perfectly competitive market at price P and that the firm can hire all the labor it wants at the prevailing wage rate (w). Given these assumptions, profits (π) are a function of L given by:

$$\pi = P \cdot Q - wL = P \cdot f(L) - wL. \qquad [17.1]$$

To maximize profits the firm should choose L such that $d\pi/dL = 0$. Consequently:

$$\frac{d\pi}{dL} = P \cdot \frac{df(L)}{dL} - w = 0$$

or

$$P \cdot MP_L - w = 0 \qquad [17.2]$$

or

$$P \cdot MP_L = w$$

---

[7] This analysis of Ricardian rent can be applied to a number of important situations in which rent is generated. For example, consider the urban housing market in which high rents are generated on favorably located land (*see* also Discussion Question 2 of Part V).

where $MP_L = df(L)/dL$ is the marginal product of labor. Notice that in the derivation of Equation 17.2 we have treated P and w as constants since we have assumed them to be "given" by perfectly competitive markets. What Equation 17.2 says is that labor should be hired up to the point at which the value of its marginal product ($P \cdot MP_L$) is equal to its cost (w). An extra unit of labor produces some extra output (MP_L), and what this output can be sold for ($P \cdot MP_L$) should be set equal to the wage rate. Since all other firms will make similar decisions we might say that w is determined by the value of labor's marginal productivity. Sometimes the term $P \cdot MP_L$ is called the *marginal value product* of labor.

An identical analysis of factor demand would result if there were more than one productive input. In fact, the mathematics of such an analysis have already been presented in Chapter 10. Here, however, we will adopt a slightly different derivation, which will permit further insights into a firm's input choices. Suppose that there are two inputs (the familiar capital and labor) which go into producing output $[Q = f(K, L)]$ and that Q, K, and L are all traded in perfectly competitive markets at prices P, v, and w respectively. We have seen that the firm has two different types of choices to make. First, it must choose K and L so that any output is produced at minimal cost and; second, it must choose the profit-maximizing level of output. We have already discussed the mathematics of cost minimization in some detail in Chapter 12. There (in Equation 12.2) we showed that the firm should choose L and K so that:

$$w - \lambda f_L = w - \lambda MP_L = 0$$

$$v - \lambda fK = v - \lambda MP_K = 0$$

where λ was the Lagrangian Multiplier for the minimization procedure. We also showed that λ can be given an interpretation as the marginal cost (MC) of producing one more unit. Consequently, we can rewrite the necessary conditions for cost minimization as:

$$w - MC \cdot MP_L = 0$$
$$v - MC \cdot MP_K = 0. \qquad [17.3]$$

But now we must take into consideration the firm's profit-maximizing output decision which requires that output be chosen so that $P = MC$. To arrive at both minimizing costs and maximizing profits therefore, the firm should choose L and K such that:

$$w - P \cdot MP_L = 0$$
$$v - P \cdot MP_K = 0. \qquad [17.4]$$

This is exactly the condition derived in Equation 17.2. A firm should hire any input up to the point at which the value of its marginal product is equal to its cost. The relatively tedious derivation of Equation 17.4 clearly shows the derived nature of input demand and illustrates the way in which output and input decisions are interrelated.

Given this analysis we can return to a question raised in the first section of this chapter: How will a firm react to a change in the price of an input? Specifically we will look at the demand for labor (the analysis for capital would be identical) and ask about the sign of $\partial L/\partial w$. We have indicated previously that it is likely this derivative will be negative (a decrease in w will cause more labor to be hired), but now we are in a position to give a more detailed treatment.

One reason for expecting $\partial L/\partial w$ to be negative is based on the presumption that the marginal physical product of labor declines as the quantity of labor employed increases. A decrease in w means that more labor must be hired to bring about the equality $w = P \cdot MP_L$: A fall in w must be met by a fall in MP_L (since P is fixed), and this can be brought about by increasing L. That this argument is strictly correct for the case of one input can be shown as follows. Write the total differential of the necessary condition Equation 17.2 as:

$$dw = P \cdot \frac{\partial MP_L}{\partial L} \cdot \frac{\partial L}{\partial w} \cdot dw$$

or

$$1 = P \cdot \frac{\partial MP_L}{\partial L} \cdot \frac{\partial L}{\partial w} \qquad [17.5]$$

or

$$\frac{\partial L}{\partial w} = \frac{1}{P \cdot \frac{\partial MP_L}{\partial L}}.$$

If we assume that $\partial MP_L/\partial L < 0$ (that is, that MP_L decreases as L increases) we have:

$$\frac{\partial L}{\partial w} < 0. \qquad [17.6]$$

A *ceteris paribus* fall in w will cause more labor to be hired (and, parenthetically, also will cause more output to be produced).

For the case of two (or more) inputs the story is considerably more complex. The assumption of a diminishing marginal physical product of labor can be misleading here. If w falls, there will not only be a change in L but also a change in K as a new cost-minimizing combination of inputs is chosen. When K changes, the entire MP_L function changes (labor now has a different amount of capital to work with), and an argument such as that used above cannot be made. In the remainder of this section a combination of graphic and pseudomathematical techniques will be used to suggest why, even in the two-factor case, $\partial L/\partial w$ must be negative.

Figure 17.5 The Substitution and Output Effects of a Decrease in the Price of a Factor

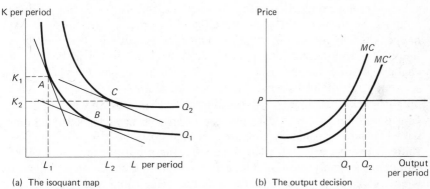

(a) The isoquant map   (b) The output decision

When the price of labor falls, two analytically different effects come into play. One of these, the substitution effect, would cause more labor to be purchased if output were held constant. This is shown as a movement from point A to point B in 17.5a. At point B the cost-minimizing condition ($RTS = w/v$) is satisfied for the new, lower w.

This change in w/v will also shift the firm's expansion path and its marginal cost curve. A normal situation might be for the MC curve to shift downward in response to a decrease in w as shown in 17.5b. With this new curve (MC') a higher level of output (Q_2) will be chosen. Consequently, the hiring of labor will increase (to L_2) also from this output effect.

In some ways analyzing the two-factor case is similar to the analysis of the individual's response to a change in the price of a good which was presented in Chapter 5. When w falls we can decompose the total effect on the quantity of L hired into two components. The first of these might be called the *substitution effect*. If Q is held constant at Q_1 there will be a tendency to substitute L for K in the productive process. This effect is illustrated in Figure 17.5a. Since the condition for minimizing the cost of producing Q_1 requires that $RTS = w/v$, a fall in w will necessitate a movement from input combination A to combination B. Because the isoquants have been assumed to exhibit a diminishing RTS, it is clear from the diagram that this substitution effect must be negative: A decrease in w will cause an increase in L if output is held constant. Therefore it has been shown that:

$$\text{Substitution effect} = \left.\frac{\partial L}{\partial w}\right|_{Q = Q_1} < 0 \qquad [17.7]$$

in exactly the same way that the individual's substitution effect was shown to be negative.

It is not legitimate to hold Q constant. It is in considering a change in Q (the *output effect*) that the analogy to the individual's utility-maximization problem breaks down. The reason for this breakdown is that consumers have budget constraints, whereas firms do not. Firms produce as much as the available demand allows. In order to investigate what happens to the quantity of output produced, it is necessary to investigate the firm's profit-maximizing output decision. A change in w, because it changes relative factor costs, will shift the firm's expansion path. Consequently, all the firms' cost curves will be shifted, and probably some output level other than Q_1 will be chosen. In Figure 17.5b what might be considered the "normal" case has been drawn. It has been assumed that with this new expansion path the marginal cost curve for the firm has shifted downward to MC'. Consequently, the profit-maximizing level of output rises from Q_1 to Q_2.[8] The profit-maximizing condition ($P = MC$) is now satisfied at a higher level of output. Returning to 17.5a, this increase in output will cause even more L to be demanded, providing L is not an inferior input (*see* below). The result of both the substitution and the output effects will be to move the input choice to point C on the firm's isoquant map. Both effects work to increase L in response to a decrease in w.[9]

Although we have assumed that the marginal cost curve shifts downward in response to a decrease in w, this does not necessarily have to be the case. It is clear that the average cost of producing Q_1 must decrease

---

[8] Price (P) has been assumed to be constant. If all firms in an industry were confronted with a decline in w, all would change their output levels; the industry supply curve would shift; and, consequently, P would change. So long as the market demand curve for the firm's output is negatively sloped, however, the analysis of this chapter would not be seriously affected by this observation.

[9] From the diagram it should be clear that no definite statement can be made about the sign of $\partial K / \partial w$. The quantity of capital demanded may be either increased or decreased by a change in w. The precise outcome will depend on the relative strength of the output and substitution effects. By geometric reasoning it appears that the relative size of these effects depends on (among other things) the elasticity of substitution.

since the input combination at point B costs less than that which previously minimized costs at point A. However, what happens to marginal cost is a more difficult question which depends on the shape of the isoquant map and its related expansion path. The particularly complicating element here is the possibility that L may be an inferior input (*see* Chapter 12). In this case it is possible that MC could shift upward for a decrease in w. Despite this complication, it can be shown unambiguously that in all cases the output effect induced by a decrease in w causes L to increase.[10] Consequently we have:

$$\text{Output effect} = \frac{\partial L}{\partial w} \text{ (from } dQ) < 0$$

and therefore: [17.8]

$$\frac{\partial L}{\partial w} = [\text{Substitution effect} + \text{Output effect}] < 0.$$

By centering attention on the derived nature of the demand for L we have been able to show that the quantity demanded of any input is inversely related to its own price. In the theory of the firm a situation analogous to Giffen's Paradox (in which the quantity of a good purchased by an individual increased when its price increased) cannot occur. The marginal productivity theory of factor demand therefore yields an unambiguous comparative statics "theorem." Any firm's (and presumably any industry's) demand curve for a factor must be negatively sloped.

---

[10] A "proof" of this assertion can be briefly indicated. We are interested in $\partial L/\partial w$ brought about through a change in Q. There are three stages in calculating this change: (1) the change in MC from a change in w, $(\partial MC/\partial w)$; (2) the change in Q from this change in MC, $(\partial Q/\partial MC)$; and (3) the change in L in response to this change in Q, $(\partial L/\partial Q)$. The total effect is then the product of these three effects:

$$\text{Output effect} = \frac{\partial L}{\partial w} \text{ (from } dQ) = \frac{\partial MC}{\partial w} \cdot \frac{\partial Q}{\partial MC} \cdot \frac{\partial L}{\partial Q}.$$

Now $\partial Q/\partial MC < 0$. A shift upward in marginal cost will (assuming a negatively sloped market demand curve) decrease output and vice-versa. It can also be shown (by totally differentiating the optimal conditions of Equation 17.2) that $\partial MC/\partial w$ and $\partial L/\partial Q$ are *identical*. They are either both positive (which is the normal case as illustrated in Figure 17.5) or they are both negative (which would be the case for an inferior input). The product of effects (1) and (3) must be positive, and so the total output effect is negative. For a more detailed proof of these assertions *see* C. E. Ferguson, *The Neoclassical Theory of Production and Distribution* (Cambridge, Mass.: Cambridge University Press, 1969), pp. 136–153.

Some Extensions of the Marginal Productivity Analysis: The Determinants of Factor Shares

As was indicated by the quotation from Ricardo in the introduction to Part V, the analysis of the determinants of the share of total output accruing to each factor of production has been of central concern in the development of economic theory. An early policy question which provided the impetus for much of this analysis was the debate in England over the repeal of the "Corn Laws." These Laws placing tariffs on the importation of grain into England were instituted during the Napoleonic Wars. The debate over repeal centered attention on the fact that under these Laws protected land owners in England received a larger share of the nation's income than would be the case were the Laws repealed. In order to discuss the possible effects of repeal on the factoral distribution of income adequately, it was necessary to develop a theory of factor shares. The examination of this problem relied on Ricardo's analysis of land rent. As the Industrial Revolution proceeded, however, more attention came to be devoted to the determinants of the distribution of income between capital and labor.[11] In part, this emphasis was a response to the Marxian assertion that an increasing amount of capital in the economy would lead toward the impoverishment of the working class (labor). Because capital, unlike land, is not in fixed supply Ricardian rent analysis was inappropriate for discussing these questions of factor shares. A new analytical tool was needed. The *marginal productivity theory of factor demand* provided this tool.

Although the marginal productivity theory of factor demand can be used to analyze the distribution of income between any arbitrary number of factors, it will be convenient here, as before, to assume there are only two: labor and capital. We will also assume that there is only one firm (perhaps "the economy") producing a homogeneous output using labor and capital. The production function for the firm is given by $Q = F(K, L)$,

---

[11] In recent years discussion of the division of income between capital and labor has become less important than it once was. There are two reasons for this. First, some of the most important inequalities in income distribution which exist today are inequalities in the distribution of what is ostensibly labor income. A discussion of the incomes of "Capitalists" and "laborers" may obscure these inequalities. A second, related reason for the irrelevance of this distinction is an increasing lack of precision in defining what is "labor" income and what is "capital" income. This occurs because of the large increments to "human capital" which have been made in recent years. For example, are the wages of doctors to be regarded as examples of differential labor incomes or as a return on the capital invested in medical education? The final chapter of this book takes up a more general analysis of the distribution of income by centering attention on inequalities in the ownership of wealth, both "human" and "nonhuman."

and this output sells at price P in the market. The total income received by labor from the productive process during one period is wL, whereas the total income accruing to capital is vK (where v is now used as the rental rate on capital). Since the total value of output is given by $P \cdot Q$, *labor's share* of output is given by the ratio wL/PQ and *capital's share* is given by vK/PQ. Sometimes it is convenient also to talk about the *relative shares* of labor and capital: wL/vK.

If the firm in question is a profit maximizer and if it operates as if it were in a perfectly competitive market, it will choose capital and labor so that the marginal value product of each factor is equal to its price. Hence:

$$\text{Labor's share} = \frac{wL}{PQ} = \frac{P \cdot MP_L \cdot L}{PQ} = \frac{MP_L \cdot L}{Q}$$

and   [17.9]

$$\text{Capital's share} = \frac{vK}{PQ} = \frac{P \cdot MP_K \cdot K}{PQ} = \frac{MP_K \cdot K}{Q}.$$

The shares of capital and labor are therefore determined by purely technical properties of the production function relating the quantities of these inputs used and their respective marginal physical products. If we knew the exact form of the production function we could predict the behavior of the factoral shares.[12]

Before proceeding to discuss changing factor shares, however, it is important to clear up one theoretical point. Although we have been speaking rather loosely of the "shares" of income, it is not clear that this usage is necessarily consistent. A basic fact of bookkeeping is that the total value of output must equal the total costs of factor inputs.[13] But it is not obvious that the relationships embodied in Equation 17.9 will insure this.

---

[12] The competitively determined factor share can also be given an interpretation as the elasticity of output with respect to the input in question. For example, in the case of labor:

$$E_{Q,L} = \frac{\partial f}{\partial L} \cdot \frac{L}{Q} = \frac{MP_L \cdot L}{Q} = \text{Labor's share.}$$

This fact is often used in empirical studies of economic growth (*see* the Appendix to Chapter 11, especially Equation 11A.3).

[13] For the economy as a whole this is a statement of the income-output identity implicit in the *National Income and Product Accounts*.

Mathematically, it is required that:

$$P \cdot Q = w \cdot L + v \cdot K$$

or

$$1 = \frac{w \cdot L}{P \cdot Q} + \frac{v \cdot K}{P \cdot Q} \qquad [17.10]$$

or

Labor's share + Capital's share = 1.

Total product must be exhausted between those factor payments assigned by the marginal productivity theory to labor and those factor payments assigned to capital. An important question then is whether or not the marginal productivity theory of factor demand will insure this.

In the late 1930's considerable theoretical controversy surrounded this question. If there were no reason why the shares should "add up" properly, it was argued, then perhaps the whole marginal productivity apparatus should be abandoned. One way that was proposed for answering this problem was purely formal. It can be shown that the marginal productivity theory is consistent (in the sense of Equations 17.10) if (and only if) the production function, $f(K, L)$, exhibits constant returns to scale. If this is the case, competitively determined factor payments will exactly suffice to exhaust total output.[14]

[14] *Proof:* If $f(K, L)$ exhibits constant returns to scale, we know that:

$$f(tK, tL) = t \cdot f(K, L) \qquad \text{for any } t > 0.$$

Differentiating this with respect to t gives:

$$f_1 K + f_2 L = f(K, L).$$

But, as was shown in Chapter 11, the partial derivatives f_1 and f_2 depend only on the ratio of K to L, not on the scale of output. Hence f_1 is equal to the marginal product of capital with inputs K and L, and f_2 is equal to the marginal product of labor. Therefore:

$$Q = MP_K \cdot K + MP_L \cdot L$$

as is required by Equation 17.10.

This proof is one case of a more general mathematical theorem, *Euler's theorem*, which states that if $f(X_1,..., X_n)$ is homogeneous of degree m [that is, if $f(tX_1,..., tX_n) = t^m f(X_1,..., X_n)$ for every $t > 0$] then:

$$f_1 \cdot X_1 + ,..., + f_n \cdot X_n = m \cdot f(X_1,..., X_n).$$

A less formal approach must somehow rely on the above observation about the relationship between constant returns to scale and total product exhaustion. For example, it has been mentioned in several other places that a perfectly competitive, constant cost industry behaves as if it had a constant returns to scale "production function" in the sense that output is doubled in the long run by simply doubling the number of optimally sized plants.[15] If we believe that "most" industries are of this type, the factor shares dictated by the marginal productivity theory do indeed add up properly. Another way of seeing this result is to note that the zero profit condition requires that total revenues be exactly equal to total factor costs in the long run. There will be no excess revenue left unaccounted for if each input is paid the value of its marginal product.

Although it would be possible to go more deeply into different aspects of the adding up problem (perhaps to encompass increasing returns to scale, or to consider the possibility of technical progress), we will not do so. Rather, several important aspects of the competitive determination of factor shares can be investigated using those tools which have already been developed. More specifically, we will be interested in examining how certain technical features of the production function may cause factor shares to change over time. In this discussion it will be assumed, in the light of what has gone before, that $f(K, L)$ exhibits constant returns to scale and that we may therefore talk about competitively determined factor shares which do exhaust total output.

Factor Shares and the Elasticity of Substitution

A fact of modern industrialization is that capital-labor ratios tend to rise over time. This seems to be true for all industries, although capitalization may proceed at different rates in different industries. One important question which might be asked is how will this increasing use of capital affect the distribution of income between capital and labor: Will vK/wL rise or fall over time? If v/w falls more rapidly than K/L is rising, capital's relative share will decrease; whereas if v/w does not change greatly in response to major changes in K/L, capital's share will increase. In a sense the question is: Which changes more rapidly, relative prices or relative quantities? It might be possible to analyze the theory of factor pricing to gain some insights into the rates of change in these magnitudes.

If we are willing to assume that factor markets are perfectly competitive (or perhaps a reasonable approximation thereof), the concept

[15] For a more detailed summary of the "adding-up controversy" *see* Appendix B of E. Chamberlin, *The Theory of Monopolistic Competition,* 8th ed. (Cambridge, Mass.: Harvard University Press, 1962).

of the elasticity of substitution (*see* Chapter 11) can be quite useful in analyzing the behavior of factor shares. Recall that the elasticity of substitution was defined as:

$$\sigma = \frac{\text{Percent } \Delta(K/L)}{\text{Percent } \Delta RTS}. \qquad [17.11]$$

This parameter gives us some information about the shape of the production function's isoquant map. It measures the percentage change in K/L relative to the percentage change in the rate of technical substitution (RTS — the slope of the isoquant). Information about this shape will indicate how "easy" it is to substitute capital for labor and will therefore be helpful in investigating the consequences of an increasing K/L.

Because the firm (or the economy) in question obeys the conditions of the marginal productivity theory of factor demand, the RTS (of L for K) will be equal to the ratio w/v. Relative factor rewards will be determined by relative marginal productivities (and therefore by the RTS). Definition Equation 17.11 can then be rewritten as:

$$\sigma = \frac{\text{Percent } \Delta(K/L)}{\text{Percent } \Delta(w/v)} \qquad [17.12]$$

and we can use this parameter to study changes in relative factor shares. If $\sigma = 1$, Equation 17.12 says that w/v will change in exactly the same proportion that K/L does. In this case, therefore, the relative shares of capital and labor (vK/wL) will stay constant. Any increase in the capital-labor ratio over time will be exactly counterbalanced by an increase in MP_L/MP_K ($= RTS$), and this will be manifested by an identical increase in w/v.

For $\sigma > 1$ the percentage increase in K/L will exceed the percentage increase in w/v, and hence the share of capital in total income will rise as the capital-labor ratio increases. The opposite result occurs when $\sigma < 1$ (when substitution is relatively "difficult"). Capital's share will tend to decline in this case because the relative price of labor is rising rapidly in response to an increasing amount of capital per worker.

The elasticity of substitution is therefore a useful conceptual tool for understanding the effect of changing input proportions on factor shares. If factor substitution is relatively easy, the more rapidly expanding input will increase its share of total income. But this need not be the case. If substitution is difficult, the changing relative factor rewards which result from changed input proportions can reverse this result.[16] Empiri-

---

[16] *See* Problem 2 in Part V for an application of the elasticity of substitution to the policy question of wage-price "guideposts."

cally, it seems to be the case that the shares of labor and capital income in total income have been relatively constant over time. This is one reason why the Cobb-Douglas production function is of considerable interest. Since this is the production function for which $\sigma = 1$, it is in general accord with the observed constancy of income shares.

Using these observations permits the development of an interesting "back-door" proof that the factor shares are constant ($\sigma = 1$) for the Cobb-Douglas production function with constant returns to scale. Suppose the production function is given by:

$$Q = K^\alpha L^{1-\alpha}$$

then

$$MP_K = \frac{\partial Q}{\partial K} = \alpha K^{\alpha-1} L^{1-\alpha} = \alpha \frac{Q}{K} \qquad [17.13]$$

and

$$MP_L = \frac{\partial Q}{\partial L} = (1 - \alpha) K^\alpha L^{-\alpha} = (1 - \alpha) \frac{Q}{L}.$$

Hence, according to the marginal productivity theory of factor pricing, capital's share is given by:

$$\frac{P \cdot MP_K \cdot K}{P \cdot Q} = \frac{MP_K \cdot K}{Q} = \alpha$$

and labor's share by: $\qquad\qquad\qquad\qquad\qquad\qquad$ [17.14]

$$\frac{P \cdot MP_L \cdot L}{P \cdot Q} = \frac{MP_L \cdot L}{Q} = 1 - \alpha.$$

These shares sum to 1 as they should for any constant returns to scale production function. It is obvious from Equation 17.13 that if a Cobb-Douglas function prevails, the shares will be constant. In fact, the magnitude of these shares is given by the exponents of the production function. This explains the reason why α is usually taken to be approximately 1/4 since this is about the share of capital in total income. Similarly, about 3/4 of total income accrues to labor, and this share seems to have remained relatively constant over time.

From these examples it is clear that the concept of the elasticity of substitution can be useful in examining the way in which changing input ratios affect income shares. Initial suppositions about the effect of increasing capitalization, for example, may be inaccurate if they do not take account of the possibility of changing factor prices. These models are of only limited value in discussing the actual evolution of factor shares over time, since we have assumed a fixed production function. In a more complete examination it would also be necessary to consider the possibility of technical progress and how this would affect competitive factor shares. Even in such a study, however, it would be necessary to investigate the ease of substitution of one factor for another.

Conclusion

The perfectly competitive theory of factor demand provides a complete model for the examination of factor pricing. Use of this model would seem to be an obvious place to begin any examination of supply and demand in factor markets. One interesting (and perhaps limiting) feature of the model is its mechanical nature. The demand for any factor is determined solely by the nature of the production function and by the demand for the output which the factor produces. The assumption that firms hire factors in relation to the value of their marginal productivities makes intuitive sense and it gives us several ways of understanding why factor rewards may differ between various employments. Wages, for example, may differ either because marginal productivities differ or because the output which the labor produces may be valued differently in the goods market. When these notions of demand are combined with the supply side of the market we have a "reasonable" picture of the way in which productive inputs fit into an overall model of pricing.

As we saw in Part IV, however, the perfectly competitive model is only one way in which markets may be organized. In the next chapter we will see that although the marginal productivity theory is useful it may not be strictly appropriate in many situations.

CHAPTER 18

Pricing in Imperfectly Competitive Factor Markets

Introduction

Departures from the perfectly competitive model may affect factor pricing in three different ways. First, the firm hiring a particular factor may sell its output under imperfectly competitive conditions. If the factor market is itself competitive this aspect of imperfect competition can easily be handled as an extension of the analysis of the previous chapter. Second, the factor market may diverge from the perfectly competitive assumption if there are only a few [or perhaps only one] demanders of the factor. This is the case of *oligopsony* or *monopsony* in the factor market, and is discussed in the section "Monopsony in the Labor Market" below. Third, a departure from the competitive model can occur if the sellers of a factor are able to form an effective monopoly. In this case the analysis is much the same as that which was developed in Chapter 15 for any monopoly seller. All three of these departures from the assumptions of perfect competition may occur simultaneously, and this is perhaps the most realistic and interesting case to study.

Conditions of imperfect competition can (and undoubtedly do) occur in any factor market. In this chapter, however, it will be useful to center attention on the labor market. This choice is made not only for the sake of concreteness; although it will be easier to speak of "labor" and "wages" rather than some undefined "factor" and its "reward." The primary reason for centering attention on labor, however, is that all three types of imperfect competition are prevalent in this market, and many theoretical and practical issues are raised by this fact. It would be a simple matter to rephrase the results of this chapter so that they would be relevant to any factor of production.

The first way in which imperfect competition affects factor pricing can be discussed in this introductory section. Remember that a profit-maximizing firm will hire any input, say labor, up to the point at which the extra revenue from hiring one more unit of labor is equal to its extra cost. If it is assumed that the labor market is perfectly competitive, the extra cost of an additional unit of labor is the wage rate: The firm is faced by a horizontal supply of labor curve. However, if the firm sells its product in an imperfectly competitive market the analysis of the demand for labor differs slightly from that presented in the previous chapter. The extra revenue from hiring one more unit of labor is given by:

$$\frac{\partial R}{\partial L} = \frac{\partial R}{\partial Q} \cdot \frac{\partial Q}{\partial L} = MR \cdot MP_L. \qquad [18.1]$$

The firm uses its extra labor to produce some extra output. It then sells this extra output and, as always, receives some additional (marginal) revenue. The total magnitude described in Equation 18.1 is sometimes called the *marginal revenue product* of labor (MRP_L). The profit-maximizing firm which buys labor in a perfectly competitive market (at a wage rate w) will therefore hire labor up to the point at which:

$$w = MR \cdot MP_L = MRP_L. \qquad [18.2]$$

It is easy to see that the analysis of Chapter 17 is really a special case of Equation 18.2. If the firm sells its output in a perfectly competitive market marginal revenue would be equal to price and the condition of Equation 18.2 would reduce to that already derived in Equation 17.2, namely that in equilibrium the wage will equal the marginal physical product of labor times the price of the good. Regardless of whether the firm sells its product in a perfectly competitive market or not, input decisions will be based on a computation of the marginal revenue product. The analysis of Chapter 17 is only slightly modified by introducing the possibility of imperfect competition in the output market.

Figure 18.1   Substitution and Output Effects of a Change in w when Output Is Not Sold in a Perfectly Competitive Market

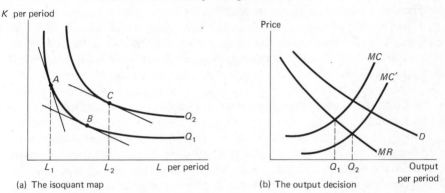

(a) The isoquant map   (b) The output decision

This figure is identical to 17.5 except that the firm faces a negatively sloped demand for its output. The profit-maximizing choice of L in response to a decrease in w changes from L_1 to L_2. The output effect differs slightly from that presented previously because the firm now recognizes that marginal revenue is less than market price.

The firm's demand curve for labor can be constructed for this case in much the same way as that used in Chapter 17. Again a change in w will induce both substitution and output effects. The sum of these two effects will determine what happens to the quantity of labor demanded. Such a comparative statics analysis is presented in Figure 18.1. A reduction in w will cause the optimal input combination to shift from point A on the Q_1 isoquant to point B in Figure 18.1a. As before, this is the substitution effect. An analysis of the output effect is somewhat different from that presented previously because now we must consider the possibility of a negatively sloped demand curve for the firm's output. Such a curve is drawn in Figure 18.1b together with its associated marginal revenue curve. The initial profit-maximizing output is Q_1 where $MR = MC$. A reduction in w will, however, shift this MC curve. Again the normal case must be considered to be a downward shift (we will not discuss the other possibility here) in this curve to MC'. At MC' the new profit-maximizing output is Q_2, and this output will be produced with the input combination

C shown in 18.1a. The substitution and output effects work in the same direction causing an increase in L in response to a decrease in w. Consequently, any firm which acts as a price taker in the labor market (even if it sells its output in an imperfect market) will have a negatively sloped demand curve for labor.[1] This curve will be the locus of (w, L) combinations for which the profit-maximizing condition of Equation 18.2 holds.

Monopsony in the Labor Market

There are many situations in which the supply curve of labor faced by a firm is not a horizontal line at the prevailing wage rate. It may frequently be necessary for the firm to offer a wage above that currently prevailing if it is to attract more employees. In order to study such situations it is most convenient to examine the polar case of *monopsony* (a single buyer) in the labor market. If there is only one buyer in the labor market this firm faces the entire market supply curve. In order to increase its hiring of labor by one more unit it must move to a higher point on this supply curve. This will involve not only paying a higher wage to the "marginal worker" but also paying additional wages to those workers already employed. The marginal cost of the extra unit of labor (MC_L) therefore exceeds its wage rate.[2] In order to maximize profits the firm should choose its labor input so that:

$$MC_L = MRP_L. \qquad [18.3]$$

In the special case of an infinitely elastic labor supply $(MC_L = w)$ Equations 18.2 and 18.3 are identical. However, if the firm faces a positively sloped labor supply curve Equation 18.3 dictates a different level of input choice.

The monopsonist's choice of labor input is illustrated in Figure 18.2.

[1] In a sense it might be said that a firm faced by a negative sloped demand curve for its product has a "less elastic" demand for labor than if this output were traded in a competitive market. This can be seen in Figure 18.1 because an increase in output means a decrease in MR, whereas in the perfectly competitive case MR is constant at the prevailing market price. The output effect is then "smaller" in the case illustrated in Figure 18.1 than it was in Figure 17.5.

[2] The total cost of labor is wL. The cost of one more unit of labor is:

$$\frac{\partial wL}{\partial L} = MC_L = w + L\frac{\partial w}{\partial L}.$$

If the firm buys labor in a perfectly competitive market w is constant $(\partial w/\partial L = 0)$ for the firm and hence $MC_L = w$ as we have assumed previously. If, however, the firm faces a positively sloped supply curve, $\partial w/\partial L > 0$ and $MC_L > w$.

The firm's demand curve for labor (D) is drawn negatively sloped as we have shown it must be. Here also the MC_L curve[3] associated with the labor supply curve (S) is constructed in much the same way that the marginal revenue curve associated with a demand curve can be constructed. Because S is positively sloped, the MC_L curve lies everywhere above S. The profit-maximizing level of labor input for the monopsonist is given by L_1, for at this level of input the condition of Equation 18.3 holds.[4] At L_1 the wage rate in the market is given by w_1. Notice that the quantity of labor demanded falls short of that which would be hired in a perfectly competitive labor market (L^*). The firm has restricted input demand by virtue of its monopsonistic position in the market. The formal similarities between this analysis and the monopoly analysis presented in Chapter 15 should be clear. In particular, the "demand curve" for a monopsonist consists of a single point. In Figure 18.2 this point is given by L_1, w_1. The monopsonist has chosen this point as the most desirable of all those points on the supply curve S. A different point will not be chosen unless some external change (such as a shift in the demand for the firm's output or a change in technology) affects labor's marginal revenue product.

There are several real-world labor markets for which the monopsony model may be considered appropriate. For example, consider professional baseball, football, and hockey. The major leagues in each of these sports are the only hirers of highly skilled athletes. The "reserve" clauses in these leagues effectively prohibit interteam competitive bidding for players, so the monopsony model is appropriate. One buyer (the league) is free to choose that point on the players' supply curve which is most advantageous. In any detailed analysis one would want to go considerably further than the simple monopsony model. Particularly important in this regard would be consideration of the differences in players' abilities which cannot be captured in the previous models which assume homogeneous labor.

---

[3] Some authors refer to this curve as the *marginal expense curve*.

[4] Figure 18.2 is intended only as a pedagogic device and cannot be rigorously defended. In particular, the curve labeled D, although it is supposed to represent the "demand" (or marginal revenue product) curve for labor, has no precise meaning for the monopsonist buyer of labor, since we cannot construct this curve by confronting the firm with a fixed wage rate. Instead, the firm views the entire supply curve, S, and uses the auxiliary curve MC_L (and the condition of Equation 18.3) to choose the most favorable point on S. There is in a strict sense no such thing as the monopsonist's demand curve. This is analogous to the case of a monopoly where we could not speak of a monopolist's "supply curve."

When firms have some effect on the prices of the inputs they buy another complication arises. The rule for the choice of minimum cost input combinations must be revised to take these price effects into account. It should be easy for the reader to show that inputs $(K$ and $L)$ should be chosen so that the RTS (of L for K) is equal to MC_L/MC_K, and that this ratio is no longer equal to the ratio of the inputs' prices (w/v). We will not, however, analyze this explicitly here.

Figure 18.2 Pricing in a Monopsonistic Labor Market

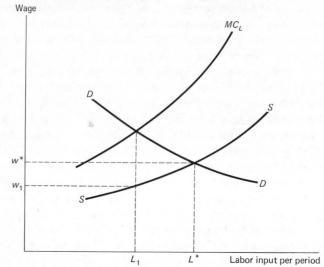

If a firm faces a positively sloped supply curve for labor (S) it will base its decisions on the "marginal expense" of labor curve (MC_L). Because S is positively sloped, MC_L lies above S. The curve S can be thought of as an "average cost of labor curve," and the MC_L curve is marginal to S. At L_1 the equilibrium condition $MC_L = MRP_L$ holds (but *see* Footnote 4) and this quantity will be hired at a market wage rate w_1. Notice that the monopsonist buys less labor than would be bought if the labor market were perfectly competitive (L^*).

Other examples of monopsonistic behavior in the labor market occur because of geographical considerations. In many mill towns the local firm is the only source of employment. Since moving costs are high for the local residents, the monopsony model is appropriate. Other monopsony positions may arise because only one firm hires a particular type of labor which has a unique technical knowledge. In this regard the government is in many situations a monopsony buyer. For example, consider the market for park rangers or the market for astronauts. In such situations the limited availability of even remotely substitute jobs creates the monopsonistic position.

Exploitation

The term "exploitation" has a long history in economic discussions. Perhaps the most important use of the term was developed by Karl Marx in *Capital*. One of the principles underlying Marx' analysis was that ownership of the means of production (what we have called capital) permitted

Capitalists to syphon off a portion of income which rightfully belonged to labor. To Marx, laborers were "exploited" by Capitalists who extracted some payment for the services of the capital they provided. As was the case for many of Marx' theories, this argument provided a challenge to future economists to propose some alternative theory which explained factor pricing. The theory which emerged from these investigations was in fact the marginal productivity theory, which we have already examined. In this theory the share of income accruing to capital is treated symmetrically with that which accrues to labor, and both are determined by the workings of the price system. There is no place in the marginal productivity theory for Marxist type of exploitation (but *see* the Appendix to Chapter 19 for possible modifications to this statement).

Even to an economist who believes that the marginal productivity theory is an adequate representation of reality, however, there is a sense in which exploitation can occur. Suppose we adopt the principle that a worker deserves the "fruit of his labor" and make this more precise by defining the "fruit of his labor" to be the value of his marginal product. The principle adopted is that a worker deserves to be paid an amount equal to what he contributes (at the margin) to the value of output. Under this principle a worker who is not paid $P \cdot MP_L$ is being "exploited."

Using this definition, it is a simple matter to apply the analysis presented earlier in this chapter to demonstrate two situations in which exploitation may arise. First, if the output of the firm hiring labor is sold in a noncompetitive market, labor will be paid its marginal revenue product. Since, for a negatively sloped demand curve $MR < P$, this means that:

$$w = MRP_L = MR \cdot MP_L < P \cdot MP_L. \qquad [18.4]$$

In this situation our definition would say labor is being exploited. Whether this is very serious is open to question because labor is paid what it is "worth" to the firm in question, even though this falls short of the value of its marginal product.

Exploitation in our sense also occurs when the firm in question is a monopsonistic buyer of labor services. In this situation the firm intentionally cuts back its employment of labor to the point where the marginal expense of an extra unit is equal to the marginal revenue product. Even if the associated goods market is perfectly competitive, exploitation can arise in this situation since:

$$w < MC_L = MRP_L \leq P \cdot MP_L \qquad [18.5]$$

where the last relationship will be an equality in the case of a perfectly competitive goods market. This type of exploitation is in a sense more serious than the previous type because here the marginal worker is actually being paid less than he is worth to the firm. The firm is able to "get away" with this by virtue of being the only employer in the market. Presumably, if other employers were competing in the market, wages would be driven toward the value of a laborer's marginal productivity.

Because the definition of exploitation we are using is based on the competitive model as a norm, the recommended policy action by which to combat exploitation is obvious: One should enforce competition in both the goods and factor markets. This remedy is, in itself, rather sterile because it provides neither suggestions for concrete action nor does it describe how close an approximation to perfect competition is required. Two more common policy proposals for dealing with the second (and more important) type of exploitation are minimum wage laws[5] and the creation of unions (*see* below). Each of these remedies provides a way of counteracting the power of a monopsonist in its hiring practices. There may, however, be an inconsistency between the greater equity brought about by these policies and their interference with the "efficiency" with which the market works. A more complete discussion of this inconsistency will be presented in Parts VI and VII.

The economist's definition of exploitation is therefore precise and suggestive of remedies. It is not, however, a sufficiently broad definition to cover many situations which are termed "exploitation" in everyday conversation. For example, neither type mentioned above seems to be relevant to the case of migrant farm workers, although many people would agree that these workers are exploited in some social sense. What the economic analysis of this situation would suggest is that the low incomes of farm workers represent a problem in income distribution rather than a problem of the hiring policies of firms per se. Therefore, this type of exploitation might be more effectively handled by (perhaps lump-sum) income transfers than by "solutions" (such as minimum wage legislation) which attempt to affect the equilibrium price of labor.

Labor Unions: Definitions and Goals

Labor unions are organizations of the suppliers of certain types of labor who have banded together in order to achieve goals which are more effectively pursued as a group. In that association with a union is volun-

[5] See Problem 1 of Part V in which the reader is asked to analyze the possible effects of minimum wage laws under different organizations of the labor market. Notice in particular that in a monopsony market an imposed minimum wage may *both* increase wages and increase employment.

tary it can be assumed that the union member derives some net benefit from his membership. Compulsory membership (the "closed shop") is, however, frequently enforced in order to maintain the viability of the union organization. If each worker were left on his own to decide on membership his rational decision might be not to join the union (and hence avoid dues and other restrictions). He would, however, benefit from the higher wages and better working conditions which have been won by the union. What appears to be rational from each individual worker's point of view may prove to be irrational from a group point of view since the union is undermined by "free riders." Compulsory membership may therefore be a necessary means of maintaining an effective union coalition.[6]

Unions play important roles in the labor markets of many Western countries. They are often condemned (and occasionally praised) for their effects on these economies. Most of the assertions about the effects of unions necessitate empirical evidence and are usually conducted on a macroeconomic level. For these reasons a complete treatment of labor unions is outside the scope of this book. It is important, however, to understand the microeconomic foundations of theories of labor union behavior, and a discussion of these foundations is the purpose of the remainder of this chapter.

As was the case for our discussion of the theory of the firm a logical starting place for an analysis of union behavior is to define the goals toward which a union strives. A first assumption which might be made is that the goals of a union are in some sense an adequate representation of the goals of its members. This assumption avoids the problem of union leadership and disregards the personal aspirations of those leaders which may be in conflict with rank-and-file goals. Union leaders are therefore assumed to be conduits for expressing the desires of the membership.[7] In the United States union goals have tended to be oriented toward "bread-and-butter" issues. The promotion of radical social change, except briefly in the early 1900's, has not occupied an important position in the programs of major unions. Rather, unions have attempted to exert an effect solely in the labor market to which they are a supplier, and in this they have had some success.

---

[6] For a more complete discussion of the issues raised in this and later sections *see* J. Dunlop, *Wage Determination under Trade Unions* (New York: The Macmillan Co., 1944). A more analytical approach to many of the same issues can be found in Allan M. Cartter, *The Theory of Wages and Employment* (Homewood, Ill.: Richard D. Irwin, Inc., 1959).

[7] An alternative treatment might assume that union leaders attempt to maximize their own utility subject to the constraint that they must be able to win re-election. For a further discussion of this concept of leadership behavior *see* Chapter 23 and the fascinating book by A. Downs, *An Economic Theory of Democracy* (New York: Harper & Row, 1957).

In many ways strong unions can be treated in the same way as a monopoly firm. The union faces a demand curve for labor and, because it is the sole source of supply, it can choose at which point on this curve it will operate. The point which is actually chosen by the union will obviously depend on what particular goals it has decided to pursue. Three possible choices are illustrated in Figure 18.3. The union may, for example, choose to offer that quantity of labor which maximizes the total wage bill ($w \cdot L$). If this is the case it will offer that quantity for which the "marginal revenue" from labor demand is equal to 0. This quantity is given by L_1 in Figure 18.3, and the wage rate associated with this quantity is w_1. The point E_1 is therefore the preferred wage-quantity combination. Notice that at wage rate w_1 there may be an excess supply of labor and the union must somehow allocate those jobs which are available to those workers who want them.

Figure 18.3   Three Possible Points on the Labor Demand Curve which a Monopoly Union Might Choose

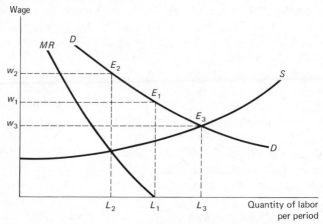

A union has a monopoly in the supply of labor. It may therefore choose that point on the demand curve for labor which it most prefers. Three such points are shown in the figure. At point E_1 total labor payments ($w \cdot L$) are maximized; at E_2 the economic rent which workers receive is maximized; and at E_3 the total amount of labor services supplied is maximized.

Another possible goal which the union may pursue would be to choose the quantity of labor so as to maximize the total economic rent obtained by those members who are employed. This would necessitate choosing that quantity of labor for which the additional total wages obtained by having one more employed union member (the marginal revenue) is equal to the extra cost of luring that member into the market. The union should therefore choose that quantity L_2 at which the marginal revenue curve crosses the supply curve.[8] The wage rate associated with this quantity is w_2, and the desired wage-quantity combination is labeled E_2 in the diagram. Again, this combination requires that some workers who desire to work at the prevailing wage are left unemployed. Perhaps the union may "tax" the large economic rent earned by those who do work in order to transfer income to those who don't.

A third possibility[9] would be for the union to aim for maximum employment of its members. This would involve choosing the point w_3, L_3 which is precisely the point that would result if the market were organized in a perfectly competitive way. No employment greater than L_3 could be achieved since the quantity of labor that union members supply would contract for wages less than w_3.

Frequently it happens that a union does not face a large number of relatively small demanders of labor but faces a monopsonist. In this situation both the union and the firm have a substantial degree of market power and the outcome of the wage negotiations is indeterminate: It will depend on the bargaining skills of the two parties. This possibility is illustrated in Figure 18.4.[10] If the monopoly union can get the firm to act in a "naïve" way (to take wage rates as given), it can then choose points E_1, E_2, or E_3 as before. On the other hand, if the monopsonist can force the union to take wage rates as a given, it would choose the wage-quantity combination dictated by E_4 (*see* Figure 18.2 where the monopsonist's choice is diagrammed). Since it is not likely that either the union or the firm will behave in such naïve ways the actual wage bargain which will be decided upon is indeterminate. For example, if it is assumed that the union's desired point is given by E_2 and the firm's by E_4 the actual w, L combination which emerges from negotiations can be anywhere "between" these two points. Since this situation should be regarded as fairly typical in any economy (such as the economy of the United States) char-

---

[8] Mathematically, the union's goal is to choose L so as to maximize $wL - $ (Area under S) $= wL - \int_0^L S(\ell)d\ell$. The first-order condition for a maximum is then:

$$\frac{dwL}{dL} - S(L) = MR_L - S(L) = 0.$$

[9] The three union goals shown in Figure 18.3 are those which are most easily diagrammed, but the list is by no means inclusive. For example, one important union goal which cannot be easily fitted into the traditional supply-demand model is the issue of job security. Unions may often seek some measure of "rights" to the jobs they hold for their members and thereby hope to isolate these workers from fluctuations of supply and demand in the labor market. An appreciation of this aspect of union behavior would be a necessity for any detailed examination of pricing in union-dominated labor markets. This would be especially true if job-security goals conflicted with wage-employment goals.

[10] Figure 18.4 is applicable to the more general case of *bilateral monopoly*, in which a monopoly seller of any product faces a monopsonist buyer.

acterized by powerful forces on both sides of labor negotiations, it is important to turn now to a brief discussion of bargaining.

Figure 18.4 Bilateral Monopoly in the Labor Market

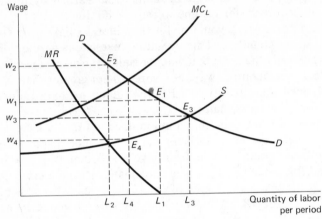

If a monopoly union sells its labor to a monopsonist firm the w, L combination which results will be indeterminant. The union may desire points such as E_1, E_2, or E_3, whereas the firm prefers point E_4. These goals are in conflict, and the ultimate outcome must be determined by bargaining.

The Economics of Bargaining

In this section a formalized analysis of the bargaining process will be presented. This presentation is not intended to be in any sense a realistic picture of the kinds of negotiations which take place between powerful firms and unions. Rather, the intent here is to present a useful conceptualization of the bargaining process upon which the reader can build by reference to institutional detail.

A logical place to start is to inquire what bargaining is all about. In reality labor negotiations involve a multitude of issues ranging from wages and employment practices to the length of coffee breaks and the type of piped music provided on the job. It will be convenient to combine all such features which are subject to negotiations into one magnitude: *utility*. Unions are then assumed to strive for the highest level of utility, and firms are assumed also to pursue a similar goal. Bargaining situations arise because utility cannot be increased for both parties simultaneously. Rather, concessions to labor unions are costly to firms, and vice-versa.

The possible combinations of firms' and unions' utility levels which can technically be achieved are represented by all points on and inside the curve UU in Figure 18.5.[11] Only a small subset of these possible points can be regarded as likely to emerge from the successful completion of bargaining—those on the outer periphery. For example, consider a point such as A which promises outcomes $U_A{}^f$ and $U_A{}^u$. This point will not be a likely result of successful negotiations because both participants could be made better off. The firm's utility could be increased to $U_{A'}{}^f$ without causing any loss to the union. The union will therefore not fight strongly against this movement. A similar argument can be made about any point not on the "utility frontier" UU. Hence UU can be regarded as the set of outcomes which will emerge from favorable and efficient negotiations. The choice among points on UU is a true bargaining problem, in that the firm can be made better off only at the expense of the union.

Figure 18.5   The Possible Utility Outcomes from Bargaining

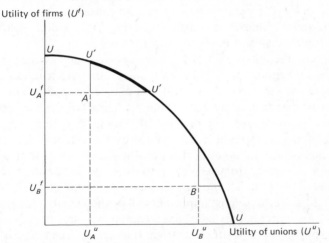

All points under the curve U are technically feasible outcomes of the bargaining process. If bargaining is successful, however, only points on the periphery of this curve will be chosen. Indeed, if the participants can establish bargaining floors they can further narrow the range of outcomes. For example, if point A is selected as an initial point only outcomes on the arc $U'U'$ will result from bargaining. Where on $U'U'$ the final settlement occurs will depend on the bargaining strength of the parties.

The set of possible outcomes from negotiations can be further narrowed by considering the utility levels from which the bargaining starts. If each participant can commit himself to accepting no utility outcome

---

[11] The analysis in this part is greatly extended in the book by Luce and Raiffa, *op. cit.* (*see* especially Chap. 6).

below a certain level, these levels will be the starting point for negotiations. For example, if the firm can commit itself to accept no solution less than $U_A{}^f$ and the union can commit itself to no level lower than $U_A{}^u$, point A becomes the origin for the negotiations. The set of possible outcomes has been narrowed to the arc $U'U'$.

The choice of initial position in negotiations can have an important effect on the outcome. Starting from a position such as A is relatively favorable to the firm, whereas if the initial point could be made to be B the union would be in an attractive position. It is no trivial matter how one starts a negotiation, and in many cases this may be the most important aspect. Consider the pledges which are made by union leaders to their constituents. These may form a commitment which presents an effective utility floor for the union. By staking their careers on a particular settlement, union leaders may be able to establish such a floor.[12] Firms may also strive for beneficial initial positions by pleading poverty or by invoking the public's fear of "union-caused" inflation. There are other possible scenarios of initial jockeying for position which are far more complex than those which have been suggested.

Suppose the initial point A has been decided upon by the participants in the labor negotiations. Then bargaining amounts to choosing some point from the set $U'U'$. How will this choice be made? The outcome obviously depends in some way on the "strength" of the bargainers. One possible way to quantify the concept of "strength" is to assume that the strength of any participant is determined by the extent of the costs he is able to impose on the other party. For a union the costs it is able to impose on a firm stem from its ability to interrupt the productive process by means of a strike. The costs that such an action will entail depend on many factors. Perhaps most important will be the extent of the firm's fixed costs. Firms with high levels of fixed capital investment may suffer substantial short-term losses from a strike. If lost sales are immediately made up after the strike the costs of the strike consist only of the shift in timing of receipts (a dollar tomorrow is worth less than a dollar today) and the (presumably slight) physical depreciation on the firm's capital stock during the work stoppage. However, if sales lost during a strike are lost forever—say there are close substitutes for the product produced by the struck firm—the cost of even a short stoppage can be substantial. The costs of a strike may also depend on its timing. For example, the threat of a strike in the early fall is a very effective weapon available to the United Automobile Workers. The costs imposed on a struck automobile company at the start of a new model year can be exceedingly high.

---

[12] For an insightful discussion of the benefits of making binding commitments and taking rigid positions prior to negotiations *see* T. Schelling, *The Strategy of Conflict* (Cambridge, Mass.: Harvard University Press, 1960).

Firms, on the other hand, may also be in a position to impose high costs on a union at times. Perhaps the most effective weapon is to threaten to go out of business. If this threat can be made to appear realistic it will affect the bargaining outcome in the firm's favor. Other actions which threaten the jobs of union members may also impose costs. For example, the threat of further automation may appear very real to a worker unable to shift his occupation easily. Threats to change plant locations, to hire replacement workers, or to change work rules can be similarly effective — particularly if the union does not represent the total supply of available labor.

Bargaining is therefore an important and complex aspect of pricing in the labor market. Whereas the theory presented here has been rather formal and a priori, the reader may be able to apply the concepts which have been developed to particular aspects of real-world negotiations.

Conclusion

Although this chapter has centered on questions of pricing in the labor market, it should be clear that the tools are applicable in any factor market characterized by imperfect competition. The pricing of large units of industrial equipment (paper machines, atomic power plants, large aircraft) is often characterized by elements of imperfect competition on both the supply and demand sides of the market. The monopsony and bargaining models in this chapter are equally relevant to these situations.

Again only the two polar cases of perfect competition and monopoly (monopsony) have been analyzed in any detail here. In many situations neither of these models may be strictly appropriate. It is particularly likely that a monopoly union may face several firms rather than only a single one. In such a situation the study of bargaining becomes even more complex than that discussed. Account must then be taken of interfirm strategy and of attempts by the union to "divide and conquer." The examination of polar cases can, however, throw some light on these more complex forms of market organization.

CHAPTER 19

The Theory
of Capital

Introduction: What Is Capital?

Probably no branch of economics is at the same time so important and so controversial as is capital theory. The study of capital allocation and accumulation plays a central role in modern theories of economic growth, therefore an understanding of the nature of capital as a factor of production is essential to understanding the growth of any economy. The study of capital theory is, at the same time, engulfed in controversy. Primarily this controversy revolves about the question of whether or not the owner of a piece of productive equipment has any "right" to obtain a rent for its use. In the final analysis the answer to this question must be regarded as one aspect of the broader question of the nature and desirability of private property as a social institution. A brief economic discussion of this issue will be presented in various sections of Part VII. In addition, an appendix to this chapter will give some attention to the particular controversies which surround the theory of capital. In the chapter itself these controversial questions will be avoided in order to build an understanding of the nature of capital and why the allocation of capital is an important issue. A first step toward discussing more complex social issues would seem to be to understand the economics of the matter.

In this chapter three questions will be investigated: What is "capital"? What is "the" rate of return on capital and how is it determined? Finally, how can the answers to the first two questions be used to develop a theory of capital accumulation (investment) by integrating the theory of capital and the theory of the firm. A partial answer to the first of these questions can be presented in this introduction, although any deeper understanding can only come from a much more detailed study.

When we speak of the capital stock of an economy we mean the sum total of machines, buildings, and other man-made, nonlabor resources which are in existence at some point in time. These assets represent some part of an economy's output in the past which was not consumed. This output was set aside to be used for production in the future. All societies, from the most primitive to the most complex, engage in capital accumulation. A bushman's taking time off from hunting to make arrows, individuals in a modern society using part of their incomes to buy houses, or governments taxing citizens in order to purchase dams and post-office buildings are all engaging in essentially the same sort of activity: Some portion of current output is being set aside for use in producing output in future periods.

This process of capital accumulation is pictured schematically in the two panels of Figure 19.1. In both panels society is initially consuming level C_0 and has been doing so for some time. At time t_1 a decision is made to withhold some output (amount s) from current consumption for one period. Starting in period t_2 this withheld consumption is in some way put to use producing future consumption. An important concept connected with this process is the *rate of return,* which is earned on that consumption which is put aside. In 19.1a, for example, all of the withheld consumption is used to produce additional output only in period t_2. Consumption is increased by amount x in period t_2 and then returns to the long-run level C_0. Society has saved in one year in order to have an orgy in the next year. A measure of the (one-period) rate of return from this activity would be:

$$r_1 = \frac{x}{s} - 1. \qquad [19.1]$$

If $x > s$ (if more consumption comes out of this process than went into it) we would say that the one-period rate of return to capital accumulation is positive.

Figure 19.1   Two Views of Capital Accumulation

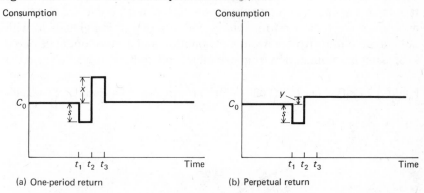

(a) One-period return   (b) Perpetual return

In 19.1a society withdraws some current consumption (s) in order to gorge itself (with x extra consumption) in the next period. The one period rate of return would be measured by $x/s - 1$. The society in 19.1b takes a more long-term view and uses s to increase its consumption perpetually by y. The perpetual rate of return would be given by y/s.

In 19.1b society is assumed to take a more long-term view in its consumption decisions. Again an amount s is set aside at time t_1. Now, however, this set aside consumption is used to raise the consumption level for all periods in the future. If the permanent level of consumption is raised to $C_0 + y$, we define the perpetual rate of return to be:

$$r_\infty = \frac{y}{s}. \qquad [19.2]$$

If capital accumulation succeeds in raising C_0 permanently, r_∞ will be positive.

When economists speak of the rate of return to capital accumulation, then, they have in mind something between these two extremes. Somewhat loosely we will speak of the rate of return as being a measure of the terms at which consumption today may be turned into consumption tomorrow (this will be made more explicit below). A natural question to ask is how is the economy's rate of return determined. Again, the answer must somehow revolve around the supply and demand for present and future goods. The next section will present a simple model in which this supply-demand interaction is demonstrated.

The Determination of the Rate of Return

The previous section hints at the way in which the rate of return is determined. Capital accumulation is productive, but people are impatient, and hence the rate of return acts as both a signal to individuals to withhold some output from current consumption and as a rationing device to keep capital accumulation from expanding indefinitely. It would seem that

Figure 19.2 Technical Possibilities for Trading Current for Future Consumption

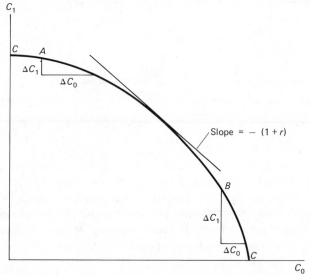

The curve CC shows the alternative combinations of consumption today (C_0) and consumption tomorrow (C_1) which are technically feasible. The slope of this curve [defined to be $-(1 + r)$] shows how one unit of consumption today may be traded for consumption tomorrow. Such a slope is a measure of the rate of return to capital accumulation.

the rate of return, if appropriately chosen, would be able to generate an equilibrium between individual tastes and the available technology. This equilibrium can be demonstrated by means of a graphic argument originally presented by Fisher.[1] In Figure 19.2 the technical possibilities for transforming consumption today (C_0) into consumption tomorrow (C_1) are represented by the concave curve CC. Given the available resources

[1] See I. Fisher, *The Rate of Interest* (New York: The Macmillan Co., 1907).

of society the points on CC represent the possible combinations of C_0 and C_1 which might be produced in these two periods. This curve is directly analogous to the production possibility frontier first discussed in Chapter 12. It is drawn as a concave curve on the assumption of a decreasing rate of trade-off of C_0 for C_1 as the production of C_0 is increased. The slope of the curve CC can be regarded as a measure of the rate of return to capital accumulation. At any point on the curve the slope dC_1/dC_0 shows how consumption can technically be traded between the two periods. At a point such as A relatively little C_1 would be gained by withholding some output from current consumption, whereas at B a great amount of extra C_1 could be achieved by similar abstinence. If we let r be the rate of return on capital investment, then the slope of the curve CC is defined to be $-(1 + r)$. If a one-unit sacrifice in C_0 yields more than one extra unit of C_1, r is positive; whereas if this sacrifice yields less than an extra unit of C_1, r is negative. Consequently, r is a direct measure of the productivity of capital accumulation.

Individual tastes between C_0 and C_1 can be represented by a set of indifference curves similar to those which were used in Chapter 8. Such curves show those combinations of C_0 and C_1 with which individuals are equally well off. If it can be assumed that there are curves which are representative of *all* individuals' tastes,[2] these curves can be superimposed on the production possibility curve of Figure 19.2 to demonstrate the determination of the rate of return. In Figure 19.3 this construction is shown. The highest utility for society is achieved at point E. At this point of tangency the rate at which individuals are willing to trade C_0 for C_1 is exactly equal to the rate at which they can be technically traded. The common tangency at point E has a slope given by $-(1 + r^*)$. This value of r^* is the equilibrium rate of return for which individual tastes and productive technology are in agreement as to their rates of trade-off between consumption today and consumption tomorrow. The rate of return therefore plays an important allocative role on both the supply and demand side of the market.

It is likely that the equilibrium rate of return (or *interest rate*)[3] which emerges from the interaction pictured in Figure 19.3 will be positive. At

---

[2] The construction of "community" indifference curves has not been discussed in detail here. It is sufficient for our purposes that the curves in Figure 19.3 are in some way broadly representative of the tastes of society as a whole. For example, it might be assumed that society is composed of one million identical individuals and that their common indifference curve map has just been blown up for use in the figure.

An example similar to that in Figure 19.3 is taken up in more detail in Chapter 20.

[3] The terms *interest rate* and *rate of return* can be used interchangeably only if it is kept clearly in mind that we are talking about the possibilities for trading C_0 and C_1 and not about the various monetary interest rates which occur in the real world. In the simple model of allocation being examined here no such distinction need be made, since the definition of r is unambiguous.

Figure 19.3 Determination of the Equilibrium Rate of Return

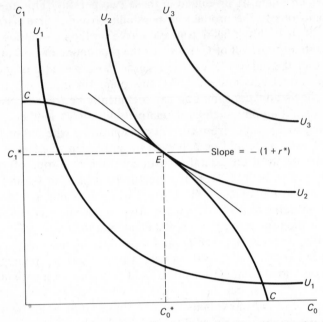

The equilibrium rate of return is determined by the interaction of tastes (as represented by the indifference curve map in the figure) and the technological possibilities for transforming goods over time. Given the productive possibilities (curve CC), the highest level of attainable utility occurs at point E. The common tangency at this point is defined to be $-(1 + r^*)$, and r^* is called the rate of return on capital. It is quite likely that r^* will be positive.

the equilibrium point E it is likely that one unit of C_0 will trade for more than one unit of C_1. To see this it can first be argued that C_0 and C_1 will be of approximately equal magnitudes. It is unlikely that society would choose to specialize in consuming in one of the periods at the expense of the other. Rather, consumption will probably only change slowly from one period to the next. But tangencies which occur at relatively equal values for C_0 and C_1 will exhibit a positive r for two reasons. First, on the demand side, individuals tend to be impatient. Because the future is uncertain and "far away," individuals will require some inducement in order to get them to trade a unit of C_0 for some C_1. In particular, they will probably require that more than one unit of C_1 be offered as a reward for abstinence. Only if individuals were relatively satiated with C_0 would they be willing to give up one unit today for less than a unit tomorrow.

A similar argument can be made about the supply side of the market.

It is likely that for relatively equal values of C_0 and C_1 the productive process will permit one unit of C_0 to be transformed into more than one unit of C_1. In a sense, time is productive (*see* the next section), and letting C_0 "age" for a period will increase its quantity. Only if capital accumulation were pushed to an extremely high level (a high C_1 relative to C_0) would it be expected that the rate of return on capital accumulation would be negative.

This a priori proof suggests that peculiarities in both tastes and technology will cause r to be positive. The precise value of r will depend on the specific nature of the equilibrium in the supply and demand for present and future goods. Numerous real-world examples[4] seem to imply, however, that the rate of exchange of present for future consumption will be greater than one-for-one. In the section called "The Rental Rate on Machines and the Theory of Investment" we will examine the way in which this positive interest rate (r) affects firms' decisions on capital usage. First, however, it will be useful to discuss a few other conceptualizations of the demand for capital in a more abstract setting.

Capital, Time, and the Rate of Return

In the previous section we avoided any specific discussion of something called "capital" by focusing attention on trade-offs between present and future consumption. It was not necessary to specify exactly how C_0 is to be transformed into C_1 in order to make the essential conceptual point. Using the notion of the rate of return permitted us to avoid difficult issues about how to add up a stock of rather different pieces of capital. In the late nineteenth-century economists were similarly interested in finding some way of abstracting from real-world complexities in order to isolate the "essence" of capital. The "Austrian" capital theorists[5] were particularly successful in this regard for they analyzed the basic similarity between capital and time. In their theory labor was treated as the one basic, "primitive" factor of production. Any good was conceived of as having been produced by the application of various doses of labor over time. For example, in the production of a loaf of bread, labor was applied in the production process not only at the time the bread was

---

[4] Why is it, for example, that the notion of interest arises in even the most primitive societies, and that persons in economies in which the standard of living is near subsistence engage in capital accumulation? (*See also* Discussion Question 7 of Part V.)

[5] The following discussion must of necessity be greatly abbreviated. For a more complete examination and a comprehensive list of references *see* M. Blaug, *Economic Theory in Retrospect* (Homewood, Ill.: Richard D. Irwin, Inc., 1962), Chap. 12.

baked but also when the flour mill was built, when the wheat was planted (and harvested), when the flour was milled, and so forth. By regarding labor as the only nonproducible factor of production the entire productive process could be looked at as a very long and complex set of applications of labor.

Figure 19.4 Conceptualizations of the Capital Accumulation Process

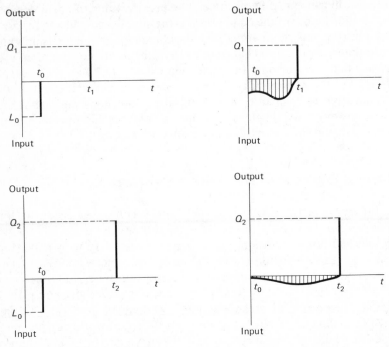

(a) Point input—point output   (b) Continuous input—point output

Capital accumulation can be viewed as a sequence of roundabout applications of labor. The longer the time elapsed between input and output, the more a fixed amount of labor will be able to produce. This is illustrated for the point input-point output case in 19.4a, and for the continuous input-point output case in 19.4b.

This conceptualization views capital as being a *period of production*. Capital accumulation is manifested by more complex and roundabout methods of production. In this way capital has been reduced to a homogeneous aggregate called *time*. The essence of capital accumulation is a lengthening of the period of production. Two versions of this process are pictured in Figure 19.4. In 19.4a, a *point input-point output* scheme of production is diagrammed. In this figure some labor (L_0) is input at time t_0. This input then grows in some way over time and "matures" by yielding output (Q_1) at time t_1. By lengthening the period of production the same amount of labor input at t_0 will yield a higher output (Q_2) at time t_2. This lengthening of the period of production is the essence of capital accumulation. By investing labor over longer periods machinery can be built and ultimately more output can be obtained.

In 19.4b, the more general case of a *continuous input-point output* method of production is illustrated. Labor is applied in varying amounts over the period t_0 to t_1, and some output (Q_1) emerges at time t_1. By applying the same total input of labor over a longer period output can be increased to Q_2 at time t_2. Making the techniques of production more roundabout has increased the output produced by this fixed quantity of labor.

Once this simplified view of the productive process is accepted, a logical question to raise is what is it that determines the length of the of production? The most direct answer which can be given to this question is that it is "the" interest rate which determines the length of the period of production. If the interest rate is high this shows a general impatience on the part of individuals (a dollar today is worth much more than a dollar tomorrow); they are unwilling to tolerate long periods of production. On the other hand, a low interest rate is indicative of a general willingness to "wait" for output; therefore the period of production will be relatively long.

This phenomenon can be demonstrated by using a simple model which examines the planting of trees. The planting of a tree for its timber output is the prototype example of a point input-point output productive process: Some labor is invested initially in the planting and then the tree is allowed to mature. The ultimate size of the tree (the output of this process) will obviously depend on the length of time the tree is permitted to grow until it is cut. It will be shown that, under certain assumptions, the optimal age for cutting down the tree varies inversely with the rate of interest.

Suppose that the value of a tree at any time, t, is given by $f(t)$ and that initially L dollars are invested as payments to the workers who plant the tree. Given these data, the tree owner must decide when to cut the tree. Assume that there has been established in the market a certain (instantaneous) interest rate,[6] r, at which the tree owner can borrow or lend all he wants. Given this assumption, the tree owner will choose his har-

---

[6] Instantaneous interest is paid and compounded at "each instant" at a rate r. This term is described more fully in the appendix to Chapter 8. There it is shown that the present value of $\$N$ payable T years in the future is $\$N(1 + i)^{-T}$ if interest is compounded yearly at a rate i and by $\$Ne^{-rT}$ if interest is compounded continuously at the rate r.

vesting date so as to maximize the present discounted value of his profits. By properly discounting the future value of the tree to take account of the interest payments he could earn on the funds he has invested (in the tree) the owner can make the correct harvesting decision. At any time, t, the present discounted value of the tree owner's profits is given by:

$$PDV(t) = e^{-rt} f(t) - L \qquad [19.3]$$

which is simply the difference between (the present value of) revenues and present costs. The firm's decision then consists of choosing t to maximize Equation 19.3. As always, this value may be found by differentiation:

$$\frac{dPDV(t)}{dt} = e^{-rt} f'(t) - re^{-rt} f(t) = 0 \qquad [19.4]$$

or after dividing both sides by e^{-rt}:

$$f'(t) - rf(t) = 0 \qquad [19.4']$$

therefore:

$$r = \frac{f'(t)}{f(t)}. \qquad [19.5]$$

Hence t should be chosen so that Equation 19.5 holds. Two features of this optimal condition are worth noting. First, observe that the cost of the initial labor input drops out upon differentiation. This cost is (even in a literal sense) a "sunk" cost which is basically irrelevant to the profit-maximizing decision. Second, Equation 19.5 can be interpreted as saying that the tree should be harvested when the rate of interest is equal to the proportional rate of growth of the tree. This is true because $f'(t)/f(t)$ is in fact the percentage increase in $f(t)$ at time t. This result makes intuitive sense. If the tree is growing more rapidly than the prevailing interest rate its owner should leave his funds invested in the tree, since the tree provides the best return available. The volume of timber in this case might be increasing at 8 percent per year, while the interest rate available in the market is only 5 percent. On the other hand, if the tree is growing less rapidly than the prevailing interest rate the tree should be cut and the funds obtained from its sale should be invested elsewhere at the rate r.

Equations 19.4' and 19.5 are only necessary conditions for a maximum. By differentiating Equation 19.4' again it is easy to see that it is also required that at the chosen value of t:

$$f''(t) - rf'(t) < 0 \qquad [19.6]$$

if the necessary conditions are to be sufficient. If we assume $f'(t) > 0$ (that the tree is always growing), then the assumption that $f''(t) < 0$ will insure that Equation 19.6 holds.[7] The necessary conditions will also be sufficient if we assume that the tree is always growing, but that this growth slows over time.

To see how the optimal choice of t (the period of production) changes in response to a change in the interest rate it is necessary to differentiate Equation 19.4' totally:

$$f''(t) \frac{\partial t}{\partial r} - rf'(t) \frac{\partial t}{\partial r} - f(t) = 0$$

or   [19.7]

$$\frac{\partial t}{\partial r} = \frac{f(t)}{f''(t) - rf'(t)}.$$

This expression will be negative in view of Equation 19.6. We have shown therefore that an increase in r will cause t to decrease (the tree will be cut sooner if the interest rate rises), and vice-versa.

These results can be illustrated graphically. In order to simplify the graph, however, we will make a few modifications in the analysis. First, it will be assumed that initial labor costs are 0. As has already been shown, this assumption will have no effect on the choice of t. Second, instead of working with the expression $PDV(t)$ given in Equation 19.3, we will work with its logarithm, $\log[PDV(t)]$. Choosing t to maximize this logarithm is equivalent to choosing t to maximize the original expression since taking logs is an order-preserving operation. Now, since $L = 0$, from Equation 19.3 we have:

$$\log PDV(t) = \log f(t) - rt. \qquad [19.8]$$

Therefore we wish to choose t to maximize Equation 19.8. In Figure 19.5 the curve $\log f(t)$ is graphed. This curve is drawn as a concave function of t in view of our assumptions that $f'(t) > 0$ and $f''(t) < 0$.[8] For any value of $f(t)$, the value of $\log(PDV)$ is found by drawing a straight line with slope r through the proper point on the $\log f(t)$ curve. The intercept

---

[7] Assuming that $r > 0$.

[8] Let $X(t) = \log f(t)$. Then:

$$\frac{dX(t)}{dt} = \frac{f'(t)}{f(t)} > 0 \text{ and } \frac{d^2X(t)}{dt^2} = \frac{ff'' - f'^2}{f^2} < 0.$$

Hence $X(t)$ is a concave function of t.

of this straight line with the vertical axis will be log (PDV). That this construction is correct may be seen from Equation 19.8, where it is shown that log (PDV) is computed by subtracting rt from the value of log $f(t)$. Consequently the choice of an optimal t consists of choosing that point on the log $f(t)$ curve for which the straight line with slope r through this point has the greatest possible intercept on the vertical axis. From the figure this value is seen to be t^* where the rt curve is just tangent to the log $f(t)$ curve. This will then be the date at which the tree owner will choose to harvest the tree in order to maximize its present value.[9]

From Figure 19.5 it is easy to see that a change in r will move t^* in the opposite direction. For an increase in r the line rt would become steeper and the required tangency would occur at a smaller value of t. An opposite result would occur for a decrease in r. There is thus an inverse relationship between the rate of interest and the length of the period of production.[10]

Figure 19.5   The Optimal Production Period for a Tree

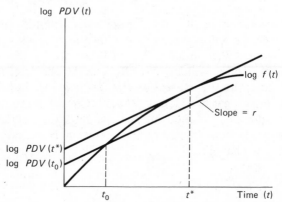

A tree should be cut down when the rate of growth of the tree is equal to the market interest rate. In the figure (which uses the logarithm of the tree's growth for graphic simplicity) this point is found to be at t^*. For time periods either greater or less than t^* the present value of the tree will be smaller.

[9] At t^*, r is equal to the slope of the log $f(t)$ curve. But this just says that $r = f'(t)/f(t)$ as was shown above.

[10] One might be tempted to conclude from this analysis that more generally there is an inverse relationship between the rate of interest and the amount of capital (relative to labor) in an economy. In many simple models this is indeed the case. It is not necessary to explore the theoretical literature very far, however, to find numerous reasonable models for which such a unique inverse relationship does not hold. Many of these "perverse" models were first developed in the attack on the marginal productivity theory of factor pricing.

Bucolic examples such as tree harvesting (or scotch bottling — *see* Problems 6 or 7 of Part V) have at best a limited usefulness in the development of general theories of capital. Because the models are simple, however, they do permit the isolation of some of the important aspects of a firm's intertemporal decisions. In the tree-harvesting model the importance of discounting future profits by the market interest rate is apparent.[11] When making decisions over time this calculation must be completed because of the opportunity cost (in terms of lost interest) on those funds which are invested during the production process. This important observation has relevance far beyond the confines of point input-point output type of models, as we shall see in the next section.

The Rental Rate on Machines and the Theory of Investment

So far in this chapter we have not talked about the firm's demand for capital. It is time to do so using the concepts already developed. Presumably a firm will rent machines in accordance with the same principles of profit maximization which were derived in Chapters 17 and 18. Specifically, in a perfectly competitive market the firm will choose to hire that number of machines for which the marginal revenue product is precisely equal to their market rental rate. In this section we will first investigate the determinants of this market rental rate; and it will be assumed that all machines are rented. Later in the section the particular problems raised by the fact that most firms buy machines and hold them until they deteriorate (rather than renting them) will be examined.

Consider a firm in the business of renting machines to other firms. Suppose this firm owns a machine which currently sells for P dollars in the market. How much will this firm charge its clients for the use of the machine? The owner of the machine faces two kinds of costs: the cost of depreciation on the machine and the *opportunity cost* of having its funds tied up in a machine rather than in an investment earning the present interest rate. If it is assumed that depreciation costs per period are a constant percent (d) of the machine's market price and that the market interest rate is given by r, then the total costs of the machine owner for one period are given by:[12]

$$dP + rP = P(r + d). \qquad [19.9]$$

---

[11] If there were no discount factor (if $r = 0$) the tree would be allowed to continue growing until growth actually stopped ($f'(t) = 0$).

[12] In the next section it is shown that this formula must be amended slightly if the price of the machine is changing over time.

If it is assumed that the machine rental market is perfectly competitive no pure profits can be earned by renting machines. The workings of the market will insure that the rental rate per period for the machine (v) is exactly equal to the costs of the machine owner. Hence we have the basic result that:

$$v = P(r + d). \tag{19.10}$$

The competitive rental rate is the sum of interest and depreciation costs. In the case of a machine which does not depreciate ($d = 0$) Equation 19.8 can be written in a more familiar way as:

$$\frac{v}{P} = r. \tag{19.10'}$$

This simply says that in equilibrium an infinitely long-lived machine is equivalent to a perpetual bond, and hence must "yield" the market rate of return. The rental rate as a percent of the machine's price must be equal to r. If $v/P > r$ everyone would rush out to buy machines, since they yield more than the prevailing interest rate. Similarly, if $v/P < r$ no one would be in the business of renting out machines, since more could be made on alternative investments. The reader may also notice that v/P is analogous to the concept of a perpetual rate of return discussed in the first section of this chapter. An amount P is given up in order to receive a return of v for every period in the future.

Generally, firms do not rent the machines they use. A firm will buy a machine and will use the services of this machine in combination with the labor it hires to produce output. The ownership of machines makes the analysis of the demand for capital somewhat more complex than that of the demand for labor. However, by recognizing the important distinction between a *stock* and a *flow* these two demands can be seen to be quite similar.

A firm uses *capital services* to produce output. These services are a *flow* magnitude. It is the number of machine hours which is relevant to the productive process (just as it is man hours), not the number of machines per se. Frequently, however, the assumption is made that the flow of capital services is proportional to the *stock* of machines (one hundred machines can, if fully employed for one hour, deliver one hundred machine hours of service) and therefore these two different concepts are used synonymously. If during a period a firm desires a certain number of machine hours, this is usually taken to mean that the firm desires a certain number of machines. The firm's demand for capital services is also a demand for capital.

A profit-maximizing firm in perfect competition will choose its level of inputs so that the marginal revenue product from an extra unit of any input is equal to its cost. This result holds also for the demand for machine hours. The cost of capital services is given by the rental rate (v) in Equation 19.8. This cost is borne by the firm whether it rents the machine in the open market or owns the machine itself. In the former case it is an explicit cost, whereas in the latter case it is an implicit cost since the firm could rent its machine to someone else if it chose to do so. The fact of ownership is, to a first approximation, irrelevant to the determination of cost. Perfectly competitive firms will therefore use that number of machine hours for which:

$$MRP_K = v = P(r + d). \qquad [19.11]$$

If a firm obeys the profit-maximizing rule of Equation 19.11 and finds that it desires more capital services than can be provided by its currently existing stock of machinery, it has two choices. First, it may hire the additional machines which are needed in the rental market. This would be formally identical to its decision to hire additional labor. Second, the firm can buy new machinery to meet its needs. This second alternative is the one most often chosen; we call the purchase of new equipment by the firm *investment*. It is an obvious, but often forgotten, fact that investment and the demand for capital services are not the same concept. Net investment (that is, investment over and above that necessary to replace what is being worn out) only occurs if the firm's demand for capital services exceeds that level of services which can be provided by its existing stock of machinery.

Investment demand is an important component of "aggregate demand" in macroeconomic theory. Frequently it is assumed that this demand for plant and equipment (that is, machines) is inversely related to the rate of interest. Using the analysis developed in this part of the text it is possible to demonstrate the links in this argument. A fall in the interest rate (r) will, *ceteris paribus*, decrease the rental rate on capital (Equation 19.10). This will prompt firms to substitute capital for labor in production. Because the new level of capital services demanded may exceed that level which can be provided by the currently existing capital stock, investment may take place.[13] The theory of investment can in this way be integrated into the theory of the firm which was developed in Part III.

[13] There may be substantial lags between the perceived demand for additional capital and actual expenditures on new machines. These lags arise both because decision making takes time and because there may be costs associated with making these decisions. In empirical work the estimation of these lags is quite important.

For an example of lagged adjustment in the demand for an input *see* Problem 5 of Part V.

The Present Discounted Value Criterion and Investment Demand

The theory of investment demand is usually stated in a rather different way from that which was discussed above. This alternative method centers attention on the *present discounted value of the future profits from owning a machine*. If this present discounted value exceeds the price of the machine, the machine should be bought; otherwise the funds should be invested elsewhere. The purpose of this section is to discuss the alternative investment criterion and to show that, under certain conditions, this theory is identical to the one developed in the previous section.

Consider a firm in the process of deciding whether or not to buy a machine. The machine is expected to last n years and will give its owner a stream of monetary returns in each of these n years. Let the return in year i be represented by R_i. If r is the present interest rate, and if this rate is expected to prevail for the next n years, the present discounted value of the machine to its owner is given by:

$$PDV = \frac{R_1}{(1 + r)} + \frac{R_2}{(1 + r)^2} + \cdots + \frac{R_n}{(1 + r)^n}. \quad [19.12]$$

If this value exceeds the price of the machine the firm should purchase it, since even when foregone interest is taken into account the machine promises to return more than it costs. On the other hand, if the price is greater than PDV more could be made by investing elsewhere at the rate r. The only point of equilibrium in a competitive market will be when the price of the machine (P) is exactly equal to its PDV. Only at such a price will those machines which are supplied be demanded by firms.

Using the equilibrium condition $P = PDV$, it is possible to demonstrate two situations in which the present discounted value criterion is identical to the rental rate criterion discussed in the previous section and shown explicitly in Equation 19.10. Suppose that all markets are competitive. The return in period i to the machine owner (R_i) will therefore be precisely the market rental rate (v_i) for the machine during that period. Competition will insure that machine owners, whether they rent their machines to others or use the equipment themselves, will earn the same return. Using the result that $R_i = v_i$ for all i, Equation 19.12 can be rewritten as:

$$PDV = \frac{v_1}{(1 + r)} + \frac{v_2}{(1 + r)^2} + \cdots + \frac{v_n}{(1 + r)^n}. \quad [19.13]$$

Now assume that the machine will last infinitely long and that it will have the same rental rate in every period (v):

$$PDV = \frac{v}{(1 + r)} + \frac{v}{(1 + r)^2} + \cdots + \frac{v}{(1 + r)^n} + \cdots$$

$$= v \cdot \left(\frac{1}{(1 + r)} + \frac{1}{(1 + r)^2} + \cdots + \frac{1}{(1 + r)^n} + \cdots \right)$$

$$= v \cdot \left(\frac{1}{1 - \frac{1}{1 + r}} - 1 \right) \qquad\qquad [19.14]$$

$$= v \cdot \left(\frac{1 + r}{r} - 1 \right)$$

$$= v \cdot \frac{1}{r}.$$

But since in equilibrium $P = PDV$ this says:

$$P = v \cdot \frac{1}{r}$$

or

$$\frac{v}{P} = r$$

as was shown in Equation 19.10′. For this case the present discounted value criterion gives results identical to those outlined in the previous section. We have again demonstrated the algebraic relationship between a machine's price, the rental rate on the machine, and the market rate of interest. In particular, a *ceteris paribus* increase in r will decrease the machine's PDV, and firms will be less willing to buy machines for the same reasons as were discussed above.

Equation 19.10 can be derived for the more general case in which the rental rate on machines is not constant over time and in which there is some depreciation. This analysis is most easily carried out by using continuous time.[14] Suppose that the rental rate for a *new* machine at any time s is given by $v(s)$. Assume also that the machine depreciates expo-

---

[14] What follows is more mathematical than are most other sections of this text. The reader may wish to accept the assertion that Equation 19.10 can be derived without pursuing the formal mathematical argument. Those who can follow the mathematical argument may find it useful in understanding more advanced topics in capital theory.

nentially[15] at the rate d. The net rental rate (and the marginal revenue product) of a machine therefore declines over time as the machine gets older. In year s the net rental rate on an *old* machine bought in a previous year (t) would be:

$$v(s) \, e^{-d(s-t)} \qquad\qquad [19.15]$$

since $s - t$ is the number of years over which the machine has been decaying. For example, suppose a machine were bought in 1960. Its net rental rate in 1965 would then be the rental rate that is earned by new machines in 1965 $[v(1965)]$ discounted by the factor e^{-5d} to account for the amount of depreciation that has taken place over the five years of the machine's life.

If the firm is considering buying the machine when it is new in year t it should discount all of these net rental amounts back to that date. The present value of the net rental in year s discounted back to year t is therefore (if r is the interest rate):

$$e^{-r(s-t)} \, v(s) \, e^{-d(s-t)} = e^{(r+d)t} \, v(s) \, e^{-(r+d)s} \qquad\qquad [19.16]$$

since, again, $(s - t)$ years elapse from when the machine is bought until when the net rental is received. The present discounted value of a machine bought in year t is therefore the sum (integral) of these present values. This sum should be taken from year t (when the machine is bought) over all years into the future:

$$PDV(t) = \int_{t}^{\infty} e^{(r+d)t} \, v(s) \, e^{-(r+d)s} \, ds. \qquad\qquad [19.17]$$

Since in equilibrium the price of the machine at year $t[P(t)]$ will be equal to this present value, we have the following fundamental equation:

$$P(t) = \int_{t}^{\infty} e^{(r+d)t} \, v(s) \, e^{-(r+d)s} \, ds. \qquad\qquad [19.18]$$

---

[15] In this view of depreciation machines are assumed to "evaporate" at a fixed rate per unit of time. This model of decay is in many ways identical to the assumptions of radioactive decay made in physics. There are other possible forms which physical depreciation might take; this is only the most mathematically tractable.

It is important to keep the concept of physical depreciation (depreciation which affects a machine's productivity) distinct from accounting depreciation. The latter concept is important only in that the method of accounting depreciation chosen may affect the rate of taxation on the profits from a machine. From an economic point of view, however, the cost of a machine is a sunk cost: Any choice on how to "write off" this cost is to some extent arbitrary.

This rather formidable equation is simply a more complex version of Equation 19.13 and can be used to derive Equation 19.10. First rewrite the equation as:

$$P(t) = e^{(r+d)t} \int_t^{\infty} v(s) \, e^{-(r+d)s} \, ds. \qquad [19.19]$$

Now differentiate with respect to t, using the rule for taking the derivative of a product:

$$\frac{dP(t)}{dt} = (r+d) \, e^{(r+d)t} \int_t^{\infty} v(s) \, e^{-(r+d)s} \, ds - e^{(r+d)t} \, v(t) \, e^{-(r+d)t}$$
$$= (r+d) \, P(t) - v(t).$$

Hence:

$$v(t) = (r+d) \, P(t) - \frac{dP(t)}{dt}. \qquad [19.20]$$

This is precisely the result shown earlier in Equation 19.10 except that the term $-dP(t)/dt$ has been added. The economic explanation for the presence of this term is that it represents the capital gains which accrue to the owner of the machine. If the machine's price can be expected to rise, for example, the owner may accept somewhat less than $(r+d)P$ for its rental. On the other hand, if the price of the machine is expected to fall $[dP(t)/dt < 0]$ the owner will require more in rent than is specified in Equation 19.10. If the price of the machine is expected to remain constant over time $dP(t)/dt = 0$ and Equations 19.20 and 19.10 are identical. The result of this analysis is to show that there is a definite relationship between the price of a machine at any time and the stream of future profits which that machine promises. It also shows how machine prices, rental rates, and interest rates are related.

Conclusion

This chapter has presented a general overview of the theory of capital as it stands today. The models presented have been based exclusively on the perfectly competitive assumptions and have been relevant only to a world without uncertainty. Even with these limiting assumptions the theory is still conceptually rather difficult. Great care has been taken to show exactly how a theory of capital can be integrated with the classical theory of the firm. For this reason the theory which has been developed might be called a "neoclassical theory" of capital. An understanding of this theory is an obvious place to begin a study of the demand for capital. The more complex factors of any real-world analysis (such as the uncertainty of future returns from a machine) can be investigated only if a well-developed model is available.

It should be emphasized that although the neoclassical model is the most complete model available it is by no means universally accepted. Some economists may choose alternative models for two rather different reasons. The first reason is essentially pragmatic. It is claimed that real-world investment decisions are based on far different criteria than those outlined in this chapter. To discuss the myriad of alternative investment models which have been proposed would, however, be to go too far afield.

A second, more theoretical, objection relates to the neoclassical model's overly simplistic assumption that there is something called "capital" which has a rate of return. The idea that we may speak unambiguously of the rate of return to capital accumulation underlies all of this chapter. This rate was first examined explicitly in the initial three sections of the chapter and, although the analysis of the last two sections was carefully centered on the nature of the demand for a particular machine (not for "capital" as a whole), it was still necessary to introduce "the" interest rate into the analysis. Some economists would object to this treatment by arguing that in a world with many different types of capital equipment to speak of an overall rate of return is misleading. Since this objection is usually raised together with the rather different question of whether capital owners "deserve" to receive a return, it will be briefly examined in the appendix to this chapter.

APPENDIX TO CHAPTER 19

Alternative Views on the Theory
of the Factoral Distribution
# of Income

Introduction

The quotation by Ricardo in the introduction of Part V stressed that the central concern of economic theory is an investigation of those factors which influence the distribution of an economy's output among the owners of productive factors. While this concern may not be so important today as it was at the time Ricardo wrote, nevertheless the study of the determinants of the factoral distribution of income is still a hotly debated issue. In the previous three chapters the marginal productivity theory of the pricing of factors has been developed. This theory is con-

385

ceptually "neat" and elegantly ties together the notions of demand for goods and demand for factors. Pricing of factors and the associated distribution of income is seen as simply one more example of the workings of an interrelated web of supply and demand relations. Because the theory is completely worked out and consistent it is the predominantly held view of the mechanisms which operate to determine factor prices. It would be a mistake, however, to conclude that economists are "happy" with the theory. Numerous complaints have been raised against the theory, some of which will be examined in this appendix. An alternative theory which originated in the writings of Karl Marx will be briefly outlined.

The major complaint which has been brought against the marginal productivity theory is that it is "too mechanical" in its explanation of the factoral distribution of income. In the marginal productivity theory the interreaction of individuals' tastes and productive technology is the sole determinant of factor shares. There is no place in the theory for distortions created by bargaining power, incomplete information, or by "exploitation." Those economists who believe that such other features of factor pricing must be accorded some consideration are therefore led to reject the marginal productivity theory as a complete theory of factor shares. Before turning to an examination of an alternative theory which has been put forth it is useful to survey some of the more specific arguments which have been made against the theoretical structure of the marginal productivity theory.

Specific Theoretical Objections to the Marginal Productivity Theory

Two major theoretical objections to the marginal productivity theory of factor demand have been debated by economists. The first of these concerns is the "adding-up" controversy. A brief discussion of this has already been presented in Chapter 17. Chapter 17 concluded that the marginal productivity theory is, under certain conditions, a consistent explanation of factor pricing in that the factor shares dictated by the theory are exactly sufficient to exhaust total output. The condition required for this result is that industries exhibit constant costs (in a sense "industry productions" must have constant returns to scale). This requirement raises numerous theoretical issues: Is it required that firms also have constant returns to scale production functions?[1] Are these

---

[1] The requirement that all firms in an industry exhibit constant return to scale raises another interesting theoretical issue: What is it that determines the actual size of firms? If constant returns to scale truly prevails, firm managers should be indifferent about the

requirements satisfied in the real world? If not, how can the marginal productivity theory of pricing be made consistent with the income-output identity? None of these questions have been unambiguously resolved, although the theoretical controversy has been dormant for several years.

More recently a second theoretical controversy has arisen over the marginal productivity theory of factor pricing. This controversy centers attention on the concept of the *marginal productivity of capital.* Some authors question whether this concept can be given any meaning when it is recognized that "capital" is in fact a very inhomogeneous mass of machines, buildings, and other equipment. Whereas it may be possible to speak of the marginal productivity of a particular machine, to speak of the marginal productivity of some aggregate "capital" at best involves circular reasoning. To demonstrate this circularity, suppose there are only two capital goods, anvils (A) and bellows (B). Let the quantity of anvils be denoted by Q_A and the quantity of bellows by Q_B. The "traditional" approach for aggregating these two different pieces of capital into a single magnitude is to use their respective market prices (P_A and P_B). By this method the aggregate capital stock (K) would be defined as:

$$K = P_A Q_A + P_B Q_B. \tag{19A.1}$$

The traditional theory would then conclude that the marginal productivity of capital is the extra output obtainable from using one dollar more of this aggregate capital. The workings of the market will insure that this extra output will be the same whether the dollar is spent on anvils or bellows. It is this marginal productivity which, in part, determines the rental rate on capital and in so doing also determines *the* interest rate.

This argument seems, at first glance, to be a reasonable one. Upon closer inspection, however, a circularity in the proof becomes apparent. Consider the prices P_A and P_B. What determines them? As we saw in Chapter 19, in equilibrium the price of anvils will be equal to the present discounted value of the future profits from owning an anvil. But this cannot be calculated until the interest rate is known. On the other hand, the interest rate is not known until some aggregate capital can be defined so that we may determine the marginal productivity of "it."[2] As Kaldor[3]

---

particular size of their firm in a perfectly competitive industry. Technically, marginal cost and price will be equal at all levels of output. The size distribution of firms in a perfectly competitive industry is indeterminate, then, if each firm exhibits constant returns to scale.

[2] Notice that this problem would not arise if there were only one kind of capital and one type of output, since we could then speak of the marginal physical product of this machine without the necessity of introducing market prices.

[3] N. Kaldor, *Essays on Value and Distribution* (London: G. Duckworth & Co. Ltd., 1960), pp. 218–223.

points out, it seems that some additional "equation" is needed in the economic system if we are to avoid this circularity. The marginal productivity theory does not provide such an equation. Therefore, if it is desired to speak of the interest rate as a payment for the productivity of an aggregate stock of "capital," some further conceptual bases must be developed.

The problem of aggregating capital has not as yet been solved in an entirely satisfactory manner. Although this question has been investigated by a number of authors[4] many of the basic conceptual difficulties remain. Indeed, since it will probably always be impossible to add "apples and oranges" in an objective (nonprice) way, it is unlikely that the aggregation problem will ever finally be resolved. Most recent work has attempted to show those conditions which must hold if the marginal productivity theory is to provide an approximately correct explanation of the rate of return to capital. Since this work is theoretical, and since the analysis will probably never convince strong anti-Capitalists in any case, no further summary will be presented.

An Alternative: The Notion of Surplus Value

A major alternative[5] to the marginal productivity theory of aggregate factor shares is based on the notion of *surplus value*. This concept was originally used by Marx[6] in developing his labor theory of value. In its most elementary form surplus value is defined to be that amount by which the price of a good exceeds the "socially necessary" costs of producing it. For Marx, socially necessary costs included only labor costs (Marx called these "variable capital," v) and costs of physical depreciation (Marx called these "constant capital," c). Hence, if the price of a good is denoted by p, surplus value (s) is defined by the famous formula:

$$p = c + v + s. \qquad\qquad [19A.2]$$

[4] A survey and bibliography of this literature is presented in G. C. Harcourt, "Some Cambridge Controversies in the Theory of Capital," *Journal of Economic Literature*, vol. VII, no. 2 (June 1969), pp. 369–405.

[5] Many recent theoretical treatments of the factoral distribution of income have been macroeconomic theories. In these it is aggregate economic factors which determine the distribution of income, not microeconomic pricing decisions. These alternative theories are not examined in this book.

[6] The major reference is Karl Marx, *Capital: A Critique of Political Economy*. There are many editions of this book and reading any of these is no simple task. The beginning reader interested in the economic aspects of *Capital* might start with the heavily edited and rearranged Modern Library version, *Capital and Other Writings*, Max Eastman, ed. (New York: Random House, Inc., 1932).

For some reason goods sell at a price which exceeds socially necessary costs $(c + v)$, and this excess is termed surplus.

The choice of the word "surplus" was appropriate for Marx's purposes. Included in this term are all factor payments to capital (rent, return to capital, and "pure" profits). Terming such payments "surplus" is not merely a matter of terminology; there is also the strong implication that these payments are undeserved. In fact, Marx concludes that labor is exclusively responsible for the creation of surplus value and that it is the nature of capital owners to expropriate this surplus. Hence Marx' theory of value gives strong ethical support to the proposition that private ownership of capital is both unnecessary and undesirable.

It is possible to develop the Marxian notion of surplus within the framework of the marginal productivity theory. While this development is very far from the methods actually used by Marx, the use of these more recent tools does permit the concept of surplus to be incorporated into the analytical structure of this book. For this purpose, then, assume that labor is homogeneous (an essential Marxian assumption) and that labor input is measured in man hours (L). In Figure 19A.1 the marginal value product of labor curve ($MVP_L = P \cdot MP_L$) is drawn with a negative slope reflecting the usual assumption of a diminishing marginal productivity.[7] If the competitive wage rate is given by w,[8] then the profit-maximizing firm will hire L^* units of labor. With this input of labor the total value of production is represented by the area under the MVP_L curve (AOL^*E). Because of the workings of the market, however, labor is only paid wOL^*E, and therefore a "surplus value" of AwE is generated. Typically, this surplus will be "expropriated" by capital owners in the form of interest and profits or by land owners in the form of rent. The actual division of the surplus will depend on a number of factors, but the most important one is the bargaining strength of the various parties competing for the surplus. Marxists would claim that Capitalists and land owners have great strength in this regard and are likely to expropriate the entire amount of surplus for their own uses. It is the private ownership of these means of production which permits this exploitation to take place. Such factors as union bargaining power and government interference have at most a small effect on the final distribution of this surplus.[9]

[7] To be strictly correct the MVP_L curve should be drawn to exclude capital depreciation which even Marx recognized as a socially necessary cost of production. The MVP_L curve then represents "net" productivity.

[8] In the argument originally presented by Marx w would be determined by the subsistence level of wages necessary to maintain a laborer. By various methods Capitalists are assumed capable of keeping w at a subsistence level.

[9] More recent Marxist writings stress that certain ostensible labor costs (for example, salaries paid to advertising men) should also be included as a part of the surplus, since these costs are also socially unnecessary.

Figure 19A.1   A Marginal Productivity Notion of Surplus

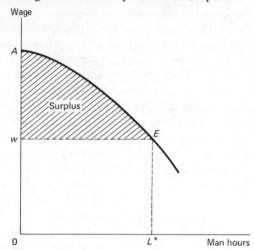

A profit-maximizing firm chooses labor input such that $MVP_L = w$. Total payments to labor are then wOL^*E. The total value of production is AOL^*E, and therefore the "surplus" is given by the area AwE.

Critical Comments on the Notion of Surplus Value

Marx's labor theory of value has a strong metaphysical aspect. The argument that labor is the only productive factor which deserves a return is one that must be taken as a matter of faith. Certainly it is possible to envision an institutional arrangement of society in which capital does not receive any payment, but a similar argument could also be made for payments to labor (at least to the extent that wages exceed some subsistence level). In this sense all factor payments which exceed "depreciation" (both human and physical) can be regarded as surplus, since all such payments could be expropriated by the state.

Such a generalized conception of surplus is made even more attractive when it is recognized that, contrary to the Marxian model, labor (as well as capital) is in fact very inhomogeneous. In modern industrial societies the wages paid for one man hour of labor differ substantially among workers.[10] It may be quite reasonable to include some portion of these differentials as part of the expropriatable surplus. This way of viewing the concept of surplus can be made Marxian by recognizing that

---

[10] If it is recognized that labor also is inhomogeneous, the same problems of aggregation arise as those which occur for the case of capital. One can no longer speak unambiguously of the supply of labor but must instead make some attempt to measure labor in "efficiency units."

in many cases wage differentials reflect a return on "human capital." The high wages of, say, a doctor are more related to his education and training than to any innate aspects of his labor power. Wage differentials are no more socially necessary than are payments to capital.

The position taken here is that the initial distinction made by Ricardo in regard to distribution of income among particular factors of production is no longer particularly useful if one wishes to study social welfare. One should instead center attention on the size distribution of income (regardless of source) and analyze whether or not the existing distribution is desirable in some social sense. This question is examined in detail in the final two parts of this book and given explicit treatment in Chapter 26.

Conclusion: The Place of the Marginal Productivity Theory

Critics of the marginal productivity theory of the pricing of factors have brought up several important objections. Unfortunately, no very adequate theory has been developed as a replacement. From the point of view of prediction these critics have shown that one should be careful in applying the marginal productivity theory. Many imperfections exist in factor markets, and in these cases bargaining strength will play an important role in pricing. The marginal productivity theory is at best a good place to start the analysis.

As is generally the case in economics, it is useful to make a distinction between the *positive* and the *normative* roles of a theory of factor pricing. A positive theory of factor pricing would seek to determine those elements of tastes and technology which affect factor productivities. The question of whether market prices adequately reflect these productivities is also an important area of investigation. In cases where market prices diverge from physical productivities it is the productivities which are important for purposes of allocating resources. As Solow[11] points out, studies of the determinants of the rate of return on capital can be properly understood as attempts to establish some measure of the social productivity (that is, the "shadow price") of capital rather than as ideological pleadings. It is important for any society to have some evaluation of the productivity of capital investment so that intelligent allocational choices can be made. For example, it would seem unwise for a society in which capital is in short supply (and therefore

[11] R.M. Solow, *Capital Theory and the Rate of Return* (Skokie, Ill.: Rand McNally and Company, 1964). This book consists of three lectures delivered in the Professor Dr. F. DeVries Lecture Series at the Netherlands School of Economics.

presumably the rate of return is high) to adopt industrial projects which use a relatively great amount of this scarce resource. Only by recognizing the true costs of building a capital intensive project (a dam, steel plant, government palace) can that capital which is available be used in a socially optimal way. Many of the tools developed in Chapter 19 aid in understanding this aspect of capital allocation.

An understanding of the forces determining factor productivity does not, however, answer the normative question of who "should" receive the returns generated from factor employment. This question can only be answered as part of a more general investigation of the economics of social welfare. It is the purpose of Parts VI and VII to shed some light on these difficult philosophical questions.

DISCUSSION QUESTIONS AND PROBLEMS FOR PART V

Discussion Questions

1. Doesn't it somehow seem rather crass to speak of a man's wages being determined by such impersonal forces as "supply" and "demand"? Shouldn't we take more account of human needs and individual personalities?

2. Often one reads an advertisement for a store in the newspaper which asserts that its prices are low because it operates in a low-rent area and does not have to pay the high costs associated with more prestigious locations. Using Ricardo's analysis of rent, how would you evaluate this assertion?

3. Is there a sense in which Kareem Abdul Jabbar (formerly Lew Alcindor) is more exploited by the workings of the labor market than are migrant farm workers? If so, isn't the concept of "economic exploitation" a somewhat useless one from the point of view of social policy?

4. The study of bargaining offers the possibility for the construction of many interesting scenarios. For example, under what conditions would the two parties agree to the appointment of an "impartial" arbitrator with absolute power to set the final contract terms? Once he was appointed, how would each side treat the arbitrator? What sorts of proposals would they present? Finally, is there anything the arbitrator himself might do to make the bargaining more "serious"?

5. Can you develop any additional theories of the determinants of labor's share of total income which are consistent with the facts? Perhaps a hybrid of some of the theories discussed in the appendix to Chapter 19 would be useful in this regard.

6. The objections raised by Joan Robinson, N. Kaldor, and others to our attempts at measuring capital apply with equal force to the measurement of "labor," "land," and "output." Since it will always be logically impossible to add apples and oranges, some common measuring rod must be found in order to talk about these aggregates. Can you think of any possible measuring rods other than market prices?

7. It is very costly for trains to go up and down grades; a level track bed is far more economical in terms of operating costs. Since railroad planners probably assume their roadbeds will last forever (or at least for an extremely long time), it would seem that the cost

savings from flattening a roadbed would be so great as to warrant this in almost all circumstances. If flattening a hill will save only $1000 per year in operating costs, but the roadbed will last forever, the total cost savings would be infinite. Nonetheless, railroad roadbeds do in fact go up and down grades. Why?

8. Proudhon said "property is theft," and Marx concentrated on one aspect of this "theft": the private ownership of productive capital. Comment on the assertion that there is absolutely no reason why the owners of capital deserve a monetary return. Could such an argument also be applied to one's labor power, particularly in that one's productiveness may depend on ownership of human capital?

9. In Chapter 19 we discussed the fact that a firm will invest in a machine so long as its rate of return from this machine exceeds the cost of capital to the firm. In the real world a firm has many ways of raising capital: by selling stock, selling bonds, getting bank loans, or reinvesting corporate profits. In this complexity of financing methods what in fact is its "cost of capital"?

Problems

1. Under what conditions would you expect the imposition of a minimum wage to:
   (a) have no effect on wages or on the number of workers employed?
   (b) increase wages and leave the number of workers unaffected?
   (c) increase wages and decrease the number of workers?
   (d) increase both wages and the number of workers?
   Use your knowledge of the American economy to argue on a priori grounds which of these outcomes (or possibly others) seems, on the whole, the most likely.

2. Explain each of the following observations about the labor market by using a supply-demand analysis:
   (a) Women are often paid less than men for the same job.
   (b) Wages of doctors and construction workers have risen rapidly in recent years whereas general manufacturing wage rates have not.
   (c) The United States in the early 1960's had a "shortage" of engineers and scientists.
   (d) There now appears to be a "surplus" of persons in the academic job market.

3. In the early 1960's President John Kennedy's Council of Economic Advisers recommended the institution of "Wage-Price Guideposts."

The basic idea of the guideposts was to require wages in all industries to increase at the rate at which the national level of output per worker increases (about 3.2 percent per year). Some industries would have had rates of productivity increase of less than 3.2 percent. These industries were to be permitted to increase prices to the extent that their productivity increase fell short of the national average. On the other hand, firms which had productivity increases in excess of the national average were expected to reduce their prices to the extent of this excess.

Adherence to these rules were to keep prices constant on a nationwide basis. There were numerous exceptions to these general principles, but assume for the purposes of this problem that these were not important. If the Wage-Price Guideposts were legislated as an unbreakable law, answer the following questions:

(a) What would happen to the relative factor shares in each industry over time?

(b) What does this implicitly assume about the elasticity of substitution in all industries?

(c) What effect would this legislation have on the investment of new capital if industries do not obey the assumption discussed in (b)?

(d) In regard to your answer to (c), what effects do you think the Guideposts would have on economic growth?

4. Suppose a union has a fixed supply of labor to sell. If the union desires to maximize the total wage bill what wage rate will it demand? How would this answer be changed if unemployed workers are paid unemployment insurance at the rate u per worker and the union now desires to maximize the sum of the wage bill and the total amount of unemployment compensation?

5. We have always assumed that there are no costs other than the wage rate associated with adding (or subtracting) workers to the work force. In fact there are substantial costs to hiring and firing which are not directly reflected in the wage rate. For example, costs of fringe benefits, such as health insurance, make hiring costs greater than the wage rate. Analogously, severance pay makes it relatively unattractive to fire a worker. The effect of these costs is to make firms unwilling to change the previous period's level of employment (L_{t-1}).

Suppose the costs of changing from L_{t-1} to L_t are given by:

$$c_1 = b_1(L_t - L_{t-1})^2.$$

There are also costs involved in not having the desired level of employment (L_t^*) at period t. These costs are given by:

$$c_2 = b_2(L_t^* - L_t)^2.$$

(a) Show that if a firm desires to minimize $c_1 + c_2$ it will adjust its labor force "proportionally," that is:

$$L_t - L_{t-1} = \lambda(L_t^* - L_{t-1})$$

where:

$$\lambda = \frac{b_2}{b_1 + b_2}.$$

(b) Interpret mathematically and in words how the firm would adjust its labor force if $b_1 = 0$, $b_2 = 0$, or if $b_1 = b_2$.

(c) Because the firm adjusts its labor force slowly toward L^*, at any point of time it is likely that L will not equal L^*. Suppose that the firm chooses L^* in accord with the marginal productivity theory of factor demand. More specifically, suppose the firm has a Cobb-Douglas production function with constant returns to scale and that the ratio of the firm's output price to the wage rate of labor stays constant over time (that is, P/w is constant over time). Show that this implies: $L_t^* = kQ_t$ where Q_t is output in period t and k is a constant.

(d) If $L_t^* = kQ_t$ and the firm adjusts L_t slowly toward L_t^*, how will the *average productivity* of labor (Q_t/L_t) change over time as output fluctuates over the business cycle? Does this kind of change occur in the real world?

6. As in the example of Chapter 19, suppose trees are produced by applying one unit of labor at time 0. The value of the wood contained in a tree is given at any time (t) by $f(t)$. If the market wage rate is w and the instantaneous rate is r, what is the *PDV* of this production process and how should t be chosen to maximize this *PDV*?

If the optimal value of t is denoted by t^* show that the no-pure-profit condition of perfect competition will necessitate that:

$$w = e^{-rt} f(t^*).$$

Can you interpret what this expression means?

A tree sold before t^* will not be cut down immediately. Rather, it will still make sense for the new owner to let the tree continue to mature until t^*. Show that the price of a u-year-old tree will be we^{ru} and that this price will exceed the value of the wood in the tree $[f(u)]$ for every value of u except $u = t^*$ when these two values are equal.

Suppose a land owner has a "balanced" woodlot with one tree of "each" age from 0 to t^*. What is the value of this woodlot? (*Hint:* It is the sum of the values of each tree in the lot.)

If the value of the woodlot is V show that the instantaneous interest on V, $(r \cdot V)$, is equal to the "profits" earned at each instant by the land owner, where by profits we mean the difference between the revenue obtained from selling a fully matured tree $[f(t^*)]$ and the cost of planting a new one (w). This result shows that there is no pure profit in borrowing to buy a woodlot, since one would have to pay in interest at each instant exactly what would be earned from cutting a fully matured tree.

. As scotch ages, its value increases. One dollar of scotch at year 0 is worth $e^{2\sqrt{t}-.15t}$ dollars at time t. If the interest rate is 5 percent, after how many years should a man sell his scotch if he is to maximize the *PDV* of this sale?

PART VI
General Equilibrium and Welfare

Introduction

In previous sections of this book we have examined the operations of single markets in isolation. This simplification is necessary if we are to comprehend in any detailed way the determinants of supply and demand. In order to understand the workings of the market system some narrowing of focus is imperative. Nonetheless, the "partial equilibrium" (single market) method of analysis has one major weakness: We can never conceptualize how the system works as a whole. Clearly, an increase in demand in one market will affect prices not only in that one market; the effects of this shift in demand will reverberate throughout the economy. For example, consider the effects of an increase in the demand for automobiles. This increase will affect pricing in the automobile market. The increased demand for autos will also create an increased demand for steel, glass, chromium, and so forth. These increased demands will similarly affect demands in other markets for goods which these industries use. But the story does not stop there; in fact, it has only begun. The increased demand for production in various industries will also increase the demand for factors of production, notably labor. This increased demand for labor may raise wages, thereby increasing purchasing power and increasing the demand for all those goods which individuals buy. It is possible to extend this story indefinitely, but the essential point is clear. The economic system is tied together by a vast web of interconnected markets. A disturbance in one market generates ripples which spread through many others. In fact, by starting the discussion with an "increase in the demand for automobiles" we have probably obscured some aspects of the interwoven nature of the economic system since such "increases" don't just happen. Rather, an ideal theory would attempt to understand the forces which caused the increase.

Economists have, naturally, been aware of the need for a *general equilibrium* approach to the economic system. At the same time that the Marshallian analysis was being developed in England a different mode of analysis was being considered by several Continental economists. This second analytical system represented an attempt to understand the workings of the economic system as a whole. Foremost among the individuals engaged in these investigations was the French economist Léon Walras (1834–1910). In his *Elements of Pure Economics* Walras demonstrated a model for looking at the economy (in a formal way) as a set of *simultaneous equations* which determine the quantities and prices of all those goods and services which are traded among individuals. The essential concept in this analysis was that of simultaneity. Just as the solutions to two equations in two unknowns studied in high-school algebra depend simultaneously on both equations, so do the equilibrium prices and quantities determined by the economic system depend simultaneously on the workings of all markets. The Walrasian system attempts to represent this interwoven nature of the economy's allocative mechanism.

Except for a brief appendix (to Chapter 22), this part will not investigate the general Walrasian model in any detail. Although Walras' concepts (or their modern successors) will underlie much of the analysis, it is not necessary to develop a detailed general equilibrium model here. Rather, these chapters will deal with only a few simple cases, although the results which are presented can easily be made more general.

In Chapter 20 the concept of economic efficiency will be examined. It is important to be precise in defining what it means for an economic system to allocate scarce resources "efficiently"; the purpose of this chapter is to develop such a definition. Since the notion of efficiency is examined for an economic system as a whole, it is clear that general equilibrium analysis is the proper tool for these investigations.

Efficiency is only one aspect of the more general question of welfare. Given scarce resources, efficient use of these resources is an obvious necessary condition for maximizing societies' "welfare." However, we will see in Chapter 21 that there are many ways of efficiently allocating resources.[1] To choose among these efficient allocations it is necessary to make some value judgments about social welfare. In Chapter 21 formal approaches to welfare decisions will be examined. An understanding of the abstract ideal of social welfare provides a valuable frame of reference for examining more policy-oriented questions.

In Chapters 20 and 21 no mention is made of how efficient, socially optimal allocations of resources can be brought about. It is important to make a careful distinction between the ends which an economic system might achieve ("social welfare") and the means which might produce these ends. Conceivably a government could, if it were omniscient, dictate to each agent the behavior which is required if society is to operate as efficiently as possible. Or, alternatively, perhaps some mechanism might be found which does not require such autocratic methods. One mechanism which has been intensively studied is the price system. In Chapter 22 it will be demonstrated that under certain conditions a price system can be devised which, by relying on the self-interest of individuals and firms, will cause resources to be allocated in an efficient manner. It will also be demonstrated that a suitable price system can be found which will bring about any particular efficient allocation of resources. Specifically, a set of prices which will (again, under certain conditions) yield a "socially desirable" allocation exists.

The discovery of the interrelationship between the optimal allocation of resources and the "correct" pricing of goods was one of the most important in theoretical economic analysis. This is true

---

[1] There are many more ways in which to allocate resources inefficiently.

not so much because of the policy implications which can be derived from this theorem (in fact, we will see that the policy implications are meager) but because of the insights into the workings of the economic system which are provided by this way of looking at the world. The "duality" relationship between pricing and allocation has an importance which transcends the mathematical framework within which it was developed.

Although from a social point of view Part VI takes a broader view than earlier sections of this book, it is still rather limited in its approach to social welfare. Two features of any truly universal conception of social welfare are conspicuously absent. First, the analysis of this part deals only with economic matters. Esthetics are not really adequately discussed. For an economics text this is perhaps as it should be and no apologies will be made. Second, more pragmatically, social behavior and welfare are not examined in Part VI in relation to the role of government in the economic system. Because the government has come to exercise a large role in most economies of the world, any analysis which omits this agent is in many ways deficient. Since most of the tools which have been developed in other sections of this book can be applied to a study of government decision making Part VII consists of a brief investigation of this rather different aspect of social welfare.

CHAPTER 20

The Concept of
Economic Efficiency

Introduction

The word "efficiency" is used in many different economic contexts. It is frequently argued that American workers are "more efficient" than their foreign counterparts; that the steel industry is plagued by "inefficient" technology; that an electric motor is "more efficient" than a steam engine; and, perhaps, that monopolies and labor unions create "inefficiencies." Each of these notions of efficiency is important to a variety of policy issues. The tools developed in this text are useful in quantifying and understanding these issues. The concept of efficiency to be discussed in this chapter is, however, both more far-reaching and more abstract than any of those mentioned. Here, the term *economic efficiency* will be used in the context of investigating the general question of whether resources are allocated optimally. To describe what economists mean by the term "optimally" is the purpose of this chapter.

Traditionally, the investigation of economic efficiency has been carried on by using a restricted model. This model examines the question of efficiency in a static context. The allocation of resources at one point in time is examined and the question is posed whether conditions might be "improved" if these resources were reallocated. This analysis is therefore one more example of the comparative statics approach. While it is possible to generalize the analysis a bit,[1] such generalizations will not be attempted in this book. The basic static model illustrates most of the properties found in advanced models. More important, many questions of optimal allocation cannot be analyzed at all using traditional "marginal models." These questions have been mentioned briefly earlier and are considered again in Chapter 21. The purpose of the present chapter is, however, to provide a clear understanding of economic efficiency in its most elementary form.

A definition of an efficient allocation of resources is difficult because there is no single magnitude which is being maximized. For example, it is impossible to talk about the output of the economic system as a whole because there is no unambiguous way of adding up all the different goods which are produced. Similarly, since we have no means for making comparisons of individuals' well being, we have no way of measuring society's "utility." For these reasons it is clear that optimality must be a multidimensional concept; problems of aggregation can therefore be avoided. Using this multidimensional idea, it is possible initially to introduce the concept of efficiency in an abstract setting. If there are a number of beneficial activities a situation is said to be *efficient* if one of these activities cannot be increased without decreasing some other activity. It is perhaps easiest to see why such a situation is called efficient by observing what *inefficient* situations might be. By the definition a situation is inefficient if some beneficial activity can be increased without necessitating a cutback on any other activities. In inefficient situations conditions can be made unambiguously better. On the other hand, if we are to move from one efficient situation to another, this would require reducing one activity in order to increase other activities. Without a way of comparing these activities it is impossible to know whether or not conditions have improved.

---

[1] For example, generalizations to consider time or uncertainty can be easily (if rather formally) made to the static, certain model presented here. All that is necessary is to redefine the concept of a "good" (and its "price") in the ways discussed earlier.

This general definition can be made more transparent by considering the examples which will arise in this chapter. We will consider an *exchange economy* in which certain amounts of various goods exist and the problem is to allocate these goods among individuals in an efficient way. An allocation of the existing goods is said to be efficient if *no one can be made better off* (by reallocating the available goods) *without making someone else worse off*. This concept of efficiency avoids the problem of interpersonal comparison of utility. Rather, individuals decide for themselves whether a particular change makes them better off or not. If one individual were made worse off by some allocational change, even if everyone else were made better off we could not say that the change was an unambiguous improvement. Since we have no way of comparing individuals' utility levels, we cannot pass judgments on changes which make some individuals better off and others worse off.

A first step toward creating an economic model having production possibilities is to investigate the conditions for efficiency in production. In this case an allocation of resources is said to be efficient if no more of one good can be produced (given present technology) without the necessity of cutting back on the production of some other good. By using this definition the problem of comparing the levels of output of different goods has been circumvented.[2] It is not necessary to add together "apples and oranges" in order to be able to talk about efficiency in production. Instead, a situation would be described as inefficient if more oranges could be produced without the necessity of cutting back on apple production: Apples are compared only to apples and oranges only to oranges.

Productive efficiency is not an end in itself. The ultimate end of an economic system is presumably to provide for the well being of its citizens, not simply to produce goods. Insofar as individuals are not satiated with goods, however, productive efficiency can be seen to be a necessary condition for any more general achievement of efficiency. If more apples could be produced without cutting back on orange production these extra apples could be given to someone, thereby increasing his well being (without affecting the well being of anyone else). Since this kind of argument could be made whenever production is inefficient we have shown that general efficiency in a *production and exchange* economy must entail productive efficiency. These ideas also suggest that for a definition of efficiency in a society in which both production and exchange take place a simple modification of the definition for an exchange economy will suffice.

---

[2] The most usual way of aggregating commodities is to use their market prices. Because no mention will be made in this chapter of a price system such an avenue is not open. Indeed, even if aggregation of commodities by market prices were permissable it is not at all clear whether a prescription such as "maximize GNP" would be in any way related to economic efficiency.

A particular allocation of resources and the associated production plan is defined as efficient if no one individual can be made better off (by some possible reallocation of resources or final goods) without making someone else worse off. This definition serves to tie together individuals' tastes and productive technology into a general conception of efficiency. The conditions which are required for such efficiency are discussed in the section "Efficiency in Production and Exchange" below.

The definitions of economic efficiency are therefore quite similar to one another. In the remainder of this chapter we will discuss the allocative requirements which achieve the goals of efficiency as so defined. It should be mentioned at the outset that efficiency is not necessarily an end in itself. Efficiency in production and exchange is, however, a possible means for achieving an even more ethereal goal: "social welfare." This point will be greatly expanded on in Chapter 21.

Efficiency in Exchange

In an exchange economy the quantities of all goods are fixed. By starting our discussion with this simplified case it is possible, for the moment, to ignore problems raised in the theory of production. Our goal is to allocate these goods among individuals in an efficient way. The necessary conditions for an efficient allocation can easily be stated: For an allocation of the available goods to be efficient the goods should be distributed so that the marginal rate of substitution (MRS – remember that this is a measure of how an individual is willing to trade one good for another) between any two goods is the same for *all* individuals. To show this, suppose there are only two goods (guns and butter, to use familiar examples) and two individuals (Smith and Jones) in society. Assume also that there are 50 guns and 100 pounds of butter to be allocated. Would an equal allocation of these commodities to each individual be efficient? The answer to this question depends on the individuals' tastes. Suppose that the MRS (of guns for butter) for Smith is 2/1 when he gets 25 guns and 50 pounds of butter. Smith is willing to give up 2 pounds of butter to get 1 more gun under the proposed equal allocation. On the other hand, suppose that Jones' MRS (of guns for butter) is 1/1: Under the equal allocation scheme (with 25 guns and 50 pounds of butter) he would be willing to trade 1 pound of butter for 1 gun. Under these assumptions it is easy to see that the proposed allocation is not efficient. Take 2 pounds of butter from Smith. Trade 1 of these to Jones for 1 gun (notice that Jones is willing to make this trade). Now give this gun to Smith so that he will be as well off as he was before the 2 pounds of butter were taken. We have now found a new allocation in which Smith (with 26 guns and 48 pounds of butter) and Jones (with 24 guns and 51 pounds of butter) are each as well off as they were under the original equal allocation. With this new allocation, however, there is 1 pound of butter left over. It may be given to either Smith or Jones, making the lucky recipient better off than he was before. What we have shown, therefore, is that the initial (equal) allocation was not efficient: There exists some alternative allocation in which Smith, say, could be made better off without making Jones any worse off.[3]

It should be clear that the numbers in this example were purely arbitrary. Any allocation in which the *MRS*'s of two individuals differ can be shown to be inefficient. There may be many different allocations which are efficient, however, and these can be most easily demonstrated by using a graphic device known as the *Edgeworth Box*.[4] The construction of this diagram is shown in Figure 20.1. The Edgeworth Box has dimen-

---

[3] The reader is reminded that "proofs" such as this are not strictly correct in that they use discrete ("whole unit") analysis to show what are essentially continuous (calculus) results. For this reason the proof in the text should only be considered to be a nonrigorous, pedagogic device.

A "correct" calculus proof can be demonstrated as follows. Let B_S and G_S be the quantities of butter and guns received by Smith in some allocation. Then Jones will receive $(100 - B_S = B_J)$ pounds of butter and $(50 - G_S = G_J)$ guns. Let the individuals' utility functions be given by $U_S(B_S, G_S)$ and $U_J(B_J, G_J)$. The definition of efficiency requires that these goods be allocated in such a way that if Jones' utility is fixed at some level $(\bar{U}_J)$, Smith's utility should be as large as possible. Setting up the Lagrangian expression:

$$L = U_S(B_S, G_S) - \lambda[U_J(100 - B_S, 50 - G_S) - \bar{U}_J]$$

and taking partial derivatives with respect to B_S and G_S gives:

$$\frac{\partial L}{\partial B_S} = \frac{\partial U_S}{\partial B_S} + \lambda \frac{\partial U_J}{\partial B_J} = 0$$

$$\frac{\partial L}{\partial G_S} = \frac{\partial U_S}{\partial G_S} + \lambda \frac{\partial U_J}{\partial G_J} = 0$$

as the first-order conditions for a maximum. These can be rewritten as:

$$\frac{\frac{\partial U_S}{\partial G_S}}{\frac{\partial U_S}{\partial B_S}} = \frac{\frac{\partial U_J}{\partial G_J}}{\frac{\partial U_J}{\partial B_J}}$$

or, since these ratios in fact are equal to Smith's and Jones' marginal rates of substitution, this equation says that the *MRS* (guns for butter) of Smith should equal the *MRS* (guns for butter) of Jones, as was to be shown.

One aspect of this proof which seems obvious should be stated explicitly: All of both goods must be given to either Smith or Jones. Leaving some amount unallocated would obviously be inefficient.

[4] Named for F. Y. Edgeworth (1854–1926) who derived the concept of a contract curve in his *Mathematical Psychics: An Essay on the Application of Mathematics to the Moral Sciences* in 1881 (New York: August M. Kelley, 1953).

sions given by the total (fixed) quantities of the two goods (call these goods simply X and Y): The horizontal dimension of the Box represents the total quantity of X available, whereas the vertical height of the Box is the total quantity of Y. The point O_S is considered to be the origin for Smith. Quantities of X for Smith are measured along the horizontal axis rightward from O_S; quantities of Y along the vertical axis upward from O_S. Any point in the Box can then be regarded as some allocation of X and Y to Smith. For example, at the point A Smith gets X_S^A and Y_S^A. The useful property of the Edgeworth Box is that the quantities received by Jones are also recorded by any point such as A. Jones simply gets that part of the total quantity which is "left over." In fact, we can regard Jones' quantities as being measured from the origin O_J. The point A therefore also corresponds to the quantities X_J^A and Y_J^A for Jones. Notice that the quantities assigned to Smith and Jones in this manner exactly exhaust the total quantities of X and Y available.

Figure 20.1 The Edgeworth Box Diagram

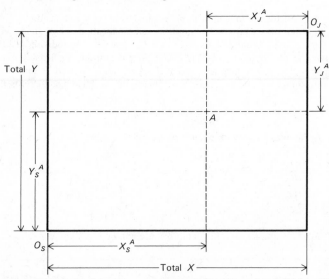

The Edgeworth Box diagram permits all possible allocations of two goods (X and Y) to be visualized. If we consider the corner O_S to be Smith's "origin" and O_J to be Jones', then the allocation represented by point A would have Smith getting X_S^A and Y_S^A and Jones would receive what is left over (X_J^A, Y_J^A). The purpose of this diagram is to discover which of the possible allocations within the Box are efficient.

Any point in the Edgeworth Box represents an allocation of the available goods between Smith and Jones, and all possible allocations are contained within the Box. To discover which of these points are efficient we must introduce tastes. In Figure 20.2 Smith's indifference curve map is drawn with origin O_S. Movements in a northeasterly direction on this map represent higher levels of utility to Smith. In the same figure Jones' indifference curve map is drawn with the corner O_J as an origin.[5] Movements in a southwesterly direction represent increases in Jones' utility level.

Figure 20.2   Edgeworth Box Diagram of Efficiency in Exchange

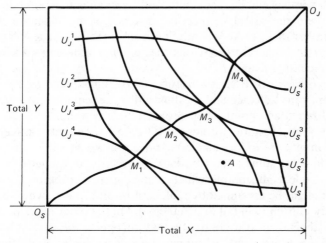

The points on the curve O_S, O_J are efficient in the sense that at these allocations Smith cannot be made better off without making Jones better off, and vice-versa. An allocation such as A, on the other hand, is inefficient since both Smith and Jones can be made better off (by choosing M_2, for example). Notice that along O_S, O_J the MRS for Smith is equal to that for Jones. The line $O_S O_J$ is called the contract curve.

Using these superimposed indifference curve maps it is possible to find the efficient points in the diagram. Consider any fixed utility level for Jones, say, $U_J{}^3$. The definition of efficiency requires that Smith's utility level be maximized for this given level of Jones' utility; not to do so would be inefficient. The point of maximum utility for Smith in this case is point M_2 where Smith's indifference curve $(U_S{}^2)$ is just tangent to the curve $U_J{}^3$. At this point of tangency the MRS (of X for Y) for Smith is equal to that for Jones; hence the efficient condition discussed earlier holds.

Within the Edgeworth Box there are a number of tangencies such as M_2. A few of these are labeled M_1, M_3, and M_4 in Figure 20.2. Each of these points has the property that Smith's utility is as large as possible given some preassigned level for Jones' utility. The locus of all these ef-

---

[5] It may help the reader to picture this construction as taking Jones' indifference map in its usual configuration, rotating the whole diagram (axes included) by 180°, and "fitting" this into Smith's map.

ficient allocations is called the *contract curve*. In Figure 20.2 this locus is given by the line running from O_S to O_J.[6] Every allocation on the contract curve has the property that Smith cannot be made better off without making Jones worse off: The utilities of Smith and Jones are directly in conflict at such points as is required by the definition of efficiency. This is not true for points off the contract curve. For example, an allocation such as point A, which is off the contract curve, is distinctly inefficient in that both persons can be made better off by moving to a point on the contract curve. This would be true, for instance, if the allocation M_2 were chosen rather than A. At M_2 both Smith and Jones are better off than they were at A; it is therefore obvious that point A represents an inefficient way of allocating X and Y.

The Edgeworth Box is a useful tool for understanding the meaning of efficiency in exchange and for illustrating the requirements that MRS's be equalized. Each point in the Box represents a different allocation of the same total quantities of goods. It is surprising that relatively "few" of these points are in fact efficient. Indeed, it would appear to be a very difficult task for some authority (lacking precise knowledge of individual tastes) to select allocations which just happened to be on the contract curve. It might be presumed that allocations of X and Y, which are rather arbitrarily chosen, will fail to be efficient. On the other hand, individuals, if left on their own to trade freely, may recognize the mutual benefits of being on the contract curve and may be able to choose an efficient point. We will return to this discussion on how efficient allocations might be discovered in Chapter 22.

While the proofs in this section have considered only two individuals and two goods they are general. Given any number of individuals and any number of goods to be exchanged, it is still true that the necessary condition[7] for efficiency is that the MRS between any two goods should be the same for all individuals. Efficient allocations which satisfy this condition will lie on a many-dimensional analogue of the contract curve. Along this curve the available goods are allocated so that no one person can be made better off without making someone else worse off. Such efficient allocations are sometimes called *Pareto optimal allocations* after the Italian scientist Vilfredo Pareto (1848–1923) who pioneered in developing the concept of economic efficiency.

---

[6] Because we have assumed that neither Smith nor Jones can become satiated with those goods which are available O_J will be Smith's most desired point and vice-versa. Hence O_S and O_J are points on the contract curve. If Smith is at O_J his utility level must be reduced if Jones is to get anything.

[7] These conditions may not be sufficient to insure efficiency if individuals' indifference curves are "oddly" shaped. It is important, therefore, to make a careful distinction between the locus of points of tangency of the individuals' indifference curves and the locus of efficient allocations. It is clearly the latter concept which is important for this chapter; it is this locus which is termed the contract curve.

Exchange with Initial Endowments

In this discussion fixed quantities of the two goods in question were assumed to exist, and these could be allocated in any way conceivable. A somewhat different, more restricted analysis would hold if various quantities of the goods in question started out in the possession of the individuals participating in exchange. A typical example of such a situation would occur if two men were marooned on an island and each had certain basic commodities in his possession. There is a very definite possibility that each man can benefit from voluntary trade (suppose force is ruled out by social conventions), since it is unlikely that the initial allocations would be efficient ones. On the other hand, neither man would engage in a trade which would leave him worse off than he would be without trading. Hence only a portion of the contract curve can be regarded as efficient allocations which might result from exchange.

Figure 20.3 Exchange with Initial Endowments

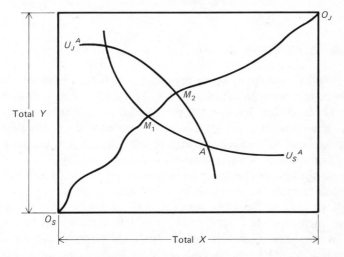

If individuals start with initial endowments (such as those represented by point A) neither would be willing to accept an allocation which promised a lower level of utility than point A does. Smith would not accept any allocation below U_S^A and Jones would not accept any allocation below U_J^A. Therefore, not every point on the contract curve can result from free exchange. Only the efficient allocations between M_1 and M_2 are eligible if each individual is free to refrain from trading, and we require that the final allocation be efficient.

These ideas are illustrated in Figure 20.3. The initial endowments of Smith and Jones are represented by point A in the Edgeworth Box. As before, the dimensions of the Box are taken to be the total quantities of the two goods (X and Y) available. The contract curve of efficient allocations is represented by the line O_S, O_J in Figure 20.3. Let the indifference curve of Smith which passes through point A be called U_S^A and, similarly, let Jones' indifference curve through A be denoted by U_J^A. Neither Smith nor Jones will accept trading outcomes which give them utility levels of less than U_S^A and U_J^A, respectively. It would be preferable for an individual to refrain from trading rather than accept such an inferior outcome. Thus only those efficient allocations between M_1 and M_2 on the contract curve can occur as a result of free exchange. The range of efficient outcomes from voluntary exchange has been narrowed by considering those initial endowments with which individuals enter into trading.

Exactly which allocation on the segment M_1, M_2 might be chosen by the participants in exchange is difficult to predict. Obviously Smith would prefer points closer to M_2, whereas Jones desires points close to M_1. The desires of the two individuals are in conflict, and bargaining between the two will determine the final allocation. It is clear, however, that if point A is not on the contract curve both parties can benefit from trade by moving to some point between M_1 and M_2.

Efficiency in Production

A society with fixed amounts of productive resources is said to have allocated those resources efficiently if more of one good cannot be produced without cutting back on the production of some other good. Three separate questions must be investigated in order to detail the conditions which must hold to achieve productive efficiency. First, on the level of a single firm resources must be allocated efficiently among those goods which that firm produces. On a society-wide scale, two additional problems in allocation must be solved: How should resources be distributed among firms making the same product; and how should the firms decide which of their feasible output mixes they will actually produce? These questions are taken up in turn below. It should be pointed out, however, that dividing up the general allocational problem in this way is only for pedagogic purposes, since in reality all three specific problems of allocating resources must be solved simultaneously.

Optimal Choice of Inputs for a Single Firm

Suppose a firm has fixed quantities of capital (K) and labor (L) inputs to devote to the production of two outputs (X and Y). The firm will be producing efficiently if, for a given level of Y output, it allocates its resources so as to maximize the output of X. The necessary conditions for insuring this efficiency are similar to those discussed above in the theory of exchange and are summed up by:

Allocation Rule 1.   A firm with fixed resources should allocate these resources among various uses in a way such that the rate of technical substitution (RTS)[8] of any two inputs is the same in the production of every output which the firm produces.

Figure 20.4   Box Diagram of Efficiency in Production

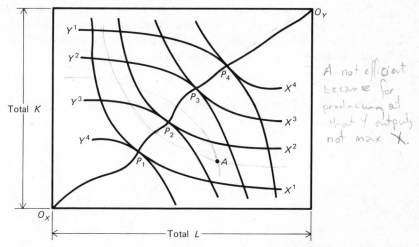

A not efficient because for producing at that Y output is not max X.

This diagram is analogous to Figure 20.2. It shows various efficient ways in which a firm can allocate a fixed amount of K and L between the production of two outputs $(X$ and $Y)$. The line joining O_X and O_Y is the locus of these efficient points. Along this line the RTS (of L for K) in the production of good X is equal to the RTS in the production of Y.

This rule is demonstrated in Figure 20.4 by using a diagram similar to the Edgeworth Box. The dimensions of this box are given by the total quantities of inputs available. The vertex O_X is used as the origin for an isoquant map for good X, and the vertex O_Y is used as the origin for an isoquant map for good Y. Any point within the Box represents an allocation of the available resources between the production of X and the production of Y. As before, it is obvious that the locus of efficient points is

[8] Remember that the RTS was defined (in Chapter 11) to be the rate at which one input can be traded for another in the productive process while holding output constant.

given by the points of tangency of the various isoquants. For any allocation such as point A, which is not on the O_X, O_Y locus, there exists an efficient point, such as P_2, at which the output of both goods is increased. Allocation Rule 1 holds everywhere along the O_X, O_Y locus, as is clear from the figure.[9]

The efficiency locus derived in Figure 20.4 can be used to derive the *production possibility frontier* which was first discussed in Chapter 12. By considering different efficient allocations ranging from point O_X to point O_Y the firm's production possibilities are traced out in Figure 20.5. Moving along this efficiency locus, resources are being transferred from the production of Y into the production of X. The production possibility frontier is therefore negatively sloped reflecting the efficiency notion that more X can be produced only by giving up some Y. The reader is reminded that the slope of the production possibility frontier shows the rate at which Y can be traded for X in the productive process. This slope is called the *rate of product transformation* (*RPT*).

Figure 20.5   Production Possibility Frontier Derived from Figure 20.4

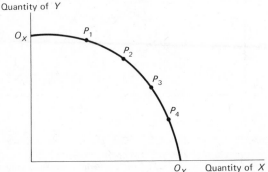

The production possibility frontier shows those alternative combinations of X and Y which can be produced by a firm with fixed resources. The curve can be derived from Figure 20.4 by varying inputs between the production of X and Y while maintaining the conditions for efficiency. The slope of the production possibility curve is called the rate of product transformation (*RPT*).

[9] A mathematical proof of Allocation Rule 1 would be identical to that given in Footnote 3 and will not be repeated here. The reader may also wish to construct a written proof of this rule — the proof would be similar to that which was presented at the start of the second section of this chapter.

It should be pointed out that the conditions required in Allocation Rule 1 are necessary conditions only for a true maximum. For these conditions to be sufficient the isoquants must have "normal" shapes such as those shown in Figure 20.4.

Efficient Allocation of Resources among Firms

If society has a fixed stock of resources these must be allocated in some efficient way among firms in order to insure overall productive efficiency. Intuitively, resources should be allocated to those firms where they can be most efficiently used. More precisely, the condition for efficient allocation is given by:

Allocation Rule 2. If production is to be efficient resources should be allocated so that the marginal physical product of any resource in the production of a particular good is the same no matter which firm produces that good.

To show the necessity of this rule, consider a situation in which it does not hold.[10] Suppose that the marginal physical product of labor (MP_L) in the production of corn is 3 bushels per extra man hour on farm A and only 1 bushel on farm B. Then a transfer of one unit of labor from farm B to farm A would increase total output by 2 bushels of corn. Clearly the initial allocation of labor was inefficient and this transfer of labor should be continued until Allocation Rule 2 is fulfilled. A similar result holds for any other productive input. For example, machines suitable for producing yo-yos should be allocated among producers so that their marginal productivities are identical for each user, otherwise yo-yo output could be increased. Allocation Rule 2 shows one more reason why the concept of *marginal* productivity is the important definition of productivity for economic problems.

Efficient Choice of Output by Firms

Even though resources may be efficiently allocated both within a firm and among all firms there is still one other condition of efficient production which must be obeyed: Firms must produce efficient combinations of outputs. Roughly speaking, firms which are good at producing hamburgers should produce hamburgers, and those which are good at producing cars should produce cars. The necessary conditions for efficient choices of outputs are summarized in:

Allocation Rule 3. If two (or more) firms produce the same outputs they

---

[10] A mathematical proof of this assertion is extremely simple. Suppose there are two firms (A and B) each producing X with labor alone. Suppose further that there is a total amount of labor given by $\bar{L}$ and that the firms' production functions are given by $X_A = A(L)$, $X_B = B(\bar{L} - L)$. The object is to choose L to maximize $X_A + X_B = A(L) + B(\bar{L} - L)$. The first-order condition for a maximum is $A'(L) - B'(\bar{L} - L) = 0$ or $A' = B'$ as is to be shown.

must operate at points on their respective production possibility frontiers at which their rates of product transformation are equal.

Consider two firms (A and B) which each produce both cars and trucks. Let their production possibility curves be given by those in Figure 20.6. Suppose firm A chooses to produce at point P_1^A (100 cars and 50 trucks) where its RPT (trucks for cars) is 2/1. At this point firm A must give up 2 cars if it is to produce 1 more truck. Suppose also that firm B chooses to produce 100 cars and 50 trucks, but that at this point its RPT (trucks for cars) is 1/1. In this case productive efficiency can be improved by having firm A produce more cars (since it is relatively efficient in this), and firm B produce more trucks. For example, firm A could produce 102 cars and 49 trucks, whereas B could move to producing 99 cars and 51 trucks. By this reordering of production the total output of cars has been increased without decreasing the total output of trucks. Hence the initial choices of firms A and B were inefficient. Only if Allocation Rule 3 holds is it impossible to make such a beneficial reallocation. This result is particularly interesting in that it shows that output may be increased (even if the inputs to all firms are fixed) by having firms produce the "correct" output combinations.[11]

These three rules summarize the conditions which must hold if production is to be efficient.[12] The operation of the rules can be visualized as follows: Rule 2 determines the size of each firm's production Box (and hence the "size" of its production possibility frontier); Rule 1 determines the shape of these frontiers; Rule 3 determines where on the frontiers production will take place.[13] It is important to repeat that all three Allocation Rules must hold simultaneously: It is not true that having two Allocation Rules hold is necessarily better than having none at all. How

---

[11] The reader may recognize Allocation Rule 3 as the basis for the theory of *comparative advantage* in international trade. The production possibility curves in Figure 20.6 can be taken to be those of two different countries (each with fixed resources), and points P_1^A and P_1^B may represent these countries' before-trade production choices. If the RPT differs between the two countries the opening of trade relations can increase total world output and (presumably) make both countries better off. In the famous "wine" and "cloth" examples of comparative advantage proposed by Ricardo, the production possibility frontiers were taken to be negatively sloped straight lines: The RPT in each country was constant for all output combinations. If these RPT's differ, each country should completely specialize its production in that good which it produces relatively efficiently (at least within limits set by "demand").

[12] One additional condition of efficiency is at least implicit in the three rules: Resources must be fully employed. So long as a resource has any positive productivity it would be inefficient to leave it idle.

[13] The three Allocation Rules are not independent of one another and any one of them can be derived from the other two. All three were presented here, however, for illustrative purposes.

Figure 20.6   A Graphic Demonstration of Allocation Rule 3

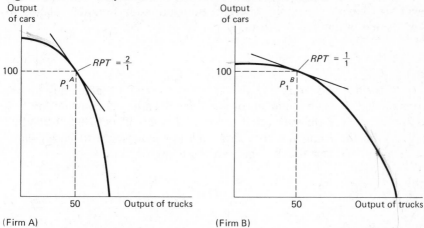

(Firm A)   (Firm B)

If two firms' rates of product transformation differ, total output can be increased by moving these firms toward equalization of those rates. In the figure Firm A is relatively efficient at producing cars and Firm B is relatively efficient at producing trucks. If each firm were to specialize in its efficient product total output could be increased.

efficiency in production might be achieved is an important question which is taken up in later chapters.

Lerner's Rule as a Summary of Efficiency in Production

The three Allocation Rules in the previous section may be difficult to remember. They can be conveniently summarized in one equation: *Lerner's Rule*.[14] Consider any firm, say firm A. This firm is characterized by a _transformation function_ which states the technical relationship between the firm's inputs and its outputs. The function can be written in implicit form as:

$$T^A(X_1^A, X_2^A, ..., X_n^A) = 0 \qquad [20.1]$$

where some of the X's are inputs and some are outputs. All Equation 20.1 says is that there is some function relating these inputs and outputs. The production functions studied in Chapter 11 are a special case of a transformation function which has only one output. Here we are gen-

---

[14] Named for Abba P. Lerner who carefully laid out the rules for efficiency in production in his book *The Economics of Control: Principles of Welfare Economics* (New York: The Macmillan Co., 1944).

eralizing to allow for multiproduct firms. Similarly, any other firm (B) will also have a (possibly different) transformation function relating its inputs and outputs in the form:

$$T^B(X_1^B, X_2^B,..., X_n^B) = 0. \qquad [20.2]$$

Consider allocating any two X's, say X_1 and X_2, efficiently among firms A and B when the levels of the other X's are held constant for each firm. Lerner's Rule states that the rate of trade-off between X_1 and X_2 should be the same for both firms if these goods are to be allocated efficiently. Mathematically, this can be summarized as:

$$\frac{dX_1^A}{dX_2^A} = \frac{dX_1^B}{dX_2^B}. \qquad [20.3]$$

Allocation Rules 1, 2, and 3 are special cases of Equation 20.3. For example, if X_1 is an output and X_2 is an input Equation 20.3 states that the marginal physical product of X_2 in the production of X_1 should be equal for the two firms. This is exactly what was required by Rule 2. If X_1 and X_2 are both outputs Equation 20.3 says that the *RPT* (of X_2 for X_1) should be equal for the two firms. This is Rule 3. Finally, if X_1 and X_2 are both inputs Equation 20.3 says that the *RTS* (of X_2 for X_1) should be equal between any two firms in the production of any output. Rule 1 is then simply a special case of this more general requirement.

Equation 20.3 summarizes all the necessary rules for allocative efficiency. It is also instructive in that it clearly demonstrates the general nature of trade-offs in the production process. Only if rates of trade-off are identical for all firms will production be efficient. Impediments in an economy which interfere with the equating of these rates of trade-off can make allocative efficiency impossible to achieve.

Efficiency in Production and Exchange

The goal of an economic system is to satisfy human wants. Being efficient in production may not be at all desirable if the "wrong" combination of goods is being produced. As the definition of efficiency in a production and exchange economy we will adopt the Pareto definition which was used in the case of exchange: *An allocation of goods and resources among both firms and individuals is efficient if no one can be made better off without making someone else worse off.* In this section we will examine those conditions which are required to achieve such an efficient allocation.

As a starting point it should be obvious that all the conditions for both exchange efficiency and productive efficiency must hold if we are to have overall efficiency. For example, if production is inefficient then there exists some good the production of which could be increased without decreasing the production of anything else. This extra output would increase the utility of the person to whom it is given without decreasing anyone else's, and thus the original situation could not have been efficient. Hence Allocation Rules 1, 2, and 3 must hold in any allocation which is to be efficient in an overall sense. Graphically, we must be on the economy's production possibility frontier. Similarly, those goods which are produced must be exchanged efficiently. If this were not so two individuals could both be made better off by trading goods among themselves.

For both production and exchange to be efficient is not a sufficient condition for overall efficiency. It must also be the case that the right goods are being produced. It does little good for an economy to be an efficient producer of yo-yos and xylophones if no one wants these goods. In order to assure overall efficiency we need some way to tie together tastes and productive abilities. The condition which is necessary to insure that the right goods are produced is that the *marginal rate of substitution* for any two goods (these rates should be identical for all individuals if we are to have efficiency in exchange) must be *equal* to the *rate of product transformation* of these two goods (these rates are identical for all firms by Allocation Rule 3). Simply phrased, the psychic rate of trade-off between the two goods must be equal to the rate at which they can be traded off in the productive process.

[margin handwritten: $MRS = RTS$]

This requirement can be demonstrated graphically for a very simple case. Suppose there are only two goods (X and Y) which are produced and suppose there is only one individual (perhaps Robinson Crusoe) in society. Those combinations of X and Y which can be produced are given by the production possibility frontier PP in Figure 20.7. Any point on PP represents a point of efficient production. By superimposing the individual's indifference map on Figure 20.7, however, it is clear that only one point on PP provides maximum utility.[15] This point of maximum utility is at E, where the curve PP is tangent to the individual's highest indifference curve, U^2. At this point of tangency the individual's MRS (of X for Y) is equal to the technical RPT (of X for Y), and hence this is the required condition for overall efficiency. Notice that point E is preferred to every other point which is efficient in a productive sense. In fact, for any point such as F on the curve PP (other than point E) there exist points which are inefficient but which are preferred to F. In Figure 20.7 the "inefficient" point G is preferred to the "efficient" point F. It would be preferable from

[15] Figure 20.7 is identical to Figure 19.3 in which it was shown how an interest rate is established; only the interpretations to be given to the graphs are different. Figure 19.3 shows how efficiency in allocation over time can be discussed using identical tools to those developed in this chapter.

the individual's point of view to produce inefficiently rather than be forced to produce the "wrong" combination of goods in an efficient way. Point E (which is efficiently produced) is superior to any such "second best" solutions. We will return in later chapters to investigate why it might be desirable to choose points such as G.

Figure 20.7 Efficiency of Production and Exchange in a Robinson Crusoe Economy

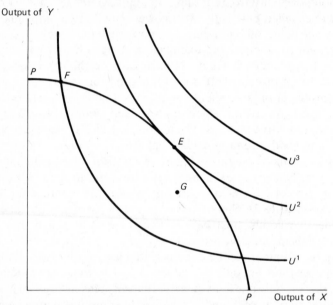

In a single-person economy the curve PP represents those combinations of X and Y which can be produced. Every point on PP is efficient in a productive sense. However, only the output combination at point E is a true utility maximum for the individual. At E the individual's MRS is equal to the rate at which X can technically be traded for Y (the RPT).

Although we have only shown the conditions of efficiency in a simple case they are general. It is the equating of individuals' marginal rates of substitution to firm's rates of product transformation which ties together tastes and technology. It is necessary to have such an interconnection if resources are to be allocated in a truly efficient way.

Efficiency in the Supply of Productive Inputs

Although this analysis has assumed that the quantities of productive inputs available in the economy are in fixed supply, it is a simple matter to incorporate variable input supplies into a model of allocative efficiency. The Allocation Rules for productive efficiency are unchanged by the observation that some inputs are not in fixed supply. During one period some amount of labor, for example, will be offered by individuals and the Rules apply equally well for whatever level of this input is supplied. The important question though is what is the efficient quantity of labor for households to offer. An analysis of this question necessitates looking at the interaction of tastes and technology in the provision of labor services. Specifically, a necessary condition for efficient allocation is that individuals' psychic rate of trade-off between leisure (the act of not offering labor services) and some good should be equal to the technical rate at which labor services can be transformed into that good.

As an example of this aspect of efficiency consider again the Robinson Crusoe economy. Suppose Crusoe's psychic trade-off rate between leisure and coconuts is 2/1: He is willing to give up 2 hours of leisure for 1 more coconut. On the other hand, assume that his marginal physical productivity in the harvesting of coconuts is 1/1: By working 1 more hour (giving up 1 hour of leisure) he can harvest 1 coconut. This situation is clearly inefficient. Robinson could give up 2 hours of leisure and harvest 2 coconuts. But he only requires 1 additional coconut to keep him indifferent. The extra coconut is a net addition to his utility and he should put forth the effort. Only when the two trade-off rates are identical will he be allocating his time efficiently.

This result is depicted in Figure 20.8. Crusoe's quantity of leisure is shown on the horizontal axis of the graph and his quantity of coconuts is shown on the vertical axis. The curve TT shows those alternative combinations of leisure and coconuts which can be obtained by Crusoe. Although the curve is negatively sloped in most regions (implying that additional leisure may be obtained only by sacrificing some coconut production), it has been assumed that choosing a level of leisure less than H_1 actually causes fewer coconuts to be produced (perhaps Crusoe loses his proficiency from lack of sleep). Also drawn in Figure 20.8 is Crusoe's indifference curve map between leisure and coconuts. It is clear from the figure that the optimal quantities of leisure and coconuts (H^*, C^*) occur at the point E where Crusoe's MRS (of leisure for coconuts) is equal to his marginal productivity in picking coconuts (the rate at which he can technically transform leisure into coconuts). A similar result could be shown to hold for any other productive input which Robinson Crusoe might supply.

These results are perfectly general, although only a single-person example has been used for graphic simplicity. Efficient factor supply requires that every supplier equate his psychic rate of trade-off between providing the factor service and consuming some good to the technical rate at which the factor service can be transformed into that good. There is consequently a notion of efficiency in factor supply which is in many ways identical to the efficiency condition required in the choice of outputs by the economy. In this regard the close similarity between Figures 20.7 and 20.8 should be noted.

Figure 20.8   Robinson Crusoe's Optimal Labor-Leisure Choice

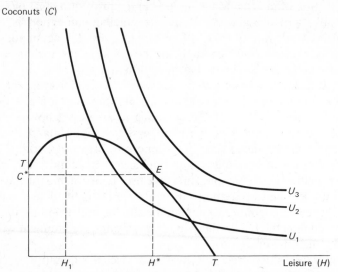

The curve TT shows those combinations of leisure and coconuts which Robinson Crusoe can technically achieve. To maximize utility he should choose that combination on TT, (H^*, C^*), for which the technical rate of trade-off (the marginal productivity of labor in the picking of coconuts) is equal to the rate at which Crusoe is psychically willing to trade H for C. Notice in particular that no point to the left of H_1 would ever be chosen since there the marginal productivity of labor is negative, implying that Crusoe could have more of both leisure and coconuts.

Although this section on factor supply has been presented more-or-less separately from the other analyses of efficiency in this chapter, the separation has been for ease of exposition only. It should be clear that all the requirements for efficiency discussed in this chapter are interconnected, and no one set of conditions is more important than any other. The economy is truly a *circular flow* between the individuals who consume goods while providing resources and firms which use resources to produce goods. This flow, although it may be broken down into its various components for analytical simplicity, must be considered as a whole for any investigation of efficiency. For example, one would not want to call a highly regimented society of forced labor "efficient," even though this labor might be used efficiently and might even produce the "correct" combination of final goods. In such a society individuals' labor-leisure choices will be coerced, and it is likely that at least one good, leisure, will be produced inefficiently. Similarly, it would be misleading to claim that the shrinkage in the length of the work week during the twentieth century has been a manifestation of "inefficiency." Rather, this reduction has undoubtedly reflected the changing nature of the technical possibilities for transforming leisure into consumption goods.

Conclusion

In the myriad of marginal rules for allocative efficiency presented in this chapter two facts are likely to be lost. Therefore these bear repeating. First, the chapter has dealt only with physical quantities of goods and with individuals' tastes for these quantities. No mention has been made of prices, incomes, or profits. Efficiency in allocation is a physical, not a monetary, problem.

Second, there is an essential similarity in all the conditions for efficiency which have been derived. If the reader has an occasional feeling of *déjà vu* as he reads some of the examples, this is no accident. The study of optimal allocation is a study of marginal trade-offs. The "benefits" and "costs" of any reallocation must always be examined. Only when the trade-off rates for certain benefits (or costs) are the same for all economic agents will resources be allocated efficiently. This result, because of its wide applicability, is perhaps the most important in microeconomic theory. It should be clear that much of the analysis of this chapter is similar to that presented earlier when we discussed the problem of agents' equating rates of trade-off to rates which are determined by the market. In Chapter 22 we will examine the specific relationship between these two types of problems and will show that relying on perfectly competitive markets is one way in which efficiency might be obtained. Before going on to this task, however, it will be useful to continue (in Chapter 21) using the present abstract model (which lacks prices, markets, and profits) in order to investigate some problems in social welfare theory which transcend efficiency. By proceeding in this way the discussion of those ends which an economy might pursue can be effectively separated from the distinct question of possible means for achieving those ends.

CHAPTER 21
Welfare Economics

Introduction

Welfare economics concerns the examination of all those allocations of resources which are feasible for a society and the establishment of criteria for selecting among these allocations. The basic question which is raised is "what is the best allocation of resources from a social point of view." As should be clear from this definition welfare economics is the most normative branch of microeconomics. The subject ultimately comes down to the necessity for making hard choices about the welfare of different individuals; with limited resources not everyone can achieve "bliss" (indeed perhaps no one can). In assessing the desirability of one possible organization of society, say A, in comparison with another feasible organization, B one is faced with the problem that some individuals prefer A whereas others prefer B. In some way interpersonal comparisons must be made between individuals. Not surprisingly, economists have been no more successful in postulating universally agreed upon rules for making these decisions than have other social philosophers. In this sense the study of welfare economics has been a failure: Most of the basic philosophic questions remain to be answered. It is in demonstrating its inability to establish such universal ethical principles, however, that welfare economics is in some sense a success. To learn why there are no easy answers is an important intellectual achievement. The purpose of this chapter is to examine the intrinsic difficulties inherent in questions of social welfare and to demonstrate some important conceptual issues which have been raised. The chapter is rather abstract in nature. A somewhat more "down-to-earth" approach to social welfare is taken in Part VII when the role of government is examined in detail.

An initial assumption to be made here in defining social welfare is that individual tastes are to "count." The measure of social welfare is how well off the individuals in society feel. Some authors refer to this as the *individualistic assumption*.[1] Using this definition of social welfare, it is clear that a Pareto optimal allocation of resources (one in which no one can be made better off without making someone else worse off) is a necessary condition for a *social optimum*. If resources were allocated in a way such that someone could be made better off without necessarily lowering the utility level of anyone else this allocation could not have been socially optimal. On the other hand, there may be many Pareto optimal allocations and the purpose of welfare economics is to establish criteria for choosing among these.

The Need for Welfare Criteria in an Exchange Model

The model of efficiency in exchange developed in the previous chapter is useful for demonstrating the problems involved in establishing welfare criteria, and we shall use that model exclusively in this chapter.[2] Con-

---

[1] This assumption is by no means universally accepted. A brief discussion of possible alternatives is presented in the section "The Social Welfare Function" below.

[2] Production can be integrated into the discussion of welfare economics. *See,* for example, F. M. Bator, "The Simple Analytics of Welfare Maximization," *American Economic Review,* vol. 47 (March 1957), pp. 22–59. Although no new conceptual problems would be created by such an addition several graphic difficulties do arise. Because goods can be produced (rather than being in fixed supply as they are in the exchange model), any contemplated change in the utility levels of individuals in society will also necessitate a change in the whole production plan (society's production possibility frontier would change). We will not investigate these analytic complications here.

Figure 21.1   Edgeworth Box Diagram of Exchange

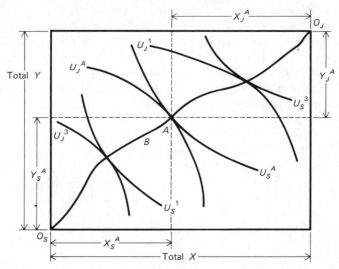

This diagram is simply a redrawing of Figure 20.2. The curve O_S, O_J is the locus of efficient allocations of X and Y between Smith and Jones. Allocations off this locus are dominated by those on it in that both individuals *can be* made better off by moving to the contract curve.

sider the Edgeworth Box diagram in Figure 21.1. Only those points on the contract curve are eligible to be considered as possible candidates for a social optimum. Points off the contract curve are dominated by points on the curve in the sense that both individuals can be made better off, and in so doing social welfare could be improved. Along the contract curve the utilities of the two individuals (Smith and Jones) vary and these utilities are directly competitive: Smith's utility can be increased only by decreasing Jones'. Given this set of efficient allocations, we now wish to discuss possible criteria for choosing among them. For this purpose it will be convenient to assume for the moment that utilities are measurable and that they may be compared on a common scale. Obviously this assumption is in direct contradiction to the warnings expressed in Chapter 3 about the measurability of utility, and later in this chapter the assumption will be reconsidered. Initially, however, making such an assumption will permit the conceptualization of certain problems. From the assumption of measurability the possible utility combinations along the contract curve in Figure 21.1 can be used to construct the *utility possibility frontier* shown in Figure 21.2.[3] The curve O_S, O_J records those utility levels for

[3] This construction is identical to that used in Chapter 20 to derive the production possibility frontier.

Smith and Jones which are obtainable from the fixed quantities of those goods which are available. Any utility combination (such as point C) which lies inside the curve O_S, O_J is inefficient in the sense that utilities *could* be unambiguously improved (for example, by moving to any point on the arc $C'C'$). This is simply a reflection of the way in which the contract curve is constructed. Using the utility possibility frontier, the "problem" of welfare economics can now be rephrased as being the development of criteria for selecting a point on this frontier.

Figure 21.2   Utility Possibility Frontier

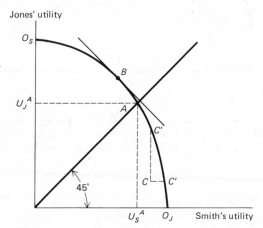

Assuming measurability of utility, the utility possibility frontier can be derived from Figure 21.1. This curve (O_S, O_J) shows those combinations of utility which society can achieve. Two criteria for choosing among points on O_S, O_J might be: Choose "equal" utilities for Smith and Jones (point A); or choose the utilities so that their sum is the greatest (point B).

Two simple criteria for choosing a point on O_S, O_J can be shown on Figure 21.2. One possible principle would require complete equality: Smith and Jones should in some sense enjoy the same level of welfare (again remember the dubious nature of the assumption of measurability here). This social welfare criterion would necessitate choosing point A on the utility possibility frontier. Since point A corresponds to a unique point on the contract curve the socially optimal allocation of goods has been determined by this choice. In Figure 21.1 this allocation is seen to require that Smith gets X_S^A and Y_S^A, whereas Jones gets X_J^A and Y_J^A. Notice that the goods X and Y are not necessarily distributed equally. It is equality of utilities which is required by the criterion not equality of goods. If individuals have rather different tastes for the two goods these goods could be very unequally distributed at point A. It might even be the case that one of the individuals would get more of both goods at the socially optimal point. This would be true, for example, if Smith were ascetic by nature, whereas Jones were materialistic. To equalize utilities, therefore, Jones should be given more goods with which to satisfy his cravings.

A similar (though not necessarily identical) criterion would be to choose that point on the utility possible frontier for which the *sum* of Smith's and Jones' utilities is the greatest. This would require that the optimal point (B) be chosen to maximize ($U_J + U_S$) subject to the constraint implied by the utility possibility frontier. As before, point B would imply a certain allocation of X and Y between Smith and Jones, and this allocation could be derived from Figure 21.1.

These two criteria represent extremely simple notations of social welfare. If it has been decided that society should follow one of these principles these tools provide a method for finding the socially optimal allocation of goods. Exactly how the specific goods are to be allocated in the socially optimal way is a more difficult question. One way to achieve the optimal allocation would be for all goods to be directly allocated by the government. This would require perfect knowledge about individuals' tastes. It is highly unlikely that such knowledge will be readily available. Another possibility would be to allocate one of the two goods "correctly" (for example, give Smith $X_S{}^A$ and Jones $X_J{}^A$) and then let Smith and Jones trade only in the other good until they reach the contract curve. It will be shown that this approach will work even when more than two goods are being exchanged: The correct allocation of one of the goods and the requirement of efficiency in exchange can assure that the desired allocation is achieved. A third method which relies on a price system will be discussed in Chapter 22. In some ways this final method is the most practical of those which have been mentioned.

The Social Welfare Function

A more general approach to social welfare (which includes the two criteria discussed above as special cases) can be obtained by examining the concept of a social welfare function.[4] If we assume that individual tastes are to count, this function might depend only on Smith's and Jones' utility levels:

Social welfare $= W(U_S, U_J)$.   [21.1]

---

[4] This concept was first developed by A. Bergson in "A Reformulation of Certain Aspects of Welfare Economics," *Quarterly Journal of Economics,* vol. 52 (February 1938), pp. 310–334.

Figure 21.3 Using a Social Welfare Function to Find the Social Optimum

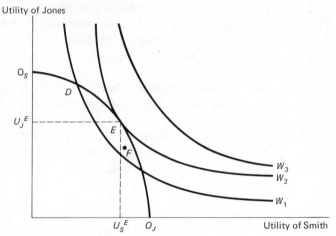

If we can postulate the existence of a social welfare function having the indifference curves W_1, W_2, and W_3, it is possible to conceptualize the problem of social choice. It is clear that efficiency (being on O_S, O_J) is necessary for a welfare optimum, but this is not sufficient, as may be seen by comparing points D and F.

Society's problem then is to allocate X and Y between Smith and Jones so as to maximize W. This procedure is pictured in Figure 21.3. The curves labeled W_1, W_2, and W_3 represent *social indifference curves* in that society is indifferent about which utility combination on a particular curve is chosen.[5] These indifference curves for the function W are drawn convex on the normative assumption that "society" exhibits a diminishing rate of substitution of Smith's utility for Jones. This assumption would seem to be a reasonable one if society is basically egalitarian, although we will attempt no further justification. The assumed shape of the indifference curves is convenient in that Figure 21.3 closely resembles other figures in this book.

Point E is the optimal point of social welfare in that this is the highest level of W achievable with the given utility possibility frontier. As before, it is necessary to go from point E to the Edgeworth Box diagram in order to determine the socially optimal allocation of goods. Any of the methods already mentioned might be used to obtain this allocation.[6]

[5] Under the "equality" criterion the social welfare function would have L-shaped indifference curves, whereas under the "maximum sum of utilities" criterion the indifference curves would be parallel straight lines with slope of -1.

[6] Suppose there are n goods in fixed supply: $X_1,..., X_n$. Then society's goal is to allocate these between Smith and Jones so as to maximize:

$$W[U_S(X_1{}^S, X_2{}^S,..., X_n{}^S), U_J(X_1{}^J, X_2{}^J,..., X_n{}^J)].$$

Figure 21.3 demonstrates the conceptually correct way of choosing a distribution of utilities so as to maximize social welfare. Before turning to a more detailed examination of the nature of the function W, it is interesting to use this figure to illustrate an important economic principle: the possible *inconsistency between equity and efficiency*. All of the points on O_S, O_J are efficient by the Pareto definition. But some of these points are far more equitable than others when the function W is used to judge equity. There are in fact inefficient points (such as F) which are socially preferred to some efficient points (such as D). This obser-

---

The first-order conditions for a maximum are:

$$\frac{\partial W}{\partial X_1{}^S} = \frac{\partial W}{\partial X_1{}^J}$$

$$\frac{\partial W}{\partial X_2{}^S} = \frac{\partial W}{\partial X_2{}^J}$$

$$\vdots$$

$$\frac{\partial W}{\partial X_n{}^S} = \frac{\partial W}{\partial X_n{}^J}.$$

All this says is that the goods should be allocated so that welfare cannot be increased by redistributing any good from Smith to Jones. Notice that the allocation of any particular good affects welfare only through its effect on individuals' utility levels:

$$\frac{\partial W}{\partial X_1{}^S} = \frac{\partial W}{\partial U_S} \cdot \frac{\partial U_S}{\partial X_1{}^S}$$

and similarly for all the other derivatives. It is therefore easy to show that these optimality conditions require efficiency in exchange. Rewriting the first-order conditions as:

$$\frac{\partial W}{\partial U_S} \cdot \frac{\partial U_S}{\partial X_1{}^S} = \frac{\partial W}{\partial U_J} \cdot \frac{\partial U_J}{\partial X_1{}^J}$$

$$\frac{\partial W}{\partial U_S} \cdot \frac{\partial U_S}{\partial X_2{}^S} = \frac{\partial W}{\partial U_J} \cdot \frac{\partial U_J}{\partial X_2{}^J}.$$

And dividing one by the other gives:

$$\frac{\dfrac{\partial U_S}{\partial X_1{}^S}}{\dfrac{\partial U_S}{\partial X_2{}^S}} = \frac{\dfrac{\partial U_J}{\partial X_1{}^J}}{\dfrac{\partial U_J}{\partial X_2{}^J}}$$

or that the MRS between X_1 and X_2 must be equal for the two individuals. This is precisely the necessary condition for efficiency in exchange. It is also easy to see that if the second equation holds for all pairs of goods (if exchange is efficient) and if one good, say X_1, is allocated optimally as in the first equation, then (by substituting the second equation into the first) any other good can be shown to be optimally allocated.

vation suggests that it may sometimes be in society's interest to choose inefficient points if socially desirable allocations are not achievable.

As a practical example of this sort of inconsistency consider the debate in the United States over the desirability of adopting a guaranteed annual income. Opponents of this proposal assert that its acceptance would lead to great inefficiencies because, once the necessity to work was mitigated, individuals would withdraw from the labor force. Without examining either the logic or the actual size of this purported effect it is possible to show on a priori grounds why it is not necessarily a damning assertion. For example, suppose that without income transfers only points such as D could be achieved. Perhaps initial endowments of the goods are so skewed that even perfectly efficient trading would insure a relatively unequal outcome of utilities. On the other hand, perhaps income transfers could cause the "inefficient" point F to be achieved.[7] What has been sacrificed in efficiency has therefore more than been compensated for (in terms of social welfare) by increased equity. We will discuss this example in more detail in Chapter 26. Here, however, the discussion of welfare economics will continue on an abstract plane.

The function W we have been using is in reality nothing more than some lines which were rather arbitrarily drawn. Although having a social welfare function is in some ways the "ideal" solution to the problem of making social decisions, it must be admitted that this solution is only a conceptual one. In the remainder of this chapter various questions about the form of the function W and about problems in the establishment of such a function will be discussed.

One important assumption about social welfare which has been made is that individual tastes are to count. The allocation of X and Y affects social welfare only through the utility that Smith and Jones obtain from these goods. Although this assumption is convenient because it permits the use of the various efficiency ideas developed in Chapter 20 there may be reasons for abandoning such an individualistic view of society. Perhaps society (the government?) knows what is good for its members better than the members themselves. Individuals' choices may be so distorted by conspicuous consumption and other materialist yearnings that any serious view of social welfare would disregard individual

---

[7] For example, the withdrawal of persons from the labor force may cause the total quantities of X and Y available to contract (not so much can be produced when income transfers are introduced). Graphically, the size of the Edgeworth Box would be contracted, and perhaps F is the "best point" which can be obtained within this new, smaller Box.

tastes.[8] Instead, goods should be allocated with "higher motives" in mind.

This "anti-individualistic" argument undoubtedly has some merit. It is in proposing alternative criteria that difficult problems arise. If individual tastes are not to be the measure of social welfare what is? The idea of an allocation imposed by a dictator or by a panel of cultured "experts" brings forth images of numerous potential injustices. It is not clear what is meant by the statement that the allocation resulting from central direction is socially preferred to that which individual tastes might dictate.

Even if it were decided that individual tastes are relevant components of a social welfare function it could be argued that other variables should also be included. Certain esthetic goals might be included even though these are not reflected in individual tastes. For example, it might be argued that goods such as education should be allocated equally regardless of people's tastes. Similarly, true social welfare may depend also on the well being of future generations, and therefore it may not be desirable only to look at the tastes of individuals currently in society. This list of other influences on social welfare could be extended indefinitely. When a function of the form of Equation 21.1 is used, it should be clear that all other factors affecting social welfare are treated as being held constant. Optimal allocation decisions can be regarded as an optimization problem in which the *ceteris paribus* assumption is made about factors not explicitly considered.

A final problem in applying a function of the form of Equation 21.1 to actual social decision making is that we have no way of measuring utilities in the first place.[9] Although the idea of a social welfare function

---

[8] The arguments of this part are probably more relevant to an economy with both production and exchange than to only an exchange economy. It is in the allocation of resources to producing "unnecessary" commodities that the individualist assumption of social welfare may be the most unwarranted.

[9] A "natural" answer to the measurability problem was proposed by several welfare economists (principally Kaldor and Scitovsky) in the late 1930's under the general heading of *Bribe Criteria*. Simply put, these criteria stated that a move from situation *A* to situation *B* is socially desirable if those who gain by such a move *can* bribe those who lose so that they would accept the change. In this way it was thought that comparisons could be avoided by letting each individual decide when he is better off.

The bribe principle embodies two rather different criteria depending on how the word *can* is interpreted. If compensation must actually be paid, the Bribe Criterion is simply a rephrasing of the desirability of efficiency. If both individuals can be made better off in situation *B* by exchanging goods (or by transferring money with which to buy goods) then an application of Pareto's principles would rank *B* as a social state which is preferred to *A*.

The bribe principle is therefore most interesting (and controversial) when compensation need not be paid: All that is required is that it *could* be paid. If this principle were

may have some conceptual value, as a policy tool it is hopelessly inadequate. The most promising answer to this dilemma is to use available measuring quantities in the belief that these may serve as an adequate proxy for utility. Family income or wealth, for example, may provide such an indicator. Society's welfare function might therefore depend on the level of income per family and the distribution of income among families. In an even more aggregated sense the welfare function might be approximated. by a function whose arguments are such macroeconomic variables as the unemployment rate, the rate of inflation, and the level of per capita income. It would be quite useful to have such a function explicitly stated as a matter of social policy. On the other hand, it should be clear that such a function is at best an extremely crude approximation of the theoretical ideal of a welfare function.

The Nature of Social Decisions

It is possible to envision the role of society as being the establishment and enforcement of a suitable social welfare function (or a "constitution"). Economists have studied two aspects of this issue. First is the positive question of how social decisions are made. A study of this question is similar to investigations of how allocative decisions are made: The "markets" in which social decisions take place are closely related to the markets in which resource allocation decisions are made. This aspect of the social decision-making process is examined in Part VII (especially Chapter 23). A second, more theoretical and philosophical area of interest to economists is whether it is in fact possible to conceive of a social welfare function which in some way mirrors the preferences of the individuals in society. The pioneering work in this field

---

acceptable it would seem that a reasonable rule for social choices had been found. However, inherent in the bribe principle without compensation is a hidden, and perhaps undesirable, ethical premise: that we can compare individuals' monetary evaluations of their well being. To see that this may be untenable consider the following situations: In situation A Jones has $1 million and Smith has $100; in situation B Jones has $1.1 million and Smith has $80. Compensation could be made (Jones could give Smith, say $25, and both individuals would be better off than they were in situation A). But would we want to rank B as socially preferred to A given that compensation need not be made? Adopting the bribe principle would in this way disagree with many persons' conception of equity. One cannot subject utility to the "measuring rod" of money.

For a further discussion of complications raised by Bribe Criteria *see* E. J. Mishan, *Welfare Economics: Five Introductory Essays* (New York: Random House, Inc., 1964), pp. 38–52.

was undertaken by Arrow in the early 1950's.[10] Because Arrow's work clearly demonstrates the intrinsic difficulties in conceptualizing social welfare an elementary discussion of his results is presented below.

Arrow views the general social problem as choosing among several feasible "social states." It is assumed that each individual in society can rank these states as to their desirability to him personally. The question Arrow raises is: Does there exist a ranking of these states on a society-wide scale which fairly records these individual preferences? Symbolically, assume there are three social states (A, B, and C) and two individuals in society (Smith and Jones). Suppose Smith prefers A to B (we will denote this by $A\ P_S\ B$, where P_S represents the words "is preferred by Smith to") and B to C. These preferences can be written as $A\ P_S\ B$ and $B\ P_S\ C$. If the individual is to be "rational" it should then be the case that $A\ P_S\ C$: The individual's preferences should be *transitive*. Suppose also that, among the three states, Jones has preferences: $C\ P_J\ A$, $A\ P_J\ B$, and $C\ P_J\ B$. Arrow's *Impossibility Theorem* consists of showing that a reasonable social ranking of these three states (call this ranking P) cannot exist.[11]

The crux of this theorem is to define what is meant by a "reasonable social ranking." Arrow assumes that any social ranking (P) should obey the following seemingly unobjectionable axioms (here P is to be read "is *socially preferred to*"):

1. It must rank all social states: Either $A\ P\ B$, $B\ P\ A$, or A and B are indifferent ($A\ I\ B$) for any two states A and B.

2. The ranking must be transitive: If $A\ P\ B$ and $B\ P\ C$ (or $B\ I\ C$), then $A\ P\ C$.

3. The ranking must be positively related to individual preferences: If A is preferred to B by Smith and Jones then $A\ P\ B$.

4. If new social states become feasible this fact should not affect the

---

[10] K. J. Arrow, *Social Choice and Individual Values,* second ed. (New Haven, Conn.: Yale University Press, 1951), published in 1963. In his second edition Arrow makes clear that his notion of a social welfare function is also to be taken as representing the process of social choice. It is always implied that the social welfare function is not only a scheme for identifying the most preferred social state but also a process for achieving that state. Hence "majority rule" might be regarded as a social welfare function whose properties are worth investigating.

[11] What follows is a great oversimplification of the richness of Arrow's result. The interested reader should consult Arrow's book (*op. cit.*) for a more detailed description.

social ranking of the original states. If, between A and B, A P B then this will remain true if some new state (D) becomes feasible.[12]

5. The social preference relation should not be imposed, say by custom. It should not be the case that A P B regardless of the tastes of individuals in society.

6. The relationship should be nondictatorial. One person's preferences should not determine society's preferences.

Arrow was able to show that these six conditions (all of which seem ethically reasonable on the surface) are not compatible with one another: No general social relationship obeying Conditions 1 to 6 exists. Using the tastes of Smith and Jones among A, B, and C it is possible to see the kind of inconsistencies which can arise in social choice. Since B P_S C and C P_J B, it must be the case that society is indifferent between B and C $(B$ I $C)$. Otherwise society's preferences would be in accord with only one individual (and against the other) and this would violate Axiom 6 requiring nondictatorship.

Since both Smith and Jones prefer A to B, Conditions 3 and 5 require that A P B. Hence, by transitivity Axiom 2, A P C. But, again, this is a violation of the nondictatorship assumption since A P_S C but C P_J A. Thus, in this simple case an inconsistency arises in the attempt to construct a social preference relationship. Admittedly, this example is a bit contrived, but it does clearly illustrate the problems of trying to aggregate divergent patterns of individual preferences into some reasonable social pattern. The importance of Arrow's more complex *impossibility theorem* is to show that any social decision rule which is chosen must violate at least one of the ethical postulates embodied in Axioms 1 to 6.

The making of social choices can be shown to be a theoretically

---

[12] Condition 4 is sometimes called the axiom of the *independence of irrelevant alternatives*. More controversy has arisen over this axiom (and similar ones in the Von Neumann-Morgenstern list) than any other. To see the sort of functions which are ruled out by the axiom consider individuals voting for candidates in an election. Suppose each individual can rank these candidates in order of their desirability. An election somehow combines these individual lists into a society-wide list. According to Axiom 4 the social list must have the property that if candidate x is preferred to candidate y this should remain true even if other candidates enter or leave the race. The most common election procedure in which each man votes *only* for his *most* preferred candidate may not obey the axiom because of the presence of "spoilers" in the race. For example, it is conceivable that the presence of George Wallace in the 1968 presidential election caused Hubert Humphrey to lose (Richard Nixon was shown to be socially preferred). With the "irrelevant alternative" Wallace out of the race, Humphrey might have won. The presidential election system therefore might not obey Arrow's Axiom 4. Many authors have examined the consequences of relaxing the axiom.

difficult and perhaps contradictory exercise. Other authors have investigated sets of ethical postulates which are somewhat less restrictive than Arrow's, but in many of these cases consistency problems remain. Economic theorists have had great difficulty in developing a theory of social choice which is neither completely subjective (that is, one which generally disregards the tastes of individuals in society) nor totally rationalizes the status quo.

Conclusion

To anyone familiar with the works of Smith, Marx, Schumpeter, or any of a number of other political economists the approach to social welfare taken in this chapter will be seen to be extremely limited. The tools developed here have sacrificed philosophical and descriptive richness for analytical simplicity. Obviously anyone interested in an understanding of the nature of a "good" society should not only pursue the analytical tools mentioned in this chapter but should, more importantly, take a broader perspective. There is no substitute for the insights provided by general political philosophy.

That is not to argue, however, that conceptualizations such as the social welfare function are useless because of their formality. Many subtle aspects of the problem of social choice can only be appreciated through an acquaintance with these tools of analysis. An eclectic approach utilizing both the formal concepts of the theoretical economist and the breadth of the social philosopher is necessary if a start is to be made in examining social issues in some systematic way.

CHAPTER 22

The Efficiency of Perfect Competition

Introduction

The two previous chapters have examined the notions of economic efficiency and social welfare without mentioning prices. Achieving efficiency and choosing among efficient allocations has been regarded as a purely physical problem in relating individual (and societal) tastes to the available productive technology. Presumably a desirable allocation of resources could be brought about by an omniscient central government. All that would be needed is complete information about individuals' tastes and the productive possibilities of all firms.

Even if it were in principle possible to gather such detailed information it would undoubtedly be prohibitively costly to do so. Because both tastes and productive technologies are constantly changing, much of society's resources would be devoted to information gathering with little left over for the satisfaction of basic wants. Consequently, alternative, less costly allocational methods would have to be investigated. The allocational device which has received by far the greatest attention is the price system. By relying on the self-motivation of many decision makers the price system permits the decentralization of allocational decisions. Relative to perfect central planning an interconnected market system provides a method for relating individual tastes and productive technology in a low-cost way. The natural working of the market mechanism generates information about tastes and technology in the form of prices. These prices act as signals to economic agents in guiding their supply and demand decisions. Changes in preferences or in productive techniques will require a reallocation of resources and, again, the price system can quickly disseminate information relevant to this new allocation. It is clear from previous chapters that in a market economy the price system does allocate resources. The question to be investigated in this chapter is whether or not this allocation can be efficient.

The Perfectly Competitive Price System

In order to study the efficiency of a price system it is necessary to have a well-formulated model. The model chosen is the perfectly competitive price system which has been examined throughout the earlier sections of this book. Choice of the perfectly competitive model is no accident. It will turn out that a perfectly competitive price system yields an efficient allocation of resources. Indeed, the correspondence between a Pareto Optimal Allocation of resources and a perfectly competitive price system is exact: Every perfectly competitive allocation is Pareto Optimal; and every Pareto Optimal Allocation has an associated perfectly competitive set of prices. The allocational problem and the establishment of competitive prices are, in a formal sense, "dual" problems.

Two warnings about this conclusion (which will be taken up in detail below) should be briefly mentioned at the outset. First, it should be kept in mind that not every Pareto Optimal Allocation is a social welfare optimum. Consequently, although a competitive price system may bring about an efficient allocation of resources some care must be taken in assessing the social desirability of such an allocation. It may be that the efficient allocations which are generated by the price system are inequitable. Second, one should be extremely careful in drawing any policy conclusions from the formal theorem of equivalence between perfect competition and Pareto optimality. Many of the requirements of a perfectly competitive price system may not hold in the real world. This point is examined in the last three sections of the chapter.

Having recorded these caveats it is now necessary to specify exactly what is meant by a *perfectly competitive price system*. It is assumed that there are in the economy under investigation some number, say *n*, of well-defined, homogeneous goods. Included in this list of goods are not only consumption items but also factors of production and intermediate goods. Each of these goods has an *equilibrium price* which is established by the action of supply and demand in the markets for *n* goods.[1] At this set of prices each market is cleared in the sense that suppliers are willing to supply that quantity which is demanded and vice-versa. It is assumed that there are no transaction or transportation charges and that both individuals and firms have perfect knowledge of these prices. Hence each good obeys the *law of one price:* A good trades at the same price no matter who buys it or which firm sells it. It is therefore legitimate to speak of *the* price of a good.

Given the prices of *n* goods, economic agents react to these prices in specific ways:

(a) There are assumed to be a large number of individuals buying any one good. Each individual takes all *n* prices as given. He adjusts his behavior so as to *maximize utility,* given these prices and his budget constraint. Individuals may also be sellers of productive services and in such decisions they also regard prices as fixed parameters.[2]

(b) There are assumed to be a large number of firms producing each good, but each firm produces only a small share of the output of any one good. In making input and output choices firms are assumed to operate so as to *maximize profits.* The firm treats all prices as fixed parameters in its profit-maximizing decisions: The individual firm's activities, either as a supplier of goods or as a demander of factor inputs, have no effect on market prices.

---

[1] Some technical questions regarding the ability of "the market" to establish these *n* prices are examined in the appendix to this chapter. One aspect of this market interaction should be made clear from the outset. The perfectly competitive market only determines relative (not absolute) prices. In this chapter, therefore, we will only speak of relative prices. It makes no difference whether the prices of apples and oranges are 10¢ and 20¢ respectively, or $10 and $20. The important point in either case is that 2 apples can be exchanged for 1 orange in the market.

[2] Since one price represents the wage rate the relevant budget constraint is in reality a time constraint. This is the way in which individuals' labor-leisure choices were treated in Chapter 7.

These assumptions characterize a perfectly competitive market. Using the assumptions it is possible to show that such a perfectly competitive price system will allocate goods efficiently.

The Equivalence between Perfect Competition and Pareto Optimality

The essence of the relationship between perfect competition and the efficient allocation of resources can be summarized in a very simple way. In Chapter 20 the conditions of efficiency were shown to require that the rate of trade-off between any two goods, say X and Y, should be the same for all economic agents. For a perfectly competitive market the ratio of the price of X to the price of Y provides this common rate of trade-off to which all agents will adjust. Because prices are treated as fixed parameters in both individuals' utility-maximizing decisions and firms' profit-maximizing decisions all trade-off rates between X and Y will be equalized to the rate at which X and Y can be traded in the market (P_X/P_Y). Since all agents face the same prices all trade-off rates will be equalized and an efficient allocation will be achieved.

To examine this proof in more detail we will now investigate in turn the conditions for efficiency in exchange, efficiency in production, efficiency in production and exchange, and efficiency in the provision of inputs. First, consider efficiency in exchange. The required condition is that the MRS for any two goods, X and Y, should be the same for all individuals. But utility maximization requires that each individual equate his MRS (of X for Y) to the ratio P_X/P_Y. In so doing he will be equating the rate at which he is willing to trade X for Y to the rate at which these can be traded in the competitive market. Since every individual faces the same price ratio the utility-maximizing decision of each individual will succeed in establishing the conditions for efficient exchange. Mathematically, consider any two individuals. Each faces the price ratio P_X/P_Y and will choose X and Y such that:

$$MRS \text{ (individual 1)} = \frac{P_X}{P_Y}$$

and

$$MRS \text{ (individual 2)} = \frac{P_X}{P_Y}$$

hence

$$MRS \text{ (individual 1)} = MRS \text{ (individual 2)}.$$

This is the condition required for an efficient allocation of X and Y which was derived in Chapter 20.

The simplicity of this proof may obscure some of its important features, and it is therefore worth dwelling a while on some aspects. First, remember that the prices P_X and P_Y are assumed to be equilibrium prices. This means that supply will be equal to demand in both markets. While it is true that any arbitrarily chosen price ratio would insure that individuals would equate their MRS's to one another, such arbitrarily chosen price ratios would not assure equilibrium: Both individuals may be oversupplied with X (and undersupplied with Y) if an incorrect price ratio were arbitrarily set. For example, suppose two individuals were stranded on a desert island with few sources of water and that each arrived on shore with some diamonds and some water (to rephrase an example from Chapter 1). They might initially adopt a "price ratio" of diamonds for water which approximated that in the world from which they had just come: Perhaps 1 diamond would exchange for 100 gallons of water. As time wore on, however, both individuals would find they were more than willing to trade diamonds for water at this price ratio. There would be an excess supply of diamonds and an excess demand for water at the price ratio that had been brought from the outside world. For this island society the price ratio of 1 diamond to 100 gallons of water is not an equilibrium, and it would be expected that some other price ratio would be decided upon by the two men. The mechanics of arriving at equilibrium prices are discussed in the next section.

A second important feature of the proof is the way in which it illustrates the remarkable information-gathering ability of the market. Not only does the market assimilate all relevant information about individuals' supply and demand functions (and with this information establish prices) but also the market creates a societal rate of trade-off of X for Y which is a correct reflection of every individual's trade-off rate. Information which could only be gathered at great cost by, say, governmental investigative bodies can be costlessly generated by the interaction of supply and demand.

Proofs similar to the one presented above can be used to demonstrate that perfectly competitive prices will lead to efficiency in production. To show this we will examine the three Allocation Rules developed in Chapter 20. Allocation Rule 1 requires that a firm have identical rates at which it can trade one input for another (the rate of technical substitution, RTS) in all those outputs which it produces. But this is assured by the existence of perfectly competitive markets for inputs. In minimizing costs the firm will equate the RTS between any two inputs, say capital and labor, to the ratio of their competitive rental prices (v/w). This will be true for any output which the firm happens to produce and hence the firm will be equating all its RTS's to the common price ratio

v/w. In this way the firm will be led to adopt efficient input proportions in a decentralized and low-cost way.

Allocation Rule 2 will hold for a similar reason. This rule requires that every firm which produces a particular good, say X, have identical marginal productivities of labor in the production of X $(MP_L{}^X)$. In Chapter 17 it was shown that a profit-maximizing firm will hire additional labor up to the point at which the marginal value product $(P_X \cdot MP_L{}^X)$ of labor is equal to the competitive wage rate (w). Since both P_X and w are given by the market, each firm will equate its $MP_L{}^X$ to w/P_X. Consequently, every firm will have the same marginal productivity of labor in the production of X. Again the market has succeeded in bringing about an efficient allocation.

Finally, Allocation Rule 3 requires that the rate of product transformation $(RPT-$this is the rate at which one output can be traded for another in production) between any two goods, say X and Y, be the same for all firms. That a perfectly competitive price system will insure this can be most easily shown by recalling (from Chapter 12) that the RPT (of X for Y) is equal to the ratio of the marginal cost of X (MC_X) to that of Y (MC_Y). But each profit-maximizing firm will produce that output level for which marginal cost is equal to the market price. Therefore, for every firm $P_X = MC_X$ and $P_Y = MC_Y$, and hence $MC_X/MC_Y = P_X/P_Y$ for all firms. Allocation Rule 3 is therefore satisfied.[3]

This discussion demonstrates that the profit-maximizing, decentralized decisions of many firms can achieve efficiency in production without any central direction. Competitive markets act as devices to unify the multitude of decisions which firms make into one coherent, efficient pattern. Relying on the motivations of entrepreneurs proves to be a workable and low-cost way of prompting the production sector to act efficiently.

Proving that perfectly competitive markets lead to efficiency in the relationship between production and exchange is even more straightforward than the proofs already presented. Since the price ratios quoted to consumers are the same ratios which the market presents to firms, the MRS shared by all individuals will be identical to the RPT which is shared by all firms. This will be true for any pair of goods. Consequently, an efficient mix of goods will be produced and exchanged. Again, notice the two important functions which the market performs. First, the market

---

[3] An interesting example of the ability of a perfectly competitive price system to satisfy Allocation Rule 3 occurs in the theory of international trade. If world prices are set by the supply-demand mechanism, and if all markets are competitive, each country's RPT will be equated to these prevailing world prices. But this will insure that world production is allocated efficiently between countries. Each country will specialize in producing those goods of which it is a relatively efficient producer. This "theorem" forms the basis for a belief that free trade is the best policy.

assures that supply and demand will be equalized for all goods. If a good were produced in too great amounts a market reaction would set in (perhaps its price would fall) which would cut back on the production of the good and shift resources into other employment. The equilibrating of supply and demand in the market therefore assures that there will be neither excess demand nor excess supply. Second, the resulting equilibrium prices provide market trade-off rates for both firms and individuals to use as parameters in their decisions. Because these trade-off rates are identical for both firms and individuals efficiency is assured.

Finally, it is easy to see that factors of production will be supplied in an efficient manner. Each individual will choose his hours of work so that his MRS between leisure and consuming a particular good is equal to the ratio of the price of labor (w) to the price of the good, say P_X. But, as has been discussed, each firm equates its marginal products of labor to the ratio w/P_X. Hence the individual's psychic rate of trade-off between additional leisure and consuming more of some good is equal to the rate at which his labor services can technically be transformed into this good.[4] The perfectly competitive market again assures both that the amount of any factor which is supplied by individuals will be demanded by firms and that the quantities supplied will be those which are efficient given the prevailing tastes and technologies in society.

It has been shown that perfectly competitive markets (and their associated equilibrium prices) can bring about efficiency in the allocation of resources. It should be clear that this "proof" can be reversed to show

---

[4] If this condition holds for one good for the individual, and if he is allocating his income so as to maximize utility, the condition will hold for every good. Consider two goods, X and Y, and suppose the individual has equated the MRS (of leisure for X) to the ratio w/P_X. This says that:

$$MRS \ (L \text{ for } X) = \frac{\partial U/\partial L}{\partial U/\partial X} = \frac{w}{P_X}$$

where L represents hours of leisure.

For the individual's expenditures to be allocated optimally between X and Y it is required that:

$$MRS \ (X \text{ for } Y) = \frac{\partial U/\partial X}{\partial U/\partial Y} = \frac{P_X}{P_Y}.$$

Multiplying the first equation by the second gives:

$$MRS \ (L \text{ for } Y) = \frac{\partial U/\partial L}{\partial U/\partial Y} = \frac{w}{P_Y}.$$

Hence the efficient conditions for labor supply hold with respect to any other good (Y). This is why we can speak unambiguously of the MRS of leisure for "consumption."

that any Pareto Optimal Allocation can be reproduced by a perfectly competitive price system. Any optimal allocation involves a number of trade-offs. By setting price ratios equal to these trade-off rates, and by so distributing goods among individuals that supply and demand are in equilibrium, this allocation can be achieved by the workings of the price system. In principle, then, a price system is a low-cost way of achieving an efficient allocation of resources. The impersonal workings of the market and the maximizing decisions of numerous economic agents combine to produce this result. Demonstrating this theoretical duality between allocation and pricing is one of the major achievements of microeconomic theory. In a sense this finding provides "scientific" support for the laissez-faire position taken by many economists. For example, Smith's assertion that:

> The natural effort of every individual to better his own condition, when suffered to exert itself with freedom and security, is so powerful a principle that it is alone, and without any assistance, not only capable of carrying on the society to wealth and prosperity, but of surmounting a hundred impertinent obstructions with which the folly of human laws too often encumbers its operations . . .[5]

has been shown to have substantial validity if we can assume (as was surely the case) that Smith had in mind a perfectly competitive market. It is a remarkable feature of a perfectly competitive price system that a single-minded pursuit of self-interest on the part of each economic agent is in fact capable of producing an efficient overall result.

The equivalence theroem raises many more issues than it resolves. These questions are of two rather different types. First are relatively theoretical questions about how a perfectly competitive set of prices is to be obtained. These issues will be discussed briefly in the next section and in more detail in the appendix to this chapter. A more important set of issues raised by the equivalence theorem, however, is whether the theorem should be assigned any importance from a policy point of view: Is the theorem a guide for governmental action or simply an interesting theoretical construction? A start toward answering this question will be made below in the last three sections and will, to some extent, be the principal subject of the entire final part of this text (Chapters 23-26).

One important theoretical point should be mentioned here. The entire discussion of efficiency in Chapters 20-22 has examined only the first-order conditions for a maximum. This procedure is in agreement

<hr />

[5] Adam Smith, *The Wealth of Nations* (New York: Random House, Inc. 1937), Modern Library ed., p. 508.

with the decision stated at the outset to minimize the use of mathematics associated with second-order conditions. It has generally been assumed that individual tastes and productive technologies are of such an "obliging" nature that the necessary conditions for a maximum are also sufficient. Hence it was assumed that indifference curves are convex, that isoquants are convex, and that production possibility frontiers are concave. All of these assumptions are based on the general principle of *diminishing marginal effectiveness*. The rate of trade-off of X for Y decreases in all these applications as the ratio of X to Y increases. These assumptions, which seem reasonably supported by both a priori logic and by real-world observations, insure that the necessary conditions for a maximum do indeed yield a true maximum. It is important therefore to recognize the role played by these *convexity assumptions* in models of the efficiency of perfect competition, and to note that many of the proofs developed in this part are incomplete in the absence of these assumptions. In some applications it is possible to relax the strict convexity assumptions which have been made and still achieve efficiency. Such theoretical extensions will not be examined here.

An Example of the Efficiency of Perfect Competition in an Exchange Economy

A graphic proof of the efficiency of perfect competition can be presented for the case of a two-person, two-good (X and Y) exchange economy. In order to diagram this proof it is helpful to introduce the concept of an *offer curve*. This curve shows the quantities of X and Y which an individual desires at various price ratios.

To construct the curve consider the set of individual indifference curves shown in Figure 22.1. Suppose the individual has an initial endowment of goods X and Y which is denoted by point A. If "the market" quotes a price ratio (P_X/P_Y) to the individual then the trades which he can make from his initial endowment are along a straight line with slope $-P_X/P_Y$ passing through point A.[6] Given this budget constraint, the individual's preferred point is B where the tangency conditions for a maximum are satisfied. To reach this point by trading in the market the individual will trade some of his initial endowment of X, ($X^A - X^B$) for an additional amount of Y, ($Y^B - Y^A$). The ratio in which these two quantities can be traded is given by the market price ratio of goods (that is, by the slope of the budget constraint).

---

[6] The individual can afford any combination of X and Y such that:

$$\frac{P_X}{P_Y} \cdot X + Y \le \frac{P_X}{P_Y} \cdot X^A + Y^A.$$

Figure 22.1   Construction of an Individual's Offer Curve

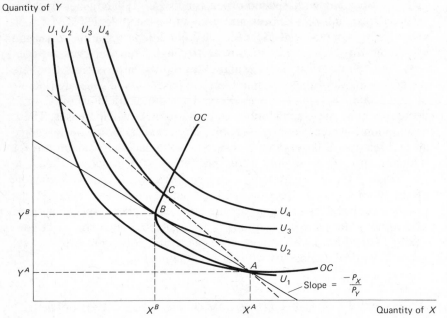

An individual's offer curve shows the quantities of X and Y, for particular initial endowments, that the individual would choose when presented with different price ratios. For example, if a price ratio of P_X/P_Y were quoted by the market the individual would choose point B. In so doing he would be willing to trade $(X^A - X^B)$ of good X for $(Y^B - Y^A)$ of good Y. By varying the price ratio all points such as B can be traced out as the offer curve.

The individual's offer curve can now be constructed as the locus of the trade points, such as B, which result from presenting him with all possible price ratios. For example, an alternative budget constraint arising from a different price ratio might be represented by the dashed line in Figure 22.1, and the utility-maximizing position would be at point C. The locus of all points such as A, B, and C would be the offer curve.[7] This curve is labeled OC in the figure.

The offer curve concept is a useful graphic device for demonstrating

---

[7] Notice that the initial point A is included on the offer curve. There is some price ratio at which the individual's optimal choice would be to abstain from trade. Also notice that the offer curve never passes below the indifference curve passing through point A. An individual would never choose to trade if he were forced to accept a utility level lower than that available from his initial endowment.

the reactions of an individual being presented with fixed market prices and an initial endowment of the two goods. By using offer curves for the two individuals in an Edgeworth Box diagram it is possible to demonstrate how a perfectly competitive price system can lead to efficiency in exchange. In Figure 22.2 the indifference curves of the two individuals (Smith and Jones) are drawn together with the offer curves (OC_S and OC_J) associated with the initial endowments represented by point A.

Figure 22.2 Demonstration of the Efficiency of Perfect Competition in an Exchange Economy

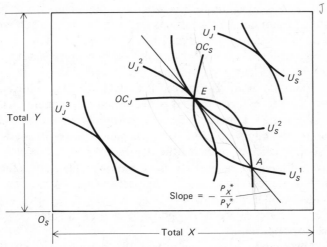

In this Exchange Box diagram the initial endowment is given by point A. The offer curves through point A are drawn; the intersection of these curves at point E represents an exchange equilibrium since what Smith is willing to trade Jones wants, and vice-versa. The price ratio P_X^*/P_Y^* will be able to bring about this equilibrium point. It can also be seen that E lies on the contract curve since Smith's and Jones' indifference curves are tangent at E. Hence the price ratio P_X^*/P_Y^* will also promote efficiency.

These curves record the responses of Smith and Jones to all possible price ratios. At the points of intersection of OC_S and OC_J exchange is in equilibrium: The demands of Smith and Jones exactly exhaust the total quantities of the two goods available. For example, point A is an exchange equilibrium since both individuals could choose to keep their initial endowments. If the offer curves intersect at a point other than A, say E, it can be shown that this new equilibrium point is on the contract curve and hence is an efficient allocation of X and Y. Consider the straight line joining A and E. The slope of this line ($-P_X^*/P_Y^*$) represents an equilibrium price ratio since Smith and Jones react to this ratio by demanding combinations of goods which exhaust the total quantities of X and Y. At E the line AE is tangent to Smith's indifference curve U_S^2 since this is the way the offer curve was constructed (*see* Figure 22.1). Similarly, the line AE is also tangent to an indifference curve of Jones (U_J^2) at E. Hence Smith's and Jones' indifference curves must be tangent to each other at E. Providing that the indifference curves have the normal convex shape, this point of tangency will be on the contract curve; it will represent an efficient allocation of X and Y between the two individuals. The market's generation of equilibrium prices has insured both that what is demanded will in fact be supplied and that the resultant trade will be Pareto Optimal.

Figure 22.2 shows graphically what was demonstrated in the previous section. If individuals take prices as given by the market, an equilibrium set of prices can generate an efficient allocation of goods in an exchange economy. It is important to point out, however, that the efficient allocation which is achieved may not be optimal from a social welfare point of view. The point on the contract curve which is "chosen" by the price system is necessarily related to the initial endowments with which the individuals start. Different initial endowments would result in different points on the contract curve being chosen. A government desiring to achieve some particular point on the contract curve by means of a price system would have to insure that initial endowments permit the desired point to be achieved. This might necessitate some reallocation of initial endowments prior to the start of trading. Although the price system can generate an efficient allocation of goods it may need some help if it is to yield a welfare optimum.

This observation is just one aspect of a more general principle: Efficiency is only a necessary condition for a social welfare optimum. The allocation of resources which is generated by a perfectly competitive market may not be equitable (by some standards) even though it is efficient. This point cannot be underemphasized, for it has relevance throughout this book. For example, in Chapter 6 it was shown that market demand functions depend not only on all prices but also on the distribution of income among the members of society. Consequently, the final output mix decided upon by the workings of a price system will depend on how purchasing power is distributed. If the income distribution is very skewed, a final output mix of only luxury yachts and subsistence food might result from the workings of supply and demand. Although this mix might be efficient in that marginal rates of substitution are indeed equal to rates of product transformation, this mix may be far from that which is socially optimal. Perhaps some form of income redistribution could move society toward a more equitable allocation of resources. This possibility is examined in Chapter 26.

Some Limitations of the Equivalence Theorem

The equivalence between an optimal allocation of resources and the workings of a perfectly competitive price system depends crucially on the assumptions which underlie the competitive model. When one moves beyond the confines of this model and examines possible real-world allocative problems certain difficulties become apparent. In this section some of the impediments which may prevent free markets from generating an efficient allocation will be examined. It will be seen that many of these are quite likely in view of our knowledge of the real world. Some observations about the lessons to be drawn concerning optimal resource allocation in the presence of these impediments will be taken up in the next section.

The number of impediments to perfect competition which might be discussed is practically infinite. These can, however, be classed into three general groupings which include most of the cases occurring in the real world. Each of these broad classes of impediments is discussed separately below.

a. *Imperfect competition.* We will use the term "imperfect competition" in a broad sense to include all those situations in which economic agents exert some market power in determining price. Markets which are organized as oligopolies or in which there is a monopsony on the demand side are therefore also considered in this category, in addition to the usual case of monopoly. The essential aspect of all such markets is that marginal revenue (or marginal expense in the case of a monopsony) is different from market price. A profit-maximizing firm, by equating marginal revenue to marginal cost, will not produce where price is equal to marginal cost. Because of this behavior of firms relative prices will no longer reflect relative marginal costs, and the price system no longer carries the information necessary to insure efficiency.

As an example consider the efficient conditions for production and exchange in the Robinson Crusoe economy diagrammed in Figure 22.3. Point E represents an efficient allocation in that at this point the MRS (of X for Y) is equal to the RPT (of X for Y). A perfectly competitive price ratio of P_X^*/P_Y^* could generate this allocation. Suppose, instead, that one of the goods, say X, is produced under monopoly conditions, whereas Y is produced under conditions of perfect competition. The profit-maximizing output choice then is that combination of X and Y for which:

$$RPT \ (X \text{ for } Y) = \frac{MC_X}{MC_Y} = \frac{MR_X}{P_Y} < \frac{P_X}{P_Y} \qquad [22.1]$$

where the final inequality holds because $MR_X < P_X$ for the monopolist.

Figure 22.3 The Production of Good X under Monopoly Conditions Prevents Efficiency in Production and Exchange

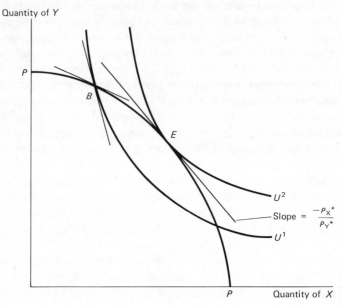

If good X is produced in a monopoly market the profit-maximizing firm will choose that output combination for which the RPT (of X for Y) is equal to MR_X/P_Y and this will be less than the ratio of these goods' market prices (P_X/P_Y). Production will take place at a point such as B where the RPT is less than individuals' marginal rates of substitution. Too little X will be produced as a result of the monopolization of its market.

But this will entail a choice of outputs such as that represented by point B with less X and more Y being produced than is optimal, given the existing tastes and technology.[8] The existence of a monopoly, by creating a divergence between price ratios and technical trade-off rates, has caused the efficiency of the price system to fail. No longer do individuals and firms equate their rates of trade-off to the same market-determined magnitudes. It is marginal revenue which is relevent to firms' decisions and price which is relevant to individuals' decisions; under conditions of imperfect competition these two will differ.

A similar proof would hold for other circumstances in which markets

[8] This is a "general equilibrium" proof of the result first illustrated in Figure 15.4 where the differential effects of monopoly and perfect competition were demonstrated in a partial equilibrium framework.

are imperfectly competitive. Market power by an agent creates a divergence between market price and that marginal figure which is relevent to the agent's decision. Because of this divergence, market prices will not play the role of fixed parameters in every agent's choices; therefore efficiency in allocation by the price system is no longer possible.

b. _Externalities._ A second way in which the price system can fail to allocate resources efficiently occurs when there are interactions among firms and individuals which are not adequately represented by market prices. Examples of such occurrences are numerous. Perhaps the most common one is the case of a firm which pollutes the air with industrial smoke and other debris. This situation is termed an _externality_: It is an interaction between the firm's level of production and individuals' utilities which is not accounted for by the price system. While a more complete discussion of the nature of externalities will be presented in Chapter 25 it is possible to describe why the presence of such nonmarket interactions interferes with the ability of the price system to allocate resources efficiently.

The conditions for efficiency which were discussed in Chapter 20 must be defined in a "social" sense when the possibility of externalities is recognized. For example, it is required that the _social rate of product transformation_ (the rate at which society can transform one good into another) be equal to the _social marginal rate of substitution_ (the rate at which society is willing to trade one good for another) for an optimal allocation of resources. The problem which arises in the presence of externalities is that economic agents only pay attention to _private_ rates of transformation and substitution in their decisions. If private and social rates diverge, the perfectly competitive price system will not generate an efficient allocation.

As an application of this logic imagine two goods in an economy: steel and balloons. Assume that the private marginal cost of balloons (MC_B) is identical to the social marginal cost (SMC_B), that there are no externalities in balloon production. On the other hand, suppose the production of steel entails the pollution of water and air and thereby imposes costs (such as the cost of cleaning one's clothes or the additional costs to cities of removing the pollutants from drinking water) on society in addition to production costs. Hence the social marginal cost of steel (SMC_S) exceeds the private marginal cost of steel (MC_S). The social rate of product transformation of steel for balloons ($SRPT$) is then defined as:

$$SRPT = \frac{SMC_S}{SMC_B}.$$ [22.2]

It is easy to see that this rate will exceed the private rate of product transformation:

$$SRPT = \frac{SMC_S}{SMC_B} > RPT = \frac{MC_S}{MC_B} \tag{22.3}$$

because of the externalities associated with steel production. This equation says that the rate at which society can trade balloons for steel exceeds the rate at which they can be traded privately. In giving up 1 ton of steel production additional resources for balloon production come from two sources: those resources which were previously used in steel production and those resources which were used in combating the effects of air and water pollution. The social RPT records the additional balloons which can be produced with the resources from both these sources. From the firm's point of view, however, the RPT reflects shifting only those resources which move directly from steel production into balloon production: The external effects are ignored in a firm's private decisions.

In this example the required condition for efficiency is that:

$$SRPT \text{ (Steel for balloons)} = SMRS \text{ (Steel for balloons)} = \frac{MU_S}{MU_B}. \tag{22.4}$$

But the price system, by relying on the private motivation of firms, will generate an allocation in which:

$$RPT \text{ (Steel for balloons)} = \frac{P_S}{P_B} = SMRS \text{ (Steel for balloons)}. \tag{22.5}$$

Since the social and private rates of product transformation differ, this allocation will not obey the conditions for an optimal allocation. The private market will tend to produce too much steel and too few balloons. In this situation decentralized decisions, because they ignore externalities, have led to an inefficient allocation of resources.

Many more examples of this failure of the perfectly competitive price system could be investigated. Firms may, for example, produce beneficial externalities: Building a dam to produce hydroelectric power involves the construction of a reservoir which provides recreational and esthetic benefits to local residents. Because private firms may not take this beneficial effect into account in their profitability calculations resources may be underallocated to dam building.

Externalities can also occur *in consumption* if one individual's consumption behavior affects another individual's utility. Suppose, for example, that my neighbor is a motor-cycle enthusiast with very little desire for a muffler. It is quite probable that his comings and goings at all hours will have a negative effect on my utility. Any assessment of the social marginal utility of motor cycles should consider not only the utility derived by the neighbor but also the external effect that his consumption has on me. In giving up one motor cycle the social loss would be less than the private loss to its owner, since I would in fact be made better off. The price system, again because it reflects only private utilities, will not adequately register this fact, and it may be that motor cycles will be overproduced. Since this type of interpersonal externality is probably quite prevalent in densely populated countries the motor-cycle example is by no means a trivial one.[9]

Although this brief discussion of externalities raises many more issues than can be investigated here, the essential point should by now be clear. Externalities create the possibility of a divergence between private and social rates of trade-off. The rules for optimal allocation apply to social trade-off rates, whereas the price system equates only private rates. Hence the allocation brought about by relying on the private decisions of firms and individuals under a competitive price system may not be efficient.

c. _Indivisibilities._ A third possible failure of the price system to produce an optimal allocation of resources can be illustrated by examining the logic of the notion of efficiency more closely. The various marginal rules for individuals' and firms' choices require that all quantities be infinitely divisible. Marginal rates of trade-off are well defined only when marginal adjustment is in fact possible. If some goods can only be consumed or produced in large units such marginal adjustments are impossible. Only a "few" of the points in our two-good graphs are attainable through production and exchange, and the precise tangencies required by the marginal rules may not be attainable. A particularly important type of indivisibility problem occurs in the allocation of resources to the production of goods which are used by more than one person. The most famous example of this is the problem of whether an optimal amount will be spent on the maintaining of a road. Suppose many people use a particular road. Each of these persons consumes the services of the road but there is no obvious way in which maintenance charges on the road will be shared by them. In fact, it is likely that each person will adopt

---

[9] It may be possible in many situations for individuals to resolve these problems of externalities by bargaining among themselves. For example, I might be able to bribe the neighbor to wheel his cycle down the street before starting it. This possibility raises several issues about the proper way of defining externalities which are examined in Chapter 25.

the principle of "let the other guy do it" in regard to road repairs, and consequently few resources will be devoted to this task. As we will see in Chapter 23 this type of indivisibility problem is prevalent, and it makes government interference necessary to assure the efficient operation of the price system.[10]

The Theory of the Second Best

It must be admitted that the three general types of impediments mentioned are present in any economic system. A freely operating price system will therefore probably be incapable of generating a true Pareto Optimal Allocation of resources. It is tempting to reason that a competitive price system could still be advocated for those sectors of the economy in which these impediments are unimportant. By using the price system in these sectors the Pareto rules for allocational efficiency would be satisfied there, and this would be a *second-best* solution to the problem of optimal allocation. Unfortunately, this intuitive answer to the problem of finding a second-best solution is not correct. In a 1956 article Lipsey and Lancaster addressed themselves to this general question and reached a rather devastating conclusion.[11] If certain constraints within the economic system prevent some of the Pareto conditions from holding, then, given these constraints, it will generally not be desirable to have the optimum conditions hold elsewhere. It is not true that having more (but not all) of the optimum conditions hold is necessarily superior to having fewer hold. One must analyze each individual situation rather than attempt to draw such broad, all-inclusive policy recommendations.

While a technical proof of the assertions made by Lipsey and Lancaster is rather difficult, the basic point can be made using a simple graphic argument. Suppose that society's production possibilities for two goods are represented by the frontier PP in Figure 22.4, and that tastes are given by the indifference curves. Assume also that there is a constraint in the economic system which makes the true optimal point (E) unattainable. Let this constraint be represented by the line AB; combinations of goods to the northeast of line AB cannot be achieved because of the constraint. Society's optimization problem is to maximize

[10] For a more complete discussion of the question of indivisibility *see* T. Scitovsky, *Welfare and Competition,* rev. ed. (Homewood, Ill.: Richard D. Irwin, Inc., 1971), Chaps. 12 and 13.
[11] R. G. Lipsey and K. Lancaster, "The General Theory of Second Best," *Review of Economic Studies,* vol. 24, no. 63 (1956–1957), pp. 11–32.

welfare (as represented by the indifference curves) subject to the constraint AB. The figure makes clear that this optimal point need not be on the PP frontier; the point C is definitely preferable to the "efficient" point D. This then demonstrates the principal negative result of the theory of the second best: If all the conditions for a Pareto Optimum cannot be satisfied, it is not necessarily true that to fulfill some of them is the best policy.

This discussion of second-best choices at least casts some doubt on the advisability of advocating competitive pricing in particular sectors of the economy, when it is recognized that the Pareto conditions may not hold elsewhere. Whether or not such "partial" competitive solutions are in fact optimal will depend on the particular situation and on the nature of the constraints present in the economic system. In a theoretical sense the attainment of a Pareto Optimum must be approached as a problem in constrained maximization rather than by piecemeal application of general optimal rules. With complete knowledge of society's tastes and technology it may in fact be possible to derive some optimal departures from perfectly competitive pricing.

Figure 22.4   A Graphic Demonstration of Theory of Second Best

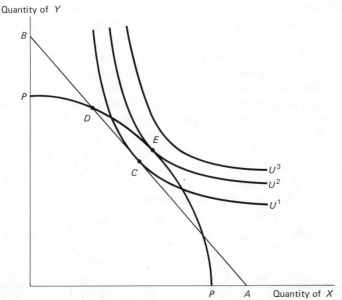

In the diagram the constraint AB prevents the optimal point E from being achieved. It is not true that, given this constraint, a society should strive for productive efficiency. Points such as C are preferred to those efficient points, such as D, which are obtainable. Second-best points are therefore not necessarily efficient points.

So Why Study Perfect Competition?

By now the perplexed reader might legitimately ask why such great attention has been devoted to the optimal properties of a perfectly competitive price system if such a price system is unlikely to be attainable in any case. This is a valid question which, unfortunately, can only be answered in a rather vague and conceptual way. A study of the ideal of competitive allocation provides a pedagogic device for understanding how a price system allocates resources among alternative uses. The relationship between market trade-offs and technical trade-offs is forcefully brought out by such an examination. Through a study of the competitive world one can achieve a feeling for how the economic system hangs together and gain an understanding of the notion of general equilibrium. A comprehension of the interrelationships between pricing and allocation is an integral part of any economic education.

On a more practical level the competitive model provides insights into how a price system ought to operate and into the nature of decentralized decisions. The most important application of these principles to date has been in the examination of the possibilities for decentralization in a centrally planned economy. Early writers claimed that an optimal allocation of resources would be impossible to achieve in a Socialist state because of the vast amount of information and infinite computations which would be necessary. It was argued that no central planning board could possibly assimilate all the information which is provided in a market economy by the price system. Without the free operation of a market, resource allocation would be hopelessly inefficient. These views were challenged by the Polish economist Oscar Lange in a series of articles in the late 1930's.[12] Lange suggested that a Socialist economy could achieve an efficient allocation of resources (at least in theory) by utilizing the desirable properties of markets in permitting decentralized decision making, while at the same time having social ownership of the means of production. Because an examination of Lange's proposals exhibits as much about the problems of resource allocation in a market economy as it does about resource allocation in a centrally planned one, we will outline his scheme in some detail.

Under Lange's system the central planning board is charged with setting prices which are to be regarded by all economic agents as fixed. Individuals are free to make consumption decisions given these prices, and presumably they will do so in a utility-maximizing way. Firm managers are under strict orders to minimize the costs of producing any

---

[12] The principal article appears in edited form in *On the Economic Theory of Socialism* (New York: McGraw-Hill Inc., Paperbacks, 1964), originally published by the University of Minnesota Press.

level of output, and are to produce that output for which price equals marginal cost. In other words they are to approximate the decisions which managers of perfectly competitive firms would make in order to maximize profits. What Lange's model attempts to do is to approximate the efficient features of the perfectly competitive model.

From a theoretical viewpoint there are three interesting questions which might be raised about the Lange model: How is equilibrium between supply and demand assured? How are factor supplies regulated? How are possible externalities treated?

The first of these problems is perhaps the most important. If the central planning board sets nonequilibrium prices chaos is certain to result. A price set too high will mean that an excess supply of the good in question will be produced. Similarly, a price set below equilibrium will have the result of bringing about long shopping queues and other manifestations of excess demand. In a market economy such problems are avoided by relying on the interactions of supply and demand to establish an equilibrium price. Because this market interaction would not take place in a planned economy the central planning board is under a strict mandate to raise prices of those goods in excess demand and lower the prices of those which are being oversupplied. Hopefully, by closely observing inventories and other indicators of market equilibrium, the central planning board would be able to adjust prices so as to respond to any possible discrepancies between supply and demand.

In the Lange model labor is allocated in the same manner assumed to operate in a market economy. Wage rates are set by the central planning board and individuals make their labor-leisure choices and their occupational choices based on those rates. Similarly, firms demand labor based on the marginal productivity principle because of the requirement that they "maximize profits." The board must be careful to set equilibrium wage rates.

It is in the supply of capital that Lange's solution differs markedly from the perfectly competitive model. Since capital is not privately owned in a Socialist economy no interest payments are made to individuals. At this zero interest rate there may be "insufficient" incentives to save.[13] The central planning board is therefore charged with the responsibility of deciding how much output to withhold from current production for purposes of capital accumulation. Firms are, however, charged a rental rate for the capital equipment they use in order to insure that the supply of capital available is allocated in an optimal way. Although this procedure will (in principle) insure that capital is efficiently allocated at any one point in time, very real questions might be raised about the

---

[13] It is possible that some saving may take place even at a zero interest rate. Individuals may still wish to transfer some current purchasing power into the future.

board's decisions regarding the total amount of capital accumulation for society as a whole. The most important of these questions is whether the decisions of the board will adequately reflect the tastes of individuals for present versus future goods. In fact, there is some evidence that planners in Socialist countries may allocate too large a portion of current output to capital accumulation. The chronic "shortage" of consumer goods in the Soviet Union and some Eastern European countries is one sign of this possible misallocation. Such economies might be considered to be inefficient in an intertemporal sense.

A final ingenious solution to the problem of achieving an efficient allocation of resources was proposed by Lange to deal with externalities. The suggestion made was that external costs of production should be imposed (in the form of taxes) on the responsible firms. This would shift the firms' marginal cost curves up and would reduce the quantities they were willing to supply at the prevailing price. Then a shortage would appear in the market at the current price, and the central planning board would respond to this excess demand by raising prices. Finally, this action would presumably cut back on the demand for those products which are produced with harmful external side effects. Lange's suggestion insures an allocation of resources which adequately reflects true social costs. We will see in Chapter 25 that a similar solution might be desirable in a Capitalist economy as well.

Lange's notion of "market" socialism has never been applied in practice, although recent actions in some Socialist countries suggest a movement in that direction.[14] The rather lengthy discussion of Lange's ideas has been presented more because of the light it sheds on allocation in a market economy than as a practical guidebook to Socialist planning. Clearly exhibited in this model is the importance of relying on decentralized decision making and the central role which a price system can play in unifying the actions of the decision makers. In certain circumstances these interactions may be able to achieve a socially desirable result.

The use of decentralized responses to a price system in order to achieve a desirable allocation is not confined to Socialist economies. Many modern corporations have adopted programs of decentralized decision making and the optimal pricing of intracompany resources (such as capital or the use of sales staff) in order to promote efficiency in their organizations. Several of the management tools used in this process were

---

[14] These experiments have progressed furthest in Yugoslavia, where much of the economy is directed by (modified) Lange rules [see B. Horvat, "Survey of Yugoslavian Economic Policy," *American Economic Review,* Supplement (May 1971) for a detailed summary]. Similar experiments are being conducted in the Soviet Union under the intellectual leadership of Yevsei Liberman.

developed in the study of allocational efficiency. The problems of making a corporation perform profitably and making a society utilize its resources efficiently have many conceptual and technical similarities.

All of these examples really skirt the crucial issue of whether it makes sense to adopt governmental policies which attempt to duplicate competitive behavior in some sectors of the economy while recognizing that great divergences exist in others. One might, for example, want to say that it is desirable that the agricultural industry is competitive even though steel production and automobile production obviously are not. What the analysis of the previous sections showed was that in order for such an assertion to be theoretically correct "second-best" considerations must be relatively unimportant. Whether this is indeed the case, and we may therefore recommend a selective policy of enforcing competition, is an empirical question which economists are only beginning to investigate.

It is important to keep in mind that the discussion of perfect competition which has been presented in this chapter has been of a normative nature. We have been asking about the type of allocational devices a society should adopt. The discussion has been only tangentially related to the positive question of whether the competitive model explains reality. It would be perfectly legitimate and consistent for an economist to adopt the competitive model for predictive purposes while at the same time recognizing the many ways in which real-world markets may fail to achieve an efficient allocation of resources.

Conclusion

This chapter has examined in some detail the relationship between a price system and the efficient allocation of resources. It was shown that these two concepts are closely related. In many ways a price system is a desirable way, and perhaps the only way, to achieve any approximation to a Pareto Optimum. One issue raised by thoughtful economists of the "New Left" has not, however, been investigated. Whereas it may be true that a price system is in some sense efficient, it is argued by these economists that a price system also has certain concomitant undesirable features which should be considered in any total social assessment. For example, it could be argued that a price system instills socially undesirable motives of greed and avarice in the members of society. Unpriced "goods" (such as love, beauty, serenity) are likely to be "underproduced" when a price system is instituted. In this view a price system has important negative effects on the development of individual values. The search for alternative, relatively efficient allocative mechanisms which are considered to be less costly in a social sense will therefore undoubtedly continue.

Whether or not alternative mechanisms can ever be developed is open to question. The price system is such an excellent conveyer of information that it is hard to imagine any other device which would be even remotely so efficient. Smith noted in individuals a basic "propensity to truck barter and exchange one thing for another."[15] In those situations in which an alternative to the price system has been established, this "propensity" seems to have a remarkable degree of perseverance. In practically all social organizations the price system tends to appear despite elaborate precautions to avoid this phenomenon. For example, Soviet collective farms were established to isolate the agriculture industry from the workings of the price system. Yet in a short time collective farm workers were producing output in their own small garden plots to sell in the produce markets. The price system had come into being as a way of permitting individuals better to utilize their productive energies to their own advantages.

To take another example, tickets to major sporting events are often allocated on a first-come, first-serve basis, but are then reallocated by "scalpers." This is another example of the indomitable nature of the price system. Any allocation which leads to a situation in which two parties can recognize the benefits to be derived from further exchange sets the stage for the emergence of a market. Only if the costs to establishing this market are very high (if, for example, it is illegal to trade) might the market system be kept down.

To an economist, the price system appears to be a low-cost, relatively efficient allocative device which is likely to be a major feature of any economic system (at least in some form) for a long time into the future. Recognizing this, the most important question for social policy becomes how to take advantage of the beneficial aspects of the price system. Utilizing the efficient features of decentralized decision making can be an important tool for promoting social goals. At the same time any price system will exhibit shortcomings both in achieving efficiency and (perhaps more important) in achieving equity. In dealing with these shortcomings the government can be assigned a central role. Because much economic analysis is relevant to understanding these functions of government, the final part of this book will examine this economic agent.

---

[15] Adam Smith, *The Wealth of Nations* (New York: Random House, Inc., Modern Library ed., 1937), p. 13.

A Mathematical Proof of the Existence of General Equilibrium Prices

Introduction

In Chapter 22 it was shown that a perfectly competitive price system can bring about an efficient allocation of resources. The proof of this assertion requires that equilibrium prices exist for each of the goods and factors being allocated. Presumably these prices will be established by the operation of supply and demand in the market. The question to be investigated in this appendix is whether, in fact, markets will be able to generate these prices. In a sense this appendix represents a test of the consistency of the supply-demand models developed throughout the book.

The question of the existence of general equilibrium prices was first rigorously investigated by Walras in the late nineteenth-century. Walras made the important observation that all prices must be thought of as being determined simultaneously. It is not legitimate to argue that equilibrium prices are established in one market at a time. The equilibrium price in, say, the market for bread will depend on the price of meat and vice-versa. The establishment of an arbitrary price at which supply and demand are equal in the bread market may disturb the equilibrium in the meat market, whereas equilibrating the meat market may result in disturbing the equilibrium in the bread market. Since the demand and supply functions in every market will depend on all prices, it is not possible to solve for one price as distinct from all others. Rather, a whole set of equilibrium prices must be established by the workings of all markets. Walras attempted to formalize those conditions which must hold if such an equilibrium is to exist.

In order to investigate the question raised by Walras it is necessary to develop a rather formal mathematical model. General equilibrium theory is probably the most sophisticated area of economic theory in terms of the mathematics used, and several extremely powerful tools have been introduced in recent years. The purpose of this appendix is to provide a very brief introduction to the kind of mathematical reasoning that is used in this field. Unfortunately, many of the analytical results which have been derived are either too formal (being purely mathematical) or too advanced to be covered within the scope of this book. The interested reader is therefore directed to the excellent survey recently presented by Quirk and Saposnik.[1]

A Simple Mathematical Model of Exchange

The essential aspects of the modern solution to the Walrasian problem can be demonstrated for the case of an exchange economy. Suppose that there are n goods in this economy, that these goods are in absolutely fixed supply, and are distributed in some way among the individuals in society. Let S_i $(i = 1,..., n)$ be the total supply of good i available, and let the price of good i be represented by P_i $(i = 1,..., n)$. The total demand for good i depends on all of the prices,[2] and this function represents the sum

[1] J. Quirk and R. Saposnik, *Introduction to General Equilibrium and Welfare Economics* (New York: McGraw-Hill Book Company, 1968).

[2] Labor (and hence income) can be treated as one of the goods in this model. Each individual can be assumed to possess an initial stock of labor, and an equilibrium price (wage rate) for labor will be determined by the market.

of each of the individuals' demand functions for good i. This total demand function is denoted by:

$$D_i(P_1,\ldots, P_n) \qquad\qquad [22A.1]$$

for $i = 1,\ldots, n$.

Since we are interested in the whole set of prices $P_1,\ldots, P_n$ it will be convenient to denote this whole set by P. Hence the demand functions of Equation 22A.1 can be written as:

$$D_i(P). \qquad\qquad [22A.2]$$

Walras' problem can then be stated formally as: Does there exist an *equilibrium set of prices* (P^*) such that:

$$D_i(P^*) = S_i \qquad\qquad [22A.3]$$

for all values of i. The question posed by Walras is whether or not there exists a set of prices for which supply is equal to demand *in all markets simultaneously*.

In what follows it will be more convenient to work with excess demand functions. The excess demand for good i at any set of prices (P) is defined to be:

$$ED_i(P) = D_i(P) - S_i. \qquad\qquad [22A.4]$$

Using this notation, the equilibrium conditions can be rewritten as:

$$ED_i(P^*) = D_i(P^*) - S_i = 0. \qquad\qquad [22A.4']$$

This condition states that at the equilibrium prices excess demand is to be equal to 0 in all markets.[3]

Walras himself noted several interesting features about the system of Equations 22A.4'. First, it can be assumed that demand functions (and hence the excess demand functions) are *homogeneous of degree zero*. If all prices were to double (including the wages of labor) the quantity demanded of every good would remain unchanged. A second assumption made by Walras was that the demand functions (and therefore the excess demand functions) are *continuous:* If prices were to change by only a small amount quantities demanded would only change by a

---

[3] This equilibrium condition will be amended slightly below.

small amount. This assumption and the previous one are both direct results of the theory of consumer behavior which was presented in Part II.

A final observation which Walras made is that the n excess demand functions defined in Equations 22A.4 are not independent of one another. The equations are related by the formula:

$$\sum_{i=1}^{n} P_i \cdot ED_i(P) = 0. \qquad [22A.5]$$

Equation 22A.5 is usually called *Walras' Law*. The equation states that the "total value" of excess demand is 0 at *any* set of prices. There can be neither excess demand for *all* goods together nor excess supply. Proving Walras' Law is a simple matter, although it is necessary to introduce some cumbersome notation. The proof rests on the fact that each individual in an exchange economy is bound by a budget constraint. A simple example of the proof is given in the footnote;[4] the generalization of this proof is left to the reader.

Walras' Law, it should be stressed, holds for any set of prices, not

---

[4] Suppose there are two goods (A and B) and two individuals (Smith and Jones) in society. Let $D_A{}^S$, $D_B{}^S$, $S_A{}^S$, $S_B{}^S$ be Smith's demands and supplies of A and B, and use a similar notation for Jones' demands and supplies. Smith's budget constraint may be written as:

$$P_A D_A{}^S + P_B D_B{}^S = P_A S_A{}^S + P_B S_B{}^S$$

or

$$P_A(D_A{}^S - S_A{}^S) + P_B(D_B{}^S - S_B{}^S) = 0$$

or

$$P_A ED_A{}^S + P_B ED_B{}^S = 0$$

where $ED_A{}^S$ and $ED_B{}^S$ represent the excess demand of Smith for A and B respectively. A similar budget constraint holds for Jones:

$$P_A ED_A{}^J + P_B ED_B{}^J = 0$$

and, therefore, letting ED_A and ED_B represent total excess demands for A and B, it must be the case that:

$$P_A \cdot (ED_A{}^S + ED_A{}^J) + P_B \cdot (ED_B{}^S + ED_B{}^J) = P_A \cdot ED_A + P_B \cdot ED_B = 0.$$

This is exactly Walras' Law as it appears in Equation 22A.5.

just for equilibrium prices. The Law can be seen to apply trivially to an equilibrium set of prices, since each of the excess demand functions will be equal to 0 at this set of prices. Walras' Law shows that the equilibrium conditions of Equation 22A.3' are not independent. We do not have n independent equations in n unknowns (the P's). Rather, Equation 22A.4' only represents $(n - 1)$ independent equations, and hence we can only hope to determine $(n - 1)$ of the prices. But this is what would have been expected in view of the homogeneity property of the demand functions. We can only hope to determine equilibrium *relative prices;* nothing in this model permits the derivation of absolute prices. The "price level" is indeterminate in this system since multiplying all equilibrium prices by any positive constant will maintain equilibrium.[5] This feature of equilibrium prices was reflected by the Edgeworth Box diagram in Figure 22.2 in which only relative prices were determined by the intersection of individuals' offer curves.

Having recognized these technical features of the system of excess demand equations, Walras turned to the question of the existence of a set of equilibrium (relative) prices. He tried to establish that the n equilibrium conditions of Equation 22A.4' were sufficient, in this situation, to insure that such a set of prices would in fact exist, and therefore that the exchange model had a consistent theoretical framework. A first indication that this existence of equilibrium prices might be assured is provided by a simple counting of equations and unknowns. The market equilibrium conditions provide $(n - 1)$ *independent* equations in $(n - 1)$ unknown relative prices. Hence the elementary algebra of solving simultaneous equations suggests that an equilibrium solution might exist.

Unfortunately, as Walras recognized, the act of solving for equilibrium prices is not nearly so simple a matter as counting equations and unknowns. First, the equations are not necessarily linear. Hence, the well-known conditions for the existence of solutions to simultaneous equations are not particularly relevant in this case. Second, from consideration of the economics of the problem it is clear that all the equilibrium prices must be non-negative. A negative price has no meaning in the context of this problem. To attack these two difficulties Walras devel-

---

[5] An important theoretical question which will not be touched on in this appendix is how the level of absolute prices is determined. The usual assumption made is that there exists some good (perhaps money) which is used as a *numéraire* in the sense that all prices are determined relative to the price of this good. If good n is this *numéraire* then the relative prices P_1/P_n, P_2/P_n,..., are determined by the conditions of equilibrium. Absolute prices can then be calculated once P_n is established by some "outside" force. A common assumption made in this regard is that P_n (the "price of money") is determined by the quantity equation of the demand for money which is discussed in macroeconomics courses.

oped a very difficult and tedious proof which involved solving for equilibrium prices in a series of successive approximations. Without presenting Walras' proof in detail it is instructive to see how he approached the problem.

Start with some initial, arbitrary set of prices. Holding the other $(n - 1)$ prices constant, find the equilibrium price in the market for good 1. Call this "provisional" equilibrium price P_1'. Now, holding P_1' and the other $(n - 2)$ prices constant, solve for the equilibrium price in the market for good 2. Call this price P_2'. Notice that in changing P_2 from its initial position to P_2' the price initially calculated for market 1 need no longer be an equilibrium price. This is a reflection of the fact that the system of equations is indeed simultaneous. Using the provisional prices P_1' and P_2', solve for a provisional P_3'. The proof proceeds in this way until a complete set of provisional relative prices has been calculated.

In the second iteration of Walras' proof $P_2', \ldots, P_n'$ are held constant while a new equilibrium price is calculated for the first good. Call this new provisional price P_1''. Proceeding as outlined above, an entire new set of provisional relative prices $(P_1'', \ldots, P_n'')$ can be calculated. The proof continues to iterate in this way until a reasonable approximation to a set of equilibrium prices is achieved.

The importance of Walras' proof is in its ability to demonstrate the simultaneous nature of the problem of finding equilibrium prices. It is, however, a cumbersome proof and cannot easily be reproduced here. More recent work has utilized some relatively simple tools of advanced mathematics to demonstrate the existence of equilibrium prices in a formal and elegant way. In order to demonstrate such a proof one mathematical theorem must be discussed in detail.

Brouwer's Fixed-point Theorem

Since this section must of necessity be purely mathematical, it is perhaps best to plunge right in by stating Brouwer's Theorem:

> Any continuous mapping $[F(X)]$ of a closed, bounded convex set into itself has at least one fixed point (X^*) such that $F(X^*) = X^*$.

Before analyzing this theorem on a word-by-word basis, perhaps an example will aid in understanding the terminology. Suppose $f(x)$ is a continuous function which is defined on the interval $[0, 1]$, and suppose that $f(x)$ takes on values also on the interval $[0, 1]$. This function then obeys the conditions of Brouwer's Theorem; it must be the case that there exists some x^* such that $f(x^*) = x^*$. This fact is demonstrated in Figure 22A.1. It is clear from this figure that any function, so long as it is continuous (so long as it has no "gaps"), must cross the 45° line somewhere. This point of crossing is a *fixed point* since f maps this point (x^*) into itself.

Figure 22A.1   A Graphic Illustration of Brouwer's Fixed-point Theorem

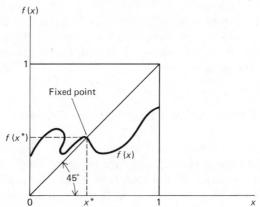

Since any continuous function must cross the 45° line somewhere in the unit square, this function must have a point for which $f(x^*) = x^*$. This point is called a "fixed point."

To study the more general meaning of the theorem it is first necessary to define the terms "mapping," "closed," "bounded," and "convex" used in Brouwer's Theorem. Definitions of these concepts will be presented in an extremely intuitive, nonrigorous way, since the costs of mathematical rigor greatly outweigh the possible benefits for the purposes of this book.

A *mapping* is simply a rule which associates the points in one set with points in another (possibly the same) set. The most commonly encountered mappings are those which associate one point in n-dimensional space with some other point in n-dimensional space. Suppose F is the mapping we wish to study. Then let X be a point for which the mapping is defined: The mapping associates X with some other point $Y = F(X)$. If a mapping is defined over a subset of an n-dimensional space (S), and if every point in S is associated (by the rule F) with some other point in S, the mapping is said to map S *into* itself. In Figure 22A.1 the function f maps the unit interval into itself. A mapping is *continuous* if points which are "close" to each other are mapped into other points which are "close" to each other.

The *Brouwer Fixed-point Theorem* considers mappings defined on certain kinds of sets. These sets are required to be closed, bounded, and convex. Perhaps the simplest way to describe such sets is to say they look like (*n*-dimensional analogies of) soap bubbles. They are *closed* in the sense that they contain their boundaries; the sets are *bounded* because none of their dimensions is infinitely large; and they are *convex* because they have no "holes" in them.[6] A technical description of the properties of such sets can be found in any elementary topology book.[7] For our purposes, however, it is only necessary to recognize that Brouwer's Theorem is intended to apply to certain types of conveniently shaped sets. In order to use the Theorem to prove the existence of equilibrium prices, therefore, we must first describe the set of points which has these desirable properties.

Proof of the Existence of Equilibrium Prices

The key to applying the Brouwer Theorem to the exchange model just developed is to choose a suitable way for "normalizing" prices. Since only relative prices matter in the exchange model it is convenient to assume that prices have been defined so that the sum of all prices is 1. Mathematically, for any arbitrary set of prices $(P_1, \ldots, P_n)$ we can instead deal with *normalized prices* of the form:[8]

$$P_i' = \frac{P_i}{\displaystyle\sum_{i=1}^{n} P_i}. \qquad [22A.6]$$

These new prices will retain their original relative values $(P_i'/P_j' = P_i/P_j)$ and will sum to 1:

$$\sum_{i=1}^{n} P_1' = 1. \qquad [22A.7]$$

---

[6] A more technical definition of a convex set was given in Chapter 3, where a set was defined to be convex if a line connecting any two points of the set is completely contained within the set. The fixed-point theorem is one additional example of the importance of this concept of convexity in economic theory.

[7] For a development of the mathematics used in general equilibrium theory *see* G. Debreu, *Theory of Value* (New York: John Wiley & Son, Inc., 1959), Chap. One.

[8] One additional assumption must be made here, that at least one of the prices is non-0. In economic terms this means that at least one good is scarce. Without this assumption a normalization of prices would not be possible.

Because of the homogeneity of degree 0 of all the excess demand functions, this kind of normalization can always be made. Hence, for the remainder of this proof, it will be assumed that the feasible set of prices (call this set S) is composed of all possible combinations of n non-negative numbers which sum to 1.

This set, S, is the one to which we can apply Brouwer's Theorem. The set S is closed, bounded, and convex.[9] To apply Brouwer's Theorem it is necessary to define a continuous mapping of S into itself. By a judicious choice of this mapping it is possible to show that the fixed-point dictated by the Theorem is in fact a set of equilibrium relative prices.

Before demonstrating the details of the proof it is necessary to redefine what is meant by an "equilibrium set of prices." We do not really require that excess demand be equal to 0 in every market for an equilibrium. Rather there may exist goods the markets for which are in equilibrium, but for which the available supply exceeds demand; there is negative excess demand. For this to be the case, however, it is necessary that the price of this particular good be 0. Hence the equilibrium conditions of Equation 22A.4' may be rewritten to take account of such *free goods:*

$$ED_i(P^*) = 0 \qquad \text{for } P_i^* > 0$$
$$ED_i(P^*) \leq 0 \qquad \text{for } P_i^* = 0. \qquad [22A.8]$$

Notice that such a set of equilibrium prices continues to obey Walras' Law (Equation 22A.5).

Using this definition of equilibrium and remembering that prices have been normalized to sum to 1, it is now possible to construct a continuous function which transforms one set of prices into another. The function to be defined builds on the Walrasian idea that in order to achieve equilibrium, prices of goods which are in excess demand should be raised, whereas those in excess supply should have their prices lowered. Hence, define the mapping $F(P)$ for any (normalized) set of prices, P, such that the ith component of $F(P)$, denoted by $F^i(P)$, is given by:

$$F^i(P) = P_i + ED_i(P) \qquad [22A.9]$$

for all i. The mapping then performs the necessary task of appropriately raising and lowering prices. If, at P_i, good i is in excess demand $[ED_i(P)$

---

[9] In two dimensions the set would simply be a straight line joining the coordinates (0, 1) and (1, 0). In three dimensions the set would be a triangle with vertices at (0, 0, 1), (0, 1, 0), and (1, 0, 0). It is easy to see that each of these sets is closed, bounded, and convex.

> 0] the price P_i is raised, whereas if excess demand is negative P_i is reduced. Because the excess demand functions are assumed to be continuous this mapping will also be continuous. Two problems with the mapping of Equation 22A.9 remain. First, nothing insures that the new prices will be non-negative. Hence the mapping must be redefined to be:

$$F^i(P) = \text{Max } [P_i + ED_i(P), 0] \qquad [22A.9']$$

for all i. The term "Max" here simply means that the new prices defined by the mapping F must be either positive or 0; prices are not allowed to go negative. The mapping 22A.9' is also continuous.

A second problem with the mapping 22A.9' is that the recalculated prices are not necessarily normalized; they will not sum to 1. It would be a simple matter, however, to normalize[10] these new prices so that they do sum to 1. To avoid introducing additional notation assume that this normalization has been done and therefore assume that:

$$\sum_{i=1}^{n} F^i(P) = 1. \qquad [22A.10]$$

With this normalization, then, F satisfies the conditions of the Brouwer Fixed-point Theorem. It is a continuous mapping of the set S into itself. Hence there exists a point (P^*) which is mapped into itself. For this point:

[10] In order to accomplish this normalization it is first necessary to show that not all of the transformed prices will be 0; it is necessary to show that $P_i + ED_i(P) > 0$ for some i. This can be proved by contradiction. Assume $P_i + ED_i(P) \leq 0$ for all i. Multiply this expression by P_i and sum over all values of i giving:

$$\sum_{i=1}^{n} P_i^2 + \sum_{i=1}^{n} P_i ED_i(P) \leq 0.$$

But:

$$\sum_{i=1}^{n} P_i ED_i = 0$$

by Walras' Law. Hence:

$$\sum_{i=1}^{n} P_i^2 \leq 0$$

and this implies $P_i = 0$ for all i. This conclusion, however, contradicts our earlier assumption (see Footnote 8) and therefore we have proved that at least one of the transformed prices must be positive.

$$P_i^* = \text{Max } [P_i^* + ED_i(P^*), 0] \qquad\qquad [22A.11]$$

for all i.

But this says that P^* is an equilibrium set of prices—for $P_i^* > 0$:

$$P_i^* = P_i^* + ED_i(P^*)$$

or

$$ED_i(P^*) = 0 \qquad\qquad [22A.12]$$

and for $P_i^* = 0$:

$$P_i^* + ED_i(P^*) \leq 0$$

or $\qquad\qquad\qquad\qquad\qquad\qquad\qquad\qquad\qquad$ [22A.13]

$$ED_i(P^*) \leq 0.$$

Therefore it has been shown that the set of excess demand functions does in fact possess an equilibrium solution consisting of non-negative prices. The simple exchange model developed in this appendix is consistent in that the market supply and demand curves necessarily have a solution. The homogeneity and continuity properties of the demand functions and the ability of Walras' Law to tie together supply and demand are jointly responsible for this result.[11]

Conclusion

Most readers will probably wish to skip this appendix and take its results on faith. It seems intuitively plausible that the simultaneous operation of n markets can establish n equilibrium prices. After all, since market prices obviously exist, markets must be capable of establishing them! The model developed in this chapter tells us something about the mathematical consistency of supply and demand models, but it provides little information about economic activity in the real world.

The points made in this paragraph are well taken. General equilibrium theory has found little practical application. Although the sophistication of the tools used and the breadth of questions asked have both expanded tremendously in recent years the studies which have been

[11] The proof used in this section represents a simplified (and considerably vulgarized) version of a proof first presented by J. Kemeny and J. L. Snell in *Mathematical Models in the Social Sciences* (New York: Blaisdell Publishing Company, 1962), pp. 35–41.

undertaken must still be classified as "pure" research. This is not to imply, however, that these results have been uninteresting from a conceptual point of view. Much valuable information has been generated about the forces which determine equilibrium prices, and these results have illuminated many aspects about the behavior of large groups of individuals. The primary obstacle in applying these models to investigating real-world policy problems has been a lack of data in anything approaching the quantity necessary. Considering the rapid development of statistical techniques and the increasing availability of reasonably accurate microeconomic data, it would seem premature to judge such research as wasteful from the point of view of economic policy.

DISCUSSION QUESTIONS AND PROBLEMS FOR PART VI

Discussion Questions

1. Some authors argue against the use of the Pareto criterion of efficiency because, by focusing attention only on mutually desirable allocational changes, it tends to preserve the status quo. The essence of welfare judgments is that some individuals must be forced to accept a position of lower utility. Can you propose any efficiency criteria which are at the same time more flexible than the Pareto definitions and are generally agreeable to "most" members of society?

2. Use the Allocational Rules for efficiency in production to discuss the mutually advantageous nature of totally free world trade. One problem in this application is the requirement of Rule 2 in regard to the allocation of factors of production. Since factors of production (notably labor) are not very mobile on an international scale, will it generally be possible to fulfill Rule 2? Can sufficient trade in goods bring about equality of marginal products without the necessity of transferring factors?

3. The "Bribe Criterion" proposed by Kaldor and Scitovsky was discussed in a footnote to Chapter 21. This welfare criterion states that a movement from social state A to state B is an improvement in social welfare if those who gain by this move are able to compensate those who lose sufficiently so that they would accept the change. Compensation does not actually have to be made; it is only necessary that it could be paid. If the compensation is actually made, this criterion reduces to the Pareto definition (some individuals are made better off without making anyone worse off). Hence the Kaldor-Scitovsky criterion is novel only in that compensation is not paid by the gainers to the losers. In such a situation does the Bribe Criterion seem a "value free" one, or does the criterion seem somehow to favor those who are initially rich?

4. How do you assess the Arrow result? Are his axioms reasonable and are social decisions therefore impossible to make? Or, on the other hand, is Arrow's approach to social choice too pure and is it likely that satisfactory social decisions will emerge from "the political process"?

5. The general equilibrium models discussed in Part VI are not readily applied to problems of real-world prediction. In terms of practical application, current Keynesian macroeconomic models are prob-

ably the closest approximation to a general equilibrium model. Do such models really capture the simultaneity of the market system?

6. In the appendix to Chapter 22 the Brouwer Fixed-point Theorem was used to demonstrate the existence of equilibrium prices. While this theorem is an extremely powerful tool, much of what is economically important is obscured when the Theorem is applied. Can you develop an economic argument in words which shows the interrelationships among markets and indicates how equilibrium prices might be discovered?

Problems

1. Smith and Jones are stranded on a desert island. Each has in his possession some slices of ham (H) and cheese (C). Smith is a very choosy eater and will only eat ham and cheese in the fixed proportions two slices of cheese to one slice of ham. His utility function is given by $U_s = \text{Min } (H, C/2)$.

   Jones is more flexible in his dietary tastes and has a utility function given by $U_J = 4H + 3C$. Total endowments are 100 slices of ham and 200 slices of cheese.

   (a) Draw the Edgeworth Box diagram which represents the possibilities for exchange in this situation. What is the only price ratio which can prevail in any equilibrium?

   (b) Suppose Smith initially had $40H$ and $80C$. What would the equilibrium position be?

   (c) Suppose Smith initially had $60H$ and $80C$. What would the equilibrium position be?

   (d) Suppose Smith (much the stronger of the two) decides not to play by the rules of the game. Then what could the final equilibrium position be?

2. On the island of Pago-Pago there are two lakes and twenty fishermen. Each fisherman gets to fish on either lake and gets to keep the average catch on his particular lake. On Lake X the total number of fish caught is given by:

$$F^X = 10L_X - \frac{1}{2} L_X^2$$

where L_X is the number of men fishing on the lake.

For Lake Y the relationship is:

$$F^Y = 5L_Y.$$

Under this organization of society what will the total number of fish caught be?

The chief of Pago-Pago, having once read an economics book, believes he can raise the total number of fish caught by restricting the number of men allowed to fish on Lake X. What is the correct number of men to fish on X in order to maximize the total catch of fish? What is the number of fish caught in this situation?

Being basically opposed to coercion the chief decides to require a fishing license for Lake X. If the licensing procedure is to bring about the optimal allocation of labor what should the cost of a license be (in terms of fish)?

Does this example prove that a "competitive" allocation of resources may not be optimal?

3.   In an economy with two individuals (A and B) discuss the results of exchange in the following situations:

  (a)   Perfect competition in which A and B accept prices as given by "the market."

  (b) A is a monopolist and can set any price he chooses.

  (c) A is a perfect price discriminator and can charge a different price for each unit traded.

Does each of these lead to a Pareto efficient solution? It would be useful to work with an Edgeworth Box diagram to present your solution.

4.   The country of Podunk produces only wheat and cloth, using as inputs land and labor. Both are produced by constant returns to scale production functions. Wheat is the relatively land-intensive commodity.

  (a)   Explain in words, or with diagrams, how the price of wheat relative to cloth (p) determines the land-labor ratio in each of the two industries.

  (b)   Suppose p is given by external forces (this would be the case if Podunk were a "small" country trading freely with a "large" world). Show, using the Edgeworth Box, that if the supply of labor increases in Podunk, the output of cloth will rise and the output of wheat will fall.

5.   Use an Edgeworth Box diagram and/or excess demand curves to illustrate several possibilities of an exchange economy in which equilibrium prices will not exist.

6.   "Convexity" in tastes and in production is necessary for the Pareto Optimality-perfect Competition Theorem to hold. Can you present a few simple examples where nonconvexity causes this theorem to fail?

7. Two types of goods which cause difficulties for the theorem of the equivalence between Pareto Optimality and Perfect Competition are "joint products" and "public goods." These are defined as:
    (a) Joint products are goods like leather and beef which are produced together in fixed proportions; their production cannot be separated.
    (b) Public goods are consumed by everyone at the same level (for example, national defense). Once the good is produced, no one can be excluded from its use.

    How must the Pareto Optimal conditions be rephrased in the presence of these types of goods (think primarily about the condition $MRS_{X \text{ for } Y} = RPT_{X \text{ for } Y}$)?

    Is perfect competition likely to bring about these revised conditions?

PART VII
The Role
of Government

Introduction

The previous parts of this book have examined the way in which
markets act to integrate individuals' tastes with the productive
techniques available to a society. Markets permit the decentralized decisions of millions of economic agents to be unified into
an overall allocation of resources. In a sense the benefits to be
derived from the operation of markets are related to the differences
among economic agents. If Smith and Jones have similar
resources but rather different tastes great benefits will accrue

479

to each man by trading with the other. If two firms have different productive capabilities total output can be increased by having each firm specialize in the production of that output in which it is most efficient. Although many qualifications were expressed throughout the first six parts of this book, generally the analysis sought to demonstrate these benefits of market interactions.

There are many ways, however, in which markets may fail to produce beneficial results. Some goods which are universally desired may not be produced by the free operation of the market. For example, even though police protection and public health services may be desirable goods free markets may not provide them in as large amounts as would be considered "optimal" by most members of society. On the other hand, the private market may overproduce other types of goods. As discussed in Chapter 22, this would be the case if detrimental externalities were associated with the production of some good, and these externalities were not reflected in firms' output decisions. Finally, and perhaps most important, the unfettered operation of the market may produce a distribution of income which is considered to be undesirable from the point of view of overall social welfare. Some movement toward greater equality may be desired by most of the individuals in society, but the market does not provide a way to translate this desire into action.[1]

In each of these cases of *market failure* it may be necessary to have governmental interference in the market system if socially beneficial results are to be achieved. This part will examine the reasons for such failures and will develop a framework for government action. A discussion of such issues is central to understanding modern microeconomic theory. As modern society has become more complex, examples of market failure have become more apparent. Matters which were previously treated as mildly interesting textbook examples (such as air pollution) have today become matters of major social concern. In response to these market failures the role assigned to government in the operation of the economy has been progressively enlarged in practically all countries. For this reason it is important that the economic foundations for governmental behavior be examined. Only in this way can a true picture of how all economic agents interact to determine the allocation of resources be presented.

---

[1] The reasons why private philanthropy fails to achieve a desirable distribution of income will be discussed in Chapter 26.

A general discussion of the rationale for government inter-ference will be presented in Chapter 23. The purpose of this chapter is to examine possible definitions of public (government provided) goods and to detail certain problems which arise in the provision of such goods. In this sense Chapter 23 provides a framework within which to consider the various applications presented in the following chapters. Most of the analysis of Chapter 23 is of a normative nature: An attempt is made to describe the kinds of activity governments *should* undertake. A final section of the chapter does, however, present a brief summary of some positive (predictive) theories of governmental behavior.

Chapter 24 represents an extension of many of the ideas developed in the previous chapter. The conceptual problems which arise in attempting to measure the benefits and costs of providing particular public goods are examined. In recent years this type of analysis has become increasingly important to governmental decision making. The application of some of the basic price-theory concepts developed elsewhere in this book permits a clearcut demonstration of the principles which underlie modern *cost-benefit analysis*. The notion of opportunity cost is stressed in this chapter.

One important function of government is in the definition of property rights for the members of society. Goods are by their nature neither privately owned nor publicly owned. Rather, the government and its associated legal system must establish certain "rules of the game" that specify who owns what and outline the rights that this owner has to exchange his property for that of someone else. Chapter 25 examines these questions about the nature of property rights in some detail. It is shown that the question of property rights and the problems raised in a market economy by the existence of externalities are closely related issues. In a sense the existence of detrimental externalities (such as air pollution) is a manifestation of the absence of property rights (people don't own the rights to the air they breathe). The major purpose of Chapter 25 is to make this rela-tionship more precise and to demonstrate the implications that the assignment of property rights have for the way in which resources are allocated.

All major governmental decisions effect the distribution of income among the members of society. In some situations (such as the payment of Aid to Families with Dependent Children) this effect may be a primary purpose of the program, whereas in other cases (such as the government providing for national defense) these effects may be secondary to the major purposes of the program. In either case it is important that some attempt be made to measure these distributional effects and to judge whether or not they are desirable. In Chapter 26 several concepts are developed which permit the government's role in affecting the distribution of income to be viewed as one more example of the provision of a public good. In this regard a brief analysis of the idea of an "optimal" distribution of income is presented. A principle purpose of the chapter is to point out the complexities inherent in defining such a concept. Because decisions about the distribution of income in society are in many respects *the* central concern of normative economics, Chapter 26 represents a natural conclusion to the book.

CHAPTER 23

Government as an Economic Agent

Introduction: Government and Public Goods

To define in any detail exactly what a government is would seem to be
both tedious and unnecessary. It should be clear that a government
consists of a set of laws or customs and a procedure for establishing these
laws. In large, complex societies a government also consists of certain
individuals who act as leaders. For the major part of this chapter (and
for all of Chapters 24, 25, and 26) we will abstract from the individual
motivations of government leaders and will instead treat government as
a single economic agent. In the section "Aspects of a Positive Theory

of Government," however, a brief discussion of the individualistic nature of government leadership will be presented.

If government is to be treated as one distinct agent then a natural way to define it would be to describe what it is that a government does. Economists might class all such activities under one general heading: A government *produces public goods*. The term "public goods" in this definition refers to all those effects which a government has on the members of society. This includes all the tangible goods and services provided by the government and also is intended to include the various intangible benefits (or costs) of citizenship. In a sense governments are not very different from other organizations (such as labor unions, professional associations, or the American Legion) which provide benefits to, and impose obligations on, their members. The distinguishing characteristic of government is its ability to affect practically every aspect of the lives of the individuals in society.

The definition of public goods given above is of necessity circular. Governments were defined as producers of public goods, and public goods were defined to be the "stuff" which government produces. Many economists (most notably Friedman[1]) have tried to attach a more specific, technical definition to the term public good. The purpose of such a definition is to differentiate those goods which are public by nature from those which are private.[2] In the most common of these definitions the *nonexclusive nature of public goods* is stressed. Once a public good is provided, it is impossible (or very costly) to exclude individuals from deriving benefits from it. The most straightforward example of a nonexclusive good is national defense. It is impossible to exclude particular members of society from obtaining the benefits of defense protection. Once the good has been provided, it has been provided to everyone.

A closely related definition of public goods stresses their *nonrival* nature. Once the good is provided, additional persons may use the good without reducing the benefits that those currently using the good are receiving. A private good, say a pork chop, is either consumed by Smith or Jones. Consumption of the pork chop by Smith precludes its consumption by Jones. On the other hand, public goods do not have this property. For example, Smith may enjoy the prevailing level of public health without detracting from the level Jones enjoys. There are many similarities between this definition and the nonexclusive definition. Since the nonexclusive definition is somewhat more common it will be used for the remainder of this chapter.

By using the definition of public (or *collective*) goods it is possible

---

[1] *See* Milton Friedman, "The Role of Government in a Free Society," in *Capitalism and Freedom* (Chicago: The University of Chicago Press, 1962), Chap. 2.

[2] Usually the implication is that governments should not produce private goods since the free market will do a better job of this.

to see why the free market will not provide such goods in adequate amounts. In the case of a private good the purchaser of that good can expropriate the benefits of the good entirely for himself. Smith's pork chop, for example, yields no benefits to Jones. The resources which were used to produce the pork chop can be seen as contributing only to Smith's utility and he is willing to pay whatever this is worth to him. The resource cost of a private good then can be "attributed" to a single individual. For a public good this will not be the case. An individual in buying a public good would not be able to expropriate all the benefits of the good for himself. Since others cannot be excluded from benefiting from the good, society's utility obtained from the resources devoted to the public good will exceed the utility which accrues to the single individual who pays for the good. The resource cost cannot be attributed solely to the one purchaser. However, the potential purchaser will not take the benefits that his purchase has to others into account in his expenditure decisions. Consequently, private markets will tend to underallocate resources to public goods.

As an example of the allocational problems raised by the nonexclusive nature of public goods consider an individual choosing between two goods, an automobile and an open field for use as a park. Suppose that both the automobile and the field have the same resource cost (and hence the same price), but that the automobile yields slightly more utility to the individual. The automobile will be purchased since this is the utility-maximizing decision for the individual to make. Resources will then be devoted to automobile production (perhaps an automobile plant will be built in the open field). From a social point of view this may not be the best allocation of resources. In producing the automobile social utility is increased only to the extent that the individual derives a private benefit from his purchase. Had the field been turned into a park, social utility would have been increased not only by the utility of the purchaser but also by the additional utility which accrues to all those who live near or walk past the park. In his decisions the individual will not recognize this external effect of his actions and hence the free market may cause resources to be underallocated to the provision of parks.

These ideas will be made more precise below. First, however, it will be useful to survey those types of public goods which are provided and to demonstrate the pervasive nature of the nonexclusion property.

Kinds of Public Goods

It is customary to divide the economic activities of government into three branches: the Allocative Branch, the Distributional Branch, and the Stabilization Branch.[3] The name of each branch is intended to indicate the type of public good which it produces. Hence the Allocative Branch is concerned with general problems relating to the allocation of resources; the Distributional Branch engages in activities which promote a desirable distribution of income; and the Stabilization Branch is involved with the formulation and execution of macroeconomic policies to effect full employment. The "outputs" of each of these branches are characterized by the nonexclusion property in the sense that no one in society can be excluded from the benefits of the branches' activities. Since we are not concerned here with macroeconomic policy, however, only the Allocative and the Distributional Branches will be explicitly considered.[4] It should be clear though that the activities of each of the branches are closely interconnected and that no policy affects only a single branch to the exclusion of the other two. Hence the distinctions made here are of a purely conceptual nature.

From the point of view of microeconomics the allocative function is the most important of the activities of governments. The government is charged with modifying "undesirable" results which may be produced by the free operations of markets. This function would then include the provision of collective goods (national defense, parks, public health facilities, and so forth) to which resources would be underallocated by a competitive market. The Allocative Branch is also given the responsibility of insuring that those goods which are produced in private markets are produced efficiently. Again, since everyone in society can benefit from efficiency this is a proper governmental function. In this regard there are two general types of market imperfections which face the government. The first of these involves markets that diverge from the competitive assumptions because of the way in which they are organized. Since the profit-maximizing decisions of firms that face negatively sloping demand curves will cause a discrepancy between marginal cost and price inefficiency in allocation can result. Hence the government may in some way wish to regulate "monopolies."[5]

---

[3] This classification was first developed by R. A. Musgrave in his classic, *The Theory of Public Finance* (New York: McGraw-Hill Book Company, 1959).

[4] It is interesting to see how macroeconomic policy can be regarded as a public good. It is impossible to exclude any member of society from the benefits of full employment. Similarly, although it is conceivable that a single individual could undertake his own fiscal policy, say by spending a larger fraction of his income on consumption goods than he had previously, the individual undoubtedly would not do so since he could expropriate only a small part of the total benefits of his actions. Again, there is a need for some degree of general government coercion if an active full-employment policy is to be pursued by the entire society.

[5] This book is not the proper place to survey the vast literature which surrounds the

A second major type of market imperfection with which governments must deal is the existence of externalities. Because the presence of externalities causes a divergence between private and social rates of trade-off, markets will work improperly if left on their own. A government by adopting suitable taxation and subsidy programs may be able to modify the allocation of resources in a way which takes account of significant externalities. We shall return to this question in more detail in Chapter 25, when the subject of externalities is examined in the general context of the specification of property rights in society.

---

economic theory of government regulation of monopolies. Some central aspects of this theory might, however, be mentioned.

1. The theory is usually presented in a partial equilibrium framework. It is generally assumed that the economy is perfectly competitive except for the industry under investigation. The wisdom of enforcing marginal cost pricing in this industry is then analyzed. Some attention has been paid to "optimal" departures from marginal cost pricing, although these discussions have also usually been conducted in a partial equilibrium framework. The choice of such a model is certainly necessary on pragmatic grounds, since no adequate general equilibrium model is available. By making this choice, however, it must be recognized that second-best type of considerations (*see* Chapter 22) have been assumed to be unimportant.

2. Once the allocational goals of regulation (perhaps marginal cost pricing) have been decided upon there remains the problem of finding a suitable regulatory mechanism for achieving the desired results. Although absolute price regulation is the mechanism frequently chosen, some theoretical attention has also been paid to schemes of subsidy and taxation which might achieve the same results. The reader should be able to show that by imposing taxes on a monopolies' product (hence shifting the demand curve relevant to the firm), and by imposing profits taxes, practically any desired output level can be imposed on a profit-maximizing monopoly.

3. Although concepts of optimal taxation and subsidy schemes have been debated by economists for most of this century they have never played an important role in the methods of real-world regulatory commissions. Rather, regulatory commissions have tended to emphasize price regulation. The most common such scheme has been to set prices in a monopolistic industry at a level which "insures" a "fair rate of return" on invested capital. Recently a great deal of attention has been paid to analyzing how such regulation actually affects the allocation of resources. The obvious questions to ask in this regard are: How does regulation affect the regulated firm's output? Will it use more or less resources than would be optimal? And how does regulation affect the input choices that a firm makes since the regulatory commission, by stressing a fair rate of return doctrine, affects the input costs which are relevant to the firm.

One of the seminal articles in recent microeconomic theories of regulation is H. Averch and L. L. Johnson, "Behavior of the Firm under Regulatory Constraint," *American Economic Review*, vol. 52 (December 1962), pp. 1053–1069. A valuable summary of other recent developments is W. J. Baumol and A. K. Klevorick, "Input Choices and Rate of Return Regulation," *The Bell Journal of Economics and Management Science*, vol. 1. (Autumn 1970), pp. 162–189.

Although the allocational function of government is the most important insofar as the microeconomic theory of government activity is concerned, this aspect can be overemphasized. Many activities of government are undertaken for distributional rather than allocative reasons. Public housing and surplus food distribution programs are two important examples of this emphasis. Indeed, many governmental activities which seem to be allocative in nature (such as the regulation of banks and railroads) have significant distributional aspects to them, and at times these distributional benefits may conflict with the pursuit of efficient allocation. In a sense government pursuit of distributional goals agrees with the nonexclusion definition of public goods. Everyone benefits from a more equal society[6] and no one can be excluded from this benefit. The knowledge that society is relatively "just" is a public good in the same sense that national defense is.

The Efficient Production of Public Goods

The distinction between "pure" public goods and "pure" private goods can be made in a simple way by considering the conditions for efficiency which must hold in the two cases. We know that for the case of any two private goods marginal rates of substitution must be identical for all individuals and that this common *MRS* must equal the rate at which the goods can be technically transformed. There is no ambiguity when we say that the social *MRS* must equal the social rate of product transformation. For the case of a (nonexclusive) public good it is still possible to speak of the rate of product transformation of this good for some private good. Exactly the same kind of resource reallocation takes place between private and public producers as takes place between two private producers when the composition of output changes. In producing more national defense some automobiles, say, will have to be given up, just as they would if society decided to produce more trucks. It is in defining the social marginal rate of substitution between a public good and some private good that important differences arise.

Because public goods are provided on a nonexclusive basis to everyone,[7] the social marginal utility of an additional unit of a public good is the *sum* of the marginal utilities of each person benefiting from the public

---

[6] Whether increasing equality is a socially desirable goal will be discussed in detail in Chapter 26.

[7] Because public goods are not exchanged (they are instead provided in "equal" amounts to everyone), there is no need to discuss the conditions for optimality in exchange here. Questions about the exchangeable nature of certain goods will be discussed in more detail in Chapter 25.

good. If SMU_P denotes the social marginal utility of the public good and $MU_P{}^i$ (for $i = 1,\ldots, n$) represents the marginal utility of the public good to each of the n individuals in society, then (assuming that we can somehow compare utilities):

$$SMU_P = MU_P{}^1 + MU_P{}^2 + \cdots + MU_P{}^n. \qquad [23.1]$$

On the other hand, all the additional benefits of the production of one more private good accrue to the individual receiving the good, say individual i. The social marginal rate of substitution ($SMRS$) of the public good (P) for the private good (G) is therefore defined as:

$$SMRS \ (P \text{ for } G) = \frac{SMU_P}{MU_G{}^i} = \frac{MU_P{}^1}{MU_G{}^i} + \frac{MU_P{}^2}{MU_G{}^i} + \ldots, + \frac{MU_P{}^n}{MU_G{}^i} \qquad [23.2]$$

and the condition for an efficient allocation of resources requires that:

$$RPT \ (P \text{ for } G) = SMRS \ (P \text{ for } G) \qquad [23.3]$$

where $RPT \ (P \text{ for } G)$ is the rate of product transformation of the public good for the private good.[8]

The efficiency condition of Equation 23.3 cannot be achieved by the workings of the price system. Free operation of even an "ideal" perfectly competitive market will only insure that:

$$RPT \ (P \text{ for } G) = MRS \ (P \text{ for } G) = \frac{MU_P{}^i}{MU_G{}^i} \qquad [23.4]$$

$$< SMRS \ (P \text{ for } G)$$

where the final inequality sign holds as long as the public good provides some positive benefits to other individuals in addition to those provided to individual i. Hence the free market will tend to underallocate resources to the production of public goods. Equation 23.4 is simply a formal statement of the ideas which were examined earlier in this chapter when the automobile-public park example was considered.

Problems raised by the nonexclusive nature of public goods can also be demonstrated with partial equilibrium analysis by examining the demand curve associated with such goods. In the case of a private good the market demand curve (*see* Chapter 6) was found by summing individuals'

---

[8] These conditions are clearly demonstrated in P. A. Samuelson, "The Pure Theory of Public Expenditure," *Review of Economics and Statistics,* vol. 36 (November 1954), pp. 387–389; and in several later articles in the same journal.

demands horizontally. At any price the quantities demanded by each individual are summed to calculate the total quantity demanded in the market. The market demand curve shows the marginal evaluation which individuals place on an additional unit of output. For a public good (which is provided in fixed quantity to everyone) individual demand curves must be added vertically. To find out how society values some level of public good provision we must ask how each individual values this level of output and then sum these valuations. This idea is pictured conceptually in Figure 23.1. Here the total demand curve for the public good (DD) is the vertical sum of each individual's demand curve. Each point on the DD curve represents the social marginal evaluation of the particular level of public goods' expenditure.[9] Producing one more unit of the public good would benefit everyone. To evaluate this benefit it is necessary to sum each individual's personal evaluation of the good. Because markets, by their nature, sum demand curves horizontally rather than vertically, Figure 23.1 again indicates why free markets may fail to provide public goods in adequate amounts.

Problems in the Definition of Public Goods

It would be inappropriate to infer from the theory of public goods already presented that the dividing line between private and public goods is clearly drawn. Rather, the technical property of nonexclusion is only a conceptually convenient way to illustrate why markets may fail to produce certain goods. To use this technical definition as the sole criterion for government action would be misleadingly precise in an area which defies precision. There are at least three reasons why the nonexclusion

---

[9] If MC_P and MC_G represent the marginal costs of a public and a private good respectively, then (somewhat loosely) the conditions for optimality in the production of a private good are given by:

$$MC_G = MV_G{}^1 = MV_G{}^2 = \cdots = MV_G{}^n$$

and for the public good by:

$$MC_P = MV_P{}^1 + MV_P{}^2 + \cdots + MV_P{}^n$$

where $MV_G{}^i$ and $MV_P{}^i$ are the "marginal valuations" (that is, the amount an individual is willing to pay for one more unit of the good in question) of the two goods. This idea of marginal valuation was used, at least implicitly, to construct demand curves in Part II. Technically, $MV_X{}^i = MU_X{}^i/\lambda_i$ for any good X (where λ_i is the marginal utility of income for individual i).

Figure 23.1   Derivation of the Demand for a Public Good

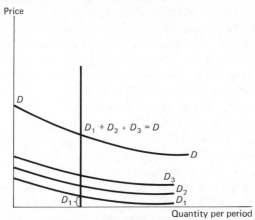

Since a public good is nonexclusive the price that individuals are willing to pay for one more unit (their "marginal valuations") is equal to the sum of what each individual would pay. Hence, for public goods market demand curves are derived by a vertical summation rather than the horizontal summation which is used for the case of private goods.

principle may not be a sufficient description of those activities government should pursue: There are many goods which fall between the two poles of private and public goods; leaving goods which are exclusive in nature to be produced by the free market assumes that this market will work "correctly" — this may not in fact be the case — and if a broader view is taken, the nonexclusion principle may become simply a matter of opinion. Each of these difficulties will be illustrated in this section. The list of difficulties is not, however, intended to be exhaustive. Rather, it is intended only as an indication of the large dose of subjectivity which is inherent in any definition of public goods.

As an example of a good which falls midway between the public and private categories consider the case of education. There are many ways in which everyone in a society benefits from an educated population. Education may lead to technical progress which benefits everyone. An educated electorate may make democracy work "better." Finally, it may just be "nice" to have educated people around to talk to. Each of these benefits is nonexclusive; it is technically infeasible to exclude some members of society from benefiting from the general educational level of their fellow citizens. On the other hand, many of the benefits of education are private in nature. An individual may, by virtue of his education, obtain a higher income; he may derive enjoyment from the cultural aspects of education; and education may permit the individual to enter social circles from which he would otherwise be excluded. Each of these benefits has no important externalities—the individual can expropriate the benefits to himself. Since it is technically feasible to exclude persons from gaining these benefits (you can keep certain people out of the schools if they don't pay for the services they receive), this aspect of education does not differ in a fundamental way from the purchase of any other private good.

The problem raised by education then is "how much" of it is a public good and how much a private good. If there were some way to decide this the government could provide only that portion which is truly public.[10] In practice such a distinction is extremely difficult to make and the decision of the correct amount of government support for education is left up to the political process to decide.

The suggestion that all goods which are not public in nature should be left up to the private market to produce seems, on the surface, desirable. This rule of thumb provides a way to keep the bureaucratic tentacles of government under some control. In fact, Friedman suggests that keeping government out of most activities of exchange among persons will preserve our "freedom." Without commenting on the truth of these assertions (such speculation is really a matter of opinion which is left to the reader to decide for himself), it is important to point out a central presumption which underlies this logic: It is implicitly assumed that the free market will function in a desirable way. This requires not only that markets be relatively free of monopolistic elements but (perhaps more important) that the other conditions of perfect competition (such as perfect knowledge on the part of all agents) also hold. To see that this may not be the case it is useful to examine two examples of goods which have exclusion properties but are nonetheless usually classed as public—education (again) and wilderness parks.

Consider education. Suppose all college education were left for the free market to provide; would it be provided in optimal amounts? Even if the benefits to education are regarded as exclusively private, there are reasons why individuals may not buy this good in sufficient amounts. One primary problem, not accounted for in the perfectly competitive model, is that investing in education is a risky proposition. Not only is the income gained from educational expenditures subject to uncertainty but also human capital, because it cannot be sold, is a most illiquid investment to make. Both of these features of education suggest that risk-averting individuals will not buy education in sufficient amounts and that lenders will not be willing to accommodate a borrower wishing to finance his education. The peculiar nature of the good makes it dubious therefore that the free market is totally suited for producing it.

---

[10] It might be argued, for example, that elementary and secondary education have important public good aspects and should therefore be provided by the government. On the other hand, the benefits of college education may be essentially private, and provision of college education should be left to the private market.

Similar problems arise in considering the government's provision of wilderness parks. It might be argued that such parks are not truly public goods. The benefits of a park are derived almost exclusively by those who use them. Whereas it may be impossible to exclude city residents from benefiting from urban parks, the exclusion principle would seem to be operative for wilderness parks.[11] A private company could, after all, build a fence around Yellowstone and charge admission. It might thus be argued that the government should not be in the wilderness park business. Again, however, this argument assumes that the workings of the free market will produce desirable results. In particular it assumes that future demands for park land will be adequately reflected in present market interactions.[12] If this is regarded as unlikely there is justification for governmental interference even though the principle of nonexclusive benefits is not strictly applicable.

A final reason why a narrow definition of public goods may not be sufficient requires that a broader view be taken of the function of government. Suppose it is decided that the function of the government is to be a morally and culturally up-lifting force for its citizens. In this role the government may justifiably interfere in any productive activity because every aspect of the economy has some effect on the moral virtue of the population. The government might, for example, legitimately engage in the production of toys (an exclusive type of good) because it is determined that the type of toys produced has significant effects on the overall nature of society. This justification would involve only a slight extension of the notion of externalities to include the possibly detrimental effects that free market-produced toys have on all the members of society. Any reader who is familiar with the assortment of toys which are available today will recognize that this example is not far-fetched.

These instances of the ambiguity of the nonexclusion principle in many important cases point out the essential subjectivity of any definition of the proper economic role of government. Instead of relying on rigid technical definition it would seem more appropriate to weigh the total benefits and costs of private versus public production. Many of these benefits and costs cannot, however, be readily estimated, since most of these are of an esthetic nature. Nonetheless, a careful enumeration of

---

[11] This argument assumes that the benefits of just knowing that the park is there are small. For parks such as the Grand Canyon this is probably unwarranted, since virtually everyone in the country benefits from the knowledge that this park exists. On the other hand, at present National Parks exist in the United States which only a small minority of the population has ever heard of and which even fewer are likely ever to visit. The externalities of such parks are (at least to the present generation) probably insignificant.

[12] This is particularly important in the case of parks because of the irreversibility of decisions. Once it is decided, say, to strip mine an area the possibility of using it for a park in the future is not available.

benefits and costs, even if these are not quantifiable, may provide some policy guidance.

Problems in the Provision of Public Goods

Even in the case of a well-defined public good (national defense, for example) there are significant problems in deciding how much of this good to produce. Efficiency considerations would suggest that additional amounts of the public good should be produced up to the point at which the social marginal cost of production is equal to the marginal utility evaluation placed on the good by the members of society. Assuming that the resource costs of production can be calculated, the problem of optimal provision of public goods then becomes one of estimating the relevant social demand curve (*see* Figure 23.1). This problem is the central concern of this section.

A first difficulty with estimating the demand curve for a public good is that there is usually no good measure of output: We don't know what to put on the horizontal axis in Figure 23.1. For example, how can the quantity of national defense be defined? The defense establishment provides something which might be called "protection," but there seems to be no natural units in which to quantify this concept. This problem is not unique to national defense (as another example consider how one might measure the quantity of education provided by a school system). Rather, the problem is a general one for public goods because these goods are not traded in organized markets and, consequently, natural price-quantity measures are not available.

Even if a suitable quantity measure could be defined, there would still be substantial problems in discovering the demand curve for a public good. If it were decided, for example, to ask individuals how much they value a particular public good the results of this poll might be extremely inaccurate. In answering the question each individual may feel that he should understate his true preferences for fear he will ultimately have to pay what the good is worth to him in the form of taxes.[13] From the individual's point of view the proper strategy is to understate his true preferences in the hope that others will bear the burden of paying for the good. Since for a traditional public good no one can be excluded from enjoying its benefits, the best position to occupy is that of

---

[13] Taxation based on the value of benefits received has been extensively studied by economists. The determination of benefits is a difficult matter, and in practice governments often divorce expenditure decisions from taxation decisions. It should be recognized that any movement away from the *benefit principle* of taxation necessarily involves some element of redistribution.

a "free rider."[14] Each individual by acting in his own self-interest may insure that society underestimates the demand for public goods and hence underallocates resources to their production. Only if there is a strong degree of social cohesion and some concomitant negative sanctions to discourage "nonsocial" behavior can the true demand for public goods be appraised.

Much of the discussion of welfare economics which was presented in Chapter 21 is relevant to the problem of the provision of public goods. For example, even the most well-meaning government may give up on the task of consciously calculating the demand for public goods and let the political process determine the level of these goods to be provided. The question of whether or not this level of goods will be desirable can then be answered only with some ambiguity. All of the problems of social choice, such as the Arrow Impossibility Theorem, interfere with an assessment of the desirability of any particular political procedure. As is generally the case in political questions a final assessment ultimately comes down to being a matter of opinion.

Aspects of a Positive Theory of Government

The previous discussion in this chapter has been primarily normative. We have investigated a few aspects of the question how governments *should* behave in their economic functions. Although the answers to this question were necessarily vague the analysis which was presented did raise some interesting conceptual issues. This normative approach is rather different from that which was taken in Parts II-V. In these we were more interested in developing theories to explain observed economic behavior without attaching value judgments to this behavior. Economists have recently attempted to adapt this positive methodology to the study of government and its functioning. In this section we will examine a few of the steps which have been taken in this direction.

As was the case for the theory of the firm a logical place to start a positive analysis is to examine the motives of government leaders. It might, for instance, be proposed that government leaders act so as to maximize social welfare. At least two realities argue against assuming such benevolent motivations. First, the notion of "social welfare" is extremely ill-defined. It is just not true that everyone in society has the same view of the way things should be and is simply waiting for

[14] In free markets individuals are forced to "reveal" their true demands and this problem does not occur. For a complete and thought-provoking discussion of the problems in providing public goods in many types of groups *see* M. Olson, *The Logic of Collective Action* (Cambridge, Mass.: Harvard University Press, 1965).

governmental action to bring this desirable state into being. Second, the assumption of a benevolent leadership would be in marked contrast to the self-interest assumption which underlies both the theory of the individual and the theory of the firm developed earlier. There seems no very persuasive reason why men should change their basic motivations upon elevation to a political office. Consequently, in order to be consistent with the other positive theories of this book some less socially virtuous theory is necessary.

One interesting theory of leadership motivation has been put forward by Downs. In his book, *An Economic Theory of Democracy*, Downs hypothesizes that "parties in democratic politics are analogous to entrepreneurs in a profit-seeking economy. So as to attain their private ends they formulate whatever policies they believe will gain the most votes, just as entrepreneurs produce whatever products will gain the most profits...."[15] In other words parties[16] act so as to *maximize political support*. In order to pursue this goal parties must contend with uncertainty in many respects. It is uncertain how any particular policy choice will affect political support. This is true not only because it may be hard to ascertain who benefits from government action but also because policies must be adopted before the policies of the party (or parties) out of power are known. This strategic advantage of those out of power is significantly modified, however, by the control that the party in power has over the public's access to information.

It would be impossible to summarize the numerous insights and testable hypotheses which follow from Downs' basic assumption. Perhaps the most interesting general conclusion which the author draws is that the party in power will generally adopt a *majority principle* in its policy decisions. It will pursue only those policies for which more votes are gained than are lost, and it will pursue such policies up to the point at which the marginal gain in votes from those benefiting from the policy equals the marginal loss in votes from those being hurt by the policy. The analogy between party motivation and profit maximization is quite close. It is by examining corollaries to the majority principle that Downs is able to arrive at many of his most interesting results.[17]

---

[15] Anthony Downs, *An Economic Theory of Democracy* (New York: Harper & Brothers, 1957), p. 295.

[16] Downs devotes some space also to examining the relationship among individual members of a party coalition and to investigating how these intraparty relations effect the policies ultimately chosen. This subject will not be pursued here.

[17] For the purposes of this book the most interesting implication of the majority principle is that the allocation of resources achieved by a government acting on this principle is unlikely to be efficient by the Pareto criterion. One reason for this is that the distribution of votes (absolutely equal in an ideal democracy) undoubtedly differs from the initial distribution of purchasing power, and hence public goods will not be financed in strict accordance with the benefit principle. The other aspects of Downs' proof of this assertion are too detailed to repeat here, and the interested reader is directed to the original source.

It is worthwhile to contrast Downs' view of the nature of the political process with another, more commonly held view. This alternative conception examines the *pluralistic* nature of democratic government. Social decisions are assumed to be made by the interaction of many powerful special interest groups. Presumably these groups wield some influence over political leaders by virtue of campaign contributions, friendship, superior knowledge of special issues, or perhaps by direct measures of corruption. Whatever the avenues of control it is assumed that pressure groups are the primary molders of the legal system.

Two assessments of pluralism have been put forward. The first optimistically predicts that the interaction of numerous pressure groups will, in some sense, produce a socially desirable outcome. Laws which are ultimately passed represent an equilibrium among numerous groups. Because no one group has significant power (at least not on all issues), the resultant equilibrium will generally be representative of the society as a whole.

This beneficial assessment of pluralism has been questioned by many authors. One of the most interesting objections was put forward by Olson.[18] This author pointed out that there is a systematic bias in a pluralistic society which causes only certain kinds of pressure groups to exercise political power. In particular, Olson argues, only pressure groups which represent narrow special interests will arise; pressure groups representing the "public interest" will be weak or nonexistent. The reason for this tendency, Olson explains, lies in the nature of the collective good provided by a pressure group to its members. For a close-knit group each member can recognize the benefits of his group action and there may be strong sanctions against being a free rider. Consequently, groups such as the "oil lobby" would be expected to have considerable success because each member of the group will find it in his interest to engage in pressure group activity.[19] On the other hand, diffuse public-interest groups will have minimal success because individual members of such groups cannot hope to obtain for themselves any major part of the benefits of their activity. The collective goods provided by public-interest groups, say consumer legislation, have significant nonexclusion properties (everyone will benefit whether or not they join Nader's Raiders), so the natural tendency is for such groups to be weak. Olson's assessment of pluralism is therefore not particularly

---

[18] See Mancur Olson, *The Logic of Collective Action, op. cit.,* especially Chapters V and VI.

[19] Other important examples of special-interest groups are found within the government. For example, the Pentagon lobby and the "welfare" lobby may be quite powerful in distorting government expenditure decisions away from those which are socially optimal. For this reason certain kinds of public goods may be overproduced.

positive. He foresees a serious absence of effective pressure groups to represent broad questions of public interest.

By combining Downs' and Olson's theories of government action an interesting third alternative can be constructed. It is undoubtedly true that pressure groups exercise considerable influence over legislation, and Olson is probably right when he theorizes that the public interest will be underrepresented. However, Olson's model does not take sufficient account of the motives of political leaders. Lobby groups probably do give "utility" to political leaders in many ways, and these leaders may therefore follow the dictates of the lobbyists. But the legislator does not have an unconstrained utility-maximization problem. Rather, he must operate subject to the *constraint of re-election*. The legislator must therefore pay some attention to what Downs calls the majority principle, although this attention will by no means be absolute. The purpose of public-interest lobby groups can then be seen as attempting to make individual voters aware of the benefits and costs of certain governmental action. Such an awareness on the part of voters may make a legislator's re-election constraint more binding and may mitigate the void of power on public issues noted by Olson.

It would be possible to extend this brief treatment of the positive theory of government behavior, but that would be to exceed the purposes of this section. Rather, it is hoped that this analysis will indicate some of the flavor of current forays by economists into the field of political science. The possibility for examining alternative behavioral assumptions is wide open.

Conclusion

This chapter describes various bits and pieces of a theory which is still very much incomplete. For many years economists avoided political questions because of an unwillingness to get involved with "unscientific" normative issues. Consequently, except for some aspects of macroeconomic theory the general foundations of an economic theory of government are relatively underdeveloped. Our understanding of the allocation of resources in a free market economy is considerably more advanced than our understanding of the allocation of resources between the private and public economy. Perhaps this lack of development is intrinsic in the nature of the subject. Political questions will probably always be a matter of opinion and the most we can hope to obtain from theoretical investigations is a variety of perspectives and conceptualizations within which to develop an informed opinion of our own.

One central message does, however, emerge from the various

discursive developments of this chapter: that it is in some sense desirable to have a consensus on what sorts of public goods (broadly defined) should be produced. As Olson[20] points out, an ideal society would be one in which individuals had rather different tastes for private goods and rather similar tastes for public goods. Such a society would benefit both from the markets' ability to accommodate different tastes efficiently and from a general agreement on the proper allocation between the public and private sectors. Such a normative prescription says little about how such an ideal might be achieved in practice.

[20] Mancur Olson, "Economics, Sociology and the Best of All Possible Worlds," *The Public Interest*, no. 12 (Summer 1968), pp. 96–118.

CHAPTER 24

Cost-benefit Analysis and the Provision of Public Goods

Introduction

It is possible to approach the study of government decision making in two ways. The first of these, utilized in the previous chapter, is philosophical in nature and stresses the necessary ambiguity which must be attached to any prescription about what a government should do. A second (and equally thought-provoking) area of inquiry is more pragmatic in nature. This area, which might be termed "applied welfare economics," emphasizes the fact that governments must make many important day-to-day decisions which can have significant effects on the allocation of resources in an economy. In making these decisions it would seem important that governmental leaders be apprised of as much information as can reasonably be gathered on the questions under investigation. The framework within which such information is coordinated has come to be known as *cost-benefit analysis*. As the name implies, this mode of analysis represents an attempt to calculate all the benefits and costs of any proposed project. Using the results of such a study an informed judgment may be made about the overall desirability of the project.

In recent years the methods of cost-benefit analysis have become practically a universal language within United States government agencies for the analysis of specific projects. With the introduction of the Planning-Programming-Budgeting System (PPBS)[1] into the federal budgetary process in the 1960's, a common framework was established for the accumulation and reporting of data. The purpose of this chapter is to examine this framework and to demonstrate the usefulness and limitations of microeconomic tools in the making of governmental decisions.

The chapter also has a broader purpose: to emphasize the economists' concept of *opportunity cost*. While this concept has already been mentioned (in Chapter 12), it would be hard to overemphasize its importance to economic analysis. The notion that the cost of any action can only be measured by the value of the opportunities foregone by taking the action is at the same time trivial and profound. Every child recognizes that the cost of an ice-cream cone is, say, two packs of chewing gum. With limited resources (here 10¢), the child may choose only one of these alternatives, and consequently the cost of the choice actually made can be measured by the utility of the alternative which was not chosen. If the child, for example, chooses the ice-cream cone, presumably the benefits of the cone (the utility from consuming it) exceed the costs (the loss of utility from not being able to consume two packs of gum). The opportunity cost doctrine expresses no more than this simple observation.[2]

As is the case for most simple observations the opportunity (or "alternative") cost concept has many important ramifications. To recognize that the cost of any action is the value of the foregone alternative

---

[1] For an extremely valuable survey of the theory and practices of the PPBS *see The Analysis and Evaluation of Public Expenditures: The PPB System*, published by the Joint Economic Committee (Washington, D. C.: U.S. Government Printing Office, 1969).

[2] There are basic philosophical issues involved with a proper definition of cost which are not considered here. A brief examination of these issues is presented in Chapter 26.

not only emphasizes that very few activities are in any sense "free" (any activity uses scarce time if nothing else) but also provides a conceptual method for computing the cost: All that is necessary is to compute the value of the foregone alternative. In the next section we will see how this basic principle underlies the tools of cost-benefit analysis.

The Conceptual Framework

Suppose the government is considering undertaking a particular project. This project will change the consumption level of society both in this year and for years into the future when compared to the stream of consumption which would have prevailed in the absence of the project. Probably the most common example would be the government's taxing the population (reducing current consumption) in order to build an investment project which would raise consumption levels in future periods. Benefits of the project would then be these future consumption levels, whereas the costs would be foregone consumption in earlier periods.

Notationally, when the project is undertaken, a stream of consumption levels $(C_0', C_1',..., C_n')$ is generated over n future time periods and this stream must be compared to the stream $(C_0, C_1,..., C_n)$ of consumption levels which would prevail in the absence of the project. For the investment example it would be the case that $C_0' < C_0$, but that eventually $C_i' > C_i$ after some number of years. We now need some way to compare these two streams. The common way to do this would be to compare the present discounted value of one stream to that of the other. Let:

$$PDV_{C'} = C_0' + \frac{C_1'}{1+r} + \frac{C_2'}{(1+r)^2} + \cdots + \frac{C_n'}{(1+r)^n}$$

$$PDV_C = C_0 + \frac{C_1}{1+r} + \frac{C_2}{(1+r)^2} + \cdots + \frac{C_n}{(1+r)^n}$$

[24.1]

be these two present discounted values where r is society's rate of return (or "rate of time preference"). By taking account of this rate of time preference it is possible to compress the consumption streams into two figures which can be compared. Our decision rule might then be to undertake the project if $PDV_{C'} > PDV_C$ and omit the project if this were not the case. Since:

$$PDV = PDV_C' - PDV_C = C_0' - C_0$$

$$+ \frac{C_1' - C_1}{1 + r} + \frac{C_2' - C_2}{(1 + r)^2} + \cdots + \frac{C_n' - C_n}{(1 + r)^n} \qquad [24.2]$$

this criterion can be viewed as evaluating the present discounted value of the project's *net benefits* (consumption levels in the presence of the project less consumption levels in the absence of the project). Only if this discounted sum were positive would the project be considered desirable.

Equation 24.2 is the conceptual cost-benefit criterion. In reality no one ever tries to compute these two alternative streams of society's consumption. Rather, emphasis is placed on estimating a stream of benefits from a project $(B_0, B_1, ..., B_n)$ and a stream of project costs $(V_0, V_1, ..., V_n)$ and then computing the PDV of these two streams:

$$PDV_B = B_0 + \frac{B_1}{1 + r} + \frac{B_2}{(1 + r)^2} + \cdots + \frac{B_n}{(1 + r)^n}$$

$$\qquad\qquad [24.3]$$

$$PDV_V = V_0 + \frac{V_1}{1 + r} + \frac{V_2}{(1 + r)^2} + \cdots + \frac{V_n}{(1 + r)^n}.$$

The criterion adopted is to compare PDV_B to PDV_V and if their difference (PDV):

$$PDV = PDV_B - PDV_V = B_0 - V_0 + \frac{B_1 - V_1}{1 + r}$$

$$+ \frac{B_2 - V_2}{(1 + r)^2} + \cdots + \frac{B_n - V_n}{(1 + r)^n} \qquad [24.4]$$

is positive the project "should" be undertaken.

The cost-benefit criterion outlined in Equation 24.4 might also be used to discriminate between possible projects. In fact, this is probably the most important real-world application of the criterion, since often total government funds are treated as fixed and a decision must be made about how to allocate these funds. One method of applying the criterion might be to calculate the *benefit-cost ratio* (PDV_B/PDV_V) and select those projects for which this ratio is the greatest.

In calculating real-world benefits and costs many problems arise in deciding exactly what should be included in these estimates. By comparing the actual formula in Equation 24.4 to the conceptually correct one in Equation 24.2 many computational ambiguities can be cleared up. It is important to keep the opportunity cost notion clearly in mind in cost-benefit calculations.[3] Even though we cannot estimate the consumption streams required in Equation 24.2, it is important that the calculations which are made in Equation 24.4 be in accord with those which are theoretically correct.

Applications of this opportunity cost doctrine of cost-benefit analysis are presented below. Since there are three distinct types of data needed in Equation 24.4, the discussion will examine benefits, costs, and *the* interest rate separately.

Project Benefits

Because they usually occur at more distant dates in the future and because they are generally less tangible, project benefits are more difficult to compute than costs. Consequently, it is in the evaluation of benefits that cost-benefit analysis is perhaps most controversial. Project benefits can be classed into three categories: *marketable, external,* and *esthetic.* Of these types marketable benefits are the most easily estimated. For example, one benefit of a dam is the hydroelectric power produced. The value of this benefit can be taken to be the market value of the electric power generated.[4] The market provides a convenient way of measuring society's evaluation of some of a project's benefits.

Many of the benefits of government projects are nonmarketable, however. As was pointed out in the previous chapter government will be called on to produce those goods which by their nature have relatively small marketable benefits. One important type of nonmarketable benefit of a project is the external effects that the project may have on production possibilities elsewhere in the economy. To return to the dam example, it is possible that this project will improve the productivity of other enterprises along the river on which the dam is located. By regulating the annual water flow, for example, the dam may permit such enterprises to utilize their present plants more efficiently. Although this type of benefit is not marketed, it could in principle be evaluated, since the increased productivity will be reflected by the price system. The

---

[3] In the context of cost-benefit analysis with fixed government expenditures the opportunity cost doctrine is sometimes used to argue that the true costs of any project are in fact measured by the benefits of the best project which cannot be undertaken because of lack of funds.

[4] Problems may arise if a project is large enough to affect the prevailing price structure. For example, the dam may be large enough to affect the prevailing price of electricity and one must decide whether to evaluate this benefit at the "before project" price or the "after project" price. There is no easy answer to this problem of *nonmarginal effects.* It is really just a further manifestation of the index number problem discussed in the appendix to Chapter 5.

value of land along the river may rise, for example, and this increase in value would be indicative of the land's increased productivity.[5]

Finally, the esthetic benefits of a project must be considered. The evaluation of these benefits is difficult even in principle because the price system cannot act as a guide. If people derive pleasure from looking at a reservoir behind a dam that is clearly a benefit of the project. To make this benefit commensurable with other benefits, however, it must be assigned a price and this assignment will always be to some extent arbitrary. Esthetic benefits may also be negative (suppose the dam destroys places of natural beauty) and some attempt should also be made to evaluate these costs of a project. Because esthetic benefits and costs are not measurable in a monetary sense there may be a systematic tendency to underestimate them, although we have no very good idea what "underestimation" in fact means.

One particularly important "esthetic" benefit of any project is the effect which that project has on the distribution of income. Some projects (such as the Tennessee Valley Authority) may promote equality, whereas others (such as the supersonic transport) may benefit only the rich. Any overall assessment of a project must include some statement as to the desirability of its distributional effects. It is extremely difficult to assign a monetary value to distributional effects in order to make them comparable to other types of benefits.

Costs

In a sense costs are simply "negative benefits," and therefore it is not really necessary to add anything to the comments of the previous section about them. Indeed, project costs are usually easier to estimate because they are more tangible, more certain, and occur closer to the time plans are actually made than do project benefits. There are, however, certain aspects of costs which should be specifically mentioned. Particularly important is the conception of opportunity cost, which must be used to evaluate the costs of a government project. Generally, what is required is a measure of the reduction in output elsewhere which

---

[5] It is important not to double count or miscount these external benefits. It would be totally inappropriate to calculate the total increase in production along the river that follows its construction as benefits from a dam. Such a calculation would involve both double counting (since the electricity used in production has already been enumerated as a marketable benefit) and miscounting (since the additional resources, such as labor and capital, drawn to the river imply that production has been cut back elsewhere). It is also generally true that the employment generating attributes of a project are not added as benefits. The reasoning here is that any government project will generate employment, and hence such benefits cannot be uniquely assigned to one particular undertaking.

comes about as a result of shifting resources to a project. In some cases this reduction can be estimated by the market prices of the resources used in the project. However, there may be situations in which market prices do not reflect true costs in terms of foregone output. The purpose of this section is to examine such situations.

In an ideal, perfectly competitive world the price of any input hired for a project would be equal to its marginal value product in alternative employment. Hence the cost of the input exactly reflects the amount by which the value of output is reduced elsewhere by the transferring of the input. For the perfectly competitive case then the market price of an input is identical with its opportunity cost, and there is no ambiguity in calculating direct project costs.[6]

When there are elements of imperfect competition present in the markets for the inputs to be used for a project some care must be taken in calculating costs. It is the opportunity cost of these inputs which is relevant, not the market price. In Chapter 18 several situations were analyzed in which imperfect competition in factor markets may create a divergence between factor prices and marginal value products. Similarly, for manufactured inputs (such as steel, concrete, glass, and so on), the presence of monopoly elements in these markets can bring about a divergence between price and marginal cost. In both of these cases market prices of project inputs will not reflect true opportunity costs and some adjustments must be made if the true spirit of cost-benefit analysis is to be maintained. In practice, however, adjustments for divergences from perfect competition are seldom calculated.

Externalities also represent important divergences from the competitive model which should be accounted for in proper opportunity cost calculations. If the social marginal cost of a project input differs from the private marginal cost it is the social marginal cost which is relevant to cost-benefit calculations, even though this cost may not be reflected in prices determined by the private market. For example, it might be argued that resources drawn away from the steel industry should not be valued at their market prices. Since there are significant negative external effects of steel production the private marginal value product of these inputs will exceed that marginal value which is socially relevant. In withdrawing inputs from steel production there will be less steel output (an opportunity cost) but there will also be less pollution (an "opportunity benefit"), and only the net result of these two effects should

---

[6] Sometimes the cost-benefit criterion is simply restated to be that projects should be chosen on the principle of making the present discounted value of future total "output" as large as possible. In a perfectly competitive model the cost-benefit criterion can indeed be represented by this prescription, although much of the rationale of opportunity cost calculations is obscured by a naïve application of this principle.

be calculated as the cost of shifting the input. It may be that the planned project will produce some detrimental externalities of its own, and this should also be considered in the cost calculations.

Finally, there are situations in which market prices may have been artificially affected by government regulation and will no longer reflect true opportunity costs. For example, minimum wage legislation may necessitate high labor costs on a project even though the drawing of labor into the project does not reduce output elsewhere in the economy. This would be the case if the labor hired in the project were previously unemployed. Such labor input should be valued at 0 (its opportunity cost in terms of foregone output) rather than at the artificial minimum wage.[7] Another example of this kind of divergence occurs in underdeveloped countries when planners must value the amount of foreign exchange needed to complete a project. The market exchange rate may not reflect the true opportunity cost of foreign exchange, since foreign exchange is a vital and scarce input into many developmental projects. Consequently, it may be necessary to evaluate the "hard" currency requirements of a project at a rate above the prevailing exchange rate.

All of these examples are simply corollaries of the general opportunity cost principle. Once the full importance of this doctrine has been demonstrated, further applications become obvious. The gathering of data to estimate divergences between market prices and true opportunity costs may, however, be quite difficult, and frequently rather gross approximations must be used.[8]

The Interest Rate

The choice of an appropriate interest rate with which to discount future benefits and costs is important for two related reasons. First, the interest rate chosen will determine which government projects can profitably be undertaken. Since the benefits of projects usually accrue over a longer time horizon than do costs, it is likely that higher interest rates will mitigate against the government's undertaking a project. With a high interest rate distant benefits will be discounted to a much greater extent than are nearby costs, and consequently many projects will fail to meet the cost-benefit criterion. On the other hand, low interest rates will favor the adoption of many government projects including those with a long-time span of benefits. If a governmental policy of always under-

---

[7] This argument ignores the value of leisure to the unemployed worker. Leisure has traditionally been imputed a 0 value in most cost-benefit studies (but *see* the section "Two Different Problems of Valuation" below) and also has a 0 value in the *GNP* accounts.

[8] In this regard the calculation of "dual" variables as a way of evaluating certain economic constraints is an important empirical tool for estimating opportunity costs.

taking those projects for which benefits exceed costs is adopted, which interest rate is used for discounting will have a significant effect on the number of such projects to be undertaken: The choice of interest rate will affect the allocation of resources between the public and private sectors of the economy.

Even if the size of the governmental sector of the economy is fixed by political forces the choice of interest rate can have a second important effect in deciding what sort of projects are favored. If a low interest rate is used, programs with a long pay-off period will be relatively more attractive, whereas the choice of a high interest rate will mean that distant benefits are discounted significantly and "fast pay-off" projects will be favored. Consequently, the choice of interest rate by which to discount benefits and costs can determine whether a government takes a long-term or a short-term view in its allocational decisions.

Choosing a proper interest rate is therefore an important policy question. In looking at the real world one is faced with a bewildering assortment of interest rates ranging from rates on very liquid short-term assets (say 0 percent to 6 percent) through the rate of return on capital in very profitable industries (which may be higher than 40 percent). Even if these extremes are disregarded, a "reasonable" choice of interest rates would include rates from the 6 percent that is standard on government bonds through the 15-20 percent which Solow estimates as the social rate of return on business investment in the United States during the 1950's.[9] Clearly, choosing among these will have major implications for governmental allocation of resources.

For guidance in the proper choice of rates it is necessary to return to examining the logic of the cost benefit formula.[10] The reason future period's consumption levels are discounted is that a dollar of consumption today can be transformed into more than a dollar of consumption tomorrow. This basic aspect of capital investment was illustrated in Chapter 19, where it was shown that the rate of product transformation between present and future consumption is equal to 1 plus the rate of return. The opportunity cost doctrine argues for discounting in order to make consumption levels in various time periods commensurable. This doctrine also argues that it is the rate of return[11] on capital which is drawn into the government project that should serve for discounting

---

[9] R. M. Solow, *Capital Theory and the Rate of Return, op. cit.*, pp. 92–97.

[10] The analysis of this part draws on W. J. Baumol, "On the Discount Rate for Public Projects" in the *PPBS* volume, *op. cit.*, pp. 489–503. It should be pointed out that many of Baumol's conclusions are still regarded as controversial.

[11] The rate of return used should be calculated before payment of corporate profits taxes since pre-tax earnings are the relevant measure of the social rate of return on the actual capital investment.

benefits and costs. Only by this choice will the logic of the opportunity cost concept be obeyed.

This result may seem rather surprising in that it recommends a much higher discount factor (say 10 percent or perhaps even 15 percent) than has been traditionally applied to government projects (5-6 percent is the common range[12] used). Several authors have attempted to justify the use of a lower discount rate on government projects than prevails in the private economy. Many different reasons have been put forward for such a choice, but these can be classed under three general headings: monopoly, risk, and private hedonism. Each of these contentions will be summarized briefly below:

1. *Monopoly.* It is argued that calculated rates of return on industrial capital investment include a substantial element of monopoly rent. Since such rent arises as a result of market organization and not from the productivity of capital per se, rates lower than private rates should be used for government projects.

2. *Risk.* Private rates must compensate for some uncertainty in the return on investment. This is reflected in interest rate differentials between risky and secure assets. It is argued that to use "risky" rates in the evaluation of government projects would be unwarranted since the government, by virtue of its size, will be able to spread its risk over a large number of projects. Government investment as a whole therefore should be regarded as "riskless," and should be evaluated at a lower rate than prevails in private markets.

3. *Private hedonism.* In this version of the argument it is claimed that the private economy will generally tend to underinvest since people are basically selfish and don't care about future generations.[13] As a result interest rates in the private sector will be higher than they "should be." In governmental decisions the selfish nature of private citizens should not be taken into account, and consequently a lower rate is required.

To comment on each of these allegations in detail would be inappropriate for the purposes of this book. Some of the points (such as 1)

---

[12] The use of different discount rates on different government projects would, in general, seem to be a mistake. Only if projects draw capital from sources with rather different rates of return would there be a convincing argument for varying the rate used.

[13] This argument essentially says that investment is a public good in that there are important externalities of investment which cannot be captured by the individual investor. Whereas there may be some truth in this, given the great growth in output levels in developed countries during the twentieth century, it would be hard to argue that underinvestment is a pervasive phenomenon.

seem essentially correct, whereas others (most notably 2) are probably mistaken.[14] Whatever the truth of these claims, the opportunity cost doctrine can act as the basic foundation upon which to base any final assessment. Specific instances will require detailed empirical examination.

Two Difficult Problems of Valuation

It would be inappropriate to infer from this analysis that the evaluation of the costs and benefits of a project is an exact science. It is often the case that rather subjective values must be placed on certain project effects. One obvious area of subjectivity occurs in the attempt to place monetary values on esthetic benefits. Even more important problems may arise in the evaluation of certain "tangible" benefits. In this section we will discuss two benefits, time saving and life saving, which characterize many projects and have proved particularly difficult to quantify with a dollar magnitude. It will be shown that for these benefits the opportunity cost doctrine does not provide a clearcut solution to the question of valuation.

Consider first the problem of assigning a value to individual's time. For many projects a primary benefit is time saving. For example, an urban transit system may substantially lessen commuting time, and some attempt should be made to place a value on this benefit. The most common method of evaluation consists of theorizing that an individual equates his *MRS* of leisure for income (*see* Chapter 7) to the prevailing wage rate, and that time savings should therefore be evaluated at this wage rate. Implicit in such reasoning is the presumption that time saved can be utilized in some productive way and that this productivity can be measured by the wage rate. Other authors have questioned this assumption by pointing out that the usual alternative to commuting time is increased leisure, and therefore we should only evaluate time savings at some arbitrarily determined price of leisure. For instance, from comparing the traffic usage of toll versus nontoll roads there is some evidence that individuals implicitly place a very low value on their time. Consequently, the use of a market wage rate to evaluate time savings may be to overvalue potential benefits. Some choice, however, must be made, and the value of time which is chosen will be a significant determinant of the worth of many projects.

[14] By the opportunity cost doctrine risk capital should be evaluated at the rate it actually earns. The fact that higher earnings are necessitated by risk aversion in the private market is irrelevant to assessing its productivity. For a further discussion of this point *see* J. Hirshleifer and D. L. Shapiro, "The Treatment of Risk and Uncertainty" in the *PPBS* volume (*op. cit.*), pp. 505–530.

An even more important problem of valuation arises in attempting to assess the economic value of a human life. Many projects have life-saving as a principle purpose and there must be some way to make this benefit commensurable with other benefits. For example, the question of whether the government should devote more resources to cancer research or more to education is an important one which cannot be answered unless some value can be placed on the benefits of the cancer program. Economists are not bashful about proposing possible methods for estimating a value for the benefit of saving one life.[15] Nonetheless, it is difficult to be content with any such definition even though it may be phrased in the best tradition of the opportunity cost doctrine.

Ideally, one might like to adopt all those projects with any chance of saving even one life. However, resources (especially those for saving lives) are scarce and some rules must be established for allocating these scarce resources among competing ends. The problem of valuation is inescapable, although it must be admitted that any value chosen is essentially arbitrary.

Conclusion

If the preceding section succeeds in casting some doubt on the precision of cost-benefit calculations it has served its purpose. Most costs and benefits have significant unmeasurable components which can only be estimated in a subjective way. Recognizing this does not imply that cost-benefit analysis is worthless. It is important to think precisely about the overall effects of projects and the cost-benefit framework is a helpful unifying device. The notion of opportunity cost is, in a broad sense, certainly the correct conceptual approach for considering difficult problems of choice, and the problem of valuation is unavoidable. Any actual analysis which is undertaken will, however, of necessity reflect the subjective views of its author. It may in many instances be the case that the political process of "muddling through" will produce decisions which are in some sense better than the most exact and ingenious cost-benefit analysis. It is important, however, that those doing the muddling be as well informed as possible.

---

[15] For example, it might be suggested that the value of a life is the present discounted value of a person's productivity less the costs of keeping him alive. Obviously this definition ignores the utility society derives from having the person around, and ignores the value the person places on his own life.

CHAPTER 25

Externalities and Property Rights

Introduction

The idea of externalities has been mentioned in many places in previous chapters. The reader should therefore have a general conception of what the term means. Externalities refer to interactions among economic agents which are not adequately reflected in markets. To analyze why markets may fail in this way is the purpose of the present chapter. Hopefully an explanation of why failures take place will also be indicative of the possibilities for efficient and equitable solutions.

More generally, a study of externalities provides insights into the nature of and problems associated with private and public property, and to examine the issue of property rights is an underlying theme of this chapter. Before launching into a detailed analysis, however, it will be helpful to be more precise in defining exactly what an externality is, since there has been substantial confusion over this point in many economic investigations.

It is best to define externalities as technical features of tastes and technology without initially referring to markets at all. Broadly speaking then an externality is said to be *Pareto relevant* (that is, to have important allocative significance) when the activities of one agent directly affect the tastes or technological abilities of another agent. To make this abstract definition more transparent it is necessary to present a few examples. Consider two firms—one producing good X, another producing good Y—where each uses only labor as an input.

The production of Y is said to have an external effect on the production of X if the output of X depends not only on the amount of labor chosen by the X-entrepreneur but also on the level at which the production of Y is carried on. Notationally, the production function for good X can be written as:

$$X = f(L_X; Y) \qquad [25.1]$$

where L_X denotes the amount of labor devoted to good X, and Y appears to the right of the semicolon in the equation to show that it is an effect on production over which the X-entrepreneur has no control.[1] As a concrete example suppose the two firms are located on a river with firm X being downstream from Y. Suppose firm Y pollutes the river in its productive process. Then the output of firm X may depend not only on the level of inputs it uses itself but also on the amount of pollutants flowing past its factory. The level of pollutants, in turn, is determined by the output of firm Y. Consequently, $\partial f/\partial Y < 0$, and we would say that there exists a negative external effect between the output of Y and the production function for good X.

In the next section we will return to analyze this case more fully as it is representative of all types of externalities. First, however, it will be useful to detail a few more examples of external interactions.

The relationship between two firms may be beneficial. Most examples of such positive externalities are rather bucolic in nature. Perhaps the most famous, proposed by J. Meade,[2] involves two firms, one

[1] We will find it necessary to redefine the assumption of "no control" considerably as the analysis of this chapter proceeds.

[2] J. Meade, "External Economies and Diseconomies in a Competitive Situation," *Economic Journal*, vol. 62 (March 1952), pp. 54–67.

producing honey (raising bees) and the other producing apples. Because the bees feed on apple blossoms an increase in apple production will improve productivity in the honey industry. The beneficial effect of having well-fed bees is a positive externality to the beekeeper. By contrasting this example to the previous one it can be seen that the usual perfectly competitive case is simply the middle ground between positive and negative externalities. In such a middle ground the productive activities of one firm have no direct effect on those of other firms.

Externalities may also occur between individuals or between a firm and an individual. These possibilities were discussed briefly in Chapter 22 and they will not be repeated here. The reader can certainly dream up additional cases of interpersonal or firm-person externalities on his own. A principle feature of all such examples is that tastes, or tastes and technologies, are related in some direct way, not simply through the market.[3]

Externalities and Markets

It has traditionally been argued that the presence of externalities such as those described earlier can cause a market to operate inefficiently. The reasons for this were discussed in detail in Chapter 22, but will be repeated here by using the example outlined above of the two firms located on a river. Suppose the production function of the pollution-producing firm is given by:

$$Y = g(L_Y) \qquad [25.2]$$

where L_Y is the quantity of labor devoted to Y production. The production function for good X (which exhibits an externality) was given by Equation 25.1. By the Pareto conditions for an optimal allocation of labor it is required that the social marginal value product of labor $(SMVP_L)$ be equal in both occupations. If P_X and P_Y are the prices of good X and Y respectively, the $SMVP$ of labor in the production of good X is given by:

$$SMVP_L{}^X = P_X \frac{\partial f}{\partial L_X}. \qquad [25.3]$$

---

[3] This might be denoted mathematically in the interpersonal case by observing that the utility level of one individual (U_i) would depend on the utility level of some other individual in addition to depending on the goods he himself consumes: $U_i = U_i(X_1,..., X_n; U_j)$. For firm-person externalities utility would depend on goods consumed and on the level of productive activity of the firm, say Y: $U_i = U_i(X_1,..., X_n; Y)$.

Because of the productive externality the statement of the *SMVP* of labor in the production of Y is somewhat more complex. An additional unit of labor employed by firm Y will produce some extra Y. But it will also produce some extra pollution, and this will reduce the production of X. Consequently:

$$SMVP_L{}^Y = P_Y \cdot \frac{\partial g}{\partial L_Y} + P_X \cdot \frac{\partial f}{\partial Y} \cdot \frac{\partial Y}{\partial L_Y} \qquad [25.4]$$

where the second term represents the effect that hiring additional workers in plant Y has on production in plant X. This effect will be negative if $\partial f/\partial Y < 0$. Efficiency then requires that:

$$SMVP_L{}^X = SMVP_L{}^Y. \qquad [25.5]$$

The decentralized calculations of the two firm managers will not bring this condition about if only "normal" market reactions are allowed. Firm X will hire labor up to the point at which its private marginal value product (MVP_L) is equal to the prevailing wage rate:

$$w = MVP_L{}^X = P_X \frac{\partial f}{\partial L_X}.$$

Firm Y will follow a similar course of action:

$$w = MVP_L{}^Y = P_Y \frac{\partial g}{\partial L_Y}. \qquad [25.6]$$

The market will therefore cause:

$$MVP_L{}^X = MVP_L{}^Y. \qquad [25.7]$$

Now it is readily seen that the condition of Equation 25.7 will insure Pareto efficiency only if $\partial f/\partial Y = 0$ in Equation 25.4. In other words so long as the externality exists, the managers' decisions will not bring about an optimal allocation. In our example we assumed $\partial f/\partial Y < 0$, so this implies that labor will be overallocated to the production of good Y. Labor's social marginal value product in the production of Y will fall short of its value in the production of X. The value of output could be increased by shifting labor from the production of Y into the production of X.

To investigate possible solutions to this failure of the market it is useful first to assume that production techniques are fixed, and that the externality is a necessary fact of life.[4] Under this assumption, then, prescriptions such as "ban pollution" or "force Y to use alternative production techniques" are outside the frame of analysis. There are still two approaches which may bring about improved efficiency. First, the government could impose a suitable *excise tax* on the firm generating the external diseconomy. Presumably this tax would cause the output of Y to be cut back and would cause labor to be shifted out of the production of Y. This classic remedy to the externality problem was first lucidly put forward in the 1920's by Pigou[5] and, although it has been somewhat modified, it remains the "standard" answer given by economists. The central problem for regulators becomes one of obtaining sufficient empirical information so that the correct tax structure can be enacted.

The taxation solution is illustrated conceptually in Figure 25.1. Suppose firm Y's marginal cost curve is given by MC and that the market demand curve for Y is given by D (ignore the curve D' for the moment). Assume also that Y's marginal social cost curve is represented by MC'. This curve differs from MC by the amount of extra costs which the production of Y imposes on others (here only firm X) in the economy. From a social point of view the optimal output of Y would be Y_2. At this output level the marginal benefit of Y's production (what people are willing to pay for the good) is exactly equal to the marginal social cost. However, the market will[6] cause output level Y_1 to be produced since, at this output, market price is equal to private marginal cost. Consequently, Y will be overproduced as was indicated previously.

An excise tax of amount t (*see* Chapter 14) would cause the effective demand curve for Y to shift to D'. With this new demand curve the private profit-maximizing output will be Y_2, and this will indeed be that level of output which is socially optimal. At Y_2 the marginal external damage done by producing Y is given by the distance ad and this is pre-

---

[4] It is also assumed that the detrimental effects of the production of Y do not affect any other agent in the economy other than firm X. Similarly, the discussion of externalities usually takes place within a partial equilibrium framework in which "second-best" problems are assumed to be unimportant.

[5] A. C. Pigou, *The Economics of Welfare*, 4th ed. (London: Macmillan & Company, Ltd., 1946). Pigou also stresses the desirability of providing subsidies to firms which produce beneficial externalities.

[6] It will be convenient to assume that firm Y acts as a *perfectly price discriminating monopolist* in the market by selling each unit separately at the highest price it will bring. Consequently, in Figure 25.1, at the initial equilibrium total revenue will be $ODbY_1$ and private profits will be Deb. The assumption of a perfect price discriminator eliminates the need for introducing the notion of consumer surplus into this analysis since there is in fact no such surplus (*see* Chapter 15). The results would not be materially changed if firm Y were a perfectly competitive firm. In such a case, however, it would be necessary to discuss consumer surplus in detail.

Figure 25.1   A Graphic Demonstration of the Costs of an Externality

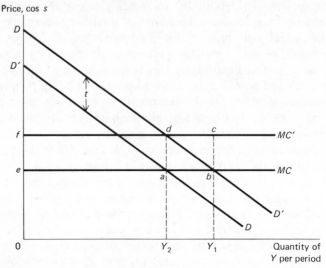

The demand for Y is given by the curve DD, and the private marginal cost curve for Y by MC. The curve MC' records the social marginal cost of Y production. From society's point of view, therefore, Y_2 is the optimal output. However, the normal workings of the market will cause output level Y_1 to be produced. One way to force the market to allocate goods correctly would be to adopt an excise tax of amount t on the production of Y. The effect of the tax is to reduce the demand curve facing the firm from DD to $D'D'$ and this will shift the profit-maximizing level of output from Y_1 to Y_2.

cisely the amount (t) paid by the consumers of Y in the form of excise taxes.

A second possible cure for allocational distortions brought about by the external relationship between firms X and Y would be for these firms to merge and thereby *internalize* this externality. Since it has been assumed that the only relevant external effect of firm Y's action is on firm X, the merging of the two firms under a single management would eliminate the problems associated with decentralization. Following the merger the marginal cost curve for the production of Y would be MC', since now the effect of Y on the production of X would be taken into account. The manager of firm $(X + Y)$ would consequently produce output level Y_2, which is the socially optimal position. Internalizing the externality corrects the allocational distortion.

Property Rights, Allocation, and Equity

One important question might still be asked about this analysis. If firm Y's actions impose a cost on firm X, why doesn't firm X bribe firm Y to cut back on its output? Presumably the gain of such a cutback to firm X (area $abcd$ in Figure 25.1) would exceed the loss of profits to firm Y (area abd) and some bargaining arrangement might be worked out which would monetarily benefit both parties. Both firms would be irrational not to recognize such a possibility and it would seem that the benefits of internalization could be obtained without the necessity of a merger.

This observation can be made even more general by introducing the concept of property rights. Simply put, *property rights* are the legal specifications of who owns what, and what rights an owner has to trade those goods which he owns. Some goods may be defined as *common property* which are owned by "society at large"; others may be defined as *private property* which are owned personally by individuals. Private property may either be *exchangeable* or non-exchangeable, depending on whether the good in question may or may not be traded. In this book we have been primarily concerned with exchangeable private property,[7] and these are the type of property rights which will be considered here.

For the purposes of the two-firm externality example it is interesting to consider the nature of the property right which might be attached to the river shared by the firms. Suppose property rights were defined so as to give "ownership" of the river to one of the firms, but that the firms were free to bargain over how the river might be used. It might be thought that if the ownership of the river were given to firm Y, pollution would result; whereas, if the right were given to firm X, the river would remain pure. This might not be the case, however, because such a conclusion disregards the bargains which might be reached by the two parties. Indeed, several authors[8] have argued that if *bargaining is costless* the two parties left on their own will arrive at the Pareto Optimal output (Y_2), and that this result will be independent of who "owns" the river.

If, for example, firm Y owns the river it must then impute some cost of this ownership into its cost function. What are the costs associated with river ownership? Again the opportunity cost doctrine provides the answer: The costs are what the river would bring in its next best alternative use. In the problem only firm X has some alternative use for the river (to keep it clean), and the amount that this firm would be willing to pay for a clean river is equal to the external damage done by the pol-

---

[7] Two important examples of privately owned goods which are not exchangeable are an individual's human capital (this could only be sold in a society which permitted slavery) and an individual's vote (a private good which is provided by the state). These examples clearly point out that the nature of the property right attached to a good is determined within the legal framework of society.

[8] This argument is presented along with numerous interesting legal illustrations in R. Coase, "The Problem of Social Cost," *Journal of Law and Economics,* vol. 3 (October 1960), pp. 1–44.

lution. Consequently, if firm Y calculates its costs correctly its marginal cost curve (including the cost of river ownership) becomes MC' in Figure 25.1. Firm Y will therefore produce Y_2 and sell the remaining rights of river use to firm X for a fee of some amount between abd and $abcd$.

A similar allocational result would occur if firm X owned the rights to the river. In this case firm Y would be willing to pay any amount up to the total profits it earns from production for the right to pollute the river. Firm X will accept these payments so long as they exceed the costs imposed on it by the river pollution. Hence the ultimate result of bargaining will be for firm Y to offer a payment of at most $eadD$ to firm X for the use of the river in dumping pollution associated with output level Y_2. Firm X will not sell the rights to dump any further pollution because what firm Y would be willing to pay falls short of the cost of additional pollution to firm X. Again the Pareto Optimal point can be reached by relying on free bargaining between the two firms. Notice that in both situations some production of Y takes place, and hence there will be some pollution. Having no Y output (and no pollution) would be inefficient in the same sense that producing Y_1 is: Scarce resources would not be efficiently allocated. The example shows that by relying on the opportunity cost doctrine there is some "optimal" level of pollution and that this level may be achieved through bargains between the individuals involved.

The effect of this demonstration is startling. Traditional arguments, at least within this simple model, have been shown to be wrong in their assertions that free markets cannot accommodate externalities. When a broad enough view of the possibility for free exchange is taken, the allocation difficulties raised by the externality are readily handled by bargaining between the individuals involved. Even more interesting is the fact that the free market allocation of the use of the river is independent of the actual ownership of the river. The description of the allocation process is completely symmetrical and the results are identical to those which would prevail if an "ideal" merger were to take place.

There are distributional effects which do depend on who is assigned ownership of the river. If both firms appear in court demanding property rights to the river, the court's decision on how these rights should be assigned will have important distributional effects. If firm Y is given ownership of the river its owners will be better off than they would be if firm X were the owner. Because, in our example, allocation will be unaffected[9] by the way in which property rights are assigned, any as-

---

[9] This conclusion requires that the changing distribution of wealth implied by different assignments of property rights has no effect on the allocation of goods. Loosely speaking, it is assumed that the demand and cost curves of Figure 25.1 will not shift in response to the changing distribution of wealth. It is assumed that "income effects" are unimportant.

sessment of the desirability of certain assignments must be made on equity grounds. For example, if the owners of firm Y were very wealthy and those of firm X poor we might argue that ownership should be given to firm X on the basis of distributional equity. The price system may, in principle, be capable of solving certain simple externality problems of allocation but, as always, the price system cannot deal with problems of equity.[10]

It should be pointed out, however, that the issue of equity in the assignment of property rights arises in every allocational decision, not only in the study of externalities. The issue of which firm should be assigned ownership of the river is not essentially different from the question of which individual has the right of ownership to a particular house. In either case a government could decide that the prevailing system of property rights is undesirable and might therefore redefine these rights. The issue of income distribution is no more intertwined with the problem of externalities than it is with any other allocational question.

The analysis of this section depends crucially on the assumption of zero bargaining costs. If the costs (real or psychic) of striking bargains were high, the workings of the free exchange system may not be capable of achieving allocational efficiency. Similarly, if transactions costs were high the allocation of resources would probably not be independent of the way in which property rights are assigned. In the next section we will examine an important type of externality for which bargaining costs are indeed quite high: environmental externalities. Considerations of equity will also enter this discussion, as it is possible that prevailing ownership rights are distributed in an equitable way.

Environmental Externalities

The example developed in the preceding two sections is extremely artificial. Two aspects of the problem are particularly unrealistic. First, the assumption that only two parties are involved in the externality does not adequately represent the vast majority of situations in which externalities arise. A far more common case occurs when the production of one

[10] Matters of equity cannot be established here on a priori grounds, but require a detailed examination of the welfare level of each agent. It would be inappropriate to argue, for example, that firm Y has an inalienable right to the use of the river or, conversely, that firm X has a basic right to clean water. Since firm Y's actions only affect firm X, no such a priori conclusions are possible. The desires of the two firms are strictly competitive and any arguments about the intrinsic rights of one party can symmetrically be applied to the other. For some fascinating examples of this symmetry in legal cases *see* the article by R. Coase (*op. cit.*).

good has external repercussions on numerous other agents, including both firms and individuals. Second, although the assumption of a fixed technology was valuable in its ability to isolate certain important aspects of the allocational problems raised by externalities one has only to look at the increasing proliferation of pollution control equipment to recognize that technology is not fixed. Rather, the technical methods of production should be treated as an additional variable in the firms' productive decisions. In this section we will examine each of these observations in the context of the "environmental crisis." Before beginning such an examination, however, it will be useful to describe how the notion of the environment fits into traditional economic models of production and exchange.

Figure 25.2   Schematic Diagram of the Relationship between the Environment and the Market Economy

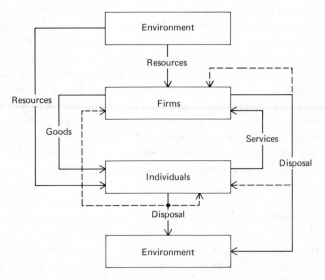

The economic system is embedded in a larger environment. Disposal activities of firms and individuals may have important effects on other firms and individuals. These effects are denoted by the dashed arrows in the figure.

In a sense, the entire economic process begins and ends with the environment.[11] All agents draw resources (air, water, raw materials) from the environment, transform these resources by productive processes, consume those "final" goods produced, and then return resources (CO_2,

[11] This section draws on the recent work of A. V. Kneese. *See,* for example, A. V. Kneese and R. C. d'Arge, "Pervasive External Costs and the Response of Society" in the *PPBS* volume (*op. cit.*), pp. 87–115.

used water, and rusting cans) to the environment. This process is pictured schematically in Figure 25.2. This figure clearly shows that the circular flow of goods and man-made inputs is in fact embedded in more general environmental surroundings. The entire system is a general equilibrium one, and only the simplest kinds of interactions are illustrated in the figure.

One interesting aspect of the interaction of the economic system with the environment is that physical mass is preserved throughout the productive process. Generally, the total flow of materials from the environment must eventually return to the environment. Resources may be transformed and physically transported by the productive process, but they do not disappear. As the total flow of output, say *GNP*, increases, then the total flow into and out of the environmental sector will also increase, and this trend creates an increasing potential for environmental externalities.

To examine the nature and causes of environmental problems it is interesting to examine the nature of the markets which exist for the flows pictured in Figure 25.2. The markets for goods and human services are relatively well developed. The operation of these markets has been intensively studied in this book. Markets involving the flow of resources from the environmental sector into the productive sector are less well developed. Although certain natural resources (petroleum, iron ore, bauxite) do have complex market structures, other resources (notably air and water) usually have been treated as common property and hence have not been allocated by markets. This failure of markets to develop may in part be attributable to the relative abundance of these resources and in part to the technical difficulties of actually establishing markets.

It is in the return of resources to the environment, however, that the most serious deficiencies in market organization can be seen. Disposal of goods into the environment has traditionally been considered to be "free," and few markets have been associated with such flows. Even though markets have not developed, the disposal flows may have great allocative significance. Disposal activities may affect both individuals and firms; such effects are shown by dashed arrows in Figure 25.2. The environment can act as a conduit for carrying the disposal activities of one agent into interaction with someone else. Firms may discharge smoke into the air and this may affect individuals' welfare. Firms may also affect the productive capabilities of other firms (as was shown in the earlier example). Not only firms may produce such external effects. Individuals may litter the landscape, produce vast quantities of trash and sewage, and make noise; each of these activities may affect other agents. Because there are no markets regulating the flow of goods through the disposal sector there is a very real possibility that "too much" of these activities will be carried on. Each agent will regard his disposal costs as zero and will use the environmental sector so long as this use permits him to improve his own welfare. Because the environment is common property each agent will act as if he "owned" it. This then is the prototype of environmental problems which will be investigated here.

In view of the analysis of the previous two sections a natural first question to ask would be why markets for disposal activities have not developed. If a firm's activities harm a group of individuals, for example, why don't these individuals band together and force the firm to internalize the social costs of its disposal programs into its decisions. Using the analogy of the previous section it would seem these costs could be internalized by suitable bribes to the firm or use charges placed on the firm. A principal reason this does not happen is the *high bargaining costs* which are associated with most environmental externalities. It is frequently difficult to identify those injured by, say, air pollution. It is even more difficult to organize these individuals into an effective bargaining unit[12] and to calculate the monetary value of the losses suffered. Finally, our legal system has been set up primarily to adjudicate disputes between two agents, rather than to represent the rights of diffuse groups. Each of these factors makes bargaining costs extremely high in most cases of environmental spillovers. Indeed, the lack of effective group action in the real world would seem to imply that these transaction costs may exceed by a substantial amount the possible gains which can be obtained by successful action.

In cases characterized by high bargaining costs the assignment of (private or common) ownership rights can have significant allocative effects. If, as is normally the case, disposal of refuse into air and water is treated as a common (and free) activity, this in effect assigns ownership rights to each agent. The agent may use the air and water around him in any way he chooses, and high bargaining costs will prevent him from internalizing any external costs into his decisions. For this reason pollution-producing activities may be operated at a higher level than would be optimal in a Pareto sense. On the other hand, government regulation (that is, asserting public property rights) might ideally limit the use of the environment in ways which would impose full social costs on an agent's cost structure and, consequently, external effects would be reflected in the outputs and prices of pollution-producing commodities.

The assignment of ownership rights can also have important distributional effects when environmental externalities are considered. These

---

[12] Many of the problems which arise in the provision of public goods are important impediments to group antipollution action. Once pollution is abated, it is abated for everyone: The benefits are nonexclusive. Consequently, it may be to the advantage of each individual to adopt the position of a free rider.

effects will be of a more significant nature than those discussed in the previous section. In the environmental case not only will there be transfers between agents depending on ownership (as in the previous section) but also cost curves will differ depending on how ownership is assigned. Consider, for example, a firm producing automobiles and some concomitant amount of air pollution arising from this production. Because this air pollution affects a diffuse group bargaining costs are high and social costs will not be internalized into the firm's cost structure. Consequently, if air is treated as a free good (if "ownership" is assigned to the firm), cars will be produced at relatively low cost and in great numbers. Pollution will also be produced in great amounts. In such a situation those who consume automobiles will be better off than if prices reflect social costs, and those who are affected by pollution will be worse off than if fewer cars were produced. Consequently, in assessing the desirability of this particular assignment of air-use rights it is necessary to determine whether or not these distributional effects are desirable. If it is decided that the welfare effects are unfavorable, transfer of air ownership rights to a public agency may be an improvement.

Specification of ownership rights may also be an important determinant of the productive technology which is adopted. Because cost curves will be affected by the way in which these rights are distributed, incentives for adopting different techniques of production will be generated. If the full social cost of pollution-producing techniques can be imposed on the polluters these techniques will appear less profitable than they otherwise would. It is even possible that a judicious choice of schemes to internalize social costs may succeed in prompting pollution-saving technological innovations, since these innovations would become more profitable than if resource use were to remain free. When a dynamic view is taken of the economic process the assignment of property rights may have significant effects on the evolution of productive technology. For example, it was not until strong anti-air-pollution laws were imposed on electric utility generation that low-sulphur fuels came into general use. Similarly, development of geothermal and solar electric generation may proceed more rapidly than would have been the case had the external costs of more traditional methods of generation not been imposed.

Property Rights and Private Ownership

It is in the study of property rights that the two subjects of law and economics are most closely interwoven. Legal decisions about the nature of property rights will have important implications for economic efficiency and equity. In this section we will use the previous analysis of the relationship between property rights and externalities to investigate one of the most important legal questions which faces every society. What goods should be privately owned? To discuss this question it will be useful to examine only one alternative to private ownership. This alternative, previously mentioned, is common or communal ownership.[13] One way of illustrating the difference between private ownership and common ownership is by examining the type of *exclusion restriction* which each type connotes. With private property the owner has a total right of exclusion. The owner may determine how the good is to be used and may exclude others from use of the good. For common property there is no exclusion restriction. Anyone may use the property to his own advantage, but may not exclude others from doing the same. The purpose here is to see how this difference affects the overall desirability of the two forms of ownership.

It is important to recognize at the outset that goods are neither private nor communal by their own nature. Society must decide which goods will fall in each category and this decision will depend on the moral and social climate of the time. Many goods which were at one time commonly owned (most land, for example) have become privately owned in more recent years. Other goods which were privately owned in the past (some roads, bridges, fire companies, and national "shrines") have come to be primarily communally owned. The ownership rights attached to particular goods, therefore, are not constant but may be related to benefits and costs of private versus common ownership and to how these benefits and costs change over time.[14] A brief description of these benefits and costs is presented below.

The benefits to private ownership (relative to communal ownership) have already been mentioned. Private ownership permits bargaining to take place. The exchange of property rights may permit social costs to

---

[13] A third type of ownership, government ownership, will not be examined here. For a good under government ownership it is the state which exercises the right of exclusion. The state may choose to provide some goods (such as national defense) in a nonexclusive way. In other instances (with education, for example) the state may choose to exclude certain people from the good's use. Once an exclusive, state-owned good is distributed to the population it becomes privately owned, although quite often (as in the case of votes, food stamps, or public housing) these goods are not exchangeable. We will return to this example in the next chapter.

[14] The analysis of this section draws heavily on the work of H. Demsetz. *See*, for example, "Toward a Theory of Property Rights," *American Economic Review, Papers and Proceedings* (May 1967), pp. 347–359. A particularly interesting section of this paper discusses the changing nature of ownership rights among various American Indian tribes in response to changing benefits and costs of private versus common ownership.

be internalized and hence to be taken into account in individual decisions. Private property rights have definite allocational advantages. In the case of common property social costs will not be internalized and communal property may be overused.[15] Private ownership also reduces the costs of reaching some bargains because it is not necessary to obtain agreement from every member of society in order to use a good in a particular way. As an example of this, suppose I decided that I wanted to plant one hundred acres of wheat. Under private ownership I would merely have to contact the owner of the land and bargain about price. Under communal ownership it would be necessary to obtain agreement from every member of society, otherwise I might wake up some morning and discover that someone had built a gas station in my (nonexclusive) wheat field. Finally, private ownership permits a degree of specialization of goods to suit individual tastes which would be impossible given communal ownership. For example, it is no accident that privately owned clothes are more varied than institutionally provided clothes (such as military uniforms and gym clothes). When goods are communal there must be a degree of homogeneity (a "least common denominator") which would not be the case with private ownership.

There are also substantial costs associated with private ownership. A principal cost is the necessary policing which is required for a viable private-property system. Private contracts must be enforceable and the exclusion restriction must be enforced. For example, in a world of common property (if such a world is conceivable) there would be no crime called "theft," since no individual uniquely owns anything. Fishermen, for example, are not considered to be stealing when they take fish from the common oceans for private use. In a world of private property, however, resources must be devoted to theft prevention in order to maintain the viability of the system. Resources devoted to the mechanics of bargaining and information gathering may also be considered a cost of private ownership. Most of the resources devoted to surveying, recording of deeds, and operation of real-estate agencies would be unnecessary if land were communally owned. Finally, some of the benefits of private ownership may be, from a somewhat different perspective, social costs. For example, it might be argued that the variety of types of goods brought about by private property also leads to undesirable feelings of envy on the part of individuals. Similarly, an emphasis on bargaining may mean

---

[15] In the air pollution example of the previous section, air would be such an overused resource. Other interesting examples of the overuse of common resources are ocean fishing grounds and the cutting of timber on "public" lands. For a forceful example of a scientist's discovery of the problem of common ownership *see* G. Hardin, "The Tragedy of the Commons," *Science,* vol. 162 (December 13, 1968), pp. 1243–1248.

that a private-property society will be inhabited by individuals who are callous, calculating, and unfeeling. The quantification of such costs (or indeed the question of whether they exist at all) remains a matter of opinion.

This list is far from comprehensive. However, it clearly points out that there are benefits and costs to private ownership which must be considered in any overall assessment. There are some goods for which it is undoubtedly true that the benefits of being privately owned are greater than the costs (for example, consider the case of dentures). On the other hand, other goods will always be more or less communal. This is probably true for some environmental resources, especially those (such as air) for which policing costs are high. Most goods (houses, cars, land) fall into a middle ground, and for these goods it is interesting to debate the relative merits of common (or perhaps state) versus private ownership.

Conclusion

As with all the chapters in Parts VI and VII, this one has been concerned with the optimal allocation of resources. A somewhat broader view of the allocational problem was taken here so that the pervasive nature of externalities could be examined. It was shown that externalities often have allocative significance and that, in cases where bargaining costs are high, external costs may not be reflected in individual agents' decisions. This problem was shown to be particularly important in the case of environmental spillovers, and it was shown that the way in which the economic system interacts with the environment makes it likely that such problems will increase over time.

The way environmental spillovers were treated here, however, was rather different than the way they might be treated by an ecologist. Such effects were considered to be just one more aspect of the general problem of how best to allocate resources in order to satisfy human needs. This view of the environment is very man-centered. It argues that pollution is an evil only in that it affects (no matter how indirectly) individuals' welfare. It is necessary that these costs be taken into consideration in allocational decisions, but it should be pointed out that such *costs are not infinite*. Prescriptions such as "ban all pollution" have no place in a study of optimal allocation, since the "optimal" level of pollution is quite likely positive. Again, resources are scarce and they must be allocated to fulfill a vast variety of final end uses; the opportunity costs of alternative allocations must be carefully weighed.

Finally, the role of private ownership was discussed. It was shown that private ownership provides an important means by which externalities with low bargaining costs may be internalized into decentralized allocational procedures. The chapter clearly points out that the assignment of property rights is an important social question and that there may be an "optimal" way to go about assigning such rights.

CHAPTER 26

The Distribution of Income

Introduction

The previous six chapters have been primarily concerned with allocational questions. Efficiency in allocation was described and many problems associated with attaining efficiency were investigated. Since microeconomic theory was primarily developed for the purpose of studying the allocation of resources, this extended coverage is undoubtedly warranted. However, there are other desirable ends which an economic system might pursue in addition to efficiency in allocation. One of the most important of these is achieving an equitable distribution of income. Indeed, equity in the allocation of resources is a goal which might be assigned equal importance with that of efficiency,[1] although it may be more difficult to analyze because any definition of "equitable" necessarily involves making interpersonal comparisons. Such comparisons between individual levels of welfare were not required in our discussions of efficiency. In those chapters we were only concerned with how to make the "pie" (output) as large as possible, not with how to divide it up. Many questions of economic importance cannot, however, be judged only on efficiency grounds. In this chapter we will be specifically concerned with definitions of equity, with making interpersonal comparisons of welfare, and with showing how the goals of efficiency and equity may be in conflict. Because these problems of equity concern all economic systems, this chapter provides a natural way for concluding the book.

Before beginning a detailed discussion, however, it is important to clear up one possible source of confusion. When we speak of equity we are presumably interested in the distribution of welfare (utility) among the members of society. The distribution of income per se is a significant indicator of equity only if income differences are a true reflection of utility differences. This may not be the case. Everyday adages ("poor, but rich in the things that count," "money can't buy happiness") and more scientific studies suggest that income and utility are not synonymous. Even in a society characterized by total equality of utility (if it were possible to define this) differing individual tastes might require that incomes be distributed unequally. Persons with a strong craving for yachts and gourmet food should, in the interest of true equity, be permitted a higher income than persons like Thoreau who are devoted to the simple life. In this chapter, however, we will not deal with such problems and will instead treat the distribution of income as being an adequate proxy for the distribution of utility.

In a market economy the distribution of income is determined simultaneously with the allocation of resources. Governments may attempt to affect the way that after-tax income is finally distributed, but the market acts as the principal distributing mechanism. Here we will be interested both in how the market distributes income and in developing a framework for redistributional policy. One aspect of the distribution of income will, however, receive relatively little attention. This aspect concerns the other side of the simultaneity between resource allocation and income distribution: the fact that the way in which income is distributed will affect what is ultimately produced and what relative prices prevail. Since this

---

[1] Sometimes growth is considered to be a third major goal of any economic system. Since the study of growth is in many ways a "macroeconomic" problem, and since much of the static analysis of this book can readily be applied to questions of growth, this subject is not explicitly examined here.

facet of general equilibrium analysis is often ignored, it may be instructive to present a few observations on this matter here.

In Chapter 6 it was clearly demonstrated that market demand depends not only on all (relative) prices but also on how income is distributed. In a free market it is "dollar votes" which ultimately determine the demands for different commodities. To repeat the example of Chapter 6, the market demand for pizza will be rather different depending on whether total income goes primarily to pizza lovers or primarily to pizza haters. This phenomenon is pervasive—far more so than the triviality of the pizza example may imply. For example, some underdeveloped countries show a remarkably high demand for imported luxury goods (cars, air conditioners) despite the fact that the *average* income in these countries is far below luxury standards. The reason for this, as suggested by the pizza example, is that data on average income do not tell how income is distributed in these countries. If income is very unequally distributed, there may be a substantial demand for luxuries on the part of the rich because they exercise most of the dollar votes.

It is equally true that relative prices will be affected by the way in which income is distributed. This is so not only because market demand curves are affected by the distribution of income but because supply curves also are. Suppose, for example, that the government adopted a massive taxation-subsidy program of income redistribution. The end result of this program would be to introduce both income and substitution effects into individuals' factor (labor and capital) supply decisions. This would, in turn, induce changes in factor prices, and consequently it would induce shifts in firms' cost and supply curves. It is clear, therefore, that the distribution of income affects the goods market on both the demand and supply side. Relative prices will reflect these effects. Prevailing relative prices are therefore not necessarily "correct," "just," or "technically necessary." Rather, the set of relative prices (and the accompanying allocation of resources) which exists at any time will reflect all those forces which interact in a truly general equilibrium system including the prevailing distribution of income and wealth.[2]

No detailed quantitative estimate of how the distribution of income

---

[2] The recognition that a variety of factors, in addition to technological considerations, go into determining relative prices raises some fundamental questions about the opportunity cost doctrine. To argue that the opportunity cost of an ice-cream cone is two packs of gum implicitly accepts this market-determined trade-off rate as being the "correct" one. This is not true, since the relative prices of these two goods could have a different relationship to one another if different demand and supply conditions prevail. Consequently, when opportunity cost analysis is conducted (as in Chapter 24) it is important to recognize that existing supply-demand relationships are implicitly accepted as given. For a detailed statement of the basic subjectivity of any notion of cost *see* J. M. Buchanan, *Cost and Choice* (Chicago, Ill.: Markham Publishing Company, 1969).

affects the overall allocation of resources has as yet been made. Until precise general equilibrium models are developed, it may be impossible to obtain such estimates. It would be fruitless, therefore, to pursue this question further. We will instead turn to the investigation of an area where somewhat more quantitative and conceptual information is available: the study of the determinants of the distribution of income.

Determinants of the Distribution of Income

Any theory which purports to explain the distribution of income must be fairly comprehensive if it is to explain the vast differences in income among individuals. The two homogeneous factor models of distribution discussed in Part V are clearly inadequate for this task. For example, such simple models do not really help us understand why two individuals both working forty-hour weeks may have incomes from this work which differ by a factor of ten or even twenty. One way to generalize the simple capital-labor model of distribution would be to disaggregate these factors into numerous smaller groupings. We might then examine pricing in the market for "very skilled" labor, for "unskilled labor," and for several categories in between. The marginal productivity theory of distribution could undoubtedly be generalized in a fairly straightforward way to take account of this more detailed list of factors of production.

In this section, however, we will not take this traditional route but will instead adopt an approach which is very similar to the two-factor model, but permits somewhat more flexibility. This approach is based on the simplification that there are only two sources of income: income from capital and income from labor. We will modify the concept of income from labor slightly, however, and term such income a *return on human capital*. Consequently, all income will be regarded as a *return on capital* —some portion arising from *human capital* and the other portion arising from *nonhuman capital*. Under the heading of income from human capital would be included all those payments (either monetary or payments "in kind," such as the food that a farmer grows for his own use) which individuals receive for their labor services. Wages, salaries, and fringe benefits would be the most important such payments. Income on nonhuman capital would include all payments received by an individual from his physical and financial investments. The most important sources of this type of income would be interest, dividends, profits, rent (including imputed rent on owner-occupied homes), and the "income" which accrues to an individual in the form of services on the durable goods he owns. Although the distinction between income from human and nonhuman capital may be conceptually clear, in the real world problems of classification will always exist. For example, how should the income earned by a small shop owner be allocated to the two sources? There seems to be no clearcut way of dividing up the shop owner's total income. Because we are not particularly interested in such problems of classification, however, we will assume that income can be classed into one of the two groups in some unambiguous way.

An individual's total income (Y) then comes from two sources: income from human capital (Y_H) and income from nonhuman capital (Y_N).[3] Consequently,

$$Y = Y_H + Y_N. \tag{26.1}$$

We may further examine these two components by assuming that each in fact represents a return on some stock of capital. In particular Y_H can be taken to be the product of the rate of return the individual earns on his human capital (r_H) times the stock he employs (K_H):

$$Y_H = r_H K_H \tag{26.2}$$

and, similarly, income from nonhuman capital can be regarded as the product of the rate of return the individual earns on this type of capital (r_N) times the stock of capital (K_N) he has invested:

$$Y_N = r_N K_N. \tag{26.3}$$

Combining these two equations shows that total income depends on both rates of return and on the amount of capital which the individual has "invested":

$$Y = r_H K_H + r_N K_N. \tag{26.4}$$

From Equation 26.4 it is clear by our definitions that income differentials can arise either from differences in the rates of return which individuals are able to obtain on their two types of capital or from the amount of capital they in fact have. In the remainder of this section we will examine the relative importance of these two sources of income differences.

On a priori grounds it might be thought that the rates of return available to individuals on their capital would not differ very much from one person to the next. Because both labor and capital are relatively mobile

---

[3] A third source of income, "gifts," is not explicitly considered here but will be taken up in later sections.

it might be assumed that both factors would move into that employment which offers the highest reward. This action would tend to equalize the rates of return obtainable throughout the economy. Once uncertainty is recognized, it is possible that some rates of return may be, *on the average,* higher than others because of the differences in risks attached to certain ways that capital might be employed. For example, a given quantity of nonhuman capital invested in common stock might yield a higher return (on the average) than if it were invested in a savings account. Similarly, a given quantity of human capital might earn a higher return if it were invested in a relatively risky occupation (such as steeple-jacking) than if it were employed in a safe, secure job. Such differentials would represent normal market reactions to risk and higher average returns would be available to anyone willing to assume the risk. Differences in returns could then be assumed only to represent differences in risk taking.

This conclusion about the equalization of rates of return must be modified to take account of market imperfections. There are many impediments in real-world markets which prevent the same rates of return from being available to everyone. For example, there is some evidence that the rate of return obtainable from a given quantity of human capital is lower for black Americans than for whites.[4] Job discrimination may prevent equalization of returns from taking place. Other impediments in the employment of human capital may occur because of restrictive trade union practices (a higher return on a given amount of skills can be achieved by those able to get into the union), restrictive professional practices, or as a result of worker immobility (for example, workers trapped in the Appalachian region may earn a lower return on their skills). Impediments can also cause unequal rates of return to be available to owners of nonhuman capital. For example, it has been calculated that government-imposed ceilings on savings account interest rates have discriminated against small savers while the wealthy can find ways to circumvent these ceilings. Although such impediments to equalization may exist for nonhuman capital it is likely that they are of somewhat less quantitative importance than are impediments in the labor market.

Rate of return differentials may therefore have a considerable effect on the distribution of income even though, if markets were working perfectly, this might not be the case. The second cause of income differen-

---

[4] The distinction made here attempts to hold constant any possible difference in human capital between blacks and whites. The assertion is that for a given level of "education" blacks still earn less than whites. This fact has been documented in many places. Perhaps the most detailed quantitative analysis is L. C. Thurow, *Poverty and Discrimination* (Washington, D. C.: The Brookings Institution, 1969).

tials, differences in capital ownership[5] (both human and nonhuman), may be of even greater significance. Whereas there are some factors at work tending to equalize the rates of return different individuals receive, there is no such mechanism working to equalize capital ownership. In fact, the existing mechanisms for obtaining capital may preserve or even exacerbate inequalities. The two principal ways of obtaining capital, inheritance and individual savings, are briefly discussed below.

When one thinks of inheritance visions of vast quantities of (nonhuman) wealth being transferred from one generation to the next come immediately to mind. While this sort of transferring of great fortunes undoubtedly has some effect on income inequality, it is the inheritance[6] of human capital which may have a far greater quantitative significance. An individual may pass on human capital to his heirs in a variety of ways. In the United States children of upper-income families tend to have higher educational levels and (perhaps more important) a higher quality of education than do children of poor families. The choice by parents to spend for their children's education is undoubtedly a cause of differentials in the ownership of human capital. Other types of inheritance may be equally as important as formal education in determining income differences. Various cultural traits (work habits, attitudes toward material values) are aspects of a broadly defined notion of human capital which may be passed from one generation to the next. These might be one more factor tending to preserve inequalities in the distribution of capital. It would be possible to go into far more detail about how wealth (both human and nonhuman) is transferred from one generation to the next, but the basic point should by now be clear: Inheritance is in many ways responsible for the preservation of income inequalities.

Inheritance is not the only way in which capital can be accumulated, however. As was discussed in Chapter 8, individuals have considerable freedom in making savings and investment decisions. An individual's decision to accumulate capital — especially human capital — may have significant effects on his income. A major question then is whether this freedom to accumulate increases or decreases equality in capital ownership.

---

[5] Individuals may also differ in the amount of capital they choose to employ in income-producing ways. Probably the most important such choice is in the individual's labor-leisure decision. If an individual has a strong "taste for leisure" he may choose to employ his human capital in ways which do not yield monetary income. Such decisions will not only lead to observed income differentials but may also affect the total income available in society. We will return to this point in the section "Redistributional Programs" below.

[6] The possibility for inheriting physical differences is not specifically examined here. While such inheritance may possibly lead to differences in the distribution of human capital the evidence on this point is ambiguous.

There is no unambiguous evidence on this point. Some authors have suggested, on the basis of a priori argument, that it may be more "imperative" for the poor to consume all their income than for the rich to do so. Consequently, the rich may be free to engage in additional accumulation, and by so doing will increase existing inequalities. Several arguments have been brought forth against this view[7] and the issue is still very much unresolved.

This analysis, while it provides a conceptual framework for examining income inequalities, certainly leaves many important questions about the determinants of the income distribution unanswered. It was shown that the distribution which actually prevails is importantly determined by both market and nonmarket factors, and that any more precise answers must await more detailed quantitative investigations. In the remainder of this chapter we will take the privately determined distribution of income as a "given" and ask what the government can do and should do to change it.

The Distribution of Income as a Public Good

We will begin our discussion of the government's role in the distribution of income by asking the normative question of whether the government should do anything about the distribution which comes about as a result of the private market. One way to approach this question would be to argue that the government has a "moral duty" to promote equality, or at least to eliminate abject poverty. If we adopt this principle there is little more to be said, except perhaps to argue over how much equality is dictated by this moral imperative. If, on the other hand, we adopt the principle that any government action should be undertaken only if it is favored by "most" individuals we have posed the question in a way which is conducive to gaining some insights into the problem. In this section we will show that equality is in many respects a public good and that, for reasons common to all public goods, the free market may tend to "underproduce" it.

---

[7] One argument might be that our progressive tax system makes it more difficult for a rich man to accumulate nonhuman capital than for a poor man to do so. Consequently, the freedom to accumulate capital might work to mitigate inequality. An analysis with a similar conclusion could be made about human capital. It might be argued that since time is more valuable to a rich man than to a poor one, and since acquiring human capital is a very time-intensive activity, the poor will be more willing to accumulate additional amounts of this type of capital than will the rich.

Suppose every individual in society is of a philanthropic nature and believes equality is a good thing. We might then ask why equality will not be achieved by the workings of the free market. After all, any individual is free to give all the money he wants to any other individual. Private philanthropy could therefore be relied upon to produce equality. Under this reasoning it might be concluded that the absence of equality is *prima facie* evidence that people are not really very philanthropic after all.

Such a conclusion would be similar to the argument that if the free market does not provide adequate public health facilities perhaps people don't care about being healthy. The fallacy in both these arguments is that they ignore the public good nature of the two activities. If I decide to give money to a poor person everyone in society who favors equality will benefit. My own personal calculations will not take this externality into account, however. Because I am not able to exclude others from gaining a psychic benefit from my generosity, I may not give as freely as would be desirable from a social point of view. By this argument then I, as well as everyone else, will refrain from giving, and inequality will persist even though no one wants it. This is precisely the public goods "problem" which was discussed in detail in Chapter 23.

In fact, not everyone *does* agree on what the proper degree of equality should be. Some individuals have benevolent attitudes toward others and favor an egalitarian society. Other individuals may derive some utility (status) from knowing that there are persons on the economic ladder below themselves, and therefore would prefer that inequality be maintained. One might choose to pay no attention to such malevolent "tastes," but this would involve imposing a moral principle over and above those dictated by individual tastes. One might as well start out with the premise that equality is a good thing in the first place. Alternatively, a government could adopt the benefit principle of providing equality by taxing each individual to the extent he benefited psychically from knowing that he lived in a more equal society. Under this procedure only the philanthropists of society would engage in redistributional programs, and governmental coercion would insure that no true philanthropist was a free rider. Gathering information on individuals' attitudes would be a tricky problem, however, as was mentioned in Chapter 23, since each individual would know he would be taxed in accordance with his professed beliefs. In short, there seems to be no easy way to base an answer to the question of redistribution on the tastes of individuals in society just as there is no easy way to find out how much of any public good should be produced. The public good aspect of the problem does indicate, however, why governments attempt to redistribute income, and why the free market may produce a distribution of income which is considered undesirable by almost everyone.

These thoughts conclude the conceptual aspects of the distribution of income to be discussed in this book. It would be inappropriate, however, to conclude without investigating some of the more down-to-earth problems associated with any redistributional scheme that is agreed on by a political consensus. In the next section we will take up these problems.

Redistributional Programs

Every activity of government will have distributional consequences. Because governmental decisions affect the allocation of resources they cannot avoid at the same time affecting the distribution of income. In this section, however, we will be concerned with those activities which the government undertakes with the express purpose of "improving" the distribution of income.[8] It is possible to class these activities into two different groupings: *market oriented programs* and *pure distributional programs*. In the first category would be included governmental attempts at equalizing those basic determinants of income which were discussed in the second section above. Government action to promote equal opportunity in hiring practices, for example, would be an important such activity. Many regulatory functions of government which appear based on allocational considerations (such as action against monopolistic practices) could also have important distributional effects. Finally, governments could adopt educational and work training programs with the purpose of equalizing the stock of human capital. All of these traditional measures involve the government in trying to get the market to produce a more equitable distribution of income than would result if the market were left to operate freely.

A second general class of government distributional programs are of a direct subsidy nature. These programs seek to supplement income directly, rather than working indirectly through the market. In this category would be included both plans which subsidize the purchase of certain commodities (food stamps, low-income housing) and plans which redistribute generalized purchasing power (Aid to Families with Dependent Children, Social Security, and "negative income tax" type of proposals).

---

[8] It is assumed in this section that the government's goal is to increase equality. The cynical reader could reverse many of the arguments made here to show how, in fact, real-world governments may promote inequality.

Although all of these direct programs have the same general goal of re-distribution they may differ substantially in the efficiency with which they achieve this goal.[9, 10]

The principal benefit of either of the two classes of redistributional programs is, naturally enough, increased equality. If the population as a whole desires equality this benefit will be of some value, and scarce re-sources should be devoted to achieving it. Market-oriented redistribu-tional programs may have the additional benefit of improving the opera-tion of various labor markets and perhaps raising the productivity of some workers. Such programs might therefore insure not only that the output of the economic system is distributed more equitably but also may increase the total output to be distributed. Pure redistributional programs may also have this benefit — for example, eliminating malnutrition would undoubtedly have a positive effect on productivity — but this would seem to be a less-important aspect of these programs than to the market-oriented programs.

The costs of redistributional plans are not the dollar costs of such programs. These dollar costs represent transfers from one member of society to another and are therefore not costs in a social sense. It is an obvious but frequently obscured fact that although billions are spent on "welfare" these payments are not a net cost to society (total output is not necessarily reduced). One should not, however, conclude that redis-tributional programs are costless. The raising of revenues, say by taxes, with which to finance transfer programs can induce important distortions into the allocational process. If taxes could be imposed in some "lump sum" way (so as to decrease the purchasing power of the individual taxed without biasing his decisions) these distortions might be minimized. However, as we saw in Chapter 7, all existing taxation schemes violate this lump sum principle and will in fact distort individuals' decisions.

---

[9] Here we use the word "efficiency" to refer to allocational efficiency. In the study of redistributional programs some authors refer to a narrower concept of efficiency by dis-cussing, for example, how a fixed sum of money might best be spent on "eliminating pov-erty." In this sense an antipoverty program might be inefficient either because it did not benefit large segments of the poor population or because it did benefit substantial segments of the nonpoor population.

[10] Among pure subsidy-type of programs economists have an inherent bias toward pro-viding cash income rather than providing particular goods. For example, laymen may see starving people and suggest that the obvious remedy is to provide them with food. An economist's instinctive reaction, on the other hand, is to argue that they should be provided with general purchasing power. They may then buy food if they like, or they may choose to buy something else which presumably has more value to them. An interesting view con-trary to this and favoring a more equal distribution of specific goods (although not neces-sarily a more equal distribution of general income) is presented in J. Tobin, "On Limiting the Domain of Inequality," *The Journal of Law and Economics,* vol. XIII, no. 2 (October 1970), pp. 263–277.

In particular an income tax, because it affects the wage rate relevant to an individual's decisions, will cause a reaction in the labor-leisure choices of those taxed.[11] It may be that the progressive income-tax rates needed to carry out adequate redistributional programs will encourage the most highly paid (and possibly most productive) workers to choose more leisure. The concomitant reduction in output occasioned by this withdrawal from the labor force would be the true cost of any transfer program. Undertaking a redistributional program may therefore involve a very difficult choice between allocational efficiency and equity. One must, as is always the case for any project, weigh the relevant benefits and costs.

The possible inconsistency between the goals of efficiency and equity shows up even more strongly in the cases of current government programs which interfere in certain markets with the ostensible purpose of making the prices in these markets "more equitable." Such programs include minimum wage laws, rent controls, interest rate regulation ("usury" laws), and farm price support programs. Whether any of these programs have their intended effect of promoting equity is an empirical question,[12] but there can be no doubt that these do indeed interfere with the efficiency with which these markets operate. In all these cases the ability of the market to allocate resources efficiently has been distorted in the interest of increased equity. It is an open question whether this supposed benefit of these programs exceeds their allocational cost.

Conclusion

Any conclusion to a chapter on equity must of necessity be vague. Much of what has been presented merely represents ways of conceptualizing

[11] Recipients of transfer payments will also have their labor-leisure choices affected since most conceivable subsidy programs affect the relevant take-home wage rate. In this regard it may be important to differentiate between the income and substitution effects of transfer programs on income recipients. For example, if income transfers were to increase total purchasing power without affecting wage rates, it might be claimed that labor-leisure choices were not distorted. If individuals choose more leisure in such a situation this would only be a manifestation of the superior nature of the "good" leisure. On the other hand, if transfer schemes really do affect the relevant wage rate (as they most surely will) labor-leisure choices would be distorted. Using an analogy to the graphic analysis of Chapter 7: Economists are less concerned with increases in the demand for leisure, which stem from a shift outward in the individual's budget constraint, than they are in changes which come about from artificially varying the slope of the constraint.

[12] There is some evidence that each of these programs may in fact have inequitable effects when a comprehensive view of supply-demand interaction is taken. For one empirical investigation of such programs *see* Y. Brozen, "The Effect of Statutory Minimum Wage Increases on Teen-age Unemployment," *Journal of Law and Economics,* vol. 12 (April 1969), pp. 109–122.

what ultimately comes down to being matters of opinion. One conclusion does emerge, however, from applying economic reasoning to these problems: There may be an "optimal" degree of inequality for society. We may wish to stop short of a perfectly egalitarian society even though everyone unambigously feels equality is a good thing. It may be necessary to adopt programs which preserve work incentives[13] to assure that a "reasonable" level of output is produced. In many respects the production of equality uses scarce resources and we must therefore consider how much in resources to devote to this purpose.

---

[13] Incentives do not necessarily have to be monetary. Appeals to patriotism, the awarding of medals, or the careful doling out of warm handshakes may be equally capable of producing utility differences and concomitant work incentives.

DISCUSSION QUESTIONS AND PROBLEMS FOR PART VII

Discussion Questions

1. At many points in Chapters 23–26 possible conflicts between equity and efficiency were mentioned. Are there really such conflicts, or don't we understand enough about what "equity" and "efficiency" mean to be able to draw such conclusions with any degree of certainty?

2. Is inheritance a "legitimate" cause for differentials in incomes? Should individuals be allowed to leave bequests and should other individuals be allowed to receive them? How might a law forbidding all bequests affect the allocation of resources?

3. How might political leaders be chosen in an "ideal" society? Would the same types of problems in making these choices occur as were mentioned in connection with Arrow's Impossibility Theorem in Chapter 21?

4. How valid is the dichotomy between labor and nonlabor income? Can you construct an argument which indicates why, in a world of inhomogeneous factors of production, individuals have a "right" to one type of income, but the other type is undeserved and exploitative? Is your argument symmetric in that it can be applied to either type of income?

5. What economic principles might be invoked in order to decide on the "optimal" level of property rights in society? Could these principles be decided on in a "scientific" (that is, objective) way?

6. In Part VII the concept of optimality was brought up in many contexts. Is it possible that economists have carried this concept too far, and by so doing have weakened what should be considered "moral absolutes"? For example, how do you react to the suggestion that there may be an optimal level of pollution or an optimal level of injustice?

7. Is the providing of information, say about the quality of certain consumer goods, a public or a private type of good? More specifically, should the government evaluate products or should this be left up to Consumers' Union?

Problems

1. Suppose the government decided to regulate monopolies by permitting them to earn a fixed "fair" rate of return on their capital invest-

ments. How would this decision affect the rental rate of capital to the monopoly? Given this effect, how might the monopoly's input choices be affected, and how would its profit-maximizing choice of output be changed? How might a regulator commission set the rate of return so as to make desirable those changes which are brought about?

2. The demand curve for public goods in Chapter 23 was rather casually drawn. Can you think up a way of deriving such a demand curve from more basic data on individuals' tastes? What problems would arise in such a derivation?

3. An investment criterion which is closely related to the present discounted value criterion discussed in Chapters 19 and 24 is the internal rate of return criterion. In using this criterion, the present cost of an investment (P) is equated to:

$$P = R_0 + \frac{R_1}{(1 + i)} + \frac{R_2}{(1 + i)^2} + \cdots + \frac{R_n}{(1 + i)^n}$$

where R_j is the net return from the investment in year j, and i is treated as an unknown. The resulting equation is then solved for i, which is termed the internal rate of return. This rate of return is that interest rate which, when used to discount the returns from the investment, will cause this discounted value to equal the investment's current price exactly. The investment criterion consists of undertaking the investment of $i > r$ and refusing to do so if $i < r$ (where r is the market rate of interest).

   Show that this criterion is equivalent to the present discounted value criterion if all the R_i's are positive, but that these may not agree if some of the R_i's are negative.

4. Interpret Problem 2 of Part VI as an example of externalities. How does this problem reflect the difficulties of communal ownership?

5. Develop an example of interpersonal externalities similar to that illustrated for interfirm externalities in Chapter 25. Show how the assumption of zero bargaining costs permits exchanges among the two individuals to bring about an optimal allocation of resources even in the presence of this type of externality.

6. Develop an hypothetical production function for human capital. If this function adequately describes the way in which human capital is distributed among people how might income equality be brought about? Specifically, would equality of governmentally determined inputs (the amount spent per pupil on education, for example) insure equality of output, or would it be necessary to adopt some more remedial programs? Develop your arguments using an isoquant map if possible.

Glossary of Frequently
Used Terms

Some of the terms which are used frequently in this book are defined below. More complete descriptions of these concepts can be found in the relevant sections of the text. Each of the terms is also listed in the Index which follows this section.

Contract Curve   The set of all the efficient allocations of goods among those individuals in an exchange economy. Each of these allocations has the property that no one individual can be made better off without the necessity of making someone else worse off.

Convexity Assumptions   Assumptions which are made about the shapes of individuals' utility functions and firms' production functions. These assumptions are based on the presumption that the relative marginal effectiveness of a particular good or input diminishes as the quantity of that good or input increases. The assumptions are important because they insure that the application of first-order conditions will indeed yield a true maximum.

Decreasing Cost Industry   An industry in which expansion of output generates cost-reducing externalities which cause the cost curves of those firms in the industry to shift downward.

547

Economic Efficiency   A condition which exists when resources are allocated so that no activity can be increased without the necessity of cutting back on some other activity.

Elasticity   A measure of the percentage change in one variable brought about by a 1 percent change in some other variable. If $y = f(x)$, then the elasticity of y with respect to x ($E_{y,x}$) is given by $dy/dx \cdot x/y$. This concept is most often used to describe how the quantity of a good demanded responds to a change in its price.

Equilibrium   A situation in which supply and demand are in balance. At an equilibrium price the quantity demanded by individuals is exactly equal to that which is supplied by all firms.

Expansion Path   The locus of those cost-minimizing input combinations which will be chosen at all levels of output when relative input costs are held constant.

Externality   An effect of one economic agent on another which is not taken into account by the first agent when he decides on his actions.

Fixed Costs   Costs which do not change as the level of output changes in the short run. Fixed costs are in many respects irrelevant to the theory of short-run price determination.

Income and Substitution Effects   The two analytically different effects which come into play when an individual is faced with a changed price for some good. Income effects arise because a change in the price of a good will affect an individual's purchasing power. Even if purchasing power is held constant, however, substitution effects will cause individuals to reallocate their expenditures. Substitution effects are reflected in movements along an indifference curve, whereas income effects entail a movement to a different indifference curve.

Increasing Cost Industry   An industry in which the expansion of output creates cost-increasing externalities which cause the cost curves of those firms in the industry to shift upward.

Indifference Curve Map   A contour map of an individual's utility function showing those alternative bundles of goods from which the individual derives equal levels of welfare.

Inferior Good   A good which is bought in smaller quantities as an individual's income rises.

Inferior Input   A factor of production which is used in smaller amounts as a firm's output expands.

Isoquant Map   A contour map of the firm's production function. The contours show the alternative combinations of productive inputs which can be used to produce a given level of output.

Marginal Cost (MC) The additional cost incurred by producing one more unit of output.

Marginal Expense The cost of hiring one more unit of a productive input. The marginal expense of hiring one more unit of labor, for example, is denoted by MC_L.

Marginal Physical Product (MPP) The additional output which can be produced by one more unit of a particular input while holding all other inputs constant.

Marginal Rate of Substitution (MRS) The rate at which an individual is willing to trade one good for another while remaining equally well off. The *MRS* is the absolute value of the slope of an indifference curve.

Marginal Revenue (MR) The additional revenue obtained by a firm when it is able to sell one more unit of output.

Marginal Revenue Product (MRP) The extra revenue which accrues to a firm when it sells the output which is produced by one more unit of some input. In the case of labor, for example, $MRP_L = MR \cdot MPP_L$.

Marginal Utility (MU) The extra utility which an individual receives by consuming one more unit of a particular good.

Marginal Value Product (MVP) A special case of Marginal Revenue Product which applies when the good being produced is sold in a perfectly competitive market. If the competitive price is given by P ($= MR$ in this case), then $MVP_L = P \cdot MPP_L$.

Opportunity Cost Doctrine The simple, though far-reaching observation that the true cost of any action can be measured by the value of the best alternative which must be forgone when the action is taken.

Output and Substitution Effects The effects which come into play when a change in the price of an input which a firm uses causes the firm to change the quantities of inputs which it will demand. The substitution effect would occur even if output were held constant, and is reflected by movements along an isoquant. Output effects, on the other hand, occur when output levels change and the firm moves to a new isoquant.

Perfect Competition The most widely used economic model in which there are assumed to be a large number of buyers and sellers for any good and in which each agent is a price taker.

Prisoner's Dilemma A problem which was originally studied in the theory of games but which has widespread applicability. The crux of the Dilemma is that each individual, faced with the uncertainty of how others will behave, may be led to adopt a course of action which proves to be detrimental for all those individuals making the same decision. A strong coalition might have led to a solution preferred by everyone in the group.

Production Function A conceptual mathematical function which records the relationship between a firm's inputs and its outputs.

Production Possibility Frontier The locus of all the alternative quantities of several outputs which can be produced with fixed amounts of productive inputs.

Rate of Product Transformation (RPT) The rate at which one output can be traded for another in the productive process while holding the total quantities of inputs constant. The *RPT* is the absolute value of the slope of the Production Possibility Frontier.

Rate of Technical Substitution (RTS) The rate at which one input may be traded off against another in the productive process while holding output constant. The *RTS* is the absolute value of the slope of an isoquant.

Returns to Scale A way of classifying production functions which records how output responds to proportional increases in *all* inputs. If a proportional increase in all inputs causes output to increase by a smaller proportion the production function is said to exhibit decreasing returns to scale. If output increases by a greater proportion than the inputs the production function exhibits increasing returns. Constant returns to scale is the middle ground where both inputs and outputs increase by the same proportions.

Short Run-Long Run Distinction A conceptual distinction made in the theory of production which differentiates between a period of time over which some inputs are regarded as being fixed and a longer period in which all inputs can be varied by the producer.

Social Rates of Transformation and Substitution When externalities are present private rates of trade off and social rates of trade off will differ. To study the optimal allocation of resources it is necessary to examine social rates.

Utility Function A mathematical conceptualization of the way in which individuals rank alternative bundles of commodities.

Variable Costs Those costs which change in response to changes in the level of output being produced by a firm. This is in contrast to fixed costs which do not change.

Author Index

Subject Index